I WANTED TO WRITE

"No author deserving of the name can work alone and unassisted. Many a writer's fame and fortune have been built upon the unseen sympathy and efforts of one whose very existence sometimes remains forever unknown; and many a man who might have been a novelist of note has gone unproductive to his grave because he lacked the encouragement, the protection or the help of understanding friends or of a woman.

"Whether I could have finished *Civil War in America* without the help of friends, I cannot say. What I can say is that those friends gave me the inner warmth that keeps an author's pen from freezing, and spurred me to my dreary task on those oft-recurring occasions when I feared and freely said I'd never write another line."

—*Oliver Wiswell*

KENNETH ROBERTS

I Wanted to Write

GARDEN CITY, N. Y.

Doubleday & Company, Inc.

1949

To

CLARA CLAASEN

who labored unceasingly
in preparing for publication
Arundel, The Lively Lady, Rabble in Arms,
Captain Caution, Northwest Passage,
Oliver Wiswell, Lydia Bailey,
Moreau de St. Méry's American Journey
and
I Wanted to Write

"I have a friend who wants to write. If you could spare a few moments to give him a little advice, I know it would be a great help to him."

—Quotation from innumerable letters

KENNETH ROBERTS TO THEODORE ROOSEVELT

A LETTER OF PROTEST

"I got a whole lot of entertainment out of one other book, the title of which I have forgotten. I can't recall even the author's name, but the story was mighty good."

—Theodore Roosevelt, in an interview

I had intended, sir, to write
  A book—a novel, say—this summer:
Something exciting, gripping, bright:
  In short, a hummer;

But, sir, your statements in the news
  Have filled my heart with hesitation
And made me think I'd better choose
  A new vocation.

In fact, to all us writer chaps
  Who'd fain be Tarkingtons or Trollopes,
Your words are worse than thunderclaps
  Or numbing wallops;

For how can we preserve our poise
  And keep undimmed the flame Ambition
If we're to be denied the joys
  Of recognition?

No book can possibly succeed
  Unless the public knows its title
And author, too. These things, indeed,
  Are almost vital;

For with his book unsought, unsold,
  The author cannot know Fame's blessing;
And that, combined with lack of gold,
  Is most depressing!

And if you, sir, forget these things,
  Won't lesser minds forget them also?
Indeed they will! 'Tis that which stings,
  And stirs my gall so!

So, speaking for the writing crew,
  I pray that henceforth you'll be heeding
The author and the title too
  Of what you're reading.

New York Sun, April 1918

(Colonel Roosevelt, after cross-examination by his daughter, Ethel Derby, rapturously replied that the book was *The Lone Wolf* by Louis Vance, adding, "be sure you let me see you when you come back.")

I WANTED TO WRITE

"It is remarkable that there is little or nothing to be remembered written on the subject of getting a living; how to make getting a living not merely honest and honorable, but altogether inviting and glorious; for if *getting* a living is not so, then living is not. One would think, from looking at literature, that this question had never disturbed a solitary individual's musings. Is it that men are too much disgusted with their experience to speak of it?"

—HENRY D. THOREAU, *Civil Disobedience*

I'D LIKE to have it understood in the beginning, and remembered until the end, that these chapters have been written solely because of the staggering number of would-be authors who seem to labor under the delusion that I know a routine, formula or diet that in a half hour's time will transform any aspiring young person who admires his own letter-writing ability into a competent and successful novelist.

Since there is no such diet, formula or routine, I have mournfully found it almost impossible to talk to these eager aspirants who want to write—impossible because I also must write, and nobody can produce anything worth printing while talking.

Wilbur Wright, called on to utter after two dreary speakers had benumbed a roomful of diners assembled in Paris to do him honor, reportedly excused his own brevity as a speechmaker by saying, "The most talkative bird in the world is the parrot, but he is a poor flier."

If Wright said this, which I doubt, he was wrong, but he was working on an idea that was basically sound. In the West Indies one winter, engaged in carrying out my long-standing desire to write, I was so constantly disturbed by the monotonous screams of three small caged parrots that I took steps to have them banished to other parts. During the banishment, they escaped from their cage and for two days swooped dazzlingly about the scene of their captivity. Their flight strongly resembled that of wild pigeons or kingfishers; and if they had relied on their wings to remain at liberty, they could have defied us forever. Their mental processes, fortunately, were not as well developed as their wings; and when they felt the pangs of hunger, the sight of a ripe banana held them goggle-eyed and motionless, and so intent on emitting a flux of parrot talk that they were easily picked up and once more caged.

Wilbur Wright might more truthfully have said, "One of the best fliers in the world is the parrot, and he's also a good talker; but not even a parrot can afford to talk if he wants to keep on flying."

§

It's impossible, too, to converse helpfully with those who have the writing urge, because most of them (and this is also true of many authors who have attained eminence) welcome only suggestions they wish to hear. It's embarrassingly difficult to hint to a dewy-eyed young lady panting to plunge into a deathless novel that she needs, to say the least, about five years' experience on a newspaper. Knowing that Jane Austen served no such apprenticeship, she scorns the hint.

A friend once insisted that I see a young man wishful of embarking on a powerful piece of fiction, determined, in spite of my protests, that I advise him how to do it. I protested because I was in a frenzy of bewilderment, working fourteen hours a day on a long novel that I couldn't seem to control. So the young man appeared, and I asked him what he had already written. He was merely a Wanta Writer, and had written nothing. I could only say helplessly that the way to write is to write; then rewrite. If, I foolishly added, he would write something and bring it to me in a year's time, I might be able to make concrete suggestions.

A year later he returned with nine neatly typed chapters of a novel and asked to be told frankly whether or not they were good. I begged him not to press me, telling him honestly that no professional writer can speak frankly to a Wanta Writer without bruising the greater part of his most delicate sensibilities.

It made no difference, he said. Frankness was what he wanted. How, unless he knew the truth, could he ever become another Tolstoi?

My fears were justified. I read the nine chapters with care, then had to tell him that there was no way of finding out what he was driving at: that if an author couldn't make himself clear in his first chapter he probably would never make himself clear. I assured him that no publisher would for a moment consider publishing his chapters, since everything in them was wholly inconsequential and trivial. I pointed out that the basic motivation of his protagonist was the unworthy desire to build up a fortune by selling a daily two dollars' worth of frankfurters to a small and excessively uninteresting group of his social and mental equals; that the narrative was inept, confused, incapable of interesting even the somewhat limited membership of the frankfurter industry—and I had to say brutally that the sooner he destroyed his manuscript and forgot it, the better off he'd be.

The young man took it well. His reply was restrained but not satisfactory. It didn't repay me for the time and thought I'd put on his efforts, for it ended: "Just to prove you're wrong, I'm going to keep right on with it."

That partly explains why I regretfully avoid invitations to attend writers' conferences in Colorado, Wisconsin, Oregon and other far-flung places, for the purpose of appearing haltingly for two-hour periods before groups of eager and intelligent young men and women, in order to explain clearly and comprehensively how it's done. There's no way of telling how it's done, either in a two-hour address or by any other sort of demonstration.

I have been accused of hermitcy or recluse-ism because I stay at home and work while others sit in the sun on a beach: because I shun cocktail parties and large gatherings of distractomaniacs. If that's being a hermit or a recluse, I plead guilty. I'm also a writer, and it's my unalterable belief that writers should stick to writing: not argue world affairs over radio programs, or act as ballyhoo men (and most offensively so) during presidential campaigns, or kill valuable hours at noisy gatherings of gin drinkers who have nothing better to do, or try to collaborate with the editorial staffs of moving picture companies. In addition to wasting time, such things are ruinously destructive to a writer's peace of mind.

Years before I wrote *Northwest Passage,* the *Saturday Evening Post* sent me to California to assemble a series of articles on the oddities and novelties of life in Movieland. Under the guidance of the Will Hays Office, I carefully scrutinized the infant Art, as it was then called. I was deeply impressed by the manner in which wealthy producers imported well-known writers at great expense, allowed them to remain idle for months on end, and finally mangled their books so sadistically that the original stories and characters were unrecognizable on the screen. There was no question in my mind that authors who catered to the checks and calls of fantastic, unpredictable and too often unreliable motion picture companies should have remained at home writing, with minds at rest and hackles smoothly in place.

With the publication of *Northwest Passage,* I had my first direct—and profoundly depressing—contact with cinema circles. Since journals accessible to those circles had reviewed the book favorably, a studio executive was smitten with the thought that I should be summoned to Hollywood—not to help on *Northwest Passage,* with which three years of intensive research had made me familiar; but to prepare a movie version of an unnamed novel dealing with longhorns, shootin' irons, six-guns, the range, hoss wranglers, caow rustlers, little dogies, ten-gallon hats, the Bar-Hairpin Ranch and the purple sage, all of which could have been better interpreted by any ten-dollar-a-week cow hand than by me. Consequently an agent telegraphed: would I be interested in coming to Hollywood for a month at a thousand dollars a week?

I replied that I would not.

The agent promptly telegraphed that Paramount would pay me fifteen hundred dollars a week for ten weeks.

This offer stirred no pulse in me, and I said so.

Quickly came another telegram: "How much will you take to come to Hollywood?"

I replied, with none of the evasiveness of a presidential candidate jockeying for position, "Not coming to Hollywood."

The agent tried again, offering two thousand dollars a week for ten weeks, plus all transportation and hotel accommodation for myself and my family.

This time I replied that if Paramount would send one man, authorized to make final story decisions, to Maine to work with me, I'd do what they wanted in half the time, and for half the amount per week.

This put an end to the negotiations, as cinema executives were revolted by the idea of sending a man to Maine. Apparently they thought of Maine as being somehow poisonous and infectious, as did a ponderous British professor, Arnold J. Toynbee, who wrote a history of his idea of history, representing Maine as populated by "woodmen, watermen and hunters."

Incidentally, when the screen version of *Northwest Passage* was in production at the Metro-Goldwyn-Mayer studio, those in charge found themselves lacking in technical knowledge concerning the uniforms and behavior of Rogers' Rangers.

In such a circumstance, one would naturally suppose that the possessors of even rudimentary brains would consult the book's author for the information. But the artists engaged in distorting *Northwest Passage* turned to Miss Dorothy Vaughan, librarian of the Portsmouth, New Hampshire, Public Library.

Being considerably at sea herself about the details, Miss Vaughan appealed to me for the answers. I told her, and she told the Metro technicians, only to have them disregard my accurate replies and use their own conceptions, which were nauseatingly incorrect.

Months later I ran into John Ford, who, in spite of having been born and reared in the destructive climate of Maine, had somehow contrived to become Hollywood's outstanding director. I told him about the Paramount offer and asked him why, in his opinion, the Paramount officials hadn't taken advantage of my proposal to do the work in half their stipulated time and at considerably less than half their stipulated price. Mr. Ford was quick to reply that they were merely exercising their inalienable right to make damned fools of themselves.

I know of nothing that could make me alter my opinion that a writer able to support himself by writing should remain at his desk and write: not go running off to Hollywood or after strange gods. Conceive of the mental unrest of writers caught in the Hollywood spider web, when things of this sort happen:

The first motion picture version, or treatment, of *Northwest Passage,* unless I was misinformed by heads of the Authors' League, was done by the extremely capable scenarist Frances Marion, who was paid twenty-five thousand dollars for her script. This script was not used. Another scenarist or group of scenarists evolved a second script which proved unsatisfactory. Mr. Robert Sherwood was then called in, at the going rate, and wrote a script that miraculously adhered closely to the book as written. Doubtless it was this startling fact that caused Mr. Sherwood's script to be thrown away. Mr. Laurence Stallings had a hand in the fourth, final and equally expensive effort.

I cannot vouch for the accuracy of the foregoing paragraph, and my experience has taught me that participants in the Hollywood scene are frequently unreliable in their utterances and promises. I can, however, vouch for the exact truthfulness of the statement that when the director, the cutters, the producers and the producers' relatives had finished with the film and released it as one would release a wounded duck, the dauntless and hard-boiled leader of the original Rangers had horribly turned into the sort of person who bursts into tears at a crucial moment of an arduous expedition; a woman character, shrewish and a harridan, had become a sweet and mealy-mouthed nonentity; all motivation had been discarded; the book's thesis had ceased to exist; its essential portion, on which the name of the book and the film were based, was ignored; and a Hollywood flavor was added by introducing a sequence stolen from *Arundel.*

So I stick gladly to writing; and though I repeat that it's useless to travel here and there, disseminating unpalatable facts to would-be authors, I have tried to demonstrate why no professional writer can explain adequately any part of his never-ending apprenticeship in a two-hour interview—or in two days, two weeks, two months or two years. The point is that it's a lifetime task. For me that task began at

Cornell. With some delightful exaggerations, its commencement has been described by an old friend, Romeyn Berry, for many years the editor of the *Cornell Alumni News,* and before that, when an undergraduate, the editor-in-chief of the Cornell humorous magazine, the *Widow.*

CHAPTER

2

For some years [wrote Romeyn Berry in the *Cornell Alumni News* late in 1941], there was a wooden box with a glass front firmly attached to the stonework in front of Morrill Hall. It had a postman's slot in its lower half. It bore the name of *The Widow*—nothing more —and was used both to display proofs of that publication's next cover by André Smith or Willard Straight, and as a place where such timid souls as Hendrik Willem Van Loon might deposit their youthful contributions to Literature and Art without disclosing their identity.

In my time, this box was opened periodically by the paper's business manager, George Jean Nathan, for the purpose of changing the poster, and occasionally by your reporter in the exercise of his editorial functions, to see if some unknown Gigadibs had miraculously turned up.

On one occasion in the fall of 1904, a mass of copy, all by the same hand, fell out of the box at our astonished feet. There was verse which both scanned and rhymed; light prose written in English that echoed the King James version of the Holy Bible rather than the Campus jargon of the period; editorials that flayed the policies of the University's Administration with a stark courage scarcely to be expected in a Freshman but two weeks out of the egg. This copy was written neatly in legible script fit to go without change to Messrs. Andrus and Church, the printers, and each piece bore the utterly meaningless name of Kenneth Lewis Roberts '08.

Somewhere in the years between, the author of *Rabble in Arms* and *Northwest Passage* has deftly dropped overboard and lost the middle name of "Lewis," but there abides with him yet the same lust to flay hypocrisy, double-dealing, stupidity, sordid self-interest, laziness, and everybody else who disagrees with him that he possessed in the fall of 1904. The critics who now regard this author as a flayer of some note are witnessing but the attenuated efforts of a weary artist. They should have seen Mr. Kenneth Roberts at flay when he was a Freshman!

The *Cornell Widow* announced Mr. Roberts's election to the board at the bottom of the editorial page in the Junior Week issue of February, 1905. That was pretty quick action on a Freshman, but the editors of that period were sufficiently astute to realize that it might be expedient to get this boy inside the fold, and working for glory, before he found out he could sell his stuff to somebody else for cash.

This reporter takes no credit for the discovery of a distinguished novelist. It is our only claim that without us to intercept his copy, and to chuck most of it in the wastebasket before it found its way up the back stairs to the Andrus and Church composing room and thence into print, Mr. Roberts would never have received a college education. He would have been fired to hell out of there by a maddened Faculty in the first three months of his career.

The late Teefy Crane[1] had been a practicing lawyer before he became a university professor, and he knew the law governing free speech and a free press in its applications to undergraduate journalism. Often have we heard him state it after one of Mr. Roberts's milder efforts had managed to squeeze through the editorial mesh: "I doubt if I, as Dean, possess the power to abolish the *Cornell Widow*. But there can be no doubt of my full power—nor of my present inclination to exercise it—of my full power, I repeat, to abolish you and every other member of the board, including the unlicked cub who wrote that peculiarly offensive attack on the management of the Forest City Livery and Boarding Stables."

But this article started out with the intention of becoming a review of Kenneth Roberts's latest novel, *Oliver Wiswell,* a story of the American Revolution written from the Tory angle. It's too late for that now, nor is another review necessary. The book had an advance sale in the trade of over 100,000 copies before its official date of publication, and doubtless the figure will have gone to double that before this notice appears in our little paper. Any praise that we could pile on that record of popular approval would be a work of supererogation.

Suffice it for the intimate family circle of Cornell that *Oliver Wiswell* does to the Third Reader's version of the Revolution's history, its portraits of the heroes and villains thereof, its sentimentalized romances, just what Mr. Roberts's Freshman opus did to the local reputation of the Forest City Livery and Boarding Stables: hauls off and kicks it in

---

[1]Dean, in 1904, of the College of Arts and Sciences of Cornell University.

the stomach; chokes it to death with authenticated facts. It's a pretty terrible book. All the time we were reading it, we felt frightened over what Teefy Crane might do to us about it; thankful, for his sake, that Mr. Roberts had now passed on to a point where the Faculty Committee on Student Conduct couldn't lay a hand on him any more, or beat him to a pulp with a blunt instrument.

§

I don't question Mr. Berry's veracity. Maybe it all happened that way. I'm sure of only one thing: even as a Cornell freshman I "wanted to write"; but what to write, or how to do it, was wholly beyond my understanding.

To evolve little short verses, little short paragraphs, little short burlesque playlets for the *Cornell Widow,* wasn't difficult. One who aspired to that form of expression needed only to go to the university library six nights a week and sedulously peruse the back files of the *Cornell Widow, Life, Puck* and *Judge:* then go ahead and do something along the lines suggested by that reading. This took time—so much time that I never understood how I contrived to accumulate sufficient information on the side to cope with examinations and acquire a degree. It proved to me, however, that almost any undergraduate in any American college of liberal arts ought to be able to do twice as much work as he *does* do, and do it in three years instead of in four. If not, he shouldn't be in a college at all. It seems to me that I learned practically nothing in college; but I learned enough to be wholly certain that my editorial duties on the *Cornell Widow* bore no faint resemblance to any form of writing that would satisfy my inner craving.

Thanks to Mr. Berry, I perpetrated a few acts of a musical comedy that he had started but, because of complications, not finished. It was performed with considerable éclat by the Cornell Masque before crowded houses during the Junior Week festivities; but the enthusiasm with which it was received was due, I am sure, to the muscular and astoundingly hard-faced chorus girls, and the manner in which the heroine, played by Mr. Lee Miller, looked yearningly into her lover's adoring eyes and soulfully bellowed, in a deep colorado maduro voice, "With love my maiden heart . . ."

I even wrote the words for two football songs. In 1946 Mr. Douglas Black, president of Doubleday and Company and a trustee of Columbia, took me to see Columbia play Cornell, and I found that those two songs were still being melodiously rendered by the Cornell band and somewhat raggedly sung by the Cornell cheering section. I ran over the words in my mind and shuddered in spite of the warm sun that made my overcoat oppressive. They were atrocious!

When I received a degree from Cornell, proving to doubters that I had what is familiarly known as an education, I knew no more about writing than I did about climbing Mount Everest.

ONE of the many bad features of the form of occupation known as writing is the painfully small return, even in the best of times, to most of those who practice it. The Authors' League has repeatedly published the figures. The average yearly earnings of ninety-five per cent of those who write for a living is two thousand dollars—and as a rule those favored with this magnificent reward are no tyros. They have been at it for years and know their way around.

As an undergraduate I had not concerned myself with the problem of keeping home and bank balance together while engaged in the calling on which I thought I had set my heart. A young man reared on the shores of Puget Sound drew cartoons for the *Widow* while I was its editor, and claimed to have considerable standing in the city of Seattle. He knew nothing whatever about writing, and so was quick to give advice about it. It was his belief that if a person was determined to be a teller of tales he could tell about the great Northwest with more vitality and élan than about anything in the effete East. He had, he claimed, access to persons of importance on the business and editorial staffs of the *Seattle Post-Intelligencer*. If I would come to Seattle, he said, he would use his influence, I could join the reportorial staff of the *Post-Intelligencer,* and we could go onward and upward in our profession, I penning powerful (as he put it) yarns about the Royal Northwest Mounted Police or some breed of Alaskan dog that had eluded the notice of Jack London, and he illustrating the—loathsome word—yarns with pen-and-ink drawings of the Frederic Remington school.

College undergraduates of all eras have been given to sketchy and short-circuited thinking; and undergraduates of my day were no exception.

They were sure that anyone with one thousand dollars in cash could make a million during a stock market crash.

The publication of a book, they thought, brought wealth and fame to the author.

Frequently they discussed the amount of income a college graduate should achieve before essaying the fatal march to the altar.

Few of the young men had ever earned enough to keep themselves in cigarettes, but their forums usually resulted in the agreement that no self-respecting college graduate could possibly venture into the field of matrimony unless he were earning five thousand dollars a year.

College men had all sorts of odd ideas: one of my roommates for a time was Mr. Joseph Newton Pew, Jr., later the eminent oil executive and political leader. Mr. Pew, as an undergraduate, was frequently the vortex of violent argument because of his thesis that if a man were within half a mile of the North Pole and saw a bear moving to the eastward, the bear was in reality east of the North Pole and not south of it.

So I saw nothing strange in considering myself practically a member of the staff of the *Post-Intelligencer*—until, while recuperating in Maine from the arduous undergraduate labors of my senior year, I discovered that my friend from Seattle was making no response to queries concerning my prospective duties as a reporter, and that time was passing with startling rapidity, hustling me toward the day when I must cease being a dependent and get down to earning my bed and board.

I never did receive an answer from him, and I had to do some straight thinking as to whether or not I would be wise to travel three thousand miles to a place I'd never seen on the chance of obtaining employment on a newspaper I'd never read.

The more I applied my college-trained mind to this problem, the more dubious it looked. After all, I had to eat, and I wasn't sure I could eat in Seattle; whereas in Boston I had friends who had attained prominence in leather circles—friends who would probably loan me a slice from a newly killed cow if I were starving.

So I abandoned all thought of literature and art, went to Boston, and immediately found myself an assistant office boy in a wholesale leather house, drawing the munificent sum of four dollars a week.

Leather, I think, would have been the last thing to which I'd have turned if I hadn't had a friend with whom I'd played baseball and golf. His father was the head of a leather business—not the one in which I had, as fond mothers sometimes put it, accepted a position. And he had a sister who had agreed to become Mrs. Roberts. Thus, in a vaguely collegiate manner, I visualized myself as the head of a rival leather house, effecting a union of great leather interests, laudably engaged in

supplying America and Europe with footgear, and incidentally brows-
ing among my books and tossing off chapter after chapter of a trenchant
study—*Leather Through the Ages.*

Almost the first thing I learned in the leather business was the falsity
of that accepted undergraduate belief that a college graduate has no
right to be married until he is earning five thousand dollars a year.
When I found myself on a salary of two hundred and eight dollars a
year I quickly lowered my sights from five thousand to twelve hundred.

The reasoning behind that barbarous Boston custom of forcing an
educated neophyte to start working in a bank, brokerage firm, leather
house or wool office at nothing—sometimes less than nothing—a week
was always obscure to me.

Ordinary office boys whose education had ceased at the end of their
first year in high school were employed at the princely wage of fifteen
dollars a week; but anyone with the advantage of a college education
was seldom paid more than four dollars a week when undertaking to
learn, as the saying went, the business.

Thus newly employed young men at Lee, Higginson & Company,
Kidder, Peabody & Company and other important Boston business institutions were often heard to say: "Come on, let's eat: the barrels must
have been put out at the Touraine."

No Bostonian was ever able to explain that custom to my satisfaction.
I think Boston just liked to make things as difficult as possible for as
many people as possible.

The four dollars a week wasn't the only thing I didn't like about my
leather venture. I particularly loathed the Shoulder Book. In leather
circles, the finished product is divided into sides, shoulders and rough
bellies, and the amount of those commodities remaining in stock at the
end of each day must be reported to the front office and entered in
ledgers, so that the salesmen may know how much they can dispense
on the following day.

It was my daily duty to post all those ledgers, and the head shipper
never got around to counting up his shoulders until late in the afternoon, when everyone else had gone home; and I, eager to be off and
think confused thoughts about wanting to write, damned the Shoulder
Book with scorching ferocity.

I intensely disliked the odor of leather, which seemed to linger in the
garments at all times, and even to flavor everything I ate; the daily
lunches of kidney beans and coffee at the nearby Waldorf Lunch were
repellent; and the problem of existing on four dollars a week was not
only painful: it was maddening.

I break out in a sweat, even now, at the recollection of the inner fury, the flaming resentment, that filled me, night after night, when I dwelt upon that miserable four dollars a week, and upon a state of society too witless to force employers to pay more than four dollars a week for even the most rudimentary and unintelligent form of labor.

I think that weekly four-dollar pay check so infuriated me that my yearning for a literary career evaporated for a time. Then I learned that the *Bohemian Magazine* was contemplating a series of stories on humorous journalism in American colleges; and when I wrote persuasively to its editor, he readily consented to let me do the one on the *Cornell Widow*. It was to be four thousand words long, and the emolument was to be seventy-five dollars. Since I was, to put it mildly, unripe, the production of four thousand words seemed to me almost as laborious a chore as evolving *War and Peace*—and almost as important; and I'm speaking conservatively when I say I made hard going of it.

Once a person begins to have a faint understanding of writing, he thinks nothing of sitting at a desk for eight or ten hours every day, and for months on end; but of course I was ignorant of that. Like most of those who yearn to be Kiplings, I had a vague idea that people wrote when they felt like it, or on rainy afternoons, or when they were "inspired"; so I niggled and twiddled with that four-thousand-word piece for three months before I considered it fit to print—and even then I was a bad judge.

For a long time I had the impression that this was the only form of composition I did during my association with the leather industry; but long years afterward I received a letter from a young lady secretary who had worked in the same leather emporium, and had sympathetically observed my writhings and fumings.

She had recently seen, she wrote me, one of the Shoulder Books in which I had entered endless and wearisome columns. The book was on display in the office which had so grudgingly paid me four dollars a week, opened to the flyleaf, on which I had inscribed:

> Bitterly I sit and wonder,
> With each day that I grow older,
> Why the Lord in Heaven didn't
> Make the cow without a shoulder.

In a month or two I was given an assistant, a companionable young man recently graduated from Amherst. He also, by a series of accidents, had stumbled into the leather business with the idea of learning it; so he became assistant office boy at the conventional weekly four dollars, I was raised to head office boy at six dollars, and the former head office boy was made clerk, with a desk of his own and the regal salary of sixteen dollars.

My assistant and I were united in our detestation of the odor of leather, and I made no secret of my growing desire to abandon it and devote all my time to the formation of sentences. This feeling even persisted when the company for which I worked decided to open an office in St. Louis and recklessly proposed sending me there to take charge.

My friend from Amherst gave this state of affairs considerable thought, and then bluntly said that if I were out of his way he would certainly be in a position to draw down six dollars instead of four, and might even get the St. Louis position for himself. His family, he said, were long-time friends of Mr. Edwin A. Grozier, who owned the *Boston Post*. Mr. Grozier, he told me, was a nice man: one who, if tactfully informed that he could further the fortunes of a family friend by merely allowing a newly graduated collegian to become a reporter on his newspaper, would probably prove agreeable and I would be in a better position to become an author than I'd be if I remained among shoulders and rough bellies.

I embraced his suggestion instantly and with fervor; and that night, when I had made my last entry in that accursed Shoulder Book, my friend and I threaded our way through the paper trucks that blocked Newspaper Row, mounted a worn flight of stairs to an office bearing the sign "Editor and Publisher," brashly knocked upon the door of the supreme authority of the *Post,* and walked in on Mr. Grozier as if he were no one out of the ordinary.

Mr. Grozier was a small, brownish man who sat at a large desk, looking down at the roaring traffic of lower Washington Street and across at the chalk-written blackboard bulletins of the *Post's* deadly rival, the *Boston Globe.*

Since I knew nothing about newspapers or writing, Mr. Grozier at that time seemed to me just another undersized party, rather delicate and plaintive-looking, perhaps because he wore a straggly mustache, had a rug over his knees, and peered benevolently at me over the tops of his glasses.

Later, when I had become aware that he was a newspaper genius, an ex-secretary to the great Joseph Pulitzer, and the creator of a newspaper property whose miraculous circulation baffled the most astute New York circulation managers, I found it impossible to enter his presence without shivering slightly at the shocking ignorance and temerity I had displayed on the occasion of our first meeting.

But, as my friend had said, Mr. Grozier was a nice man; and instead of having me tossed out on my ear, or brusquely telling me to see the city editor or Sunday editor, he inquired blandly as to my reasons, if any, for thinking I was qualified for newspaper work; listened as though I were saying something worth hearing; then amiably observed that if I cared to accept a position on the staff of the *Sunday Post* at eighteen dollars a week, he felt sure his Sunday editor could find a place for me.

If I cared to! Would a drowning man care for a life preserver? Would a starving man care for a T-bone steak? I lost little time in bidding farewell to my friends in the leather district, shaking the odor of leather from my clothes, and repairing to the offices of the *Sunday Post;* for at last, instead of "wanting to write," my heart's desire was about to be realized—or that's what I thought.

§

The offices of the *Post* at that time were a sort of rabbit warren of ancient, dusty houses joined by labyrinthine passages, the whole underlain by subterranean chambers tunneled deep into the rock to hold the presses; and of all the dark and dingy rooms in those dark and dingy buildings, the Sunday Room was the darkest and dingiest.

Somehow, too, the type of news stories to which the Sunday editors of those days were addicted struck me as even darker and dingier than the room.

The *Sunday Post* was convinced (it seemed to me) that its readers were passionately interested in such things as giant squashes, two-headed calves, hundred-and-five-year-old women who ascribed their longevity to the daily chewing of an ounce of tobacco or the currycombing of a horse.

I was completely uninterested in such manifestations; and when I sat before a battered typewriter and painstakingly tried to describe them in a fascinating manner and at unwarranted length, I found myself oppressed by an overwhelming feeling of futility. The deadline on a Sunday paper, too, isn't twelve or half past one o'clock in the morning, as on a daily paper, but comes only on Friday night. Thus a reporter for a Sunday newspaper doesn't work under pressure, as he would on a daily: he dallies over his assignments and has too much time to brood over the insignificance of himself and the so-called "Sunday features" for which forests must be destroyed.

I felt hampered, too, by the frequent warnings I received from the assistant Sunday editor against intruding humor into my accounts of two-headed calves and four-yolked eggs. If I persisted, I'd be labeled a "one-armed man," fit to deal only with frivolous subjects. Then no city editor would work me on Big Stories.

For me the brightest day in the week was Saturday, when the Sunday staff was instructed to report to the City Room and put themselves at the disposal of the city editor.

I quickly made several important discoveries during those Saturdays in the City Room. Word seemingly had got out that I had gone to work on the *Post* by direct orders of Mr. Grozier; and the deduction had promptly been made by those in authority that I was not only somehow related to Mr. Grozier, but probably dined with him several times a week to dispense office chitchat. Thus I was viewed with alarm and suspicion: I might, perhaps, be a stool pigeon.

I found, too, that there was a deep-seated distrust, in Boston newspaper offices, of persons with college educations. They were thought to be afraid of hard work: lacking in reportorial stamina. I never wholly understood the reason for this aversion to college graduates, and it faded, eventually, to such a degree that Dartmouth and even Harvard men came to be tolerated in all Boston newspaper offices; but for a year or so I couldn't pass the den in which the staff photographers played with their pans, stinks and chemicals without hearing ironic shouts, within that noisome cave, of "Rah, rah, rah; college!"

This alarm and suspicion, however, did not extend to the assistant city editor, a young man who had bounced almost straight from office boy to the city desk by virtue of locating the rammed steamship *Republic* in a fog off No Man's Land and scooping the town with an account of the disaster. This young man was Mr. John F. Royal, who later became Midwest director of the Keith-Albee interests: then went on up to high office in the National Broadcasting Company.

Mr. Royal was in no way interested in my supposed relationship to Mr. Grozier or anyone else, but he seemed puzzled by the almost unheard-of spectacle of anyone from the Sunday Room coming without complaint to the City Room on Saturday and working until the paper went to bed. He soon requested the loan of a fuzzy tweed overcoat I had recently acquired; and on the following Sunday he introduced me to the unrivaled Sunday onion soup and conventional Raines Law sandwiches at the old Province House—British Headquarters during the early days of the American Revolution. The sandwiches were for display only, but we braved the displeasure of the waiters and ate them, along with the soup, in the same room from which Tom Buell stole Sir William Howe's wine and telescope in *Oliver Wiswell*.

Mr. Royal pointed out to me that he officiated at the city desk from 10 A.M. until 1 P.M. each day, after which the regular city editor appeared on the scene, and that during those three hours reporters were scarce as hen's teeth, since few of them deigned to rise from their couches until high noon. Yet if any sort of story broke while he was on the desk, he explained, he couldn't wait for the arrival of the city editor; he had to lay hands on a reporter by fair means or foul and jump him out on the story.

I took his words to heart, and every Saturday thereafter I was in the City Room promptly at ten o'clock, eagerly anticipating the fifteen-hour day before me. Thanks to Mr. Royal's habit of finding stories that couldn't wait for the city editor, and to his repeated admonition of "Don't be afraid to josh 'em," I spent the first five days of the week looking forward to Saturday, and all day Sunday dreading my return to the dreary purlieus of the Sunday Room.

This unhappy situation was complicated by a difficulty with the Business Office. The Business Office, in addition to selling advertising space to various organizations and amusement enterprises, gave away additional space in the form of stories about the advertised product, right in among the reading matter. Miss Jane Cowl was then at the beginning of her brilliant career; and when the *Post* sold space to the management of the theater at which Miss Cowl was playing, it did so with the understanding that an interview with Miss Cowl would be printed just as if it were genuine news; so the advertising manager sent up to the Sunday editor and requested that I be assigned to this Business Office Must.

I went to Miss Cowl's hotel and had a long and pleasant chat with her, after which, in line with Mr. Royal's suggestion, I joshed Miss Cowl for a column and a half. When the results were delivered to the Business Office, there were dark looks and head shakings. At that period no soubrette had feelings as susceptible or as easily hurt as Boston advertisers. When accidents took place in department stores or hotels, no Boston newspaper ever, ever ventured to publish the names of the hotels or stores. Any disconsolate or introverted unfortunate who wished to disappear completely and unrecorded from Boston's tribulations and repressions needed only to cut his throat or swallow a tot of arsenic in one of the thronged aisles of Jordan Marsh & Company or William Filene's Sons & Company; for the affair would be completely ignored by all Boston newspapers. And for a Boston newspaper to mention an advertiser or anyone connected with an advertiser in a tone that even hinted at levity was almost as unthinkable as to speak slightingly of any form of religion. But eventually a representative of the Business Office timorously conferred with the theater management about the Cowl interview, and since the management saw nothing harmful or libelous about it, the story was reluctantly printed.

A few days later I was again summoned to the Business Office. My story on Miss Cowl, the business manager said, hadn't been at all bad. Miss Cowl had liked it: the theater had liked it: *Post* readers had liked it. Consequently he had decided to let me do more of the same; and as a starter would I step up to the Touraine and interview the gentleman now playing at the Tremont Theater.

Somewhat to my surprise, and certainly to the business manager's annoyance, I refused the assignment on the ground that this was a press agent's work, that press agents too often had to misrepresent their wares, and that I didn't want to be a press agent. The business manager, huffy at finding his generosity unappreciated, complained bitterly to the Sunday editor, who also seemed to think my attitude was unreasonable and incomprehensible.

They were so unpleasant about it that I thought a little about attempting to storm that frowning Boston newspaper citadel, the *Transcript;* but I hesitated to do so because I felt that I was congenitally unfitted to write ponderous columns about supremely uninteresting subjects—and all *Transcript* reporters had to be able to do that.

My restless mood was at its height when I had a call from an acquaintance of long standing, the head of an investment firm on State Street, asking if I'd come in to see him. When I did so, I found that he was one of a group entrusted by New York, New Haven & Hartford magnates with the task of acquiring as unostentatiously as possible a controlling interest in the stock of the Boston & Maine Railroad. He needed the assistance of someone who could keep his mouth shut. Newspapermen, he'd heard, had learned to do that, and he wondered whether I could get a three months' leave from the *Post* and help him out. If so, he said, he'd double my *Post* salary.

The opportunity of seeing State Street from the inside was so tempting that I went at once to the Sunday editor, Mr. Wingate, told him all about it, and asked for a three months' leave. Mr. Wingate said sourly that he wouldn't stand in the way of my going but that he couldn't promise I'd be taken back at the end of the three months.

That didn't seem wholly reasonable to me, so I bade him a polite farewell, went next door to Mr. Grozier's office, and apprehensively laid the situation before him. Mr. Grozier, kind as ever, told me to go right ahead; come and see him, he said, when I was ready to return: he was sure Mr. Wingate would have a place for me.

When I did come back, at the end of the three months, I presented myself before Mr. Wingate at an early hour, long before Mr. Grozier had arrived to blanket his knees and scan the *Globe's* blackboards. I wasn't at all surprised when Mr. Wingate eyed me owlishly and said there was no vacancy at the moment on the staff of the *Sunday Post*. I wasn't even sufficiently interested to tell him that Mr. Grozier had authorized my leave of absence. Instead of that I hurried to the City Room and asked the city editor, Mr. Charles H. Lincoln, whether he could use me as a reporter.

Mr. Lincoln eventually became my good and staunch friend; but in those days he had little use for soft-handed, soft-headed young squirts who had done practically nothing except be a vast expense and doubtless severe cross to their parents; so he stared at me coldly and asked why I wasn't working for the *Sunday Post*.

I told him I'd been on a leave of absence for three months and that Mr. Wingate no longer had room for me on the *Sunday Post*.

Mr. Lincoln raised his eyebrows. "In that case," he said, "I can't do anything for you. If I did, I might hurt Mr. Wingate's feelings. It would be going over his head."

To my way of thinking, this made no sense. I liked reporting, and I was willing to work hard at it; and, having learned how to coax a battered typewriter into grinding out column after column of copy without disintegrating, I saw no reason why a quick-tempered editor with a temporarily distorted sense of justice should keep me from that far-off goal I hoped to reach.

One of the first things a reporter learns in a City Room is the uselessness of arguing with a city editor; so I did what I should have done in the beginning: went down the dark and narrow stairs to Washington Street, drew a deep breath, went up the slightly more spacious stairs leading to Mr. Grozier's office, and was admitted by his charming and sympathetic secretary, Miss Louise Marston, who seemed to sense that I brought my troubles to Mr. Grozier with profound reluctance.

My three months' leave had finished yesterday, I told Mr. Grozier, and I had come back to the Sunday Room only to find that there was no vacancy: that I'd then gone to Mr. Lincoln, and found he couldn't take me on, because if he did, Mr. Wingate's feelings might be hurt.

He sighed and said, "You should have come to see me before you went to Mr. Wingate."

I said I knew it, but hadn't wanted to bother him.

"Well," he said, "don't make that mistake when you're on a story. Always follow instructions. By the way, you don't want to go back to the Sunday Room, do you?"

When I said I certainly didn't, he reached for a slip of copy paper and wrote, "Dear Mr. Lincoln, Please put Mr. Roberts on the city staff at eighteen dollars a week. E.A.G."

I felt pretty uncomfortable about the whole thing, but I was determined not to be thrown out of the sort of work I wanted to do unless there was a better reason than one man's personal dislike. So I had no option except to climb those dusty stairs to the City Room and place Mr. Grozier's note before Mr. Lincoln.

He looked at it and then at me, and I never saw a face grow red so quickly.

I averted my eyes and waited tensely for the explosion. When none came, I went softly to the far end of the City Room, straightened the tangled keys of a typewriter, reversed its tattered ribbon, and hammered out a few paragraphs for the "Observant Citizen" column.

I don't know whether Mr. Lincoln ever mentioned that note to anyone. He certainly never mentioned it to me, and I never spoke of it myself—since I wanted to stay as close to the linotype machines as I possibly could.

CHAPTER

4

THAT little passage with Mr. Lincoln had its beneficial side. Mr. Royal gave me regular news assignments early every morning; and if I unearthed the necessary information and returned in time to write it before five o'clock in the afternoon, Mr. Lincoln took good care to see that I didn't remain idle. He chased me right out on another story—and those he picked for me, in the beginning, weren't the things a reporter would have chosen if he had any say about it.

I sensed almost immediately that the labor expended in tracking down insignificant items dealing with matters of supreme dullness would be completely wasted unless sufficient detail could be introduced to make them lively.

For example: Mr. Lincoln eyed me satirically late one winter afternoon and handed me a classified advertisement clipped from the *Transcript*—an advertisement offering a reward for the return of a pair of trousers.

As a piece of news it wasn't overly promising, but I felt there must be some way in which I could extract more from it than Mr. Lincoln's derisive eye seemed to think I could.

On the following day Mr. Lincoln expressed neither surprise nor resentment when he found the pants story starting on page 1 and breaking over onto page 6 for a column and a half. It read:

LOST—*A pair of pants, on Linden or Harvard Sts., Brookline. Finder will be rewarded by returning them to 15 Linden St.*
                                                        —(*From Sat. and Sun. papers.*)

George E. Page, who resides at 15 Linden Street, Brookline, has lost his pants, and doesn't know where to find them; but the mystery of the lost Page pants is greater now than it was on Sunday morning; for

Mr. Page, still minus his pants, is loath to have the world further acquainted with his loss.

In order that Mr. Page might be assisted in tracing the elusive but necessary pants, a *Post* reporter called his home on the telephone yesterday.

Mr. Page spoke into the transmitter and was questioned regarding his lost pants. But Mr. Page said that he really did not care to say anything about the pants, since he had already paid for as much publicity as he desired. He accordingly hung up the receiver.

In order that the mystery of the missing pants might be solved, the *Post* reporter took a car and journeyed to the Page home. On a telephone pole at the corner of Harvard and Linden Streets, where an inquirer disembarks to reach the residence of the Pages, was an oblong white card. On this card, which was surrounded by several amateur detectives, was again set forth the tale of the missing Page pants, together with the promise of reward, should return of same be made to 15 Linden Street. The amateur detectives ventured the information that they had looked everywhere for clues, such as pants buttons, but that the neighborhood was singularly unproductive of traces.

Passing further along Linden Street, in the direction of the Page home, the investigator encountered a large policeman.

"How about the robbery?" the policeman was asked by the investigator.

The investigator was rewarded by a searching stare from the policeman, who finally queried: "Do you mean them pants?"

On being told that "them pants" were those concerning which the question was asked, the policeman expectorated disgustedly and said: "Say, ain't he got another pair?"

Leaving the policeman, or "bull," as he is designated in Brookline parlance, the investigator proceeded to the Page home, where he rang the bell and hunted vainly for a doormat bearing the word "Welcome."

Mrs. Page appeared at the door to answer questions; but on learning that the investigator represented a newspaper, she informed him that Mr. Page had left the house for a time, and that in his absence she thought that it would be better for her to say nothing, especially regarding the subject of Mr. Page's lost pants.

"Do not think, though, that Mr. Page hasn't another pair of pants," said Mrs. Page, "because he has. He does not want anything more said about his lost pants, so you will please excuse me if I say nothing about them."

Mrs. Page was asked why it was that neither she nor her husband was willing to utter concerning the pants.

"Well," said Mrs. Page, "I know you want to write something sensational about them, and put big headlines over it. That is just what neither George nor I wants to happen."

"You are in error," Mrs. Page was told. "Nothing is wished except to write something regarding the pants—something heart-throbby and serious that will call them to the attention of the people of Brookline, and start them looking around for stray pants resembling those which Mr. Page lost."

Mrs. Page, however, continued to reiterate that somebody wished to write something sensational about the pants; then to place the sensational writings upon the front page of a newspaper under large, black headlines.

When asked whether she would prefer to have something humorous written about the pants rather than something sensational, Mrs. Page intimated that there was nothing humorous—particularly to Mr. Page —in the loss of his pants, and that it would be next to impossible to write anything humorous regarding them.

Mrs. Page then wished to be promised that, in case anything was written concerning the pants, the names of all persons connected with the loss would be suppressed. Seventeen minutes were thereupon utilized by the investigator in showing Mrs. Page the futility of writing anything concerning the loss of pants and not mentioning the name of the person who had possessed the pants prior to their loss.

The pros and cons of the case were thoroughly argued, and Mrs. Page finally consented to relate the story of the loss of the pants, in the hope that some reader of the *Post* might encounter and recognize the pants, and thereby effect their return to the Page home at 15 Linden Street, Brookline.

It seems that the pants, which were of the striped worsted variety commonly worn with a dark coat and vest, were comparatively new, and essential to the successful wearing of the dark coat and vest. "They were expensive pants," explained Mrs. Page, "and they were part of a suit. With them the suit was a very good one; but without them——" And by a gesture of her arms, Mrs. Page suggested the worthlessness of the coat and vest without the pants.

On Friday evening, directly after dinner, Mr. Page inspected his wardrobe and found a pair of shoes in need of repair. He also found that his dark coat and the fine, nearly new worsted pants which went with it could stand pressing.

It was snowing.

Mr. Page put on his overcoat, and took his shoes in his right hand—the shoes which needed repairing—and over his left arm he hung his dark coat and the striped worsted pants.

Then he set forth through the snow from his home at 15 Linden Street, walking directly to the corner of Harvard and Linden Streets. At Harvard Street he turned to the right and proceeded to the shop of the cobbler on Harvard Street. Arrived there, he gave the cobbler the requisite directions for the proper repair of his shoes.

When he emerged from the cobbler's, the dark coat and the pants—the lost pants—were hanging over his left arm. At least Mr. Page had no reason to think otherwise. The pants, to be accurate, were hanging over the coat in such a position as to blow unrestrainedly in the light breeze which accompanied the snow.

On emerging from the cobbler's, he turned to the left and walked down Harvard Street toward Brookline Village, intending to leave the dark coat and the striped pants at the tailor's. But just as he was about to step into the tailoring establishment, he noticed a lightness about the bundle over his arm which aroused his suspicions. Looking down, his suspicions were confirmed.

The pants—the striped worsted pants so essential to the well-being of the dark coat and vest—was, or were, gone.

Immediately Mr. Page retraced his steps in the snow, looking for the pants; but the snow revealed no traces of the pants.

He re-entered the cobbler's shop and asked for the pants. The cobbler knew of no pants except those draped upon his own limbs.

Mr. Page returned observantly along Harvard Street to the little home on Linden Street, but still no trace of the pants greeted his eager eye.

And despite advertisements in the greatest papers of Boston, the whereabouts and the manner of disappearance of the lost Page pants are still a mystery.

§

I think Mr. Lincoln had no intention of embarrassing me when he handed me another small clipping late one rainy afternoon—so late that he must have known that the Quincy Market and Faneuil Hall fish stalls would be closed for the day.

I suspect he was merely tired of seeing me seated at a reporter's bench, doing nothing, and thought a little brisk exercise on wet pavements would be beneficial to both of us. The clipping was an ordinary bit of

waterfront news from the *Boston Globe* stating that a record-breaking
codfish weighing seventy-one pounds had been landed at T Wharf by
the schooner *Manomet,* Captain Price, and was on display at Quincy
Market.

"Here," Mr. Lincoln said, as he handed me the clipping, "just run
down and get the details on this."

As I had anticipated, the Quincy Market fish stalls were dark and
deserted, so I returned to the office wondering what details, other than
those published in the *Globe,* I could have found out about that
seventy-one-pound cod, even if the fish stalls had been open and the
fish itself displayed upon an outsized cake of ice.

I could see that Mr. Lincoln was in a choleric mood when I re-
entered the City Room, and I suspected that if I admitted I hadn't seen
the fish and consequently had no story, I'd find myself catching the six
o'clock train from the North Station and spending the night in Manchester, New Hampshire, or Ascutney, Vermont, interviewing someone reputed to have a method for inducing hens to lay square eggs.

So when Mr. Lincoln said, "Did you get it?" I said, "Yes," and sat
down before my rattletrap typewriter to bring the *Post's* clientele up to
date on large codfish.

On the wall before me was tacked one of a score of similar signs
displayed in all parts of the City Room. It read, in 80-point capitals,
"ACCURACY, ACCURACY, ACCURACY."

As I contemplated the sign and thought about that tiresome cod, the
time seemed ripe to touch lightly on the subject of accuracy as well
as on that of fish.

Thanks to Mr. Lincoln, a closed fish market and the prying nature
of Mr. John Royal, wavelets from that story lapped up on many people
and in unexpected places.

About half a column, I thought, would adequately cover the codfish;
but after I'd finished two paragraphs I found Mr. Clarence Finn, the
copy and office boy, sighing behind my ear and saying, "Mr. Lincoln
wants to know how long that story's going to run."

Still mindful of Ascutney, Manchester and the square egg, I told him
that, in the immortal words of John Paul Jones, I had just begun to
write.

It seemed to me that Clarence was breathing down my neck at the
end of each paragraph, asking if I was almost finished; so I kept on and
on until Clarence made the firm announcement, "Mr. Lincoln says he'll
take that story the way it is."

This was what he got:

A codfish measuring five feet three inches from snout to tail and weighing 71 pounds dressed was caught by the fishing schooner *Manomet* and pitchforked into Boston yesterday.

So far as is known, this codfish is the largest ever caught and brought home. It is on exhibition at Quincy Market.

The eminent authority on fish, Professor Morton Kilgallen, estimated the age of this enormous cod as forty-seven years.

"I base my estimate of this fish's age on the length of his whisker," said Professor Kilgallen to a *Post* reporter. "I would unhesitatingly give him ten years per inch."

The cod's whisker was four and seven-tenths inches long and was slightly mossy around the edges.

When Professor Kilgallen was approached by the *Post* reporter for an interview on this large cod, he expressed himself as being unwilling to talk for publication.

"I have a fear of being misquoted," said he, "and especially of being misquoted concerning codfish, which have been the object of my deepest study during the past few years. What I do not know about the codfish, from infancy to maturity, is not worth a hoot. Consequently I would not care to be misquoted."

"You need have no fear," Professor Kilgallen was assured. "Accuracy is the watchword of the hour, and everything that you say regarding this enormous fish shall be faithfully transcribed."

"Very well, then," said Professor Kilgallen, filling his pipe with tobacco seaweed from the Farallon Islands, and scratching a match on one of the clamshell seahorses with which his vest was appliquéd, "Very well, then; I will consent to give you an interview regarding this very interesting large codfish.

"Unlike the human race, the cod weighs more when undressed than when dressed. This being the case I should say that if this unusually large cod weighed 71 pounds dressed, it must have weighed nearly 100 pounds when undressed, or at the moment of being drawn from its native element."

Professor Kilgallen here blew a smoke ring and thrust an emphatic forefinger through it. "If you do not believe me," said he, "you can confirm my statement from the man who caught the cod in question."

Captain Price of the schooner *Manomet* later confirmed the statement of Professor Kilgallen.

"To the best of my knowledge," Professor Kilgallen resumed, "this is the largest codfish ever caught. In 1871 James Thornton of the schooner *Isobel,* while fishing off the Georges Banks, connected with a codfish. Mr. Thornton was asleep at the time and had the line fastened to his wrist. He was awakened by a terrific blow on the head and found he had been pulled into the bow of his dory, which was forging through the water at a stupefying rate. He removed his vest and shoes and battled with the monster for twenty-eight minutes.

"The leviathan was at last hauled to the surface, fastened to the bow of his dory by a short rope, and forced to draw the dory seven miles back to the *Isobel.*

"When hoisted to the deck, the fish was found to be a cod weighing 77 pounds undressed. This fish, so far as I know, led the league up to the time of the capture of the very large cod of which we are speaking.

"We have many records of men making unusual catches, some of which I myself have investigated. I have often heard of the catching of a 100-pound cod, and have looked into the matter, only to find that the cod escaped before it could be drawn into the boat, or else that the man who caught it had been somewhat soused and had been so staggered by the struggles of his enormous catch that he let it go free before it could be weighed.

"Contrary to general opinion, the age of a codfish is not told from looking at his teeth, although some old salts claim that they can, and with a certain amount of reason, tell the age of a cod by examining his molars.

"I, personally, am strongly of the opinion that the age of a cod can only be determined by the length of his whisker. This is, of course, a precarious method, but the only infallible one. It is a well-known fact that when two codfish are battling for the possession of some particularly fine kelp patch, each cod will attempt to affix himself to the whisker of the other, and to remove it if possible.

"The loss of the whisker seems to outlaw the cod among his kind. I have known instances of codfish who deliberately committed suicide by swimming up on a beach and exposing themselves to the air, after suffering the loss of their whiskers.

"The codfish, from earliest infancy, is adorned with the whisker. The mother cod lays her eggs and keeps them warm by constantly breathing warm water upon them. Since the cod is a cold-blooded fish, this is one of the hardest things that the mother cod has to do. She is always successful, however, and soon the little codfish peck their way from their eggshells, each adorned with a tiny whisker.

"While the cod's whisker can, generally speaking, be regarded as developing at the rate of one inch every ten years, it should never be forgotten that the juvenile cod seldom becomes a ground-feeder until its twelfth year. So for the first twelve years, cod-whiskers are untrammeled and may be overdeveloped for their owners' age.

"After the twelfth year, however, the cod clings close to the bottom of the ocean, and the whisker is constantly worn down. Consequently, at the age of twenty, the whisker is exactly two inches long, so far as I have been able to determine from my experiments. At thirty it is three inches long, the growth during the third decade and subsequent decades varying almost not at all.

"Since, therefore, the whisker of this enormous cod is four and seven-tenth inches in length, I deduce that he is exactly forty-seven years of age. If I am in error regarding this, I would be glad to enter into a debate with any competent authority concerning it.

"A codfish which has attained the age of forty-seven years has acquired many unusual habits, as I have determined. For one thing the old cod acquires the habit of carrying a small stone in its mouth at all times when not eating. This habit becomes as confirmed as the opium or smoking habit among the human race. It results merely from a wish to keep the teeth and the interior of the mouth in good condition.

"When about to seize its food, the big cod drops the stone to the bottom. After it has eaten, it will return to the spot where it dropped the stone and hunt for it, sometimes for days at a time. This was twice proved by the Duca degli Abruzzi, in his study of ocean life. He marked the stones and released the fish. Three years later he dragged that locality with nets, and captured both of the cod. Each one was carrying the same loose stone in his mouth.

"The aged cod also acquires the habit of eating seaweed. Each cod may have a preference for a certain sort of seaweed. A cod will travel miles for a snack from his favorite seaweed bush. This is a well-known fact.

"I should say that a cod weighing 71 pounds dressed could be made into 821 fish balls. Its head alone would make enough rich fish chowder for 27 persons.

"If my remarks are not misquoted, I shall be glad at any time to tell the readers of the *Post* about the habits and customs of any sort of fish except the purple toble fish, which arouses in me an intense antipathy."

From where I sat I could see Mr. Lincoln angrily accept the codfish story from young Mr. Finn and fumingly peruse it.

Mr. Lincoln was obviously exasperated by Professor Kilgallen, and by the professor's opinions on accuracy and on marine flora and fauna, because his face grew redder and redder as he turned over sheet after sheet. When he'd finished, he glared at Mr. Royal, who was nonchalantly pretending to search the *Evening Transcript* for expandable items at a nearby desk.

Then Mr. Lincoln, seeing the night city editor approaching, contemptuously dropped the story in the wastebasket, put on his coat and hat and went frowningly home.

When Mr. Royal had given the night city editor a résumé of the day's activities, he reached into the wastebasket for the wad of copy paper tossed there by Mr. Lincoln.

I watched him read it. He looked dissatisfied, as he usually did when in repose; but as he neared the end he set off toward the night desk and the managing editor's office.

I was consumed, as the saying goes, by curiosity; but Mr. Royal was in one of his more remote moods and did nothing to enlighten me.

I was left in darkness until the first edition began to roll. Then I learned that Mr. Royal had taken the story to Mr. Carberry, the managing editor, and sat on the corner of his desk until he'd read it. Having read it, Mr. Carberry wrote across the upper right-hand corner, "Must— C.B.C.," and tossed it to the night desk for a head and crossheads.

Thanks to that potent "Must—C.B.C.," the night desk withheld its murderous blue pencil; and when Mr. Carberry went to the composing room around midnight, Professor Kilgallen hit the front page, along with a murder, Governor Foss, a two-headed calf and other important matters.

§

The *New York World,* at that time, was even more interested in stories of five-legged calves and showers of fish in Winsted, Connecticut, than was the *Sunday Post* in elderly widows who had reached the age of one hundred and seven by virtue of chewing plug tobacco.

When the *Post* containing the Kilgallen story reached New York, the *World's* Boston correspondent received a sharp telegram from his paper's city editor, rebuking him for letting the *Post* beat him to Professor Kilgallen.

The *World* representative was naturally distressed. He failed to find the professor listed in the telephone directory or the city directory; so he went to the Lagrange Street Police Station for help, having deduced from something in the professor's narrative that his habitat was in that station's purlieus.

The police lieutenant in charge at Lagrange Street at once issued instructions to his men to scour the district for Kilgallens, male or female.

But when the *World* man returned to his office, he found another brusque telegram from New York, listing a set of questions to be propounded to Professor Kilgallen, the answers to be the exclusive property of the *New York World*.

The correspondent, in desperation, turned to Mr. Carberry, who assured him that the entire output of the professor had been contracted for by the *Boston Post*.

When the *World* man showed signs of dissatisfaction and hinted that he would, if pressed, obtain the professor's address from Mr. Grozier, since Mr. Grozier had once worked for Mr. Pulitzer, Mr. Carberry broke down and revealed the truth.

The *World* man was justifiably annoyed because of the telegraphic rebukes he had received, and because of the additional tart messages that would reach him before the matter was satisfactorily explained to his superiors in New York.

Two days later Mr. Carberry, small, slender, deaf and a little stooped, came softly from his office to prowl through the City Room, according to his nightly custom.

He stopped beside me, looking absent-minded and apologetic. "The Chief liked that piece about the old professor," he whispered. "He wants some more. He wants about three a week for a while. I told Lincoln not to work you on news on Mondays, Thursdays and Saturdays."

So Professor Kilgallen developed a number of peculiar attributes. He was elected a Fellow of the Royal Geographical Society and lengthened his name to Professor Morton Kilgallen, F.R.S., of Balliol College; he was addicted to indulging secretly in small hookers of cod-liver oil; he possessed a pet sculpin to which he had grafted a set of human dentures, thus enabling the sculpin to eat ham and eggs; he smoked a pipe made from sturgeons' scales that gave off an effluvium which his wife found obnoxious; he wore vests of Bahama flax embroidered with a motley array of denizens of the deep; he connected electric eels to his lighting system, thereby cutting down his electricity bills; he became the author of several monographs, the most noteworthy being *The Pollywogs of Kappadokia;* he maintained a private aquarium-hospital in his home in which he treated sick halibuts for sunburn, practiced phlebotomy on sculpins with gastric ulcers, and studied the love life of the lobster.

CHAPTER

5

PROFESSOR KILGALLEN was helpful to me in more ways than one. Some months before his first appearance in the *Post,* in the autumn of 1910, I had hesitantly broached to Mr. Carberry the delicate matter of increasing my weekly stipend. I was modest about it, merely hinting that I could eat more nourishingly and work more energetically if I were to receive twenty dollars a week instead of eighteen.

Mr. Carberry, who had been a great reporter before he became managing editor of the *Post,* was more than a little deaf, but with surprising frequency he miraculously contrived to catch remote whisperings in their entirety. He had difficulty in hearing my suggestion until I'd repeated it several times; and when he finally seemed to understand a little, he shook his head doubtfully, as if implying that the *Boston Post* might be bankrupted if forced to bear any such additional financial burden.

I found out later, however, that he added my name to the list of reporters and editors who were constantly clamoring for raises, and took it to Mr. Grozier. He had indicated to Mr. Grozier the names of those whose requests should be partially or wholly satisfied unless the *Post* wished to dispense with their services; and in the interests of economy he indicated those who might be kept waiting for yet a little while. I was one of the latter.

Mr. Grozier, it seemed, had looked mournfully at Mr. Carberry when he came to my name and said, "Well, Carberry, I guess you'd better give it to him. You remember what happened when we didn't give Lorimer that two-dollar raise he wanted."

George Horace Lorimer, in 1900, had been a reporter on the *Post* staff at eighteen dollars a week. When his request for a raise to twenty dollars was ignored, he went to Philadelphia and persuaded Mr. Cyrus Curtis to make him editor of his newly acquired, sick-looking *Saturday*

Evening Post, which was then a moribund affair with only five thousand circulation.

In the next ten years Lorimer's editorial genius made it the greatest of American magazines, and Cyrus Curtis wouldn't have traded him for the Philadelphia mint. It wasn't exactly a sore subject with Mr. Grozier, but it lingered in his memory.

Mr. Carberry might reasonably have argued that I couldn't follow Mr. Lorimer's example, since there was no undeveloped *Saturday Evening Post* for me to edit; but it may have occurred to him that the two dollars wouldn't have to come out of his own pocket. At all events, I got the two-dollar raise, but it didn't come easy.

The creation of Professor Kilgallen resulted in a few changes. Mr. Grozier and his academically-minded Cambridge neighbors were sympathetic toward the professor's utterances, but there were other *Post* subscribers who felt that the professor was imposing on the *Post.*

Some of the serious-minded readers ventured to question his statements. They did not, in fact, believe the professor's assertion that oysters, in lieu of dentifrice, draw sand into their mouths and force it between their teeth.

That tunneling crabs progress underground for great distances by biting into the earth and blowing it backward through their ear passages.

That jellyfish could be used to make jellied rabbit, and produce their young by breaking off small pieces of their bodies.

That a scarcity of herring during the autumn of 1910 was due to a small organism, *Clingator irritens,* which originated in refuse thrown out by summer hotels along the New England coast.

They were also suspicious of other statements. They thought Professor Kilgallen had studied the wrong textbooks, and they conveyed that impression to Mr. Grozier in no uncertain terms.

Consequently Mr. Grozier ordered that every Kilgallen story should be prefaced with a mattress or shock-breaker:

> The *Post* has a deep regard for the remarkable scientific theories put forth by Professor Morton Kilgallen, F.R.S.; but as the subjects are beyond the lay editor, the responsibility for the assertions must lie with Professor Kilgallen.

Seemingly it occurred to Mr. Grozier, when he ordered the addition, that the professor's feelings might be wounded by this intrusion on his

privacy; for my next pay envelope held twenty-five dollars and the nota-
tion: "My compliments to your friend from Balliol. E.A.G."

§

The *Post,* on February 13, 1911, carried a two-column interview with
Professor Kilgallen on the subject of his approaching marriage, starting:
"A flutter of excitement was sent through the scientific world by the
announcement, made early last evening, that Professor Morton Kilgallen, F.R.S., of Balliol College, was to be married on the evening of
Tuesday, Feb. 14, since scientists the world over, knowing that Professor Kilgallen was a bachelor, had thought him wedded to science."

On his honeymoon, the professor explained, he intended to study the
action of green bananas on the voracious greetle fish of the Gulf Stream.
He then touched lightly on the outstanding features of his busy and
useful life, from the day he was born on a neck of land in the Orkney
Islands; including his school days in Cheltenwisholm (pronounced
Chisel), where he first learned to love fish; through his college life in
Balliol, which he had chosen because the name of the college somehow
—though he never understood exactly why—reminded him nostalgi-
cally of cod-liver oil; and thence to his first shipwreck, caused when his
professorial mind led him to bore a hole in the bottom of a schooner for
the purpose of studying the habits of the deadly ghit fish.

I had arranged with Mr. Lincoln for a three weeks' vacation; and
when I went to the Business Office the day after the professor's marriage
intentions appeared in the *Post,* the pay check was for thirty dollars, in
addition to which there was an additional and unexpected check for an
extra three weeks; and enclosed was another little note: "Please extend
my felicitations to the professor and the bride. The *Post* will miss him
and will be glad to have him back. E.A.G."

Mr. Lincoln, when I bade him good-by, looked exasperated and said
it was the first time he'd ever heard of a reporter turning in two columns on his own marriage, and it all went to prove what he'd long
suspected: that newspapers were going to hell.

So I have always had a warm spot in my heart for Professor Kilgallen. Some years later Houghton Mifflin suggested that I persuade my
friends Booth Tarkington and Hugh MacNair Kahler to collaborate
with me on a burlesque volume on antiques, to be called *The Collector's
Whatnot.* It was far from being a serious book, so we used fictitious
names instead of our own. A brother of Professor Morton Kilgallen,
F.R.S., of Balliol College, was called in and made chairman of the three
experts on antiques; and I took the same pleasure in renewing the pro-

fessor's acquaintance that I'd have taken in a visit from an old and dearly loved friend—which is exactly what the old professor had come to seem.

§

When I returned from my three-weeks' vacation, however, the professor was necessarily less active; for in addition to Mr. Royal's willingness to find printable assignments for me, Mr. Lincoln decided to let bygones be bygones. This was due to an inexcusable blunder on my part—one that might have worked out in such a way as to lead Mr. Lincoln to stab me to the heart with the office shears.

Cardenio F. King was a Boston banker who, convicted of illegal banking practices, had been incarcerated in the state prison at Charlestown, the inmates of which are not available to reporters.

In Boston there was considerable interest in King's future prospects, especially among a multitude of small investors whose finances had been materially impaired by King's misfortunes. Understandably they hoped that somehow, some day, a part, if not all, of the savings lost through King's activities might be restored to them.

King, in prison, was perforce silent—and now here was a bolt from the blue: a notification that King was seriously ill and had unexpectedly been transferred from the Charlestown prison to the state hospital in Bridgewater. The notification added that reporters from all Boston newspapers would be allowed to see Mr. King if they would take the seven-ten train to Bridgewater on the following day.

Mr. Lincoln handed me the note, and I thought his look was grimly commiserative—perhaps because he knew prisoners seldom have an opportunity to talk freely to reporters.

The tip about King's transfer mentioned that his doctor was the distinguished Boston surgeon, Dr. Maurice Richardson; so I spent the evening hunting for Dr. Richardson to find out whether King really was ill, or whether Influential Circles were claiming illness as an excuse for the transfer.

Eventually I located Dr. Richardson and learned from him that King's case was not only bad, but the worst of its kind he'd ever seen.

It was late when I left Dr. Richardson, and even later when I got to bed—which is no excuse for the dreadful thing that happened. I wouldn't care to say that I overslept; but I didn't reach Boston's South Station the next morning until seven-ten and a half, and the last car of the train bearing the representatives of every other Boston newspaper was vanishing in the direction of Trinity Place.

There was no other train to Bridgewater until nine-ten; so I fumed and fretted within the banana-scented South Station for two long hours, well aware that to go to Bridgewater was a waste of time, since I could hardly ask Cardenio F. King to repeat an interview which had already been uttered.

How, I wondered and wondered and wondered, could I ever explain this contretemps to Mr. Lincoln?

When, around noon, I descended to the deserted station platform in Bridgewater, I had come to the conclusion that if I couldn't persuade one of the other reporters to share his King interview with me—and Boston reporters of that period frowned grimly upon such procedure—I might as well reconsider my long-abandoned project to favor the *Seattle Post-Intelligencer* with my services.

My depression increased when I jolted toward the state hospital in Bridgewater's lone taxi, for the driver revealed the unhappy news that all the reporters who arrived at half past nine had returned to Boston on the ten o'clock train.

Since no other train returned to Boston from Bridgewater until six that night, I hopelessly understood that my chances of prying the story from another reporter in time for tomorrow's *Post* were worse than dim.

So a dejected reporter punched the bell at the state hospital and told a keen-eyed matron that he wanted to see Mr. Cardenio F. King. She nodded and asked, "Relative?"

Almost any reporter soon learns to be as silent as possible when not asking questions, and this seemed to me a moment when silence was imperative.

I looked unhappily at the floor. The matron nodded understandingly, called an attendant, who led me to an elevator; and a few moments later I was ushered into a small, sunny room mostly filled by a bed. The bed was completely filled by Mr. King, who was long and extremely large, especially around the middle. On the single small chair beside the bed was a steel brace the size of a potato barrel.

King stared at me, baffled, puzzled, half offended, while I stood waiting for the attendant's footsteps to fade away. Then he asked, "How'd you get in here?"

I said I had apparently been mistaken for a relative, though I'd made no such claim: that I was a reporter from the *Boston Post* who had missed the seven-ten train from Boston, and that I must have his help if the *Post* wasn't to be scooped by every other paper in Boston.

"Put that brace on the floor," he said, "and sit down."

The brace was as heavy as three typewriters.

King stared at me as if he couldn't believe his eyes, and said, over and over, "By gracious, how'd it ever happen? How'd you get in? By gracious, it's like a miracle! Who let you in?"

Then he told me that the other reporters, arriving together two hours earlier, had been refused admittance.

They never even saw Cardenio F. King, to Cardenio F. King's inexpressible disgust; for he ardently longed to talk about himself and his plans for obtaining a pardon and reimbursing everyone who had lost through investment in his enterprises.

He talked and he talked and he talked.

When lunch was brought to him, he shared it with me.

"Just think," he kept repeating, "for almost two years and a half I've been alone in Charlestown. Nobody to talk to! Nobody! But now I'm here and talking to you. I've been here only a day, and in that time something has happened that never happened in Charlestown—I'm talking to somebody! Talking to somebody who can tell people what I want 'em told!"

I was glad, for many reasons, and for King's sake as well as my own, that mishaps had dogged my steps that day.

When I returned to the *Post,* I found Mr. Carberry making one of his nightly catfooted prowls through the City Room.

He looked at me wanly and sighed, "Didn't get anything, did you?"

I said I'd got plenty and it was good. King wanted to pay in full and knew how to do it. Carberry's eyes gleamed whitely. "You didn't get in to *see* him, did you? We heard nobody got in! Do you mean to say you talked to King himself?"

When I said I'd talked to him for three hours, he took me by the arm, paternally escorted me to a typewriter, and breathed delightedly in my ear: "Give us all you've got! Pour it on! Lay it on thick! Give it a by-line! Fix each take[1] to go straight to the machines. I'll pick 'em up myself and write the heads! We'll run no risk of having this spilled outside!"

His eye caressed me and he went happily away, comfortingly reappearing at the miraculously exact moment to remove each take, paragraphs all awry, from the scarred platen of my junk-pile typewriter.

The King story led the paper the next morning, a four-column head in the upper right-hand corner.

When Mr. Lincoln had a chance to speak to me, he smiled that

---

[1] A "take," in newspaper parlance, is slightly less than half a typewriter page, cut crosswise. Custom, habit, experience, God-knows-what, causes a newspaper "take" always to average 150 words.

peculiarly ironic smile of his and said, "Come on, now, how'd you do it?"

I told him I'd promised King I wouldn't tell. He frowned darkly and shook his head. "There's something mighty queer about the whole business! What I can't figure is how the others let you get away from 'em!"

His glance reverted to me, suspicious still, and yet relieved because the *Post* had scooped the town. I think he may have had an inkling of the awful truth, but was willing to let sleeping dogs lie.

§

I found myself receiving longer and longer assignments—political swings around the state with gubernatorial candidates; the Glover murder case and the return to Cape Breton, for Christmas Eve, of pretty Hattie LeBlanc, who had been acquitted of Glover's murder; the transcontinental walk of seventy-two-year-old Edward Payson Weston, during which, to the intense interest of everyone over sixty years of age, he walked 3,883 miles in seventy-six days and twenty-three hours; Theodore Roosevelt's return from Africa; Harvard-Yale boat races; Columbus Day parades; the dedication of the Provincetown Monument.

The last story was one that made every *Post* editor quiver with apprehension, for Mr. Grozier was a Provincetown product who took a deep interest in Provincetown's welfare, and was sharply responsive to public opinion in that isolated community.

The residents of Provincetown, too, were sensitive in the extreme to any reference to Provincetown that could possibly be construed as unfavorable; and when any such unintentional slip of the typewriter appeared in the *Post*, Provincetown's social, political and business leaders dipped indignant pens in vitriol and violently assailed Mr. Grozier, complaining that they knew you couldn't believe *anything* you read in the papers, but that they had always thought Eddie Grozier was above letting such a terrible lie be printed.

And now here was a monument to the Landing of the Pilgrims, erected right smack in the middle of Provincetown, to be dedicated by the President of the United States, senators, governors, battleships, army, navy, editors and what not, all present in person in that proud and soubrettish community.

To the residents of Provincetown, naturally enough, the monument and its dedication were of far greater moment than even the discovery of America; and they made their feelings clearly known to Mr. Grozier.

Mr. Grozier, therefore, directed that a reporter be sent to Provincetown eight days in advance, and that the dedication be given full coverage, along with a front-page display every day until the final day, when the story, and accompanying photographs of Provincetown and national dignitaries, would spill all over everything except the financial, editorial and sporting pages.

When Mr. Carberry told me that I was the lamb selected for the slaughter, he gave me a briefing that left me almost as apprehensive as he was himself.

"This story is dynamite for all of us," he warned. "Just one slip and every Tom, Dick and Harry in Provincetown will telegraph the chief, demanding the scalps of everyone connected with the dastardly outrage. You know how the chief is about Provincetown: if he gets a squawk from two ministers and the old lady that runs the candy store, he'll probably fire Lincoln and the night city editor, and I'll land back on the copy desk. God only knows what'll happen to you! We'll send the whole staff down to help you on the final day, but you've got to handle the first seven days by yourself. Don't put in a fact or a name you haven't verified ten times; because if anything's wrong, those Provincetown prima donnas'll start screaming as if they'd been stabbed. No wisecracks, either, because if they suspect anybody's getting any sort of laugh out of 'em, they'll burn you on top of a mountain of lobster pots. Now good luck, and remember we're all a lot scareder than *you* are."

I can imagine nothing drearier than just one account of the dedication of a monument, no matter how beautiful or how important. To try to maintain interest in such an affair for eight days in succession is purely nauseating.

By the grace of God no slips were made, no feelings were hurt, and no complaints went hurtling from the tip of Cape Cod to char the top of Mr. Grozier's desk. I was so unnerved by the experience, however, that I asked for a three-day rest when it was over. Mr. Grozier graciously gave me six days and raised me to thirty-five dollars a week.

Boston was fertile ground, in those days, for an inquiring and aspiring reporter, even though financial rewards were insignificant. The city was almost as small as the rewards, and a reporter could get around in it nearly as easily as he could make a tour of Kennebunkport, Maine.

Newspaper Row, home of the *Globe, Post, Transcript, Record, Journal* and *Herald,* was contained within a few cozy, grimy blocks on lower Washington Street, a section decorated by tall newspaper blackboards on which employees wrote, in chalk and at considerable length, the news of the day.

Those chalk writers had a profound attraction for me, yet filled me with discomfort. They seemed symbolical of something I disliked to contemplate: scrawling, scrawling, scrawling, day after day after day after day after day, only to have their work destroyed each night, wiped from existence, washed out—never a word saved, ever. Before I'd grow old and gray, covering a blackboard that would have to be covered again and again, tomorrow after endless tomorrows, I'd—ah, well . . . !

One who descended those dusky *Post* stairs and paused a moment to look up at the clock and weather vane on the drab steeple of the Old South Church, diagonally across the street, was in the center of a host of fascinations, all as readily reached as the eighteenth floor of an office building. Just to the right was Childs, behind whose window a white-capped chef deftly poured and turned flapjacks by the dozen, by the gross, by the thousand, by the million, for the insatiable maws—ah, well! once more.

That was a good Childs. It achieved the best pork chops in Boston. They were cut thin, always, and the fatty portions were crisp, in contrast to flabby pork chops elsewhere. Late at night, when the morning papers had been put to bed, strong-minded desk men vacillated pitiably between Childs pork chops and succulent three-to-the-portion sausages with mashed potato and brown gravy.

A little to the right of Childs was half-portion, uphill School Street, abbreviated drooping tail of Beacon Street. DeWolfe and Fiske's admirable bookstore was on the corner, until crowded out by cigar stores, hatshops and shoeshine parlors; and right around the corner was City Hall.

Opposite City Hall was Province Court and the old Province House, haunt of light ladies either with or without their dubious escorts, but source of the best onion soup in Boston or anywhere else. I cursed the numskulls who let it be torn down, that ancient seat of military pomp and power, in which General Gage, General Howe, General Clinton, General Burgoyne, Lord Percy and their glittering, scarlet-jacketed subordinates had gathered on the steamy hot morning of June 17, 1775, and issued the incredibly stupid orders that sent a thousand helpless soldiers to dreadful mutilation on a hilly cow pasture above Charlestown —the Province House, long the true heart and hub of Boston, whose walls had seen more great and famous men than any other building in America; where, through a long and cheerless winter, harried and hungry Loyalists from every hole and corner in Massachusetts had shuffled through snow and slush for the meager rations doled out to them by their fellow Loyalist, Benjamin Thompson, who became Count Rumford and one of Europe's foremost scientists.

But the Province House was torn down so a street could be widened. It was in the way of City Hall. Yes, the British who met in the Province House were often stupid, but Boston has had City Fathers who were stupider—much, much stupider. Much!

Just beyond Province Court was the Parker House, where the leaders of Boston's Republican party were to be found every noon, sipping old-fashioneds, preparatory to reveling in the Parker House's justly famed broiled tripe, and discussing ways and means of ousting from power the knaves who blackened every horizon.

Only a little farther uphill was the Bellevue, where the flower of Boston's Democratic giants, brimming with confidence, celebrated their impregnability with astounding quantities of hard liquor.

Next door to the Bellevue was the State House; and the State House looked down on the Common and half-portion Park Street, steep highway of publishers, jewelers, bookstores and the Union Club, all as convenient as could be, and loaded with stories for a reporter who wasn't wasting a lot of time wanting to write.

But let us return to Washington Street and the white-capped chef pouring, pouring, pouring his batter; turning, turning, turning his flap-jacks in the window of Childs.

Before looking to the left on Washington Street, look straight ahead, through the secondhand bookshop in the basement of the Old South Church. There, on Arch Street, was John Fennel's wine cellar with sawdust on the floor, a diminutive bar facing a few small tables, and open bookshelves against the wall beside the bar. Instead of books the shelves held bottles, privately owned by the élite of Boston, and tagged with their names. John Fennel was a wine merchant who had stocked innumerable cellars for wealthy Bostonians. He blended and aged, in sherry casks, a special rye called O.F.R.—Old Fennel's Rye—which was dispensed in black bottles on which the letters O.F.R. were roughly lettered in white.

Reporters seldom had recourse to O.F.R. except on special occasions, for it was staggeringly priced at $2.25 a bottle. But on special occasions it was pleasant to visit John Fennel's for a shot of O.F.R., and incidentally to observe the almost secret comings and goings of distinguished Bostonians, somewhat different in quality from those to be found in the bars of the Parker House and the Bellevue. Like ghosts, or men in a dream, they materialized before the bottle-bookcase, unobtrusively reached for their personal bottles, downed a quick snort, and drifted silently away without demeaning or torturing themselves by speaking to the bartender or suffering the indignity of being addressed by casual barflies.

Turning now to the left on Washington Street, we encounter Pie Alley, dim and dank, redolent of printing ink, scorched matrixes and beer. The beery smell emanated from a door above which protruded a carved ham-like hand grasping an upraised bell. This was the ancient Bell in Hand, resort of composing-room inmates seeking surcease from the parched tongues induced by heat waves from linotype and hellbox.

Inside the Bell in Hand, usually, was Jocko Cairns, King of Pie Alley, who (considering that he seldom left the Bell in Hand) was gratifyingly conversant with the movements of such characters as hopheads, detectives (both headquarters dicks and private eyes), molls, gamblers and the Scollay Square crowd of queer ones. Jocko appointed himself my staff representative after I injudiciously favored him with a five-dollar loan by way of assisting him in a recovery program he had outlined to me. For a dollar, thereafter, Jocko could usually produce an item susceptible of elaboration into half a column.

Beyond Pie Alley was Thompson's Spa, almost across from the Old State House. Every male from every bank and bond house on State

Street assembled at noon in Thompson's Spa to converse in muted
tones with the sympathetic young ladies who presided over each horse-
shoe-shaped counter, and deftly dispensed sardine sandwiches, graham
crackers and half-and-half (half milk and half cream), oyster stew,
minced chicken with green peppers, pumpkin pie, crullers, and a superior
quality of coffee to a semi-circle of admirers born to the purple of the
broad (or Harvard) A and the flattened R.

If Thompson's Spa had been named Thompson's Spar, its habitués
would still have called it Thompson's Spa.

The position of waitress at Thompson's Spa was avidly sought by
Boston working girls. Nine times out of ten a Thompson's Spa girl
could confidently count on marrying a Harvard man and moving to
Newton or Brookline. Since tipping, at Thompson's, was forbidden,
those who remained unmarried were assured of being showered with
daily theater tickets, books, candy and costume jewelry during their
tenure of office. That wasn't tipping.

Behind Thompson's Spa was Young's Hotel (now, alas, no more),
whose broiled scrod and broiled tripe with mustard sauce surpassed any
ambrosia ever concocted in the kitchens of Mount Olympus: whose
bartenders were surely earmarked by Jove himself for elevation to his
Olympian nectar lounges.

Behind Young's, in turn, was the Court House, and a few steps
beyond Thompson's and Young's was Adams Square. If one stood in
Adams Square and looked uphill, he looked past the secondhand book-
shops and loan shops of Cornhill to Scollay Square, home of Austin and
Stone's Museum, which in turn was only a stone's throw from the Old
Howard burlesque theater, where Charley Hoyt, another graduate of
the *Boston Post,* first tried out his tuneful extravaganzas, such as *The
Milk White Flag* (all of them written for his beautiful wife, Caroline
Miskel), before convulsed audiences.

The Old Howard appealed to a refined clientele in its earlier days:
Senator Hoar and his lady occupied a stage box on opening night, and
John B. Stetson, its manager, made a flowery speech: "We are proud
to have you with us, Senator Hoar, sir, on this happy occasion, and
hope to have the honor of welcoming you and Mrs. W. within these
portals at many another performance."

In later days the customers of the Old Howard grew impatient of
overcultivation and repression: performances were dominated by come-
dians who beat each other over the head with flour-filled bags, affected
amorous dalliance with chorus girls who wore no tights and had mot-
tled legs, especially during the winter months, and made great play

with bawdy jests and gestures that would have been intolerable to
Boston's censors if delivered from the stages of the Colonial, Tremont
or Hollis Street theaters.

If, on the other hand, one looked down the slope from Adams Square,
he looked into the square brown face of Faneuil Hall and the long gray
bulk of Quincy Market behind it, both of them housing, in cubicles,
scores and scores of prosperous marketmen, all wearing the official
Faneuil Hall market uniform: a long white duster and battered straw
hat.

Gourmets, chefs who ruled the justly celebrated kitchens of the Touraine, the Thorndike, the Adams House, the Parker House, the Somerset Club, the Union Club, haunted Faneuil Hall market to rub speculative thumbs across the surface of marbled beef and plethoric chops;
dreamily to sniff strange cheeses; for in that market were displayed the
choicest cuts, the tenderest chops, the ripest cheeses, the freshest butter,
the crispest vegetables and juiciest fruits, the most luscious asparagus,
and incomparable shad, scrod, soft-shelled crabs, oysters and clams.

One of the fish stalls specialized in boning shad, and he who has
never eaten a boned shad baked twenty minutes on a hot oak plank
has been deprived of the most delicious morsel that the ocean yields.

For each bone found in one of their boned shad, maintained the
owners of that fish stall, they would refund twenty-five cents. In a
transparent envelope they displayed a solitary shad bone, returned by
one Bostonian who insisted that they make good on their promise, and
who got his quarter back. (Incidentally, I have heard tell that Faneuil,
in Boston, is pronounced Fannel, but in newspaper circles it was always
Fan'-yew-ull.)

On Saturday nights a reporter with a commodious green baize bag
could accumulate a wealth of bargains in Faneuil Hall market; for its
proud marketmen disdained to stoop so low as to carry perishable odds
and ends over Sunday.

Green baize bags were common to Boston lawyers and Harvard
undergraduates in that era. Practically every male in Boston had one,
and carried it with him daily. Clearly as I remember mine, I cannot
remember how or where the bag was carried when empty. When
stuffed with Ginters' Rye, early pink Bermuda potatoes, a bunch of
Jersey asparagus, a nice little scrod, and a copy of Charles Stuart Calverley's poems, it was unnoticeable. The carrier might be any respectable Boston lawyer, banker, politician, bond salesman or safe-cracker
returning to his adoring family with Important Papers. When empty,

it must have been embarrassing, since it was only slightly smaller than a folded parachute.

§

So Boston held a store of easily seized treasures for a reporter who was willing to use eyes, tongue and pen; and the city held good reporters, too, to say nothing of the Gentlemen from the *Transcript*.

The Gentlemen from the *Transcript* were thorns in the flesh of reporters from other papers, because of their habit of turning out three or four columns of intricate copy concerning an occurrence that any other reporter would cover in three quarters of a column—and that three quarters doomed to be cut by one third.

Anyone had to be on his toes in order to compete with Mr. Henry T. Parker of the *Transcript,* or Mr. John P. Marquand, or Mr. Burton Kline. Not that Mr. Parker ever demeaned himself by covering a murder case or a five-alarm fire. His province lay in the realm of music and the theater, but ordinary reporters frequently had to tangle with the theater too; and when they did, they had to remember that Mr. H. T. Parker could write three columns of the most philosophical, elegant and enigmatic language about theatrical performances of any sort, from the *Rogers Brothers in Central Park* to *Cyrano de Bergerac.* The readers of the *Transcript* venerated Mr. Parker, and never dared express an opinion on a play until they could find the time to read what H.T.P. thought about it—though it was often difficult, even after reading Mr. Parker, to know what he had thought.

At all events, *Post* reporters couldn't afford to take chances on underwriting when Gentlemen from the *Transcript* were on the prowl, unless they wished to run the risk of being summoned to the city desk and flayed alive by Mr. Lincoln for seemingly slovenly observation and reporting. If I learned that a Gentleman from the *Transcript* was working on a job on which I was also engaged, I was ill at ease until I had hammered out twice as much as I figured any *Transcript* Gentleman could possibly write.

The boys from the *Globe* and *Herald* and *American* were good, too, but deceptive-looking. There was none of the sharp, ferret-faced, tough-talking newshawk of stage and fiction about them. Cliff Carberry, managing editor of the *Post,* had an appearance of gentle helplessness that made everyone sorry for him; but in his reportorial days he was usually about three jumps ahead of everyone. It was he who solved the Susan Geary murder case by deducing that the murderer had dismembered Susan, packed the body in three bundles and sunk them in Boston

Harbor; then by further deducing where the murderer would have sunk the bundles. He backed up his deductions by hiring a tugboat and a diver and showing the diver where to dive—and the diver came up with all of Susan Geary.

His brother John was a veteran reporter on the *Globe,* and my good friend. I don't know what a reporter looks like: John looked like a courteous, smiling, studious businessman. He worked on the wreck of the *Portland,* which disintegrated at the height of the big blizzard of 1898, and eventually got the story on the tip of Cape Cod at a moment when all telegraph wires to Boston were down. Carberry solved the problem and scored the beat of the year by cabling the story from Cape Cod to England for relaying back to Boston.

Eddie Park of the *Globe,* large, sedate, gray-haired, slow-moving, resembled a reporter less than he did one of the custodians of the First National Bank's safe deposit vault; but he was a fast worker on a news story—a careful worker, too. In his suitcase, when engaged on an out-of-town story, he carried a rope in case he should be obliged to escape from a burning hotel in the still watches of the night.

I worked often with Bert Ford, of the *American;* and there was something about Bert, much as I liked him, that disturbed me. In New York, in Bermuda, in Springfield I'd see a man who reminded me of Bert Ford. Within three or four hours, to my delight, I'd meet Bert Ford.

I was annoyed, while working on the Hattie LeBlanc murder trial, by an extremely large reporter from the *Boston American,* who sat mountainously between me and the witness stand, moving restlessly on his overburdened chair, so that my view of the witnesses was constantly interrupted. Later I got to know him well, and found he wanted to write too. He was Ben Ames Williams; and after a lapse of thirty years, when he was at work himself on his 1500-page *House Divided* and snatching an occasional day's rest to help me struggle with the seemingly insuperable problems of *Lydia Bailey,* we often spoke ironically of those days when we were young and gullible, and thought it must be fun to have a book published.

§

There were many others: all good newspapermen; and a reporter had to work hard if he didn't want his inadequacies made painfully evident to his city editor. These men were understanding and sympathetic, and I had a great affection for all of them. In fact I was constantly amazed by the unfailing kindness of editors and reporters, as well as of the victims subjected to the attentions of reporters in the performance of their daily tasks. I can think of only two persons, during those newspaper days, who struck me as being—let us say—difficult.

One was the *Post's* Sunday editor; the other President Lowell of Harvard; but even then I knew there is no such thing as an uninteresting or unlikable person. I knew the Sunday editor and President Lowell had adoring families and circles of loyal and admiring friends: knew my failure to hold them in high esteem was emphatically due to some reprehensible fault in myself.

I can clearly see now where I was at fault about President Lowell. During my undergraduate days at Cornell, I acquired a piece of costume jewelry known as a Kappa Beta Phi key. The Kappa Beta Phi Society was largely composed of seniors who had signally failed to live up to the requirements of the more venerable and honorable society of Phi Beta Kappa, whose members must have unimpeachable scholastic standing. Kappa Beta Phi's aims were avowedly the opposite of Phi Beta Kappa's: candidates for admission were required to prove they had been ejected (busted, in Cornell phraseology) from at least one collegiate course, and were obliged to drink a bottle of Younger's Scotch Ale (as effervescent as it was potent) through a straw; then display sufficient control over the churning fumes within them to walk one hundred feet along a curbstone without stumbling. As an added irritant to the more refined Phi Beta Kappa Society, Kappa Beta Phi adopted as its insignia a gold key similar to that worn on the watch chain by Phi Beta Kappas, except that the face of the Kappa Beta Phi key, in lieu of a hand pointing to three stars, as on the Phi Beta Kappa key, displays a reversed hand pointing to a beer mug. Only a close scrutiny reveals the difference.

During the 1910–15 era, watches were frequently carried in the breast pocket of young men's jackets, the chain being affixed to the lapel buttonhole by a gold bar. A shorter chain also hung from the bar, and carried a collegiate symbol of some sort—a gold football, baseball or Porcellian Club pig, say, such as those that dangled from watch chains draped more conventionally across the vests of the upper crust of Boston bond salesmen. My whim was to wear a Kappa Beta Phi key attached to the shorter chain, a seeming advertisement of erudition and reliability.

Thus decorated, I was summoned to the city desk by Mr. Lincoln on the evening of the hottest July 3 ever to have been recorded by the Boston weather bureau. "We just got a tip from New York," Mr.

Lincoln said. "The Gaekwar of Baroda left the Plaza and took a train for Boston this morning to see President Lowell. Hop out to Lowell's house and find out what's going on. If the Gaekwar's still here, get hold of him. He's richer than Carnegie and Morgan and Rockefeller put together, and if he's going to drop any of his dough around here, we ought to know it."

When I pressed the doorbell of President Lowell's house, Mrs. Lowell graciously admitted me. The dinner hour was approaching, and she had been sitting with a guest in the living room. When I asked whether I might see President Lowell for a moment, she glanced at my Kappa Beta Phi key; then cordially asked me to come in, adding that President Lowell would be downstairs shortly. She probably figured that a Phi Beta Kappa wouldn't be calling on the president at such an ungodly hour, and in such heat, on any trivial matter.

So I sat down and we talked about the temperature, and how all the Boston stores had sent their employees home at midmorning—and then President Lowell appeared on the staircase. I got up to meet him, and he came toward me with his hand outstretched—a courtly Harvard president greeting, as an equal, one of his Phi Beta Kappa boys.

Before he reached me I said, "I'm from the *Post,* President Lowell."

He withdrew his hand as from the flame of a welding torch. "I never talk to reporters," he said coldly.

His conversational reactions to reporters was a minor matter: if he wouldn't talk, he wouldn't talk; and I was free to pick up some sort of story through other sources. His social reaction, however, interested me profoundly, and his instantaneous revelation of overwhelming revulsion to a specimen from a lower layer of society gave me almost uncontrollable pleasure—pleasure, because it confirmed what I had long suspected.

With Mrs. Lowell and her guest in the room, I couldn't, of course, mention that aspect of things. Since I was a reporter, however, I had every reason to ask questions, and I asked several, openly examining my scorned right hand, front and back, as I did so. What was the reason for the visit of the Gaekwar of Baroda? Was his visit planned or unexpected? Did it have anything to do with the fact that the Gaekwar's son was an undergraduate at Harvard? Was the Gaekwar's son in trouble? Had the son been expelled? Was it true that the Harvard Corporation was urgently in need of funds?

The president, of course, maintained an icy silence; so after I had embarrassed him as much as I could, I bowed to Mrs. Lowell, who was looking thoughtful, and went out considerably refreshed.

The Gaekwar's visit was duly chronicled on the front page of the *Post* the next morning, to the extent of a column of type and a two-column line drawing of the Gaekwar, who looked something like an angry Herbert Hoover with a waxed mustache. President Lowell, owing to Mrs. Lowell's error in mistaking my call for a social one, got off easy; but I could never feel sorry for him, afterward, when he occasionally put his foot in it, inadvertently publicized Harvard's anti-Jewish subterfuges, lost his driver's license through inexcusably clumsy driving, or otherwise suffered minor mishaps.

Perhaps President Lowell, if I had encountered him under other auspices, would have proved companionable, as almost everyone else proved to be—and I made contact with an invaluable diversity of types while working for the *Post*. Librarians, peddlers, side-show freaks, governors, insane asylum attendants, tramps, art directors, orchestra leaders, gypsies—I should have been able to write about them, it seemed to me, but I couldn't; end-of-the-world believers, senators, mayors, jockeys, bankers, flat-earth advocates, French chefs, perfume manufacturers, photographers, judges, artists, polo players, sculptors—I could produce a column or so about them, but I couldn't make them go together; headwaiters, doormen, degenerates, elevator boys, professors, policemen, pimps, compositors, law students, murderers, shyster lawyers, dress designers, opium sellers, brewers, surgeons—fascinating characters, but somehow flat, cut from cardboard and pinned for a moment to the pages of a morning newspaper; counterfeiters, ward heelers, actors, actresses, mind readers, princes of the Church, bartenders, gamblers, astrologers, press agents, Sir Ernest Shackleton, Theodore Roosevelt, Buffalo Bill, Buffalo Jones, Sarah Bernhardt, divorcees, confidence men—I can't begin to name them all; and all, once they started to talk, told me a thousand things I had never known or suspected; but the things they told me refused to blend in the sort of consecutive narrative to which I blindly aspired.

§

Frequently, when things were slack on a Monday, I'd walk up to Scollay Square for an instructive conference with my old friend Professor Hutchins, the lightning calculator and lecturer at Austin and Stone's Museum; and into my attentive ear he'd pour information that would be handed on, next day, to the readers of the *Post:*

"They're going one by one," said Professor William Street Hutchins with moist eyes, when told of the death of his old friend, Thomas

Holmes, the last of the "elastic-skinned men." "All the great ones are dead and gone—dead and gone. Last week it was the Wild Man of Borneo—cute little man—and today it's the elastic-skinned man."

Professor Hutchins gazed unseeingly at Mlle. (pronounced "Mil-lie") Christine, who was scrutinizing her crystal ball for the benefit of a bashful bridegroom, and sighed deeply as he summoned memories of those dear dead days when he extolled to spellbound millions the strange attributes of the human rarities assembled by P. T. Barnum for the Greatest Show on Earth.

Professor Hutchins has known them all. Some of them he has held in his arms when they were children. Others he has visited in their homes.

"Dead and gone," he repeated, "dead and gone. They were a great band, all of them, and Holmes was one of the greatest. He was the last of the elastic-skinned men, and none was greater.

"Well do I remember the first elastic-skinned man. He was Henry Haas, who came across the sea from Munich, in Bavaria, and his skin was like the sheet of rubber that the dentist crams into your mouth when he goes into action. He could take hold of the skin on his chest and pull it up around his ears. He was a blond man, with blue eyes, and tall—oh, very tall—and very handsome.

"Elastic skins are very rare—oh, very rare. The elasticity results from a peculiar omission or oversight in the assembling of the human frame. As you may have read in books, the outer skin is known as the epidermis, from the Latin *derma—derma,* Latin—skin. Then there is the *cutis vera—vera* meaning true—true skin. And then there is *reta mucosa,* or inner skin—inner. When there is an intermediate tissue between these layers the possessor is just like you and me. But when there is no intermediate tissue the possessor is elastic-skinned and can get lots of money from letting people look at him. Lots and lots of money. It is very rare—oh, very rare—like the little hairless dog from Mexico—very rare.

"Then Holmes, who has just died, was the second and last elastic-skinned man in the world. He could tie knots in his skin and was very accomplished—very. His entire family was accomplished. He had two brothers. One of them was an actor and the other was a barber. Both were very accomplished, and both made lots of money, as did Holmes. He called himself Maurice—pronounced Mawrees. This was his stage name.

"He married Marie Clifford, and he taught her to swallow swords. Under his teaching she became very accomplished. She could swallow a sword twenty-eight inches long. And she could swallow electric light bulbs, so that you could see them shining through her skin, way down—way down. She was a beautiful girl, and attained great eminence in her profession.

"And now poor Holmes is dead. And he was the last. Ah, well, they are going one by one—one by one. But he was very rare—very rare."

The cracked squeak of the Punch and Judy show rang loud in his ears, and the roar of the African lions in the big cage beat relentlessly against his tympanum, but still the professor meditated sadly upon his accomplished friends.

"There was Barnum's first great 'What-Is-It?'" he went on. "She was a cute little girl, although she didn't look cute. Harmless and quiet as a dove. And very dopy. Very dopy. She didn't have any hair on her head. Bald, sir. Bald as a loon. And strange in other ways. Two men found her in North Carolina, and sold her to Barnum. More of a wonder than Zip, but not so accomplished. Zip had hair all over him, a head like an egg, and could play the violin. A very accomplished person. There have been fakes—good fakes, too. The pair called Tom and Hattie were the best fakes. They were called the Wild Children. But they weren't wild—not really wild. Sometimes they were wild because they couldn't go out on the street and play, but that was all. Just ordinary children with funny bodies and twisted brains. They were born in civilization."

A voice broke in upon him. "These four large lions," it said, "these four very large lions are African lions. Roar? You can hear them forty miles at sea! Leap? They will leap forty feet in the air!"

The professor continued: "And Bearded Ladies. Ah, there have been some great ones! Well do I remember the first one—the wife of the Swiss warbler. And what hair she had! Covered with it! And she had a son, whom she named Hairy Esau—not Harry—Hairy. He had hair all over him—born with it. When he was three years old, they put him in a cage and called him a wild man.

"Then there was Annie Jones. I held her in my arms when she was three weeks old. She was very beautiful. And very hairy. And there was Madam Lyons, who was covered with hair and had a beautiful beard and a son on the police force of New York city.

"And Madam Montague—ah, she was a bearded lady who *was* a bearded lady. When I knew her she was thirty years old and very beautiful—very, very beautiful. She had a very long golden beard and a beautiful figure. Her arm was lovely. She was married to Joe Montague, who was one of the most successful living skeletons ever exhibited, weighing only forty-two pounds. They were a rare pair—very rare. But now they are dead and gone. All gone. And how many times I have had skeptics come to me and point over to these prodigies and say: 'Say, Hutch, how about the dame with the whiskers?' But they were all real. All real.

"I have known some great fat women. I have known the greatest of them, but they are all gone. Hannah Perkins was the greatest. She came from Augusta, Me., and she tipped the scales at 603 pounds. She was very tall—six feet—and very beautiful. Her flesh was as cold as ice; but then, all fat women are that way. It is a gift of nature, I suppose, to keep them from suffering in the hot weather. The ordinary person has 27,000,000 pores in his body, but I feel sure that Hannah Perkins and the other fat women had more than that—many more than that. And fat women are always thirsty—very thirsty. They'll drink anything at any time of day or night.

"I have known some very fine ossified men—very fine. And very rare. Of them all—and there have not been many—Jonathan Richardson Bass was the most accomplished. He was hard as a rock. If anyone had wanted to dent him he would have had to use a file. He was fifty-two years old when he died. He was in a very healthy condition, too, and would have lived to be sixty easily, but his manager dropped him on the floor one day.

"Yes, it was very sad. He dropped him. Something must have cracked in him, because he died immediately after.

"Ossified men—from the Latin *os,* meaning bone—are the direct result of living skeletons. If a living skeleton lives long enough, he grows into a true ossified man. And of course an ossified man is much rarer than a living skeleton—much rarer. They are very rare, anyway, and there is only one in existence. They are all going—all going.

"Of the living skeletons, the two best known ones were Calvin Edson and Isaac Sprague. Sprague's manager dropped him, I remember, one day when he was carrying him up a flight of stone steps. Sprague wasn't entirely ossified; but he was brittle, and the drop made him angry—very angry. He hardly said a civil word after that happened, because no matter what he said, he always managed to get in a few words which were not at all complimentary to the man who dropped him. He weighed forty pounds; but eat! That man ate like a trooper. You wouldn't think a man weighing forty pounds could eat much; but believe me when I say that Sprague always ate more than the giant who occupied the platform beside him.

"Speaking of giants—which, by the way, are very rare—the finest I knew was Colonel Goshen, an Ay-rab. He was a fine, large man, being seven feet eight inches high and weighing 602. He was a very handsome man, too, with big black eyes. Around his abdomen he measured triple the distance around the waists of three ordinary men with big abdomens. But he was a dreadful liar—dreadful.

"It seems too bad—too bad. They are all going—all dead. First the cute little wild man from Borneo and then the elastic-skinned man. There are only a few left. But that's the way it goes. Everybody dies; everybody dies!"

And Professor Hutchins blew his nose loudly and gazed sadly and unseeingly at the Arab magician from Mecca, who was making a rabbit come out of the corner of a silk handkerchief.

§

On the editorial page of the *Boston Post,* at this period, was a column written by Mr. Newton Newkirk, titled "All Sorts."

Mr. Newkirk was a genial and seldom seen gentleman who had joined the staff of the *Post* when Mr. Grozier became its owner, and from the beginning had conducted the "All Sorts" column on the editorial page. He had invented a character named Stealthy Steve, a supersleuth; and the Stealthy Steve of Newkirk's column was as popular with grownups and children alike as were the funnies of a later day. There was little question that Stealthy Steve had contributed largely to the *Post's* rapid jump in circulation. The only other thing to which it could be attributed was the *Post's* early guessing contests, in which the contestants' cupidity was aroused by important awards to those who came nearest to guessing the number of beans in a glass jar—a form of endeavor that seemed to appeal tremendously to the intellects of many Bostonians.

Stealthy Steve had appeared only sporadically; and the "All Sorts" feature at the time of which I write was suffering from a sort of jungle rot or athlete's foot. Mr. Newkirk had taken on, as a sideline, the editorship of a Boston magazine devoted to hunting and fishing; and the "All Sorts" column had faded to half size, and read as though written while riding to work on the subway. It was skimped, slovenly, and wholly lacking in originality, humor or good taste.

On several occasions when Mr. Newkirk, fatigued by his onerous duties, took a vacation, I was elected to fill his column with odds and ends of a frivolous nature. I was allowed a full column, and although my weekly stipend was about one tenth of Mr. Newkirk's, I was at first elated, not only because I might build up an army of contributors, as had Franklin P. Adams, Bert Leston Taylor and Eugene Field, so that I would have a lot of time to myself in which to put my thoughts on paper, but also because I was allowed to hobnob with proofreaders, compositors and typesetters, and to experiment with colophons, 6-point blackface, 8-point italics, De Vinne and other queer types.

Finally Mr. Newkirk went on a long hunting trip to the Rockies, and again I was assigned to the "All Sorts" column. This time I saw clearly that there was too much sameness to it by comparison with the daily uncertainty of reporting; too much danger of ending one's days compiling little paragraphs, little parodies, little playlets, little verses with a humorous twist at the end. Such unrelated items, it seemed to me, had small relation to the sort of thing I nebulously contemplated—a form of endeavor that would let me sprawl all over the place.

A daily column did, however, have one advantage: the work could be done at home—a matter to which I gave more than a passing thought; for although I still had no idea of what to do, I subconsciously knew that anything I did would have to be done after-hours; and a reporter on a morning newspaper has no after-hours.

So when Mr. Newkirk returned, I again made my way up the dimly lighted stairs to Mr. Grozier's office and tremblingly made a request: Mr. Grozier had been kind enough to express approval of my work: wouldn't I be of more value to the paper if I could have a daily stint that readers might come to expect in a given spot: couldn't I have a column of my own—a news column to run on a fixed page each day, with the assignments to be furnished by myself? I outlined to him exactly the sort of column that was handled so successfully, several years later, in the *Boston Post* by Mr. Bill Cunningham, and subsequently syndicated by the *Boston Herald*.

Mr. Grozier looked mournful and said he hoped I'd understand his position, but he just couldn't do it. Another humorous column in the *Post* would be a reflection on Mr. Newkirk and would hurt Mr. Newkirk's feelings; and Mr. Newkirk had been with the *Post* so long, had been so instrumental in the *Post's* early success, that the thought of offending Mr. Newkirk was too dreadful to contemplate.

I said I didn't want a column even vaguely resembling Mr. Newkirk's; cared nothing about having it on the editorial page: I'd be equally content to see it on the page opposite the editorial page, or any other page: back page, sporting page, page 2. I also pointed out that if such a column were indeed painful to Mr. Newkirk, it would almost certainly improve the quality of his work—a state of affairs that couldn't possibly be harmful to Mr. Newkirk or to the *Boston Post*.

Mr. Grozier continued to shake his head sadly. "I can't do it," he said, "but I'll tell you what I *will* do. I'll give you a page to yourself on the Sunday paper. That doesn't mean you'd be under the Sunday editor. I'll give you an office with Olin Downes in the new building. You can work out your own page and have it illustrated by Norman [the *Post* cartoonist]. You can make it up yourself without any interference from anyone, and I'll start you off at forty dollars a week."

Mr. Grozier was as understanding as he was kind. He knew, because I'd told him so repeatedly, that I wanted to write; and I think his offer of a Sunday page was his way of subsidizing me until I had more experience. I think he was doing the same thing for Olin Downes. Olin was a music critic whose brilliance was appreciated by few members of the *Post* staff and almost as few *Post* readers. His criticisms were kept within enragingly circumscribed bounds, were wholly beyond the understanding of most people who bought the *Post,* were so entangled among advertisements as to be unseen except by the most observant eye. Yet Olin was paid what I was paid: enough to live on—if we were careful.

But there were many who considered that the *Post* had the same need for Olin that a débutante would have for a wart on her nose: they were sure that unless he were related to Mr. Grozier, he'd have been liquidated years ago. Yet when the *New York Times* lost its distinguished music critic, Mr. Richard Aldrich, the *Times* instantly summoned Olin Downes to take his place, and Olin's genius was recognized and given full scope.

As a roommate, Olin, much as I admired him, was a harrowing experience. He would return from a concert or an opera, place the score of the performance on his desk, set a metronome to clacking noisily, and, intense and oblivious to his surroundings, rehash the orchestration with mumblings, mutterings, hummings, arm wavings and desk rappings. He forced me to work at home. I could no more have toiled in his vicinity than in an old Dutch windmill engaged in pulverizing flint corn.

EACH WEEK, from early 1912 through the better part of 1915, I produced a full page of verse, paragraphs, essays, satirical political sketches, parodies of the poems of Swinburne, Hood, Moore, Tennyson, Calverley, Villon, Longfellow, Poe, W. S. Gilbert, Felicia Hemans, Browning, Chaucer; ballades, rondeaus, sonnets, villanelles, rhymes royal, triolets; burlesques of Laboulaye's, Grimm's, Andersen's, Andrew Lang's fairy tales; of Aesop's Fables, Bulfinch's Mythology, Legends of the Rhine, Stories of Great Operas. None of it was easy work; verse that reads smoothly requires considerable struggling; burlesques can be exhausting.

It had one enormous disadvantage: because of lack of time, none of the prose material could be adequately rewritten; and any humorous ventures that aren't repeatedly rewritten are inevitably painful. The work had two advantages. It couldn't be done unless the person who did it worked at it every day, all day, and occasionally all night. It wasn't the sort of writing that I vaguely hoped to do; but it was sustained work, and it's my conviction that no one can become a writer of any standing unless he learns to drive himself incessantly and ruthlessly. Such driving, as a rule, is beyond the comprehension of those whose desires arise from their belief that writing is an easy form of work, and that authors can be idlers.

Perhaps doctors have to slave at their professions to a somewhat similar degree, since they're on call at all hours of the day and night; but good newspapermen, and those who really want to write, pay no attention whatever (when engaged on anything they consider important) to Christmases, holidays, Sundays, eight-hour days, forty-eight-hour weeks (let alone forty-two), vacations or proper mealtimes. A newspaperman's day off is as likely to fall on Tuesday as on Sunday; but no competent reporter ever let a day off interfere with a good story. Perhaps that's one of the reasons why things which seem important to most people seem highly unimportant to newspapermen and to authors, who as a rule have been subject to newspaper discipline at some time or other.

The work's other advantage was that I could do it at home, and I had come to the conclusion that the only place to do any sort of writing was in the home.

Consequently two offers from New York left me unmoved. One was from the old *Hampton's Magazine,* of which Harris Merton Lyon had been drama critic. When he died, Mr. Ben B. Hampton suggested that I have a try at filling his place. Since I wanted to write, I said No.

Later I received a hushed call from the publisher of the *Boston American.* Would I call on him for a moment? I did. Would I, in return for my expenses, go to New York to see Mr. S. S. Carvalho—the Guiding Light, the Grand Panjandrum, the little round button on top of Mr. Hearst's *New York American* and *Journal?* I would indeed! Perhaps he had a magic opening that would suddenly and miraculously turn me into a writer.

Unfortunately he had something else in mind. He had chosen me to compose the limpid phrases, the philosophic utterances, that issue in the shape of balloons from the lips of those comic-strip characters, the Katzenjammer Kids. Mr. S. S. Carvalho—whose name was pronounced to rhyme with snarl-yo—was a foxy-appearing, baldish, brownish man in mouse-colored habiliments. He fondled a roan Vandyke beard and eyed me in a way that I found irritating—probably because of the realization that my long and arduous labors had only fitted me, in his eyes, to produce such literary gems as "Awk!" "Eek!" and "Vere is der fedders fum der olt vomman's shdummick?"

He offered me five thousand dollars a year to manufacture the awkings and eekings of the Katzenjammers. That sounded gratifyingly large; but I said I couldn't, because I wanted to write. He asked if I'd do him two full-page Katzenjammer Kid conversation pieces as an experiment. Since I wondered whether I was actually capable of producing such a form of entertainment, and since I wanted to end the interview on a happy note, I agreed and returned to Boston.

I found I could do two Katzenjammer episodes in a day; but they frightened me. There seemed to be something dangerous about them—something that might affect me like a poisonous outbreak of skin trouble. Mr. Carvalho sent me a check for one hundred dollars, hinting that he could do a little better than a yearly five thousand dollars if I could put the Katzenjammers ahead of my desire to write.

I found no difficulty in refusing the five thousand plus; but the hundred Katzenjammer dollars seemed such a fantastically large return for so worthless a product that I felt guilty about taking them. And for months those Katzenjammer Kids came unbidden to mind, mongoloid morons horribly suggestive of the doom awaiting anyone who devoted his life to them.

Having refused Mr. Carvalho's offer, I mentioned to Mr. Grozier, without comment, the fact that I had done so. He raised me to forty-five dollars a week, also without comment.

§

In 1916, after three years of wrestling with that weekly page of verse, parody, burlesque and unpolished essays—roughly the equivalent, in wordage, of twenty average-length novels—I made a startling discovery.

From a New York newspaperman who professed familiarity with goings-on in that literary center, I learned that *Life,* which at that time was a weekly magazine of about the same format and quality as the English *Punch,* was in the habit of running special issues dealing with certain holidays or trends, and advising a coterie of steady contributors to submit their offerings by a given date.

Thus steady contributors might concentrate on Christmas quips, poems, sentiments and what not as early as mid-August, getting a three months' jump on those who did their writing on rainy afternoons, or when inspired.

Here it was only New Year's, said that New York reporter, yet *Life* was already planning a spring fashion number and was sending out notifications to its regulars.

If he had the time, he said, he'd toss off a few odds and ends and send 'em along to Tom Masson.

He was confident and superior, but it was clearly apparent that he wouldn't have the time. He was too busy talking.

I had the reading habit when I learned about *Life's* editorial quirks; I had been free to go to work at 6 A.M. if I chose to do so—and I had so chosen—and spend my nights in delightful contemplation of the insufferable Mrs. Proudie, or the exciting stodginess of the Five Towns, or J. H. Fabre's investigations into the love life of the wasp, the ant and all the other insect inhabitants of southern France. When I found an author I liked, I gobbled him. On discovering Charles Reade, I read his books straight through. Trollope, too, and Sienkiewicz, Dickens, Dumas, Jules Verne, Rider Haggard, Kipling, Hugo, De Morgan, Doyle, Mark Twain, Wells.

I didn't, however, *have* to read—not if that New York reporter knew what he was talking about. He hadn't struck me as unusually talented; yet he had appeared completely confident of writing acceptable contributions for *Life* if he had only had the time.

Well, I had the time; and if he could do it, which I doubted, I could do it. Anyway, I had all the time there was. I could work on my Sunday page from 6 A.M. to 4 P.M. every day and then, for the next fourteen hours, do as I pleased. If I neither ate, read nor slept, I could work all fourteen hours. If I frittered away two hours on eating and exercising, and slept five hours, I'd still have seven hours left in which to engage in any desired activity.

So that same day I sat down with all the Boston and New York newspapers and studied them closely for ideas or items that would serve as foundations for verses, paragraphs, little one-act plays or short editorials.

As I clipped each item, I pasted it at the top of a sheet of copy paper. When I had finished clipping and pasting, I did something about each excerpt. I didn't know or care what I did, so long as I did something —anything: something like:

HOW HISTORY REPEATS ITSELF

"New York Fashion Experts Condemn Latest Slit Skirts"

> When Homer thumped his little lyre
>   In semi-prehistoric ages,
> The fashion of his wife's attire
>   Disturbed the matrons and the sages.
> They shrieked: "Her peplum's laced with string!
>   There's too much danger of it busting! !
> It's too risqué for anything! ! !
>   Disgusting! ! ! ! "
>
>
> When Arthur ruled in Camelot,
>   A Camelot Protective Leaguer
> Became extremely wroth and hot,
>   And claimed that styles were far too meager.
> "Observe," he moaned, "our gracious Queen!
>   She says her wimple is de rigger!
> She can't fool me; for I have seen
>   Her figger!"

When Montespan and Pompadour
  Created styles and acted haughty,
From countless throats there rose a roar,
  Declaring that their gowns were naughty.
When hoopskirts later came to view,
  A million voices thundered "Shocking!
We see an inch—and sometimes two!—
  Of stocking!"

Each time there comes a shift in style,
  To change the contour of the ladies,
Some prude will always call it vile,
  And tell us that it looks like Hades.
Although his words may bear a sting
  For some, do they affect me? Never!
Nice girls look nice in anything
  Whatever!

That disposed of the fashion experts, so far as I was concerned; and I turned to the report of a new intelligence test that had achieved widespread publicity at an American Psychologists' Convention.

AS IT MIGHT HAVE BEEN
(If the Psychologists Are Correct)

January 30, 1854.—At the American psychologists' convention last night an interesting demonstration was given of the Whipple system of determining a person's intelligence. An ordinary-looking man was selected.

"Name, please?" the man was asked.

"Abraham Lincoln," he replied.

"Well, Mr. Lincoln," remarked the psychologist-in-charge, "will you be kind enough to define the word 'chamfer'?"

" 'Chamfer'?" drawled Lincoln in a puzzled manner. "I can't say that I know what—ah—it hasn't anything to do with a horse, has it?"

"No, nothing to do with a horse," replied the psychologist with a cold smile. "Perhaps you can define 'dibble' for us."

"That's a new one on me," replied Lincoln regretfully, "but that reminds me of a story about——"

"Just confine yourself to the questions, please," interrupted his questioner. "Can you define 'mitosis'? 'Synecdoche'? 'Peneplain'? 'Gambit'?"

Lincoln's dejected features were lightened by an expression of relief. " 'Gambit'?" he cried joyfully. "Yes, yes! A gambit is an opening
in a chess game in which an advantageous attack is obtained by sacri-
ficing——"

"Quite right," broke in the psychologist impatiently and with a
trace of annoyance. "And now can you define 'testudo'?"

" 'Testudo'?" ruminated Lincoln. "That reminds me of a little story
regarding——"

"Gentlemen," interrupted the psychologist, rising abruptly to his
feet and dismissing the abashed Lincoln with a wave of his hand,
"gentlemen, it gives me great pleasure to report to you that the person
who has just appeared before us is 82 per cent unintelligent. He is
mentally equipped for no tasks higher than sheep-tending or potato-
picking. If you will now pass into the Main Hall, we will demonstrate
that everyone, with the exception of psychologists, is mentally unsound."

By midnight that night I had five or six small pieces. By the fol-
lowing midnight I had seven or eight more. By the third midnight
I had six or seven more. By the fourth midnight I had another eleven.
I put them all together and read them.

They weren't bad. In fact I thought they were better than some of
the things I'd seen in *Life,* which had occasionally struck me as painfully stodgy.

At all events, I selected eighteen, put them in a long container with
a return envelope, wrote Thomas L. Masson's name on it, carried it
in person to the central post office in Boston to make sure it caught the
I A.M. mail to New York. The remaining pieces I reserved for my page
in the *Boston Post.*

On the following Thursday, Mrs. Roberts brought me the return
envelope that I'd sent off with my eighteen little odds and ends. It
was addressed in my handwriting, so there could be no mistake about
its contents. She was reluctant to give it to me: that was apparent; and
when I felt the fatness of the envelope, I felt unhappy, too, but did my
best to cheer her up.

Don't give it a thought, I told her: it wasn't wasted work! We ought
to regard it as a sort of windfall—one that would let me fritter away a
whole evening! Sure! We'd knock off and go to the Touraine for
dinner. I'd stand up Joe Di Pesa for a couple of seats to DeWolf
Hopper or somebody. In fact, we'd go right now, hey? To hell with it,
kid! Forget it!

And I opened the envelope.

There were the pages I'd typed the week before, but there also was a blue slip and a penciled account sheet. The sheet read: "How History Repeats Itself," $16.00; "As It Might Have Been," $28.70; "Cradle Song," $5.00. Forty-nine dollars and seventy cents for two verses and one small conversation piece! Ten cents a word for prose, they'd paid, and fifty cents a line for verse! Well, say! What do you know! Oh boy, oh boy, oh boy!

"Did you ever *hear* of such a piece of luck!" Mrs. Roberts said.

"Luck be damned!" I told her. "If I can do it once, I can keep on doing it! Do you realize what this means? It means we might be able to add five or six hundred dollars a year to our Travel Fund! We might even be able to add a thousand!"

Our Travel Fund was intended to carry us to some remote spot in Europe—some warm, quiet, quaint bower set amid grapevines, fig trees, olives, lemons, oranges and Sabine farms.

From its windows one would see Lake Como, the Adriatic, the Alps, and picturesque islands studded with cypresses and Etruscan ruins. There I could settle down and really write, taking no time off except to dig occasionally for urns, bronze figurines and relics of the Augustan Age.

We were meticulous about our Travel Fund.

By walking three miles each morning, Mrs. Roberts was able to buy cream and unsalted butter for eight cents less than she would have had to pay at the nearest creamery; so she walked three miles each morning, and the saved eight cents went into the Travel Fund.

She had also consistently abstracted five dollars a week from my pay envelope, even when I was only getting twenty-five dollars a week, and allocated it to the Travel Fund. When I was raised to thirty dollars, she abstracted eight dollars. Whenever the emolument was increased, the Travel Fund benefited. The hundred dollars from Mr. Carvalho went into the Fund. The forty-nine dollars and seventy cents from *Life* went into it.

Occasionally, when friends or relatives dropped in for an evening of idle chatter, a game of poker would ensue. As I contemplate the financial aspects of those far-off poker games, they seem fantastic—dreamlike. Always a receptacle labeled "Travel Fund" was in evidence; and a percentage of every jackpot, by common consent, was contributed to the Fund by the winner. Aside from that, players were allowed to keep their winnings, and were even supplied with rye highballs made of Ginters' Rye, obtained from Ginters', near Newspaper Row, one bottle

at a time, ninety-five cents a bottle, and carried home in the green
baize bag.

§

That check from *Life* altered my working schedule considerably. Up
to now I had risen at six, worked until two, ridden to the office to
listen to Olin Downes's metronome from three until five; gone home
and busied myself with thesaurus and rhyming dictionary until we
had dinner at nine; then read until one. And I'd taken Sunday off. ˎ

But with this lush new field unfolding before my eager eyes, I abandoned lethargic habits. I went to the office only to leave copy in the
composing room, to work with the cartoonist, read proof, play with the
type as it went on the stone,[1] and stretch or cut the type to make it
exactly fit the page.

Instead of reading at night, I worked. Each day I held out a verse
or an idea in which I saw possibilities. On Sundays I crouched over
my desk from sunrise to midnight, elaborating those ideas, polishing
them, twisting them, rewriting them, typing them. At the last possible
moment I packed them up, caught a streetcar for the big post office in
Boston, and put them on the last train for New York, getting back
home around 2 A.M., exhausted but pleasantly speculative.

Mrs. Roberts's account book, in which she recorded the title and
wordage of everything I wrote and its ultimate fate, as well as all our
investments and all our expenditures, shows the exact result of those
added hours of work. Any of my outpourings rejected by *Life* were
sent to *Puck*. If returned by *Puck,* they went to *Judge*. When *Judge* sent
them back, they were fitted into my Sunday page. Monthly returns in
1916, from *Life, Puck* and *Judge,* were: January, $49.75; February,
$111.67; March, $155.75; April, $182.95; May, $141.25; June, $96.70; July,
$116.40; August, $186.70; September, $200.85; October, $150.40; November, $167.75; December, $201.00. The total was $1,861.17, and all of it
went into the Travel Fund.

---

[1]A newspaper page is assembled, in the composing room, on a sturdy wheeled table
with a soapstone top on which the type slides easily until locked in position.

CHAPTER

8

Bostonians frequently find themselves enveloped, around January and February, by dark depression, probably because of a surfeit of snow, slush, gray skies, east winds and cold feet.

When, early in 1917, I was submerged in the prevalent Boston gloom, I regarded myself with a morose and critical eye. I was eight years out of college; and during all those eight years I had wanted to write, but I wasn't doing it the right way. I was hurriedly and frenziedly filling a page a week in a newspaper, and the page wasn't improving; consequently it wasn't helping the *Post*.

So far as I could see, the *Post* was helping me, but to its own detriment—a situation strongly in need of correction. Unless I took radical steps, and soon, I clearly saw that I'd finish exactly where I started: wanting to write and with nothing written.

I had been confirmed in my belief that, although I wanted to write, I wasn't doing so, by Professor George Pierce Baker, who at that time conducted a course at Harvard for budding or would-be playwrights.

Mr. Howard Brock, night city editor of the *Post*, had enrolled in Professor Baker's course; and Mr. Brock suggested that I enroll in it, too, not only as company for him, but to familiarize myself with the technicalities of another branch of the great Independent Order of I Want to Write.

The requirements, Mr. Brock said, were simple: all that was necessary was to submit one act of an original play, or an episode from an original play, to Professor Baker, along with a signed request to be enrolled. Anybody, Mr. Brock assured me, could get in.

A few months previously, Mr. John Royal had approached me with a plea from Mr. Bart Grady, leader of the orchestra of B. F. Keith's Boston Theater.

Every year the employees of Keith's Theater presented, upon that theater's generous stage, a midnight frolic, attended only by the Keith staff and their friends. I had earlier interviewed Mr. Grady at some length concerning anguished moments in the life of an orchestra leader in a vaudeville theater, and Mr. Grady had not been displeased by the result.

Now, wishing a one-act skit that might be enacted at the Keith Frolic by the members of his orchestra, he thought of me. Since the orchestra had little or no time to rehearse anything but music, Mr. Grady visualized a playlet or skit that would be practically wordless —purely pantomime.

In view of Mr. Royal's many kindnesses to me, I gladly fell in with Mr. Grady's desires, and evolved a wordless one-act play. This had already been presented on the stage of Keith's Theater before a fondly appreciative audience of friends and relatives.

So when Mr. Brock brought me an application blank for Professor Baker's course, I filled it out and attached, as the required dramatic episode, a copy of the Keith one-act skit; and for good measure I included a shorter playlet in which Mars, Jupiter, Vulcan and their Olympian colleagues enviously discussed the progress made by warring humans toward the total obliteration of everyone, whether concerned or unconcerned. The latter had already been accepted, though not yet printed, by *Life*.

A week later my samples were returned, accompanied by an almost undecipherable scrawl from Professor Baker. Its gist, however, was clear. In Professor Baker's opinion, my attitude toward the writing of plays was not sufficiently serious; and the space I sought to occupy in his Workshop would be better allotted to another. Consequently—and he expressed no regrets—he could not grant my request for enrollment.

So my desire to write was getting me nowhere, and something had to be done about it. After considerable thought, I reviewed the situation with Mrs. Roberts. What, I asked her, would be her reactions if I applied for a six months' leave of absence, without pay, from the *Post,* for the purpose of investigating our ability to keep our heads above water by just trying to write?

She not only said she heartily favored the idea, but she elaborated on it. We were the fortunate owners of a solidly constructed stable, conveniently located in southern Maine, that had been purchased on easy terms from a favorite aunt. We hopefully called it Stall Hall, but our resources hadn't allowed us to make extensive alterations, though it already boasted a bathroom, a cookstove, a bed, and a commodious set of living-room furniture I'd made myself out of white birch.

We could, Mrs. Roberts said, give up our apartment, live in Stall Hall, pay into our Travel Fund the same amount of rent we'd paid for the apartment, hold our food budget to one dollar a day, and get along *somehow,* no matter what the outcome.

There are, as I have implied, no rules arbitrarily laid down for those who want to write. If there were, I'm inclined to believe that one of the cardinal rules would be "Marry the right woman"—one who will never suffer from quietophobia or be cowed by uncertainty, by a precarious income, by late and irregular hours: one who accepts short rations as a matter of course rather than as merely a war or patriotic measure: a good cook willing to make beds, manipulate a typewriter, keep the household accounts, pay the bills, lose track of her friends, go anywhere at a moment's notice, forswear social functions, keep her mouth shut when urged by relatives to persuade her husband to stop being a disreputable reporter and accept a responsible situation in a respectable business.

When, on the following day, I ascended for the last time the dim staircase leading to the office of Mr. E. A. Grozier, two inner and austere guardians, New England Frugality and Eagerness for Security, dozing until now, came suddenly to frenzied life within my brain and uttered anguished screams of protest.

"Stop!" they squalled. "Think! Reconsider! Forty-five dollars a week sacrificed for what? Possibly for nothing! Fool! Wastrel! Idiot! Think of your Travel Fund! Contemplate threadbare pants: frayed shirt cuffs: worn-out shoes!"

Even after I had tapped upon Mr. Grozier's door, I could feel Frugality and Eagerness for Security kicking inside my skull and hissing bitter imprecations at my stupidity.

Mr. Grozier looked benevolently unhappy when I told him I was deeply appreciative of his sympathy and generosity, but not at all satisfied with the work I was doing for the *Post,* and would like to have, if agreeable to him, six months' leave of absence without pay.

At first he misunderstood me, and thought I was again making an effort to coax from him the daily column for which I'd previously pleaded. He regretted—he regretted very much—*very* much! He hoped I understood his position. Mr. Newkirk had——

When I said I just wanted to escape entirely from that weekly page for six months, and find out whether I could perform more satisfactorily without its uninspiring bulk looming perpetually over my shoulder, Mr. Grozier was distinctly relieved.

"That's an excellent idea," he said. "Excellent! I won't agree to six months. It's dangerous. I'll tell you what we'll do. We'll give you three months on full pay, and then you can have another three months on yourself. After that, if you want to come back, we'll have something for you. How's *that?*"

When I attempted to tell him how it was, he flapped a deprecatory hand. "Not at all," he said. "Nothing! I've always been sorry we let Mr. Lorimer go the way we did. If you ever meet him, I'd be glad to have you tell him so."

I never saw Mr. Grozier again, though he wrote me several times. Each letter was an encouragement, and each expressed regret that he hadn't been able to consent to the daily column I'd suggested. It was obvious that he was wedded to the old newspaper belief that nothing about a successful newspaper should be altered: equally obvious that he was genuinely and generously pleased whenever this superstition proved to be a help rather than a hindrance to those it affected. And it also seemed obvious to me that I'd never meet Mr. Lorimer.

§

God help writers if they're ever forced to keep union hours; for if they're to help themselves adequately, they must devote more time to their work than would be countenanced by any union.

With the certainty of a weekly pay check slowly fading as 1917 wore on, holidays and Sundays ceased to exist. Every day was a work day, and each work day usually began an hour or two before breakfast and frequently continued until midnight.

The results were gratifying, and yet I suspect they were far below the flamboyant ideas of those who interpret any small success as being permanent security.

One of the greatest disservices ever done to would-be writers, it seems to me, was done by Edith Wharton in *Hudson River Bracketed,* a book in which her protagonist, a callow youth, achieves acclaim and fortune by having one short story published in an obscure magazine.

Life is not like that; and Mrs. Wharton's young man was as absurdly unreal as any of the knights, damosels, dragons, giants and sorcerers in the early tales of knight-errantry that befuddled Don Quixote's brain and sent him blundering in search of fame and glory, only to encounter disillusionment and disaster.

Somewhat similar misrepresentations were made in Laura Z. Hobson's widely circulated *Gentleman's Agreement,* which dwelt heavily on the sensational impact made on the public, the publishing world and an unknown author's fortunes by the publication, in an imaginary

Smith's Magazine, of five articles resulting from a two months' study of what is loosely known as the Jewish problem.

I had a number of things in my favor during that year: I had already contributed to *Life,* so that I was no newcomer; I was able to write verse as well as prose; I was kept informed as to the dates of special issues, so that I was often spared the anguish of racking my brain for subjects about which to write; and above all, I could work on *Life* material all day and every day. As a result, my name appeared in *Life* with almost painful frequency—three times as often as that of any other contributor. I set down these facts for one reason and only one: just to show that it's not as easy to make a living by writing as most people think.

I could see, as time passed, that I was far from my goal, but that I was nearer to it than I'd have been if I were still turning out a page a week for the *Boston Sunday Post;* so I wrote Mr. Grozier that I couldn't be content to go back to regular newspaper work until I'd gambled on another sort of writing—just what sort I didn't know—and that I wasn't returning to the *Post* at the end of the six months' leave.

His reply, as ever, was considerate. Again he hoped that I understood his position about that daily column—he was sure my gamble really wasn't a gamble at all; but if things didn't work out for me the way he trusted they would, I should come in and see him again.

To my great regret, I never had another opportunity to see that kind and generous man.

At all events, I had now crawled out on a limb, and with genuine apprehension understood that I was poised precariously over an abyss.

My course seemed clear: I had to work harder. So I rose even earlier every morning and embarked on a short story—a luscious, whimsical fantasy with a slender golden-haired heroine and an O. Henry twist—sandwiching my labors on it between my work for *Life.*

When I finished it, I sent it to a New York literary agent and instantly started another, halting every little while to dally with a playlet for *Life,* or a cubist poem, or a page of satirical comment on anything that seemed to deserve satirical comment—and in 1917, as in all other years, there were few things that didn't deserve it.

Just as I finished the second story, I had a telegram from the New York agent saying the first story had been bought by the *Saturday Evening Post* for three hundred dollars. So I sent off the second and feverishly went at a third, keeping right on with my *Life* attempts.

Again came a telegram, saying that the second had been bought by the *Saturday Evening Post* for three hundred and fifty dollars.

I sent off the third. Nothing happened to the third—not for some time. The *Saturday Evening Post* and all other magazines rejected it. A new magazine sponsored by W. C. Clayton offered forty dollars for it, but the offer was spurned. Then I turned to a new agent and eventually *Collier's* bought it for four hundred dollars.

Now let me recapitulate, and show the tangible and exact results of all this labor and success—for, thanks to Mrs. Roberts's records, I can be exact about it. And make no mistake: it *was* success: success far beyond that which falls to the lot of most persons who want to write.

I understand that some circles regard any specific mention of the rewards of writing as somehow reprehensible or demeaning. That seems to me unfortunate. Government agencies have been known to reward farmers for dumping potatoes, for killing hundreds of thousands of little pigs, or even for not allowing hundreds of thousands of little pigs to be born, or for failing to plant millions of bushels of grain; but no government agency has ever paid authors for not writing books, or bought up and plowed under millions of copies of books to which book buyers are unresponsive.

Consequently he who wants to write must either support himself on the proceeds of his writings, or have independent means, or marry a wealthy woman and accept her bounty, or be subsidized by his family while trying to write, or earn a living in some other trade or profession while devoting his spare moments to writing something worth printing. Of the foregoing, the ones who are chiefly in need of accurate knowledge are those who hope to exist on the returns from their writings; and they, unfortunately, are the ones who are almost never told the exact truth about magazine payments, book royalties, agent's fees or anything else. They struggle along in an Edith Wharton dream world, which is a miserable place of frustration and agonizing disappointments, not conducive to straight thinking or permanent literature. Since this book is for those who want to write, and not for literary coteries who are revolted by brutal and open association of Letters and Finances, I must risk seeming revolting and reprehensible whenever this narrative calls for plain speaking.

The number of verses, playlets, sketches and essaylets sent off, in the successive months of 1917, were: January, 57; February, 51; March, 29; April, 44; May, 57; June, 27; July, 56; August, 72 (plus a never completed short story); September, 42 (plus two completed short stories); October, 36; November, 36 (plus one short story); December, 51 (plus an unsalable short story).

Some two fifths of those effusions never found homes, and were destroyed. The monthly returns from those that did find homes were, January, $299.25; February, $247; March, $140; April, $320.89; May, $291.80; June, $244.80; July, $378.80; August, $393.30; September, $1,064.01; October, $486.76; November, $742.29; December, $321.06.

Life's checks had amounted to $3,070.01; *Puck's* to $980; *Judge's* to $65.45; those from the three short stories to $914.50.

I learned a lot from that hard work in 1917. The most important thing I learned was that I knew far too little about anything, and that I must thoroughly investigate everything about which I wanted to write, just as a reporter might cover a news story, only more exhaustively. I learned that I'd never be content to go on turning out verse or playlets or editorial paragraphs, no matter how remunerative they might be, because half of them were rejected, which meant that half the effort spent on them was wasted effort, and because those not wasted were necessarily as impermanent as chalked letters on a blackboard—and I'd long had a deep-rooted aversion to chalked letters on a blackboard.

I learned that any sort of writing was the most absorbing pursuit in which I could indulge: that I'd been having too good a time, for too long a time, playing at writing, and that I couldn't delay much longer if I intended to get anywhere.

I had an excellent opportunity and abundant leisure to brood over these discoveries, because there was a war on, and I went in the army. I went in because I was distinctly and unmistakably told that the army was urgently in need of investigators trained to collect accurate and unbiased information of a military nature, and to report it quickly in such a way that it could be understood by even the lowest mentality. The fact that I believed what I was told should have proved to me that I wasn't yet ready to write.

CHAPTER

9

PROPERLY developed, that part of the army—the Military Intelligence Division—in which I found myself would have functioned as General Donovan's Office of Strategic Services functioned in a later war.

It was cluttered with authors, poets, historians, editors and reporters, most of them eager to go somewhere and do something; but the unfortunate truth was that only a few of them went anywhere, and practically none of them did anything, because nobody in authority was competent to tell them where to go or what to do when they got there.

Everything has its compensations, and the compensations for the uselessness of life in Military Intelligence during the first World War were the associates who fumed and fussed on every side, begging to be used in France, in Belgium, in Russia, in Turkey—in any place where their ability to investigate and report could be used.

It was my great good fortune to have as a commanding officer Major Rupert Hughes, who had held a commission in New York's Fighting 69th until deafness made it impossible for him to go overseas with that redoubtable regiment. If Major Hughes could have been given as free a hand with Military Intelligence as General Donovan was later given with O.S.S., the United States would long ago have had a genuine Intelligence Section. Unfortunately it was controlled by agencies deficient in flexibility; and the frustration among the highly imaginative personnel of Military Intelligence was intense.

The existence of an emergency made it impossible for this explosive personnel to voice opinions concerning Military Intelligence before outsiders or before their Regular Army superiors; but in private conversations behind locked doors they blew off furious clouds of highly concentrated steam.

Among the records preserved by Mrs. Roberts I find the constitution of a Military Intelligence organization known as General Hind Quarters, drawn up and signed by Herbert Quick, Holworthy Hall (Harold E. Porter), First Lieutenant, Air Service, and Kenneth Roberts, Captain, National Army. On its back are endorsements by Rupert Hughes, Rear Admiral, and Will Irwin, Vice-Admiral, General Hind Quarters, entrusting Captain Roberts with the task of establishing in Siberia, Manchuria or the Pacific islands a chapter or a chain of chapters of General Hind Quarters.

The members of General Hind Quarters messed together frequently, usually in the cloistered chambers of Washington's Cosmos Club; and the aims and duties of the organization, as outlined in its constitution, bore a striking similarity to the apparent aims and objectives of the Military Intelligence Division.

For example, "The object of General Hind Quarters is to have no object except . . . to encourage the physical, moral and intellectual development of the world . . . to foster among its members a love for all that is beautiful, spontaneous, and soporific in the realm of literature, art, science, veterinary surgery, psycho-analysis, kinetic stability, free lunch, optometry and military intelligence."

The direction of the affairs of General Hind Quarters was vested in a rear admiral, a vice-admiral or censor, and a Privy Council.

The rights and obligations of the Privy Council were "To direct and govern in their own minds all business affairs of General Hind Quarters, and to be empowered to buy and sell chattels, to lease or rent property of any description, to make or rescind contracts and make collections and payments of every kind; to suspend or expel from General Hind Quarters any member for (1) bad conduct, (2) good conduct or (3) no conduct."

Membership in General Hind Quarters was restricted to "any person of the male persuasion" who was "the author or parent of a published book, pamphlet, brochure, broadside, dodger, three-sheet, General or Special Order, proper to literature or sufficiently improper to insure a general circulation. Technical publications and newspapers, as such, shall not be considered literature for the purposes of this section, unless the author can produce vouchers to substantiate his claim of payment therefor."

The insignia of General Hind Quarters was ordered to be "a slight trace of soft-boiled egg, $3\frac{3}{8}$ inches by $1\frac{7}{16}$ inches, the eastern dimension to be $\frac{5}{8}$ of an inch equidistant from the most prominent frontal elevation of the tunic or blouse, and extending thence in a southwesterly direction along the property now or formerly occupied by huckleberry

stains in season: thence to any other point at the convenience or idio-
syncrasy of the wearer."

General Hind Quarters' rules adhered closely to those in vogue at the
Army and Navy Club and other Washington military centers—"No
visitor shall be introduced to General Hind Quarters oftener than once
in any war, express or implied; children under four years of age will
not be admitted to the Club Rooms unless accompanied by a member of
the Committee on Public Information; skating will not be permitted
in the club, whether ice, roller or alcoholic; no gambling shall be permitted in the club rooms except with rich and unsuspicious guests; no
member shall bestow any gratuity upon any servant or employee of the
club. Tips permitted."

Since the Military Intelligence Division was addicted to secret meetings to consider matters that could have been publicized in Berlin without arousing the slightest interest in any branch of the Imperial General
Staff, General Hind Quarters also provided for similar protective meas-
ures: "During the green corn season, all meetings of the club shall be
secret and held behind closed doors."

§

A uniform, I found, deprives its wearer of a large part of his efficiency
and energy. He bows to restrictions that he would never accept when
wearing civilian garb; and during the first months of my connection
with the Military Intelligence Division, I never thought of questioning
the order forbidding members of the armed forces to write or to publish
anything anywhere, under penalty of being promptly and dishonorably
divested of his rank and discharged from the service.

Major Hughes, it's true, was working furiously on galley proofs of a
novel, but he was doing it by permission of the Chief of Staff, or General Pershing, or another of those remote beings who wore stars on their
shoulders, instead of ordinary leaves, bars or eagles—and star wearers
seemed as inaccessible to lowly captains as Mars itself.

I couldn't see what harm could possibly result to anyone if I continued to write for *Life;* but I accepted the anti-writing order, just as I
accepted the futility of the Military Intelligence Division, and the devastating effect of high rank on subordinates.

When I'd been a reporter, everyone had looked alike to me. I walked
unabashed into the presence of governors, generals, bankers, opera singers, admirals, mayors, university presidents, millionaires, newspaper

owners, magazine editors, and freely asked embarrassing questions; but I had no sooner donned a uniform than I found myself quivering internally and short of breath when confronted by shoulder straps bearing eagles or stars, even when the wearers were opinionated bores. In the beginning I blenched at the mere thought of setting in motion the countless military wheels that would need to turn if I were to have permission to write.

That peculiarly military affliction didn't last forever. I think it received its death blow, late on a hot night, when I let myself into Military Intelligence Headquarters on F Street to do some work on an important-sounding but silly suggestion concerning the utilization of newspaper personnel in war work—a suggestion which, if followed, would make it obligatory for me to travel extensively and unhampered all over the United States, completely detached from desks, stars, eagles and the exasperating secrecies of Military Intelligence.

To my surprise, when I reached the lair in which I carried on my pseudo-military activities, I found it already occupied by a restless and uneasy-looking officer, Colonel Coxe, adjutant or chief assistant to the head of Military Intelligence, Marlborough Churchill himself. In the ordinary course of events I would never have seen Colonel Coxe except over the heads of several aides and sentries; and if I had had occasion to approach him in person, I would probably have been unable to speak except in a trembling whisper.

The sight of him fluttering helplessly among the desks of MI-4, however, somehow fogged and obliterated his shoulder insignia, so that I was able to ask him, as one ordinary human being to another, whether I could help him.

He said No: he'd dropped in on the chance that Captain Ruth might be here: Captain Ruth couldn't be reached by telephone, and he wanted to see Captain Ruth as soon as possible. His voice faded, and he uncupped his left hand to disclose a typed list which he worriedly studied.

Carl Ruth, Washington correspondent of a Cleveland newspaper, had been commissioned in Military Intelligence only a few days before, entirely as a result of recommendations made by me to Major Hughes. If his name was on a list, there was something afoot, because lists of Intelligence officers weren't put together by the general's adjutant for the mere fun of the thing. As a rule, any listing of Intelligence officers was preliminary to sending those officers somewhere.

"I know where Captain Ruth lives," I told Colonel Coxe. "If it's anything important, I can see him tonight. Is it important?"

"Well," he said, "it is, in a way. Someone mentioned him as being a good man to send to Siberia with General Graves's expeditionary force, and he won't have much time to get ready."

Siberia? Did he say *Siberia?*

Siberia!

Something to write about!

I could feel subjects whirling in my brain—a veritable Siberian salt mine of subjects ranging from droshkies and icons through samovars, rubles and serfs to steppes, vodka and caviar.

"Colonel," I said, "Captain Ruth's the newest man in MI-4. I got him in myself. If anyone's going to Siberia, what's the matter with me going?"

"You're needed here," the colonel said.

"I am like hell," I told him. "What am I needed for? Who said I was needed here?"

"Major Hughes," the colonel said.

"Listen, Colonel," I said, "Major Hughes needs me here as much as he needs a cigar store Indian. If you don't believe it, I'll have him in your office at nine o'clock tomorrow morning and make him tell you so himself!"

The colonel looked doubtful. "Major Hughes," he protested, "gave the matter considerable thought, and——"

"Colonel," I said, "don't send Captain Ruth. He's got two children, and I haven't any. He'd have a fit if he were sent to Siberia. He'd die of homesickness. I've had more experience than he's had. I can do anything that he could do in Siberia; and he can do anything I'm doing here, because that's mostly nothing. Listen, Colonel——"

"Yes, yes, yes!" Colonel Coxe said. "I'd hoped to go to France myself, but I can't. I get your point, but I can't stand here all night while you elaborate on it. I have other things to do. I'll consider what you say. I can't promise anything, but I'll take it under advisement. Meanwhile, you're not to discuss the matter with anyone. Understand? Say nothing to Major Hughes. Say nothing to Captain Ruth. Say nothing to anybody! Is that clear?"

It wasn't; but he was a colonel, so I said it was, and he took himself discontentedly off. The next day I quietly busied myself with futilities, and tried to conceal from Major Hughes the tumult churning in my vitals; but he wasn't a novelist for nothing. Late in the afternoon he fixed a casual eye upon the ceiling and said, with elaborate carelessness, that he assumed, from my strange and unaccustomed repression, I had been in contact with Colonel Coxe and had been instructed by him not to mention the Siberian expedition to anyone, Major Hughes included. If his suspicion was correct, he said, he felt he ought to tell me that he, too, had been instructed by Colonel Coxe to say nothing to me about the Siberian expedition, and that these admonitions about secrecy were childish. At all events, he said, he insisted on having one piece of information: did I really want to go to Siberia?

When I said emphatically that I did, he smote his brow with his open hand and said, "My God, I thought I was doing you a favor!"

He hurried away in the direction of the section devoted to Top Secrets and Top Brass.

I got my orders that night:

> The following named officers are relieved from their present duties, and will proceed to San Francisco, California, and report to the Commanding General, American Expeditionary Force, Siberia, for duty in the intelligence section of his command:
>
> Capt. Montgomery Schuyler   Capt. Maximilian Elser
> Capt. Frederick F. Moore   Lieut. Robert J. Scovell
> Capt. Francis Bayard Rives   Lieut. James E. McKenna
> Capt. John A. Powell   Lieut. Ben Stinchfield
> Capt. Kenneth Roberts   Lieut. Lawrence Packard
> Capt. Harold Van Vechten Fay   Lieut. Max P. Cushing
> Capt. Roger Straus   Lieut. Lawrence Richmond
> Capt. Frederic Vieweg   Lieut. Ralph L. Baggs
>
> The travel directed is necessary in the military service.
>
> By order of the Secretary of War:
>
> PEYTON C. MARCH,
> General, Chief of Staff
>
> Official:
> H. P. McCAIN,
>   The Adjutant General

The first person to whom I showed the orders was Captain Ruth. "Carl," I said, "I don't know for sure how you're going to feel about it, but I persuaded Colonel Coxe to put me on this list in your place. I hope you won't be sore."

"Siberia!" he said. "Sore? Siberia? Gee, thanks!"

§

I had no time to think about writing in the three days before that detachment of officers set off for San Francisco and Siberia. Typhus, typhoid and paratyphoid injections helped to drive most thoughts from the brain, and those remaining were shattered by the shock of discovering the high cost of Siberian equipment, which necessitated heavy uniforms, fur hats, fur gloves, bulletproof underwear, sheepskin jackets, extra heavy trench coats, knee-length stockings, eight-foot mufflers, felt boots, bedding roll, camp cot, camp chair and five so-called blankets, product of a manufacturer more interested in feathering his nest than in keeping soldiers warm.

If I wasn't to leave Mrs. Roberts financially crippled, I had to find some way of buying that Siberian equipment with funds over and above my army pay: yet I was fettered by fear of army regulations. In desperation I wrote Mr. Masson of *Life,* explaining the dire punishments visited on any officer who defied the anti-writing regulation, and telling him that during the ensuing ten days (at the end of which time a certain transport would leave a certain place for a certain destination) he would receive contributions signed Laurence Kane, and that I was Laurence Kane—a name whose syllables, if separated and slurred, were a sort of acrostic of the letters L-R-K—K.L.R.—but please keep it dark.

I scribbled industriously during a hurried trip to Maine and an equally hurried return trip to Washington: labored over a blankbook from morning to night on the long train ride across the continent, except when being instructed by experts on the perils of attempting to follow the devious workings of the oriental Russian mind while still retaining an occidental manner of thought. In San Francisco I toiled (and Mrs. Roberts knitted two pairs of three-foot-long stockings) while brother officers and their devoted families made merry in Chinatown and on the Barbary Coast. As a result, *Life's* pages for the next three months were freckled with contributions from a hitherto unknown Laurence Kane—and the bills for my Siberian equipment were met in full.

The act of putting words on paper almost necessitates the use of the head; and as I struggled to evolve those little pieces for *Life,* my mind turned with increasing resentment to the army's anti-writing regulation, and to the patent absurdity of signing a fictitious name to harmless verses. My brain, torpid from association with Military Intelligence, stirred lethargically. If Major Hughes had received permission from Higher Up to correct proofs, perhaps something could be done about my case as well.

But what sort of case did I have? my inner self demanded, and promptly replied, No case at all! I was merely one of two million uniformed men, and why should I be given permission to write when nobody, myself included, had any idea of what I wanted to write? Following that thought, I dispatched a telegram to the editor of the *Saturday Evening Post,* Mr. George Horace Lorimer, whom I'd never met. It read:

CONFIDENTIAL EXPECT IMMINENT TRIP TO SIBERIA REPRESENTING LARGE RESOURCEFUL ORGANIZATION. IF YOU INTERESTED IN REPORT WILL REQUEST PERMISSION TO MAKE ONE.

A reply was waiting for me when I reached San Francisco:

THANKS FOR MESSAGE. HOPE YOU CAN GET DESIRED PERMISSION. AM VERY MUCH INTERESTED IN ARTICLES ON SOCIAL, POLITICAL, ECONOMIC SITUATION.
GEO. H. LORIMER

Social, political and economic situation, egad! The earth, the sea, the sky! The sun, the moon, the stars! The whole wide world and all that moves upon it, above it and within it! Get going! Turn every stone! Invoke all Influence!

I wrote passionately to Major Hughes concerning the military order forbidding officers or enlisted men in the United States Army to write professionally. What, I wanted to know, was the big idea? Was it an effort on the part of the General Staff to deprive the American Army of the means of expressing itself, in addition to having done its best to strangle all intelligent and independent thought? Here I had the chance to write something for the *Saturday Evening Post*—articles that an army ought to be willing to *pay* to have written. Instead of that, I was throttled: couldn't write anything at all unless I had special permission. How could I get the permission?

I went so far as to submit to Major Hughes a revision of the entire anti-writing order. The revision actually encouraged writing. By its terms any soldier, sailor or marine in a United States uniform was permitted to write for any newspaper, magazine or publishing house in existence, so long as his manuscript was submitted for approval to any responsible superior officer. Since I had great affection for Major Hughes and an abiding faith in his enthusiastic willingness to attack stupidity wherever he found it, I spoke my mind freely on the botched complexion of military affairs.

I was momentarily shocked, therefore, to receive, a few days later, a long official telegram signed by Marlborough Churchill. At the sight of that potent name, fountainhead of all Military Intelligence, my heart rolled over.

Orders rescinded? Dishonorably discharged? Court-martial ordered for disrespectful letter?

But no! Not with Major Hughes on the job! The telegram read:

LETTER TO MAJOR HUGHES RECEIVED, AMENDMENT CONCERNING AUTHOR-
SHIP APPROVED IN PRINCIPLE, BUT DIRECTED TO MAKE COMPLETE REVISION OF
ENTIRE ORDER. THIS WILL PROBABLY BE APPROVED. COMMANDER FOREIGN
FORCES HOWEVER IS EMPOWERED TO ESTABLISH MODIFICATIONS AND REGULA-
TIONS OF HIS OWN. PERSHING HAS GIVEN PERMISSION TO SIX OFFICERS TO
WRITE WHAT THEY PLEASE, SUBMITTING IT TO CENSOR. PLEASE EXPLAIN THIS
TO GENERAL GRAVES. SEND YOUR MANUSCRIPTS TO MAJOR HUGHES AND HE
WILL GIVE THEM PERSONAL ATTENTION.

Explain to a general? Send manuscripts? Was it really going to be as
easy as that?

I THINK writing would have been easy if all the officers of the Siberian
Expeditionary Force had been of the same quality as Major Samuel I.
Johnson of Honolulu, commanding officer of troops on the transport
Sheridan, on which, in company with the transport *Logan,* we slipped
silently away from the Presidio on a dark autumn evening. The major
didn't care who wrote what, or about whom.

My close association with Major Johnson began on the second day
out, when some minor mishap caused him to stop just outside the door
of the cabin in which Captain Vieweg and I, stretched on our bunks,
were supposedly studying *Russian Self-Taught* and learning that the
word for "yes" is *da;* for "no," *nyet;* for "certainly," *sceechas;* for "cigarettes," *pappirossi;* for "who cares," *nitchevo;* for "waiter," *chelovyek;*
for "money," *dengi;* for "howdy," *zdras';* for "be seeing you," *do
svidanya;* for "breakfast," *zahvdrahk;* for "how much," *skolkostoit;* for
"please," *pazholst;* for "thanks," *spasibo;* for "I love you," *ya vas lu blu.*
In reality I was commenting bitterly and at length to Captain Vieweg
on the fact that the *Sheridan* was armed only with 37-millimeter Vickers Maxims, as effective against raiders or submarines as bean blowers,
and that there wasn't even a single crate of gas masks for the four thousand men sardined in the holds of both ships.

At the conclusion of my comments there was a rap on the door, and
a moment later Major Johnson stepped in, sat down, and examined us
carefully, while we stared apprehensively at him over the tops of our
copies of *Russian Self-Taught.* The major was short, flat-backed, big-
muscled, high-chested, swarthy, with a little black mustache, hair cut
en brosse, and the sharpest black eyes that ever were. "I heard you
speaking about those gas masks," he said. "That is nothing. This is only
the beginning. Later, perhaps, you will see things so stupid that you
will be speechless." He eyed me sardonically and added, "Maybe."

He slapped his arched chest. "Look," he said, "in Honolulu I was brigadier general of Hawaiian Militia. Nothing was happening in Honolulu, so I resigned my commission and went to training camp in the States, in order to be recommissioned and sent to France, where I could pot a few Krauts. So I am made a major and sent to Siberia, where there are no Krauts: only a few relatives. You should talk about gas masks!" He laughed satirically and abruptly got to his feet.

"You have relatives in Russia?" I asked.

"A few," he said. "Three brothers were killed by Germans in this war. Another lives in Odessa, blinded by Germans. My uncle was governor of Irkutsk. Before that he was commander in chief of the Russian armies. Maybe later I tell you everything. It takes time. I told it all to Jack London when he visited me, and he would have made it into a book, only he died." He nodded brusquely. "I stopped for just a moment, merely to tell you not to think about those gas masks too much. You will have other and bigger mistakes to speak about."

He slammed our cabin door behind him and went clattering off down the passageway.

On the following day he ordered all officers to the afterdeck for target practice with their .45 automatics. The vessel was rolling atrociously, and accurate shooting under such circumstances was plain luck, so I was neither surprised nor elated to find that my score was a trifle better than the major's. Later that day he sent for me to come to his cabin, handed me a cigarette, and from his locker trunk took a black velvet roll.

The roll was a strip three feet long and one foot wide, completely covered with medals. One, from the Sea Girt Rifle Association, was to cause me considerable embarrassment at a later day. Another was for the twenty-five-mile swimming championship of Honolulu. Several were for rifle marksmanship. One with a number of bars attached proved that Samuel I. Johnson had held the rifle championship of Hawaii for eighteen years. Others were for lifesaving, sprint swimming and excellence in pistol shooting. He rapped the latter with a stubby forefinger and asked, "What do you think of those?"

I said they proved what I'd known only too well: that my bull's-eyes had been accidental.

"Maybe," the major said, "but perhaps you like to think about something." From a field desk he took the pretty little design prepared for General Graves's edification by Intelligence Headquarters in Washington, showing the make-up of his Intelligence Section—the sort of design in which oblong plates or panels descend from a single cap like the stones of a pyramid. The uppermost panel bore the name of Major David I. Barrows, General Graves's Chief Intelligence Officer, who was already in Siberia, awaiting our arrival. The panel directly under Major Barrows's bore my name with the added legend, "administration, co-ordination and dissemination."

The major tapped that subordinate panel. "Executive officer," he said. "Nobody ever did anybody any good by being executive officer. You don't get a chance to shoot pistols when you're executive officer, not at anybody but yourself."

I said I was painfully aware of that fact, but could only let nature take its course.

"You ride some?" the major asked.

I said I did.

"I teach you tricks you never heard of," he said. "I am a Cossack. I was born in a Cossack camp. For two years I went to a Russian military college for officers and then into the Cossack cavalry. Some day I tell you how I change into an American. I think our army and our country knows less about Russia than about the moon. I think I could do somebody some good if I took one officer and two orderlies and went across Siberia and into Russia, south of the railway, on field Intelligence. Perhaps we have a little trouble, but not much, I think. I am accustomed to being in trouble and getting out of it. Maybe we ride across the Urals and see my brother in Odessa. How would that sound to you?"

I said it would sound like a newspaperman's dream of heaven.

The major rolled up his medals and put them in his trunk. "When we get settled," he said, "I ask for you and two orderlies and four horses. Then we go quickly away from headquarters. Headquarters is always hell. Always there is some nervous old woman to drop things in the machinery."

I made an effort to get Major Johnson's complete story, but I was hampered by rough weather off the Aleutians, by the major's duties as commanding officer of troops, and by unfortunate complications resulting from the simultaneous eruption, in the Northern Island of Japan, of a Japanese typhoon and four thousand intoxicated American soldiers—as well as by the major's proclivities as an entertainer.

I have seen noted magicians publicly at work upon the stage—Herrmann, Kellar, Thurston, Houdini—but none of them ever achieved the mystifying effects obtained by Major Johnson when, after performing a score of lesser impossibilities, he stood in the center of the *Sheridan's* crowded and brightly lighted smoking room, extended a deck of cards behind him for any haphazard officer to select, expose and replace a card, then violently hurled the deck on high. Fifty-one cards fell in a shower about him: the back of the remaining card—the one selected by the baffled officer—remained plastered to the ceiling.

He had learned his illusions, he said, from Brooks, an English magician, and from Herrmann and Kellar. In return for a favor he did for Herrmann in Odessa, Herrmann gave him his best trick. What was the favor? Private matter! He later traded that particular mystifier to Brooks for four of Brooks's best tricks.

One thing led to another when he spoke of his dexterity with cards. A fakir in Singapore had once undertaken to make a laughingstock out of him by pretending to find cards secreted on the major's person, only to be so discomfited by superior tricks that he left Singapore permanently. This naturally led to the occasion when the major performed before the Sultan of Johore, which of course brought up his visit to the wilds of the Malay Peninsula and his capture of monkeys, a crocodile and a bear. Out of this developed the details of his return to Honolulu, when the bear escaped from its cage into Honolulu Harbor, as a result of which Johnson was obliged to dive in and get a rope around his neck—a chore that resulted in a row of deep scars in the heel of one of his hands, caused by the bear's teeth. The major had, as the saying goes, got around. He considered Palmyra Island in the South Pacific, by the way, the nearest thing to heaven he had encountered in his rambles.

§

I had always been attracted by the sketchy account of the life of Ivan Petruski Skavar, as narrated in the all-too-short song which casually mentions that Ivan could imitate Irving, tell fortunes at cards, and perform on the Spanish guitar. Skavar's life, however, was mere milk and water by comparison with the major's—whose original name had been a mélange of Russian characters that defied American tongues. Anyway, the major said, his former name was of no importance because he had formally taken the name Johnson when he became an American: for him the other name had ceased to exist.

He seemed to have a soft spot in his heart for writers. He had been greatly attached to Jack London, as well as to Mrs. London, and had furnished material for several of London's Hawaiian stories. Richard Walton Tully, the playwright, had been welcome in his home, as had been Tully's wife, Eleanor Gates, author of *The Poor Little Rich Girl*. During one of Tully's visits, Johnson supplied him with the material for *The Bird of Paradise,* which Tully wrote then and there.

In the end I accumulated a notebook full of material on Sam Johnson's fantastic life,[1] and I often wondered what Jack London would have done with it. I know that whenever, in after years, I found myself struggling with a character who was constantly in trouble—Cap Huff, say, or Robert Rogers or Tom Buell—I always found it helpful to recall Major Johnson and imagine what he would have done in similar circumstances. To have traveled with him over the Urals would have been like traveling with Eugene Leitensdorfer, that singular character in *Lydia Bailey.*

---

[1] See p. 375, Appendix.

I was mildly surprised that we got to Japan at all; even more surprised that we got away alive.

Our transport, the *Sheridan,* was hampered on the trip by the strange behavior of her sister ship, the *Logan,* whose speed, for unknown reasons, was reduced at times to zero.

The captain of the *Logan* sent repeated messages to us insisting that we slow down sufficiently to stay within reach; but never, during that tedious three weeks' voyage, did the captain of the *Logan* condescend to reply to our demands to be told the reason for her slow and erratic course.

Thus there was no way of knowing whether we might be called on to rescue two thousand soldiers from a sinking ship, or whether the *Logan's* steering gear had gone so completely to pot that we might eventually have to take her in tow—and neither prospect was alluring; for we were burning more coal than had been expected, and we were so close to the Aleutians that we caught frequent glimpses of their frowning bulks and their fringes of frothing breakers through the everlasting fog and rain. They were strikingly unappealing.

When the *Logan* wabbled through Tsugaru Strait and dropped her mud hook two miles out in the harbor of Hakodate (rhyming with ratty and looking the same), at the southern tip of the Northern Island of Japan, she was almost completely out of coal and listing dangerously.

No effort had been made by either the War Department in Washington or the Siberian Expeditionary Force in Vladivostok to notify Japanese authorities of the arrival of our ships, what the ships were, what was in them, or where they were bound—gross oversights, all, on the part of official America, and disturbing evidence that the wits of several persons in high position had wandered and would probably continue to wander.

That failure was bad enough, but the events that followed our landing were unimaginably worse—a true harbinger of what we might expect in days to come.

I was delighted to have this first glimpse of those interesting little
people, the Japanese, our honored and supposedly honorable Allies; and
Major Johnson, knowing that coaling was a tedious process in Japan,
since coal is handed aboard ship in small baskets by women long past
the age of sprightliness, sent our troopless detachment off in sampans
with his benisons, and with orders to be back by midnight.

As we went happily ashore, barges were assembling to carry almost
four thousand enlisted men to a day's freedom in batches of five
hundred.

Hakodate was a fishing, shipping and factory town as slightly endowed with beauty as it was rich in dirt and stenches. Still, it was picturesque—good background for a story, perhaps, if I ever got around to
writing one—so we went up one street and down another and out into
the country, examining temples, shrines and curio shops.

We were suspicious of the eating houses we saw because of their
dreadful stinks and the fringe of coryza-afflicted children who wandered in and out of them at will; also because of their English signs,
which had apparently been furnished by playful American sailors.

The Tomé House displayed a sign reading: "Notice!!! Having lately
been Refitted and preparations have been made to supply those who
give us a look-up, with Worst of Liquors and Food at a reasonable
price, and served by the Ugliest Female Savants that can be Procured.
The Establishment cannot boast of a proprietor, but is carried on by a
Japanese lady whose ugliness would stand out even in a crowd. The
Cook, when his face is washed, is considered the best looking of the
company."

In the end we halted an amiable-looking postman, addressing him
with some of the Japanese phrases we had studied on shipboard when
not immersed in *Russian Self-Taught*—such phrases as *Ryoriya wa
doko desuka* (Restaurant where is); or *Kono michi wa doko ye iki-
masuka* (This road where to goes)?

Controlling by an heroic effort his obvious desire to yield to mirthful
convulsions, the postman escorted us to the Go-To-Ken Restaurant,
where he obligingly consented to be our guest and to introduce us to
the dishes most highly favored by residents of Hakodate. These all
proved to be various sorts of slices of raw or half-cooked fish floating
in watery sauces.

Time passed swiftly and on silent wings: partly because of our exotic surroundings; partly because of our determination to make ourselves understood by the postman and the restaurant staff; partly because of our mistaken notion that the Japanese drink called "saki" and spelled *sake* (which is vaguely like warm diluted sauterne) was as wishy-washy and ineffectual as it seemed. It was midafternoon when Major Johnson poked his head in the door of the Go-To-Ken, spied us, and came to our table wearing his usual saturnine smile.

We urged him to join us in raw fish, *sake,* and Japanese badinage, but he shook his head. "Pay up fast," he said. "You've got a hard night ahead. There's no coal in town, and we've got to get everyone back to the ships, and quick."

"Would the major be kidding?" someone asked.

"Listen," the major said, "the quartermasters didn't take the trouble to ask whether we could get coal in this dump. They just bulled in, trusting to luck to find it, and we thought they knew what they were doing. Nearly everyone on both ships has shore leave till midnight, and now the quartermasters tell us there isn't a lump of coal in Hakodate. We've got to hustle out of here and around to Otaru before a storm hits us. If we run into a typhoon before the *Logan* is coaled and ballasted, she'll capsize. Nothing can keep her afloat. She'll blow right smack over, and there'll be two thousand men trying to swim in the middle of a typhoon. Did any of you ever see a typhoon strike?"

While the postman helped us settle our account with the affable proprietor of the Go-To-Ken, the major spurred us on. "All the cheap bars have scotch whisky made in Japan," he told us. "If you come across any, don't touch it. It's called Queen George, and it's more bitched up than its name. It must be eighty-six per cent corrosive sublimate proof, because thirty-five hundred enlisted men were stinko fifteen minutes after they got ashore. I never saw so many get so drunk so fast."

Probably the Go-To-Ken had escaped the attentions of that mass of American soldiery only because of its distance from the waterfront, center of the bars, grogshops, pothouses and brothels that catered to the uncultivated tastes of the polyglot mariners who frequented that unsavory port. When we reached the more congested parts of town, the tumult was deafening. American enlisted men, blouses unbuttoned and caps askew, sat tipsily on curbs, careered wildly along muddy highways in jinrikishas, waving bottles and shouting, embraced each other or any convenient Japanese with abandon, leaned against flimsy buildings to steady themselves while arguing and drinking. Some declaimed in the center of throngs of fascinated Japanese; some slept in doorways; some reeled in alleys, offering to share bottles with kimono-clad admirers.

The noise that surged from all those garish, paper-walled structures was unending—a sort of concentrated drunken squealing.

Among those fuddled thousands moved American M.P.s, endlessly reiterating orders: "All leave is canceled. Return at once to the ships. No coal here and the ships sail tonight. Pass the word along. Return to the ships. Go to the dock and get back to your ship. Do not try to take liquor aboard. Anybody caught with bottles will get five days in the brig. All leave is canceled. Both ships will sail tonight. Return at once to your ship."

The situation was complicated by the quality of many of the infantry officers. Some, newly commissioned, had been sergeants in the Philippine Scouts, or enlisted men from the Regular Army who had only recently been graduated from training camps. Unable to divorce themselves from earlier habits, they had inexcusably joined with their men in their diversions, so that the men could hardly be considered under their control.

We went to work with the M.P.s, clearing out bars, scouring bordellos from top to bottom, policing alleys, dragging roisterers from jinrikishas, commandeering jinrikishas to carry unconscious drunks to the docks, stacking other helpless enlisted men like cordwood on two-wheeled handcarts and starting them toward the waterfront. Intoxicated soldiers seemed to have the flowing quality of water, able to seep through doorways, down chimneys, up through floors. When we slowly edged a score of khaki-clad tosspots from a dive and started them toward the ships, then turned to see whether we had overlooked anyone, the room would unbelievably be filled with unsteady doughboys, sprung from God knows where, drunkenly negotiating for the changing of American money or the purchase of juss one more boll of Queen George.

The dark bedlam went on and on, as endless as a nightmare: endlessly we entered dimly lighted rooms; endlessly heard Major Johnson's icy voice repeat, "What is your name and outfit? Return at once to your ship with these men and consider yourself under arrest."

The courts-martial resulting from that day's diversion in Hakodate went on for weeks after we reached Siberia. Eighteen captains and lieutenants were found guilty of conduct unbecoming officers and gentlemen, and confined to their quarters until they could be returned to the United States and dishonorably discharged.

It was almost dawn before the *Sheridan* followed the listing *Logan* out of Hakodate Harbor. The holds of both ships were nearly filled with sick, snoring and unconscious specimens of Our Boys Over There:

nearly, but not quite, since twenty-seven Americans had apparently vanished from the face of the earth, and a lieutenant and two M.P.s had been left in Hakodate to track them down, round them up, and conduct them overland to Otaru.

The lieutenant had a tough time, for all twenty-seven were not only disorderly when located, but openly reluctant to rejoin the ships on which they had already spent so many uncomfortable days. If there had been any place to which they could have escaped, they probably would have done so; but places to go, on the Northern Island of Japan, are practically non-existent; so they permitted themselves to be dragged and driven to Otaru, albeit with violent protests and a monotonous flow of profane cursing and swearing.

§

Twenty-four hours later the *Sheridan* and the *Logan* steamed into the harbor of Otaru, a town as beautiful and cultured as Hakodate was hideous and barbarous. We'd been lucky, for the sunrise was red—bright bloody scarlet—and the typhoon arrived a few hours after we did. From the lee of a temple high above that hill-encircled harbor, four of us saw it arrive in the form of a thousand miniature waterspouts that rose like a regiment of howling ghosts from the surface to hurl themselves toward the *Sheridan* and the *Logan*.

There were men working on flatboats alongside the *Logan*. Some saved themselves by hugging the deck: others, blown overboard, rose birdlike and turned grotesquely as they fell. Life preservers, cut from the *Logan's* rail and thrown to those unfortunates, soared up and away on that appalling, squalling wind.

At a shattering crash we peered cautiously from the shelter of the temple to discover that the roof of a house had flopped and buckled, accordion-like, beside us. Since the temple itself looked fragile, we got ourselves away from there and warily descended to the more sheltered streets of the town, where roofs billowed ominously, and occasionally exploded into geysers of shingles and kindling wood. Not until then did we discover that one hundred enlisted men who had failed to receive shore leave in Hakodate had been granted a day in the open at Otaru, and were relieving the tedium of inclement weather as do most idlers with more money than brains.

The streets were patrolled by M.P.s, however, and the small numbers of roisterers, by comparison with the roaring mob that had inundated Hakodate, seemed harmless. For a time an American professor, a teacher in the Otaru Higher Commercial School, kept us busy salvaging parts of his house, an American-type building which was coming apart in the high wind.

When we returned to the business section of Otaru to study the shops, the singular odors and the incomprehensible things we had observed earlier while hurrying to the professor's residence—among them women with enormous blue clown lips, who proved to be female Hairy Ainus —we found that schools had closed to allow students to observe at close range and no cost the strange-appearing human curiosities blown in by the typhoon. From then on we were attended in our outdoor movements by staring throngs of small, medium and large runny-nosed children in kimonos, and by a number of solemn young men in dark blue uniforms devoid of insignia.

Whenever we stopped to examine a shopwindow, they stopped, too, and studied us. When we went on, the clattering of their wooden clogs, as they hurried on with us—alongside, behind, often close in front, walking backward to see us better—made speech almost impossible. When we entered a store, they entered with us, filling the place to suffocation. They got in our way: they snuffled and coughed and sneezed on us. At length one of the young men in the dark blue uniforms—a young man who stood out among all the others because he was six feet tall, and endowed with a profile no more Japanese than that on a Greek coin—made a little bow and said, "You excuse I speak badly English. You like better they go not here, iss not?"

Our expressions answered for us, so he spoke sharply to the staring children, who rushed from the shop with the hoofy clatter of Gadarene swine.

"My name is Y. Mino," the young man said, and he sucked in his breath as if suddenly aware of spilling soup on his uniform. "I am student at Otaru Commercial College, very good Japanese college. You go somewhere fight on side of Japanese Army, I think yes, iss not?"

He haltingly apologized for intruding, but said a woman shopkeeper had asked him to show us a gold coin she had received from another American that morning, in return for which she had given the American twenty-one yen and a fountain pen. The American had told her the coin was the equivalent of twenty-five yen; but in contemplating the transaction in retrospect, she was stricken with a premonition that all was not well. Could we—and he sucked soup—do her the honor of confirming the value of the coin?

The coin was a Philippine nickel five-centavo piece, gilded. So we went with Y. Mino to the shop of the unfortunate woman; then took her with us to police headquarters. There we were passed, with bows, sips and hisses, to the number one policeman, to whom we outlined a course of action for the recovery of both the twenty-one yen and the fountain pen.

Lesser policemen brought teapots and cups, and we sat cross-legged in a circle on the floor of a barren room, sipping the tea and admiring our host's easy mingling of hisses and belches in equal proportion. We, too, hissed and belched, and word went around in police circles that we were privileged characters.

Our education in Japanese customs advanced rapidly that night, for the wind howled, the rain descended in torrents, and Y. Mino hunted up a colleague at Otaru Commercial College, G. Matzumoto, a chunky and amiable young man; and the two of them, accompanying us to a restaurant patronized by Otaru's *haut monde,* introduced us to the mysteries of the geisha chart—a printed sheet like a racing form, on which were the names, accomplishments and general descriptions of geisha available to patrons of that restaurant.

Y. Mino and G. Matzumoto discussed and argued geisha values as closely as two railbirds arguing the merits of entries in the Kentucky Derby, and we were shortly thereafter joined by a fourteen-year-old geisha named Okatsu, or Little Victory. Another, Mayo, or Pine Tree Play, was the possessor of a face capable of stopping a clock. Her specialties were thrumming the samisen and deftly handling *sake* jugs. A third, Koyakko, called for convenience Three Rousing Cheers, was pleasing to the eye, and rendered Japanese popular ballads in a voice almost unbearably lugubrious and unmelodious.

That was a pleasant evening up to a certain point. Little Victory was useless; but Pine Tree Play, after endless instruction and intense application, contrived to render a passable version of "I've Been Working on the Railroad" on her samisen: Three Rousing Cheers half mastered the words, but her voice quavered painfully in unexpected places. Y. Mino and G. Matzumoto were apt vocal pupils, and all our guests were delighted at our progress in the use of chopsticks and the art of the hiss and the belch.

It was apparent to all of us that the Japanese were a fascinating and charming people—wonderful characters for a novel. Lafcadio Hearn had utilized them, hadn't he? And look at Puccini! Not a bad place to live, Japan, either, while trying to write. Y. Mino and G. Matzumoto assured us that there were delightful towns overlooking the Inland Sea where one could live for a yen or two a day.

By nine o'clock the beating of rain against the front of the restaurant

35488

was a steady roar, so we left our kimono-clad friends and splashed toward the waterfront, affectionately guided by Y. Mino and G. Matzumoto. As we neared the landing stage and customhouse through driving sheets of rain, we were stopped by a medical officer from the *Sheridan,* Lieutenant Robert Garland, who had been lying in wait for us. The police, he told us, had closed the harbor to transportation; and all enlisted men who had come ashore had repeated the Hakodate *tour de force* and were now uproariously drunk. The Japanese police, understandably nervous lest the Americans dismantle the town barehanded if permitted to remain at large, had rounded them up and lodged them free of charge in the customhouse. During the roundup, one of the Americans, resentful of being pushed around by a Japanese jerk in a monkey suit, had not only defied him but brought a Queen George bottle down on his head with stunning efficiency.

The Japanese policeman, Garland said, had been removed horizontally in a two-wheeled ambulance drawn by coolies; the situation was delicate because Japanese police are a part of the army; and for an American soldier to strike a Japanese police officer is the same as assaulting a Japanese Army officer—which automatically creates an International Incident. The Japanese police, Garland told us, were so annoyed at the catastrophe that if we weren't careful, we might ourselves land inside the customhouse. This, Lieutenant Garland assured us, we wouldn't like; and he suggested that we retire inconspicuously and seek refuge elsewhere.

We listened to the howls, bellowings and crashings within the customhouse: then, accompanied by Garland, Y. Mino and G. Matzumoto, we unobtrusively slipped away to Otaru's leading hotel, a paper-walled affair that supplied each guest with slippers in place of boots, and a blue kimono in case he wished to fraternize *en déshabillé.* The remainder of the Intelligence detachment was already in residence, and as we assembled informally in our blue kimonos to consume fried eggs and *sake,* and discuss the day's occurrences, we agreed without exception that the Japanese were truly a delightful people.

Ah, yes, delightful! In the morning the paper inner walls of the hotel were slid apart: the building echoed to splashing sounds as fertilizer carts picked up the liquefied contents of the hotel's *benjos,* or toilets; and the frightfulness of the resulting stink was almost paralyzing.

American officers were directed to the bathing facility, a room some twenty by thirty, in the middle of which was a deep wooden tub, eight by five. They were relieved of their kimonos and stood embarrassedly around the wall, naked, staring at their feet or at the ceiling, while a youngish woman and her sixteen-year-old daughter, also nude, squatted facing each other in the steaming tub and soaked. There were fortunately pails in the room, so the Americans, rather than wait their turns in the tub, filled the pails, threw water on each other, dried themselves fumblingly and came away, leaving the mother and the daughter still in soak, seemingly oblivious of the presence of eighteen large, pallid, unclothed Americans.

When we returned to the ship that morning, the customhouse contingent were returning, too, greatly the worse for wear, and were being rudely searched for liquor by unsympathetic M.P.s. We gave the major a hand at the top of the ladder, and watched the approach of a Philippine Scout officer, proudly erect in the bow of a sampan, arms folded, like Washington Crossing the Delaware.

As the sampan nosed under the landing stage, the officer stepped unsteadily upon it, on which the sampan at once pushed off a few feet. The officer swayed perilously, focused his eyes on Major Johnson at the head of the ladder, saluted elegantly, and shouted, "Sir, is this the *Logan?*"

"It's the *Sheridan,*" Major Johnson replied coldly.

"Thank you, sir!" the Scout officer said thickly. Again he saluted smartly, executed a soldierly about-face—and marched off the grating, landing face down in Otaru Harbor, to the almost uncontrollable delight of his audience.

Through five long autumn days the *Sheridan* and *Logan* lay in Otaru, waiting for Tokyo to decide whether the Japanese Army could demand the right to punish the miscreant who had defiled the sacred person of a Japanese cop, or whether the American Army, as Major Johnson insisted, should be allowed to do its own punishing. Shore leave was reduced to a minimum; but when the major went for his daily conferences with top police officials who had hastened to Otaru from all parts of the Land of the Rising Sun to investigate this outrage against their honor, he took us along, knowing us to be persona grata with the police.

"I want you to see that American whose roof blew off," Major Johnson told me, "and get from him the name of an American who can speak Japanese like a native—one who'll go to Siberia with us. We'll make him an officer. We'll use him to talk to these little bastards: otherwise they'll claim they can't understand what we say. You may think they're nice now, but wait till you're up against their army! So get busy and dig up someone, but don't let anyone know what you're doing. If you do, the Japs might arrange to have him fall overboard and drown."

On the fourth day of our stay I located the right man—a professor in the American College in Sapporo; and on the morning of the fifth day I caught an early train for Sapporo. I performed my mission, and dusk was falling when I returned to Otaru to find an anxious-looking sergeant, his fist tightly clenched, waiting for me on the station platform.

"Sir," the sergeant said, pushing the fist at me, "the major said for the captain to put these on and go right over to the Kaiyote Restaurant. You have to go in a sampan, Captain, and I've got one waiting."

He opened his fist to reveal two medals, one bearing the words "Sea Girt Rifle Association: First Prize," the other reading, "Honolulu Athletic Club: Two Hundred Meter Swim: First Prize."

When I made no move to pick them up, the sergeant carefully attached them to the left breast of my tunic, stepped back and saluted with exaggerated punctiliousness. Then he led me to a wharf, explaining as we went that the Incident of the Stricken Cop had been adjusted to Tokyo's satisfaction, that permission for the *Sheridan* and *Logan* to sail had been granted, and that an official farewell banquet was being tendered for the fifteen top officers on the transports. Major Johnson, however, had decreed that the *Logan's* personnel were congenitally unable to keep out of trouble: that the *Logan,* therefore, must sail at once, leaving officers from the *Sheridan* to attend the banquet. To lend martial splendor to his comrades in arms, the major had further ordered that each officer don two medals from his velvet roll. A Japanese officer who had less than two medals, the major said, was almost a social outcast and was encouraged to use the servants' entrance. It was my misfortune to have been absent when the medals were distributed, and naturally no one had felt a yearning for those Sea Girt Rifle Association and Honolulu Athletic Club medals, which were the only two remaining.

The honors at the hilltop Kaiyote Restaurant were done by the mayor of Otaru, the heads of Hokkaido's police, three Japanese Army officers covered with medals, some eighteen of Otaru's leading citizens in kimonos, and fifty-five geisha in their best obis—among them our companions on previous evenings. We sat cross-legged on mats, in our stocking feet, Japanese and Americans alternating, with geisha before to fill our *sake* cups and geisha behind to ply us with raw fish; and police officers circulated constantly before us to clink their cups against ours and drink in *sake* the customary Japanese health to those going away to war. Captain Vieweg and I, with Koyakko before us to keep the *sake* bottles hot, found ourselves on the best of terms with the amiable gentleman between us—Tachu Morioka. He haltingly spoke

English, and carefully examined my medals with many an admiring hiss.

"For bravery?" he asked politely.

"They were nothing," I told him modestly. "Just small battles."

After we had joined in innumerable *sake* toasts, he confided to me in fluent English that he had spent fifteen years in New York, conducting an antique shop on Fifth Avenue. Fifteen years! For bravery! Sea Girt Rifle Association! Two Hundred Meter Swim! Small battles! O Koyakko San! *Sake kudasai!*

When the *Sheridan's* foghorn sounded at nine o'clock, hosts and geisha, all bearing paper lanterns on sticks, accompanied us down the rough path to the waiting police launch. *"Sayonara"* they called after us as the police launch moved out. *"Sayonara! Sayonara!* Come back again! Come back again!"

Two weeks later, in Siberia, I received a letter from Y. Mino:

DEAR CAPTAIN ROVERTS:

How do you do? As soon as I got up early in the morning on the 27th last month, I stretched out my face from the window and looked the harbor, for my despair, I could not find your large boats, and I felt something lonely. . . .

No question about it! Certainly anyone ought to be able to write about those interesting little people, the Japanese!

MY PROSPECTS for writing, after we reached Siberia, looked doubtful, and as the days went on they looked even more so.

We had no sooner tied up at the innermost end of the long, dog-leg-shaped harbor of Vladivostok on the twenty-ninth of September, 1918, than General Graves's senior aide, Captain Roger Merriman, came aboard to brief us on the situation. He painted a picture so dark that we thought he must be indulging in that fashionable Harvard affectation of overrestraint and airy understatement. He wasn't, though. He was telling the exact truth, and he was well equipped to do so. Later, known to thousands of Harvard graduates as "Frisky" Merriman, he was Gurney Professor of History and Political Science, as well as exchange professor from Harvard to France.

The Japanese, he said, had agreed, in Allied councils, to send seventy-five hundred men to Siberia to protect the Czechs in their retreat before the Bolsheviks. The United States had agreed to send the same number. We had done as agreed, but the Japanese had sent in seventy-five thousand instead of seventy-five hundred. Thus the Japanese held the whip hand in Allied councils, and were determined to hold it; and so successfully had they blocked the Americans that the whole American expedition had become nothing but an idling party, and its members did nothing but drowse away the long days and longer nights.

Major David I. Barrows, Chief of Intelligence and our commanding officer (later to become president of the University of California), came aboard the next day, not only to confirm all that Captain Merriman had said, but to add a few disheartening words of his own.

The Japanese, he told us, had made millions out of the war, wiping out their national debt and piling up an enormous surplus. If they permitted themselves to be drawn into actual fighting, a large part of that surplus would be destroyed and they would lose their present financial superiority. Consequently they were determined to allow no fighting that might embroil Japanese troops—no fighting against Germans: no fighting against Bolsheviks: no fighting against anyone.

Perhaps, Major Barrows added, he would be able to send Intelligence officers out on station to the interior of Siberia to act as observers: until then we could break out our bedding rolls and go to living in barracks at the American base, originally built by the Baldwin Locomotive Works as a repair shop.

The base was three miles from the central part of Vladivostok, so I thought to cheer myself a little by catching an army launch and viewing this peculiar-looking city to which we had apparently been sentenced for no adequate reason. I was even more depressed by what I saw. There were Japanese sentries everywhere: groups of squat Japanese soldiery off duty, moving slant-eyed, blank-faced, four abreast, along the sidewalks, shouldering aside those in their way. The streets were crowded with Manchus, Koreans in miniature horsehair hats and baggy white trousers, Ussuri Cossacks, Amur Cossacks, Don Cossacks, Terek Cossacks, unidentifiable Cossacks, some in elegant uniforms and some in rags, Russian soldiers from the old imperial army in an infinity of threadbare regimentals; Czechs, Tartars, British soldiers and sailors, Canadian troopers, French poilus; Chinese soldiers in gray bedquilt uniforms; American soldiers and sailors.

It was a warm day, the stench of the crowd was oppressive, and to cap it all, I was increasingly aware of a ringing in the ears, a painfully sore throat and a stiffness in every joint—doubtless acquired from the pestilential drippy-nosed Japanese with whom we had mingled in Hakodate and Otaru. I was also acutely conscious of a wave of homesickness.

So I left those seething crowds and strange uniforms and went far out Vladivostok's Svetlanskaya—Main Street—to the deserted section where it dips down into the tangled mazes of the Chinese-Russian bazaar. There I stood looking numbly into the window of a Japanese shop, packed with cheap toys of fossil ivory, cheap fans, cheap bed jackets. I unbelted and unbuttoned my trench coat and dazedly wondered whether or not to take it off. I couldn't even decide that, and just stood there, glassy-eyed, hands in pockets, staring into the window.

When, from the tail of my eye, I caught sight of two American officers walking briskly toward me, I looked harder than ever into the window, pretending to be unconscious of them, and waited for them to go by.

They did go by; then one of them came back and moved around to my left elbow, forcing me to look at him. He was a tall, slender, hawk-faced major, and he eyed me disapprovingly. I withdrew my hands from my pockets as quickly as I could and saluted.

"You ought to police yourself up," he said. "Snap into it! Button your coat and keep your hands out of your pockets. We've got standards to maintain in this area!"

I snapped into it and made myself presentable, noticing as I did so that the other officer had stopped and was regarding me with distaste.

"Another thing," the major said, "you want to keep your eyes open so you can salute your commanding general."

I must have been sicker than I thought, because I said, "Jesus, is that the general? I thought it was only a major!"

The general turned away in disgust, and the red-faced major re-joined him; while I, perspiring and in despair, made myself scarce up a side street and lurked there until the major and the general had gone marching back on the last lap of their constitutional.

That was the first step in my long friendship with Robert L. Eichelberger, the red-faced major. He went home to become superintendent of West Point; then, with three stars on his collar in the second World War, he led the Eighth Army from Australia to Tokyo, to become, under General MacArthur, the at first feared and then deeply admired "Aikerubaga," boss of American occupation forces in Japan. Knowing my love for the Japanese Army, he found time, throughout that long heroic journey, to write me every ten days or so, and send me odds and ends he'd taken from our fascinating little friends—invasion currency, samurai sword, personal flag, an ancient opulent God of Happiness, scotch whisky made in Japan for the Emperor's household, a pair of temple dogs . . .

At the moment I neither knew nor cared who the major was. I only knew I had been guilty of a dreadful gaucherie, and had grossly insulted General Graves—and that in the inner pocket of my blouse I carried a telegram from Marlborough Churchill instructing me to explain my personal desires to that same General Graves!

§

Major Eichelberger was General Graves's assistant chief of staff, his chief of staff being Colonel O. P. Robinson. Both were West Pointers.

I trailed Major Eichelberger and General Graves back to headquarters, in a state of perturbation; then hurried to the base and explained my faux pas to Captain Montgomery Schuyler, who had spent some years in the diplomatic corps and was not impressed by military rank.

The shoe, in fact, seemed to be on the other foot—perhaps because word had got around in higher circles that Schuyler was the New Yorker who had collected and presented to the New York Public Library a set of the off-color parodies which all great Japanese artists whimsically made of their best-known prints.

Schuyler soothed me by saying he would go with me to see Captain Merriman in the morning. Merriman, he assured me, would explain matters to Eichelberger and Graves in his most cultured and offhand Harvard manner. "You'll find," Schuyler said, "that the incident enlivened their day. Generals seldom have a chance to bawl out a captain, and both Eichelberger and Graves will have a kindly feeling toward you because they had to give you hell."

Captain Merriman performed as Schuyler had promised, but I couldn't seem to stay out of trouble with officers almost as powerful as our commanding general.

The general called the entire Intelligence Section to his office two days later, lined them up in a half circle and gave them a lugubrious outline of the situation as he saw it. He had, he said, attempted to obtain permission from Washington for the American Expeditionary Forces to go straight in along the line of the Trans-Siberian Railway until it made contact with the Bolsheviks, its headquarters to move with the train echelons; but Washington had refused permission and told him emphatically that he was to remain quietly in Vladivostok. He was not—repeat not—to fight anyone.

Our instructions, he told us, were that nothing should be done to offend the Russians—nothing. Suspicious characters, even, must not be molested. Any discouragements encountered must be patiently endured, and discouragements would be the common lot of everyone in the expedition. Those unable to work at the tasks for which they had been trained must work on any little job that came to hand.

He dismissed us by dejectedly polishing his spectacles, after which Colonel Robinson requested us to meet him in his quarters. There he vehemently informed us that criticism of any sort would not be tolerated. In particular, there must be no criticism of President Wilson's refusal to let us help the Czechs fight the Bolsheviks, or to do more for them than was being done. In general, there was to be no criticism of anything at all: no criticism of barracks, of troop quarters, of equipment, of food, of staff officers, of orders, of the climate, of scenery. The penalty for any such criticism, he made it clear, would be the dismissal of the critic from the United States Army.

When queried as to why an American force—especially an Intelligence Section—should remain in Siberia at all, under such conditions, the chief of staff seemed amazed at such ignorance. "In the army," he said, "you obey orders."

Disliking the chief of staff's pronunciamento as much as I had the general's severely parental warning, I hunted Major Johnson to see whether he had done anything about his proposed jaunt into the interior. He hadn't, because he had been made Allied provost marshal, and was hard at work deciding just where, in the red-light district, he should station his M.P.s. He was the personification of criticism, and listened with a sardonic smile to my complaints.

"They'll put you to doing something you won't like," he assured me. "That's the way it always happens. Me, I could go easily to Samara, to Tashkent, finding out everything; so they put me on Kopeck Hill, observing houses of ill fame. That professor you found for us in Sapporo, the one who speaks Japanese like a native, they have refused to make him an officer, as we promised him, so he has gone home. Why should you expect to make reports on Russia? If they want reports, they will send out those who neither read nor write."

I was stunned by the speed with which Major Johnson's prophecy came true.

Captain Powell, whose skill at breaking codes and ciphers was almost miraculous, cried to Major Barrows for help. Censorship at the post and telegraph office was not operating properly: at the moment it was in the hands of the Czechs: the Czechs weren't able to cope with it; and Bolshevik agents were copying American messages, military and naval, and sending them back to Bolshevik headquarters in Moscow for censorship.

Powell had also learned that the Japanese, as a part of their plan to swallow all Siberian industries, intended to seize the telegraph and cable offices and install their own censors: that if they did so, they'd be almost impossible to dislodge. Those offices, Powell argued, should be immediately occupied by Americans; but he was so overburdened with his codes and ciphers that he couldn't possibly reorganize the office himself. Would Major Barrows be so kind as to make me chief Allied military censor, and assign me to reorganize the telegraph and cable offices?

I reminded Major Barrows of his intimation that Intelligence officers would be sent into the interior on station, and made the specific request that once the censorship office was running smoothly I be allowed to turn the position over to the British and go out on station in case any Intelligence officers *were* so sent.

The major said yes, I would be among the first to go out; so Captain

Powell and I went to work, rounding up American and Russian translators and Morse code experts and hustling them to the cable and telegraph offices. We were just in time; for our translators were no sooner installed than a Japanese detachment, including Colonel Sakabe, a captain and three interpreters, marched briskly in to take command.

We had little trouble with Colonel Sakabe or Japanese headquarters when American, Czech and British headquarters joined in insisting that I was to be chief military censor; but simultaneously with the arrival, a few days later, of Carl Ackerman of the *New York Times* and Herman Bernstein of the *New York Herald,* I found myself deep in trouble far closer to home than Japanese headquarters.

Immediately on Bernstein's and Ackerman's appearance, Colonel Robinson sent for me to say he wished it clearly understood that censorship must be political as well as military: he had, he said, voted twenty-five times, when he was in the War College, against sending this expedition to Siberia: he considered the establishment of an eastern front impossible, and he refused to permit any criticism of our nonfighting policy.

I pointed out that political censorships were usually imposed for political purposes—to keep a political party in power or to prevent any criticism of it, and that such censoring, not being military, should be no part of an army's duties.

Colonel Robinson couldn't see it. Correspondents, he held, had no call to come uninvited into the sphere of influence of an expeditionary force and criticize things they didn't understand; and he, as chief of staff, wouldn't tolerate such criticism. And my orders were to see that no such criticism was sent. That's all, Captain! He dismissed me with West Point abruptness.

I have never felt any of the aversion to West Pointers so frequently encountered among temporary officers; and my differences of opinion with Colonel Robinson had no effect whatever on our relations outside the affairs on which we differed. Those relations were always amiable; and for years after the war I heard regularly from Colonel Robinson —as I did from Major Eichelberger, General Graves, his son Major Sidney Graves, Colonel Morris, Colonel Winfree: West Pointers all.

Colonel Robinson, however, had a military mind, and a military mind can be stubborn in thinking that it alone knows what is good for the world.[1] I brooded for a night over Colonel Robinson's insistence

---

[1] In 1947 the *U. S. Weekly* carried the paragraph: "General Omar Bradley, Veterans' Administrator, is clamping an army-style censorship on specific information concerning details of how more than $7,000,000,000 of taxpayer money is being spent each year. The theory is that the less the public knows about what is going on, the fewer questions it will ask."

on political censorship; then went again to see him. Against my wishes, I told him, I'd accepted the post of chief military censor. In that capacity, I was responsible only for preventing the sending of information concerning troop or naval dispositions or movements that might be of value to the enemy. His request for a political censorship required me to muzzle legitimate expressions of opinion—something that not only shouldn't be done, but usually can't be done without disastrous results for those who attempt it.

Colonel Robinson contented himself with remarking, "You've got your orders." He also said amiably that he saw I would have a hard time getting from the base into Vladivostok and back to the base each day, now that the harbor was on the verge of freezing and the Siberian winter close at hand; so he'd arranged for me to be transferred to headquarters. I would hereafter occupy a room with Colonel Morris, the inspector general of the expedition—and we might as well celebrate the occasion by having the merest touch of scotch whisky, which he had contrived to retain after issuing orders that no intoxicating liquors should be brought to, or consumed in, headquarters at any time or for any purpose. I gratefully joined Colonel Robinson in disobeying this order: then went to Major Barrows.

Colonel Robinson, I told him, insisted on a political censorship. Since I considered political censorship indefensible, I refused to take the responsibility for a political censorship; and if there was to be political censoring, Colonel Robinson himself would have to do it, and newspaper dispatches would have to be submitted to the chief of staff and not to me. Major Barrows heartily agreed, and we then and there drew up a set of censorship rules for American correspondents. Paragraphs 5 and 6 read:

> 5. The Military Censor will confine his activity to military censoring. Discussion of political conditions in Siberia or of the policy of the Allied Nations here will be censored or changed only by the direction of the chief of staff.
> 6. Any exceptions to the above rules will have the personal approval of the chief of staff.

When I took these rules to Colonel Robinson, he cholerically refused to allow them. This, he said, was the Old Army Game, and I was passing the buck. I readily admitted that I was passing the buck. If he continued to insist on political censorship, somebody else had to do it. Dispatches filed by Ackerman, Bernstein or any other correspondents in Siberia would, so far as I was concerned, be untouched except in such parts as gave information about troop or naval movements.

The colonel fell back on that ancient military method of ending a dispute: "You've got your orders."

As I understood the situation, my commanding officer was Major Barrows, and I *did* have my orders. They were from Major Barrows: not from Colonel Robinson; and the orders clearly said I was not to censor politically.

Shortly thereafter Bernstein and Ackerman went on a tour of inspection to Khabarovsk with General Graves and his staff. Bernstein, who was a good reporter, returned with a story dealing with the activities of the Swedish Red Cross in Khabarovsk. Swedish Red Cross representatives, acting as German agents, said his story, were forwarding information in Red Cross tins with the connivance of Red Cross headquarters. I passed it uncensored. Such things, unfortunately, *do* happen in wartime. An American captain of a non-military organization returned from the Urals to headquarters in Vladivostok with a satchel containing fifty thousand dollars' worth of platinum to be used in making shell fuses.

Ackerman and Bernstein, who had somehow got wind of my differences of opinion with Colonel Robinson, agreed between themselves that I would almost certainly find myself in hot water if I stayed around headquarters. They had learned that a Red Cross relief train was about to leave for Omsk and the Samara front, had obtained permission to accompany it; and now, unknown to me, they put in a request to the chief of staff that I be allowed to go with them.

The request was refused.

Not that Colonel Robinson didn't seem amiable at all times: his attitude toward me was always friendly—so friendly, in fact, that I showed him General Churchill's telegram about writing. Colonel Robinson read it: then said perfunctorily that he didn't know what the general's attitude would be on the matter, but that he himself was irrevocably opposed to allowing anybody in the army to write professionally. He made it evident that he regarded himself as the actual commander of the expedition, and General Graves merely as a figurehead, and that it was immaterial to him what General Pershing, General Graves, General Churchill or anyone else thought about anything.

Ackerman and Bernstein had sized up the situation correctly; for the Swedish Red Cross dispatch had scarcely gone on its way when a code cable arrived from the office of the Secretary of War stating frostily that press dispatches from Vladivostok bore no sign of having been censored. Who, it demanded, was doing the censoring and what system was being followed?

This resulted in a hurried consultation between General Graves and Major Barrows. The evasive reply, signed by General Graves, read, "I am doing the censoring of press dispatches. It cannot be wholly effective as messages can be sent from stations outside Vladivostok."

That reply struck me as an invitation to further embarrassing messages. If he had said, "I am doing the censoring of press dispatches and wish no outside interference," there would probably have been no further protests. But when he admitted that his censorship could be ineffective, he was asking for trouble.

Who was ineffective and why? From what stations outside Vladivostok could messages be sent? Why aren't the stations covered? How do you mean you're doing the censoring? Snap into it, Graves!

At all events, I was in bad odor: no doubt of that. Obviously the Secretary of War was finding, in Ackerman's and Bernstein's dispatches, embarrassing references to the uselessness of President Wilson's Siberian policy; and equally obviously—unless the Secretary of War was put in his place—somebody was in peril of getting it in the neck as a result. Since I couldn't speak up to the Secretary of War, since I was the one who insisted that political censorship was improper, and since the Secretary of War himself apparently considered political censorship not only proper but necessary, the simplest way to disembarrass my superiors would be for me to ask to be supplanted.

So I notified Ackerman and Bernstein that no messages would be passed until okayed by the chief of staff. At the same time I told Major Barrows that if a political censorship were enforced or continued, I wished to be relieved at once.

Major Barrows' reply was to notify the general that he was sending seven Intelligence officers on station to strategic points in the interior, and that there was no reason why I shouldn't be released from my duties as military censor and sent out as one of the seven. The orders came through from Barrows on the following day: "Captain Schuyler to Harbin; Captain Roberts to Chita; Captain Straus to Blagoviestchensk, Lieutenant Scovell to Omsk, Lieutenant Baggs to Tomsk, Lieutenant Cushing to Verkhneudinsk; Lieutenant Stinchfield to Krasnoyarsk. Officers may select orderlies and requisition supplies."

Chita! I had hit the jackpot! Harbin, crossroads of Asia, was noisier, more flamboyant, richer in diversions, aristocratic Russian refugees and iniquity; but Chita was the heart of Siberia: just short of the southern end of Lake Baikal; headquarters of two Japanese divisions—the

12th or Okura, and the 3rd or Nagoya—both of which were in the mysterious situation of not being under General Otani, Chief of the Japanese General Staff in Siberia. Why? How come? What Japanese skulduggery was afoot? Let me at it!

Chita, too, was the lair of the Cossack Semeonoff, leader of cavalry squadrons that did dark deeds in return for Japanese gold, a hetman whose violence and viciousness might have served Sienkiewicz as a model in *With Fire and Sword*. And Chita was a hunter's paradise, for the prairies roundabout swarmed with ducks and geese from Lake Baikal, innumerable pheasants and those succulent little Siberian partridges known as rabchik.

I sent for Handley, a Chicago enlisted man who had been plucked from the ranks to act as one of the translators in the cable office. He was able and willing, spoke five languages, was a first-class mechanic, and regarded me with favor because I had got him a sergeantcy. So far as I knew, Handley could do everything.

"Can you cook, Handley?" I asked.

"I sure can, Captain," Handley said. "I cooked on a ninety-foot yacht once, and did good."

"How'd you like to go to Chita as my orderly?" I asked. "We might have to do our own cooking occasionally."

"Captain," Handley said, "I'd do pretty near anything to go to Chita with the captain. Those barracks—well, Captain, they throw me! They've got me down!"

"Make out a list of supplies you'll need," I told him, "and I'll requisition 'em. I'm putting in for two shotguns and two Springfields. Make it snappy, and maybe we can get out of this damned censorship mess before someone changes his mind."

Handley disappeared, running, and I went hunting for Major Buckmaster, the officer in charge of British censorship. He had imported a British civilian censor, Erving, from Hong Kong, to handle the British end of the cable office. Erving was a civil servant who took an almost sensuous delight in censoring; but since the British apparently thought highly of him, he seemed the logical one to take charge of everything. I suggested to Buckmaster that since I was going out on station, we call an inter-Allied censorship meeting and have Erving officially confirmed in the position—with the strict proviso that he attempt no political censorship and keep his hands off newspaper dispatches except as they revealed troop movements. The meeting was duly agreed to, and six of us—Americans, Czechs, British and Russians—impatiently waited nearly two hours for the Japanese representatives. The last hour was spent in a cold-blooded discussion, by all present, of the duplicity, offensiveness, untrustworthiness and contemptibility of the Japanese Army. The Japanese representatives never did appear, and we returned raging to our respective headquarters.

I find in my diary the entry: "The Russians and the Allies are unanimous in their detestation of the Japanese. Major Buckmaster's resentment of them is so bitter as to be almost un-British: he is certain that it won't be many years before they are shown their place, and most emphatically jammed into it. When asked who was going to do it, he refused to commit himself; but he was certain that the Japanese themselves would force *somebody* to do it."

§

My preparations were wasted. Barrows, gaily unconcerned because he had just been made a full or bird colonel, called me in to say that when he sent the list of Intelligence officers to the chief of staff, Colonel Robinson had crossed off my name on the ground that I was needed as chief censor. I knew better, and Barrows knew better; but military formality made it impossible for me to do anything but ask permission to put my case before the chief of staff.

Barrows reluctantly agreed; but when I reached the chief of staff and asked him to reconsider his withdrawal of my name on the ground that I'd been a professional observer for ten years, and could be of more value in Chita than as a censor, he looked at me coldly and said, "I okayed you as censor. When I okay anyone for a position, I leave him in that position till moss grows on his back! I don't pull him off every time the wind changes and some smart aleck wants to send him somewhere else."

I reminded him that we didn't agree about political censorship, and that he'd be happier if I were out from under his feet.

"It was only yesterday that I cut your name off the list," Colonel Robinson said, "and I don't change my mind that quick. Some day you can go out on station, maybe. Right now I want you here in headquarters, and that's where you're going to stay."

§

There were times during the next few weeks when I thought everyone on that expedition, including myself, had become abnormal from cold, inaction and inertia.

I was called to the chief of staff's office one morning, and shown a dispatch to the *Times* from Ackerman describing the fall of Ufa. General Graves was present, and regarded me owlishly while I read it. The dispatch was short and harmless. It contained one inaccurate statement; but that, as I saw it, was no concern of anyone except Ackerman and the *New York Times*. When I said so and handed it back to the chief of staff, General Graves said, "I guess we'll kill it."

On the following day I was again called to the chief of staff's office, and this time the general wasn't there. Colonel Robinson handed me a long dispatch from Ackerman, sent from Krasnoyarsk, describing the desperate plight of the Czechs and urging help for them.

"What do you think of that?" he asked.

I said I thought it shouldn't be touched.

To my amazement Colonel Robinson marked it okay and sent it to the cable office. Since General Graves had killed the short dispatch of the previous day, he would most certainly have refused to release the dispatch about the Czechs; and the chief of staff must have known it. I felt sorry for General Graves.

I felt even sorrier for him when he called me to his office on Armistice Day, twenty-four hours before we got the news that the war was over—though it had been apparent for some time that we were near the end. The general handed me several Herman Bernstein dispatches, saying he wished a frank opinion as to whether or not I thought Washington had objected to previous messages for political reasons only.

I asked him whether he would abrogate rank, so that I could speak freely, regardless of military formality, and whether he would consider my remarks as confidential.

He said Yes to both requests.

I told him I had been against political censorship from the beginning, because I knew it to be both stupid and wrong. I said that from the beginning, too, the Secretary of War, the State Department, and the understrappers who supplied those departments with opinions, had obviously been eager for a political censorship, but hadn't cared to say so openly. All they had done was to squeal that censorship was inadequate, probably hoping that the general would lose his nerve and impose a political censorship, thus bolstering their pretended importance. So far as military censorship was concerned, I told the general, the United States was engaged in no military movements in Siberia, and the war was unmistakably near its end, so there was no longer occasion for even military censorship; and political censorship would be sheer nonsense. More than that, I said, no commanding officer of the army of any civilized country had ever imposed a political censorship without eventually finding himself immersed in Trouble up to his eyebrows.

"If I were in your position," I said, "I'd never allow a word to be censored from any dispatch unless I had definite orders signed by somebody who'd have to shoulder the blame for inexcusable meddling: an order signed by Wilson or George Creel or Newton Baker or Marlborough Churchill; and *that* you'd never get. Nobody would be such a damned fool as to sign such an order. Your chief of staff, even, wouldn't sign it, because he'd know that when correspondents had escaped the army's jurisdiction, they'd write the truth, and he'd be lucky not to lose his scalp. As for Bernstein's dispatches, anybody who censored them would censor the Book of Job or the Flaxie Frizzle books."

"I think so too," he said. "I think so too"; but he looked helpless, as if he didn't know what he thought.

He seemed so open to the truth that I took General Churchill's telegram from my pocket and laid it before him. "Would the general have any objection," I asked, "if I took advantage of this suggestion from General Churchill and tried to write something about this expedition?"

He read it and looked even more helpless. "Oh, I suppose not," he said. "I suppose not, but all these messages from Washington have disturbed me more than I can tell you. I scarcely know what to say about anything."

§

The final act in that all-too-frequently-encountered tragicomedy of military fumbling came a month later, when a staff sergeant came to me in a lather. "Colonel Barrows says you're to report to the general at once," he said. "The colonel says it's good news, Captain."

Good news? Were they going to let me write? Was I to be sent out on station at last? Perhaps—oh, consummation most devoutly to be wished—perhaps I was to be ordered home!

At headquarters Colonel Barrows waylaid me and shook my hand. "Congratulations," he said heartily. "Congratulations! I can't tell you how pleased I am! Go right on up. The general expects you."

The general's satellites exuded an unwonted camaraderie as I approached the inner sanctum. The adjutant general abandoned his usual chilly imperturbability to smile urbanely. Major Eichelberger favored me with a stare of placid contentment. The general's two young West Point aides for the first time didn't turn away as though from a noxious vapor. One even sprang to open the general's door.

The general himself beamed upon me, and his spectacles glistened. "Sit down, sit down, Captain," he said. "This is going to please you as much as it did me. Here, read these." He pushed two messages across his desk.

The first,[2] signed by Marlborough Churchill, stated that the censorship situation in Siberia was simplified almost to the point of extinction, but that in view of General Graves's cables and the protests of Naval Intelligence in New York, his queries had been submitted to General Peyton March, Chief of Staff. The second, signed by Peyton March, stated that the War Department had no objection whatever to the publication of the protested news articles or any other articles that didn't reveal military operations, and that General Graves's attitude concerning censorship had been wholly correct.

"Well," General Graves said, and his whole face seemed to shine, "what do you think of *that!*"

I thought a number of things. I thought it was clear that General Graves, Colonel Barrows and everyone else in a position to know anything had been cravenly certain that my attitude on censorship was wrong. I thought that if the whippersnappers in Naval Intelligence had been allowed to write the opinion on Siberian censorship for Peyton C. March, I would be headed for a court-martial and a dishonorable discharge for refusing to countenance stupidity. I thought that the sooner I got out of what was known as "This Man's Army," the better it would be for everyone. I thought—I knew—that I would never again allow myself to be coaxed or coerced into donning the uniform of an organization that so earnestly persisted in wasting men and material. I thought that General Graves, in expecting me to clap my hands and caper with joy, showed that he felt I must have doubted the advice I gave him as much as he had.

Above all, I knew that this was the psychological moment to press my desire to write, and to ask for promotion. The general was so happy about the whole affair that he probably would have been willing to recommend me for a majority. But by this time I was dubious about writing until I had escaped from the army. Not for anything would I have asked to be made a major: the mere asking would have stopped me from putting in a request for immediate discharge.

I thought all these things, but when I looked into the general's happy countenance, I couldn't utter any of them. I could only thank him for letting me see the correspondence, and tell him how interesting I found paragraph 8 of General Churchill's letter—"This simplifies the censorship situation almost to the point of extinction."

---

[2]For complete dispatches, see pp. 380–83, Appendix.

CHAPTER

13

In the end it was Colonel Robinson who effected my release from the office of chief censor. The colonel was a close follower of exchange rates, which fluctuated from day to day. On our arrival in Vladivostok, a dollar could be exchanged for seven and a half rubles, but almost immediately the rate slipped to eight and a half for a dollar, rose to eight, slipped back to nine and a half and finally reached ten rubles to the dollar.

Newspaper correspondents met their heavy cable tolls with the help of the American consul general, who accepted American dollars from their respective newspapers and turned the dollars over to the chief of staff for exchange into rubles. The rubles were then delivered to me.

On November 18 Colonel Robinson returned from Khabarovsk, to which he had traveled in a private car which had once belonged to the president of the Chinese Eastern Railway, General Horvath. His private car was luxurious, and Colonel Robinson had enjoyed his trip immensely. He seemed eager to tell me about it, and generously said he'd like me to make the trip, too, not only to see the beauties of the Ussuri Valley and the enormous Amur River, but to pick up information that nobody in Khabarovsk had been able to give him.

He had been fascinated by the exchange situation in Khabarovsk. The dollar, it seemed, was worth more there than in Vladivostok. If I wanted to go, he said, he'd arrange it. I could go on a troop train scheduled to return enlisted men from officers' training school to their regiment in Khabarovsk, the training school having been abandoned when the armistice was declared. I jumped at the opportunity.

Two days later Colonel Robinson turned over to me fourteen thousand six hundred rubles to be applied to Herman Bernstein's cable tolls. The colonel had received two thousand dollars in gold from the American consul general and had converted it all at 7.3 rubles to the dollar—a noteworthy exchange, since I had never heard of anyone getting less than 7.5 to the dollar. The colonel made an interesting statement when he delivered the rubles: within the next two weeks, he said, he was sure the rate would be ten rubles to the dollar, and anybody who didn't make a little money on the tumble would be pretty stupid. I made a note in my diary to the effect that if he was so sure, he could have saved Bernstein fifty-four hundred rubles by waiting two weeks before changing the two thousand dollars.

Two days later Colonel Robinson called me to his quarters, gave me three hundred dollars, and told me to buy rubles with them at the Khabarovsk Post Exchange, provided the rate was nine for a dollar or better. Since there had already been considerable murmuring among higher officers about Colonel Robinson's ruble transactions, I accepted the three hundred dollars without comment, but later handed them to Colonel Morris to hold until my return. Colonel Morris, a West Pointer, was a splendid officer who never cared to criticize any other officer. He bore patiently with me whenever I spoke my mind concerning those who had committed obnoxious military stupidities; and when I had finished, he would blink and smile in amused exasperation, and shoot me a quizzical glance that seemed to say, "So you've finally found it out, have you?" That was how he looked at me when I gave him the chief of staff's three hundred dollars.

§

I had some trouble catching that special train for Khabarovsk—not only because I waited two days in the railway station while railway officials hunted for enough freight cars to carry the passengers, but also because Colonel Robinson had failed to consult Colonel Barrows either before or after telling me I could make the trip. Thus, when I asked Robinson for travel orders, he provided me with them, but said I must also have Barrows's permission.

As I said before, I think the utter futility of that Siberian expedition had unbalanced the minds of many of those forced to endure it. Barrows, who had not been at all disturbed when Robinson cut my name from his list of officers to go out on station, was now furious because the chief of staff dared to send me to Khabarovsk; and the resulting scene between Barrows and Robinson was both embarrassing and ludicrous; for those two full-grown, dignified officers screamed at each other like Italian ditch diggers.

Robinson, Barrows shouted, had exceeded his authority and been guilty of great irregularity in ordering me to Khabarovsk: he was thoroughly capable of administering the Intelligence Section, and he refused to recognize Robinson's authority over it. Barrows, Robinson roared, might be thoroughly capable, but by God the Intelligence Section didn't have the information he wanted and intended to have, and he knew by God that if he didn't take steps to get it himself, he'd probably never get it.

Their faces were chalk-white, and they shook with rage as they denounced each other.

Robinson stopped the argument when he saw that the hallway outside had filled with enlisted men and field clerks, all eagerly hopeful of seeing the two embattled colonels slug each other.

Robinson took a deep breath. "We can discuss this later," he said. "In the meantime that special for Khabarovsk goes out tonight and I want that information in a week."

He stamped from the room; and Barrows, breathing heavily, sat down at his desk and stared at nothing.

After an hour of intense thinking, he sent for me. He seemed as jovial as ever and, as had been his habit for almost a month, wandered off into verbal alleys and was profuse with comments on matters wholly alien to the subject under discussion.

Colonel Robinson was right about one thing, he said: we didn't have enough information on what had been going on in Khabarovsk; so I could go there as planned and get complete details on (1) the working of the Khabarovsk municipal government, (2) the manner in which the Soviet government attempted to exert influence in Khabarovsk, (3) a full set of municipal laws, (4) the names and reputations of those administering town affairs, (5) the forces and armament of the Cossack leader Kalmikoff, (6) the prisoners said to have been shot out of hand and without trial by Kalmikoff on the pretext that they were Bolsheviks, (7) the condition and morale of American troops in Spasskoi, Nikolsk-Ussurisk and Khabarovsk, (8) the relations between Japanese and American troops at those stations, and (9) further developments in the pro-German activities of the Swedish Red Cross.

§

I didn't take the same sybaritic pleasure Colonel Robinson had taken in journeying through the fabulous Ussuri Valley, which unexplainably supports palms, boa constrictors, Amur tigers, swans, geese, pheasants and innumerable ducks. The freight cars in which we rode were too deficient in windows and observation platforms.

In the center of each car was a sheet-iron stove shaped like a megaphone fastened large end down between the car's two sliding doors. At both ends of the car, midway between floor and roof, were wooden platforms. Lieutenant Duncan, who had charge of the enlisted men returning to their regiments, shared one of the platforms with me, and on it we broke out our bedding rolls. In the car with us were twelve enlisted men, who rolled up in their blankets on the other platform and in the space beneath the platforms. The temperature of the outer air was fifteen below zero, so the stove was kept cherry-red and the temperature within the car fluctuated between eighty and ninety, forcing us to remove our sheepskin coats and uniform blouses.

If we opened a sliding door for a glimpse of the scenery, the temperature plunged instantly to zero. We were two days and three long nights making that five-hundred-mile trip, and we'd have been even longer if at each stop we hadn't sent a sergeant with a gun to the engine to discourage the engineer and fireman from making long social calls in villages along the line.

Duncan and I spent a large part of our daylight hours in the cook car, which was bossed by a cook who could outcuss a mule skinner, and had been in the army so long that he had forgotten the feel of a linen shirt. His two assistants had been condemned to K.P. for minor offenses—one having received a six months' sentence for losing his overcoat and going A.W.O.L. for two days.

The vibration of the freight cars was so violent that nothing stayed on the stove unless held in place. When a stewpan fell off, as it frequently did, the cook remarked, "I see they hain't fixed that flat tire yet," at which his two time-serving assistants flattered him with hoarse laughter.

His staple culinary products were canned tomatoes thickened and enriched with crumbled soda biscuit, and canned beans to which French mustard had been generously added to provide flavor and warmth.

When Duncan produced a steak mysteriously acquired in Vladivostok, the cook sprinkled a handful of salt on a glowing stove lid and with no further formality dropped the steak upon it. "No sense dirtying up a pan," he explained when we protested at the rude treatment and the clouds of smoke that rose from the scorched meat. "Pans jounce off, but this stays where it's put. You won't have to eat *this* steak off the floor." I expected the worst; but at the end of four minutes he transferred the steak to a mess tin, and I never ate a better.

Our sergeant mounted guard over the engineer at Spasskoi and Nikolsk-Ussurisk until I could learn how the troops felt about the Japanese and about remaining in Siberia. I had never before encountered such unanimity of opinion. Every man was in a frenzy at the monotony and futility of existence: every man itched for a showdown with the Japanese, who had made no effort to endear themselves to their Allies.

In Khabarovsk the situation was even worse, because the Americans, in addition to feeling that they were at the extreme northeastern corner of nowhere, were not only irked by the Japanese, but had been irritated by the Cossack leader Kalmikoff, whose activities had been such as to make it necessary to maintain machine-gun patrols both day and night, and for officers to carry pistols in their coat pockets at all times. Kalmi-koff, I was to learn later, was a dead ringer in size, features and mus-tache for Adolf Hitler.

When I finished interviewing Colonel Styer of the 31st Infantry, the mayor and other leading citizens of Khabarovsk, and several prisoners who had lain on the floor of the jail while Kalmikoff's men blew out the brains of other prisoners, I had enough notes for a dozen reports, any one of which should have indicated to Washington that Siberia was no place for an American army. If I had been allowed to go to Chita, where there was a bigger, noisier and more offensive Cossack than Kalmikoff, and two whole divisions of those interesting little slant-eyed Allies of ours, I would have needed a special train to hold the notes I would inevitably have made.

I was glad to leave Khabarovsk. It's doubtless a pleasant place in summer, cooled by breezes from the Amur's mighty flood; but when I left it, the headquarters troop was drilling in a snowstorm, and men and horses, plastered with snow, wheeled and cantered silently like the fig-ments of a cold bad dream.

My return to Vladivostok was comparatively easy. A Russian-speak-ing sergeant had been sent to the station to get me a compartment on the train, if possible. According to his lights, he had done well; for when I joined him, my kit bag was stowed snugly in an upper berth, beside the suitcase of a pretty and agreeable Russian girl. The sergeant had already learned her name; knew, even, that she was off to spend Christmas with a school friend who lived in Nikolsk-Ussurisk, only twenty-four hours away. Perhaps I should have been grateful to the sergeant: probably I would have added gratifyingly to my store of notes if I had accepted the situation. At the moment, however, I picked flaws in the sergeant's arrangements. He was aggrieved, and said my only alternative was to talk myself aboard Major Miller's private car, which was even now being attached to the end of the train. This I did, but later I realized that it's usually unwise to reject a sergeant's judgment. Major Miller was an argumentative officer whose chief concern was the exact temperature where Réaumur and Fahrenheit thermometers coincide (15 below zero, as I recall it), and the degree of slope that constitutes a hundred per cent rise (45 degrees, I think, and to hell with it). I couldn't have helped learning more from the Russian girl —and she might have turned into a character in a book.

§

Between Thanksgiving and mid-January most of the participants in that Siberian Expeditionary Force seemed semi-insane with cold, idleness and the depression that accompanies those two curses. With those Khabarovsk notes on my hands, I went to the bazaar and for twenty-two rubles bought an old table, sent it to headquarters on the back of a Chinese coolie, equipped myself with a blankbook the size of Frye's Geography, and went to work. When the Khabarovsk reports were finished, I went right on writing about various aspects of life on the Svetlanskaya (or Main Street) Front.

There may be something about the mere act of writing that attracts onlookers as surely as a bald head lures flies. As soon as I had pinned a score of chapter headings on the wall above the twenty-two-ruble table, our quarters were in a constant upheaval, and were used as refuges by idle officers who damned Siberia, damned the War Department, damned American policy in Siberia, damned the cold, damned the food, damned the Japanese, damned President Wilson and the deal with Masaryk that had set the Siberian expedition in motion, damned the scarcity of mail, damned the postal clerks who persisted in sending to North Russia a large part of the letters and packages addressed "A.E.F., Siberia." They sat on our beds; they spread blankets on up-ended locker trunks and played interminable games of bridge; they hung over my shoulder to study the Svetlanskaya Front chapter headings and suggest additions; and through it all they damned everything over an inch high and two inches wide.

Newspaper correspondents, departing for or arriving from the interior, stopped in to say good-by or hello—Wilfrid Fleisher and Frank King of the *Japan Advertiser;* Dad Whiffen of the Associated Press; Wright of the *Chicago News;* Bernstein and Ackerman to congratulate me on having missed the Omsk trip, during which the entire party nearly froze to death, and to tell me the details of the manner in which the Bolsheviks murdered the Tsar and his family in Ekaterinburg. Major Johnson reported daily on the preceding night's occurrences among the brothels on Kopeck Hill.

On the seventh of December young Mr. Russell of the Committee on Public Information, with whom I had now and then split a bottle of peppered vodka, dropped in to say he was leaving for home that night on a fast Canadian boat, and would be glad to carry anything I hesitated to send through regular military channels. Russell knew, as did all of us, that anybody's outgoing letters could conceivably be privily opened. If the letter unhappily had made mention of some of the things that could have been told about the expedition, the writer would be in a bad spot. Consequently letter writers had to be guarded in their statements.

In Russell's hands, however, a letter would be safe, and I immediately made a personal and informal report to Major Rupert Hughes, telling him, in words of one syllable, that in spite of President Wilson's pronouncement that Bolshevism could be eliminated if we supplied Russia with food, it was a disease that couldn't be checked, and would eventually sweep all of Russia and Siberia; that if Newton Baker had told the truth when he recently said the Siberian Expeditionary Force would neither be added to nor subtracted from, there was trouble ahead for everyone, because we would certainly, unless heavily reinforced, be outnumbered and destroyed; that only by the grace of God and the skin of our teeth had detachments of United States troops repeatedly escaped clashing with and being wiped out by superior Japanese detachments —and any such clash would automatically end our so-called friendly relations with Japan; that the morale of American troops was deplorably low because of idleness and only too apparent ineffectuality, and getting lower every day; that no use whatever was being made of fifty per cent of the Intelligence detachment (two of whom were already on the verge of melancholia and four more not much better off), and no adequate use being made of the other fifty per cent. I felt obliged to touch on a few things I hadn't even dared put in my diary.

All of us, I also told him, were revolted by drawing pay we didn't deserve, wearing uniforms that prevented us from earning adequate livings, posing as soldiers in a war that had ceased to exist, and wasting government funds that would be better spent in helping to build a two-hundred-thousand-dollar high school on even such a remote and unpopulated spot as Boon Island, off the coast of Maine. I asked him for God's sake to do what he could to have us ordered home, because we all had something that really needed doing. As for me, I reminded him, I wanted to write.

"Here," I said to Russell. "You'd better read this. You oughtn't to carry it without knowing what's in it."

Russell read it; then sealed the envelope and put it in his pocket. "That's mild," he said. "I had an idea you might really blow your top."

The answer to that letter came in the form of a cable from the War Department to General Graves, asking classification of the officers under his command into (1) those wishing to be immediately and permanently separated from the service; (2) those wishing to remain temporarily; (3) those wishing to remain permanently.

On January 8 Colonel Barrows recommended to General Graves that eight Intelligence officers be returned to San Francisco for discharge; and on January 17 Lieutenant McKenna, now a captain (later to become a consul general and first secretary of legation in Yugoslavia), scratched at our door, poked his head through the opening, wagged a code-and-cipher slip at me, winked meaningly, and whispered, "We're on our way!"

So the portcullis was rising! When it had risen, perhaps I could at last do what I had always wanted to do.

CHAPTER

14

IN THE WEEKS that elapsed between the day we got our orders and the day an army transport, coated with ice from water line to crow's nest, wallowed into Vladivostok from Tientsin and Chinwangtao, suggestions as to what I might write whirled about me like snowflakes, and proved about as evanescent and weighty.

One, however, struck musically upon my ear. "You ought to take a look at Pekin while you have the chance," said Colonel Morris. "I was there during the Boxer Rebellion and made a friend who would show you plenty to write about—Princess Der-ling: a great lady."

I hastened to Captain McKenna and begged him to search the air waves for the whereabouts of all our Pacific transports, and figure the dates of arrival and departure of the *Merritt* and *Warren* on their Manila–China–Vladivostok–Nagasaki–Manila circuit: of the *Sheridan, Logan, Vera Cruz* and *Sherman* on the San Francisco–Vladivostok–Manila–Honolulu–San Francisco circuit.

The same forces that had kept me from delving into Chita, Semeonoff and the Samara front now worked willingly in my behalf. If, I told Colonel Barrows, Captain Vieweg and I could go to Pekin by rail by way of Mukden at our own expense, we could catch the *Merritt* at Tientsin for Nagasaki and board the *Sherman* when she touched there en route to Manila. "Fine," said Barrows, and he spoke to Robinson. "Good idea," said Robinson, and spoke to Graves. "Excellent," said Graves, and he gave us immediate leave and his blessing.

Unfortunately the *Merritt,* entangled in a raging storm, vanished from all air contact. While we were trying to locate her and discover whether we could safely set off for Pekin by train, the little *Warren* lurched into port, almost swamped by the tons of ice that hid her upper works. Out from the heart of the ice walked Colonel Quinlan, up from the Philippines on a sight-seeing trip, and made straight for our quarters in search of his old Manila friend Colonel Morris.

Colonel Morris introduced me to Colonel Quinlan with his characteristic head jerk. "Keep an eye on him when he reaches Manila," Colonel Morris told Quinlan. "Take him out to the Polo Club. I've written Major Doak and Shiny White to be on the lookout for him. He's going by way of Pekin—thinks he can catch the *Merritt* out of Tientsin to Nagasaki, and the *Sherman* from Nagasaki to Manila. There ought to be something in Manila that he can write about."

Quinlan protested. "If you want to write about anything in Manila, you'd better keep away from the *Merritt*. She'll never reach Nagasaki in time to make the *Sherman*. She never gets anywhere on time. She never leaves any place when she says she will. You'd better come with me on the *Warren:* then you'll be sure to get there, and I'll show you something to write about! Hell, I was the first man ashore when we landed in the Philippines in 1898, and I've been there ever since—haven't I, Morris? Me and Aguinaldo, we know everything there is to know about the Philippines—don't we, Morris? I can tell you all about Francis Burton Harrison and the ladies in the case—can't I, Morris? I know what the Moros'll do to the Tagalogs if the Tagalogs try to govern 'em. Why, say! I can even get you an interview with Aguinaldo, and that's something *nobody* ever got!"

I was touched by the thoughtful kindnesses of those we left behind. Major Eichelberger showed me a telegram from Schuyler in Omsk, asking that I be sent out to help him. "So far as we're concerned," the major said, "you're on your way home." The general and the chief of staff gave us messages to friends.

As a final farewell Major Johnson led us on a grand tour of the wretched brothels on Kopeck Hill, tendered us a midnight banquet of cold lamb and vodka at the Terek Tavern, favorite resort of thieves and spies—and at dawn on January 30, 1919, we joined Colonel Quinlan aboard the *Warren,* plowed through the ice cakes of the Zolotoi Rog— the Golden Horn—in the wake of an icebreaker; reeled for two horrifying days through mountainous billows in the Sea of Japan, and came safely into the green-rimmed harbor of Nagasaki.

If we could have gone to China, we could have cashed our pay vouchers at Pekin or Chinwangtao and thus financed our trip; so even in Nagasaki we still hoped to make a quick dash for Pekin by way of Korea—until peremptory messages from Captain McKenna and the chief of staff warned us that the *Sherman* was running ahead of schedule. We stripped Colonel Quinlan of all his spare cash, left him to go on alone in the *Warren,* and made a hurried visit to Kyoto and Kobe on the bare chance that some day I might have occasion to put them in a short story or a play or a novel.

The *Sherman* put in at Nagasaki on February 10, and on February 11 we set off for Manila and the long trip to San Francisco. Since the *Sherman* was to be our home for some weeks, I pinned my outline of the Svetlanskaya Front to the wall beside my bunk, opened the blank-book in which I had already set down a few thousand words about troikas, wolves and other Siberian products, and told myself that the time had now come to put an end to mirth and laughter: here at last was the cold gray dawn of the morning after.

§

The profession of writing has many baffling aspects. What to write and how to write, of course, are two of the most baffling; but the problem of escaping interruptions while writing is also one that requires deep consideration. Most spots, houses and rooms, no matter how sequestered, how uninviting to other activities they may appear, await only the presence of a would-be writer to develop habitués, quirks or sounds discouraging to or destructive of unbroken thought and the uninterrupted concentration needed for sustained work.

I have occupied many hotel rooms that, when I first entered them, seemed ideally situated for writing purposes; but when the writing actually started, a dance orchestra came wailingly to life a few floors below and squalled nerve-rackingly for hours, elevators rattled and banged, near-by toilets flushed unceasingly, family wrangles developed in adjacent rooms. . . .

A winter's labor in Rome was seriously imperiled by a garage mechanic who whistled the same tune all day beneath the room in which I was striving to put paragraphs together in an orderly manner. My only recourse was to retreat to an inside bathroom with my manuscript and spend practically an entire winter there.

I went so far as to build an addition to a house on an Italian cliff overlooking the Bay of Orbetello and the islands of Elba, Monte Cristo and Corsica, because it was idyllically remote and quiet—but whenever I uncapped my fountain pen, a million English sparrows surrounded the house to feud, fight and fuss from dawn to dark; and a naval aviation training station used the roof as a landmark over which innumerable planes thundered daily on bombastic missions.

And now that work beckoned on the *Sherman,* I waited tremblingly for the almost certain eruptions that would complicate my labors—and was lulled to a feeling of security when we slid quietly into ever warmer waters through the Eastern Sea, past Iwo Jima, Okinawa, Formosa, into the China Sea, raised the coast of Luzon and came to anchor in suffocating heat off the Manila breakwater, all without a daily riot, or the perpetual hammering of clangorous metals by marine plumbers and blacksmiths. Not bad, I thought: if only the *Sherman* would travel sufficiently slowly, and dawdle as she sailed, I might write on and on and on. . . .

Manila was all that Colonel Quinlan had promised—a magnificent city of stately buildings; of far distances, made beautiful by American taxpayers, and doomed from the first to inevitable destruction by Filipino incompetence or Japanese aggression; of hospitable American clubs echoing to the croakings of lizard-like geckos that crawled on walls and ceilings, bitterly uttering monotonous obscenities to the gallant soldiers and beautiful ladies gathered around the tables.

Colonel Quinlan nobly lived up to his promises. I spent hours with Aguinaldo, the little wrinkled brown man who had defied the American Army and led it such a wild chase in the mountains and jungles of Luzon. Acting Governor Yeater was liberal with information; the army's Intelligence Department opened its files to me; and Colonel Morris's Manila friends went out of their way to see that I received all the information my notebooks would hold.

When the *Sherman* sailed from Manila, her every spare nook and cranny was crammed with the families of Regular Army and Philippine Scout officers returning to the United States on furlough, a Philippine Independence Mission composed of fifty hand-picked politicians, and two hundred fragile-looking Filipino boys (known as Goo-Goos in army circles) setting off to be trained as mess attendants in the United States Navy—and I was promptly made aware of the falsity of the hopes aroused by those few quiet days on the China Sea.

No sooner had we passed Corregidor and headed south toward San Bernardino Strait than the ship became a monkey house of screams and the patter of childish feet as army darlings deserted indulgent parents to stick fingers and noses into every part of the ship. The pampered politicos of the Independence Mission had us dislodged from our allotted cabin on the upper deck and relegated to a stifling foxhole opening onto the main deck; and on that main deck, all day and all night, the two hundred Filipino mess boys squealed hysterically and fought over crap games with the ear-piercing voices of badly reared little girls.

When I tried to escape the Filipinos by retiring to a corner of the smoking room, it was filled with army urchins who pursued each other over benches, tumbled about my feet with anguished howls, and displayed an insatiable interest in my labors.

Lieutenant Garland came to sympathize with me, and tried to devise some method of intimidating those adorable angels—all of which led to a discussion of the longings that afflicted both of us. The theater had its talons in Garland, he said, and while he hadn't really written anything yet, he had evolved seven one-act plays. He had found it possible to exist while doing them by living in the town of Taormina, Sicily, where he and his mother had rented a small house near the shore for seven dollars and fifty cents a month. On the heights above the town, he said, beautiful villas could be had for thirty-five dollars a month; and in his opinion, two people could live almost regally in Taormina for twenty-five dollars a week.

Twenty-five dollars a week! Our Travel Fund hoardings had almost reached a point where, if invested at seven per cent, they would yield twenty-five dollars a week. Taormina, hey? How would I go about getting one of those thirty-five-dollar-a-month villas in Taormina?

Simplicity itself, Garland said. He had acquaintances there—Charles King Wood, the painter; Robert Hichens, the novelist; the Duke of Brontë. If he asked them to find a house for me, they would surely find one.

"Go ahead and ask 'em," I told Garland. "I want to write, and I'll go there as soon as I've caught a few fish, shot me some partridges in the autumn, and got the taste of army chow out of my mouth—that is, I will if I can think of anything to put on paper."

"Why don't you try that piece about the Tsar and his daughters and the one that escaped?" Garland asked. "It struck me, when I heard you tell it, that it would make a good play."

Mindful of Professor Baker's refusal to enroll me in his Harvard Workshop, I said there wasn't enough to it for a play, and that I knew nothing about playwrighting, and how could anybody do any sort of work, anyhow, with mopseys and Goo-Goos crawling all over the place?

Garland protested that there was enough in the incident for one act: a prologue, say, to a longer play—something about Bolshevism. "I could help you write it," he said, "and maybe two of us can hold off the little bastards better than one could."

Late that night, when slumber had stilled the cacophony of the Goo-Goos, I brooded over Garland's suggestion and wondered if a play mightn't be based on that hideous scene in Ekaterinburg. I already had a name for it—*The Brotherhood of Man*.

So the Svetlanskaya Front was laid aside, and Garland and I roamed the *Sherman* from stem to stern, from bread locker to lifeboats, seeking a spot free from that enchanting brood of army tots and those light-hearted Goo-Goos. When they pursued us, we would climb to an upper deck, settle ourselves between two lifeboats, and vainly attempt to get on with it—vainly, because crew members instantly arrived to chip paint from davits, to test falls, to grease winches.

My diary for March 2 records our difficulties: "Garland and I tried all day to work in the dining saloon. It was prolonged hell; for the blessed bairns refused to leave the pianola. Gave the dining steward five dollars to keep them out, but he wasn't equal to it. Lieutenant Hussey, learning of our troubles, came in and surreptitiously disconnected a chain inside the pianola, thinking to make it unplayable. Within five minutes a precocious seraph had dredged up the chain, readjusted it—and for the hundredth time our ears were assaulted by the tinny strains of the 'Red Dot Polka.' It played from three o'clock until the dinner gong rang at six: then from seven-thirty, when the second sitting was finished, until quarter of eleven. Advanced two pages, but don't see how we did it."

Somehow that first act was finished. It adhered closely to the evidence gathered by American Intelligence officers concerning the fate of the Russian royal family at the hands of the Bolsheviks, and the rumored escape of the Grand Duchess Tatiana on the day the Czechs captured Ekaterinburg from the Red Army.

So far as I was concerned, that first act was the last act, for I had no desire to go on with it. The characters we invented seemed unreal. They talked too much; and I had never been able to make myself believe that Tatiana escaped, anyway. So I went back to work on the Svetlanskaya Front. That at least was true, and by now I had learned that Thoreau knew what he was talking about when he said, "Any truth is better than make-believe."

CHAPTER

15

MY RETURN to the Svetlanskaya Front was simplified by a storm that incapacitated an American mine layer, the *Armistead,* so severely that the *Sherman* was forced to stand by in case she sank. Filipinos and children were laid low by the heavy seas; and in the comparative silence that ensued I wedged myself upright into a corner of our cabin in order to use my berth for a desk, and worked industriously for nine hours a day. Two days out from San Francisco I brought the manuscript to an abrupt end and went to typing my longhand outpourings. The last page was typed just as the *Sherman* tied up at the Presidio on the twenty-third of March. There were 22,000 words in the manuscript; and who, I asked myself, could possibly use a story 22,000 words long? I knew the answer. Nobody!

Somebody, somewhere, must have talked too much; for an Intelligence officer boarded the *Sherman,* before we docked, to tell me to report immediately to Captain Fisher, Chief of Intelligence in San Francisco, and supply him with information concerning the hampering of Intelligence activities in A.E.F., Siberia, by its chief of staff. There was also a telegram from the Secretary of War, demanding my presence in Washington to report on the activities of Francis Burton Harrison, governor of the Philippines. Since I knew that neither of these orders had any relation to the military well-being of the United States, I deferred acting on them until I had visited the headquarters of the Western Department of the United States Army, submitted to the attentions of the examining surgeon, collected pay through March 23, together with the sixty-dollar bonus at that time considered adequate to re-establish an ex-soldier in civilian life, and was given an honorable discharge.

Then, and not until then, I deposited the story on the Svetlanskaya Front, addressed to George H. Lorimer, *Saturday Evening Post,* in the nearest mailbox, and came to a definite decision about reporting to Captain Fisher and the Secretary of War, as ordered. Since I was no longer in the army, orders had ceased to interest me. The war was over, too, and the chief of staff would never have an opportunity to interfere with future Intelligence detachments—and anyway, I had nothing against him. Neither did I feel inclined to gossip with the Secretary of War or anyone else about the affairs of Francis Burton Harrison. So I sought the nearest Atchison, Topeka & Santa Fe office and, posing as one of our brave boys newly returned from Over There, demanded and received accommodations on that night's California Limited.

A week later I descended from the train in Philadelphia and hesitantly visited the offices of the *Saturday Evening Post,* to learn, if possible, the fate of the Svetlanskaya Front article. I was welcomed by Churchill Williams, whom I had already encountered as a major at secret conclaves of General Hind Quarters.

"Well, well," he said, "Siberia doesn't seem to have hurt you. We thought your ears would probably be frozen off. The Boss got that piece on the Svetlanskaya Front yesterday, and it went through this morning. He yelled murder—said it was so long he had to sit up all night to read it. I don't know how he's going to use anything that long unless he throws out half the ads. He's paying a thousand for it. Welcome home!"

Went through! Twenty-two thousand words! A thousand smackers! Welcome home, indeed!

Major Williams ushered me in to see George Horace Lorimer, that granite-faced but tenderhearted editorial genius, who terminated an interview with Albert Payson Terhune as I entered—not too happy an interview, apparently, as Terhune seemed to look with pronounced disfavor on both me and my uniform as he made his exit.

Lorimer greeted me cordially; then, in his characteristic way, he hrumped gruffly and eyed me suspiciously. "Well," he said, "I suppose you've got something on your mind."

I said the principal thing on my mind was something E. A. Grozier had said to me when I left the *Boston Post*—that he had always been sorry the *Post* had allowed Mr. Lorimer to get away, and that he wanted me to tell Mr. Lorimer so, if I ever met him. I added that my first two-dollar raise on the *Post* had been granted because Mr. Grozier remembered with painful clarity what had happened when the same generous salary increase had been denied Mr. Lorimer.

"Best thing ever happened to me," Lorimer said. "Probably been there yet if they'd raised me to twenty dollars. Twenty dollars! Makes me hungry to think of it! Let's eat." He summoned the heads of his editorial staff—Adelaide Neall, Churchill Williams and Fred Bigelow—and I was led with breath-taking informality to the chaste private dining room on the top floor, just as if I were an author of repute.

When we returned to the airy seclusion of Lorimer's office, he handed me a handful of chocolate buds from the lower drawer of his desk—a signal mark of favor, as I was to learn later—lit a cigarette and scrutinized me coldly. "We made the price on that last piece a thousand dollars," he said, "but don't think we're going to make a habit of any such prices. That was a long one, so I figured it was about the same as two stories."

I hastened to assure him I had anticipated no such generosity, and was only amazed he'd been able to use it at all.

Lorimer grunted. "Don't ever try to tell everything you know in just one piece. What else you got on your mind?"

I said I had little on my mind: with Lieutenant Robert Garland I had written a one-act play about the finish of the Russian royal family while coming home on the transport, but it was scarcely the sort of thing the *Saturday Evening Post* would want.

"You never can tell," Lorimer said. "Send it along and let me look at it. Anything else on your mind?"

I said I'd nosed around Manila and picked up a fair amount of information, including a long interview with Aguinaldo. The general opinion, I told him, was that there'd be hell to pay if the Philippines were given their immediate independence: that the Japanese wanted the islands and probably would take them if we got out.

"Aguinaldo, hey?" Lorimer said. "We might use something on that. Get to work on it, and let me have a look. Got anything on the way Bolshevik ideas work out in actual practice?"

I told him how we had picked up a man who had traveled through a dozen Bolshevik armies, using a homemade passport sealed with the cross-of-Lorraine device from a Uneeda biscuit box and authorizing him to travel from Wheresoever-you-arsky to Lyon Mountain, New York. From what we had seen, I told him, Communism was an aristocracy of superboobs, determined to impose their own murderous and destructive beliefs on the whole world.

"Get right at it," Lorimer said, "and don't forget we have to go to press once a week. Anything else?"

What I wanted most to tell, I said, was the story of the Japanese and their inexcusable misbehavior in Siberia and Manchuria—how they were seizing Siberian industries, testing the suitability of all East Asia for Japanese colonization, and evidently proposing to make eastern Siberia and Manchuria into a Japanese province if allowed a free hand; how contemptuous they were of American opinion and American rights, and how American detachments had narrowly escaped extermination at the hands of those supposed Allies on a number of occasions. They were doubly dangerous, I told him, because of their profound ignorance of America's size and resources—as shown by General Oi's attitude when we notified him that two million Americans had landed in France. No such number of men, he insisted, could possibly be sent across an ocean and supplied with food and arms.

"I don't know about that," Lorimer said dubiously, "but go ahead and write it anyway."

So I wasn't downhearted when I left Philadelphia for Maine. I knew, of course, I had merely hooked a precarious finger over the first rung of the writing ladder; but I also knew that with any luck at all we might actually find ourselves in Taormina on the following winter, surrounded by beautiful scenery, Sicilian warmth and rapidly growing piles of manuscript.

EDITORIAL likes and dislikes have always baffled me, as have critical likes and dislikes, but sometimes the dislikes proved extraordinarily helpful.

That was a cold spring in Maine, but thanks to the knee-length stockings, trench coat, fur hat, knitted afghan and Red Cross blankets left over from Siberia, I found no trouble in working morning, noon and night on the articles in which Lorimer had indicated an interest, and at the same time filling all interstices in my working day by commenting on the State of the Nation, and sending the comments to *Life*.

I could have kept even busier, perhaps, because the *Boston Post,* to my pleasure, hadn't forgotten me, as I learned from a telegram dated June 2:

NEWKIRK FORCED TO LAY OFF FOR TWO OR THREE MONTHS. IS THERE ANY CHANCE FOR US TO MAKE AN ARRANGEMENT WITH YOU TO DO "ALL SORTS" FOR THE SUMMER. PLEASE WIRE HOW YOU FEEL ABOUT IT. BEST REGARDS.

CARBERRY

But I couldn't have accepted unless I could have found a way to go without sleep.

The article on the Philippines, when finished, was promptly purchased. It enraged the Philippine Independence Commission and Filipinos in official life to such a degree that they brought pressure to bear on Aguinaldo—even stronger pressure than offended Provincetowners used to bring on E. A. Grozier. Aguinaldo obligingly denied my interview with him, but carelessly went so far as to say that he had never even seen me. Colonel Quinlan, who had a contract to supply Filipino schools with six thousand textbooks, was threatened with the loss of his contract unless he consented to wire the War Department that the interview had never taken place. I wasn't troubled by either denial; for Aguinaldo, during the interview, had thoughtfully presented me with an autographed photograph on which he had inscribed my name and the date, together with a number of kind words. Prominent Filipinos wrote violently to Mr. Lorimer, demanding my discharge; and Filipino societies adopted resolutions forever debarring me from the Philippines. Fortunately a number of army officers also wrote the *Post* along diametrically opposite lines, always adding: "Please do not publish my name, as the Filipinos would ruin me." A year later the *Manila Daily Bulletin* published an editorial demanding an investigation to place the blame for a rotten political situation "that Kenneth Roberts was so maligned for pointing out, and that both civil and military authorities now agree upon."

The article on the Bolsheviks was finished and accepted. At this point Mr. Lorimer demanded the play I had written with Lieutenant Garland. When I sent him *The Brotherhood of Man,* he amazingly and enthusiastically bought it, remitting a check for seven hundred and fifty dollars: five hundred for me and two hundred and fifty for Garland. Even more amazingly, he led the magazine with it.

That about exhausted my supply of Siberian material, except for those enraging investigations I had made into the activities of the Japanese in Siberia. So, although Lorimer had been dubious about using them in the *Post,* I went ahead and explained as clearly as I could how unreliable, how treacherous, how unspeakably dirty, how unbelievably cruel, how potentially dangerous we had found the Japanese Army, even as Allies—and how willing they were to be unallied to us.

Nobody on the staff of the *Saturday Evening Post* had ever encountered any part of the Japanese Army, so I was neither surprised nor annoyed when Mr. Lorimer returned it. Such an article, he wrote, might conceivably embarrass the State Department. Knowing how easily the State Department could be embarrassed, I was inclined to agree with him—though I thought a protracted series of embarrassments might prove highly beneficial to the State Department.

Just at that period the *Cosmopolitan Magazine,* under Mr. Ray Long, was brutally raiding the writing staffs of other magazines; and Peter B. Kyne and Irvin S. Cobb had been lured from the *Post* fold by startlingly liberal contracts and greatly increased pay checks. Mr. Lorimer, understandably, was annoyed. He was generous with his authors—sufficiently generous to resent having his hand forced by highjackers—and he not only held the editorial capacity of Mr. Long in low esteem, but he was revolted whenever he saw the work of one of his regular contributors in an organ that he found offensive.

By a singular coincidence, Mr. Long selected this particular moment to suggest that he would be glad to contract for a year's output of my articles for the *Cosmopolitan* at one thousand dollars apiece. I said I didn't want to tie myself down, but would be glad to supply him with an article on the regrettable behavior of the Japanese Army in Siberia. After the proper delay, I sent him the article that Mr. Lorimer had thought might embarrass the State Department. Mr. Long was most enthusiastic and asked for another; but when he received the second one, he complained bitterly because of its length, and proceeded to carve chunks from it in a manner far more whimsical than I had ever before encountered.

Mr. Long just didn't like long magazine articles, and I just couldn't say what I desired in short ones; so when he asked for a third, I handed him an extra-long one called "Food for Thought."

Mr. Long wrote me on August 15: "This is a darn difficult letter to write. In justice to you and to the *Cosmopolitan,* I have to say that in my judgment you have not hit it in the article 'Food for Thought.' Think it over and let me hear from you—quickly, because I am sailing for England on Saturday."

I acted as quickly as I could; and the *Saturday Evening Post* on August 21 wrote: " 'Food for Thought' is entirely digestible and the proper fee will be returned by our treasurer on Tuesday next."

That ended my association with the *Cosmopolitan Magazine.*

§

To me the most eventful occurrence, following my return from Siberia, was the beginning of my friendship with Booth Tarkington, brought about by a letter to him from Major Rupert Hughes. In his letter Major Hughes took it on himself to explain that I had an excitable nature, and that he felt someone (in his absence) should keep an eye on me and exercise a restraining influence when necessary (as he had so successfully done during my connection with our armed forces). Mr. Tarkington, whose summer home was near mine, immediately called upon me and examined me with a sort of sardonic interest that I found, at the time, inexplicable. Later, when Major Hughes had shown me a copy of his letter to Mr. Tarkington, I was better able to understand Mr. Tarkington's frequent and successful efforts to provoke the excitability mentioned by Major Hughes.

Mr. Tarkington was most encouraging about my aspirations. I mustn't try too hard, he said. Nobody got anywhere, in writing, by working too hard at it. If an apparently insoluble writing problem confronted him, he said—a character who wouldn't behave properly, a situation that wouldn't satisfactorily resolve itself—he put his work aside: went for a walk: went to bed. Things worked out in the subconscious. "Don't worry so much about what you're going to write," he said repeatedly. "It'll come to you when you're ready for it. Your people are people: they're in the round: they'll begin to move for you eventually."

I hadn't the slightest idea what he was talking about. I only knew that the work I was doing was somehow unsatisfactory.

He could see I had my hands full, that summer, and he had no occasion to write me as frequently as he did later. His letters were short, formal and to the point—and of course he didn't know me well enough to use the peculiar abbreviations and dialect that characterized most of his later communications. He even signed himself, almost in full, N. B. Tarkington. He seemed to have a sort of inner shrinking from the name "Booth." He never pronounced it, as did everyone else, to rhyme with "tooth." He always made it rhyme with "soothe."

DEAR MR. ROBERTS [he wrote in June, 1919],

Mr. Wellington (his daughter aged 13 says) will be here this evening & remain over Sunday.—He lives on our side of this road—the 2nd house from here.—I wish you'd buy a lot in this neighborhood.

Jewett asked me to give you his address—I enclose it. He wanted to know if you hadn't a *continuous ms* he could read—all the articles together. He was much interested.

Yours,

N. B. TARKINGTON

He was ironically amused by the lack of critical perception in *Life's* editors:

Your Mr. Metcalfe of *Life* was the only N.Y. critic who did what I was sure they'd all do to *Clarence*. His English is as faulty as usual and altogether he's up to the customary snuff. He praises *Civilian Clothes,* at the expense of *Clarence,* on the ground that the leading gentleman of the former has been a hero in France and has really done big things before the play opens, whereas *Clarence* has been a bum soldier & never got out of Texas. When you see Mr. Metcalfe I do wish you'd tell him how right I thought him about this, & how he opened my eyes to my mistake. I had ink enough for the Croix de Guerre; and *all* the leading men in plays and stories get ink enough for Croixes from their authors, except *Clarence;*—it seems, now. I must have been just blind not to make him meatier in that way.

§

I did three more pieces for the *Saturday Evening Post* before early autumn—one on dogs, one on golf, and one that I threw away; but I wasn't satisfied with any of them: they seemed to be merely enlargements of the little essays I'd written for *Life*. When Mrs. Roberts totaled our accounts, we had taken in the gratifying amount of seventy-seven hundred dollars in the seven months I had been back from Siberia; but I wanted to do something different—though I didn't know what.

I wrote the Boston artist Lieutenant Garland had mentioned in connection with Taormina—Charles King Wood—explaining my situation and saying that if Lieutenant Garland had been correct in implying that adequate housing could be had in Taormina for thirty-five dollars a month, I would greatly appreciate the opportunity of making it a base for a winter's work.

Then to myself I partly outlined a book or novel full of spies, Russians, Bolsheviks and Americans, to be called *MI-4*. The locale, of course, was Siberia. I discarded that outline, because when I was halfway through it I realized that I could never write it: knew that an overwhelming sense of falseness and futility would stop me at approximately the halfway point. I was groping for another theme or thesis when I received a letter from Mr. Lorimer, suggesting that I take the night train for Philadelphia on the following Monday to discuss possibilities for the coming winter.

I had no idea what Lorimer contemplated, but my association with him and his staff had been so pleasant during the past seven months that I welcomed his suggestion; so I shot six partridges for his delectation and took them to Philadelphia, along with a 7,000-word article dealing with my experiences while attempting to become an expert golfer.

Lorimer was never one to waste time on editorial conferences, and he wasted none on this one.

"Got anything planned for the winter?" he asked.

I said I had made tentative plans to go to Taormina with Mrs. Roberts and try to write a book.

"Taormina?" he said. "You don't have to go to Taormina to write a book."

I said I realized that, but Taormina was warmer and cheaper than Maine.

"Not much cheaper," Lorimer said, "if you count your steamship fares." He looked at me defiantly. "Now see here," he said, "a little more experience won't do you any harm. If I were you, I wouldn't be in too much of a hurry about writing fiction. Most writers start too early; then when they stumble, they're through for good. You don't know what you want to write, do you?"

When I admitted I didn't, he said sardonically, "No: most of 'em don't. My advice is to wait awhile, so you won't have to wind up by taking a job in a pickle factory. Now, how'd you like to go to Europe for us—England, Ireland, Scotland, France, Germany, Czechoslovakia, Poland, Austria, Italy . . ."

I tried to control my features and my voice. "Well," I said, "I don't know whether I could give you what you want——"

"Probably," Lorimer added, "you'd find you ought to take a little run over to Greece and Constantinople—maybe the Balkans, even, or Russia—or wherever you saw a good story. Want to try it?"

Did I want to try it! Balkans! Prisoner of Zenda! Constantinople! Ali Baba! The Magic Carpet! I could only trust myself to say "Yes!"

"You know anything about immigration?" Lorimer asked.

When I said No, he said, "Well, find out all you can about it, because that's one of the things I want you to cover."

"If I'm going to all those places," I said, "I ought to have an advance on a story or two. I don't believe I can make it on what's left of my army pay and this summer's work."

Lorimer snorted disgustedly. "The *Saturday Evening Post* doesn't expect its correspondents to pay their travel expenses," he said. He raised his voice. "Miss Davies, make out an expense check for twenty-five hundred dollars for Ken." To me he said, "How long will it take you to get ready?"

When I said I was ready then, he told me, "Better get started as soon as you can. Take the first boat out of New York—and travel alone at first. Let the Little Woman keep the home fires burning for a while. I'll give you a letter to the State Department, and maybe you can get your passport and visas in a hurry. In fact, you'd better start right now. Catch the noon train to Washington: then hop back to New York and get steamer passage. I'll send a letter of instruction to you in care of the Players Club. If there's anything you want or need, always feel free to cable."

He opened the bottom drawer of his desk, took out a handful of chocolate buds, gave me half of them, shook hands briskly, wished me good luck and shooed me from the office. I had been there slightly less than twenty minutes.

In Washington, thanks to Captain McKenna, who had gone back to the State Department when he returned from Siberia, my passport was cleared in two hours. This situation was enraging to a senator who had been waiting three days and a colonel who had waited three weeks.

Thus I had ample time to ransack the Congressional Library (which to my mind is the world's greatest, most accessible and most helpful source of information on every subject under the sun) for all authoritative utterances on immigration, and to go through the files of the *Saturday Evening Post* for the articles written from the front by the three gentlemen whom I then considered—and still consider—unrivaled as war correspondents: Irvin S. Cobb, Samuel G. Blythe and Will Irwin.

I vaguely thought that a perusal of their reports would give me some sort of idea of how they went about it. Unfortunately, their stories only confused and discouraged me, for they were magnificent. All I knew for sure about them was that all three believed practically nothing unless they saw it themselves; then viewed it amusingly and comprehensively; leaned heavily toward understatement; and avoided the sob-sister and the Oh-Gosh! manner of writing as they'd have shunned leprosy.

When I returned to New York I found Lorimer's letter of instruction. As a rule, his letters were five or six lines long; but this was elaborate:

> I have instructed the treasurer to send you a check for your golf article today and I enclose herewith the regular letter of identification that we gave all correspondents who went abroad for us during the war.
>
> The prime object of your trip is to secure a series of articles on immigration. Of course, it is not possible to lay out this series in any detail, as it will depend entirely on the character and the abundance of the material. It should, however, be approached from two slants: First, you should get in touch with as many aliens recently returned from America as possible, and get their reactions on the situation they find at home and their intentions as to settling down in Europe or returning to America. Secondly, we want to find out to just what extent aliens are planning or hoping to emigrate to America: the causes behind their decision: whether they are going to make a stake with the idea of returning to Europe and settling down there, or whether it is their plan to become citizens of the United States. Also, find out whether the larger number of these would-be immigrants hope to settle in the United States or some other country, particularly the direction that emigration from the Central Empire is likely to take, and whether they will go in big numbers to Latin American

countries. The character, trades and desirability of these would-be immigrants should be determined.

The series should, of course, be relieved by anecdotes tending to bring out the points you are trying to make. In addition to these articles, there should be several light papers on living conditions in European capitals that will give us an insight as to whether Europeans themselves are taking their problems seriously or letting them joyride; whether they are doing their utmost to relieve want and suffering, or depending on America, and to what extent. Perhaps you will be able to dig up some new stuff about the increase or the decline of Bolshevism. Anything showing how it has resulted in actual operation would, of course, be worth getting. The same thing is true of business conditions in Great Britain, France, and Italy, especially with an eye to American interests, opportunities and duties. You can always query me by cable about specific developments and make suggestions as to articles that seem important but that are not covered in this plan. The same thing is true about funds if you run low at any time. Mail me before leaving a permanent address from which letters and cables will be forwarded to you. To whom do you wish checks sent for the articles that reach us during your absence?

In a sense, you have a roving commission, as the way in which the articles shape up and their number depend entirely on what you find from actual investigation. It is, of course, important that articles be sent to us just as fast as the material for them can be assembled and they can be written. I don't want to do anything in this series unnecessarily to offend the sensibilities or to promote unnecessary antagonism between the United States and European countries. You will, undoubtedly, be frightfully irritated by a number of small happenings, but you should not let these interfere with handling or looking at your subjects in a big, broad spirit.

A week later, laden with every obtainable book on immigration, I was on the White Star liner *Lapland,* headed for Cherbourg and Southampton.

§

Emigration from Great Britain to the United States, eh? A light paper on living conditions in London, by Jove! It had sounded like nice clean work, provided I could find out what I needed to know, and then contrive to put my facts together. But the closer I came to England, concerning which I knew next to nothing, the more the prospect appalled me. On the *Boston Post,* on *Life,* in the Military Intelligence Division, I had looked into one thing at a time, and set down that one thing immediately. My reports on the Japanese, the Americans in Siberia, the Philippines, had been gathered at my leisure, and written months later.

The life and activities of a foreign correspondent, I'd always understood, were exciting, fascinating, gay, leisurely. . . . Richard Harding Davis, I'd gathered, spent much of his time in immaculate evening dress, dining with grand dukes, or devastatingly beautiful secret agents, or lovely princesses from Ruritania. Evening dress, naturally, presupposes sufficient leisure to keep the dress immaculate and get into it without tearing the shirt or ripping open a seam in the trousers.

But things were not like that, I found, and I obviously needed a plan that would take me with the utmost speed to the agencies that superintended the movement of British and Irish emigrants to America; to steamship agents and American consular officers; to emigrants' homes in England and Ireland; to American businessmen, American commercial attachés, newspapermen and all reachable persons who would be well informed on British business conditions, schools, factories, railroads, theaters, dramatists, authors, slum dwellers, upper-crusters.

By the time a hansom cab dumped me shivering on a slippery London pavement on a foggy November afternoon, it wasn't merely the penetrating quality of that bitter chill that made me shiver. It was the knowledge that I couldn't afford to spend more than ten days on any one story, and that as soon as I had accumulated the information for each story, I must write it while running down the facts for the next one. That meant fast work, and I knew only one sure way to move fast, and that was in uniform—which obviates the need of waiting for laundry and is helpful on crowded trains—and with my belongings restricted to a musette bag and a hand satchel. I had fortunately brought along my uniform, stripped of insignia and braid, and with its buttons replaced by leather buttons. Now I needed only an excuse to wear it.

The operation of getting material for a magazine article, I found, was vaguely like throwing rocks into a pond. A reporter in England, say, tosses himself into the lap of the American consul general, who then flicks him, pebble-like, at the American commercial attaché, the head of the American Red Cross, the American Chamber of Commerce, the London representatives of Standard Oil and International Harvester, the head of the Cunard Line; and wherever a pebble strikes, waves spread outward from each point of impact, each wave being another person interviewed.

Thus pebbles tossed by amiable Mr. Robert P. Skinner, the American consul general, resulted in waves that bore me onward to other consular officers in England and Ireland, Gordon Selfridge, owner of London's leading department store, the head of Astley's jewelry emporium, and a dozen other people. Major Bridges, of the American Red Cross, gave me a sort of Red Cross passport written in English, French, German and Polish, entitling me to act as courier and observer for the American Red Cross. The ripples from Major Bridges resulted in interviews with a dozen highly placed Britons. A pebble to Colonel Malone of the British Foreign Office resulted in circles that touched the Irish Office. A pebble tossed at the Irish Office resulted in waves that reached the Undersecretary of State for Irish Affairs, the police commissioner of southern Ireland, the chief of police, Sir William Johnson, England's representative in southern Ireland, and many other informative Irishmen.

Just before leaving London, I had a cablegram from Charles King Wood, saying that he had found just the thing for me—a charming villa, high on a cliff in Taormina, for thirty-five dollars a month. Should he take it for me?

I cabled him gratefully and apologetically that unexpected circumstances made it impossible to reach Italy that winter, but I would try to get there the following winter. I was as sure as ever that the sort of writing I contemplated was still far, far away. I little dreamed, however, that seven years were to elapse before I could take the step of burning my bridges behind me.

After five days in London I hurried to northern Ireland and southern Ireland, talking to emigrants in the agricultural slums of Carrickfergus and Connemara, pursuing ever-widening circles.

A pebble thrown at the Canadian Emigration Office had struck a Scot who had once been managing editor of a Belfast newspaper—Mr. Bartlett McConkey—and waves went rushing off from him to another Belfast managing editor, who proved to be a mine of information, and to the great AE, George Russell, with whom I duly talked for three long hours—and got exactly nothing worth using.

In pursuit of that plan of pebble tossing, by the time I left London for Paris, I had interviewed two hundred and eighty-two persons from every branch of society, worked, and worked hard, from twelve to twenty hours every day, developed a ringing in my ears and a feeling as though my brain were a squeezed lemon because of the endless questioning, the endless note taking, the endless questing, hurrying, listening, and trying to write.

17

December 8, 1919: Finished packing, left London at twelve-twenty, Dover two-thirty, boat sailed at three in rain and terrific sea. Nearly everybody sick: I escaped by staying on deck. Reached Gare du Nord at 3:30 A.M., groggy with weariness. This is my birthday, and I feel as if I'll never see another. Will Irwin had got me a comfortable room at the Regina—heaven, compared to England and Ireland. Wakened at 9 A.M. to see Will's bushy head of hair bent over a pad of paper on which he was listing names and addresses that would, he said, simplify my work in France.

§

Simplify? Did he really mean simplify? How could anyone or anything simplify these endless days and nights of searching, questioning, note taking, writing, packing, racing for trains?

Paris was a repetition of London, except that I had a warm bathroom in the Regina and in it, by December 15, finished the 12,000-word Irish article, in addition to getting material on Parisian life and on the flood of emigrants from western Europe who were passing through France on their way to the United States—and proving, in their passing, repulsive to the French authorities. They were a source of irritation to me, too; and when I spoke my mind to Will Irwin's wife, Inez Haynes Gillmore Irwin, she eyed me understandingly. "You're homesick," she said. "If you try to work day and night for months on end, you'll knock yourself out. Where's Mrs. Roberts and what's she doing?"

Anna, I told her, was at her mother's home in Roxbury, taking our wire-haired terrier for a walk three times a day in Franklin Park, but Lorimer had said——

Mrs. Irwin was exasperated. "That's a fine life for a woman! Get her over here and stop being homesick! Put her to work! She'll see a lot of things that you won't! She'll type your stories, too."

A light burst upon me! Paris, hitherto obnoxious in my eyes, suddenly seemed cheerful, gay, luminous. I wondered what had ailed me. Could those days in the army have done something to my manner of thought? By what right had Lorimer told me to leave Anna at home? I'd left her at home long enough, and, Lorimer or no Lorimer, I needed her! Why, sure! Nuts to Lorimer, but in a nice way. Anna! Companionship! Someone to whom I could complain, squawk, bellyache and moan! Would Lorimer's wife let *him* get away with anything like this? I should say *not*. So I cabled him that I was sending for her, cabled Mrs. Roberts to catch the next boat and meet me in Vienna, left word with our consulate general in Paris to speed her on her way, and set off for Berlin. It never occurred to me that the first boat might head for Italy instead of for France. Obviously, if I couldn't think things out better than I'd been doing, I was ill equipped to write.

Berlin was a repetition of London and Paris. On December 19, the day after I arrived, I started an article on England—"How Cousin John's Getting Along"—and simultaneously set about accumulating information with the help of my good friends Guido Enderis of the *New York Times,* Phil Powers of the Associated Press, Carl Grote of the United Press, Parke Brown of the *Chicago Tribune,* Fred Simpich, late of the consular service, Cyril Brown of the *New York Times,* and Colonel Davis, our military attaché. I interrupted the article for a Christmas celebration with Messrs. Simpich, Enderis, Grote, Parke Brown and Cyril Brown and the wives of the two latter. When one of the gentlemen of the party became slightly incapacitated, we put him in a cab with the two Mrs. Browns and formed a guard of honor on either side of the cab horse, leading it through the middle arch of the Brandenburg Gate (hitherto reserved for royalty) and attempting to introduce it into the lobby of the Hotel Adlon through the revolving door. The horse, unfortunately, lacked sufficient flexibility to let us attain our ends. In spite of this interlude, the article was finished on December 29, and on the thirtieth I left Berlin for Warsaw—a journey of startling turbulence in decrepit trains, near the end of which two Polish Intelligence officers, brothers, Jerzy and Sharl Odrovonz-Piananzek, hauled me through the window of a stranded *wagon-lit,* hoisted me aboard a platform car attached to a shunting engine, and delivered me half frozen but all in one piece to the Bristol Hotel in Warsaw.

Warsaw was a repetition of Berlin, Paris and London, though the

eating customs prevalent in Poland's hotels forced me to revise my
schedule. In other cities I had hunted all day for information, had
dinner at a seasonable hour, and spent most of the night writing. In
Warsaw, however, the dinner hour was nine o'clock, and dinner was
preceded by a staggering variety of zakuska—the inordinately hearty
Polish hors d'œuvre—accompanied by that powerful Polish aid to di-
gestion known as slivovitz. To eat and run, in a proper Polish restaurant, was practically impossible, and I was seldom able to escape from
the dining room until midnight, at which hour the orchestra turned
from dinner music to dance music and played steadily until 6 A.M. or
later. Thus in Poland I did my sleeping while the Poles danced: then
got up and went to work. Oftentimes the Poles were still dancing while
I was eating breakfast.

Vienna was vaguely like all the others: my frigid room in the
Ungarische Krone—the Hungarian Crown—held a green tiled stove
eight feet tall; but fuel was limited to one daily pailful of kindling
wood. Each morning I locked myself in that room with my pail of
wood, which warmed the stove just enough to let me write for five
hours before my fingers stiffened. In two weeks I finished a German
story, "Schieber Land," and a French story, "That Dear Paris," haunted
the kitchens of the Hoover child feeders, and by great good fortune
discovered a Cornell classmate, Arthur Du Bois, playing a lone hand in
central Europe as political investigator for the Department of State. He
put his files at my disposal; and the morning I finished "That Dear
Paris," we set off together on a disaster-haunted automobile trip through
Austria and into Czechoslovakia—one that ended temporarily in the
medieval town of Tabor, where the chauffeur chose to accelerate on an
icy downhill slope, as a result of which the car skidded, tore out two
guard posts of the military road, disemboweled itself on a third, and was
precariously arrested by a fourth on the lip of a rocky ravine. Congratu-
lating each other on being alive, we went on to Pilsen and Prague.

Prague was little different, except that I had Arthur Du Bois's company when I interviewed Czechoslovakia's Prime Minister Tusar; took
down the observations of her agile Minister of Foreign Affairs—little
Eddie Beneš, who once worked on the *Chicago Tribune;* probed into
the astounding adventures that had befallen the president of Czechoslovakia's hickish outpost, Rusinia—Gregory Satkovich, who learned slang
and learned it well at Penn State. Then, stopped by snowdrifts in the
mountains that separate Bohemia from Moravia, we turned back to
Vienna by way of Zwittau and Brünn.

The manager of the hotel in Brünn was happy to talk to two Americans. Did we know of the American writer Mark Twain? Did we indeed! Well, he himself, as manager of the Hotel Krantz in Vienna when Mark Twain lived there, had known Twain well. Twain one day received a cable that sent him posthaste to the manager's office. "I'm a happy man," Twain told him, "and you've got to help me celebrate! See this cable? It says that all my debts are paid—something I was afraid would never happen! You're the first person I've told. Let's have a drink!"

We bought him two slivovitzes, but no more; for Mrs. Roberts was due in Vienna that very evening, and I had to be there to receive her. But no sooner had we left Brünn than our automobile developed motor trouble and refused to climb the endless hills between which flow the tributaries of the Danube. Up a few of those long hills, Arthur and I pushed the car while the chauffeur drove, laboriously surmounting the slopes at a snail's pace. Then we couldn't push any more, because Arthur collapsed from inhaling the fumes of the exhaust. The chauffeur advocated stopping, but I wouldn't consent. Mrs. Roberts, I told him, was reaching Vienna that night. I wasn't worried, for I'd arranged with the head of the American Mission to Austria to meet her at the station and take her to the Bristol. Nonetheless, I had to reach Vienna. The car still ran well in reverse, I reminded the chauffeur, and if he couldn't climb the hills frontward, he could back up them. So we backed up all the remaining long, long hills that lay between us and Vienna, the chauffeur protesting vigorously.

We reached the Bristol Hotel in Vienna at two o'clock in the morning. To my horror, Mrs. Roberts wasn't there. I routed out the head of the American Mission. Where was Mrs. Roberts? He didn't know. He had sent one of his assistants to the Rome Express, but nobody with a red hat had descended from the train—and hadn't I told him she'd be wearing a red hat? Anyway, he said, he'd done as I asked and got her a room at the Bristol. I made an uproar then and later—and the next day, with the assistance of Arthur Du Bois and the Mission and Herr Schober, Vienna police chief, and my correspondent friends Charley Kloeber and Jim Smith, we found her. She had arrived in a green hat instead of a red hat, and had gone from small hotel to small hotel until one had taken pity on her and let her have a miserable room.

So life became different. Mrs. Roberts arranged with Charley Kloeber to see the manager of the Grand Hotel and persuade him to let us have a room with heat. Mrs. Roberts conferred with the headwaiter, who conferred with our room waiter, who miraculously got for us six sticks of firewood, two eggs and an ounce of butter each day. Mrs. Roberts took my notes, deciphered them and typed them: then seized each manuscript page as I finished it and typed it. Mrs. Roberts arranged with Mrs. Du Bois to kidnap Arthur and me from our joyless labors, so that we could enjoy a real dinner now and then, following it by attending Franz Lehár's sprightly operettas at the Johann Strauss Theater. Gaiety reigned once more, and between February 5 and February 24 I not only kept on gathering material, but found time to write a 14,000-word article, "Poland for Patriotism," and "Husks," a 16,000-word article on the pitiful plight of Austria. Five hours after finishing "Husks" we set off for Bratislava on the Danube, and puffed down that swollen brown stream to beautiful Budapest.

Time was running on: about three months, Lorimer had said, ought to suffice for the trip, and already I had been away more than three months. So in Hungary I wasted no time writing, and we were back in Vienna on March 9; then off at daybreak on March 11 for Italy, source of a flood of emigration that was threatening to swamp the United States.

A month later, with the Czechoslovak and Hungarian articles—"Handing It Back" and "For Over a Thousand Years"—completed, and material for two more immigration articles safely embalmed in my notebooks, Mrs. Roberts sailed for home and I crossed the Adriatic to Durazzo and Tirana in Albania for a quick look at the Balkans—a look that almost ended any possibility of further writing.

While returning to Tirana from the mountain town of Kruja with a Red Cross hospital unit, three unidentified Balkan insects in succession entered the same eye. By midnight the eye was so inflamed that sleep was impossible, and on the following morning both eyes were swollen shut. The chief medical officer ordered me to bed in a darkened room, but owing to a slight misunderstanding forgot about me for ten hours. What he saw, when he finally appeared, led him to summon two nurses to apply hot bandages to the eye every fifteen minutes for three days and nights. At the end of that time I could see a little out of one eye. The other was blind, and looked like a maraschino cherry embedded in a portion of boiled dinner.

A week later I was allowed to travel by Red Cross camion to Scutari with the eye heavily bandaged; thence, by way of Cetinje in Montenegro to lovely Ragusa on the Dalmatian coast, where I caught a little coasting steamer that gave me a quick one-eyed look at the picturesque Dalmatian ports of Curzola, Spalato, Sebenico, Zara, Lussinpiccolo, Pola, and finally dropped me in Trieste on the fourth of May.

Not until May 16, after I had been to Belgrade, returned through strike-torn Italy to Paris and Boulogne, and got myself aboard the *Nieuw Amsterdam,* would my eye stand the strain of writing; but when the *Nieuw Amsterdam* docked in New York on the twenty-third, I had completed another 15,000-word article—"Almost Sunny Italy"—and had notes for half a dozen articles dealing exclusively with immigration.

I mention all these things for just one reason: no matter what sort of writing a person wants to do, he can't afford to waste any time, or let himself be held up by little interferences like snowdrifts, broken-down trains, minor ailments or cocktail parties—not if he wishes to escape starvation.

§

My longing for a quiet spot in which I could work without interruption was still strong; but I had given up all thought of Taormina after learning, in my travels through Europe, a little about the strong attraction which that spectacular resort had for bishops, retired businessmen and artists who were lasciviously entangled with young persons of their own sex.

Mr. Robert Skinner, our admirable and capable consul general in London, having probed into my longing to write, often wrote to urge the climatic advantages of Provence, and to remind me that such captious persons as Thomas Jefferson and Lady Hester Stanhope, to say nothing of the Popes of Rome, had been deeply attached to the sweep of country lying in the neighborhood of Cette, Avignon, Nîmes and Arles.

From time to time he clipped from French papers advertisements of farms and miniscule châteaux in Provence that could be purchased for moderate sums.

Mr. Robert Haven, too, our consul in Trieste, frequently reminded me that Abbazia, not far from Fiume and Trieste, was an ideal spot for my purposes, since the chief prewar patrons of that attractive winter resort had been Germans, who were now eager to dispose of their luxurious Abbazia villas for fewer American dollars than would be needed to build a silo. Personally, I leaned toward Ragusa.

When I looked back at that winter of 1919–20 as a whole, I knew that Ragusa, Abbazia or Provence were not for me. Consular officers wrote me from every port and capital in Europe, the burden of their letters being their relief, their gratitude, that at last someone was speaking out and saying the things about immigration that they themselves had ardently longed to say for years, but could never utter because of the nature of their work. They meant what they said, too. I'd seen consular officers shed tears of fury at the unending streams of slum-stunted throngs pouring through their consulates to become added burdens to America. I'd found out a lot about immigration—enough to know where to turn for further information. I'd caught a bear by the tail, and I couldn't let go. I trust I won't be misunderstood when I say that I regarded this incredible rush to the United States as I would have regarded the advance of an attacking army; and I had to keep on saying the things that our consular officers were unable to say aloud, and describe conditions until an awakened America came to the support of senators and representatives and gave them the courage to take action.

Ignorance of European conditions, in high and low places, was almost unbelievable. Mr. Franklin D. Roosevelt, Assistant Secretary of the Navy, on August 12 made a speech at Milwaukee soliciting the Polish vote; and the *New York Herald Tribune* asked me to comment on it. Mr. Roosevelt made the ludicrously incorrect statement that if America had been a member of the League of Nations, the splendid people of Poland would not today be fighting Communist Russia with their backs to the wall. The moral force of America, Mr. Roosevelt said, would have held back the Bolsheviks, and the blame for this dreadful state of affairs lay at the door of the little narrow men who controlled the machinery of the Republican Party.

I could only say, for the *Herald Tribune's* editorial page, that the League of Nations, having no military strength to enforce its demands, had no influence whatever with Russia or any other country that was adequately supplied with arms or ammunition; that every European country had nothing but contempt for moral force; that no blame whatever attached to the Republican Party; that Newton Baker had refused to give material aid to the Imperial Russian Army against the Communist Army at a moment when the Communists could have been easily defeated; that England and France had refused, during the past winter, to furnish Poland with the arms, ammunition and supplies that she needed to keep the Bolsheviks where they belonged—in Russia.

This was the exact truth, but Mr. Roosevelt continued to blame the plight of Poland on the Republican Party, which made me even more willing to go back to Europe.

"WE'VE GOT to hammer at immigration," Lorimer said when I had finished my summer's work, "until Washington and the country at large wake up to what's happening. Go on back again, and this time start with the emigrants at their homes and go right down to the ships with them. Before you start for Poland, look around England and Scotland and find out what's being done about prohibition. And when you're through with the ports of embarkation, give us an article or two on what's happening to the Russian refugees kicked out of Russia by the Bolsheviks. Mike Cantacuzene thinks there must be a couple of million living in doghouses and chicken coops all the way from Constantinople to Berlin and Warsaw."

I could almost delude myself into thinking that I actually was writing; for Harper & Brothers just then decided to use the results of my first trip to Europe in a book to be called *Europe's Morning After*. I knew so little about it, however, that I never thought of revising the articles that had been printed in the *Post:* the little matter of wrestling with galley proofs and page proofs meant nothing to me; and Mrs. Roberts and I went blithely off to Europe, leaving the book in charge of Miss Dorothy Reed, a Kennebunkport girl on the staff of the *Ladies' Home Journal*.

I may as well say at once that the total circulation of *Europe's Morning After* was exactly 1,300 copies—so small a number that the editorial staff of Harper & Brothers for some years avoided my manuscripts as they'd have shunned a rattlesnake. I wouldn't care to say that Harper & Brothers published the book secretly, but I was almost certain that most of the Brothers had gambled that my *Saturday Evening Post* readers would become aware of its existence by some sort of second sight, and hurry to buy it—something that almost never happens.

§

That second trip took me into surroundings and among people that were almost past belief. The slums of Glasgow, Edinburgh, Liverpool and London are dreadful beyond words—so dreadful that Englishmen of standing refuse to admit they exist (a fact made only too apparent when the Duke of Windsor unguardedly expressed the thought that the barren and hopeless misery of the coal mining districts "mustn't be allowed to go on," thereby gaining the undying enmity of Stanley Baldwin and many another Briton of high degree).

Mr. Barton Currie, editor of the *Ladies' Home Journal,* was dining at London's Savage Club one evening with five eminent authors and playwrights, one of whom had that day read a *Saturday Evening Post* containing an account of a visit I had made to the slums of Camberwell and Elephant and Castle. The gentleman protested bitterly against the misrepresentations—"bloody damned lies" were the words he used—in the account.

Currie generously came to my defense, saying I had worked for the *Ladies' Home Journal* as well as for the *Post,* and *Post* and *Journal* correspondents didn't take liberties with the truth. The gentleman continued to insist that my descriptions of London slums and pubs were outrageously untrue; so Currie suggested that all present should take cabs to Camberwell and Elephant and Castle and see for themselves just how untrue they were. The five Englishmen indignantly refused. Their stubborn British brains were incapable of believing that such things could exist in Merrie England, and that was all there was to it.

A great many Americans, I later found, were equally unwilling to realize that the hordes of emigrants who were being urged and helped to enter the United States could be as undesirable as every American consular officer in Europe knew them to be—and as I emphatically found them in France, Belgium, Holland, Poland, Italy and wherever my wanderings took me that winter.

Every country into which I went seemed worse than the one before: the government of each one was in the hands of masters of knavery, chicanery, guile, misrepresentation, and ingratitude for the earnest efforts of the United States to help them back on their feet again.

Best of all, it seemed to me, was Turkey; and worst of all was Greece, where a little handful of so-called aristocrats were bungling that miserable nation's affairs with a selfish stupidity that had to be experienced to be believed.

As in all other European countries, the United States was expected to supply funds and sympathy for Greece in her wanton, unnecessary and mismanaged war against Turkey, and in the face of the corruption and determined ignorance that were stifling Greek education, agriculture, commerce and decency. This corruption could have been righted in a short time by one man, provided he was honest and had the welfare of Greece at heart. That one man was King Constantine, who was interested in the welfare of nobody but himself. He had just been brought back from exile by a dubious election in which the able and also exiled Venizelos had been narrowly defeated; and I made up my mind to stay in Athens for months, if necessary, in order to find out from the King himself why such things were allowed to exist in a nation that posed as civilized and dared to hope for American assistance and sympathy.

So I applied to Count Mercati, chamberlain to King Constantine, for an interview, and to my surprise my request was almost immediately granted. I then went into consultation with James A. Mills, Associated Press correspondent in Athens, Paul Mavrogordato, Reuter's correspondent in Athens, American Consul General Lowrie, and a few other Americans who had been sent to Greece by large American interests, and with their help compiled an exhaustive set of questions to fire at King Constantine.

The King, a handsome bald-headed six-foot-three hunk of uniformed royalty, answered them violently but inaccurately.

When the interview was over, I went to the Grand Bretagne Hotel, amplified my notes and gave copies to Mills, Mavrogordato and Consul General Lowrie for their information and by way of protection. I knew that they couldn't use any of the interview themselves—not if they wished to remain in Athens—and I was sure that the King wouldn't like the interview when he saw it in print.

It was duly published in the *Saturday Evening Post,* whereupon King Constantine officially denied that he had spoken to me or seen me. His denial was published on the front page of every large American newspaper. I learned a lot about people from King Constantine, and those who want to write can't learn too much about people.

I HAD every intention, when I returned to the United States in the spring of 1921, loaded with immigration material, of finishing that series of immigration articles and then sequestering myself in Ragusa or Provence with a plentiful supply of pens and copy paper; but when I reported to Lorimer in Philadelphia, I found he had other plans for me. Sam Blythe, he said, had made his pile and had enough of acting as Washington correspondent for the *Post,* so he was retreating to California to play golf and philosophize. The *Post,* however, needed a correspondent in Washington—somebody familiar with immigration, to keep an eye on the House and Senate committees responsible for writing and passing a new immigration law; and whether I liked it or not, I'd better resign myself to learning how to be a Washington correspondent.

So while I struggled with the mass of immigration notes, I did nothing about the advertisements of little châteaux and vineyards in Provence, which Mr. Skinner continued to send me from time to time. One of those small châteaux, inland from the seaport of Cette and available at that time for two thousand pounds, is described in *Lydia Bailey.* Late in the summer Mr. Lorimer confirmed his earlier remarks by letter—and I quote the entire letter to show why *Post* contributors regarded Mr. Lorimer as the world's most satisfying and heart-warming editor:

MY DEAR ROBERTS:

You struck twelve, and kept right on striking up to one hundred plus in this last story. It illuminated my whole evening and reconciled me to my hard life as a farmer. Check by the treasurer on Tuesday.

Don't forget our plot to send you to Washington for the winter, with perhaps an occasional excursion into the Hinterland.

Sincerely yours,
GEO. H. LORIMER

So in the autumn we took a house in Chevy Chase and I familiarized myself with the Senate Press Gallery, the House Press Gallery, the explosive General Charles Gates Dawes, the Hon. Albert Johnson of Washington, able chairman of the House Committee on Immigration, who took an almost paternal interest in me when he learned I had once thought of going to Seattle to work on the *Post-Intelligencer*. The office of the commissioner general of immigration stood open to me when rotund and cheery W. W. Husband discovered that I came from Maine. He was a Vermonter, and Vermonters usually are favorably disposed towards State of Mainers because the residents of those two states so often have to present a united front to the misguided other forty-six.

Before leaving for California, Sam Blythe appeared to view me with a skeptical eye and favor me with the benefit of his long experience on and about Capitol Hill. Sam's tongue was as caustic as his pen was brilliant—and his political articles in the *Saturday Evening Post* had repeatedly made and destroyed reputations overnight. One of my great regrets is that I couldn't have watched Sam Blythe attend a press conference in the White House during the period when Franklin Roosevelt was amusing himself at the expense of Washington correspondents, contemptuously ignoring their questions, or urging them to don dunce caps and stand in a corner. Nobody could talk that way to Sam Blythe without touching off fireworks that would have illuminated innumerable things that the offender would have preferred to keep dark.

"There's one thing you want to be mighty careful of," Sam told me. "Don't make any friends on the Hill; because if you do, they'll trim you, sure, sooner or later. They can't help it. It's just second nature to 'em. It doesn't matter how close you think they are to you: if you print something that might lose them a few votes, they'll call you a liar, just the way your pals Constantine and Aguinaldo did. Now mind what I'm telling you: make your friends among correspondents, and let the boys on the Hill alone. And be sure to see Bill Hibbs twice a week. There isn't anyone worth a damn in Washington that Bill hasn't filled with the best licker in the world, and there ain't anything about Washington that he doesn't know." And he straightway took me to Bill's penthouse apartment atop the Hibbs Building—and my political education was under way.

Sam's political philosophy in this, as in everything else, was unimpeachable. Those Washington correspondents were great reporters, and their abilities far outshone those of most senators, representatives, cabinet officers and governmental heads. Charlie Michaelson of the *World*, Dick Oulahan and Lewis Wood of the *Times*, Joe Farrington of the *Public Ledger*, Roy Roberts of the *Kansas City Star*, Herb Corey of the N.E.A., Arthur Sinnott of the *Newark News*, Fred Essary and Frank Kent of the *Baltimore Sun*, Wilmot Lewis of the *London Times*, Jack La Gorce, editor of the *National Geographic*, Charlie Ross of the *St. Louis Post-Dispatch*, Carter Field of the *Herald Tribune*, Bob Choate of the *Boston Herald*, Jim Wright of the *Cleveland Leader*, Jay Hayden of the *Detroit News*, Junius Wood of the *Chicago News*, Bob Barry of the *Public Ledger*, Frank King and Ross Bartley of the Associated Press, Henry Suydam of the *Brooklyn Eagle*, Ashmun Brown of the *Providence Journal*, Bob Norton of the *Boston Post*, Bill Brigham of the *Boston Transcript*, Mark Sullivan, Frank Simonds . . . a great crowd!

There was considerable interest in immigration that winter; and undeterred by Harper's unfruitful experience with *Europe's Morning After*, Bobbs-Merrill prepared to take advantage of that interest by publishing my new immigration articles as a book—*Why Europe Leaves Home*. The critics, except for a violent *New York Times* reviewer, spoke kindly of it, but its total circulation was 2,228 copies—a number which, when placed alongside the one hundred and twenty million population of the United States, ought to be illuminating to those who accept the unrealities of Edith Wharton's *Hudson River Bracketed*.

The winter was financially profitable, but spiritually depressing—not only because of the stumbling inability of the House and Senate immigration committees to take effective steps to slow up immigration, but because of the only too apparent determination of every government bureau and department to encourage inefficiency, duplication of effort and brazen laziness; because of the low quality of senators, representatives and government officials responsible for the carrying on of national affairs; because of the impossibility of arousing voters to a realization of these evils. Doubtless to soothe my unconcealed disgust at politicians in general, Mr. Lorimer made me a Christmas present of a month-long trip to Florida to get a series of three articles on the pleasures and pursuits of vacationists from the North—and the vacationers in Florida at that time were so few that Miami Beach was a desert waste of pumped-in sand, a checkerboard of unpopulated avenues, spotted here and there by three or four hotels and a few score houses. Bobbs-Merrill, still hopeful that *Why Europe Leaves Home* might spurt magnificently to a circulation of 3,000 or even 3,500, undertook to make a book out of the three Florida articles, calling the book *Sun Hunting;* and somewhat to our surprise it sold 4,790 copies—largely, I gathered, to weather-bound tourists in St. Augustine, Jacksonville, Miami and Palm Beach.

So I had three books on the shelf, though nobody knew it; and nobody knew better than I that I wasn't yet doing the sort of work I wanted to do. But much as I disliked the tumult, turmoil, waste, constant telephone ringing and political ineffectuality of Washington, I felt obliged to stay there until something was done about immigration restriction.

During the summer of 1922 I escaped briefly to Maine from the Washington stewpot, in order to catch up with my accumulation of Washington notes, and in the autumn returned to Washington to occupy a semi-mausoleum on Nineteenth Street, belonging to a cliff-dweller descendant of William H. Seward, Secretary of State under Lincoln. The house looked as though nothing in it had been cleaned or altered since Seward's day; and its cluttered gloom, coupled with my distaste for Washington, made me more than ever determined to repair to Avignon or Ragusa—to any sunny spot completely remote from telephones, doorbells, calling cards turned down at the corners to indicate personal delivery, luncheon parties, dinner parties, and social contacts of all sorts. I still didn't know how to do it, but I knew it had to be done.

I find that on December 28, 1922, I had a letter from an old-time friend, Arthur Somers Roche, who had been phenomenally successful, after years of existing precariously on the returns from pulp-magazine stories, in breaking into the *Cosmopolitan* and the *Saturday Evening Post*. "Loot," the story that gained him his start, incidentally, had, before going to the *Post,* been submitted to and rejected by—sometimes accompanied by indignant editorial complaints—every pulp magazine in the United States.

Mr. Roche wrote from Nice, on the French Riviera, speaking highly of the climate and the surroundings; and I at once urged him to investigate rentals in smaller Riviera resorts, such as Juan-les-Pins and Cap d'Antibes, and look for an inexpensive retreat in which I could spend the following winter writing without interference.

As a result of talking to James F. Byrnes, Simeon Fess (the House and Senate leaders of those days), Pat Harrison, John Sharp Williams of Mississippi, the brilliant George Higgins Moses of New Hampshire, and various other political leaders, I even got an idea for a novel to be called *The Corner Cutters.* Both Mr. Fess and Mr. Byrnes explained at considerable length to me that they had come to Washington as starry-eyed political neophytes, with high hopes of effecting great reforms in government, but found almost immediately that nobody could be effective until re-elected for successive terms, because only by seniority could he rise to a position of importance on any committee— and every law must be approved by a committee before it can be acted on by the Senate or the House. Thus he must constantly cater to voters in order to gain re-election, even when he knows such catering is inexcusable; and in order to stand well with his fellow committee members, he can never insist that any law which he proposes, no matter how wise or how carefully drawn, be passed exactly as written. A corner must be cut from it here to satisfy one colleague; several cut elsewhere to satisfy a dozen others, each representing a special interest with an ax to grind—and Washington is chock-a-block with special interests: a dairy bloc, determined to prevent the coloring of margarine; a silver bloc, hell-bent on keeping the price of silver where it has no business to be; and a thousand other blocs, all too many of them working feverishly against the best interests of the country. Thus the United States is governed by compromise, or corner cutting.

So I contemplated a novel about an honest, wide-eyed young politician who comes to Washington, maintains himself in office by adept corner cutting; then rises to power and finds himself entangled with European statesmen in an effort to bring peace to nations heartily sick of war. Unable to unlearn his corner-cutting lessons, he cuts corners to meet the demands of European politicians, compromises here, compromises there—until peace is impossible, and another war, bursting upon a helpless world, destroys the corner cutter's fortune, his family and his native land.

I must remark, in passing, that whenever a committee or delegation made up of senators, representatives or politicians of any other grade travels afield to act for the United States, it cuts corners abroad just as it did at home, and almost invariably makes a mess of things. Prominent corner cutters who have botched foreign relations for the United States are Woodrow Wilson, Franklin Roosevelt and James F. Byrnes. Said Stanislaw Mikolajczyk, Prime Minister of Poland, "The world has never been told what actually occurred at Teheran. Stalin easily forced Roosevelt and Churchill into appeasement . . . into one of the most infamous injustices of history."

In addition to contemplating the novel and working for the *Post*, I joined with Booth Tarkington and Hugh MacNair Kahler in producing a burlesque book on antique collecting—*The Collector's Whatnot*— a book which followed the pattern of previous books by selling 3,782 copies.

When in the spring of 1923 it became apparent that an immigration bill wouldn't be passed that year, I was so sick of Washington and of politicians that I begged Lorimer to send me away on the trip he'd half promised, suggesting that he let me cross Siberia into Russia. By way of reply he summoned me to Philadelphia, refused to consider a Siberian trip, but said I could leave Washington early in May, cover my old immigration routes in Europe for additional immigration material, look into prospective emigration from Denmark, Norway and Sweden, investigate Fascism in Italy and Germany, and once more try to enter Russia from the European end. Thus May 2 found us aboard the Red Star liner *Finland,* embarked on a trip that, so far as I was concerned, was without a peer for frustrations, the worst of them due to the mysterious activities of an American, Roy C. Woods.

In Paris I finished a story left over from Washington—"The Inarticulate Conservatives"—picked up new developments in immigration, then set off for Italy to investigate the activities of Mussolini's Black Shirts.

Our ambassador in Rome at that time was Richard Washburn Child, an author who had received his ambassadorial post as a reward for heading the Republican National Committee during President Harding's campaign. I wanted to talk to Mussolini about his offensive insistence that all Italian emigrants to the United States must permanently retain their Italian citizenship, sympathies and manner of life while living in New York, Chicago and other American centers. Consequently I made formal application, through Child, for an appointment with Mussolini. Child was amiable and helpful: an interview, of course—oh, certainly—could be arranged. He'd fix it for the following Monday.

When Monday came, the interview was postponed until Wednesday: then till Friday: then till Tuesday. Child stood high in Mussolini's favor, and I couldn't understand why he should let himself be pushed around so persistently—which proved that my political education was far from complete. I found out later that Child had no intention of helping me to a Mussolini interview, because he himself intended to write one for the *Saturday Evening Post.* Why help me get a story that would probably interfere with his?

As a matter of fact, I had already seen about as much of Mussolini as I wished; for I had sat near him at a fencing match, at which he appeared in the company of the Italian boxer Spalla. The audience applauded Spalla more heartily than it applauded Mussolini, and Mussolini unmistakably revealed himself to be a highly offensive character with the sportsmanship of a gorilla.

I stayed on and on in Rome, waiting for the Mussolini interview that

Child continued to insist he would arrange for me; and at last word came from the embassy that all was in readiness. Mr. Child made up for the delay by sending his secretary to escort me to the Chigi Palace.

To my distress I found that the interview was to be a mass interview, or audience; and among those gathered for it were Anne O'Hare McCormick of the *New York Times,* Sam Crowther of *Collier's,* Miss Auger of the *New York Herald Tribune,* and two lady lecturers on public events, whose *raison d'être* was addressing groups of ladies, and enlightening them on what was happening in the world. Both ladies wore Fascist decorations in their coat lapels, and carried large pictures of Mussolini to be autographed. I could see that the assemblages of females subsequently addressed by them might in all likelihood receive a warped estimate of Il Duce's character.

Since an interview under such conditions is no interview at all, I spoke bitterly to Mr. Child's secretary, hastened to the hotel for Mrs. Roberts, and caught the next train to Munich, where Adolf Hitler was making a spectacle of himself.

I discovered later that after the group of interviewers had waited two hours, Mussolini graciously informed them that a cabinet meeting made it impossible for him to keep his appointment.

Our consulate general in Munich was in the hands of Mr. Tracy Lay and Mr. Robert Murphy, both as helpful as they were astute. Mr. Murphy, later to become General Eisenhower's political adviser on North Africa, won my undying gratitude by taking me under his wing and briefing me comprehensively on the insanities of the Nazis. Hitler's activities were easily observed, thanks to the loud-mouthed fervor of his black- and brown-shirted adherents and the profound distrust of him then prevalent in decent German circles. He was a flannel-mouthed, blovalating demagogue and no mistake; but demagogues can be dangerous, and I was eager to spend a few hours with him in order to see how he compared with the American specimens so obnoxiously disporting themselves in the United States Senate.

On the recommendation of the consulate general, I employed a square-headed German youth named Rötser as an interpreter, and at once set him to arranging interviews with Hitler and General Ludendorff—Ludendorff at that time being Hitler's chief supporter and adviser. Ludendorff flatly refused to be interviewed. Rötser reported that an appointment was arranged for Monday with Hitler; then that the appointment was canceled. He announced a second appointment for Thursday. That, too, was canceled. On receiving a terse lesson in American profanity, Rötser hastened away and returned to report happily that a third appointment had been made for Saturday. When that in turn was postponed, Rötser was eliminated from my activities and I started after Hitler on my own by calling at the office of Hitler's newspaper, the *Völkischer Beobachter*.

My first objective was Rosenberg, the editor, who also handled Hitler's press relations. Rosenberg, I knew, had been in correspondence with Henry Ford, and would probably have an understanding of American magazines. I was received by Rosenberg's assistant, Weiss; but when I asked for Rosenberg, Weiss said it would do me no good to talk to him, since he didn't speak English.

When I said I had heard on good authority that Rosenberg had been able to get his thoughts across to Henry Ford, Weiss exclaimed, "Aha! You are Mr. Ford's secretary! He expects you today, but not until the afternoon."

Probably because of the expression on my face, Weiss said hastily that all appointments must be made through Herr Hanfstaengl. So I went to see Putzi Hanfstaengl, that tall and genial Nazi who rowed on the Harvard crew in 1908, and had become Hitler's chief jester and amusement purveyor. In fact, I talked with him several times, once taking Robert Murphy along to listen to his Nazi drivel. Putzi knew the *Saturday Evening Post* only too well, evidently; because I was never allowed to talk to Hitler.

I wrote the Hitler story in Stockholm while waiting for a Russian visa. The story, titled "Suds," spoke disrespectfully of Hitler's aims and ideals, and stated flatly that at the present stage of his development any attempt on his part to seize power would find Mr. Hitler poised at the end of a fragile limb. Mr. Lorimer, when he received the article, viewed it with doubt and apprehension, and held it several months before publishing it. As a result, it appeared in the *Saturday Evening Post* six days before Hitler's abortive Beer Hall Putsch, when both Ludendorff and Hitler were impelled to take a dive as the forces of law and order opened on beer-inflamed Nazi marchers with machine guns. Instead of shooting the machine-gunners for their failure to get either Hitler or Ludendorff, the forces of law and order sentenced Hitler to a year in a Bavarian bastille, thus providing him with sufficient leisure to write *Mein Kampf*.

In Rome I had opened negotiations for a Russian visa. I would, the Russians told me, find my permission at Russian headquarters in Berlin. In Berlin I called on Ustsinoff, the Soviet representative. He had received no instructions from Moscow concerning me, so I filled out another application, and Ustsinoff promised that a reply would be wait-

ing for me in Stockholm. In spite of knowing that Communist promises are worthless, I looked for the reply when I reached Stockholm, but
I never received it. Communists want nothing whatever to do with
anyone not heartily in favor of bringing all the nations of the world
under Communist control.

From Berlin we went on to a Danish resort town, Marienlyst, next
door to Helsingör and the ramparts on which Hamlet's father's ghost
took nightly exercise. There I wrote three articles; then caught a pint-
sized steamer from Copenhagen to Danzig. By virtue of my friendship
with Mr. Dawson, American consul general in Danzig, I obtained an
outsize ambassadorial compartment in the center of the only sleeping
car on the train from Danzig to Warsaw, and Mr. Dawson kindly
accompanied me to the station.

On the platform an elegantly dressed Charles-Dana-Gibsonish American was receiving a rousing send-off from a bevy of attractive Danzig
maidens.

Who, I asked Dawson, was the Lothario?

His name, Dawson said, was Woods—Roy C. Woods of Chicago, and
he had been moving back and forth between Danzig and Warsaw for
the past two months, though nobody could find out what he was doing,
or why. I might, Mr. Dawson added, strike up an acquaintance with
him, and look into the matter.

Thanks to my extra-large compartment and a plentiful supply of
cigarettes, I had no difficulty in meeting Mr. Woods, who was addicted
to a superior grade of perfume and carried a pearl-handled revolver
in his hip pocket.

In the beginning Woods was reticent—not uncommunicative, exactly,
but extremely cautious. In Chicago, he said, he had been assistant state's
attorney for Illinois, and the stress of successfully prosecuting some
twenty cases had proved so burdensome that he had taken a jaunt to
Poland for a rest. When I suggested that he could have found more
restful travel conditions in any other part of Europe, he contented himself with saying that he had always wondered what Poland looked like.
When I further suggested that anyone, thanks to Poland's flatness,
knew exactly what it looked like after a week of sight-seeing, he only
smiled enigmatically.

Around midnight he weakened, and admitted that he was engaged
in a venture which must for now remain a profound secret, but which
would, one of these days, intrigue, not to say startle, the world.

Around two o'clock in the morning he broke down completely. He
was in Poland, he said, because, after the newspapers of the United

States had commented admiringly on his prowess as assistant state's attorney, he had received a call from a New Yorker who represented the Russian royal family. Before the royal family had met its end in the Ekaterinburg well, the Tsar had exported from Russia a nest egg of crown jewels and immensely valuable paintings, all of which were now in a warehouse, crated and ready for shipment. Furthermore, the representative said, the Tsar's daughter, Tatiana, had been helped to escape from Ekaterinburg by a sympathetic Bolshevik officer and, in peasant garb, made her way over the Urals, across Russia and into Poland, where she was now living as a peasant with a peasant family. The Russian representative, Woods said, had commissioned him to visit Poland and arrange transportation to America for the jewels, the paintings, the girl, the Bolshevik officer who had helped her escape, and three Russian women who had accompanied her from Ekaterinburg.

It was, of course, true that American Intelligence officers in Siberia had repeatedly reported the rumor that one of the Tsar's daughters had escaped, as Garland and I had set forth in *The Brotherhood of Man;* but Woods's story struck me as fantastic. Why, I wanted to know, should a New Yorker bother to go all the way to Chicago and seek out Woods, when a thousand better-qualified New Yorkers could have been sent on such a mission?

Woods modestly said it was because of his reputation as an astute prosecutor.

Had he seen the girl? I asked.

Certainly he'd seen her. He saw her every week. He took a plane from Warsaw, landed near the village in which she lived, and went secretly by night to visit her.

How, I wanted to know, could he be sure she was what she claimed to be?

With that Woods really took down his hair. In his wallet he had a picture of the Grand Duchess Tatiana, clipped from a magazine. There couldn't be any mistake about it, he insisted. The girl he visited each week was unquestionably the girl in the picture. He had gifts that she had given him, among them a gold cigarette case decorated with the double-headed eagle of Russia in white enamel, surrounding a diamond the size of a bean. He had, he insisted, seen the packing cases containing the portraits and the jewels: some had been opened for him: he had handled the jewels, seen paintings, some by great masters, Van Dyck, Rembrandt, Holbein, Titian. If ever he could overcome the girl's fear of Bolshevik reprisal, he proposed to charter a steamer, load all the packing cases aboard it, and take Tatiana and her friends to America.

Did she speak English? Certainly she spoke English. All the Tsar's daughters had English governesses.

On the assumption that it isn't safe to overlook anything, I made a deal with him to be given the exclusive right to publish Tatiana's story serially in the *Saturday Evening Post*. I was to be taken along on the chartered steamer when Woods took her to America, and have the opportunity of interviewing Tatiana for several hours each day.

In about a month, Woods thought, he could sufficiently overcome Tatiana's fears of assassination by Bolshevik agents, and persuade her to board a ship: meanwhile he would keep in constant touch with me.

No, he couldn't take me with him to see the girl; for if the Bolshevik officer who had helped her escape learned that Woods had breathed a word to anyone concerning her existence, his life wouldn't be worth a plugged nickel. On the same grounds he swore me to secrecy.

I told him I didn't believe a word of his story. I said I thought he was junketing around Poland because he'd been in a jam in Chicago, and had been supplied with funds to make him inaccessible for a few months. To whom, I wanted to know, had the Tsar's packing cases been consigned? If there was a consignee, why hadn't they already been shipped to America? If Woods had seen them, why couldn't I see them? If he was so sure the Bolsheviks would try to kill Tatiana, why insist on calling her Tatiana? Why not call her Shura Sorokoletoff? Why not call her Mrs. Roy C. Woods? Why not claim that she was his sister Emmie? Woods preserved a sphinx-like silence.

At all events, Woods, during my stay in Warsaw, chartered a plane and was gone three days. When he returned, he insisted he had again seen Tatiana. She seemed, he assured me, more reconciled to making the trip, and he was sure he would be able to get away by the fifteenth of September.

Because of my promise to him to say nothing, I could only try to check up on him in a roundabout way through Hugh Gibson, our minister to Poland, Consul General Keena and James C. White, a former political editor of the *Boston Herald,* who was representing a Chicago banker in Poland, and by cabling America about him. From these sources I learned that Woods really had been assistant state's attorney for Illinois, that nothing whatever was known about his reasons for being in Poland; that he had made a number of airplane trips toward the Russian border; that he spent money lavishly and seemed to have plenty of it: also that he had applied to Mr. Keena for five passports in blank—an application that Mr. Keena had been forced to refuse.

It was on July 16 that I first met Woods. On July 27, when I reached Stockholm, I found a cable from Woods from Vilna:

NOTHING MORE DEFINITE REGARDING DEPARTURE. TRYING LEAVE AUGUST 17, BUT SEPTEMBER 5 LOOKS LIKELY. EXPECT ARRIVE DANZIG NEXT ABOUT TEN DAYS.

So I hurried matters in Sweden and Norway, went to London just in time to catch the *Leviathan* for Cherbourg, where Lorimer, after a short vacation, was boarding that ship to return to New York. I told him the story of Woods and Tatiana, adding that I considered it fishy. He readily agreed, however, in case Woods produced the girl, to send Princess Cantacuzene to meet the ship. Princess Cantacuzene, who was Julia Dent Grant before her marriage, had been intimate with all the Tsar's daughters, and would know whether Woods's young woman was Tatiana or a phony.

On August 11 Woods, in reply to several urgent cables from me, telegraphed:

MANY COMPLICATIONS. NOW PLAN LEAVE DANZIG 26TH LITHUANIA. WILL KNOW DEFINITELY ONE WEEK.

I investigated the *Lithuania,* and found her to be a Baltic-American liner, eighty-five hundred tons, scheduled to sail from Danzig on August 22: not August 26. Cursing Woods from the bottom of my heart for disrupting my plans and interfering with my assignments, I sent him two more cables demanding definite information; then made a hurried trip through the parts of France that had been devastated by German armies—a trip that ended in Antwerp where, at the consulate general, I found a final telegram from Woods:

TRIP STILL UNDECIDED. WILL WIRE YOU IN NEW YORK WHEN MATTERS ARRANGED AND SEE YOU GET THE STORY ON THE OTHER END.

By a burst of speed I succeeded in catching the ship on which Mrs. Roberts was sailing for America. Two months later I asked General Dawes's office in Chicago for a report on Woods, and learned that he was still at the Bristol Hotel, Warsaw, and was expected to leave for the United States in about ten days. When he finally came back to the United States, he had neither Tatiana, crown jewels nor Titians.

On February 1, 1926, when Mrs. Roberts and I were on our way to California, both of us called on Woods in Chicago, and I told him as emphatically as possible that I thought his story had been a hoax, invented by himself to conceal his real reason for leaving Chicago, and that he had maliciously and inexcusably interfered with my plans and put me to unnecessary trouble and expense. He insisted that everything he had told me was the simple truth: that he had failed to produce Tatiana only because he had been unable to persuade her to run the risk of exposing herself to the vengeance of the Bolsheviks, who would leave no stone unturned to murder any surviving member of the Russian royal family. He fully intended, he said, to return to Poland on the following summer and try again to bring the last of the Romanoffs to America. He still had no answer to my insistent queries as to why he should have considered inviting disaster by letting her travel as the Grand Duchess Tatiana when she could have safely claimed to be Ella Svoboda of Vilna—and when he could have purchased a thousand counterfeit passports for just one of those masterpieces in the Tsar's packing cases.

And yet the incident had its advantages, for it came under the head of experience.

CHAPTER

20

PRESIDENT HARDING died, that summer of 1923, while listening to a reading, by Mrs. Harding, of an article by Sam Blythe, and shortly afterward I was advised by Mr. Lorimer that he had been approached by George Christian, President Harding's secretary, who wished to dispose of a serial designed to familiarize an apathetic world with the drab experiences of Warren Gamaliel Harding in the Senate and the White House.

I knew Christian slightly, and had found him highly inarticulate. He must have, I realized, latent powers that had been carefully concealed if he was capable of assembling the 80,000 words necessary to make ten installments in the *Saturday Evening Post*. He had admitted to Lorimer that he needed help in making his 80,000 words readable; and I, said Lorimer, was to help him—and quickly, before the world forgot there had been a President named Warren Gamaliel Harding.

I reminded Mr. Lorimer that my dislike for Washington was intense, and that I wanted to get away from the place and start writing something; but my reminder left him cold. Immigration evils, he told me, were far from satisfactorily remedied, and here was this Harding job that had to be done in a hurry; and then he wanted six articles on the scurvy treatment that Navahos, Hopis, Pimas and other Indians were receiving from the government.

So once again I went back to Washington, unearthed George Christian, and asked to see the manuscript he had prepared on Harding's life.

Christian, embarrassed, said he hadn't accomplished as much as he had hoped. He had worked hard, he said, but there just didn't seem to be much of anything to write about. When I pressed him as to exactly how much he had done, he reluctantly admitted that all he had been able to wring from Harding's career, letters and papers were 3,000 words. He was depending on me for the additional 77,000.

It is, of course, possible to expand 3,000 words into 80,000 if the 3,000 are documented by facts, and deal with something of interest. Unfortunately, there were several facts about President Harding's career concerning which Mr. Christian was unwilling to be frank. In fact, he thought they shouldn't be mentioned at all, whereas to my way of thinking they were the only interesting passages in Mr. Harding's life. When I reported this in pained detail to Mr. Lorimer, he abandoned the idea of publishing Mr. Christian's estimate of President Harding's life and work.

Since there seemed to be no escape from Washington, I again rented a house there—one which Sam Blythe referred to as the ossuary. Its only recommendation was that it was across the street from the residence of the eminent and helpful jurist, Mr. Charles Beecher Warren. There I reluctantly resumed my scrutiny of the antics of the House, the Senate, the various departments of the government, and fruitlessly tried to keep clear of the almost endless round of dinners, luncheons, cocktail parties and soirees with which that peculiarly gregarious city perpetually wastes its time.

In February, true to his promise, Lorimer allowed me to break away from that fount of fat-headedness by sending me off to scrutinize the distractomaniacs of Florida, the patient Pima Indians of Arizona, the outlandish habits of Hollywood moving picture actors, actresses, directors and magnate-graduates of the clothing industry, the snake-happy Hopis of the mesas above Oraibi, the stolid Navahos around Shiprock, Beautiful Mountain and Two Gray Hills, and the admirable Pueblos of Santo Domingo and San Ildefonzo. On this journey an importunate schoolmaster decoyed me into making a trip to Los Alamos; and I think even then that inaccessible hilltop was permeated by the horror that was to emerge from it; for it was sad and soggy, cold and miserable, and I couldn't escape from it fast enough.

While I was engaged in observing the beach-sitting proclivities of Palm Beach habitués, I was discovered by an old friend, Frank Rane, whom I had frequently consulted when he was state forester of Massachusetts. Frank had become a Florida enthusiast—above all a Palm Beach enthusiast; and immediately he delivered himself of a passionate and moving address on the advantages of Florida over all the rest of the world, and of Palm Beach over all the rest of Florida.

It would, he insisted, be folly—nay, sheer criminal stupidity—if I failed to take advantage of the ineffable blessing struggling to climb into my lap. Land in this garden spot, this crowning glory of earthly

Paradises, was actually and miraculously cheaper than in the least favored of Florida resorts. Building costs were low: labor was plentiful and cheap: a boom in Florida real estate values was near at hand.

"Look," said Rane, "you cannot lose this golden opportunity! I won't allow it! Why, there couldn't be a better place in the world for a person who wants to write! Now I want you to sit right here while I get a real estate agent; then you've got to buy a house lot!"

Away he went, and in fifteen minutes returned with a brisk real estate dealer, who had already decided on the holding I was to purchase for five thousand dollars; a small, flat, weed-grown rectangle on Barton Avenue, next door to Freddie Sears and only a few houses removed from Jules Bache and Tony Biddle.

"Just the thing!" Rane said. "You'll never regret it."

"Wonderful place for inspiration," said the real estate dealer. "Sometimes I feel so inspired down here that I'd write a book myself if I only had the time."

When I protested that the land was less than a tenth of an acre, so that the asking price was at the rate of fifty thousand dollars an acre, they were cut to the heart and showered me with documentary proof that nearby lots of equal size had sold for twenty thousand dollars— for forty thousand. Why, this place was a bargain at five thousand! A pickup! A steal!

So I bought it, and instantly Rane clamored that I must build on it. I protested that I couldn't think of such a thing, as I was leaving for Arizona and the Pacific Coast early the next morning.

"It makes no difference," Rane said. "No difference at all. I've got a friend who's a contractor—fine man; reliable; enterprising; clean-cut! He's got plans ready drawn for all sorts of houses. Now you sit right here, and I'll go get him. Don't move, mind you!"

Again he hastened away and in half an hour returned with an obviously competent young man who unrolled a set of plans of pleasing Spanish-type houses and indicated one that both he and Rane seemed to consider best adapted to my purposes. That house, said the contractor, would cost me twelve thousand dollars, and he would guarantee to finish it in three months. At each sign of wavering or indecision on my part, Rane instantly poured out panegyrics on Palm Beach, its magnificent climate, its perpetually warm water, its golden sands, its tropical fruits, its charming people, its diversions, its healthfulness. . . . I just didn't have a chance to say No, and so I signed on the dotted line and went to Arizona.

Since that swing through the South and West resulted in seven articles, it made the winter endurable; but my dislike of Washington was intensified, when I returned there, by a slight contretemps with Mr. Herbert Hoover, who was then Secretary of Commerce. Mr. Hoover had a finger in a great many pies at that time, and had surrounded himself with young men supposed to be adept at getting Mr. Hoover's name in the papers. One of those amateur press agents was Alfred P. Dennis, who in years gone by had written two or three articles of a commercial nature for the *Saturday Evening Post,* which automatically made him eligible for Mr. Hoover's staff.

The Department of Agriculture, at that time, was scandalously administered, and urgently in need of a guiding hand that would ruthlessly toss out its innumerable incompetents and nincompoops, and reorganize every branch of the department, so that it would become an efficient aid to farmers instead of a disorderly catacomb of useless fuddyduddies.

Mr. Dennis came to me as an emissary from Mr. Hoover, proposing that I write for the *Saturday Evening Post* an article urging the advisability of placing a businessman, such as the head of General Motors or United States Steel or American Telephone—or perhaps Mr. Hoover himself—at the head of the Department of Agriculture, rather than handing the post to a farmer-politician from the Middle West—one who would be certain to permit the department to remain a refuge for superannuated political stumble-bums. Mr. Hoover, said Mr. Dennis, had brought Mr. Coolidge around to his way of thinking, but Mr. Coolidge was still a trifle fearful of the political anguish that would arise if he handed a political plum to one who might be characterized as a Wall Street Wolf.

I readily agreed to suggest the idea to Mr. Lorimer, and to recommend it as well; but I said emphatically that I must have the assurance that President Coolidge wouldn't absent-mindedly appoint a politician-farmer to the position before the article appeared in the *Post.*

Dennis promised me that I need have no fears on that point, since the Chief (meaning Mr. Hoover) and Mr. Coolidge thought as one concerning the need for a businessman at the head of the Department of Agriculture—understood, too, the advisability of obtaining wide publicity concerning that need. Popular clamor resulting from publicity would offset any hullabaloo from the farmer vote and Western politicians, and they would gain no sympathy by howling that Mr. Coolidge had robbed them of one of their great natural prerogatives by failing to place a dirt farmer at the head of the Department of Agriculture.

So on the following day I called on Mr. Hoover, who confirmed all that Mr. Dennis had said, gave me a comprehensive picture of the deplorable conditions in the Department of Agriculture; then arranged for me to have several talks with his top-flight economist, Dr. Dana Durand, who supplied me with facts, figures, reports, documents and balance sheets to corroborate all of Mr. Hoover's statements.

Six weeks later the article appeared in the *Saturday Evening Post,* under the title of "The Dirt Farmer Complex," carefully explaining why a businessman was vitally necessary as Secretary of Agriculture. It was a much needed article—but unfortunately, one week before it appeared, President Coolidge had named a dirt farmer-politician to that post.

When the news of the President's appointment reached me, I immediately got in touch with Mr. Dennis, and baldly pointed out to him that his promises to me and to the *Saturday Evening Post* had not been carried out; that although I had been warned by Mr. Blythe that broken faith was as common on Capitol Hill as starlings, I liked it so little that I'd accept no assignments to the Department of Commerce until its personnel had changed for the better.

I also wrote Mr. Lorimer the details, and said that if the *Post* had further occasion to publish anything about Mr. Hoover or the Department of Commerce, I would have to ask that the material be obtained by another correspondent, since I couldn't in fairness have dealings with anybody who had so signally failed to protect the *Post.*

Dennis, unconscionably irritated by my blunt remarks, didn't wait to write, but heatedly telephoned Lorimer, demanding that I be straightway banished from Washington and placed permanently on the *Post's* Index Expurgatorius.

Since Lorimer never reacted favorably to demands or threats, he found himself unable to see eye to eye with Mr. Dennis, and merely wrote me that the Department of Commerce would hereafter be out of bounds so far as I was concerned.

Some of my friends among the Washington correspondents seemed to think, at the time, that I was unduly irascible in my attitude toward Mr. Dennis and Mr. Hoover. I never understood their reasons for thinking so, and wondered how they would have preferred me to react to Hoover's failure to force Coolidge to make the planned appointment. In my position, would they, I wondered, have hurried to the Department of Commerce to kiss Mr. Dennis and Mr. Hoover?

§

By mid-1924 I could see that I was making no progress—except financially; for Lorimer had done for me what he had done for all his regular contributors: steadily raised the rate for acceptable articles. He raised it to nine hundred dollars, to eleven hundred, to fifteen hundred and now it had gone to seventeen hundred and fifty.

By now, however, I knew what I wanted to try to write. Some of my ancestors, who had settled in Kittery in 1639, had been considerably troubled by Indians as well as by fellow townsmen who objected to their willingness to help Quakers. Others, among whom were Rebecca Towne Nourse and her two sisters, had been on the losing end of a controversy with Salem witch hunters. So those two branches of the family, in 1725, moved to a less conventional neighborhood—the town of Arundel in Maine, where they were frequently engaged in fighting Indians, fighting the French, fighting the English, operating privateers, and carrying cargoes to England, Spain, Central America and West Indian ports.

I had long been curious about the ways of life of these forerunners of mine, and as time went on, I became more so. I knew from my grandmother that a sea-captain great-grandfather had done a stretch in Dartmoor Prison during the War of 1812; but when I pressed my grandmother for details, she was unable to supply them. She didn't know how he got to Dartmoor, what Dartmoor was like, what he did in Dartmoor, who his companions were, how he was clothed or fed, or anything about it. In fact, she was unwilling to discuss details, for he had been master of a privateer and she had somehow picked up the idea that a privateersman had something in common with a pirate.

Well, how about the three relatives who had gone on the expedition that captured Louisburg from the French? How had they reached Louisburg? What had they done when they got there? What sort of equipment had they carried? What was the size of a regiment in those days? How were the men fed?

Nobody knew the answer.

All right: how about the other great-and-so-on-grandpa who went to Quebec and tried to capture the city from the British; then came home and married his captain's daughter? How did he get to Quebec? Who did he go with? How long did it take? How many were killed? How was their food carried? What did they wear? Who organized the expedition?

Nobody knew.

I had three relatives from Arundel, my grandmother told me, in the retreat from Ticonderoga, the Battle of Hubbardton, both battles of Saratoga, and at Valley Forge.

I did, hey? Well, what happened at Ticonderoga to make 'em retreat? Who fought at Hubbardton, and who won, and who was there, and what was it all about, and where *is* Hubbardton, on account it ain't on any road map *I've* got? And what went on at Valley Forge outside of bloody footprints in the snow? Why didn't they move to some place where there was no snow?

My grandmother brushed me off. The rest of my family were completely in the dark.

I had tried to get some of these things straightened out in my mind by reading histories that purported to explain them; but in every case—not in most cases, but in *every* case—I found that the books explained nothing fully or satisfactorily. They were drab, dull, unconvincing, rich in omissions, and crowded with statements that couldn't possibly be true. The people in them were generals and statesmen and important personages: cardboard people, flat, unreal, bloodless, lifeless, behaving without rhyme or reason. The little people like my great-great-grandfathers and all those other men from Maine, who sailed the ships and stopped the bullets and cursed the rotten food and stole chickens and wanted to get the hell out of there and go home—they just didn't exist at all.

I understood Thoreau's complaint about historians, set down in his *Week on the Concord and Merrimack Rivers:*

> On beholding an old picture of Concord, as it appeared but 75 years ago, with a fair open prospect and a light on trees and river, as if it were broad noon, I find that I had not thought the sun shone in those days, or that men lived in broad daylight then. Still less do we imagine the sun shining on hill and valley during Philip's war, on the war-path of Church or Philip, or later of Lovewell or Paugus, with serene summer weather, but they must have lived and fought in a dim twilight or night.

It was true that one American historian had written about people who lived and fought in bright sunlight and raging snowstorms, but he was no help to me, for Francis Parkman had carefully avoided any reference to the American Revolution—though it took me years to realize why.

No historian of even half of Parkman's ability could have dealt as fully with the French and Indian Wars as Parkman had done without finding himself forced to touch on the American Revolution. Parkman, however, lived in a time when it was a crime, a sin against society, to cast doubts or aspersions on any of the asinine myths about the American Revolution that had come to be regarded as gospel. Since

Parkman was a good historian, he knew only too well that the Loyalists of America, instead of being a pack of unreasonable and contemptible Tories, had a case and a good one; and since he was by nature strongly out of sympathy with what is often called the rabble, his hands were tied and he left the American Revolution strictly alone. So, too, did William Hickling Prescott, another excellent historian of social standing in Boston, who avoided the American Revolution as he would have shunned leprosy, and confined himself to the operations of Spaniards in Mexico and Peru, concerning which he could be brutally frank without causing even a ripple on any part of Beacon Hill.

If Parkman had written the truth as he would have had to see it about the American Revolution, he would have told the Loyalist side, and in detail; and inevitably, as a result, he would have been socially ostracized by hidebound Boston—and Parkman's aversion to social ostracism was even stronger than his desire to write history.

Before the summer ended I was disgusted beyond words by the incredible dullness and scantiness of so-called histories. I realized that I could never find out what I wanted to know about those early soldiers, sailors, farmers, mothers, witches, camp followers and tavern keepers of Maine, and what they did, and where they went, and with whom they went, and how, and exactly how they did it, unless I assembled all the necessary information from every obtainable source; then put all that information together in a book in which characters acted and talked just as Major Samuel I. Johnson, or Cardenio F. King, or Professor William Street Hutchins, or Major Rupert Hughes, or Colonel O. P. Robinson, or Jocko Cairns, or E. A. Grozier, or Cliff Carberry, or Dick Oulahan, or Cal Coolidge talked and acted.

That, it dawned on me, was what I must do. Even though nobody read what I wrote, it ought to be done, because nobody had ever done it before—and there ought to be at least one book that would give the good people of Maine an honest, detailed and easily understood account of how their forebears got along. I hadn't the slightest desire then to write what is known as an historical novel, nor have I ever had any intention of doing so. In fact, I have always had a profound aversion to most historical novels, because the people in them aren't real people, and neither act nor talk like anyone I've ever known.

At all events, I looked around and took thought as to how the writing was to be done. Stall Hall was a bedlam during the summer months, and so small that a whisper at the front door penetrated clearly to every room, upstairs or down. Thinking that I knew the answer, I purchased an abandoned livery stable across the street, tore it down and with Mr. Tarkington designed a New England-Spanish workshop with a courtyard capable (I fondly imagined) of frustrating people determined to drop in for a cozy chat when I was most eager to work. Thanks to the urgings of Samuel G. Blythe, it was roofed with blue shingles and called Blue Roof.

So I now had two houses in which to work, and although both of them were unfurnished, I had a desperate feeling that it was time for me to start writing, even though I had to lie on the floor in order to do it.

When I confided to Mr. Lorimer that I thought I'd spend the winter of 1924–25 in Palm Beach, working on a novel, he was practical about it. "You can't work in that house till it's furnished," he reminded me, "and you shouldn't live in a stucco house the first year it's built, anyway. Let somebody else catch pneumonia in it. How long's that novel of yours going to run? No, don't tell me! Anybody who writes 16,000-word articles couldn't possibly stop a novel short of 200,000 words, and that's too long for the *Saturday Evening Post!* What you better do is go to Palm Beach and furnish your house; then go back to Washington for the winter and earn enough to pay for it."

He was right, of course, so there I was in Washington for another year—this time at the Wardman Park Hotel, where I strove to transfer my findings to paper despite the prattle of little children in adjoining suites; the penetrating voices of widows on the floor above and the floor below, maintaining endless social contacts by telephone; the unceasing pounding that accompanied the repointing of the cement between the hotel's innumerable bricks; the dulcet strains of its noonday, teatime and all-night orchestras; the endless churning of automobile motors conveying social butterflies to and from their morning, afternoon and evening cocktails; and the thunderous roaring of its toilets.

When I bewailed my unhappy lot to Sam Blythe, and complained bitterly because Richard Washburn Child was acting as foreign correspondent of the *Post* and, to my way of thinking, grossly misrepresenting the trend of events in Europe, Sam wrote:

Well, kid, the only thing you can do with that tempestuous spirit of yours, inherited from six generations of sea-going forebears, that leads you into these wild twenty-five share buccaneering forays on the stock market, causes to rise up in you that enormous yen to get on the expense account instead of paying your own board, and makes you tie yourself irrevocably to the land by means of building houses and sich—is to give it a dose of soothing syrup, and let it sleep. For, me lad, you must recognize that your esteemed Boss is suffering from an aggravated attack of Mr-and-Mrs-Richard-Washburn-Childitis, not made any less febrile by the fact they was once ambassador-and-ess. He'll recover in time. He always does. I've sat for twenty years and watched them come and go. They only last so long. Presently you will get a chance at the expense account joys, but not now. At present, the S.E.P. traveling representative is the Hon. Child, and you might just as well reconcile yourself to that fact and devote yourself to such good liquor as you can find.

I note that Mr. and Mrs. David Lawrence went down the river yesterday on the *Mayflower*. I trust David will write nothing about the Indian ancestry of the Hon. Coolidge.[1]

Having just walked three miles along the loud resounding Pacific Ocean in a soft haze of beneficent rain and a temperature of about 59, and contemplated the zero weather you have back there, I am about to depart for the main dining hall, having been summoned hence by the Hon. Jung Chong, who informs me he has a chicken pie, new peas and new string beans and a strawberry shortcake for my delectation, and that there are a couple of mallards in the ice box. I hardly see how I can sustain life on this until the morn. Especially as the steelheads are running up the Carmel River and the sea bass at the mouth of the Salinas River, where it crosses the bar, run from twenty to sixty pounds, and the golf is perfect. It is a hard life, of a truth, a dog's life, but I shall meekly bear my burdens as best I may.

Sam, knowing my desire for quiet, importuned me to purchase one of the few remaining lots at Pebble Beach (garden spot of the universe, both summer and winter, according to him), and participate in the delights concerning which he wrote. Blue Roof, he pointed out, was worthless in winter for writing purposes because of its arctic cold; and Palm Beach, because of the restless morons who flocked to it in winter, would be equally worthless. So rent the Palm Beach house, Sam said, and he'd buy for me, on easy terms, the finest holding I'd ever seen:

---

[1] The Republican National Committee had uttered agonized roars because I had printed, in an article on Coolidge, a fact that Coolidge himself had freely told me: one of his distant ancestors had been an Indian. The Republican National Committee, with the unfailing timidity of all political committees, tried desperately to hush the matter up.

two acres partly encircled by a deep arroyo, into which I could push unwelcome guests.

His argument seemed sound, so I bought the arroyo-encircled bit of land. Then I wrote the real estate company from which I'd bought it, asking for a topographic map, so that I could plan the house in which I hoped to work. The company sent back a map of a square and arroyo-less property, much smaller than the one I had authorized Sam to buy. When I wrote Sam, complaining about the matter, adding a few remarks about the high cost of re-roofing Blue Roof, and the offensive scent of some cigarettes he had presented to Mrs. Roberts, he rebuked me sharply:

We shall now have a short communion on the subjects of topographical maps, blue roofs and amber cigarettes, to wit:

1. You are probably the only man in Maine who owns in fee simple a topographical map of a piece of property in Pebble Beach, California; and that fact should make you very proud and superior. No doubt, many families in Maine feel keenly the need of topographical maps of bits of Pebble Beach, but you are the only one with the vision and the liberality to step out and get one. The fact that the topographical map you have is not the topographical map of the topography you thought it was, merely adds to its value. It makes it unique, being the only topographical map that does not topographize east of the Rocky Mountains. This will make a valued heirloom, and will look very nifty if framed and hung in your patio where it can easily be made to symbolize the weary trail of Padre Junipero Serra on his way to establish the Carmel Mission and to set the happy and carefree Indians to work for the Glory of God and the increment of the Padre. That you paid $27.50 for this is a mere sordid detail that will cease to pang you as time goes on. Time is a great healer of such pangs. Of course, it takes Time longer to depang a Maine man than a man from Western New York, let us say;[2] but give Time time and it will come about. My advice to you, *re* this valuable possession, is to accept it and hold it in the broad, generous, Western spirit in which it was handed to you. You are lucky that it didn't cost you $47.50, because when the earnest young topographers of the Del Monte Properties get to topographizing, they set high value on their services, especially when they topographize one lay of the land, thinking they are topographizing another and entirely foreign lay of land. It takes an elevated standard of mensuration and triangulation to make a topographical map of Lot 32,

---

[2] Mr. Blythe was born and reared in western New York.

Section B, say, and get away with it as a topographical map of Lot 56, Section F. You are so damned crass and commercial in your view of everything that you do not realize the precious possession you have. Enough of your wailings. You should look at that map every morning and say: "Well, there is one thing no one shall take from me. This is the only absolutely useless topographical map in the world. I shall tack it on the top of my most cherished Boule table, for all to see and admire." Certainly, you should do that, or something like. Anyhow, you can't hand it back to me. It is yours, implacably, irreparably, eternally.

Your groans about the high cost of re-roofing Blue Roof, because of the fading of the color, leave me cold as an ice floe six points abeam of Cape Barrow. Why, damn your parsimonious hide, have you no imagination, no artistic sense, no vision, no pride of accomplishment? Here I come along and confer on you, absolutely free of charge, save for an incidental meal or two and a night's lodging, the inestimable boon of being the only man in Maine with a house having a blue roof: I extend your horizon, establish your identity, give you a roof personality, make you an artistic pioneer, lift you up to the higher levels of decorative, structural lids—and my ears are assailed with your moanings over the cost of same. Cost hell! What does a mere matter of cost signify when you are reaching for, and attaining, the higher things? You go and spend $980 for a cheesy and probably bogus piece of furniture that you hide away in your home and only few can see; and here, with one grand gesture, I give you, free of charge, a roof that rivals the cerulean, that azures all York County, that lifts in sapphirine glory above all the commonplace, conventional canopies of those prosaic parts, that causes every passer by to stop and inquire, nasally, what the hell is biting you, and thus gives you a glittering prominence and notability among your neighbors, that is there for all to see, and your masterpiece and creation, that didn't cost you half as much and that, finally, you have cashed in on liberally through the columns of the *Saturday Evening Post* and you berate me about it. To hell with you! You probably will use that roof three times more in articles in our great family journal. I stand pat on the roof. I am a benefactor; not, as you hint, a despoiler of your purse. Cease, now, or I'll blow along and talk you into a color scheme for Stall Hall that will cause you to writhe in pecuniary agony for years to come.

Your animadversions on the scent of the amber cigarettes I brought home to you from Egypt at great personal inconvenience fall on deaf ears. They merely show your pitiable ignorance of the lures and luxuries of the East, the fabled, storied East. Your Maine nose, that sniffs the odors of a boiled dinner as the ultimate in fragrance, is not attuned to the perfumes of the harem nor the olfactory delights of the odalisque. You are so goddam Yankee that you wouldn't know an odalisque if you saw one; no, bigod, not if you smelled one. Low tide at Kennebunkport is your idea of perfume. You deserve no consideration from those of us who know the languors of the Orient, and the appurtenances thereto.

I saw Harry Wilson up at Gazelle, which is a town consisting of a post office in an abandoned box car, a general store and a filling station. He is living on a ranch and associating with 7684 Herefords, whose white faces and liquid eyes are very calming to the spirit, he says. He is doing no work save in an archeological sense; i.e., digging in an Indian mound. So far he has found nothing but an empty tomato tin, but he has hopes.

Regards to Mrs. Roberts, who can appreciate something exotic now and then, and not remain forever tied down to clams and fried pie as the limits of her horizon.

§

Life in Washington seemed to affect many people like a drug or disease: those who had sampled its pleasures for a few years were unhappy and ill at ease if forced to go elsewhere: its residents seemed somehow intoxicated by the highly press-agented people who constantly surrounded them, and shrank horrified from the thought of returning to their original homes in Wagon Wheel Gap or Tallahassee. Senators, representatives, cabinet officers clung desperately to Washington when their terms of office expired—and the post of Washington correspondent was regarded by most newspapermen as a sort of Medal of Honor. This state of affairs was so obvious and so universal that my inability to avoid Washington was almost frightening: I cravenly suspected I might become addicted to it myself and never get down to work.

And yet I couldn't seem to escape. I no sooner cleaned up my accumulated *Post* material in the summer of 1925 than America became conscious of an unprecedented mass movement from Northern states to Florida. Whole towns in Maine, Massachusetts, Vermont, were loading their belongings in flivvers, trailers, trucks, limousines, and migrating to sunshine and oranges, almost as inexorably as birds each August flit southward before approaching snow and ice.

When news of this movement reached Lorimer, he called me to Philadelphia. "As near as we can find out," he said, "those Florida stories of yours were responsible for this migration. There'll be a land boom there because of it, and the suckers rushing to Florida may lose every penny they've got unless we can stop 'em, or slow 'em up. I want you to travel along with 'em, find out how they're treated, what sort of run they're getting for their money, how many are being robbed, how much of the real estate ballyhoo is crooked, what the good real estate men down there think about it. We'll have to get this stuff in print fast, or there'll be one of the biggest bust-ups America has ever seen. Every boom has to end sometime; and the sooner this one ends, the better for Florida and everyone else."

The resulting six articles, incidentally, led the Harper Brothers to gamble once more. They had sounded out some of the more daring Florida real estate developers, such as the gentlemen who were turning a desolate expanse of scrub and sandspurs into Coral Gables, and causing the boundaries of Miami and West Palm Beach to shoot rapidly in all directions, as to the sales possibilities of a book made from these articles. Having received encouraging responses, the Brothers Harper went ahead with the volume, and broke out in a rash of grandiose estimates concerning the latent possibilities of *Florida*—as the book, with startling originality, had been named. A circulation of 20,000 was assured. . . . There was, perhaps, a possibility of 40,000 . . . of 50,000 . . .

Unfortunately, several months had to elapse before the Brothers Harper could print, proofread, bind and distribute *Florida;* and by that time the articles in the *Post* had hastened the collapse of the Florida boom. When the boom stopped, most of the developers went broke simultaneously, together with those who had dropped their money into Florida land. As a result, *Florida* sold 5,000 copies, and the Brothers Harper again lost interest in my labors.

All through 1926, too, that writing urge was held in abeyance; for Lorimer not only wanted more reports on the Washington scene, but he was in urgent need of several articles on California, and an offset to an editorial faux pas in the *Ladies' Home Journal,* which he constantly scrutinized for errors in judgment.

In this particular case the *Journal,* for some unknown reason, had published an article on the Mormons in Utah—an article that was such a masterpiece of inaccuracy and innuendo that it had brought justified screams of anguish from Mormon churchmen and laymen.

"I know the Mormons," Lorimer told me, "and they're fine people: splendid citizens: none better. Stop off in Utah on your way to the

Coast, find out what they're doing in agriculture, government and education, and give 'em a break: they certainly deserve it."

That assignment kept me busy through the summer. I had just turned to accumulating the source books that I hoped would enable me to write what I wanted to write, when a hurricane—the Great Hurricane—struck Florida and almost blew it off the map. This brought a hurry call from Lorimer to report the wreckage of that hurricane; then go from Florida to Louisiana to find out what was happening in New Orleans and the bayou country.

Early in 1927 my frantic desire to escape from city turmoil, summer vacationers, idlers, politicians and cocktail parties grew in intensity, thanks to an assignment that surpassed even the Roy C. Woods venture for complete frustration and futility—though in the end it led me to a spot where I found the full measure of solitude for which I'd longed.

I had just completed the New Orleans articles in Florida when I received a telegram from Mr. Lorimer requesting my immediate presence in Philadelphia. John Tebbel tells the story in his fine book, *George Horace Lorimer and the Saturday Evening Post:*

> One of the most unusual ghostwriting arrangements in the history of that fabulous era occurred in 1927 when S. S. McClure returned from a trip to Italy and told Lorimer that he had been in consultation with Benito Mussolini's former mistress, Margharita Sarfatti, who had agreed to act as go-between for the purpose of getting Il Duce's autobiography. A go-between was necessary, S.S. explained, because no one had ready access to Mussolini except Sarfatti, who saw him more often than most others. A ghost writer was needed because ex-journalist Mussolini was not accustomed to writing for American publications, and besides, he was occupied with the affairs of the Fascist party. However, he was willing to collaborate for forty thousand dollars—collaboration came high at that time—and McClure asked for fifteen thousand dollars, payable in three installments, for his own offices as agent. Lorimer agreed.
>
> Looking over his stable, he picked Roberts to do the ghosting, since Roberts had written two series of *Post* articles on the beginning of the Fascist party, and had many influential friends in Rome, among them Salvatore Cortesi, head of the Associated Press in Italy, and Arnaldo Cortesi, head of the Rome Bureau of the *New York Times.*
>
> Roberts, who was in Florida working on a series of articles, was recalled to Philadelphia, though Lorimer well knew that Roberts would not relish being assigned to a ghostwriting chore, even for Mussolini.

It took all the Boss's persuasive power to convince Roberts that he was elected. The doomed man protested violently that he did not want to do ghostwriting, that he viewed the whole proposition with extreme distaste, but in the end he agreed and went to New York to consult McClure, who was to act as entrepreneur in the getting and writing of Mussolini's "inside story."

McClure was in his eighties, and Roberts found him "garrulous, over-optimistic and vague" about the manner in which the story was to be obtained. The "contract" was written on a single sheet of note paper. It was merely a statement that if McClure would furnish a book Mussolini would sign it if he found it satisfactory. The statement was signed by both Mussolini and Sarfatti. Since Lorimer had instructed Roberts specifically that the *Post* didn't want the story unless Mussolini himself was willing to give plenty of time to it, Roberts telephoned Lorimer from New York and reported that he thought McClure was in his dotage and that the outlook, in his opinion, was dark, sour and smelly. He added that, since he had started, he'd keep going, but he didn't propose to travel on the same ship with McClure and be exposed to endless hours of drivel: he'd jump the *Conte Rosso,* which sailed the next day, two weeks ahead of McClure's ship.

"All right," Lorimer agreed, "but don't let them put anything over on you."

In Rome, Roberts lost no time getting in touch with Sarfatti, whom he found "a dumpy, hard-voiced, coarse-skinned bleached blonde from North Italy."

His interview with this lady confirmed his worst fears. When he pointed out to her that he would have to be allowed to have several personal interviews with Mussolini in order to do the right sort of job, Sarfatti explained that this was impossible. Mussolini was a busy man, engrossed in affairs of state. He had no time to waste on a book! The book, she said, must be compiled from a volume which she herself had written on Mussolini, from a collection of speeches and newspaper articles for which Mussolini was supposedly responsible, and from hitherto unpublished material written by Mussolini's brother Arnaldo. Moreover, when the book—eight installments of ten thousand words each—was finished, it would be thrice edited: first by McClure, then by Sarfatti, and finally by Il Duce.

Roberts snorted. Sarfatti looked offended and asked coldly how *he* thought he should be allowed to proceed. Roberts replied that he should be given at least forty personal interviews with Mussolini, of at least half an hour apiece—one interview at the end of each two thousand words of manuscript—and that he could do with considerably less editing.

Sarfatti was outraged. Roberts, she said, did not know what he was saying! Let him imagine the situation reversed! Let him imagine that she herself wished to write similarly about President Herbert Hoover. Let him imagine her, with her imperfect knowledge of English, requesting forty personal interviews with Mr. Hoover! Ha-ha! She would be ejected forcibly from the United States!

Not at all, Roberts told her. If the situation were reversed—if the United States were in Italy's position, that is, with a government open to criticism, as was the Fascist government, and wished to be placed in a favorable light before the world in a magazine as influential as the *Saturady Evening Post*—Mr. Hoover would see that Signora Sarfatti had not only forty personal interviews with him, but eighty if necessary, in addition to being supplied with all necessary interpreters and facilities.

That ended the interview and terminated any hope of a rapport between Signora Sarfatti and Mr. Roberts. The gentleman from the *Post* ignored the Roman finagler's penetrating glares and retired to his hotel, to await the coming of McClure.

Sam arrived and emerged white-faced from his first session with Sarfatti. He reported to Roberts, with masterful understatement, that the lady had assured him they had "got the wrong man." McClure urged Roberts to be reasonable, but Roberts continued to repeat Lorimer's instructions—that the story wasn't wanted unless Mussolini himself would give it his time and attention. The story, Roberts insisted further, was to be Mussolini's, and not a secondhand biography compiled from the works of brothers, ex-mistresses, press agents and special pleaders.

In desperation McClure offered to turn over to Roberts the last five-thousand-dollar installment of his *Post* payments if the story were handled as he and Sarfatti wished it handled. It was the only time Roberts had been offered a bribe in his entire experience as a correspondent.

To escape Italian censorship, Roberts went to Monte Carlo and filed a cable to Lorimer: "McClure says impossible get story way you outlined. Material necessarily got through Sarfatti; Rossoni, former editor American Socialist newspaper; Mussolini's brother Arnaldo; various officials; sundry books on Fascism; Mussolini's speeches, and Fascist press bureau. Says impossible follow your wishes as Mussolini would never agree to personal co-operation, and might revoke contract if crowded. Neither Sarfatti nor McClure dares put proposition squarely before him. Thinks with phenomenal luck might have few moments with him once a month but never his assistance in preparing material. Declares six months shortest time doing story McClure's way, subject triple supervision, maybe longer. His opinion everything handsomely covered using his methods. He will donate last 5000 installment toward expenses man writing story. Believe delays connected with McClure's method extremely trying and material far removed from your outline. Do not agree with McClure it would be Mussolini's inside story. This cannot be delivered by Sarfatti or anyone else. By time McClure and Sarfatti finish editing and Italian translation made for Mussolini's approval, story might have flavor cheese: not Mussolini. Also doubt Sarfatti able hold Mussolini in line if decided book or method of writing undesirable."

Roberts caught the next boat home. When he reported to the *Post* he found Richard Washburn Child, one-time ambassador to Italy, conferring with Lorimer. The Boss called him in to give Child a firsthand account of his experiences with McClure and Sarfatti, since Child felt that his own personal knowledge of Italy and the Italians might prevail on Mussolini to write his real "inside story." Roberts insisted that any Mussolini story would be instigated and supervised by McClure, Sarfatti and Arnaldo Mussolini, and must inevitably be worthless as inside stuff and duller than ditch water.

A week later Child sailed for Italy on the same assignment, and in a remarkably short time Mussolini's "inside story"—slightly edited translations of articles by Arnaldo Mussolini but signed by Richard Washburn Child—appeared in eight installments which bore titles characteristic of the Fascist dream: "War and Its Effects upon a Man," "The Death Struggle of a Worn-out Democracy," "The Garden of Fascism," "Toward the Conquest of Power," "Thus We Took Rome," "Five Years of Government," "New Paths" and "En Route." Two years later another pair of articles collectively titled "My War Diary" were published. The series was received with only mild interest by the *Post* audience and, published as a book by Scribner's, was a dismal failure.

The *Post* "regulars"—seasoned correspondents like Blythe, Cobb, Irwin, Roberts and Marcosson—frequently grumbled discontentedly among themselves over Lorimer's occasional weakness for "specialists" who had been diplomats; but they never suffered long. "Specialists" such as Child and Norval Richardson were unable to work as carefully and arduously as trained reporters, and inevitably, after writing a series or two for Lorimer, they vanished permanently from the *Post's* columns, thereafter to be referred to by the Boss as "soubrettes."

§

While I was waiting for that "next boat home," Mrs. Roberts's sister (who had married an Italian doctor, the head of Rome's San Gallicano Hospital) took us to see her small olive-almond-fig-and-grape holding on a Tuscan headland halfway between Rome and Leghorn. We picnicked at the holding's so-called palazzo, an unprepossessing and chilly receiving vault of a house with a magnificent view of Elba, Corsica, Monte Cristo and purple Tuscan mountains crowned with little villages. As we ravenously devoured mounds of homemade fettucini, washed down with the excellent wine that my sister-in-law had herself helped to tread out during the preceding autumn, I awoke to the fact that this was it! This, as Brigham Young said to his Mormon followers when they descended from the mountains to the shore of Great Salt Lake, was The Place!

I made a proposal to my sister-in-law and her husband: if they would allow us to occupy the house during the winter, I would have plans drawn in New York for an American Wing—a large living room with a fireplace alcove, a commodious bedroom, bath, terrace—return on the following winter to build it, beautify it with an arbor and a balcony, and provide all necessary furniture.

They agreed, and on my return to the United States I raised the funds for it by riding the Mexican border with the highly efficient Border Patrol, and writing for the *Post* a series of articles on the Mexican immigrants who had become a serious problem to scores of Southern cities.

Incidentally Mr. Wilbur Carr, a good friend who had become Assistant Secretary of State, learned that I had applied for a passport to Mexico, and asked me not to embark on that series on the ground that it might prove harmful to our relations with Latin America. I was unable to agree with him, since I was strongly of the opinion that our Department of State had already done everything possible to harm our relations with Latin America.

When I delivered the last of the Mexican articles, I told Mr. Lorimer that I dared wait no longer before embarking on the chore I'd set myself, and that Mrs. Roberts and I were returning to Italy at the end of the year to begin it. I also told him I was sure I'd have slim pickings, and that my mind would be much easier if I could look forward to doing an occasional article for the *Post*.

"That's all right," Lorimer said. "I can see you won't be satisfied until you've tried it, so go right ahead. We'll work out some light papers and a few side trips for you from time to time when the larder runs low"— a promise which, happily for me, he never failed to fulfill.

The building of the American Wing in Italy—the story of which was told in the *Saturday Evening Post* a few years later in two articles called "The Half-Baked Palace"—proved distracting. So, too, did my failure to find explanations for a discouragingly large number of details that had to be known before I could even commence the novel I contemplated. When not acting as construction foreman for the American Wing, I wrote more *Post* articles and another volume called *Antiquamania*. This, even though delightfully illustrated with drawings by Mr. Tarkington, was as unproductive as the other volumes had been. Its circulation was 1,165.

THE SUMMER of 1928 was half gone before I had accumulated, with the help of the Maine State Library, the Library of Congress, the American Antiquarian Society and a dozen bookdealers, the mass of books and diaries—some almost impossible to obtain—from which to excavate the material I needed, and had outlined a way in which to hammer it into narrative form. Mr. Tarkington had his own literary difficulties, and I consequently kept my troubles to myself. On the fourth of September, when Mrs. Roberts and I were dining with the Tarkingtons, Booth asked whether I had done anything about the Louisburg-Revolutionary novel I'd mentioned to him three years earlier. I told him I had been forced to throw away the Louisburg part of it, and concentrate on the one big campaign of the first year of the Revolution—the march of New England and Virginia troops through the Maine and Canadian wilderness to capture Quebec.

"You'd better tell me something about it," he said. "I've had a little experience at working out plots."

A little experience!

So I gave him the general idea, and told him I wanted to make the people in it behave as real people must have behaved, instead of like a lot of impossible stuffed shirts—that I was determined to avoid as much as possible the dreadful dullness that had befogged everything I had studied while trying to get my facts straight—which was something no historian had taken the trouble to do. I said I'd seen troops in different parts of the world, and I'd never encountered any considerable numbers that didn't include at least one noisy clown, constantly in trouble and eager to steal anything that he or his friends needed. Several of the diaries I had read had shown occasional gleams of humor—enough to prove that at least a few Revolutionary soldiers and officers had innumerable human attributes in spite of Fenimore Cooper's efforts to prove the contrary; so I thought I was justified in letting a genuinely rough egg play an important part in the novel.

"Have you thought of a name for him?" Booth asked.

I said I'd fumbled with several names, but hadn't found one that appealed to me. Huff seemed like a reasonable last name for the noisy oaf I had visualized, but a good first name eluded me. Gideon, or the other conventional early American names I had tried, seemed too namby-pamby, too formal, for the obstreperous party I had in mind.

"What were you thinking of calling the book?" Booth asked.

I said that since it would merely be a detailed account of the experiences and manner of life of the early residents of the town of Arundel, I felt it should be called *Arundel.*

He looked noncommittal, and I feared I had bored him; but two days later he telephoned me. For two nights he had contemplated my sketchy outline; and the more he dwelt upon it, the better he liked it. He was, in fact, gratifyingly enthusiastic—far more so than I thought he had reason to be. He even had a name for the noisy oaf. I had mentioned to him a family who had sought refuge in Arundel, and saddled their children with peculiar compound names like "Little to Depend Upon." "Why," Booth asked, "couldn't your man have been given the name of Saved from Captivity? Shorten it up to Cap Huff. I can see him now, all sweaty and smelling of rum."

The real object of his call, however, was to insist that I drop whatever else I was doing or thinking of doing, and start immediately—that very day—to write four chapters. "Dig up the biggest blankbook you own," he said, "and get going. Put down '*Arundel,* page 1, Chapter 1,' on the first page, and keep right on working until you fall asleep." He wanted no more discussion: no further brooding. He demanded action, immediate and concentrated. When the four chapters were finished, I was to read them to him.

I told him I'd gladly start immediately if I hadn't promised Lorimer to do a college series on Michigan, Illinois, Cornell and Harvard before I went back to Italy.

"Finish up those college pieces as soon as you can," Mr. Tarkington said, "and don't touch any other sort of work until *Arundel* is finished. You'd better not come back from Italy until it *is* finished, either: otherwise you'll be caught in the summer activities of idle people, and may never finish it."

How, in the ensuing three months, I contrived to travel three thousand miles through the Middle West, do four articles for the *Saturday Evening Post,* go through seventy-three biographies, diaries and other

books, including several volumes of the monumental *Force's American
Archives,* and write the first 60,000 words of *Arundel,* I can't accurately
remember. All I know is that I wrote on trains, in railway stations, in
hotel rooms, and occasionally worked all night.

Yet the preparatory work for *Arundel*—though I failed to realize it at
the time—was comparatively simple. At an earlier period I had hunted
and fished in the same sections over which Arundel men had struggled
in their march to Quebec; and local histories of Kennebunk and Kennebunkport were generous in supplying me with characters.

For example: The original of Phoebe Nason in *Arundel* was a com-
posite of Mabel Littlefield in Remich's *History of Kennebunk* and two
other young women in Bradbury's *History of Kennebunkport.* "A
daughter of Mr. Huff," says Bradbury, "was milking but a short distance from the house when an Indian, wishing to obtain the milk,
caught hold of her, but she knocked him down with her milk pail and
made her escape. The prostrate Indian was carried off by his companions. The Indians were very fond of milk, and were constantly
watching in the neighborhood of farm houses to obtain it; but were
easily frightened if discovered. One morning as a girl was milking near
Mr. Major's garrison, her father, not being able to find a bottle of rum
he was hunting after, inquired loudly of her where it was. An Indian
who had already got into the yard, thinking he was discovered, fled
with such precipitancy, as to leave his blanket, which had caught
against a stake, behind him."

From Remich, "Mabel Littlefield was quite plain, indeed she was exceedingly 'homely,' as well as masculine in her manners. Her father,
who was a trader in Wells, owned a sloop, of which she was commander. He shipped lumber, fish and other merchandise to Boston, receiving in return goods for his store and money; not unfrequently
freight was offered by parties not connected with the family, which
added to the profits of the voyage. Mabel was a merchant as well as a
sailor; she bought and sold discreetly and her management of the sloop
evidenced that she was quite proficient in seamanship. For several years
she pursued the business of coasting very successfully. But Mabel was
vain; her weakness was an inordinate fondness for jewelry, and with
this she bedecked herself extravagantly. Her friends, of both sexes, frequently bantered her on this foible, assuring her that she could never
pile enough jewelry on her person to overcome the ugliness of her
features, and that she must make up her mind to live in single blessed-
ness always. To these jokers she would good-naturedly reply that she
wore the jewelry to please herself and without any reference to 'catch-

ing a beau,' but always declared that she should in good time marry one of the best and one of the handsomest young men in town. She was agreeable and intelligent in conversation, and had laid by, for the time, a snug little property. She became the wife of Richard Boothby, a prosperous young farmer, and he never had reason to regret his choice."

I had a warm feeling for Phoebe Nason—Mabel Boothby, for Mabel's home had stood on the exact spot where my summers were spent for many years.

The original of Cap Huff's family was the Burks family in Remich's history. Burks was a private in the battle at Lovewell's Pond and in the Louisburg expedition, and on his return from Lovewell's Pond he settled in Arundel long enough to have several children, "the mother insisting upon naming them, respectively, 'Much Experience,' 'Little to Depend Upon,' and 'Great Deliverance'. How these names were abbreviated for everyday use we have not learned. All the children fell victims to a throat distemper which prevailed extensively throughout New England from 1735 to 1745."

It was therefore reasonable to change Mrs. Burks's name to Huff, and give her a fourth child named "Saved from Captivity."

The original of Steven Nason was based on Stephen Harding, who appears in both Remich's and Bradbury's histories as a notable character whose father was granted two hundred acres of upland and ten acres of marsh, "on condition that he should come into Wells, as an inhabitant, within three months, continue as such five years and do the blacksmith work for the inhabitants 'for such currant pay as the town doth produce.' He moved from Wells to Arundel about 1702 and settled near the mouth of Kennebunk River, where he built a garrison house sufficiently large to enable him to entertain travelers; also a blacksmith's shop.

"He was a man of powerful frame; an excellent marksman; a hunter, shrewd and dauntless; and was regarded as a most valuable citizen by his townsmen. He was frequently employed by the Colonial Government as a guide to expeditions, both civil and military, sent out under its authority; was licensed to keep a public house and to retail ardent spirits; and kept a stock of the luxuries and necessaries of life, such as tobacco, tea, coffee, molasses, etc. Many of these he bartered with the Indians for furs. He was popular with his red-skinned customers, for he was not only remarkably genial, but he was strictly honest; whatever he sold them was of full weight and measure; whatever he bought of them was fairly weighed and the weight correctly stated, and he never watered the liquors that he sold.

"Although conscientious in his dealings, he occasionally treated his Indian friends to stories that were tinctured with the marvelous. While cleaning his gun one day in the presence of the chief Wawa and several other red men, he explained that when he was about to go in pursuit of wolves, bears or Indians, he put in powder, shot and wadding, charge upon charge, until the barrel was filled to within an inch or two of its muzzle, and when thus loaded he was enabled, by a peculiar motion of the arm which he well understood, to send out one charge at a time and kill animals or persons widely separated. His auditors listened attentively, looked grave and uttered their often-repeated expression, 'Much man, Ste-ven.'"

When war broke out between Indians and whites, the Indians, remembering Harding's account of his repeating rifle, were so wary of him that they could never quite bring themselves to come to grips with him. He was, in short, one of the first Americans to demonstrate the value of propaganda and preparedness, and to show that honesty, in time of war, is not always the best policy.

§

The main difficulties lay in explaining the important details that historians had overlooked, or had been too slovenly to unearth. Historians have a great advantage over a novelist in that they can state a supposed fact without explaining it. A novelist, using the same fact, must explain it in order to make it clear to the reader. Historians of the Quebec expedition, for example, had been content to record that, at one point of the expedition, an entire company had suddenly run out of provisions. But a novelist who is trying to make that expedition come to life must tell why that company had ample provisions on one day, but none on the next.

The historian is within his rights when he states that smoke was seen on two occasions in the heart of an uninhabited wilderness, but makes no attempt to account for the smoke. The novelist is not within his rights if he mentions smoke and fails to explain it.

An historian can announce that a hitherto unmentioned Indian suddenly appeared in the ranks of a lost and bewildered detachment and guided it to safety; he is not required to explain how the Indian got there, or who he was, or why he hadn't acted as a guide before the detachment was lost. The novelist can't be so mysterious.

An historian can state that an army has provisions for only fifteen days; then coolly permit that army to exist for twice that length of time without explaining the miracle. A novelist must find out how the army escaped starvation, and explain it to the complete satisfaction of the reader. Otherwise his story doesn't, as the saying goes, hold water. Each omission is a hole in his tale. Most histories are filled with holes and leak like sieves.

By the time I'd plugged a few of the historians' holes and read my early chapters to Mr. Tarkington, they seemed unconscionably dull and long; but he refused to listen to my complaints. "Tell the story the way it comes to you," he said. "Later you'll change it, anyway. Just put it on paper and it'll take care of itself. You know exactly what you want to do, and that's all that matters. You've got the feel of the time and the people. I never knew any of the things you're telling, and they interest me, so keep right on going. There's nothing wrong with your opening chapters except that they were written in a hurry. Anything written in a hurry is always awkward; always has to be rewritten and rewritten. Even if it *isn't* written in a hurry, it has to be rewritten just the same. You'll always be cutting down and pointing up—taking out unnecessary words, altering awkward words, inserting pieces here and pieces there."

When *The Gentleman from Indiana* was first published, he told me, he had taken a copy to Mrs. Robert Louis Stevenson for criticism and advice. She had covered the margin of every page with annotations and criticisms. One which he most poignantly remembered was " 'Back of!' Dear me! 'Back of!' " He'd never thought about the awkwardness, the harshness of the phrase, until Mrs. Stevenson pointed it out. I'd learn such things for myself some day, he said—and when I *did* learn, I must be careful not to overdo it. His words meant next to nothing to me.

Booth was gentle, always, in his suggestions—so gentle that I failed to grasp many of them. I think he was fearful of hurting my feelings or discouraging me. As I said in the beginning, lectures, talks, advice, writers' conferences, make little or no impression on those who want to write. Writers learn to write—and always unsatisfactorily—by endless toil, and in spite of constantly recurring depression and despair; and it is my fixed belief that writing is the only form of expression that becomes increasingly painful and difficult, the more one knows about it.

§

The Michigan-Illinois-Cornell-Harvard series was finished on December 19, 1928, and since a ton of Congressional Library books, heterogeneous source material, typewriters, copy paper and garments were already packed in twenty-four weighty parcels, we climbed into the automobile and set off for Philadelphia to say good-by to Lorimer, for Princeton to say good-by to Booth, and for New York to sign the *Arundel* contract, pick up an advance of a thousand dollars, and embark for Italy. That contract, when Mr. Russell Doubleday produced it, called for an advance of a thousand dollars and royalty payments of 10 per cent to 2,500 copies, 15 per cent to 47,500 copies, and 20 per cent beyond. Since I knew that *Arundel,* when finished, couldn't possibly sell 47,500 copies, I protested bitterly that the 15 per cent should come into effect at 20,000 copies. Mr. Doubleday was equally certain that the book would never sell 20,000 copies; but a publisher never willingly agrees to any proposition from an unknown author, so he insisted that the sliding point must be 25,000 copies. Since I also was sure that there was no difference, so far as I was concerned, between 20,000 and 25,000, I signed, and on December 27 we sailed for Italy.

On January 10, 1929, when we installed ourselves in the frigid, newly built American Wing of the Half-Baked Palace, *Arundel* had progressed to the beginning of longhand manuscript page 42. Only the prologue and the first six chapters were finished, with at least thirty more chapters and two hundred manuscript pages to go, and four months—one hundred and twenty days—in which to do them.

I hung a schedule on the wall beside my bed: "Write a chapter every 4 days: write 1⅓ pages (1500 words) every day for 120 days." My heart sank whenever I looked at it.

§

That winter in Italy was a grueling one, for the American Wing had been built with door and window frames of green wood set in damp plaster, and in a bucolic Italian manner, so that spaces rapidly opened above and beneath doors, and between windows. Thus when the wintry Italian winds blew—and they were seldom still—drifts of grit, almond leaves, and almond blossoms whirled about the floor and up the trouser leg.

Our lighting system was half a dozen candles and two American kerosene lamps: our heating system two anemic stucco stoves and an inadequate fireplace that smoked villainously.

The American Wing, however, possessed one tremendous advantage: it was so inaccessible that there were no disturbances to interfere with writing: no telephones, no telegrams, no doorbells, no whistling chauffeurs, no salesmen, no golf, no picnics, no radios, no movies, no automobile horns, no callers, no luncheon guests, no cocktail parties, no dinner invitations, no autograph hunters: none of the amenities of civilization.

No sound broke the stillness of that Tuscan hilltop save the anguished brayings of distant donkeys, the shrill whistling of the never-quiet wind through casements and keyholes, the unmelodious caterwauling of the young woman who prepared our daily fettucini, *sugo di pomodoro* and fried fresh sardines, the squirpling of a thousand sparrows, the droning of Savoia-Marchetti bombers from Orbetello, and the raucous shouts of the fishermen who hauled their nets at the foot of Mont' Argentario. Perhaps I may be regarded as allergic to noise. Possibly I am—and then, again, I may merely be one of a multitude who realize that noise is a form of torture created and tolerated by idiots.

Amid groans, laments and hideous torments, interspersed with hour-long floor pacings when stubborn words, ideas and characters clogged the brain with seemingly unbreakable mental log jams, work progressed at the rate of a 7,000-word chapter every three days; and by mid-May the pile of manuscript was six inches thick—and the end, unbelievably, at hand—or so I, poor innocent, thought!

Never before had I known the meaning of the words "repression" and "exhaustion." Never again, I was sure—never!—would I have the strength to endure such mental agonies! When we climbed aboard a ship in Naples on the verge of June, such was my inexpressible relief at being freed from those interminable days of unbroken labor that often, in the privacy of our cabin, I gave tongue to explosive animal howls at my deliverance—to the consternation of our fellow passengers, whose pity for Mrs. Roberts was obvious. We were stared at surreptitiously as we entered and left the dining saloon; and we could almost hear the passengers whispering to each other that I was a mental case who took delight in beating and torturing his wife.

With the last chapter written—and typed—I could more easily revise the book once more, and I proceeded to do so to the best of my ability. Unfortunately, I had worked for so many years as a reporter that my revisions lacked the necessary care—though I didn't know it at the time. Besides, I felt by now as though that bulky manuscript had squeezed my brain dry: I wanted it out of sight—wanted to stop dreaming horridly about it and sweating in my dreams; to stop waking at daybreak to worry over that scene in the swamps of Lake Megantic—over the feelings of those men from Arundel as they blundered through a midnight blizzard to attack Quebec.

Booth returned to Kennebunkport on the sixteenth of June, and since he had completed the book on which he had been working during the past winter, he at once telephoned me to read him the chapters I had

added to those he had heard the year before. My diary tells the story of
those almost nightly readings:

June 17, 1929: Read four chapters to Booth, starting at the point
where Steven Nason and his father, halted in their effort to catch up
with the French officer, return to Swan Island. Reached the end of Book
I. He doesn't stop me as often as he did last year: says it isn't necessary:
says if he stopped me for every blemish, we'd never finish. Made three
elisions averaging a page apiece. When I suggested cutting the Indian
passages, he said to let them alone: they interested him and would interest others.

June 18: Read through Chapter 14, where Nason and Cap Huff, ordered off on a scout, leave Cambridge to return to Arundel on Phoebe's
sloop. No cutting necessary yet, Booth says.

June 19: Read through Chapter 18—the point where Arnold's army
starts up the Kennebec. Worked until three in the morning making
changes he suggested.

June 20: Read from eight o'clock in the evening until one in the
morning and damned near lost my voice. Got through Chapter 24,
where the army is lost in the swamps of Lake Megantic. Booth's enthusiasm is embarrassing.

June 21: Read through Chapter 27, reaching Book IV and the point
where the army, having descended the Chaudière, stands on the bank
of the St. Lawrence, looking across to Quebec. Booth was strongly
affected by the scenes in the swamp . . . made several suggestions as
to James Dunn's death and the scene in which Nason is put out of the
army. Home at midnight and worked until 2 A.M. making the changes.

June 22: Read six chapters, up to 34, where Nason, Cap Huff and
Hobomok work up into the Upper Town after the attack, and locate
Mary's house. Booth said to speed up the action in this part. He kept
reverting to Phoebe. He likes her and says she ought to be more openly
compassionate in the scene where James Dunn dies; also she should
enter and leave Quebec alone, instead of with Jacataqua. Rewrote these
scenes until 4 A.M.

June 23: Read to Booth what I did last night and two additional
chapters, leaving only 34, 35 and 36 to be read.

June 24: Wrote all day: then read Chapter 34, which Booth wants
entirely re-done. As it is, he thinks it's too explicit and detailed, especially in the love scene between Steven and Phoebe. He said William
Dean Howells had made the point that decent people didn't do their
love-making on park benches. Such situations, he said, should be so
handled that the reader's imagination does the work.

June 25: Rewrote and retyped Chapters 34 and 35.

June 26: Read the last two chapters to Booth, making a number of cuts and reaching the end. He was immensely pleased: says he can feel in his bones that the book will have a long and happy life. Like hell it will!

June 27: Retyped, revised and corrected the last two chapters, and corrected Books II and III.

June 28: Up at five-thirty, completed corrections at nine-thirty, packed the manuscript and sent it off to Doubleday, completed.

Completed, indeed! There have been times when I thought there was no such thing as a completed book; and certainly the writing of "The End" at the bottom of the last page of a manuscript is merely the beginning of arduous labors.

When, in a few weeks, the galley proofs of *Arundel* came back, I found to my horror—

—and why horror? I had dashed off a 250,000-word novel in nine months, spent eleven days revising it—and to my intense astonishment, the proofs weren't perfect! I still had a lot to learn about writing!

At all events, every galley cried aloud for additional revision; for alteration, rewriting, cutting, as well as correction; and when, after three readings, I returned those corrected, altered, rewritten, chopped, almost undecipherable galleys to my publishers, they tore their hair and screamed hideously. What, they wanted to know, was I trying to do? Ruin them?

I reminded them that they should be as interested as I in having things made right, and urged them to let me have page proofs as rapidly as possible. Suspecting—and rightly—that I, in my ignorance, would mangle the page proofs as brutally as I had treated the galleys, they told me coldly that there wasn't sufficient time to let me see page proofs. Since I knew less than I should have known about writing, I made only a mild protest—and mild protests get exactly nowhere with publishers. The protests must be made in anguished howls, endlessly repeated and ingeniously varied.

As a result, when I received the first finished copy of *Arundel* in Porto Santo Stefano on January 6, 1930, I found it necessary to send a cable that baffled the Porto Santo Stefano telegraph operator, who was never certain whether "Filadelfia" was in North or South America. The cable read:

IF SECOND EDITION OF ARUNDEL EVER NEEDED MAKE THE FOLLOWING CHANGES: PAGE 28 LINE 35 THEN NOT THEM; 37 TWO LINES FROM BOTTOM

INSERT AT BETWEEN US AND ALL; 84 LINE 6 HAS NOT HAD; 196 LINE 1 PRO-
TESTED NOT PROTECTED; 269 LINE 2 THERE NOT THEIR; 278 LINE 1 GRAVE NOT
GRACE; 299 LINE 17 CHOKECHERRIES NOT CHEERIES; 339 LINE 21 WORST NOT
WORSE; 356 LINE 15 MATTER NOT MATTERS; 357 LINE 2 ARNOLD NOT
ARUNDEL; 367 LINE 4 BETWEEN IT AND WAS INSERT IF ALL I HAD; 379 LINE
35 BETWEEN OF AND HEIGHT INSERT THE; 474 LINE 1 DELETE THE BEFORE
CAP; 479 LINE 9 THOSE NOT THESE; 502 LINE 14 DAWN NOT DOWN; 552 LINE
13 DELETE COMMA AFTER QUEUES; 613 TWO LINES FROM BOTTOM SABATIS NOT
SATABIS; 618 LINE 14 BETWEEN SET AND ACROSS INSERT US.

Not until the fourth or fifth edition were the typographical errors eliminated—though I don't mean to imply that *Arundel* went rapidly through many editions, or could by any stretch of the imagination be regarded as a startling success. The usual life of a novel is four or five months. It then ceases to sell in the form in which it was published, though it may dribble on much longer in paper-bound cheap editions.

Arundel, at the end of the conventional four months, seemed on the point of expiring; but it flopped gaspingly along, selling a few copies every week, and at the end of a year had sold 9,266 copies—which returned, to its happy author, a trifle more than would one article in the *Saturday Evening Post.*

Mr. Blythe, having given a copy his careful attention, delivered himself of a few remarks concerning it and book publishing in general:

You should [Mr. Blythe informed me, as of September 10, 1929] have written a book about privies, regular old-fashioned country W.C.'s, with crescents in the doors and either oval or nicely rounded seats. Then you would have had a literary sensation and a vast amount of money. Instead, you have written a book about an important and significant phase of American life, and what have you? This question is predicated on the fact, communicated to me a day or so ago by one of my agents, that Chic Sale, having put his fifteen minute spiel about privies into book form with the title *The Specialist,* has already made $1,000,000 (not so much as that—one cypher too many—$100,000) out of it, and the damn thing bids fair to last for years. And the publishers made twice as much. Now there is an absolute criterion of American taste in literature. Give them the excrement stuff and they will riot to get it; but write them a book in a decent and workman-like manner, that has few, if any, references to crap in it, and they will turn a cold shoulder to it. I fear me that you have not put any excrement in your book. I fear me.

Also, I am not so keen about the Doubleday, Doran combination. It is not so hot. They publish books like a drunken man plays roulette. They cast down a lot of chips, meaning books, letting them fall where they may; and the chip that wins is the one, and they forget the others. I trust that your book will be on seventeen when it comes up. Or some other number. Otherwise, you are out of luck.

You might or you might not be fortunate enough to have your book adopted by one of these book clubs that are raising such hell with decent publications nowadays. I saw a letter from that fellow, Kinsey I think his name is, who runs the Cosmopolitan Book Corp, and he says that these club-book things are ruination to the regular publishing game. And did you note that the Woolworth five-and-ten gents are preparing to put out a ten cent magazine for sale in their nickelodeons? Also, that *Collier's* now has 2,000,000? The pace gets hot. Be a humorist. That is the stuff, and be a humorist about excrement, and the depositaries thereof, and the genital organs, and pratt falls, and you will prosper. There is a piece in this month's *American* by Will Rogers telling how to be funny. I wonder if Bill has put any stuff about the rectum in it? I haven't read it, but crap and cans are sure fire stuff. Get a load of that book *American Colony* by Brackett. Whoopla!

§

Mr. Blythe's remarks on book circulation, coupled with the disappointingly small sales of *Arundel,* led me to investigate sales of books that had given me great pleasure—Sienkiewicz's *Fire and Sword, The Deluge* and *Pan Michael.* The most celebrated of that trilogy, *Fire and Sword,* was published in the United States by Little, Brown & Company in 1890, and that year sold 1,839 copies. In 1891 it sold 511, and continued to sell about 500 a year until 1896, when *Quo Vadis,* by the same author, was published. This book's popularity boosted the 1896 sales of *Fire and Sword* to 1,181: 1897 sales to 6,772. 1898 sales dropped back to 1,978; and in subsequent years the sales were microscopic. The sales of *Quo Vadis* were 10,000 in 1896, 56,000 in 1897, and 520,000 in 1898 and 1899; but one half of those half-million copies were not as impressive as they seem: they were paper-bound, and retailed for twenty-five cents— until even that price had to be cut and thousands of copies wholesaled at seven cents apiece.

From these figures I had no difficulty in deducing that I wasn't doing so badly, but that I must do much better if I intended to continue writing books.

WITH *Arundel* finished, I thought of taking a long rest, but Mr. Tarkington was not enthusiastic. I had been idle for only a week when he warned me against the perils of laziness, and inquired whether I had planned another book.

I said that I had tentative plans for three that really ought to be written, since there were no books, either fiction or non-fiction, capable of giving the reader an accurate and comprehensive picture of the occurrences I hoped to explain. There were hundreds of families in New England, I said, whose forebears, like mine, had fought Indians; but not one of us could turn to any volume that would make clear how those forebears had lived or what they had endured. Again, there were thousands of New England families whose ancestors had turned out for the two battles of Saratoga; but the events inextricably connected with those two difficult battles were so hidden in confused, contradictory and unattainable sources that they were nothing but meaningless words—Isle Aux Noix, for example, Valcour Island, the retreat from Ticonderoga, the death of Jennie McCrae, Burgoyne's Indians.

Again, innumerable New England families were descended from seamen who served on privateers in the War of 1812, just as had my great-grandfather and twenty-four other Arundel sea captains: yet not one of those families knew what a privateer looked like, or how she had been sailed, or where she had sailed, or how she fought the British, or what had befallen those privateersmen when they were captured, as so many were, and their crews sent to Dartmoor Prison.

So there, I told him, were three stories that ought to be written, and the one I wanted most to do was the one that dealt with the Indians. For that I had a ready-made protagonist—Major Robert Rogers—who beat any character I had ever encountered: one who had not only invented rules for bush fighters that would be standard practice as long as the world existed, but had written the first American play, two books on early America, and, if not thwarted by jealous superiors, would have been the first white man to cross the North American continent and supply the true answer to the age-old quest for a Northwest Passage to Japan, China and the Indies.

The one about Saratoga and the events preceding it, I told him, would probably be the most difficult; because the campaigns were so involved and their details so elusive that they almost defied compression into a smooth and easily grasped narrative. Those campaigns, I told him, were taught as a course at West Point, where the cadets wrestled painfully with them for month on boring month. Yet I was sure it was possible to tell them in such a way that anybody could understand them after a few hours' reading.

Booth, after contemplatively smoking half a dozen outsize cigarettes, said that under no circumstances should I attempt the story about Rogers and the Indians until I had done the other two. As for the Valcour-Saratoga story, in which Arnold would of course have to appear again, I ought to wait four or five years before attempting it. To work at it immediately after finishing *Arundel,* and necessarily using many of the same characters that had appeared in *Arundel,* might get me into bad habits. That left the privateering story, for which I already had a title—*The Lively Lady.* A good title, he said, meant a good start; so why not work out an outline of *The Lively Lady,* so that he could make sure I was on the right track before I set off for Italy?

Two weeks later I read him the outline.

I have that outline beside me. The plan for Chapter 1 reads:

Richard Nason is captain of the brig *Neutrality* at eighteen. Returning to Arundel after a voyage, his brig being in Falmouth, he encounters a coach on the road. His little white dog, brought by his father from England, discovers two women picnicking by the roadside: Lady Emily Ransome and her maid. With Richard is Jedediah Tucker, a schoolmaster-sailor, who is constantly dragging his uncle John Burbank into the conversation when drunk, and harping on the manner in which he was censured by John Paul Jones for loosing the prisoners on the *Bonne Homme Richard,* though she was sinking. Lady Ransome, an active and unconventional young lady, admires the dog and so finds herself in conversation with his master. Her husband, Sir Arthur Ransome, known as S'Roth, is temporarily absent with a fowling piece to indulge in a bit of rough shooting.

Booth heard my notes for the remaining thirty-three chapters without comment, smoking his enormous cigarettes and discarding each one, as was his custom, when only half smoked.

"That'll do it," he said, when I finished. "You want to be careful about Lady Ransome, though. She's tricky, and you'll have trouble with her, but if she's handled properly, she'll be as fetching as Phoebe in *Arundel,* though in a different way."

I scratched rough notes of his observations on the back of my outline —evidence of the pains he was willing to take to keep me from going astray:

Suppose Lady Ransome had married S'Roth because of family arrangement. He's forty: she's eighteen or nineteen. She's a fine lady who's a little girl at times—all furbelows and artificiality in first meeting—ate too much blueberry pie and got sick—snubbed Nason, then almost mashed him. Puzzled him, couldn't get her out of his mind. Husband upstage but not a villain. Husband thinks of Nason as gamekeeper or servant. Nason sore at first: later he'd see Englishman didn't know any other way. Couldn't meet without having mutual detestation: two points of view wouldn't mix: his wife's a chattel, of course: entirely subservient: English wife: he's great man of county—thinks wife ought to be damn glad to be in such a position. Now Lady Ransome finds another person of her own age—naturally congenial: pretty hoity-toity at first. Then they have a little adventure in Arundel —all disgusting to husband, though nothing compromising: his attitude offensive to Nason. Important thing is she just makes an impression on Nason: nothing more.

Suppose miniature of her left behind: lost: Nason finds it. Couldn't be returned: he didn't know where she lived. Thought about picture a good deal. Things she did had made him angry. Miniature must be valuable. Why not sell it? Why reluctant to tell anybody about it?

Quite a time later, here she is again, captured by Nason, now a privateer captain. Husband still upstage person: Nason always "my man"—Nason galled by fact Ransome didn't seem to be prisoner at all. Woman seems even more artificial than had been. Taken on manner —keeps him at distance: then not seem to be at distance at all. Nason realizes been thinking about her.

Almost seemed as though she wants him to win when he fights British ship. She seems affected by meeting him again. Treats him horribly—moony and queer—when he captured, desperate and depressed, she's angry with him—taunts him a little. He thinks she hates him—then tender—mystifies him. What does she mean?

Next time he sees her, he's a miserable figure, trying desperately to escape. He has message. Couldn't think where came from if not from her. By chance he gets to Ransome Hall and she helps him. Husband discovers she's concealing him. Says he'll give Nason up. She's determined he shan't. Probably she'd show pretty well what she feels about Nason, so husband in horror and indignation would charge her with it. She'd say if husband gave Nason up, she'd never live with him again. Tells him he *can't* give up a poor man who's at his mercy!

Think Nason would have said (when they were his prisoners) that he'd put them ashore as soon as could. Lady R. reminds S'Roth, "Going let *you* go!" Husband says can't let Nason go. "Then it's because you're personally jealous."

Suppose he threatens to discard her: Nason has to go back to prison not knowing what became of her. "Low woman—low tastes." Husband in cold fury. Outcast, and deserve to be. Sends for bailiff—wife thrown out.

Suppose Nason wounded in Dartmoor massacre. He'd be crazy with anxiety about Lady Ransome, knowing she does care for him.

Suppose Nason escaped and went back again to see what had become of her. With idea would kill Ransome. She'd tell Nason "What have we got to do with him? What do we care for English law—to hell with English law—I'm not mad at him—this is fine, maybe it's irregular marriage in England, but not irregular in America."

Jeddy Tucker's violent behavior, of course, would be due to his need to be a model while a schoolmaster. Once or twice people had observed behavior that seemed odd in a schoolmaster: these were just the faint germs of his subsequent career, and he's a hellion when his inhibitions are removed—worse than anyone because he'd so long had to practice a mild calling.

I wrote six chapters of the book, shudderingly closing my eyes to the stock market crash that sucked innumerable family fortunes into a bottomless abyss that autumn; then returned to Philadelphia where Mr. Lorimer outlined a series of articles on the stupidity and disgusting hideousness of the billboard blight that was defacing the roads of America.

In gathering material for that series, I took a route that carried me again to Quebec over the road traveled by so many Arundel men in 1775: then made a careful examination of the path they followed when they fell back and back before the British—to Lac St. Pierre, Sorel, Chambly, St. John, Isle Aux Noix, Crown Point, Ticonderoga, Whitehall (once called Skenesboro), and the battlefields of Saratoga—for I intended, while writing *The Lively Lady,* to obtain, from English and American sources, the material I must have in order to write the Valcour-Saratoga book and the Robert Rogers book.

§

With the billboard series out of the way, back we went to Italy with a wire-haired terrier to keep us company, and I embarked again on the daily grind. I find myself complaining bitterly at my ineptitude and lack of progress. Instead of producing 2,000 words a day, as I had when working on *Arundel,* I could average only a little over 1,000 a day on *The Lively Lady.* Yet I was unusually fortunate in other ways.

In the preface to *Treasure Island,* Robert Louis Stevenson admitted ruefully that although he had hoped to make the *Hispaniola* a brig, he hadn't known how to sail a brig and so was obliged to make her a schooner.

Most of the privateers in the War of 1812 were brigs, so I had to learn how to sail a brig on paper. Fortunately for me, the windows on either side of my work desk looked down on the harbor of Porto Santo Stefano and ten-mile-wide Orbetello Bay; and in and out of Porto Santo Stefano constantly passed brigs, brigantines, barques, barkentines and small, strangely rigged Mediterranean craft such as goelettes, tartanes and paranzas. Repeatedly, after a spell of stormy weather, as many as thirty brigs, caught by shifting breezes beneath the headland on which we lived, tacked and drifted for hours in their efforts to get to sea.

Armed with a first edition of Bowditch's *Navigator* and Darcy Lever's *Young Sea Officer's Sheet Anchor,* I followed the movements of those vessels and their crews through field glasses day after day—on one memorable occasion watched one of them run before a towering waterspout surging in from Monte Cristo.

Always, before approaching storms, whole fleets of square-riggers hurried for the shelter of Porto Santo Stefano's harbor, some displaying excellent seamanship, and some bungling atrociously. Nowhere else in the world, I believe, could I have learned so much about square-rigged vessels.

Fortunately, too, one of the longest-winded and dullest narratives ever perpetrated—Isaiah Cobb's *A Green Hand's First Cruise*—contained a detailed account of an American privateersman's life in Dartmoor Prison; and the dates of Cobb's imprisonment coincided exactly with my great-grandfather's Dartmoor stretch.

Then again, I had told some of my troubles to General Dawes, who had become ambassador to the Court of St. James's. I couldn't find, in the United States Navy records of Dartmoor prisoners, the names of Daniel Nason[1] and those who had sailed with him on the privateer *MacDonough*—nor were there records, in Kennebunkport, of those men, or of the circumstances of their capture. All knowledge of their efforts and tribulations had been lost. Yet I knew from my grandmother, I told General Dawes, that Daniel Nason had been captured and held as a prisoner of war in Dartmoor, and I had to have his records and those of his crew.

General Dawes promptly sent his nephew, Henry Dawes, to England's Public Record Office in Chancery Lane with instructions to unearth the records of those men from Arundel, even though he had to excavate or even blast in order to do it.

Mr. Dawes was spectacularly successful. Daniel Nason's name, it appeared, was missing from the naval records of the United States Navy because on the day he had trudged into Dartmoor Prison, footsore, rain-soaked, mud-splotched and destitute, a heavy-eyed prison clerk had entered his name, with those of his crew, in the prison ledger, but had neglected to enter it in the ledger index.

When the United States Navy obtained from the Public Record Office the names of American privateersmen prisoners, it was content to take only the names from the Dartmoor Prison Index—a sloppy piece of research, for the index contained merely names, whereas the ledger told so much about each man that he could readily be reconstructed by anyone familiar with Arundel families.

Daniel Nason, for example, was sailing master of the privateer brig *MacDonough,* 180 tons, armed with a long 24-pounder and four 6-pounders. She had been captured on November 1, 1814, after a long chase (and because both her topmasts gave way) by His Majesty's Frigate *Bacchante,* commanded by Captain Frederick Marryat, the British author who profoundly disliked Americans (in spite of having an American mother) and grossly caricatured them in his books.

Daniel Nason was thirty-four years old, six feet one half inch tall, stoutly built, had an oval face, dark complexion, black hair, gray eyes, no distinguishing marks or scars. He was received in Dartmoor on December 17, 1814, along with the other officers of the privateer; and a week later the crew arrived, all natives of Arundel and familiarly named—Abner Stone, James Fairfield, Joseph Perkins, Nathaniel Ward, John Lord, Robert Patten, George Perkins, Jesse March, Jonathan Stone, Israel Dorman, Robert Towne, James Mitchell, Eben Averill

[1]For prison record of a modern Nason see Appendix page 387.

. . . The ship's boy was Benjamin Lord, a mere five feet three inches tall, but stout, like the others. Officers and men were supplied with one hammock, one bed, and one blanket—the bed a lumpy mattress sketchily filled with something resembling wet paper; the blanket a piece of tarred canvas.

I was unable to visualize Dartmoor satisfactorily by studying the journals of the Americans who had kept records of their experiences, so I went from Italy to England and took the long road from Plymouth to the gloomy heights of Dartmoor; and that trip brought me another bit of good fortune—the discovery of a bone model of an 1814 frigate, made by Dartmoor prisoners whose skill had been such that everything about her could be operated—yards raised and lowered, guns run from the ports, davits swung out and falls released—an inestimable boon to one who needed to familiarize himself with the movements of a square-rigger. I took her back to Italy to help me evolve the sea scenes in *Lively Lady:* then carried her to America to what I hoped would be her permanent home—Mr. Tarkington's living room. She came back to me, alas, in 1947, through the kindness of Mrs. Tarkington.

The winter of 1930 was a duplication of 1929, except that my characters seemed more stubborn. They constantly wandered up side alleys, and wouldn't behave properly.

Never again, I had promised myself, would I write as long a book as *Arundel*—which showed how little I knew about writing. I didn't even know that the length of a book doesn't depend on the author's desire, but on what he's trying to do. He has no choice except to keep on writing until the task he set himself is finished, and the picture rounded and complete. I had set myself the task of making privateering and Dartmoor Prison understandable in a manner satisfactory to myself—and until that was done, I couldn't stop. As a result, the manuscript was as long as *Arundel,* but something was wrong with it. I didn't know what; I only knew I didn't like it as it was. I had worked longer and harder on it, even, than I had worked on *Arundel,* and been as sedulously at my worktable, as my diary consistently shows—as on Tuesday, February 25, 1930:

§

½ down page 100. Finished Chapter 21. A dash of Epsom salts before breakfast, more for excitement than because I need them. A *nero* day, black: *non si bono:* not so good. Again the stove started smoking. No mail. Nothing to report except general depression. Anna seems to feel elated over *The Lively Lady;* but she's only typed through Chapter

XII. *I* don't feel elated, beGod! Took Anna over the bumps at piquet for 10 lire; to bed early and read in *Journal of the Loss of the Brig Commerce;* also indulged in light repartee concerning the Torture Chamber, as my workroom is now known: how 9/10 of my life is spent in it, in three main positions—horizontal, vertical and jack-knife, the latter position being subdivided into the cross-legged, the bent-necked, the hunchbacked, the glaze-eyed, the Epsom-salts and so on. My worktable piled high with books, so that I have crowded myself off—*Napoleonic Campaigns,* Coggeshall, Maclay, *Navigation, Grand Turk, Privateer America,* Michael Scott, *National Geographic,* Blue Guide to S.W. France, *London & Paris in 1815,* 1,000 notes—and then some people think it's a cinch to write!

Wednesday, March 5: Can't find *Arundel* on any list of best sellers, but can find Zane Grey's *Fighting Caravans,* an unspeakably terrible piece of tripe; while the non-fiction list is led (for the fortieth consecutive month) by Chic Sale's 40-page monograph on privies. Fearfully depressed that *Arundel* should sell only a few hundred, while the most ephemeral drivel is bought by the hundreds of thousands.

Monday, March 10: Broke into the last stage of the sea stuff—the fight with the *Gorgon.* I hope to God this whole book isn't lost endeavor; but from the appearance of things, both this and *Arundel* are exactly that.

§

On the eleventh of June, with forty chapters finished and only two left to go, we packed our reference library and the neat 600-page manuscript Mrs. Roberts had made from the mangled pages of my longhand copybook, and on June 14 sailed from Naples for New York.

§

Aboard ship, June 16: Attacked the last chapter and a half of *Lively Lady.* It's a bum book, absolutely worthless: a year wasted. It took me a hell of a while to wake up to it. Got half down page 192, but liked none of it.

§

Just to keep the record straight on the fun-filled days of finishing a book, I quote further details from my diary:

§

June 30: Pasted up *Lively Lady* typescript in three large manuscript books, about 100,000 words to each book, and went to work on it. In despair to find how bad it seems. It's slow and wandering. Started cutting it to make it move faster.

July 1: Booth telephoned early—come over and read to him. Went back to the beginning at 11 A.M. Read till twelve. Resumed at three and read till six. Started again at eight-thirty and read till eleven. Bored almost to tears by my words. Booth says No: it's good; I've merely tried to tell too much. It's only a matter of taking out things that are unnecessary, and healing the cuts. He insists he always has the same trouble when he revises his books. Hacked out the voyage on the pink: also the louse-ish little daughter of the pink's captain—a thirty-page episode that was replaced with a single paragraph.

July 2: Joined the cut portions, wearing a motorcycle helmet to shut out the noise of firecracker explosions.

July 3: Finished reading Book I to Booth. Fifty-six pages are cut from it—about 21,000 words. Driving home, found local hoodlums tossing firecrackers under and into passing automobiles, while idiot policemen looked on, slack-lipped, and grinning. God help America.

July 4: Worked all day, joining the cuts, and almost went off the deep end at the unceasing firecracker explosions set off by infant morons and condoned by equally moronic town fathers.

July 5: Slashed chunks out of Book II amid the endless banging of firecrackers, like the senseless laughter of fools.

July 6: Cut, condensed and rewrote the start of Book II. At night read it to Booth. It will be best, he thinks, to cut straight from the burning of the first *Lively Lady* to the cruise of the second *Lively Lady,* taking out the chapters on Valençay and St. Malo. He hated to ask me to do it, he said, because the Duchess de Dino appeals strongly to him.

July 7: Cut more from Book II. Booth won't listen when I say the stuff is lousy. He insists it's a graphic, swiftly moving picture of a period and people he'd never dreamed existed.

July 8: Costain in from Philadelphia to call on Booth, and telephoned me later he wanted to see *The Lively Lady.* Told him it was too long for the *Post.* He said the *Post* would like to decide that for itself.

July 9: Cut, patched and rewrote.

July 10: Cut Talleyrand and Aunt Cynthy from Book I, smoothed and rewrote the escape from the *Gorgon,* cutting it by $\frac{3}{5}$, boiled down and speeded up the Nantes episode preceding the burning of the first *Lively Lady.* To Booth's with Book III and re-did the fight with the *Gorgon,* the capture of the second *Lively Lady* and the arrival in Plymouth Harbor.

July 11: Got a stenographer to retype the manuscript, and went on cutting and piecing in Book III. Strange that I'm unconscious of these ghastly shortcomings when I commit them!

July 13: Figured up cuts: 70 pages out of Book I's 205 pages; 132 pages out of Book II's 207 pages; 46 pages out of Book III's 195 pages. That makes it about 130,000 words long.

July 14: Took Book I away from the stenog and cut it some more. To Booth's after dinner and worked on the scene in Exeter.

July 15: Took from the stenog the first 30 pages of Book I and hacked them all to hell, so that he had to re-do them. Read the new pages to Booth, and worked till 3 A.M., mauling them so that they had to be retyped for the third time.

July 17, 18, 19, 20: Tinkered, cut and rewrote.

July 21: Finished the massacre chapter, which leaves only the last chapter to be written. Booth telephoned that he'd like to go over the opening chapters with me, as he felt they could still be improved. Over at seven forty-five, read to him, and tinkered till twelve-thirty.

July 22: Wrote the last chapter.

July 23: Threw it away and wrote another.

July 24: Rewrote it.

July 25: Rewrote it again.

July 26: Threw away the end and replaced it with a hasty one: then to Booth's and read it to him. Don't touch it, he said. Told me to go over the entire manuscript and toss out every possible "he said" and "she said."

July 28: Started to revise the entire book.

July 29: Revised Book II.

July 30: Revised some more: then wrapped up the manuscript to send to Costain. Booth telephoned we'd better do some more tinkering on Chapters 10 and 14, so unwrapped it. He offered to bet twenty-five dollars the *Post* would accept it. Took the bet in a hurry, as I know he can't win—not when *Arundel* sells only 7,000 copies in six months. A hell of a circulation builder I'd be!

July 31: Found notes for insertions I had overlooked, and wrote them in. Then once more wrapped up the manuscript and sent it off. Certain that the book will be as much of a flop as was *Arundel.*

August 1: Started revising the carbon of the manuscript to send to Doubleday. Depressed beyond words.

August 3: Carl Warton of the *Boston Herald* came to me to help him interview Booth. Took him over. He came back in a rage, saying he couldn't get Booth to talk about anything except *The Lively Lady.* Too depressed to work, so went to Ben Ames Williams' for a week.

August 16: Graeme Lorimer came to Kennebunkport to see Hugh Kahler, and telephoned that he had a message from his father—a pretty good one. His father had told him to say he had read about one third of *Lively Lady,* and if the next two thirds held up as well, it was sure-fire. His father had also told Graeme to tell me it was better than Stevenson. Hey, hey! Who would work for any other editor if he can work for Lorimer!

August 18: Lorimer telegraphed, "It's a grand book, and by cutting some of the opening fifty pages, some of the privateering stuff and a good deal of Dartmoor Prison we can get a five-part serial out of it. If this is satisfactory and you are willing to trust our surgeon, confirm. Glad to have you supervise the job if you prefer." Greatly depressed, as the book, already cut to the limit, will have to be cut in two in order to fit into five installments. Consulted Booth; he said at once that I should agree: that magazine publication was a purely temporary affair, forgotten in a matter of weeks. Only the book lives and is remembered. The book, of course, wouldn't be cut at all. Wired Lorimer, "Go ahead but please ask surgeon to be merciful."

August 20: So disturbed by thought of cutting to 60,000 words that I telephoned Lorimer and begged him to make it seven installments. He could, I told him, have it for the price of a five-part serial if he'd do so. He said he couldn't possibly spare that amount of space, but he'd try to stretch it to six—in which case, of course, he'd raise the price.

August 22: Booth offered to help me make the joints between the *Post's* cuts, at which I was squawking deafeningly. He said he was always in agony over all his books, and I shouldn't take it so to heart. He says this reading and tinkering helps to take his mind off his eyes. The eye which was operated on for cataract has begun to misbehave. The other eye is blind. A curtain seems to be lowering in the operated-on eye, so that he must throw his head farther and farther back in order to see.

August 25: Sat on the balcony in Booth's workroom and discussed the possibility of using the material we had cut from *Lively Lady.* It hadn't belonged in *Lively Lady,* he said, but it belonged *somewhere.* The work I had done on Reid's privateer fight in Fayal Roads, on Talleyrand, on his niece the Duchess de Dino, and on American prisoners in the hulks at Chatham, mustn't be lost. He is greatly concerned over his eye, and so am I, though the Wilmer people at Johns Hopkins, when phoned to, have repeatedly said there's no occasion for worry. They're cockeyed, for tonight the curtain came down completely and he couldn't see at all.

August 26: Booth went to Portland to see an eye man—just to re-assure himself, the Wilmer people say. The Portland man took one look and told Susie to get a special car and take him instantly to the Wilmer Clinic in Baltimore. The last thing Booth did before going to the train was to dictate several pages of suggestions as to how I might use the material dropped from *Lively Lady.*

August 30: A letter from Booth, dictated from the hospital, practi-cally an essay (which I'll use in a *Post* article) on people who read books, and why they read them: also why writers write.[2] And he did it while thinking he was probably doomed to blindness for the rest of his life! A great man and a great writer!

While I was finishing *The Lively Lady,* the results of the 1929 panic became painfully evident. We had borrowed from a bank to build the Palm Beach house; and just before the panic, realizing that Palm Beach is no place for one who wants to write, we had sold it at a slight profit. Unfortunately the gentleman who bought it was as much af-fected by the stock market crash as was everyone else: consequently he was unable to make payments as they came due. As a result, all the proceeds from the sale of *Lively Lady* went to the bank, and we were as broke as we had been before we sold it. Fortunately for us, Mr. Lorimer saw merit in several suggestions that I made—for an article on Tarkington, which I had long wanted to do;[3] for a true story of the amount of work that goes into the writing of a novel, and the pitifully small return when such a novel, supposedly successful, sells 9,000 copies in a year; then for a series of three articles on building problems in Italy, such as we'd had in struggling with the American Wing—the Half-Baked Palace. I cannot say too often that unless I'd been able to have the support of the *Saturday Evening Post* between and during novels, I couldn't possibly have written fiction of the sort I had set my heart on doing.

So we returned to Italy early in December; and after finishing the three articles for the *Post* and eliminating our worry over food bills, servants' wages and steamship fares, I went to work trying to plot the novel that would show how American privateers operated out of French ports, and how captured privateersmen lived in the prison ships on the Medway.

---

[2]Included in the article noted below.
[3]See p. 361, Appendix.

CHAPTER

24

As an experiment I decided to abandon the method of writing I'd used in *Arundel* and *The Lively Lady,* and attempt a compressed method that would, in effect, cut the story mentally while it was being written, thus avoiding the need of cutting it physically long afterwards. My diary shows clearly that the experiment resulted in an unusual amount of agony:

February, 1931: Corrected *Lively Lady* page proofs. Susie wrote that Booth's other eye had been successfully operated on and that he could see again. Cheering letters from readers of *Arundel* continue to arrive. They're out of all proportion to its sales, and I'd a damned sight rather just barely subsist by writing books than make three times as much doing magazine articles. But it's impossible, apparently, to avoid starving to death if I *do* stick to writing books. Wrote Page 1, Chapter 1 at the head of a blank sheet, wondering whether I'd be able to put anything underneath. Spent day after day and night after night consulting sources and writing London for more sources. Can *not* plot a satisfactory finish.

February 9: Made a start and got a quarter down page 1. These pages are blankbook pages which take almost exactly 1,200 longhand words apiece.

February 10: Got ⅔ down page 1. Haven't sufficient detail on slave ships.

February 11: ⅓ down page 2. Two barentines came into the harbor. Hurried to the port with Bowditch's *Navigator* to watch them round the headland and work up to the mooring pier.

February 12: ⅔ down page 2 and made so many insertions and alterations that Anna let her little fingernail grow long, so she can use it as a tracer to follow the insert lines that crisscross all over the pages.

February 13: ⅓ down page 3.

February 14: Cracked page 4. The story isn't planned in sufficient detail, and I'm making hard going of it. Can't see how to end it or what the climax should be. God knows whether I can ever finish it. There's something lacking.

February 15: ⅔ down page 4.

February 16: ⅓ down page 5, into Chapter 3.

February 17: Cracked page 6. Spent the afternoon studying the movements of two brigs that continually got in irons while trying to tack out in light airs.

February 18: Finished page 6, ended Chapter 3. Sent to London for more books. Tentatively adopted the title *Captain Caution*.

February 19: ½ down 7. Great difficulty in starting fourth chapter. This experiment of abandoning the first person seems awkward and unwieldy—not enough opportunity to spread out.

February 20: ¼ down 8. Room flooded by a thunderstorm, which reminded me to re-read Sienkiewicz's *Deluge. There* was a boy who could write long books without making the critics say Tut! Tut!

February 21: Finished 8. Discovered, in Coggeshall's *History of American Privateers,* a paragraph noting that the British prison brig *Emu* had been captured by an American privateer, which had deposited the *Emu's* passengers, forty women convicts, on one of the Cape Verde islands. That ought to make quite a novel. Wrote the Public Record Office in London to find out who the women were, why they had been convicted, and what happened to them.

February 22: Cracked page 9, started Chapter 5.

February 23: Letter from the *Post* asking me to write some jokes. To hell with jokes. This is no time for mirth or laughter! ¾ down page 9.

February 24: ½ down 10. In the *Paris Herald* J. B. Priestley criticized all Americans, calling them Babbitts with uncut copies of *Main Street* on their parlor tables. There isn't a British author who isn't in line for a good socking from American authors. Mr. Priestley should stand at the head of the queue, and then run back to the end and fall in for another good paste in the other eye. Struggled on in Chapter 5 with great labor. What in Kee-rist's name is the use! I should be writing the Valcour-Saratoga sequel to *Arundel.* I wonder why Booth advocated waiting five years before doing it?

February 25: ⅕ down 11.

February 26: ⅔ down 11.

February 27: Bottom of 11 and the hell with it!

February 28: To work on the terrible sixth chapter and progressed like a man striving to climb the last quarter mile of Mount Everest. ½ down page 12.

March 1: ⅕ down 13. Finished the damnable sixth chapter amid the wailing of a sirocco that rattled doors and windows like castanets.

March 2: One line on 14, enraged by the *Paris Herald's* account of Charlie Chaplin's social successes in London. People are such damned fools that I get mad at almost everything I read in the papers.

March 3: Nine lines on 14.

March 4: ⅓ down 14. Started a fight to persuade my publishers to put a better jacket on *Arundel* and let me rewrite it—which they had long before promised to do.

March 5: Finished 14 and Chapter 7.

March 6: Cracked 15, but only a few lines, as most of the day had to be spent attending the dog Serena. The local vet resembles Don Quixote with a bushy beard. He wears a magnificent gray uniform and flowing gray cape almost to his heels—a hangover from a vet-lieutenancy in the army. To us he is known as the Terror of the Balilla because he trains a group of Girl Scouts. Early in the morning Serena began to strive to toss her lunch, so we sent for the Terror of the Balilla. When he majestically appeared he said, "No worms: no pointed bones; merely a slight catarrh of the stomach which comes easily to a bitch that hasn't been bred for some time." He prescribed a red powder, rennet, to be given in a pat of butter, and a little milk. Fed her from time to time for the remainder of the day. As soon as she swallowed the rennet she began to retch and gag, keeping it up till nightfall. Then she weakly drank a little milk; then picked up a fragment of bay leaf that had been used as a buffer between two segments of broiled eel. This brought on a gagging and choking fit that lasted through the night. "All bitches," said the Terror, "should be 'covered' every two or three years to avoid nerve strain." Suggest changing the words "stud fee" to "cover charge," and vice versa.

March 7: ⅘ down 15. In a rage over a senator who staged a one-man filibuster on the last day of the Senate session, thus killing an international copyright bill and the immigration restriction bill. To hear some people talk, one might think that Benedict Arnold was the only traitor this country ever produced. There's a million of 'em!

March 8: ½ down 16. Received the *Saturday Evening Post* containing the first installment of *Lively Lady,* and perspired all day over the manner in which it had been hacked to hell.

March 9: Finished Chapter 8, page 16, but have no idea how Marvin would move from here to the hulks. The dumb bastard won't tell me.

March 10: Not a line, in spite of never leaving my desk. Just plain stuck.

March 11: Middle page 17. It dawned on me that although England passed anti-slavery laws in 1807, many British merchants continued to bootleg slaves. To raise money for a privateer, therefore, Slade would naturally go to England and blackmail the owner of one of those boot-leg slave businesses. At the same time, of course, he'd turn informer on Marvin, so to get Marvin out of his way.

March 12: ⅘ down 17. In great tribulation over *Captain Caution.* Can't seem to smooth it out. If I could have an hour's talk with Booth, I'd be all right.

March 13: ½ down 18.

March 14: Cracked page 19. Aviators from Orbetello flew around and around and around the house all day. Eighteenth-century authors needed patrons: twentieth-century authors need earmuffs or anti-air-craft guns.

March 15: Not a line, thanks to my publishers and Rebecca West. The former because their letters show a disinclination to re-do *Arundel:* the latter because she has the gall to explain America to the English through the columns of the *London Telegraph.* "Political and crimi-nal corruption in America," she writes, "is due to the exigencies of pio-neering in Colonial days. They set a cheap price on human life! Then the Civil War depraved the standards still further! America was left a legacy of rogue soldiers—who looted and killed: hence the American criminal class!" Sir John Mandeville was an accurate and skeptical reporter by comparison with these Limey interpreters of the American scene. Rebecca ought to stick to explaining the legacy left to England by the vast numbers of illegitimate children spawned in England during the seventeenth, eighteenth and nineteenth centuries by royalty, noblemen, rakes, bucks and the cream of society.

March 16: ½ down 19. Assured my publishers that my repeated attempts to make them live up to their agreements leave me feeling as though I were carrying a dead rhinoceros on my shoulders. Came across a striking analogy today: English shipowners of the eighteenth and early nineteenth centuries, trying to economize on crews, discharged English sailors in the West Indies and supplanted them with foreign-ers—who had a bad habit of mutinying. In that case the shipowners, instead of saving fifty pounds, sometimes lost ten thousand pounds. Publishers, I'm afraid, are apt to be like that.

March 17: ⅕ down 20. In despair at the chapter I'm now on. So depressed that I told Anna I thought I'd throw the book away, and

moaned querulously at my incarceration in a damned cold bedroom.
She said, "Think of prisoners who get Life." Reminded her I'd probably get Life for writing this book if I don't do better than I *am* doing.

March 18: ⅓ down 21. Started Chapter 11.

March 19: ½ down 21. Still depressed and baffled, even though we
dined on the first asparagus of the season, and an eel as big as a boa
constrictor, stewed in a red wine sauce.

March 20: Cracked 22. Struggled onward like a man wading through
clinging mud. Anna persists in saying it's swell, but what I say isn't
fit to print.

March 21: Finished 22 and Chapter 11. A terrific wind and rain,
which flooded the workroom, even though we put dams of towels
around the doors.

March 22: ¼ down 23 and started Chapter 12.

March 23: Added five lines to yesterday's, largely because I had a
reply to my letter to the Public Record Office. They had found the
records of the forty women convicts, and I tried to plot a novel to be
called *Forty on the Emu.*[1]

March 24: ⅙ down 24. Again enraged by the morning news: Chaplin returns to Paris to lunch with Briand; the Pope makes an official
squawk because Morgan invited the Archbishop of Canterbury to travel
to the Holy Land on the Morgan yacht; Dreiser and Sinclair Lewis,
two overrated authors, got into a brawl at a banquet and Dreiser slapped
Lewis' face. The world is full of people whose faces should be slapped.
Believe the brig model I saw in the Louvre Museum, the *Chasseur,* was
actually Boyle's *Chasseur.* Wrote Keena in Paris to help me get a
photograph from the director of the Louvre Museum: also for information as to her dimensions, armament and approximate price of such
a brig in 1815. Also for information as to how Marvin would have
bought such a brig from Tom Souville, the French privateer.

March 25: ⅔ down 24. Lorimer wrote, suggesting two articles in
England if I was low financially, but that they weren't particularly
important, and if I wanted to come straight home, not to bother with
them. I'll do the latter, as it would take five weeks to get those two
stories, and this book must be finished, even though it never sells. If
it doesn't sell, it'll all come under the head of training. Struggled on
in Chapter 12—a tough one. They're *all* tough ones.

March 26: ¼ down 25.

March 28: ⅙ down 26. Got Marvin and Argandeau up to the hulks,
but whether I can kick, haul and lever them aboard is something else

---

[1]See p. 430, Appendix.

again. Distressed on turning back to the hulk sections that were cut from *The Lively Lady* to discover that they were wholly unusable—clumsy and draggy. *Captain Caution* isn't nearly so badly done, so I must be learning something all the time—though I'm not conscious of it.

March 29: ½ down 26. Completely stumped by the story. Don't see how I can get anything good out of the hulk episodes, and have almost come to a complete halt.

March 30: ⅙ down 27. Squeezed through Chapter 13.

March 31: Added four lines to yesterday's work. Had a long letter from Stewart, the Louisville bookdealer, who had written to urge me to write another book like *Arundel* and had been asked whether he *really* thought it was a good suggestion, when *Arundel's* sales have been so small that they wouldn't even have kept us from starving, let alone pay our taxes and other fixed charges, and meet the needs of dependents. He admitted today that perhaps it wasn't the best of advice, so wrote him that in spite of my reply, my next book would be twice as long as *Arundel* and earn half as much. All tangled up as to how much hulk material to put in. It ought all to be in: yet if I include all of it, those who read it will go around telling each other how prolix I am. To hell with 'em! Put it all in!

April 1: ⅚ down 27. Struggled on with great difficulty.

April 2: ⅙ down 28. Rotten weather and worse progress.

April 3: Bottom of 28. There's some sort of thread missing—something to tie things together; but I can't figure what.

April 4: Cracked page 29, finished Chapter 14.

April 5: Into Chapter 15 and half down 29.

April 6: Nearly half down 30. Telegraphed London for more books on the Duchess de Dino, early English pugilism, and Bristol slave runners in 1815.

April 7: ⅞ down 30. *The Lively Lady* appeared in American bookshops today, but the results were the same as with *Arundel*. Eager booksellers trampled each other to get away from a first printing of 5,560 copies, and so far as I could tell, its publication had been Top Secret.

April 8: Finished Chapter 15, page 30.

April 9: Started Chapter 16 and cracked page 31.

April 10: ⅘ down 31. A long letter from Booth with a sketch showing Dreiser's hand meeting Lewis' face with a tremendous impact.

April 11: ⁹⁄₁₀ down 31. Discarded the ⅘ page of Chapter 16; made some progress on an entirely new 16; then threw away the new one and

cut out a block of the old 16. Exhausted and discouraged, but a little
cheered by a letter from a San Francisco sea captain assuming—because
of reading *Lively Lady*—that I was the person who had shipped on his
five-masted schooner in Callao some years ago.

April 12: ½ down 32. Had a ray of light today—a letter from R. E.
Gould, a country storekeeper in Anson, Maine:

> I feel I ought to write you how delighted I am with *The Lively
> Lady* in the *Saturday Evening Post*. On a recent trip south I met a
> teacher from Philadelphia, and I told him that the 1812 war was set-
> tled by privateers, and that their superiority over the British ships was
> due to three things: the fore-and-aft rig, the pivot gun, and the Gang-
> way Pendulum. This was the invention of a Yankee, and was hung in
> the gangway to observe the roll of the vessel. The gunner stood at the
> gangway, and when the Pendulum showed the vessel was on an even
> keel, he called "Fire"! The resulting broadsides took effect, while
> shot from the British ships, which fired on the downward roll, usually
> hit the water and ricocheted over the American vessels. Probably I
> haven't told it right, as I am no sailor, but I read this somewhere. I
> was so pleased with your story that I wrote my Philadelphia friend to
> be sure and read it. He told me he had never heard of any of these
> things, and I think it is time he did. If I get a gladiolus seedling that
> is any good, I want to name it The Lively Lady.

Later Mr. Gould—who in another fifteen years was to blossom out
as an author with his delightful *Yankee Storekeeper*—elaborated on his
first letter:

> I sent out a call for help to locate an authority for the "Gangway
> Pendulum", and as a result of my quest I received a book today from
> the Dartmouth College Library, entitled *A Treatise on Naval Gun-
> nery,* by Gen. Sir Howard Douglas, Bart., written about 1817. He
> deals with the causes of the defeat of the many British ships by Ameri-
> can vessels; and while he puts up good alibis for British ships, in the
> usual British way, he admits they were outhandled and outgunned by
> the Americans. On page 444 he speaks of the Pendulum, and also of a
> tract by Capt. Pechell, who speaks of an "ingenious expedient, viz.,
> the Pendulum". Anyone might think from reading this book that the
> Pendulum was an invention of the British; but by reading on, and
> studying what he says of the engagements between American and
> British vessels, it is plain that the Americans possessed some great ad-
> vantage that made them successful in nearly every engagement. I think

this work will give you the clue you are looking for. If you should write another book on this period, Capt. Boyle or Richard Nason could invent the "Gangway Pendulum" and so be able to defeat the British ships, and I shall be happy that I had the idea of writing you about this ancient bit of history that was tucked away in my head. I have often thought that if the stories of long ago that have been told around New England firesides in winter evenings could be preserved, they would be immensely valuable in throwing sidelights on this period. My recollections include the story of grandmother's uncle, who was attacked by Indians while mowing near Fort Popham, and killed six Indians with his scythe before they got him. Of my grandfather taking a load of salt back into the interior to swap for corn when he was nine years old, and incidentally swapping a pair of steers for a pair of oxen that the owner couldn't winter out on account of a short-age of hay. Of my great grandfather who, as a boy of eight, followed his father to the siege and capture of Quebec under Wolfe—and then to read that present-day 8-year-old boys are overtaxed when we ask them to do anything useful, such as bringing in an armful of wood!

Gangway Pendulum, eh? Hm! Sent off a score of letters—United States Naval Archives, British Admiralty, Library of Congress, H. I. Chapelle, Essex Institute—how was the Gangway Pendulum made: of what material: how did it operate: where belayed when not in use?

April 13: Gangway Pendulum! Gangway Pendulum! The end of the book begins to take form! Ain't that Douglas a typical historian? Tells people there was a Gangway Pendulum, but says nothing whatever about how it was made or rigged! ¾ down 32. Read a three-volume book on English pugilism, *Pugilistica,* and tried to reconstruct a prize fight and figure out a Gangway Pendulum. Made a wooden tripod and tried to rig one, using a bicycle bell for the gong and a mason's plumb line and bob for the striker.

April 14: ⅓ down 32b. Got going on the prize fight and did a page and a half—1,800 words—first satisfactory day's work since we've been here. Arnold Bennett died, about sixty. There was an in-and-outer. His *Old Wives' Tale* was one of the best: his *Accident* one of the worst.

April 15: Finished 32c and Chapter 16. Again did a satisfactory day's work: nearly two full pages.

April 16: ½ down 33. Back to the days of bad going: haven't a defi-nite knowledge of the last quarter of the book.

April 17: ⅓ down 34. Terrible progress, but finally got Marvin on the rope escaping down the side of the hulk.

April 18: Finished 34, plus a big pasted-in insert. Two letters from Englishmen, greatly annoyed at finding unpalatable information about England in *The Lively Lady*. It's quite all right for every British author to make scurrilous remarks about the United States, but a gross injustice when any American author has the impertinence to mention any of England's monumental present or past shortcomings.

April 19: Completed Chapter 17: ¼ down 35.

April 20: Four lines down 36. Got Slade started from Roscoff. Anna thinks it's good. I wouldn't give a nickel for it.

April 21: Finished 36. Took Slade into Whitesand Bay. I'm afraid Booth isn't going to like Slade's rawness, but that's the kind of feller Slade was.

April 22: ¼ down 38.

April 23: ½ down 38. Snagged, and had to discard my first start on the episode of Slade in Bristol. Suddenly overwhelmingly revolted by rotten European (especially Italian) politics, and in a frenzy to get back to Maine.

April 24: Cracked 38a. Squeaked through a difficult passage. Most of my time seems to be spent in just sitting.

April 25: Finished 38b and Chapter 19. Waded through Slade's interview with Sir Austin Braymore—2,000 words that came nearer to looking right than anything I've yet done.

April 26: ⅚ down 39.

April 27: Finished 40, Chapter 20.

April 28: Revised Slade's love scene with Corunna and gave it to Anna to type. Tried to go back and start Marvin and his companions on their way after their escape from the hulks, but got nowhere at all —not even a word.

April 29: Five lines on page 41. James Miles, the Leeds bookseller, sent me a rare French mezzotint of Robert Rogers and asked twenty-five pounds for it. Can't afford not to get it, as it solidifies Rogers in my mind—a big, thick-lipped, pouchy-eyed man, wholly unlike the prettied-up English mezzotints of him. Got a start on Chapter 21.

April 30: ½ down 41. All balled up. Can't figure out how Marvin would escape from England.

May 1: ⅘ down 41.

May 2: Cracked 42. The workroom in a turmoil from last-minute packing and my consultation of books on Valençay, Tom Souville, Calais, the Duchess de Dino, and so on. Made little progress and left the escapers in mid-channel.

May 3, 4, 5: Set off for Rome and Naples, sailed for New York on the *Vulcania,* and delighted to find Frank Simonds and A. Hamilton Gibbs on the ship. That made me think of Sam Blythe's story of the author who had just returned from abroad and was asked whether he'd enjoyed the boat trip, to which he replied, "Hell, no: there was another author aboard!" Sam's story, in this case, emphatically didn't apply; for both Frank Simonds and Arthur Gibbs were close and dear friends, and Arthur eventually gave many days, in Italy, Maine and the Bahamas, to reading, criticizing and editing several long and troublesome books that were driving me almost to distraction.

§

Maine, May 13–31: Cleaned up accumulated correspondence. Found that *The Lively Lady* in two months had sold 6,420 copies, about the same as *Arundel,* but brought a surprising number of excellent reviews from reviewers who understood what I was driving at. One notable exception was a review by Elrick Davis in a Cleveland paper. He had been enthusiastic over *Arundel;* but his review of *The Lively Lady* started, "I think the author of this book sold out for money." He argued that I could have made *The Lively Lady* just as long as *Arundel,* but had preferred to pander to the *Saturday Evening Post.* That, to my way of thinking, was damaging and destructive criticism at its worst—and I would have found it almost unbearable if so many reviews hadn't been wholeheartedly generous and understanding, and if letters of appreciation hadn't been so warmly enthusiastic. Wrote Davis that critical judgments were beyond my comprehension. He had glowingly praised *Arundel,* but damned *The Lively Lady,* which had been exactly as long as *Arundel* when first written, and had been edited to its present size by Mr. Tarkington and myself after months of extra labor—and only to make it more readable and understandable. At the same time Mr. Frederic Van de Water had been profoundly bored by *Arundel,* but was gratifyingly clamorous over *The Lively Lady;* whereas Arthur Staples, of the *Lewiston Journal,* strongly criticized *Arundel* when it appeared, as being too long, but now criticizes *The Lively Lady* for being too short.

Mr. Blythe, on the other hand, had still other ideas, and had no hesitation in expressing them:

The Lively Lady is at hand and I'm glad to see that it is not so tome-like as I feared it would be, but exactly the right size for a novel, save a Dreiser, of course. By the way, if you haven't seen the *New Yorker* of May 30, get it and read Dorothy Parker's piece in "Reading and Writing" at the end of the magazine on that enormous platitudinous stuffed shirt.

I'm glad to find that the Parker lady thinks Dreiser is a big bluff as a writer, for that is a lit'ry obsession of mine and I have had small support in it. It is my opinion that Dreiser is the result of a great spoof on the moron American public, deliberately foisted and fostered by Mencken. Mencken is too damned smart to think that guy can write a lick. I composed a piece about that one time, a short piece, and sent it to Harold Ross for inclusion in the *New Yorker,* and Mr. Ross sent it to both Mencken and Dreiser and asked them if this was true. So they both said No. And Mr. Ross assured me I was mistaken, as he had the word of these two that I was.

No auctorial news that I know of. Harry Wilson has finished a novel, first in three years, so it ought to be good. It is a movie-cum-Hollywood novel[2] and G.H.L. says it is good. Hugh Wiley has a $5000 advance from Ray Long for a California serial and is working to beat hell to get it done so he won't have to give back the five grand, which he couldn't do, as he has spent it. Frank Condon is starting a movie department, to run every other week. *Collier's* has 2,250,000 circulation. There is a strong demand for "American" humor for "Postscripts." Etc. Scramble these facts and see what you get.

I appreciate fully your yowl about the influx of visitors from the adjacent highway. At Sunset Hill there hasn't been a time this year when we have not had more guests than the Del Monte Hotel, and I am so damned sick of their chatter, and their yen for gin that I have had to crawl into a hideaway in a canyon and let the Jap gardener shoo them away. It does beat hell how they come in. The other day a large car arrived, containing, as I found on investigation, a chap who used to work on the *World* with me and who is high up on my private list of s.o.b.'s. And he knows it, but did that stop him from a visit nicely timed for lunch? It did not. And did he get the lunch? He did not. Nor any gin either.

That is a fine piece you have in the *Post* anent Booth Tarkington,[3] saluted by me on every appropriate occasion as the Captain General of American writers, with damned few anywhere else in his class; but I regret you were so reserved, when writing it, concerning his alcoholic days, although I concede your reticence was seemly. However, there

---

[2]*Merton of the Movies.*
[3]See p. 361, Appendix.

should be some record, somewhere, of those days for the guidance and inspiration of the younger generation of drinkers who know nothing of the art and practice of real drinking in an amusing, promethean, genial, intelligent, constructive and inventive manner.

Tales of Tark's Tanking would be a good title for it, but I suppose it will never be written.

H. Corey contributes this one: A country sparrow, living in New Jersey, flew over to visit a New York cousin.

"Marvellous city," said the Jerseyite when they had met.

"Oh, I dunno," said the New Yorker. "It ain't such a hell of a place. Let's fly around some."

So they flew up to the 89th story of the Empire State Building, Al Smith's greatest error, and looked down at the humans toiling along below, seemingly no bigger than *they* were. Presently, the New York sparrow turned tail about and dumped his load.

"My God," said the countryman, "what did you do that for?"

"Oh," the city sparrow said, "I merely wanted to show you how far a little crap will go in New York."

Ain't it the truth?

June 1–30: Impossible to work because of telephone calls and constant interruptions, so rented a cabin on Parker Mountain, New Hampshire, an hour's drive from Kennebunkport.

Parker Mountain, July 21: Despite the drawbacks of this mountain cabin it's wonderful to be where lawnmowers, golf players, crying children, gabbling old women, squawking automobile horns, mentally deficient chauffeurs and importunate telephoners aren't keeping me in a constant state of hectic jumpiness. The end of *Captain Caution* weighs on me like a thick, heavy, black fog, messy and impenetrable: all muddy in my head: nothing clear about it, either plot or people.

July 22: Tried to work, but couldn't write a line. It was a ghastly mistake to leave Italy with it unfinished. I might have finished in forty days if I'd stayed there: now it begins to look as though I wouldn't be able to finish in forty years.

July 23: 100 in the shade outdoors. In closing a window against a heavy thunderstorm, broke the window and almost cut off my right hand.

July 24: Drove to Dunbarton, New Hampshire, home of Major Robert Rogers, to look around and get the feel of the country. My mind keeps working on Rogers, who is interfering seriously with *Captain Caution*.

July 25: ⅛ down 43. Never again will I deliberately try to write a short novel. Hereafter they go as they damned please, even if they stretch to 2,000 pages. This manuscript has been at page 42 since the second day of May and I wish I'd let it stay there.

July 26: Re-started page 43, Chapter 22.

July 27–28: Terrifically hot. Lightning struck the water pipe leading from a spring into the kitchen, came out in the sink, knocked all the pans off the stove and escaped by pushing a board off the side of the cabin.

July 29: Cracked page 44. Lindbergh and his wife passed overhead, bound for Alaska and China. Wished to God I was with 'em instead of being all tangled up in *Captain Caution.*

July 30: Touched page 44a. I wonder if it's worth the struggle? It doesn't seem possible that anyone will either buy or read anything that comes so hard.

July 31: ⅘ down 44a.

August 1: ¾ down 44b. Finished Chapter 22. Drove to Concord to hunt material in the Historical Society rooms. The librarian produced for me the original sutler's accounts for Rogers' Rangers and the source of the statement that he had fought for the Dey of Algiers (in a letter from Eleazer Wheelock to George Washington).

August 2, 3, 4, 5: Cracked Chapter 23. Returned to Maine to get mail and source books, and ran into a bewildering mass of golfers, motorists, telephone calls, telegrams, callers, invitations, unanswered letters. . . . Impossible to work, so fled to Parker Mountain again.

August 6: Found that a thunderstorm, in our absence, had blasted off a corner of the roof above my worktable and ripped a twenty-foot-long trench down the mountainside. Probably my imprecations and lamentations over *Captain Caution* led Heaven to try to put me out of my misery. ⅓ down page 45.

August 7: Blistering heat. ⅔ down 45.

August 8: Heat, much as I dislike it, is preferable to golfers, automobiles, telephone bells, motor grass-cutters and squealing bathers. ⅕ down 46, and reached a scene that had been included in the original draft of *Lively Lady,* but it's impossible to use even a word out of the passage as I first wrote it.

August 9: ⅚ down 46, working in the Talleyrand scene at last—except that it's wholly different from the way I did it when I first wrote it for *Lively Lady.*

August 10: Cracked page 47 and made a hesitating start on Chapter 24. Back to Maine to get James's six-volume *History of the Royal Navy* and *The Sailor's Word Book*. Returned to Parker Mountain at 1 A.M. and read in James's *History* until three o'clock. I now understand why Theodore Roosevelt devoted half of his *War of 1812* to ripping James to pieces. James had it coming: he was a typical historian—a typical Limey, what's more, openly contemptuous of everything American.

August 11: ½ down 47.

August 12: Cracked 48. Fear I'm going astray, but can't be sure where or how.

August 13: Half down 48.

August 14: Finished 48 and Chapter 24. Returned to Maine to have it typed.

August 16: Revised earlier chapters, and made notes from source books.

August 17: To Portland and spent the day hunting Valcour-Saratoga source material.

August 18: Received *Lively Lady* book proofs from English publishers, and started correction and revision. Surprised to find that British compositors and proofreaders are worse—much, much worse—than their American counterparts.

August 19: No chance to work, thanks to summer vacationers who seem to have abandoned everything that makes life worth living: leisure, tranquillity, interest in simple things, friends, opportunity to read.

August 20: Back to Parker Mountain and cracked page 49, Chapter 25.

August 21: Half down 49, but spent most of the day trying to plot the Valcour-Saratoga book.

August 22: ⅘ down 49. Struggled onward in Chapter 25, but had to throw away some and re-do the rest. Read from 9 P.M. to 3 A.M. in Volume 2 of Rupert Hughes's *George Washington*—history at its best and most brilliant. Parkman, if he'd dared to tackle the American Revolution, might have equaled Rupert's research, but he never could have approached Rupert's humor.

August 23: ⅓ down 50. Struggled through the scene with the Duchess de Dino—the last of the incidents that had been cut from *Lively Lady*. Not a word of all those incidents as originally written can be used in *Captain Caution*. Read on in Rupert's *George Washington,* and wondered why no novelist had ever written the American Revolution from the Loyalist—the Tory—viewpoint. It's obvious that they had a case in whose soundness and worthiness they believed implicitly. I'd better start looking into this. Certainly a few, at least, of my ancestors must have been Loyalists at heart. So many of the Patriot officers were such stinkers and such blundering incompetents that many, many Loyalists *had* to be far more admirable. What were their arguments? How did they feel? What were they like? All the regular historians dismiss them as being contemptible shadows—or ignore them completely. How come Francis Parkman hadn't a word to say about them?

August 24: Finished page 50 and Chapter 25. A note from Booth says the summer infestation has begun to dwindle and we can soon come home.

August 25: ⅗ down 51. Cracked Chapter 26, and finished the day drenched in perspiration and in a state of nervous exhaustion.

August 26: Cracked page 52. Couldn't stand the heat, so returned to Maine; but could only endure the constant noise and interruption for three days.

August 30: Retreated to Parker Mountain once more.

August 31: ¾ down 52. Saw by the morning paper that Alfred P. Dennis, the one who persuaded me to write the Department of Agriculture story for the *Post,* committed suicide by taking a header into the ocean at Bailey's Island. Hope it wasn't because of brooding over the names I called him when he trimmed the *Post.* In the same paper a column by Evangeline Adams saying that persons born between December 2 and December 12 were in for the greatest year of their lives, with a special brand of luck hitting them in November and December of this year. Evangeline had better be good. I was born on December 8; and if she *isn't* good, I'll know exactly why, and can write a piece for Lorimer about the shortcomings of horoscopists.

September 1: ⅖ down 53 and finished Chapter 26. Frantic from the monotonous clanking of a cowbell. Went out with a knife to corner the cow and cut off the bell; then discovered there were six cows, all belled. Struggled on in the afternoon and am now approaching the point where Marvin can go to sea again, though what he'll do when he gets there is more than I can tell.

September 2: Cracked 54. Strange that my only productive hours seem to be between six and seven-thirty in the evening. Up to that time I just sit around and squeeze out twenty to forty words; then, when I'm thoroughly exhausted, out they pour—desperation, probably.

September 3: ¾ down 54. Struggled on in Chapter 27, making wretched going of it. Find I'm putting even more time on plans for the sequel to *Arundel* than I am on *Captain Caution.* Made a false move, killed it, revived it, re-did it, and let it ride as a temporary wind-up to Chapter 27.

September 4-9: Re-did Chapter 27. Returned to Maine, hoping to be able to work where I can get at all the old familiar source books. No good: telephones, golfers knocking balls through windows, caddies rattling clubs and screeching, cocktail parties, visitors, callers; so went north, hunting land on the Georges River on which to build a place that would give us shelter from the tumultuous anguish of a Maine summer resort. Found 250 acres at the narrows of the river, looking out to the islands that had provided shelter for Captain George Weymouth in 1605. Bought it for six thousand dollars.

September 10: Returned to Parker Mountain on the hottest day of the year. Nearly dead with exhaustion, part of it due to realizing that I have an incurable habit of trying to purchase any property, no matter where, provided I think it will be conducive to work. This, if I'm not careful, can easily be the death of me.

September 11: Too hot to work: spent the day reading *George Washington, Life on the Ocean* and *The Spanish Jade.*

September 12: Cracked page 55, Chapter 28.

September 13: Intensely hot. Tried to work, but perspiration kept running into my eyes. Added 2½ lines to yesterday's work, then read Willa Cather's *Shadows on the Rock:* a sweetly vague shadow of a novel—a series of sketches for what might have been a really substantial book.

September 14: 5 lines down 56. Struggled onward in Chapter 28. Thoroughly disgusted at everything about *Captain Caution,* and almost ready to admit that I'm so hopelessly stuck that I can never end it properly: so low that I'd burst into tears at the slightest provocation. The truth is that all my interest has become centered on that sequel to *Arundel.* That's why *Captain Caution* is proving so burdensome.

September 15: Got myself inextricably bogged in Chapter 28, and returned to Maine in disgust. Found a note from Booth asking me to read *Captain Caution* to him.

September 16: Worked from 6 A.M. to two hours after midnight, revising.

September 17: Started reading to Booth and got through five chapters. He wanted to know what I'd been squawking about. Nothing needed to be touched, he said. Real sea stuff, full of pictures, and well handled. The only thing he advised was a single paragraph at the end of the fifth chapter—one that would hold Corunna Dorman in the reader's mind. He said he could see no reason why, after *Captain*

Caution was finished, I shouldn't start on the sequel to *Arundel,* taking Cap Huff and the others through the Retreat from Canada, Valcour Island and Saratoga.

September 18: Immeasurably relieved and cheered. Rewrote the end of Chapter 5. To Booth's and read four more chapters. He insisted it was all right just as it stood—story, characters, dialogue, everything.

September 19: Re-did the end of Chapter 9.

September 20: Re-did the re-done end of Chapter 9, then to Booth's and read through Chapter 11.

September 21: Compiled a list of sixty books for Senator Moses to get for me from the Congressional Library on indefinite loan. What Indians fought for the British at Valcour Island? Who led them? Where were they from? Where did they go after the battle? How had the British enlisted their aid? Which ones killed Jennie McCrae? Haven't *any* of these historians any curiosity? Mahan says there's no way of knowing how the American ships at Valcour were rigged. He's nuts! Of *course* there's a way of finding out! Who captained those vessels? Where did they get their training in seamanship? How was food cooked aboard the vessels? How-where-what-why-when-who. . . . Can't *any* American historian write anything but dull facts with all the essentials left out?

September 22: Compiled another list of books I'll need, and sent it to Senator Moses' office.

September 23: Sent my list of sources to the American Antiquarian Society, the William L. Clements Library and the research librarian of the Library of Congress, asking them to suggest additions. Read three more chapters to Booth and took Chapter 12 from its present position and put it in another place.

September 24: Read more to Booth and rewrote the passage in which Slade returns to Corunna Dorman with a lying account of his trip to England.

September 25: Tried to help a struggling young artist by sitting for a portrait two hours a day. [The sittings continued for twenty-one days, at the end of which time the struggling young artist destroyed his work. Hereafter struggling young artists will have to pick other victims.] Read most of the day in Wilkinson's *Memoirs,* a three-volume revelation of a hundred per cent stinker.

September 26: Social activity so great that Booth could listen to only one chapter.

September 27: Read Booth two chapters, getting through Marvin's fight with Little White. Readers *had* to like it, Booth insisted.

September 28: Started with Chapter 1 and began to revise once more.

September 29: Caught in a ruinous and worthless round of letter writing, telephone calls, lunch, golf, cocktails, more cocktails, more cocktails, dinner, backgammon, idle chatter, highballs, wasted time and forced laughter.

September 30: More of the same.

October 1: Read two more chapters to Booth and found that the two post-fight chapters had to be re-done.

October 2: Rewrote and condensed the two post-fight chapters. Hampered by the after-effects of a bad oyster, so knocked off and went to call on Aunt Isabel Nason to find out whether she knew anything at all about the way in which Thomas Bickford saved Great-great-grandfather Daniel Merrill's life at the Battle of Hubbardton, as noted in Bradbury's *History of Kennebunkport*. She could provide me with nothing but wintergreen and bismuth for my stomach-ache. Nobody here knows a single accurate fact about the early days of this town and its inhabitants. Received a Michigan Commission booklet edited by Randolph G. Adams of the William L. Clements Library. It had a piece on five great historical novels describing the times in which Washington lived, naming Cooper's *Spy*, Weir Mitchell's *Hugh Wynne*, Paul Leicester Ford's *Janice Meredith*, James Boyd's *Drums*, and *Arundel*. Having tried to read *The Spy* and *Hugh Wynne* recently, can't decide whether this is an insult or a compliment.

October 3-4: Stomach-ache considerably enhanced by stock market tumbling to new lows, making outlook for next winter dubious. Unending interruptions to work. *Captain Caution* was ⅔ done when I left Italy; and after four and a half months dodging from Maine to Parker Mountain, ⅓ of the remainder is still unfinished. I can't seem to think of anything but that sequel to *Arundel,* and gosh, how I dread it! It's going to be a holy terror!

October 5: Still afflicted by the bad oyster, so read in Chase's *History of Dartmouth* and discovered Joseph Marie Verrieul and several hell-raising Indians who were thorns in the flesh of Dartmouth, but will be a great asset to me in the Valcour-Saratoga book.

October 7: Rewrote the chapter where the escaping Americans drag themselves through the mud of the Medway.

October 8: Read the revised chapter to Booth. He said not to touch it again: he could feel the mud and smell it.

October 9-10: Revised; then read to Booth, and we perspired together over the final chapters of the book. Howard Chapelle came to help me on marine scenes, and on the rig of the vessels in the American fleet at

Valcour Island. He argued that the row galleys were sloops: I maintained they had to be two-masted and lateen-rigged, because General Waterbury, in describing the action of the row galley he commanded, stated that a cannon ball had splintered his mainmast, and because lateen rigs were universal on Piscataqua-built vessels. Most of the Skenesboro shipwrights came from the Piscataqua section. I felt sure Waterbury would never have said *"main*mast" if his galley had had only one mast. We argued the matter until 2 A.M. over a bottle of bourbon. Chapelle thinks he knows how he may be able to settle the argument through a friend in the British Admiralty.

October 11–18: Revised and corrected the first 125 typed pages of *Captain Caution.* Four more chapters to go.

October 19–25: Worked over pages 126–199 of the typed manuscript, altering, transposing, building up characters, but the weather so cold I was obliged to work in front of the living-room fire and so couldn't dodge visitors, telephone calls, golfers, cocktail drinkers. Still four more chapters to go—if I can escape the madhouse.

October 26: Discarded Chapter 29 and rewrote it.

October 27: Read 29 and 30 to Booth and he insisted they were swell. Explained how I was stuck on Chapter 31, and we tried to talk out the logical way in which everyone concerned would act.

October 28: Northeaster coming, though the weather bureau, as usual, can't predict it. If we could get ten days of hard rain, perhaps these twittery idle people would stay in their homes, and I could finish the book. Typed a score of inserts for Chapters 29 and 30.

October 29: The telephone rang all day. Got a start on Chapter 31.

October 30: ¼ down page 60.

October 31: Up early and to work again on Chapter 31, making incredibly hard going of it. ⅕ down page 61. Unfortunately switched on the radio and heard a football announcer deliver a eulogy of Knute Rockne. Rockne was a successful football coach who has somehow been deified by sentimental sports writers and football addicts. Since his accidental death, his name can't be mentioned without thousands of people who have never heard of him rising and standing reverently uncovered.

November 2: Tried to crack the last chapter to a deafening chorus of banging hammers and squeaking nail-withdrawals as a nearby garage was torn down. Swore I'd never again try to work under the conditions that have been so distressing for the past five months. Got ⅝ down page 62.

November 3: Got halfway down page 63.

November 4: Worked sixteen hours on three sandwiches and three cups of tea. Finished page 66 and the book. What do I mean, "finished"!

November 5: Pasted up the typed manuscript of Chapters 21, 22 and 23 and read to Booth all afternoon. The last chapter is all wrong.

November 6: Worked all morning, all afternoon and until three-thirty in the morning, trying to make the last chapter sound right. Can't get the last three paragraphs.

November 7: Retyped the last three chapters.

November 8: To Booth's and read him the re-done chapters and the re-re-re-done ending. He couldn't see, he said, how I could improve it. I was to let it strictly alone—and to make sure I *did* let it alone, he said, I was to wrap it up at once and send it to Lorimer.

November 9: Mailed *Captain Caution* to Lorimer and then went gunning for partridges to find out whether Evangeline Adams had been correct in saying that those born between December 2 and 12 would be particularly lucky in November and December of this year. Thought I killed a partridge in the first cover, and so did the dog, but the bird couldn't be found. Shot a high bird and saw him scale to earth. Went to pick him up and he banged up under my hand, straight toward Raymond Lunge, who couldn't shoot for fear of hitting me: then missed him going away. Climax came in the Wild Cat cover at dusk when I saw the dog put up a bird, got my sights exactly right and pulled—only to find I hadn't reloaded after climbing a fence. If this is Evangeline Adams' conception of good fortune, *Captain Caution* hasn't a Chinaman's chance.

§

I have detailed the labor connected with the writing and rewriting of *Captain Caution* for one reason and only one—a reason that I think will eventually be apparent to everyone reading this book.

On November 18 Lorimer wrote:

> *Captain Caution* has gone the rounds and has finally been read by me, and the vote on the manuscript is unanimous. We all think it is good, and in some ways a better story than *The Lively Lady,* but we do not feel we can run another novel that so closely parallels *The Lively Lady* for some time to come. We now have on hand at least eight months' supply of serials. Unless you have an earlier market, or decide not to defer book publication, we shall be glad to re-consider *Captain Caution* six months from now.

When I dejectedly and despairingly handed the letter to Mrs. Roberts, she said that it made no difference: that she had figured up our finances and probable expenses, and was sure we could make out some-how during the coming winter. Booth, when he telephoned to find out Lorimer's decision, was far more distressed than I, and told me to start at once on an outline of the Valcour-Saratoga book.

§

November 19: Booth telephoned to make sure I wasn't discouraged. There was no question whatever, he said, that *Captain Caution* would eventually find a home, and a good one. If I were in dire need, and had no objection to his making a handsome thing out of it, he'd bet me five thousand dollars that he was right—and advance the five thousand, which would leave me owing him ten when the book sold. He was particularly annoyed at Lorimer's remark that *Captain Caution* closely paralleled *The Lively Lady*. It did nothing of the sort, he said. It was about an entirely different type of privateering, and about a phase of war imprisonment wholly unlike the sorry interlude of Dartmoor. The only similarity was that they were both sea stories. The *Post* perpetually published far greater similarities—the Charlie Chan series, for example, all based on murder and a Chinese detective. Had I finished the outline of the Valcour-Saratoga book? Well then—what was I waiting for? Let's get going on it.

November 22: Read the outline to Booth, but couldn't get it across to him—it's too intricate. That's because no historian has ever clearly narrated the events of those two muddled campaigns.

§

Many authors argue that there's no such thing as luck in writing, and that all writers who get anywhere do so by the hardest sort of work and persistence. This may be so, but I know that in my case luck has helped enormously. In no book or records could I find how those men from Arundel, among them Captain Daniel Merrill and Ensign Joshua Nason, had moved from Arundel to Ticonderoga and such places. I could see the men themselves, but they were flat and motion-less. They weren't sweating and fighting and shouting; I saw them as soldiers in a snapshot, silent and stiff.

And then from the Society of Colonial Wars in the State of Maine I learned of the existence of one copy of the *Maine Farmer* (Augusta, Maine) for June 29, 1872. There were no other copies, for while the issue was awaiting delivery, the print shop burned, destroying the entire issue as well as the diary. The printer had taken home the one copy. This copy contained the diary of General Henry Sewall, who had enlisted as a private in 1776 and marched to Ticonderoga, where he was transferred to Colonel Brewer's 12th Massachusetts Regiment of Colonials—the same regiment in which Joshua Nason was an ensign and Daniel Merrill a captain. In that copy were the bare bones of information I had lacked, and the moment I read it, those hitherto static figures came to life, laughing, grumbling, sleeping in the bushes, rain-soaked, mud-splashed, hungry, ragged, needy.[4]

§

November 23: Re-hashed the Valcour-Saratoga story with Booth. In all likelihood, Booth said, I'd have to give more time to it than I had to *Arundel* and *Lively Lady.* It would be longer and infinitely more involved, but the fact that it fell naturally into eleven climaxes—the retreat from St. John, the dead pits of Isle Aux Noix, the building of the fleet, the Battle of Valcour, the Indian episode, the retreat from Ticonderoga, the further retreat from Skenesboro, the holding up of the British between Fort Ann and Fort Edward, the murder of Jennie McCrae, the Battle of Bemis's Heights, and the return to Arundel of Peter Merrill and his erring brother—would make it flow more smoothly, once I was sure of all my facts. He wondered how it would be to introduce a bum, pompous, dirty, superstitious army doctor—"so dirty that by August goldenrod would be sprouting from his navel." We elaborated at considerable length on this medico, who finally took on milder characteristics and turned into Doc Means, a country practitioner who refuses to conform to the remedies, nostrums or techniques of Revolutionary army doctors.

November 24: Fished for a title of the Valcour-Saratoga book . . . "it doesn't take/A man of giant mold to make/A giant shadow on the wall . . ." *The Giant Shadow*—probably too close to *Shadows on the Rock: The Scarlet Shadow: The Dreadful Wedge: The Scarlet Web: The Sublime Rabble: Rabble Rivers: The River of the Free: Freedom's Fetters: Webs in the Wilderness: The Ragged Rabble: Shackles of Ignorance: The Webs of Ignorance: The Splendid Rabble: Rabble, A Chronicle of Arundel.*

Carl Brandt explained at some length that he was sending *Captain Caution* to the *Pictorial Review,* but that the absence of the heroine for such a long period (after the escape from the hulks) would make monthly magazines reluctant to use it. Booth said Brandt didn't know what he was talking about: that any editor with brains would know

---

[4]See p. 384, Appendix.

there was no lapse of interest anywhere. Wrote Brandt to return *Captain Caution* to me if *Pictorial Review* canned it: I'd rather leave it in the *Post* safe than have it peddled around. Blemished the first page of a manuscript book with a start of *Splendid Rabble*. That title's no good, and I don't know enough about London in 1775.

November 25: Read in American and British journals and wrote Hatchard's in London to rush books on London in 1775 and Roque's map of London, sending them to Porto Santo Stefano.

November 28: Had a letter from a descendant of Benedict Arnold, Henry Baldwin of the United Fruit Company, to whom I had written for information about Arnold's children. He was afraid I wouldn't realize that Arnold had led the American troops at Saratoga, on account of those two asses Gates and Wilkinson having conspired to withhold credit from him.

December 6: Read the first two chapters of *Rabble* to Booth. A swell start, he said: the pictures were good and the four characters stood out. I should congratulate myself on getting under way so smoothly: that with such a start, the rest of the book just *had* to go along well. Told him it sounded like tripe to me. Fine, he said: that was an excellent sign. He'd felt exactly that way about *Alice Adams*—felt nobody would ever willingly read about such God-awful people.

December 7: Carl Brandt wrote that the *Pictorial Review* couldn't use *Captain Caution*. Editorial judgment is a strange thing.

December 11: To Philadelphia to see Lorimer, and left the *Captain Caution* manuscript with Miss Neall. After lunch Lorimer spoke of *Captain Caution* as though it would in all likelihood be acceptable after the lapse of a few months; then he okayed four articles: "Country Life in Italy," "Astrology," "Dogs," and "Quiet Evenings in the Home."

§

So to New York, where Mrs. Roberts and I boarded the *Roma* for Italy, feeling considerably cheered.

§

Porto Santo Stefano, December 26, 1931: Got going again on *Rabble*, but was stopped by the arrival of the new Harper Prize novel, *Brothers in the West*, by Robert Raynolds. The Brothers Harper disgorged ten thousand dollars for it. On page 53 a character's horse flings grit from flying hoofs into his rider's face; the same character asininely thrusts a rifle muzzle in his mouth and tastes "the dull dryness of burnt powder."

Burnt black powder is wet and tastes sharp and salty. A galloping horse flings grit behind him, and the rider's face is shielded by the horse's neck and body—unless he is riding hind side to and braiding the tail, in which case he'd be fortunate if he got only grit. On page 82 Raynolds, speaking of the same wolf, calls it first "the big wolf," then "the small wolf." He tells how the eyes of one of the brothers "bored the distance." The book bored me even more, and the prize is distinctly ten thousand dollars' worth of ado over nothing. It was a Harper editor who assured me that *Arundel* wasn't worth writing, but they give this junk a ten-thousand-dollar prize!

December 27: Received Chancellor's *18th Century in London,* and must start *Rabble* all over again, re-laying the first chapter in Ranelagh. The Pope, depressed by the collapse of a wing of the Vatican library, thinks that God has forgotten the world. Well, why not? He's probably sick of seeing the bastards who control Italy, Germany, France, England, Russia and every other country, to say nothing of having to be conscious of big crooks and businessmen loafing in Florida, Maine and California, seeking distraction on a hundred thousand golf links, pouring down Niagaras of gin each day, and going nowhere in a hell of a hurry in expensive yachts and motors. The world is full of soft, spoiled loafers who need toughening, and God—if He has occasion to single out this midget world from the overwhelming solar system—has good reason to want to forget it.

December 31: Two chapters out of probably sixty-five "finished," as the saying goes, but crying to be rewritten twenty or thirty times. I feel like a golf ball lying amid a mass of rocks at the foot of the towering Matterhorn. A letter from Rupert Hughes saying "stay in Italy until you've finished your book: work is almost impossible in America because of the depression, which is so great that every telephone call, knock at the door and letter brings a call for help from someone who's down and out." Don't like to think what may happen to us before *Rabble* is finished. It makes me change with Protean rapidity from a golf ball at the foot of the Matterhorn to an ostrich with his head in the sand.

25

I HAD a vague idea, at the beginning of 1932, that the task before me couldn't possibly be more difficult than *Captain Caution* had been. I'd forgotten that at the end of every *Saturday Evening Post* assignment, I had invariably noted in my diary: "This series is the toughest I ever tackled."

One of my early distractions in the writing of *Rabble* was caused by having to familiarize myself with all the occurrences in which those relatives of mine had been entangled at Ticonderoga, Hubbardton and Saratoga. That meant finding out all about the Indian nations who had sent detachments to fight for Burgoyne; and I was forced, almost against my will, to investigate simultaneously the Indians with whom Robert Rogers had dealt at an earlier date, and to cudgel my brain about the mysteries connected with Rogers' determination to find a Northwest Passage. I thought I had the title for that Indian book—*The White Devil;* but I couldn't get the Northwest Passage out of my mind. For example:

January 1, 1932: A letter from Maynard, the little antique dealer in Dorking: "A Mrs. Rowan, an American, insisted on taking some photos of my things, so to see whether she could help me sell them in America. I cannot imagine an Englishwoman doing such a kindly thing. The more I know of the right Americans, the more I wish that I had earlier emigrated there. My experience with my own people, aside from aristocrats, is that they make me wish to wring their necks. The same experience with your people makes me want to give them things. Their absolute trust in one is the nicest thing I have met in nearly thirty-five years' experience. I have an eternal regret that I did not go to the States thirty years ago (I hadn't the fare); for the last few years have proved to me that it is my spiritual home. I've had several whiskies, so I'm telling the truth."

That put me in mind of a half-forgotten quotation, and I couldn't rest until I unearthed it. I found it in Delteil's *Lafayette:* " 'What man has not his little America?' he reflects. Each man must some day discover America, under penalty of death. To discover America means to open one's eyes: to become one's self: to be."

Maynard was right; Delteil was right! And isn't every man, too, hunting his own Northwest Passage? I put that theme on paper in a single paragraph to go at the beginning of the book I some day hoped to write about Robert Rogers, for it was peculiarly applicable to Rogers; and in the next four years I must have rewritten that paragraph a thousand times before I got it the way I wanted it.

January 2: Struck the right title at last—*Rabble in Arms.* That was what Burgoyne, writing to Lord Rochfort, called the volunteers who fought at Bunker Hill; and having a dramatist's ear, he had the exact phrase. It describes 'em perfectly. They were undisciplined, rough, ragged, insubordinate—just a rabble in arms. Heavy snowstorm. Most people are as misinformed about history as they are about things in general. Everyone in America knows that Italy is "Sunny Italy." In that dreary book by Oman from which we got our Roman history in high school, Oman had Hannibal crossing the snowy Alpine passes with his elephants, and seeing before him "the soft warm haze of the Italian plains," or something like that. Soft warm haze be damned! As I write I'm wearing woolen underwear, two sweaters, felt boots, have a comforter wrapped twice around me from the waist down, with a muffler and a heavy winter overcoat around my upper body. The task of rising and hobbling to the bookshelves for a necessary source book, then getting back under wraps again, is almost exhausting.

§

From January 5 to January 8 I rewrote Chapters 2 and 3; and thereupon for the remainder of the month *Rabble* progressed comparatively smoothly, and ten chapters were written.

§

January 31: Tomorrow I must start writing the four articles for Lorimer, as our funds will be practically exhausted by the end of next month.

§

During the first three days of February I wrote the first article, went back to *Rabble* for one day while Mrs. Roberts was typing it; on the fifth started another article—"Dogs in a Big Way"—and finished it on the eighth. On the ninth I typed it, decided it was worthless, threw it in a drawer, and on the tenth started an article on Evangeline Adams and the shortcomings of astrologers. My bedroom workroom, once called the Torture Chamber, was re-named the Rot-Haus.

At noon on the fourteenth I finished the Evangeline Adams story. After devoting an hour to angry fulminations over advices from home which revealed that Willa Cather's cobwebby *Shadows on the Rock* had sold 175,000 copies, Edna Ferber's *American Beauty* 80,000 copies and *Lively Lady* 9,000 copies, I went to work on "Country Life in Italy."

On the fifteenth, between paragraphs of "Country Life in Italy," I exhumed "Dogs in a Big Way," hacked it to pieces, and fitted it together again. It seemed slightly less revolting than when I first wrote it, so sent it off to Lorimer.

On the twenty-third, having rewritten the Evangeline Adams article and "Country Life in Italy," I mailed them to Philadelphia and returned to *Rabble in Arms*. To my distress I couldn't add so much as a line to the manuscript—perhaps because I had turned overlong to another form of writing, or possibly because of nausea induced by an advertisement in the January number of the English *Current Literature:*

THE DEVIL'S CESSPOOL

A Brilliant Historical Novel

By Margaret Flowerdew

"Catharine gripped her white shoulder fiercely.

" 'You fool!' she whispered through her shut teeth, 'control yourself—your nerves are all to pieces! Much depends upon this night, and upon you. Fail me at your peril!' "

Would you read

Of tears and laughter of beautiful women . . . of the gay and fearless Henri de Navarre, King of the Huguenots—of his cousin, the mad King of France—of the sinister Catherine de Medici, steeped in crime—of the gorgeous, arrogant Henri de Guise?

You will find them all

In these pages, together with love—hate—romance—the color and perfume of bygone days. Read of the massacre of the Huguenots, an ineffaceable deed brought about by the command of a madman!

Obtainable from all booksellers 7/6 net. Publishers, The Literary Year Book Press, Liverpool.

Devil's Cesspool! "Shut teeth! Steeped in crime! Tears and laughter of beautiful women! Gorgeous, arrogant, sinister! Your nerves are all to pieces!" That, I suspect and fear, is the stuff one has to give the troops —a good representative historical novel, well sprinkled with white shoulders, Gadzooks, Odds bodikins, Marry-come-ups and Prithees (or is it Privies). Well, let Flowerdew do it. I can't.

§

February 24: Struggled on, lost and puzzled. I've certainly tackled a stinker. Read *In the Valley* by Harold Frederic, laid in 1778 but written in a sort of pre-Cambrian style that might have been used in a 1630 narrative. Thus it's phony, for the letters written by young Evelyn (in *The Evelyns in America*) around 1775 are as simple and clear as anything written today.

§

By the end of February I had finished thirteen chapters.

§

March 3: Anna says we can't spend a penny for anything except spaghetti until we get a check from the *Post*. All writers should learn to live on spaghetti for months on end. It's delicious.[1] Stopped reading *In the Valley* when I encountered a love passage in which the hero explains how pure he is, not even allowing himself to touch the heroine's skirt. I wish it could be distinctly understood that I do *not* write historical novels.

March 6: Finished re-reading Chambers' *Cardigan*. Those who shake their heads nowadays over Chambers' stuff, and wail, "Ah, how terrible that a man who could write *Cardigan* should descend to this!" don't know what they're talking about. *Cardigan* is cheap claptrap and fustian: no more a picture of the times than tourist-catalogue pictures of Italy are pictures of real Italy. It's plain mush; and if I had to choose between being well paid for such excrement or going back to work on a newspaper, I'd unhesitatingly pick the latter.

March 10: Reached page 45 and started a new chapter. Greatly cheered by a letter from the *Post* saying the first article had been received, and that a check was on its way—and so we're saved!

---

[1]See p. 390 in Appendix.

March 12: Edged along, halfway down page 47, doing a fair amount of work, but wholly in despair as to its quality and value. I fear I've tackled an impossibility. The technicalities connected with weaving these two campaigns of the Northern Army into a novel are just too damned difficult. Slugged through to the end of another chapter.

March 14: More and more impressed with the fat-headedness of American historians and biographers. Those who have dealt with Arnold, barring I. N. Arnold, have verged on the idiotic in their lack of penetration. Instead of Arnold's "God being money"—a favorite phrase with those who manufactured evidence against him (as do the English about Americans today)—he was most generous (five thousand dollars to Lamb to raise a company; serving without pay; supporting Warren's children and those of his friend Comfort Sage; gift of money to Henry the diarist when sick on the Chaudière; openhanded hospitality; gift of two pistols to Ethan Allen—in Fort Ticonderoga Museum: an unusually beautiful pair); and sufficiently intelligent to furnish his house with Savery block-front pieces, which ultimately were among the most prized of Lorimer's magnificent collection of furniture. All those Arnold biographies clearly show that their authors haven't the slightest understanding of generosity. Arnold, instead of being choleric and arrogant, as they claim, was self-effacing in his patriotism—willing to do anything and serve under anybody for the good of the country. He was a great and farsighted leader, thwarted and baffled at every turn by a God-awful assemblage of yokels and lack-wits.

March 15: Made a false start and had to throw yesterday's work away. A letter from the *Post* saying that the dog story was good and where should the check be sent. Glory be to God!

§

Newspaper or magazine reporting, to my way of thinking, is fun; but there isn't much fun connected with the writing of a novel. Childbirth, I've heard, has its unpleasant features; but my researches into that activity have convinced me that childbirth is sheer delirious joy by comparison with the task of wrenching a novel from the brain and transferring it to paper. I know that expectant mothers are frequently afflicted with nausea during the first three months or so of pregnancy; and I have also been told that most prospective mothers, toward the end of their pregnancy, are filled with a sense of health and well-being —to such a degree, at times, that they brazenly flaunt their condition in public, wholly oblivious of bulges and distentions—and can relieve their ultimate pains by the judicious use of sodium amytal.

The novelist, however, is afflicted with nausea during the entire period of his labors. He is acutely conscious at all times—even when asleep—of the burden within him, powerless to rid himself of it, and unable to obtain relief by the use of sodium amytal or any other drug or stimulant. It's true that writers seem to be gluttons for punishment, and by choice remain at their desks, despite their sweating and groaning, for twelve or fourteen hours at a stretch; equally true that those twelve or fourteen hours pass with inconceivable rapidity. It's true, too, that the author whose screams of agony have tortured those about him during his delivery will immediately, woman-like, put himself in a position certain to result in another long period of suffering.

But for the sake of those who want to write, I cannot too often emphasize the unfortunate truth that while there are many rapturous moments during some of the preliminaries to childbirth, there are none whatever before or during the birth of a novel.

March 18: Frightfully depressed after lunch. Couldn't make progress, and what little I made was of the dullest, stupidest and most irrelevant sort.

March 20: Started a new chapter. This book is not only causing me more anguish than any of the others, but looks worse than any of them.

March 21: Made better progress today than yesterday. As I get deeper and deeper into Arnold, I can't pick up a source book on the Northern Campaign without finding myself in a fury over the shockingly raw deal he received from the military peanuts who surrounded him—and over the contemptibly raw deal he has had ever since from mentally similar persons posing as historians and biographers.

March 22: A letter from Lorimer enthusing over the Evangeline Adams piece but cutting my rate $250 per story—which is only fair, since everybody everywhere is being cut. Even so, in three weeks of February I earned more from the *Post* than I did by putting in a year writing and rewriting *Arundel,* waiting six months for its publication, and collecting royalties for two years after publication. In despair because I can't get forward. Right now the task looks impossible.

March 26: Inserted 1,000 words on page 56 and struggled partly down page 57: am rapidly approaching the moment, thank God, when I can take the army to Isle Aux Noix and out of Canada. I hate the damned place as much as I did Siberia. Maybe the action will begin to move more rapidly when the whole crew sets off for Ticonderoga—but more likely it won't. I'm afraid it's hopeless.

April 2: Inextricably tangled and at a complete loss as to how to make the transitions to Valcour and Saratoga—how to make those events essential parts of the story. I think I'd drop the whole business if it weren't that there's a possibility of accomplishing what I started to do—to give, in fiction that can be read by any schoolboy, a complete picture of a military campaign that is imperfectly grasped or understood by many advanced students of military tactics. Extremely low in mind, low at dinner, low after dinner and even lower when badly bitten by a flea I couldn't locate to save my life. To bed at nine-thirty, wholly despondent. Madame Riedesel, in her *Journal,* speaks of Burgoyne's habit of entertaining the "beautiful wife of a commissary" at champagne suppers in his quarters. Madame Riedesel clearly states that she was Burgoyne's mistress. Which commissary? Who was the lady? I've got to know. I can use her. Can't these stupid damned historians find out *anything?* Wrote a dozen letters in an attempt to get a line on her.[2]

April 3: Read before rising in Cooper's *Spy.* No words (except his own) can tell the ludicrousness of Cooper's language. Children adore him, I'm told, and grownups who haven't read him since they were twelve years old speak of him affectionately as being merely a little old-fashioned. Received an editorial from the *Boston Herald* referring to Pulitzer Prize possibilities. Willa Cather seems to have the call, in the editorial writer's mind, for *Shadows on the Rock,* a thin sketch of an episode in sixteenth-century Quebec. Ben Williams and I received "also ran" mention. Ben might get it; but nobody in literary circles will ever give me a smell of a prize. I'm damned to begin with—a mere mercenary *Post* writer.[3]

April 4: Cracked page 64. Read further in *The Spy* with an ever-growing sense of wonder at the literary ineptitudes perpetrated by Cooper and endured by his readers for over a century—still, unhappily, endured today, as *The Spy* is required reading at St. Paul's School!

April 7: Woke at six and wrote 1,000 words before rising. Two gems of American literature arrived from one of those esoteric Paris publishing houses: one called *Bubu of Montparnasse,* the other *Sanctuary* by William Faulkner. They are all about sex and syphilis: all grimness and starkness: not a ray of humor or insight: two unclothed authors committing nuisances in a public park. When I expressed myself to Mr. Tarkington about the Faulkner masterpiece, and made inquiry as to who he was and how he got that way, Mr. Tarkington replied:

---

[2]See p. 414, Appendix.
[3]See p. 435, Appendix.

From your queries about Mr. Falconer, you must be an ignorant not to say loutish person literarily. I heard of him 'way last December during which by some odd mischance I stumbled upon a copy, of all things in the world! of *Scribner's* magazine for that month, and was quite startled to find that this periodical still runs—in its own way. It has an editor, evidently, and he did a kind of trumpeting for his contents, this Mr. Falconer being what was most trumpeted. According to the noise, Mr. F. is almost officially our Leader and Hero. Subsequent to the trumpeting, Mr. F. himself appeared exuding a short story, which, as I recall it, began something like this:

"*Over in the muddy field on the edge of our town a tall man in a* . *patched overcoat glanced up toward the sky and saw (he had walked out from the town which consisted of frame houses, drug stores, etc., and was founded about 1832 by a Baptist group of pioneers and now contained every sort of people and considered itself thoroughly prosperous, having a Mayor and Council elected the preceding November) an airplane from which a peculiar dot seemed to be hanging.*"

So you can see he has some pretty original ways and would like to get lots of notice from terribly literary people, and would. Outside of being different with parentheses and things now and then, and some traces of Stephen Crane, our Leader is often satisfactorily confusing in ways that demonstrate greatness.

To return to the record of *Rabble in Arms:*

April 11: ⅙ down page 71. This is the last book of this sort I ever want to write. The labor entailed is more grueling and exhausting than anyone can possibly realize, and the returns are so small that I soon won't be able to support those dependent on me. Just to help things along, the Italian farmer on the place today purchased two sheep, both strikingly reminiscent of William Randolph Hearst, and staked them near my workroom window, where they uttered endless vacuous bleatings. The Hearst sisters die tomorrow.

April 15–26: In such a state of despair and nerves over the seeming impossibility of getting *Rabble* under control that I tossed the manuscript in a trunk, locked the door of the Rot-Haus and we took a ten-day vacation to Rapallo, across the mountains to Parma; thence to Mantua, Padua, Venice and the glass factories of Murano; then south to Rimini and the postage-stamp-supported "republic" of San Marino; and then back across the mountains to Florence, many-towered San Gimignano, Siena and Porto Santo Stefano. On my return I found a letter from Mr. Tarkington, written in reply to one of mine in which I'd complained bitterly about my progress:

> Don't get down about *Rabble in Arms* [it read]. What you've done is probably inordinately better than you think, when you think that way. Anyhow, just go ahead and it will eventually happen. We're very susceptible about writing. A written Ms. often seems horrible, looks maybe a little better or maybe a little worse when printed; and then Fanny Stringer of the Massillon, Ohio, *Herald* or Edgar Brissot of the *Saturday Review* calls it a classic and it seems to be a work of genius. *Mary's Neck* now has the appearance of almost fulsome brightness because it's coming in as top best seller on the list; but a month ago when Miss Elizabeth Smith of the *New York Herald Tribune* reviewed it, and somebody sent me the clipping, and she said the style is a combination of *Penrod* and *The Plutocrat,* I felt I hadn't made myself clear, as I hadn't intended "Mr. Massey" to speak as the author did in either *Penrod* or *The Plutocrat,* and I've always thought that the manner in which a story was told constituted the style. This is why we ought never to read reviews. Miss Elizabeth Smith was quite favorable but informative, and I find I dislike her with some virulence for the gracious things she said.

> Brandt and young Otis Wiese of *McCall's* were here for a couple of hours the other day. Wiese had a letter written to a literary agent by a young man author. The agent had transmitted to this young man an offer of Doubleday, Doran to print a new book of his, they having printed a former one, and the letter ran on something like this:

> "*Yes, tell Doubleday, Doran I'll accept, but upon the condition that they give me a Tea, guaranteeing that Edna Ferber and other D.D. authors will be present. On my part I guarantee to wear a cutaway coat and striped trousers, new, but D.D. Company must agree to take these off my hands that same evening. Also, I would like the book to be published not in the clandestine manner they used with my first. People are sure to hear somehow or other that the book has been published; it's going to leak out one way or another, and also the news that I wrote it, so why not face the facts boldly from the start and come right out with it that such a book is actually in print and I had something to do with it?*" . . .

April 29: Filled three pages with crossed-out words. For a person in my position, a vacation is not only disrupting, but entirely unneeded. To talk of "needing" one is to kid one's self. To *want* one is something else again. I constantly want one, but to succumb is the height of silliness so far as work is concerned. It results in no new ideas: no rest: no refreshment. By taking one I lose the thread of my story, impair my physical condition, get extremely tired, squander time as well as resources, and lose thoughts that invariably dodge in and out of my head before I can put them on paper: eat things I don't want at times when I don't want them: endure innumerable unnecessary discomforts, and see so many sons of bitches that I'm too often distraught. Wasted the day hunting through source books, dry-mouthed with exasperation.

May 1: Read Lamb's *American War* and Hoffman Nickerson's *Turning Point of the Revolution.* Lamb is almost as dull as an historical novel.[4] Everything about *Rabble* is a mess—the book has petered out.

May 5: Stuck on page 76. Read how the Pulitzer Prize Committee had carried out Pulitzer's wishes by awarding the prize for the "American novel which best delineated the whole American atmosphere" to Pearl Buck's *The Good Earth,* a pleasantly written story of Chinese coolies in famine years in China. Poor old Pulitzer hoped to stimulate authors to write about the true American scene; then the committee assembled to carry out his wishes proceeds to do exactly what he planned to avoid. Year before last the prize was awarded to a simple tale of an Indian whore: the year before that to *Scarlet Sister Mary,* all about a Negro whore. So that's "depicting the American scene," is it? Why not write a piece about this for Lorimer, and give the Pulitzer Prize Committee something to think about?[5]

May 7: Reached page 78 and read with horror a pile of letters describing the frightfulness of the depression that has the United States in its grip. The value of our carefully made investments has shrunk to practically nothing. Had a violent argument after dinner. What, Anna wanted to know, had become of all the money that existed in 1929? I contended most of it was hot air in an inflated balloon and never existed at all. I had to admit, of course, that our savings had most emphatically existed, and were turned into investments reputed to be sound. Now our savings had gone somewhere, and Anna wanted to know where: also who had them. I didn't know the answer, and neither does anybody else, including Andy Mellon, Henry Morgenthau, and the financial editors of the *Times* and the *Wall Street Journal.*

May 10: ⅚ down page 79. Completely bogged. I remind myself of a

---

[4] Robert Graves subsequently turned Lamb's *American War* into an historical novel titled *Sergeant Lamb.* It lacked the value of Lamb's original narrative, and was consequently even duller than Lamb.

[5] See p. 397, Appendix.

person struggling in a swamp heavily grown up to thorns and creepers. The violence of my efforts is exhausting me, and I'm forging gradually in the right direction, but tearing my pants and half blinding myself while I do it; and progress is practically imperceptible. I know I never would have been satisfied unless I had tried to write this book; and now that I've started, I must go through with it, but never again! Never, *never,* NEVER again!

May 11: Unable to move forward because of seeming impossibility of weaving together my story and the tangled mass of detail that came between the retreat from Crown Point and the Battle of Valcour.

May 12: An English publisher showed signs of interest in *Arundel,* so read it again. Horrified to find how inept and tedious so much of it seems. All things considered, the critics treated me pretty kindly. Decided to revise it, starting right now. Walked down the cliffs, through the macchia of broom (smelling of grapes), rosemary and spini di Cristo, to the little beach at Cacciarella, where we sat on the rocks, looking across the wine-dark Ligurian Sea to Elba, Monte Cristo and Corsica, and once more rewrote *Arundel's* first chapter. Just off the beach a fisherman was dabbing for an octopus with a chunk of marble on the end of a line. He caught four octopi while I worked. (In the end I re-revised it another four times, so it might be called a 20-octopus chapter—or, since the book had thirty-six chapters—a 720-octopus revision.)

May 14: Cracked page 83 and shadow-boxed with the preliminaries to the Battle of Valcour Island. Went on revising *Arundel.*

May 15: News in the *Paris Herald* of May 13 that the Lindbergh baby had been found dead—a ghastly tragedy, and one that vaguely indicates the vast number of dangerous scoundrels in the world. We will now see whether John H. Curtis, boatbuilder, Rear Admiral Guy H. Burrage, retired, and Rev. H. Dobson Peacock, all of Norfolk, at once step forward to tell who it is they've claimed to be dealing with for the past month in order to obtain the return of the child "alive and well": whether Dr. J. F. Condon, Fordham professor, will reveal the other "abductors" from whom he says he's had advances: whether Gaston B. Means takes a rap for accepting a hundred thousand dollars from Mrs. E. B. McLean in return for a promise to deliver the child! Enmeshed in the Battle of Valcour and realized only too keenly that most of the historians who tried to report that battle were as off key as Curtis, Burrage, Dobson and Peacock.

May 16: The incessant squirpling of sparrows from daybreak to dusk is dreadful beyond words. Continued making countless changes in *Arundel.*

May 21: Lindbergh landed in Paris five years ago, and maybe that young man hasn't had five crowded, newspaper-ridden years! He achieved fame in a day, and all the grief in the world along with it. He moved to New Jersey to escape the pests, newspaper and civilian, who were making his life hell; and now he's abandoning his New Jersey house for some other hell. Dr. Jenner was more than right when he said, "Never aim, my friend, at being a public character, if you love domestic peace." According to today's paper, the gullible public is beginning to realize that Professor Condon is sour as a green apple. The newspapers and police are all at sea. They always are in any big showdown. A murderer almost has to label himself and turn himself over to the police by some fool action, if he's to be caught—witness the Elwell case, the Movie Director Desmond case, the Dorothy Arnold case, the Charley Ross case, the Mate Bram case, the Lizzie Borden case: none of them solved. The world is full of false alarms: doctors, authors, lawyers, bankers, soldiers, statesmen: none worth the powder to blow 'em to hell: all posing as full of inside stuff, when they haven't a scrap of it. I saw that clearly in Washington. Politicians posing as the holders of a million state secrets; and not one of 'em with any secret at all: lobbyists "able to deliver" this, that and the other, and able to deliver nothing!

(This entry has nothing whatever to do with writing, of course, but is left in to show the tension and exasperation that envelop a writer who is trying to write one book (*Rabble in Arms*), revise another (*Arundel*), and plan a third (*Northwest Passage*).

May 24: Came to a complete standstill on *Rabble*. The sparrows are unbelievably harrowing and brain-piercing. The gentleman who bought our Palm Beach house writes he is unable to make his payments. Lorimer gave *Captain Caution* a second reading and today replied:

> At the moment the serial situation is no better. I had hoped, when last I talked with you, that advertising would pick up so that we could go back to our three serial schedule, which we maintained for some years. We have had to drop to two, with the possibility of only one during the next few months; and until business picks up I do not see how we can handle another story of the good old days. I have several serials on the list that I have been carrying for over a year in the hope that things would pick up, but I can see no immediate hope. I will talk the situation over with you at greater length when I see you in June.

Cabled my New York agent, Carl Brandt: "Get *Captain Caution* from *Post* and use your judgment."

Our financial situation is, to put it mildly, desperate. Just to keep up my spirits, wrote a sign that should be hung on our front gate in Maine if we're to keep our heads above water:

> Mrs. Roberts does the housework and marketing, and cooks the meals. Mr. Roberts is working on a novel ten hours a day. Their telephone is disconnected. They will not go to a hotel to answer telephone calls. Telegrams are delivered by mail. They do not want any sweet grass baskets, Fuller brushes, new photographs, table linen, silk hosiery or magazine subscriptions. They have heard all about the Depression. Mr. Roberts does not make public addresses of any sort under any circumstances, and has had to stop autographing books. Both Mr. and Mrs. Roberts will appreciate it if callers who have servants will give Mrs. Roberts plenty of time to run the house.

And with that we packed our manuscripts, notes, source books, journals and personal effects, and returned to America and a depression that was ruining millions, throwing other millions out of work, filling every heart with a profound fear of the future, emptying trains, taxicabs, theaters. The Grand Central Station was an empty tomb in which less than a score of gray-faced travelers wandered dejectedly across its vast floor.

Once again we were saved from disaster by Lorimer, who agreed to my proposal to write three articles for which I already had the material —"An Inquiry into Diets," "The Truth About a Novel," and the Pulitzer Prize story.

That Pulitzer Prize story is reprinted[6] as a warning to men of vision who may be tempted to establish, in their wills, worthwhile awards to authors who write about the American scene.

---

[6]See p. 397, Appendix.

WITH the Pulitzer Prize story out of the way, I went back to revising *Arundel* again, starting from the beginning. That revision, which had begun on the twelfth of May, was not finished until October 18. I re-read the book and re-read it and re-read it, with each re-reading catching repetitions, redundancies and awkward phrases—and each time, I'm not ashamed to confess, thoroughly enjoying Phoebe Marvin, Cap Huff, Steven Nason and all their friends. I have no record of the number of times that book was read in longhand manuscript, revision, typescript revision, galley proof revision, page proof revision, and then again in type, galley proof and page proof for the revised edition. Certainly it was read more than ninety times.

This is set down, not in admiration at my efforts, or amazement at my staying qualities, but solely by way of suggesting that there's more to writing than meets the eye, or than the aspiring writer can obtain from a series of lectures on How to Do It.

For the same reason, and for that alone, I keep on with the details of the slow and nauseating progress of *Rabble in Arms*:

September 19: Booth finished *Presenting Lily Mars* on the 17th. Today he telephoned to ask whether I wanted to read him the first twenty-five chapters of *Rabble*. Did I! Went immediately to the Floats [his ramshackle boathouse converted from an ancient fishhouse, overhanging the Kennebunk River] and read three chapters. His only comment was that it moved more rapidly than the version I had read him on the preceding autumn. I felt the story bored him.

September 20: Spent the day revising the first three chapters to conform to Booth's suggestion that I include more details about the exiling of American Loyalists from New England. I had already found that the story of American Loyalists had never been adequately told.

Doubted that I could tackle such a hefty job, but started today to accumulate a complete Loyalist library.

September 21: Added the Loyalist passages, revised both *Arundel* and *Rabble,* and resumed reading to Booth. He denied being bored: called it "a fine picture, filled with all the feeling of the time."

September 23: To New York to persuade my publishers to replate *Arundel.* They put me off with vague promises. To Philadelphia, where Lorimer again saved our lives by okaying my suggestion for two more stories.

September 26: Struggled on with Booth, pointed up Lanaudiere, and worked out a more sympathetic way of handling Doc Means.

September 27: Read to Booth.

September 28: Rewrote three chapters and read them to Booth.

September 29: Same thing.

September 30: Rewrote all morning and read to Booth all afternoon.

October 2: Worked on *Arundel* and *Rabble* all morning: read to Booth all afternoon, making considerable progress. Everything's all right, he says; but I greatly fear he's merely being kind.

October 3: Revised *Arundel* until 2 A.M.

October 4: Worked on both *Arundel* and *Rabble,* snatched a sandwich and a glass of milk, and to Booth's. Reached the point where the army ascends Chambly Rapids. He insists it's all interesting. Perhaps not to Mrs. Kirkby; but to him, yes!

October 5: Finished the setting copy of the revised *Arundel,* and started revising it once more before sending it to Doubleday. Scrambled ahead in my revision of *Rabble;* then to Booth's at two-thirty and pushed around a score of paragraphs.

October 7: Worked from 6 A.M. to noon on revision; then to the Floats after lunch and read the Isle Aux Noix episode. Booth couldn't have been more enthusiastic: wholly right, he said: exactly balanced between horror and the everyday humor that makes for realism.

October 8: Read two chapters of *Arundel* to Anna. Slashed more passages from the Swan Island episode and made the joints. Then ripped approximately five pages from *Rabble* and to Booth's again. He showed me how I could straighten out the Crown Point episode.

October 9: Read *Arundel* aloud again and cut some more.

October 10: Read and cut *Arundel,* and tinkered with *Rabble;* then to the Floats and pounded another chapter into shape.

October 11: Retouched *Rabble,* and to the Floats at two-thirty. Booth had me read him all the passages in which Ellen appears. He says he finds himself thinking often about her, and he'd like to see and hear more of her.

October 12: Rewrote Ellen's misunderstanding with Peter Merrill, when Merrill suspects that Ellen is being used by Marie de Sabrevois. Read it to Booth in the afternoon. He was still dissatisfied with it, so we tinkered with it and pushed it around for two hours.

October 13: Rewrote the scene in which Cap Huff and Doc Means get drunk on thistled rum; then to the Floats and read it to Booth. "Go over it again," he said, "and we'll fatten it." He takes an almost fatherly interest in Cap, but in reverse: the noisier Cap is and the drunker he gets, the oftener he steals and makes an unconscionable nuisance of himself, the more Booth likes him. This strikes me as odd, as he never permits such rough characters in any of his books. As we talked additional gaucheries into Cap's and Doc's speech and behavior, we laughed until we cried. A fine picture of the Revolution, Booth says: it has wholly changed his conception of it: I mustn't let myself be discouraged, or allow anything to stop me from going on.

October 14: Read another *Arundel* chapter to Anna, looking for repetitions and awkwardnesses. Tinkered with the pre-Valcour stuff in *Rabble*. To the Floats later and spent three hours discussing the best way of handling the episode of the building of the fleet at Skenesboro; and as a result, the fog which surrounded me in Italy almost vanished.

October 15: Read on to Anna in the *Arundel* revision; then to the Floats, and outlined to Booth the events preceding Saratoga. As we talked about it, an end for *Rabble* took shape and became clear.

October 16: Immediately after breakfast read to Anna in the *Arundel* revision. We're nearing the end and still catching blemishes. It seems as though they are like stones in a New England meadow, and work to the surface overnight. After lunch to the Floats to finish with Booth. Read him the Valcour battle. He was enthusiastic: said it made him want to get and read a factual account of Valcour, but beneath the facts he'd always see Cap Huff, Nason, Merrill and Bickford. Told him all factual accounts of Valcour are full of mistakes, misstatements, omissions and contradictions: he'd better stick to *Rabble*.

October 17: Read *Arundel* all day, eliminating many more repetitions and "very's."

October 18: Completed the revision of Chapter 33 in *Arundel,* so that's finished. Finished, he says!

October 20: Back to *Rabble* again and found I had innumerable piecings and carpenterings to perform in the earlier chapters.

October 25: Brandt today wrote that *Captain Caution* has now been to every slick magazine in the United States, and has been unhesitatingly rejected by all of them—*Pictorial Review, Red Book, Ladies'*

Home Journal, Cosmopolitan, American. As a last resort, he had sent it to *Adventure,* which doesn't pay much (we're now in a situation where we need anything we can get if we're to stick it out for another winter); but the editor of *Adventure* had written that slackening of interest in the principal characters had killed all possibility of making *Captain Caution* into a serial. As a result, Brandt thought the story should now be withdrawn. Booth, when I told him about this last refusal, made caustic comments on anyone who could talk about a slackening of interest in the action-packed pages of *Captain Caution.*

October 27: Rewrote the smallpox scene in *Rabble* and read it to Booth.

October 29: Completed the revision of the first twenty-five chapters of *Rabble,* and Anna started to type it.

October 30–November 14: This period was spent in writing articles for the *Post,* and carrying on a campaign to persuade my publishers to replate *Arundel.* I had proposed that the cost be gradually repaid out of royalties; and I was determined to have it done because *Arundel* was being used in more and more schools and colleges, and must therefore be as right as I could make it. My publishers, however, holding it to be unnecessary, shrank from committing themselves to the undertaking. My bitter complaints reached Mr. Tarkington's ears and led him to take a hand in the proceedings. He telephoned Doubleday that unless they agreed to my proposals I would certainly take *Rabble in Arms* to another publisher. Mr. Tarkington added coldly that he considered I would be justified in so doing if my demands for replating were any longer evaded, but that *Rabble in Arms* was going places some day and ought to be retained on the Doubleday list.

That ended the battle, and the rewritten *Arundel* was sent to the printers. It wasn't bad, I thought—thought, too, that perhaps, at last, I knew how to do it.

I soon found out that I didn't.

December 6, 1932: Sailed for Italy, hoping to finish *Rabble* by midsummer; but before settling down to *Rabble,* wrote two articles for the *Post* and carefully revised the 183 galley proofs of the re-set *Arundel,* which arrived in Italy on January 15—a task on which I worked day and night for eleven days. Again to my amazement, I was forced to make innumerable changes—to correct typographical errors undiscovered by proofreaders, and for purposes of clarification and strengthening. So extensive were my alterations that I felt I should somehow make up for them, so altered the proofs in such a way that all one-word lines were eliminated. This "saved" 7,200 lines and short-ened the book by twenty pages—which meant that Doubleday would in the end save the price of several tons of paper. But will Doubleday be grateful? No: they'll squawk because the changes will cost $122.49.

Anna says I'm hacking these rewritten galleys worse than I did those of the original in 1929. Why not compare writing to human rela-tionships? Young people, for example, are eager to make friends with everybody they see and meet; yearn to be with them constantly; but after they acquire wisdom and understanding, they realize that most people are silly or ignorant or malicious or futile or opinionated or wasteful or just plain damned fools, and take care to avoid most of them. Similarly, when a writer starts to write, any combination of words satisfies him; but the more he learns, the more he is revolted by words, phrases and forms of expression that in the beginning seemed harmless. Sinclair Lewis, for instance, can't write anything as simple as "he said" or "she said." It's "he jeered, she mused, she wailed, he grumbled, she sobbed, he growled, he yawned, he worried, he snarled, he muttered, he mumbled, he rumbled, he bumbled, she chirped, she caroled, he fretted, she condescended, she drawled, he blatted, he stormed, he thundered" . . . and Lewis gets the Nobel and the Pu-litzer prizes . . . and his sentences bang along like a two-cylinder motor all mucked up with carbon.

January 19, 1933: Typed for *Rabble* a chronology from May 30 to October 13, 1776, along with the plot incidents of the building of the fleet: also wrote a 2,000-word interpretation of Arnold as Arnold would have appeared to Peter Merrill. Now if anything should happen to me, my intentions will be clear and the book can be finished by somebody else. Spent the afternoon and evening on two galleys, rewriting pas-sages that may seem obscure—such as Arnold's account of being fined for whipping an informer.

January 27: Mailed the revised *Arundel* proofs to Doubleday. Stuck the chronology and outline of *Rabble* on the wall over my desk, along-side the large-scale maps of the Ticonderoga-Skenesboro-Saratoga-Albany section, threw away the start I had already made on the building of the Valcour fleet, began all over again on manuscript page 93, and wound up by writing long letters to Booth, Hoffman Nicker-son, Mother, Chapelle and a man in Hythe, England, who was walking across a common on a cloudless Sunday morning and had a fish fall through the paper he was reading—the latter in behalf of Charles Fort, who studies such phenomena. To bed at 2 A.M. and read in *War and Peace.*

January 28: Tried to work, but found myself completely befuddled and confused by the incompetence and mussiness of historians—especially those who wrote about Arnold. They read as though they had been hired to put everything about Arnold in the worst possible light, without regard to truth or the findings of military experts like Mahan, Hoffman Nickerson, General Greene, General Rogers, Justin Smith.

January 31: ¼ down 96. Attempted to straighten out the Valcour battle line-up, which is sadly misrepresented in all the histories and biographies. At Ticonderoga some years ago I found a booklet, *Ticonderoga in History* by Helen Ives Gilchrist, M.A. It has a section devoted to Valcour, and a long, imposing bibliography. Every important fact about Valcour was wrong, even to the date. It was fought October 11 and October 13. Gilchrist has it fought on the twelfth. Decker is even worse in his *Benedict Arnold.* I. N. Arnold's *Life of Arnold,* good as it is, blunders lamentably on the subject of Valcour. Admiral Mahan's account is woefully deficient. All the diarists differ, but nobody notes or attempts to explain the differences.

February 7: ⅓ down 105. Worked out the Valcour line-up to my satisfaction. A Columbia historian lists the only present-day Americans who will be remembered in the future—46 of 'em: Wilson, Hoover (for relief work), Borah, Hughes, Brandeis, Holmes, Senator Sheppard for the 18th Amendment, Senator Norris, Mellon, Baker, Edith Wharton, Leonard Wood, William J. Bryan, Governor Smith, Dawes, House, Edison, Millikan, Professor Michaelson of Chicago "who proved that the speed of light was the same in all directions"—somebody ought to prove that white is white from all directions—Steinmetz, O. and W. Wright, Irving Langmuir (chemist), the Mayos, Nicholas Murray (Stuffed Shirt) Butler, John Dewey, Lindbergh, James J. Hill (railroads), Eugene O'Neill, both Rockefellers, Morgan, Carnegie, Rosenwald, Simon Guggenheim, Pershing, General Bliss, Roscoe Pound, W. R. Hearst, Adolph Ochs, Felix Adler, Harry Emerson Fosdick, Franklin Giddings, Eugene Debs and Sam Gompers. Nuts!

February 8: ¼ down 106, bringing Arnold to Skenesboro. I suppose I'm going into this fleet-building business in too much detail, but the miracle that Arnold accomplished at Skenesboro has never been sufficiently emphasized or understood, and it can only be put across by hammering at it.

February 14: Cracked page 112 and got away from Skenesboro, which I had left partly finished last May in order to write the Valcour battle.

February 15: For the first time this winter failed to make my daily stint of 1,200 words—perhaps because I came across, in a book by one of these modern historians, some speculations about ragtime, and when and where it originated. He thought around 1901. Their inability to find out things is incomprehensible! The Negro band in Dartmoor Prison played ragtime in 1815. These pundits think that the word "flivver" originated with Henry Ford's contribution to civilization, and that the word "buddy" is derived from "bedfellow"; whereas the truth is that the verb "to fliv" has been thieves' argot for "fail" for centuries, and "buddy" has been Southern for "brother" for two hundred years.

February 22: Touched 119 and damned all historians. Hadden says the British and American fleets were 700 yards apart. His map shows them one mile apart. Jones says they were 350 yards apart. Mahan says they fought at point-blank range—150 yards.

February 28: ¼ down 123. In despair over my failure to get ahead; then counted up exactly what I'd done in the twenty-eight days of this month and found I'd progressed 32,000 words, in addition to altering and adding a great deal to what I wrote last year, so maybe it hasn't been as bad as I think.

March 10: ½ down 132. Had confirmation from Ticonderoga of my insistence that the row galleys were two-masted and lateen-rigged. Nearly finished the battle on the lake. Don't believe I'll ever have the strength to write another book of this type. Winston Churchill wrote four and as a result was comfortable for life. This is my fourth, but all four of them together have reduced us to penury and brought us nothing but depression, grief, altercations with publishers, and endless grueling toil without any letup. I suspect I've wasted two years on *Rabble.* Ah, well; may as well have a full dose to wind up on! And if I hadn't done it, I couldn't have got *Arundel* replated, since I'd have had no talking point with which to persuade Doubleday.

March 15: ½ down 138 and received page proofs of the revised *Arundel*—638 pages. Can't understand it. The revised edition's shorter by 40,000 words, and it's twenty pages longer than the original version —something like the miracle of the loaves and fishes.

March 30: Finished page 150 and feel as if I were on the verge of a complete collapse. In addition to the unending chipping of the sparrows, and the roaring of bombers and fighter planes that constantly encircle the house, a new military road is being built a hundred yards downhill from us, and the clanking of hammers as they drill holes for dynamiting has become brain-piercing.

April 4: Cracked 154. The rock drillers went on a ten-hour day yesterday and now drill steadily from sunup to 6 P.M.—a hell's tattoo in the brain. Up to yesterday I was able to work from 5 to 7:30 P.M. without mental anguish. Now we must reorganize our entire day and push our lunch hour forward to two o'clock, so to take advantage of the cessation of drilling and rock pounding between twelve and two. The airplane squadrons at Orbetello have been doubled, and buzz about us like a giant plumber's blowtorch roaring in a tin wash boiler.

April 14: Cracked page 164. This job of getting Merrill, Doc Means and Verrieul back into the war after their winter with the Sacs and Foxes, re-introducing Marie, Nathaniel, Cap Huff, the Ticonderoga garrison, the British camp followers, and explaining the army's condition, the heat, the stupidity, the blundering, and at the same time making it all seem real, believable and understandable in about 10,000 words has me hanging on the ropes. I don't wonder West Pointers find the Saratoga campaign almost impossible to understand. I suppose it can be done, but it never *has* been done, and all the books on the subject are bewildering and muddled. Ran into a snag and had to throw away half a longhand page. Made a fresh start and still got nowhere. Panicky over the Indian stuff, and want to move on to the final episode, but can't find the way to do it. Extremely nervous and upset over the whole business, and feel half off the handle—despondent and almost hopeless.

April 17: Cracked page 166. Disturbed and depressed beyond measure by the manner in which *Rabble* seems to have petered out—vanished into thin air. Certainly the only way to bridge the gap between '76 and '77 campaigns in such a way that people can have an understanding of the part played by Indians in the Revolution is by means of an Indian episode, but I seem to have made a mess of it. Yesterday and today, after dry-mouthed worrying, I've been as exhausted and useless as though I'd been on a ten-day drunk—hollow-eyed, discouraged, barely able to sit up straight. I'll never have the strength to embark on another novel of this sort. It's too agonizing.

April 23: Touched page 171. Still all at sea over the end of the Indian part. Again tried to plan ahead, but can't get things clear. The whole business is dreadfully involved, and I fear I'm effectually botching the last third of the book. Got an idea for a final chapter, and made a lot of notes on it. Also changed and added to the scene in which Merrill first meets Ellen Phipps. Anna has reached page 520 in typed pages, and page 143 in the longhand pages. Revised two chapters. The whole thing seems fruitless, boring and a waste of two years' efforts.

April 30: Started Chapter 54 and also wrote a first draft of that final chapter. Received the revised page proofs of *Arundel* and read until 4 A.M., correcting through page 130.

May 1: ⅘ down page 177. All bitched up and involved, trying to get Merrill, Huff, Means and Joe Phipps away from Langlade and back into the plot. Corrected 100 more *Arundel* page proofs, discovering innumerable typographical errors.

May 4: Started Chapter 55. Also finished the *Arundel* proofs. Anna and I between us have caught over fifty errors that the Doubleday proofreaders missed. This *Arundel* revision was started almost exactly one year ago. I used to think I had written *Arundel* in a matter of nine months, but I was wrong. Started to rewrite the beginning of the Skenesboro episode in *Rabble.* Sunk in gloom and despair over its hopelessness.

May 6: ⅕ down page 182. Bored beyond words by a *New York Times* Book Review Section carrying enormous ads of a book supposed to have strong reader appeal because it deals with "mysterious, dirty rites of naked savages"! Additionally sunk by the realization that I'm bungling the conclusion of *Rabble* and will be fighting all summer to finish it—if it doesn't finish me first.

May 8: Started Chapter 56 and squeezed myself into a meeting between Ellen, Marie, Nathaniel, Joe Phipps and Doc Means—an extremely difficult situation. If I can only get it behind me somehow, and get *on!* Get *on!* My God, I feel as though this writing might continue forever and forever. Anna is retyping the first section as insurance against loss of my corrections. Our days aren't half long enough—which is a lot better than having them seem far too long.

May 12: ⅗ down 189. Escaped from my Indians, damn 'em! Killed Verrieul and got the others into the fort. Now comes the retreat to Saratoga and the big blow-off. I need about a month and a half to block it out effectively before starting to revise—a month and a half here, I mean: not a month and a half in Maine with its daily quota of human drones. Anna has been hitting twenty-seven typed pages a day —six unbroken hours of typing, which is pretty stout going.

May 17: Finished 195. Greatly disturbed over the difficulty of making Peter Merrill's pro-Revolutionary arguments sound as reasonable as Nathaniel's Loyalist arguments. The logic lies on Nathaniel's side; it was wholly illogical for the Continental Army, at certain periods, to go on fighting. This makes things awkward when you're trying to make fiction real to the reader.

May 23: ⅘ down 200. Anna has completed the typing through page 190, Chapter 57, so we have a little additional insurance against loss.

I find myself dreaming hideously that I have lost the only existing copy of the result of two years' heartbreaking toil. Filled two large packing cases with source books from the Congressional Library and on the Burgoyne campaign, together with all the journals, diaries and Robert Rogers material obtained from London during the winter, and shipped them to Naples to be put on the *Vulcania.*

May 25: Finished Chapter 59 on page 202 and tinkered with several rough spots in the past ten pages. The whole damned thing is rough. Whether it can be sawed, planed, pounded and sandpapered into shape is highly dubious.

May 29: Finished Chapter 60 on page 205, entered a synopsis of the remainder of the book on page 206, and left Porto Santo Stefano for Naples, where Coert du Bois certified our income tax returns at the consulate general. He gave me a pain in the neck by showing me a report to the effect that J. P. Morgan had paid no income tax whatever for three years. I don't know how it's done; but I do know that if *we* tried anything like that, we'd land in jail.

May 30–June 12: Returned to New York by the *Vulcania,* completely exhausted and incapacitated by the winter's work. Unable to do anything but lie in my berth and read—*100,000,000 Guinea Pigs, Pageant* (a revolting Tasmanian story), Lewis' *Ann Vickers,* Baum's *Secret Sentence,* Delafield's *Provincial Lady in London* and *Good Man's Love,* Bromfield's *Modern Hero,* Zweig's *Young Woman of 1914, The Kennel Murder Case*—pretty punk stuff, all of it. Kept revising *Rabble* and started a campaign to find out the exact manner in which Burgoyne's camp followers, sutlers and women were disposed of when the British were moving up to attack Ticonderoga. Felt lower than ever about *Rabble:* it seems wholly rambling and diffuse.

June 15: Slightly cheered by the publication of the rewritten *Arundel,* though nobody else gives a damn. Had sent copies to the M.I.T. Department of English and to Margaret Deland, asking them to destroy their earlier editions. They, like my publishers, had not been amused. "What's the idea of doing that?" one of the M.I.T. professors asked. "It read all right the way it was."

Margaret Deland wrote:

> . . . I never heard of anything so dreadful as your suggesting that I burn my original copy of *Arundel.* Of course, I am delighted with the new book, and I *suppose* the boiling down is all right; but I am not going to take any chances of losing any old friends in the way of phrases or thoughts, or even words. In fact, I am almost afraid to read

the revised version!—for fear you will have left out anything I especially care about. No doubt it is all very well to have tightened up
pages here and there; but the first writing was good enough for *me!*
For instance, I am not going to say that I am willing to lose the
extraordinary beauty of—

*"Just after the sun had risen, and the wind had swung into the
south, my father died. It was as though all our shelter had been
snatched from us, so that we stood helpless and alone."*

Of course I admit that—

*"Just after the sun had risen, and the wind had swung into the
south, my father died"*—

is dramatically noble; but snatching away the "shelter" of Love, is a
drama of the soul.

I suppose I might as well confess that when I dipped into the new
book here and there (I haven't yet seriously begun to read it), I expected to find places where you had robbed me; but I am compelled,
in honesty—if grudgingly—to say that, except for the deletion of these
lines I quoted, I haven't yet found them. On the contrary, you have
done your boiling down beautifully, and I know that, from the stand-
point of the general reader, it will probably be thought an improvement. The trouble with me is that I love words; and when I find a
felicitous phrase, I don't want anybody, not even the author, to
monkey with it!

One of the extraordinary things about the first *Arundel,* is its unfailing psychological truth. There isn't a place which doesn't ring true
to the effect of events upon the human soul. I have a theory that
permanent literature must deal with Truth—and Truth is so much
deeper than facts! Very few historical novels do that. They just hand
out facts. Do you suppose that is because it is mighty hard for most
of us, in writing of a period—its manners, customs, happenings—to
recognize a psychology of which we have had no personal experience? *Facts* are easy enough; but their reaction upon the personality
is another matter. Did it ever strike you that the permanent books,
beginning with the *Odyssey,* deal so entirely with Truth, that the
facts, which may or may not be exact, are of no great importance to
us? We really do not *know* that Alcinous had a "tall light waggon
with a high tilt"; but we are sure of the tenderness of his heart
towards Nausicaa when he says, "My child, I do not grudge you the
mules." These words show us that eternal thing—a father's heart. In
that enchanting scene where the girls on the beach play ball, and the
salt-encrusted Ulysses, emerging from the bushes, tries to "cajole

white-armed Nausicaa with honeyed words"—is as everlastingly true as a photograph of Kennebunkport—to say nothing of being far more beautiful! It is this extraordinary feeling for the truth of things that makes me love *Arundel*—you never fall down on the relative value of fact and truth. So, if you have cut out any of these lines of beauty and value, I shall call on you and wring your neck! By the way, did I tell you what a dear, gentle old lady said to me about *Arundel,* when it first came out? She read it, every word, here by my fireside, and when she finished it, she looked up at me, with beautiful, grave old eyes, and said, "This book may not be a best seller, but it is a best liver." I hasten to add that I think she meant it might not *immediately* be a best seller; but certainly she was right about its being a "best liver" —which means, ultimately, a best seller.

One thing I must thank you for; I am so rich in having two copies of *Arundel,* that now I shall be able to reserve one for my own especial pleasure in the way of *marking things I like!* The other copy can go into my spare room, so that people who come to see Miss Annable and Roger[1] and me can turn on their midnight electricity, and not be interrupted by my marks of admiration in the margins! . . .

---

[1]Miss Annable was Mrs. Deland's secretary. Roger was Mrs. Deland's elephantine sheep dog, who had a delusion that he was a frail, sylph-like creature, able to snuggle down in anyone's lap.

Kennebunkport, June 19, 1933: Booth, who has been working on a story, "Little Marie from Kansas City," finished it today and asked me to start reading *Rabble* to him tomorrow.

June 20: Started at Chapter 25, where I'd left off last autumn, and read through Chapter 30.

June 21: Revised and rewrote all morning; then to the Floats and read half through Chapter 33. Don't see how Booth can stick it.

June 22: Revised and rewrote all morning. Extremely sunk at the prospects and outlook. The whole book seems pure tripe. Read to Booth for an hour in the afternoon, getting half through Chapter 35. Harrowing work, because of slow progress and the need of re-touching almost every sentence.

June 23: Read again to Booth, reaching Chapter 43. Too exhausted to do further work, so read Stendhal's *Chartreuse of Parma* and not particularly cheered by learning that *Chartreuse of Parma* sold about 18 copies a year for a long, long time.

June 24: Read to Booth, getting through page 500. Everything's okay, he says: stop being funereal. He refused to consider cutting any of the battle details. Heard from the Henry Baldwin who is one of Arnold's descendants. He said he had provided John Fiske with considerable Arnold material, as Fiske intended to write a book that would portray Arnold as I had, but that Fiske died before he could do it. Nice letter, but that's an ominous note about Fiske dying.

June 25, 26, 27, 28: Read to Booth each day. We tore the Indian stuff completely to pieces, threw away half of it, then rewrote it. Doubleday wants delivery of the completed manuscript in August (220,000 words having already been put in type), so that they can publish on September 13; and unless I let them have it in August, publication will be postponed until spring. Don't see how I can do the former, but if we wait for spring publication, I'll never get going on something else. Booth said to go ahead and promise August delivery. Why choose a lucky date like the thirteenth? Got my fingers on nine helpful books—*The Private Soldier Under Washington,* Fisher's *Struggle for American Independence,* Schlesinger's *Colonial Merchants in the American Revolution,* three Wisconsin Historical Society volumes, *Black Hawk,* and *France in the American Revolution.*

July 4: Revised, rewrote and to the Floats at two-thirty: reached the scene in the camp followers' camp, where Merrill finds Nathaniel, Ellen Phipps and Marie de Sabrevois. Don't see how Booth can stand it, but he seems to think it's all right.

July 5: Rewrote all morning and worked with Booth both afternoon and evening, reaching Chapter 59. It's all right, he says: if he were reading it, he'd be interested.

July 6: Read to Booth again in the evening, but got hung up on one page and rewrote it a dozen times. How in Christ's name does anyone learn how to write?

July 7: Worked all morning and all afternoon, revising and rewriting sentences that Booth hadn't quite liked.

July 8: Got Wayne's Orderly Book and Tryon's book on medicine, which lets me build up Doc Means a little. Sunk in gloom. In the evening read to Booth and finished Chapter 60, which is as far as I've gone.

July 11: Tried to get a start on Chapter 61, but prevented by a score of petty annoyances: screaming of children, hammering and banging of carpenters. This would be a wonderful world if it weren't for the people in it.

July 12: Again fruitlessly tried to embark on Chapter 61, but prevented by shouting golfers, a rattling motor-mower, unending howling and screaming.

July 13: Dan Longwell and Russell Doubleday arrived and gave me a schedule that must be followed if we're to publish on October 25. It calls for delivery of sixty-one manuscript chapters on August 1, galley proofs back on the fourteenth, galley proofs corrected August 21, and corrected page proofs to be in their hands the end of August: entire book to be in their hands September 5: entire corrected page proofs to be in their hands October 8. To add to the peace and quiet, Mr. and Mrs. Lorimer arrived for a week's visit.

July 14: Tried to write a complete outline of *Rabble* for Longwell to show Doubleday salesmen. Picked up Lorimer at Breakwater Court and took him to see Booth, from whom he'd like to pry serials for the *Post* and *Ladies' Home Journal*. *Captain Caution* seems to have slipped his mind. He did, however, show a little curiosity about *Rabble,* and asked if he could see the first part of it, so let him have the carbon copy.

July 15–16: Finished Longwell's outline, but unable to work because of having to be with the Lorimers and Longwell.

July 17: Lorimer returned the manuscript, saying merely that it was too long. I was neither surprised nor disappointed, perhaps because of numbness from overwork. Started a final revision of the typed section of *Rabble*. I must revise fifty pages a day in order to send off the first sixty-one chapters by August 1, at the same time working every night and all night on the remaining chapters. Revised 226 pages today —an enormous chore.

July 18: Lorimer said he'd planned to have me do a series for him at once; but told him I couldn't do it, as I had to finish *Rabble*. He said all right: come to Philadelphia as soon as I was through, and he'd have something for me. Asked him to give *Captain Caution* another chance, and he said he would if I'd send it to him around the middle of August. All these distractions, social activities and unending tumults, coupled with the staggering amount of work that lies ahead, make me feel like a cornered animal waiting for the club to fall.

July 19: Revised through page 470, and Anna had to retype twenty-one pages.

July 21: Corrected through page 602.

July 22: Moved from Stall Hall across the street to Blue Roof, where gates and doors can be locked against callers. Marveled at the ineptitude of Arnold's biographers. Oscar Sherwin speaks of Arnold presenting some Indians with "a Portuguese" and in parentheses after the word says "bottle of rum." That's about as near as most of them come to being right. A Portuguese, also called a Joe, was a gold coin worth sixteen dollars. I wonder how Sherwin thought Arnold materialized a bottle of Portuguese rum in a Canadian wilderness. Rewrote Doc's medical experiences at the smallpox camp, and wish I had time to rewrite the whole book.

July 24: Got going again on *Rabble,* peeling off 1,500 words in spite of carpenters next door pounding all morning and running a cement mixer all afternoon.

July 25: Discovered that the historians' (including Admiral Mahan's) references to the fleet's retreat from Ticonderoga have overlooked or ignored Colonel Udney Hay's testimony in the St. Clair court-martial, so once more rewrote the fleet's getaway from Ticonderoga. I ain't no Admiral Mahan, but Udney Hay saw it and Mahan didn't, so the hell with Mahan.

July 26: Worked all day and until 2 A.M. digging facts out of the Schuyler and St. Clair courts-martial—facts that the historians have completely ignored.

July 27: Rewrote Chapter 61 by working until 2 A.M., and sent all sixty-one chapters to Doubleday for immediate setting. Figured that Anna, in typing the original and revised versions of *Rabble,* has now typed 1,700 pages—over 600,000 words.

July 30: Worked until midnight and got ⅓ down page 211.

July 31: In the morning set Merrill and Doc to chopping trees in the valley of Wood Creek and got ¾ down page 212.

August 1: Finished Chapter 63 and feel as if I were about to explode from frustration.

August 2: Fiery hot, and I in a muck of sweat and nervousness trying to weave the events between Ticonderoga and Saratoga into the narrative. Finished page 215.

August 3: Fumbled around all day and reached page 217. The story weighs on my mind like lead: what to do, how to do it: how to compress Arnold, the facts, the story, the battle into the remaining space—what to do with Merrill, with Doc Means, with Lewis Vincent, how to dispose of the time element—how to keep sympathy for Nathaniel, how to bring Ellen back into the story, how to arrange for Merrill to miss the first battle of Saratoga, just what took place in the second battle of Saratoga—it's enough to drive anyone nuts. Maybe that's what it'll do to me, and maybe I'll be a hell of a lot better off.

August 4: Finished Chapter 64, page 218: then read Chapters 62, 63 and 64 to Booth, who made innumerable valuable suggestions.

August 5: Stumbled ahead all day, and until 10 P.M.; then threw away what I'd done and started all over again. A wrecking car went haywire outside our gate and churned explosively for hours; an airplane landed on the golf links fifty yards from the house and kept its motor running most of the afternoon while a thousand children screamed around it.[1] Almost impossible to work. Sometimes I think that because I dare to write about Arnold, I'm being dogged with

---

[1] My niece and secretary, Marjorie Mosser, after typing this sentence, confessed that she had been one of the screamers, and expressed some surprise that I had been able to work at all.

the same nemesis that pursued him. I've been fighting a sort of Revolution for five years against the sort of writing I'd been doing up to then, and now it begins to look as though I'd lost the war.

August 6: ¾ down 220. A ray of light today on the mysterious lady—the beautiful wife of the commissary mentioned by Madame Riedesel but never discovered by any of the historians. If such a lady *did* accompany Burgoyne, then Marie de Sabrevois could also accompany him, but I couldn't allow this to happen unless there were grounds for it. This I had put up to Mr. Haraszty, asking whether the commissary's wife could have been the beautiful Harriet Van Horn Foy, wife of a British officer who had arrived in Quebec in 1776 as commissary of troops. She was notoriously lax in her behavior with British officers, but I had been unable to find Foy in the records. Haraszty put his finger on the lady, deducing that she must have been the wife of J. Rousseau.[2]

August 7: ¾ down 221. Bellboys from a nearby hotel held batting practice about twenty yards from my workroom—an interminable afternoon of whacking and shouting. Read of the death of Charles H. Bangs, former head of the Sons of the American Revolution, who has written me a dozen encouraging and helpful letters, and had great sympathy for and understanding of Arnold. Oppressed and upset all day, and increasingly fearful of collapsing before I can finish *Rabble.*

August 8: ½ down 223. A note from Miss Bangs, saying that her father's last days had been cheered by the prospect of reading *Rabble in Arms,* and that he had spoken often of the difficulties I must be having with it. Anna packed up and sent off *Captain Caution* to the *Post* again—an entirely fruitless gesture that can bring us nothing but another discouraging shock along about August 15, when I'll be even more sunk in depression because of my complete frustration on this damned book. Worked until after two o'clock and fell asleep at my desk.

August 9: Scratched onward and finally got started on the Jennie McCrae episode. The New York State Historian, investigating the McCrae murder, wrote bitterly that there were as many different versions of the facts as there were people who had written them. Worked till 1:45 A.M. and got half down page 225.

August 10: Killed Jennie McCrae today, spurred on by my ardent desire to do the same to a neighbor's two children, who spend every afternoon trap-shooting in a field two hundred yards away, thus

---

[2]Complete deduction on p. 414, Appendix.

making life hell for everyone but themselves. ½ down page 227 and ended Chapter 65. Took me until 3 A.M. to kill Jennie and remove her scalp.

August 11: Abandoned the copybook to write on a pad, as I have to move from room to room in an effort to escape the perpetual outdoor din. Did a page and a half, and had a remarkable piece of luck. The second battle of Saratoga has always bothered me. Last week a trunkful of letters in a Kennebunkport attic was bought for a song by a local junk dealer. Knowing that I was addicted to such things, he wrote me that he had a letter I might like to buy. When I went to see it, I found it had been written by my great-great-grandfather immediately after that battle.[3] For the first time I saw that second battle clearly—"the Constant fire of our men and the Enemy, the Shouts and Huzzas of our army, the Cries and Groans of the wounded and Dieing men, the sight of prisoners both well and wounded, some walking with crutches or staves; some supported between two leading them in, some held in on waggons: these things were terrible to behold. . . ."

August 12: Reached the point where Peter Merrill bawls out the home-going militiamen.

August 13: Tied myself in a knot over the scene in which Schuyler orders Merrill to New England to stimulate recruiting by telling the story of Jennie McCrae. Three human lice brought a toy cannon to the practice tee of the golf links just outside my workroom and fired it steadily from five-thirty to six-thirty. Rewrote the Schuyler scene until 1:30 A.M.

August 14: Put an end to Chapter 66 by lunch time. This stuff is terrible! It wouldn't surprise me at all if critics united in giving the book a hearty, wholesale and unanimous damning. I can no longer judge how many pages I've done, as I'm writing on loose sheets and Anna is typing directly from them. She must have passed page 800 of manuscript. If it makes 850 pages, as it will, it will be considerably over 350,000 words long, and will probably bring me nothing but raucous laughter. Got a start on the return of Merrill and Doc Means to Saratoga. At eight to Booth's. Read the McCrae episode. We thought of trying to plot the end, but soon saw the details were too intricate. Just keep right on going, Booth said, and it would come out all right.

August 15: Stumbled ahead. Had a letter from Lorimer canning

---

[3]Full letter on p. 388, Appendix.

Captain Caution for the third time, but again saying that if the days of big magazines ever come back, they'll give it another reading. Worked until 2 A.M.

August 16: This is the anniversary of the Battle of Bennington, and by a singular coincidence, I find myself writing about it on the same day. Felt as if I'd been through a couple of battles myself, and was so dopey I could only work until 1:30 A.M. Reached the hiatus between the first and second battles of Saratoga.

August 17: Overcast, showery day, full of dog-choruses, garrulous caddies hunting for balls in the back yard, airplanes overhead, passing automobiles, perpetually screaming children and general agony. The first forty galleys of *Rabble* arrived. Don't dare look at them until I'm nearer the end. Worked until 3:30 A.M.

August 18: Wrote four pages before lunch, getting Merrill and Doc Means back into camp at Bemis's Heights. So groggy after lunch that I could hardly keep my eyes open, and by five in the afternoon had an overpowering feeling that I couldn't write another line, ever, as long as I live—not on *this* novel, anyway. Pulled myself together with the help of half a dozen cocktails: then to Booth's and read him all I had. Booth insists on being enthusiastic—says it's the best picture of the Revolution ever done. He gave me a long pep talk, probably because he thinks I'll cave in unless I'm encouraged—builds up like a symphony, he says—all the fear, struggle, confusion, sickness, weariness—it's all there: I've got it: done it exactly as it should be done. In spite of ascribing his words to friendship, I went home greatly cheered and had a good night's sleep for a change.

August 20: Struggled to get into the second battle of Saratoga—a hell of a job. Nobody'll ever be able to have even the faintest inkling of the tribulations and mental trials that have accompanied this book. Just another historical novel, they'll say—just another cloak-and-dagger job. Glanced at the proofs, and one glance showed me that I must stay completely away from them and from people until the writing is finished. Had a late dinner and to Blue Roof at eleven-thirty with the utmost reluctance. My back aches, my head aches, my sit-upon aches! I'm sunk in despair. Worked until 2:30 A.M.

August 21: Struggled onward with the Battle of Bemis's Heights. Several summer vacationists have protested to Anna because I don't go out oftener, and are much exercised over what they call my "failure to do my duty to society." That's a helpful attitude! Terrific dog-barking all day long. The whole book seems to be collapsing, and me with it. I'm on the next to the last chapter.

August 22: Wrote five pages before lunch. We've had to change our hours for meals and have lunch at two-thirty and dinner at eight-thirty, as this gives me more time to avoid doing my duty to society. Finished the first phase of the Battle of Saratoga at eight-thirty, to the movies from nine-thirty to eleven-thirty; then worked till 1:30 A.M.

August 23: Plowed into the battle again, made fair strides in the morning, but in the afternoon got off on a wrong lead which kept me from finishing. I doubt that I could have finished it today, anyway. To Booth's and read him the first phase of the battle. I thought it ought to be cut, but he wouldn't allow it. He keeps telling me that nothing ever written on the Revolution approaches it, but I don't believe a word he says.

August 24: Tried to finish the battle while those two neighbor's children kept up an incessant trap-shooting fusillade all afternoon. At noon received proofs through the burning of Skenesboro. Tired and despondent beyond words at everything connected with this damned book. Left the battle unfinished and horribly bitched at eight-thirty, and just couldn't drive myself to go back to it.

August 25: Logy from the unprecedented amount of sleep I had last night, but contrived to clean up the second phase of the battle—an extremely rough and sketchy job. What the critics are going to do to me is something terrible, and be damned to 'em!

August 26: Up at daybreak and tried to get going on the blow-off chapter, but bitched it all up. Have the feeling that I simply *cannot* stick through the writing, revising and proofreading of this goddam thing. To Booth's for dinner and spent all our time on the second phase of the battle, which he says must be completely clear. He gives me a lot of hot air to cheer me up: says I don't know what a big job I've done and how it's ahead of Zola's *Débâcle,* and a damn sight better and truer picture. I can only say that I wish he could write all the reviews. In that case the book might sell a few copies.

August 27: Played a game of golf—my first exercise for over a month. Weighed 166 afterwards—ten pounds lighter than when I returned from Italy. An early lunch and to Blue Roof and tried to get at that lousy blow-off chapter. Simply couldn't get anywhere with it. My nerves extremely ragged and upset, and I in a perpetual stew. Can't seem even to think, let alone write. Unable to do a damned thing after dinner, though I sat at my desk until 1 A.M. in a state of almost complete coma. To bed utterly discouraged.

August 29: Got a few inches forward in the morning, enough forward so that I could clear my desk of Lossing, Nickerson, I. N. Arnold,

Anburey, Digby, Lamb, Sparks and a few others. Finished the surrender chapter and set off on what I trust will be the last chapter. Distracted, while doing it, by a thousand infuriating noises, particularly those of airplanes and dogs. There are six planes each day each way between Boston and Portland, and all twelve pass exactly over Blue Roof. Also the place swarms with dogs—large ones with deep bass voices and a confirmed habit of indulging in orgies of protracted barking. Exhausted by eight-thirty. To the movies and saw Somerset Maugham's *Narrow Corner,* to which the Hollywood geniuses have given a new and happy end. Worked till 2 A.M.

August 30: Awakened by the incessant barking of dogs. Wired Longwell I would ship him the final chapters on Monday, and to keep the proofs coming fast. Figured that since I started on July 23, I've written over 70,000 words, and what I send Longwell next Monday will be nearer 80,000. Nobody but Booth can understand the difficulties I've had with this job. Worked till eight-forty, then had a hurried supper and to a movie abortion called *She Had to Say Yes,* which, in effect, was laid in a brothel, though supposedly depicting the cloak-and-suit trade —a story dirty, false, meaningless, plotless and without virtue. But *Arundel* or *Lively Lady* they won't do!

August 31: Lammed into work and found myself so nervous and twitchy I could get almost nowhere. Turned out a fair amount of just words, however, and kept throwing them at Anna, who today reached manuscript page 900. To Booth's with the blow-off chapter still uncompleted. Worked with Booth till ten forty-five, and he said to come over tomorrow and clean up the end. He repeatedly insists it's a magnificent job: the best picture of the Revolution ever done—worth doing even though it only sells 800 copies: worth doing if I went broke doing it: even if it doesn't sell now, it will some day. I wish he were right.

September 1: Up at daybreak to re-do the work done yesterday and finish—if you can call it that—the book. There's no feeling whatever of having finished *Rabble.* It has hung on the verge of completion for weeks, and there's always the knowledge that whatever I do must be completely rewritten. A lot of people seem to think an author can sigh with satisfaction when he writes "The End" on a book's last page; probably they'd continue to think so even when confronted with the galley proofs that now clutter all our tables. Longwell sent me a check for twenty-eight dollars—six months' royalty on *Arundel*—and observed that the next one would be bigger, thank God. I hope so, but wouldn't bet a hell of a lot on it. Kept going until seven-thirty and came to an approximate end. Snatched a hurried supper and to Booth's, where we worked until eleven o'clock, me with every nerve on edge. Booth keeps speaking of the enormous size of the book, and the big picture it presents.

September 2: Polished loose ends, and went over and over the last hundred and twenty pages. They must go off day after tomorrow, sure.

September 3: Up early and rewrote the last chapter, rewrote the first part of the Arnold chapter, stuck in bits that had been overlooked; then re-read the last hundred and twenty pages in their entirety, preparatory to wrapping them up. Squawked to Anna that they were incredibly dull, stupid and thin. Worked till midnight, inexpressibly downhearted and disgusted.

September 4: Up early, made many last-minute changes: then took the manuscript to the New York train and put it aboard the mail car myself. Back and went to correcting proofs of the first sixty-one chapters, all of which confirm my belief that the book will be a complete and irremediable flop.

September 5: Finished and sent off the first fifty galleys, then corrected through galley 73. Sunk in despair and gloom, and sure I've missed it completely: certain that my three years of work will bring me a critical bludgeoning that will make me want to blow out the gas.

September 6: Got through galley 125, nauseated by the dullness of the book—nauseated, too, by the number of typographical errors that escaped the proofreaders. Sure as hell, if I wrote it "Three cheers for old Nassau, my boys," they'd let it go "Three cheers for old Nausea."

September 7: Sent off galleys 51–125 inclusive and telegraphed Longwell to rush proofs of the final section without waiting for them to be proofread. Went on correcting proofs until my despondency drove me to having highballs with Jim Campbell. Three almost knocked me out, which indicates that I must be lower than a snake's pelvis.

September 8: Up early, feeling like the wrath of God, and had two aspirin tablets for breakfast. Lay on the couch in Blue Roof, watched a spider build a web, and corrected through galley 175 by midnight, which is pretty good going, considering my state of mind.

September 9: Removed seven large chunks from the galleys and replaced them with what may or may not be improvements. More certain than ever that *Rabble* will not only be a flop, but will get reviews that will almost break our hearts. To bed in a state of hopeless gloom.

September 10: Got through galley 220, which is all I have so far received. There should be some thirty still to come.

September 11: Up in a state verging on frenzy at the impossible working conditions of this dump. If I'm to do any more writing, I must either move away from here or go nuts. Drove to Portland and saw Royal Boston, a good small-house architect, to see what he could do about building us a reasonably priced house on our St. George land—a place where we can be free of people, and engage in some side-line activity more enjoyable and fruitful than golf.

September 12: Tinkered at galley proofs all day: then shipped them to Doubleday.

September 13: Spent the day wrapping and returning the many source books that Rupert Hughes loaned me from his Revolutionary library, and packing the Congressional Library books that Senator Moses sent me three years ago. What other library in the world would let an author keep a mass of rare and valuable books for three years?

September 14: Got the remainder of the galley proofs, corrected them all day, and after dinner to Booth's to read sections that seemed to me to need rewriting. He refused to allow alterations in the passages I read; said it was a mighty strange thing that I, having completed a splendid job, should be in despair over it and emitting squawks of distress, whereas I should be shouting and capering with glee. What I should have, he said, was a good day's rest, and I could take it tomorrow and make him a batch of my grandmother's ketchup.

September 15: Made Booth three gallons of ketchup.

September 16: A tropical hurricane struck us, so thought it was safe to sit in Stall Hall living room and work at a table in front of the fire. I'd no sooner got to work, immediately after lunch, when in walked an acquaintance accompanied by two relatives: one a pimply and stupid nephew, the other older, sober and resentful. In spite of the mass of work everywhere in evidence—nearly every chair and table covered with hacked and mauled proofs—the visitor demanded scotch, appropriated the bottle, and finally drank himself into gibbering idiocy. The nephew, aged eighteen, was destined (according to his uncle) to be a publisher. The young man, a high school student, knew all about writing, and sagely advised me to put more sex in my books if I wished them to sell. At seven-thirty my patience was exhausted, and the sober relative and I took our recalcitrant visitor by the arms, hoisted him from the front stairs on which he had collapsed, and unceremoniously deposited him in the relative's automobile. The insufferable nephew, still muttering about sex, departed unscathed, though he deserved a horsewhipping.

September 17: Second day of the hurricane: took another chance on staying in the living room, and by great good fortune was not disturbed, so finished correcting the last of the galleys and all the front matter.

Still weak from our alcoholic visitor and his consummate ass of a nephew. I'll bet, by God, he *does* get to be a publisher!

September 18: Sent off the galleys. Had word from Longwell that the first of the page proofs would arrive Wednesday. He quoted a letter from W. R. Benét, who had read uncorrected galleys for the Book-of-the-Month Club, and claimed to be most enthusiastic. All this proof-reading has turned my eyes to aching blurs. To Portland and was fitted for glasses.

September 19: Seized the breathing spell between proofs to check my topography. Made a hurried trip through Concord, Hopkinton and Bennington to Bemis's Heights. Found my reconstruction of the battle-ground okay. Pressed on to Fort Edward, Fort Ann and Whitehall (formerly Skenesboro). Scenery still okay. Hastened on to Ticonderoga and telephoned Steve Pell, who rebuilt the Fort and has been of inestimable help in supplying Valcour, Ticonderoga and armament details. Talked *Rabble* and drank highballs till midnight.

September 20: To the Fort with Pell at 8 A.M. Traced the route followed by Merrill, Doc Means and Verrieul, when Verrieul was killed. Made sure my description of the Fort was correct. Pell was extremely encouraging. Said I'd be surprised at the number of Fort visitors who had read *Arundel*. It may be so, but *Arundel,* to date, has sold 14,000 copies. Can it be that each purchaser has loaned his book to 100 friends? If not, there can't be such a hell of a lot of visitors that would surprise me. Pell said the Fort had taken 100 copies, as an experiment, and all had been sold, in spite of the depression. What, he wanted to know, were my intentions about that Robert Rogers book? When I said I was revolted by the thought of tackling another long book, he protested that the Rogers book must be written. "Why, damn it," Pell said, "think of the times Rogers and his Rangers went right out through that archway yonder and down to the lake, strapped on their skates and went skating off to put the fear of God into the French."

He took me to a parapet bristling with 18-pounders—cannon he had bought and begged all over the world. The guns pointed to Mount Independence, where the drunken French general Roche-Fermoy—known to Cap Huff as Roast-Fermoy—had burned his cabin on the night the Americans retreated before Burgoyne's forces.

"Look," Pell said, pointing to the lake shore beneath us, "Rogers must have kept his whaleboats just about there, where we found the sunken hull of an old vessel the other day—the *Trumbull,* probably. Anyway, Rogers and his Rangers might be there right now, getting the whale-boats in shape so they can sneak off up the lake to kill themselves a

mess of Indians or raise hell with the French. Can't you hear him?
Can't you see him? Sure you can, and you've got to make the rest of us
see him! He's been too long forgotten!"

If Pell feels that way about it, I'm not so positive I was accurate when
I repeatedly set down in my diary that never, *never*, NEVER again would
I tackle another long book.

Went out in a canoe with Milo King, the Fort's superintendent, and
measured the ancient sunken hull. It had only a 14-foot beam, so it
couldn't be the *Trumbull*. And the *Trumbull* was burned at Skenesboro, when Burgoyne caught up with the retreating Americans, so
both Pell and King must dream up another ship for the hull to be.

Returned to Maine through a heavy rain, during which we were
almost pushed over a precipice by a truck whose driver had fallen
asleep. Anna was driving, and I'll swear on a stack of Bibles that both
right-hand wheels were completely off the road for a moment—with a
rock-filled ravine beneath us. I was sure we were goners, and thought of
nothing except who would finish the final revision of *Rabble*.

September 21: Received the first hundred page proofs of *Rabble,* un-
proofread, and flew at them.

September 22: Kept on with the proofs. Longwell phoned that he was
sending the remainder today.

September 23: All the proofs arrived—870 pages! Booth said, "At
least no one can say about it, as a lady did about *Beaucaire,* 'I read your
little book.'"

September 24: Kept on with proofs and discovered innumerable errors, both typographical and sloppy writing.

September 25: Plowed away at proofs and found many passages that
had to be rewritten, which—since they are page proofs—necessitated
replacing the altered words with exactly the same number of letters—
the toughest of jobs. Longwell telegraphed asking permission to use
The Lively Lady in the Dollar Book Club. Refused, being against cheap
editions until those who publish them follow the English custom of
giving authors a straight ten or fifteen per cent royalty (instead of an
infinitesimal lump sum which must be divided with the publisher).
Longwell telephoned, pressing me to agree, so weakly yielded provided
he'd limit the dollar sale to three months, and advance me sufficient
funds to return to Italy and start the Robert Rogers book.

September 26: Picked up a touch of bronchitis, so stayed in bed and
read proofs, getting through page 250.

September 27: Spent the day rewriting two passages—the relation of
Wood Creek to Skenesboro, and Merrill's appeal to Long and Kidder

to hold back the British by sinking one of the vessels. I learned that latter bit from Steve Pell, and just the writing of it made me as sore as I used to be at stupidity in Siberia. Sent the two rewritten pages to Longwell to be re-set. Reached page 400.

September 28: Horrified at the number of mistakes in the page proofs. If I want to be sure that all blunders are eliminated, I must go to Garden City and do a last-minute re-revision myself.

September 29: Wired Longwell insisting I be allowed to re-revise. Had to rewrite two more passages; and a terrible task it is to take out, say, 208 letters and spaces, and replace them with exactly 208 letters and spaces. The two re-set pages mailed Wednesday came back this afternoon: snappy work.

September 30: Up early, did the last of the page proofs and wrote Lorimer that I would be happy to start on a series of articles if he still wanted them. Notwithstanding my moans and groans, these proofs don't read so badly after all. In spite of reading and rewriting that last chapter about a hundred times, I found I had a lump in my throat when I went through it again. Anna finished reading at midafternoon, and I packed the proofs, took them to the New York train, and put them on the mail car myself.

October 1: Baldwin, the Arnold descendant to whom I'd sent proofs of *Rabble,* telephoned three times and telegraphed twice. His enthusiasm is as touching as it is cheering. He had caught several errors. I had made Arnold's grandfather governor of Connecticut, whereas he was governor of Rhode Island. Wired Longwell to correct this. Later Baldwin telephoned that it was Arnold's great-grandfather, not grandfather, who was governor.

October 2: Read spare proofs for errors. Discovered I'd erred about Warren's children. I'd given him three, but he had four. Longwell wired that the publication date had been extended from October 25 to November 15. It's a wonder he couldn't have let me know sooner!

October 3: Jim Campbell offered to loan me a plane to go to Garden City in a hurry and re-revise the proofs.

October 4: Booth put down his foot on flying to Garden City. It might give me a nice case of pneumonia on top of my bronchitis, he insisted, and then he might never get to hear Rogers' story, which he felt would be good. I could damn well stay on the ground, and not go flying all over hell's kitchen. A day or two didn't matter, he said: let Doubleday send the proofs to me by special messenger. He made such a stink that I telephoned Longwell. Longwell said sure, he'd put the proofs in the mails tonight, and I could have until Monday to send them back.

October 5: First 370 pages of the revised page proofs came in, and Anna and I flew at them. The proofreaders have at last done a good job, and we caught only two small mistakes they'd overlooked. Baldwin drove down from Boston to see me, greatly excited over *Rabble*. With him he had a brooch that had belonged to Peggy Shippen Arnold. It contained a lock of Arnold's hair—a silky brown faintly touched with gray: scarcely enough gray to notice, and the brooch dated the year of his death: 1801. Consequently, those historians who call Arnold black-haired are saps, as are those who claim he was a broken-down, white-haired old man when he died. Found seven "evens" on pages 5, 6 and 7, so altered them, and rushed the pages to New York by the night train.

October 6: The second half of the revised page proofs arrived in the early mail. Had to rewrite the paragraphs about Arnold at Compo and Ridgefield, and his kindnesses to the Warren children—extremely difficult because of having to fit the words into the exact measurement of the words replaced. Came to the conclusion that the book is better than I'd thought.

October 7: Sent off the last of the proofs, so that's the end of my labors on *Rabble*. It's been bearing down on me for three years, and I thought I hated it; but now I feel lost without Cap Huff and Nathaniel Merrill and Ellen Phipps and Doc Means and all the rest of those who have so long filled me with rage and despair. Read by the morning paper that *Anthony Adverse* has just passed its 175th thousand! Poor old *Rabble* will probably be lucky to have a circulation of 7,000. Anna says I ought to have a theme song, so wrote one for her:

> I wonder what's eating him now:
> At what he is raging—and How!
> I wonder what's making him squawk and yell,
> Beef and howl, roar like hell?
> I wonder what next he'll rewrite
> All day and through most of the night?
> I wonder what tripe I will next have to type?
> I wonder what's eating him now!

28

No WORDS of mine can describe the overwhelming nerve strain and exhaustion that accompany the completion of a long book, and that duly attended the last agonized months of *Rabble*. That alone, I suspect, would have prevented me from going to work immediately on the Robert Rogers book—the one in which I hoped to dispel the fog that obscured New Englanders' understanding of the troubles of our forebears in fighting the French and Indians and the manner in which that fighting was done.

But there were other reasons why I was obliged to wait—and to me those reasons seemed insuperable. For one thing, two banks were pressing for the reduction of loans I had incurred to build the Palm Beach house, Blue Roof, the American Wing of the Half-Baked Palace, and to acquire land on the Georges River. This was unfortunate, for the purchaser of the Palm Beach house had failed to make expected payments; and as soon as I learned the size of the first printing which my publishers had planned for *Rabble*—5,000 copies—I knew that *Rabble*, like *Arundel* and *The Lively Lady*, would make so little return that we would shortly be wholly without funds. For another thing, the detail I needed, in order to start the book, seemed unobtainable. Some of it, so far as I could tell after consulting Mr. Milo Quaife, the distinguished Detroit librarian and historian, and Mr. Randolph G. Adams of the William L. Clements Library at Ann Arbor, didn't exist—though I was fairly certain that it *did* exist, and had been overlooked by historians.

Since I couldn't start until I had all available facts, the best thing for me to do, as I saw it, was to contrive by hook or crook to return to England and to that vast repository of documents and reports from England's colonial governors, generals, statesmen, navigators and public servants of every sort—the Public Record Office.

So I went to Philadelphia with a long list of suggestions for Mr. Lorimer. Three were for articles explaining the differences between a representative American university like Michigan, and an English university—Oxford. I told him my reason for suggesting this series: my need to hunt material at the University of Michigan and in England. I also told him I had received from consular friends in Germany strong hints that the Krauts were marching again to the tune of Hitler's fanatic howls, and that the Hitler Youth movement was engaged in turning out the most enormous crop of potential soldiers and murderers the world had ever seen. I wanted, I told him, to look into this by taking an automobile to Germany and going to Hitler Youth centers, labor camps, and—if I had any luck—to training centers and concentration camps.

"Go right to it," Lorimer said, "but let's have an understanding about that automobile. Gasoline's a dollar a gallon in England! What I'll do is raise your rate to two thousand dollars a story, but you'll have to buy your own gas."

He also reminded me that I had spoken disrespectfully of Mr. Hitler and his aims, years before, in the article entitled "Suds," and that I would do well to take out plenty of life insurance and make a will before setting sail for Germany.

§

That trip was a fortunate thing for me in more ways than one, and needs mention here; for it not only supplied me with material for a book, but provided the funds without which I couldn't have written it.

Not only did I find, in the Public Record Office, an unexpectedly large number of letters, petitions and reports written by Rogers himself, but I came across evidence of hitherto unsuspected villainy in Rogers' associates. I came in contact, too, with a group of living villains, perverts, braggarts, blusterers and other strange Englishmen of whose existence I would otherwise have been ignorant. Most of these were members of Sir Oswald Mosley's British Union of Fascists.

Strangely enough, the wrongs against which Mosley and his men were fighting were a disgrace to England and strongly in need of correction; but the methods advocated by Mosley to right those wrongs were as dangerous as any of Hitler's, Mussolini's or the Bolsheviks'.

During two long evenings I sat close beside the small, pale, scar-faced young man who was chief instructor to those of Mosley's adherents who had been chosen to bore from within, and heard him outline with icy ruthlessness the manner in which his listeners must go about their task of destroying Britain's ruling class. He was William Joyce, later known as Lord Haw-Haw and hanged for treason. At that time he was a lecturer at the University of London, and he somehow contrived to exude an unpleasantly exaggerated flavor of every oddity I had observed in the oddest of Oxford undergraduates. His gray slacks were stained and baggy beyond description. His loose tweed jacket, patched at sleeve-end and elbow with soiled chamois, bulged at every pocket as if filled with apples. His throat was swathed in a bulky muffler, which, stuffed into his jacket, gave him the outline of a pouter pigeon, but a pigeon suffering from a disdainful dislike of himself and all the world. His speech was even more feminine in quality, more clipped and distorted, than that of the intellectual young men who gathered each day in Oxford's Gridiron Club. His attitude was more contemptuous, more remotely condescending, than that of a sprig of British nobility portrayed on the stage by an amateur actor without taste or ability. He seemed the personification of perversion and contrariness, defying criticism and attack by sneering coldly at everything he himself lacked.

I went with many of Mosley's group leaders to Fascist rallies, and spent long hours in their company. Some were university men; some were graduates of England's best public schools; and their open depravity, their ready acceptance of what I can only call blackguardism, was manna from heaven to anyone who wanted to write. All these young men were much annoyed at President Roosevelt because he had, they insisted, stolen Mosley's ideas for his New Deal without making any acknowledgment.[1] In the end, they said, Roosevelt's plans would be abortive because he was making no effort to raise a personal army to enforce his ideas, as had Hitler, Mussolini and Mosley.

I was particularly impressed by one Mosley supporter, whose chief duty was to handle roughly any person who obnoxiously heckled Fascist group leaders at their nightly meetings. At first sight he seemed the very picture of a perfect English gentleman. He was elegantly done out in long black overcoat, white muffler, black Homburg hat; his speech was cultivated, his bearing jaunty. Yet he had just emerged from a stretch in Wormwood Scrubbs, a place of detention for those caught breaking English laws in a baser sort of way. I was indebted to him, for he had fond memories of an American wife and—on learning that I was an American—took me to his hotel on Jermyn Street and intro-

---

[1]Around that time Mr. Roosevelt had also lifted a phrase from Thoreau's *Journal* without giving credit. Under the date of September 7, 1851, Thoreau had written, "Nothing is so much to be feared as fear."

duced me to its owner and chief receptionist, whose portrait appears in *Oliver Wiswell* as Mrs. Jump.

In his room, or digs, he hospitably broached a bottle of scotch and spent the evening telling me incredible details of the behavior of his fellow lodgers in Wormwood Scrubbs.

I couldn't believe he wasn't lying, but I thought I'd better make sure by handing on the stories to an old friend who had been assigned to the Siberian Expeditionary Force by the *Japan Advertiser*—Frank King, who had now become head of the Associated Press in London. But Mr. King already knew about them. They were true, he said, but British laws of libel are as painfully severe as they are unjust, and he had thought it advisable to follow British newspaper procedure and refrain from relaying the stories to the United States.

I have always been glad, when confronted with the necessity of writing about off-color Englishmen, that I had so many opportunities of observing the wide variety of hateful characters I collected at Oxford and in the British Union of Fascists.

It is, I know, commonly said and believed that an Englishman's word is as good as his bond; but that is frequently untrue in English publishing circles. I had dealings with several English publishers, around the time when William Joyce was instructing the upper crust of the British Union of Fascists, and found all of them adept in evading written contracts, making promises they had no intention of keeping, and practicing petty meannesses that were as unnecessary as they were enraging.

As offset to that deplorable state of affairs, the fourth English publisher I had the good fortune to encounter was a gentleman and a scholar, understanding, co-operative and generous. *His* word, as I had many opportunities to discover, *was* as good as any bond.

If I, wanting to write, were to become the author of a book that might be published in England, I would try to make sure that the publisher be approved by the British Society of Authors, and that the contract used be the standard contract supplied by the British Society of Authors. If I failed to do this, I would almost inevitably find myself, to put it mildly, scurvily treated.

Doubtless Edith Wharton would have brazenly asserted that fame and fortune were certain for any American author who wrote a book that achieved British publication; but the truth of the matter is that such publication is usually unproductive—sometimes unbelievably so. The first royalty statement made by my first English publisher reported an advance sale of 287 copies of *Arundel*.

During the British Union of Fascists period I had received, from the American publisher of *The Collector's Whatnot* a check for $33.90, and so had dispatched checks for $11.30 to Mr. Tarkington and Mr. Kahler, at the same time reporting to Mr. Tarkington the loathsomeness of an English publisher who had refused to live up to any of the terms, verbally proposed by him, while lunching with (and on) me at Oxford. Mr. Tarkington replied:

> Thanks for the eleven dollars and thirty cents. I'm glad to give you and Anna as much of my foreign business as I can without hurting the feelings of my London agents, who need all they can get, I conclude, by their sending me a bill for nine shillings thruppence, which they say they've paid as my British income tax for the year, though this matter is puzzling, as I've received no British income, not even thruppence, making it more strange that the *Illustrated London News* two months ago had a half page photograph of the revival of *Monsieur Beaucaire,* this journal being my only source of information, though I have not yet written to thank it.

After several weeks' scrutiny of Oxford and its oddities, chief among which were a chill dampness more penetrating than anything I had experienced in Siberia, I moved on to London to find out why I had suddenly been afflicted with excruciating pains in my arms and shoulders—and to find a place sufficiently warm to let me limber up my writing muscles, which had stiffened in Oxford's dreadful climate.

Thanks to the advice of kind English friends, whom we had visited in Lymington before vanishing into the fog of London, we shunned hotels and turned to the purely British institution known as digs. Our Lymington friends knew of digs of high repute at 10 Berkeley Square, a mere stone's throw from that delightful Shakespearean segment of London, Shepherds Market; and they took us there.

When I saw the cheery, comfortable and quiet living room, bedroom and bath of those Berkeley Square digs, felt the warmth that radiated from the commodious fireplace, and was asked by a highly efficient butler how many there would be for dinner, and at what hour he should serve it in our living room—and when he suggested a burgundy which, though a lowly product of the British Empire (Empah, he called it), and unfortunately named Emu (Austrylian, that is to say), had given more satisfaction to discriminating patrons of No. 10 than had château wines of high repute and far greater price—when, as I was saying, I compared these interesting conditions with the stodgy discomfort of every British hotel room I had hitherto seen, I knew that never again, if I had occasion to remain for any length of time in London, would I lodge anywhere except in digs.

The house, it developed, was the one in which Lord Clive inconvenienced his household by hanging himself in the front hall; but that far-off suicide cast no shadow on the warm comfort of our digs. Without that warmth I could never have endured with equanimity my troubles with the English publisher who had sought me out in Oxford, asked to be allowed to publish *Arundel, The Lively Lady* and *Rabble in Arms* in England, and suggested royalties more generous than I had ever received in the United States.

I trustfully waited for that publisher to send me a contract incorporating those terms which he himself had proposed; but somehow they slipped his mind. My American publishers, eager to see my books published in England, cabled several times to find out the reason for the delay. I explained at length that the gentleman with whom I had been dealing had put me off, week after week, and behaved in such a way that I refused to have any further truck with him. My American publishers refused to believe my version of the affair, and cabled that I would do myself considerable harm if I offended the gentleman in question. I assured them that I had been the offended one, but they still felt the fault was entirely mine.

Fortunately the proceedings had been observed in full by Miss Winifred Nerney, once Arnold Bennett's secretary, before she had become Doubleday's extremely capable London representative, and in the course of time I received an apologetic letter from Dan Longwell, saying that he had just heard from Miss Nerney, and that she confirmed everything I said about the English publisher, and in every detail.

But in spite of that publisher, in spite of the long hours spent in the Public Record Office, in spite of visiting doctor after doctor about my aching shoulders (only to have them mistakenly blamed on infected tonsils), I succeeded in writing three more articles for the *Saturday Evening Post*—thanks to the welcome privacy of 10 Berkeley Square.

That done, we set off for Germany in an automobile laden with every book, pamphlet and newspaper I had been able to unearth in England about the rise of the Nazis. Most of them were highly uncomplimentary, and I didn't like to think what might happen if the Kraut customs inspectors at Aix took a notion to go through our luggage with care.

To my surprise and relief we were waved in with the utmost courtesy, and pressed on to Jülich for our first sight of the endless marching,

marching, marching, all day and all night, of the Brown Shirts, the Black Shirts, the labor battalions, the Hitler Jugend. . . .

§

In various ways that winter of 1933–34 in England, Germany and Italy was disappointing; for try as I would, the high-placed Nazis who had just risen to power in Wilhelmstrasse refused to let me visit the Oranienburg or any other concentration camp. Although I had an uncomfortable feeling that if I persisted in my efforts I might find myself in serious difficulties, I told Herr Voigt, the arbiter of such matters, that I had it on the best of authority that the occupants of the camps were held in slavery for nothing worse than differing with Nazi policies, or merely for being Jews, or frequently for no reason at all. Herr Voigt indignantly denied everything. The concentration camps, according to him, were almost like spas or summer resorts.

If they were as good as all that, I suggested, I should be given free access to such enlightened communities, so that all might know about them.

Herr Voigt informed me stiffly that my journal, the *Saturday Evening Post,* had recently printed articles about Germany by one Fräulein Dorothée Thompson. They were, he frostily said, wholly untrue, and he could not permit any other representative of that journal to report untruthfully on Oranienburg.

I told him I only worked for the *Saturday Evening Post:* neither owned nor edited it; and I refused to be held responsible for anything written by Miss Dorothy Thompson, who was known to me by name only. I further assured him that I would represent things exactly as they were: if, for example, I was persistently refused admission to Oranienburg and at the same time officially assured that it was a health resort, I would truthfully report those obviously unreconcilable facts to the American people.

Herr Voigt looked at me glassily through thick spectacles and wished to know what else had brought me to Germany. I told him I was eager to learn all the facts concerning that *schön und wunderbar* organization, the Hitler Youth; to examine the delightful accomplishments of the labor battalions, which we had watched tramping off to work to the tune of hoarse and sullen songs. They went to work at dawn and worked till dark, gray slaves of the Nazis. Also, I told him, I longed to witness the great strides made by Germany in the construction and development of gliders—and see, if only from a distance, the methods adopted at Treuenbreitzen to train Germany's small but magnificent Regular Army.

The truth about Treuenbreitzen was that Germany, allowed a police-force army of 500,000 men, was training 500,000: then dismissing them and training a new crop of 500,000. Thus her military strength was not 500,000, but in the millions. At my mention of Treuenbreitzen, Herr Voigt stiffened. He would not, he said, permit me to go to Treuenbreitzen, for there was nothing to see; but I could see the gliders and the labor battalions and the Hitler Youth—*warum nicht?* All these activities were exactly what they seemed on the surface—fine, healthy manifestations of Germany's well-known innocent leanings toward Turnvereining, wandervogeling, und mass beergetrinkening.

Nor was it difficult to form an opinion, for Mr. Raymond Geist, who was in charge of our consulate general, Mr. Douglas Miller, our commercial attaché (subsequently the author of *You Can't Do Business with Hitler*), and all the excellent newspapermen in Berlin—Louis Lochner, Guido Enderis, Junius Wood and others—were keenly aware of what was going on, but had to be careful about saying so if they wished to remain in Germany.

Mr. Geist smuggled me into a private office in the consulate general, where I had access to stacks of reports and figures that showed Germany to be violating the terms of the peace treaty in every conceivable way. Mr. Douglas Miller also opened his heart, in addition to reading me innumerable passages from *Mein Kampf* that proved the world must either get ready or be prepared to get it in the neck.

The glider schools and factories which I was proudly shown by Hitler Youth leaders made it painfully apparent that Germany, though deprived of an air force by the terms of the treaty, was building with furious rapidity an air force infinitely greater than the combined air forces of all the armies in the first World War.

But Oranienburg, No! I went there with a male and female Hitler Youth guide, and tried to talk them into getting me within the enclosure; but there was nothing to see, they said. We watched a battalion of concentration camp laborers march back to confinement from a day of enforced labor. A camp guard was leading them in a hoarse marching song. "Ach!" said my guides. "How they are happy und gay, *nicht wahr?*"

When I asked them who they thought they were kidding, they looked puzzled. "Vot iss, gidding?" I liked them no more than I had liked the Katzenjammer Kids, and for the same reasons.

Well, there was nothing doing, and that was all there was to it. On our way out of Germany, Mrs. Roberts and I even made a wide detour to look at Treuenbreitzen, where we saw nothing, as Herr Voigt had promised us—nothing but cavalry squads of Black Shirts drilling in the rain. But on every road the Brown Shirts, the Black Shirts, the Hitler Youth, the Hitler Maids, the Hitler Maidlets, the Hitler Booblets, were marching, marching, marching; drilling, drilling, drilling. Hitler was getting ready, and no mistake.

And yet that trip wasn't such a disappointment after all; for after Mrs. Roberts and I had journeyed from Berlin down to Porto Santo Stefano, where I proposed to write the stories I had accumulated in England and Germany, I found the reviews of *Rabble in Arms,* and a profoundly affecting mass of letters from people who had read it.

Both reviews and letters were out of all proportion to the sales of the book—which, at the end of six months, reached 16,940: not much of a showing compared with *Anthony Adverse's* 300,000; but better—far better—than I had expected.

The reviewers had been, for the most part, kinder and more generous than I had believed reviewers could be; and I could understand why so many letter writers had deduced, from the reviews, that *Rabble in Arms* must have sold a million copies, and that my fortune was made.

A number of the reviews were kind enough to express the opinion that *Rabble* might receive a Pulitzer Prize; and while I was grateful for those reviewers' kindness, I had no more thought or wish of their words coming true than of wanting the Order of the Rising Sun from the Japanese Government. I was too well aware of the strange politics that gnawed like a cancer within the Pulitzer Committee to think that any book of mine would ever be considered—knew, too, that the reviewers, encouraging though they were, were overlooking the *Saturday Evening Post* article in which I had pointed out the manner in which the committee had perverted Mr. Pulitzer's wishes.

Paris Herald Tribune, May 3, 1934: A storm of protest broke in literary circles today when it was disclosed that the Advisory Committee, headed by Nicholas Murray Butler, which makes the final decision on Pulitzer Prizes, had overridden the unanimous choices of the judges for the drama and novel prizes. The unanimous selection by the judges of Anderson's play, *Mary of Scotland,* and of the best American novel of the year, the name of which has not been disclosed, has been flatly turned down by the Committee. These prizes will go to S. Kingsley for his play *Men in White* and to Caroline Miller for her novel *Lamb in His Bosom,* neither of which received a

single vote from the judges. The rejection of Anderson's play was
due to the fact that he was last year's winner.

Off Gibraltar, May 6, 1934: Following that reasoning, Butler and his
Pulitzer Committee would have refused an award to Shakespeare for
Hamlet if he had previously been handed one for *Romeo and Juliet!*

§

May 16: Docked in New York and set off for Philadelphia as soon
as the automobile was unloaded. Lorimer said to send him *Captain
Caution* once more. He had a hole that it might just possibly fit.

New York, May 17: To Carl Brandt's office, and was told reproach-
fully that when I refused to accept $5,000 from Frank Lloyd for *Lively
Lady,* Lloyd paid $15,000 for Nordhoff and Hall's *Mutiny on the
Bounty.* Could only say that proved the stupidity of movie companies,
since Frank Lloyd could make the same movie, and without cost, from
Sir John Barrow's *Mutiny of the Bounty,* which was published in 1832
and is therefore in the public domain. Took back the *Captain Caution*
manuscript from him. He said it would never go as a serial: the *Pictorial Review* had asked to see it once more and had rejected it for the
second time: perhaps something might be done with it if it could be
rewritten.

That ain't what Booth said, so removed myself unobtrusively. Got
Brooks Brothers to wrap the manuscript for me, and shipped it to
Lorimer—the fifth time in three years.

Met Dan Longwell and Marc Connelly at the Iron Door. Dan says
he's sure *Rabble* will do better: that it's getting a lot of notice since
Alec Woollcott and Marc began to plug it, but that book buyers just
won't buy anything except *Anthony Adverse.* Connelly is leaving for
Hollywood tomorrow, and says he wants to do *Rabble* for the screen.
He claims *Rabble* has the greatest "theater" of any book he ever read.
He spoke of the bureau-and-rose-cutting incident as being the making
of *The Covered Wagon. Rabble,* he said, was crammed with such stuff.
"You'd think those movie people would see it," he said, "but they can't
see anything except the cost of production, Mother Love, the Final
Clinch and all the other old hokum." Longwell said, "There's *one* book
you won't have to rewrite."[2]

Met David Gray, the writer. He said he'd been in Ireland all winter
with E. A. Somerville, "Irish R.M." He had taken a copy of *Arundel*
with him, and all his Irish friends were nuts about it—called it a great

[2]See p. 352.

book. He asked what its sales had been. When I told him it had sold a little every week during the past three years, and had now reached 17,000, he wouldn't believe me. Dan, incidentally, had a clipping from the editorial page of the *Boston Transcript*—a box by E. F. Edgett, the *Transcript's* literary editor, listing what he considers the twenty-five outstanding novels since 1900.

They were Bennett's *Old Wives' Tale,* Blackwood's *John Silence,* Butler's *Way of All Flesh,* Churchill's *Inside of the Cup,* Ertz's *The Proselyte,* Galsworthy's *Forsyte Saga,* Philip Gibbs's *Street of Adventure,* Gissing's *Will Warburton,* Glasgow's *Barren Ground,* Johnston's *Lewis Rand,* Kipling's *Actions and Reactions,* Locke's *Beloved Vagabond,* Lowndes's *End of Her Honeymoon,* Mason's *The Four Feathers,* Maugham's *Of Human Bondage,* Maxwell's *Mrs. Thompson,* Morley's *Parnassus on Wheels,* Phillpotts' *Portreeve,* Priestley's *Good Companions,* E. M. Roberts' *The Great Meadow,* K. Roberts' *Rabble in Arms,* Sinclair's *Mary Olivier,* Snaith's *Broke of Covenden,* Tarkington's *Turmoil,* Wharton's *Ethan Frome.*

§

Maine, May 19: Collected a bag of accumulated letters from the post office, and found among them two from President Hopkins of Dartmouth, dated April 5 and April 12, offering me a Doctorate of Letters! Me a Doctor of Letters! I think our luck has turned!

May 21: Lorimer telegraphed: "Can use *Captain Caution* in five installments. Confirm if satisfactory." If satisfactory! Spent the rest of the day shouting "Oh boy! Oh boy! Oh boy!" With this we can pay nearly all we owe.

May 22: Oh boy! Oh boy! More of the same. Lyons, who bought our Palm Beach house and whom we've been carrying since the crash, wrote that he had sold the house and now would complete his payments. Oh boy, oh boy! The tide is rising and we can tackle Robert Rogers with minds at ease!

May 29: Started revising *Post* proofs of *Captain Caution,* and found innumerable places where the book must be rewritten before Doubleday publishes it next winter. That, together with letter writing and an influx of unexpected visitors, kept me going till 3 A.M. We've got to move to a quiet place.

NOTHING, I thought, lay between me and the start of that book about the French and Indian War except reading and correcting the magazine proofs for *Captain Caution* and once more revising its manuscript for book publication. The latter task was finished in thirty-seven days and nights of exhilarating toil; and just before it was finished, my publishers had another idea.

Some of the lighter articles I had contributed to the *Saturday Evening Post,* they thought, might be made into a book. Alexander Woollcott had recently compiled some of his whimsical essays in a volume, *The Woollcott Reader,* which, to the surprise of everyone, including Mr. Woollcott, had sold 175,000 copies.

Knowing that some two million people subscribed to the *Saturday Evening Post,* and that each copy of a magazine is read by a minimum of five people, my publishers were inflamed by Woollcott's amazing success, and fondly dreamed of finding themselves similarly favored. Ten million people, they reasoned, had been exposed to my articles, and many of them—many, *many* of them (not necessarily five million, even, but possibly one million) might develop an irresistible longing to purchase a collection of those articles.

So I assembled sixteen *Post* essays, scrutinized them closely—and was shocked to discover each one full of flaws and urgently in need of rewriting. Would the day ever come when I'd re-read something that I had once thought satisfactory and not agonizedly realize that it must be rewritten?

At all events, I rewrote the sixteen articles, and they were published under the title of *For Authors Only and Other Gloomy Essays.* Unfortunately the sales fell a trifle short of a million copies—the exact figure being 5,603.

With *For Authors Only* off my hands in the autumn of 1934, I surrounded myself with a rampart of diaries, journals, reports, maps and information having to do with the French and Indian War period, and prepared to delve into them; but just at that moment an English publisher expressed a desire to publish *The Lively Lady*. The terms he offered were too low to be considered, but I had been told that English publishers occasionally—not often, but once in a great while—weakly consented, when sufficiently pressed, to grant an American author a royalty so generous that the proceeds from one book might be exchanged for as much as a pair of shoes or a Harris tweed jacket. Consequently, I took a copy of *The Lively Lady* from the shelf and re-read it. To my despair I saw that it was all wrong. The facts were correct, but I knew I must revise it and—in many places—rewrite it.

Trembling with rage and frustration, I came to a reckless conclusion, in which I was encouraged by Mrs. Roberts. A part of Robert Rogers' activities, according to his own accounts, had taken place in North Africa, where he claimed to have fought in two battles for the Dey of Algiers. I knew of no way in which I could find out about that Algiers interlude except by visiting Algiers: knew, too, that if I lost any of the books and documents—many of them from the Library of Congress—which I had accumulated for the writing of the Rogers novel, I could never replace them. So, in order to be sure that they remained always in my custody, we packed them in mail sacks, wedged the mail sacks in the rear deck of our Ford, drove it to Boston and with it boarded the *Saturnia,* bound for Algiers, Gibraltar, Naples and Trieste.

Even when all those precious journals, diaries and source books were safely deposited in my chilly workroom in Porto Santo Stefano, I couldn't seem to concentrate on them.

The Lively Lady revision was only a slight handicap, for I did it in two months by allotting three hours a day to it. A worse handicap was my inner fury at the daily chronicling, in the *Paris Herald Tribune,* of the insane blunderings, the determined idiocies, the asinine blusterings, the adamant boneheadedness, of statesmen, prime ministers, legislators, rulers and other highly placed jackasses in France, Russia, Japan, England, Germany, Italy, the United States, Spain, Yugoslavia, and every other country sufficiently important to rate more than an inch of newspaper space.

I'd seen so many of those jackasses at close range that I already had a low opinion of their abilities; and each morning, on reading the *Paris Herald,* I found myself unable to work until I had delivered an impassioned speech to Mrs. Roberts, bitterly cursing everyone and everything.

While she waited patiently to get to her typing in a room whose temperature was seldom higher than 45 degrees, I pointed out to her that since the beginning of the world, nations had done their utmost to destroy every other nation and all people, and had only failed because of lacking adequate weapons. Given adequate weapons, which they were now on the verge of having, they would almost certainly be successful when they tried once more—and that once more was not far off —not with the world misguided by such dangerous characters as Stanley Baldwin, Benito Mussolini, Josef Stalin, Adolf Hitler, Franco, and the blunderers functioning in the purlieus of Capitol Hill, Pennsylvania Avenue and 10 Downing Street.

I couldn't get the thought out of my head unless I wrote it out, so I abandoned the Rogers book to write a pseudo-scientific treatise, *The Great Lice Age (Die Leiszeit)* by Prof. Ugo Furtwängler, Univ. of Braunschweig, translated by Ernest Fox, A.M. (Pratt), B.Sc. in Arch. (I.C.S.), Fellow National Geographic Society: Hinckeldreck & Krankheit, Leipzig, MMDCDXXXV.

In *The Great Lice Age,* savants from a future civilization recorded the behavior of the human lice who, as their crowning contribution to the Lice Age, had destroyed themselves and all the world with them. I perfunctorily sent it to my publishers when it was finished, though I never expected to have it published. Nor was it. Nor did I waste time revising it; for it had served its purpose. Having blown off steam in the writing of it, I felt better and could really go to work—though slightly hampered by the need of correcting newly arrived galley proofs of *For Authors Only*. These, I found, contained innumerable passages that required rewriting, and they were read six times before I was content to release them.

Then, before I could buckle down to steady work, the proofs of the rewritten *Lively Lady* arrived. A preliminary reading disclosed 122 typographical errors that the proofreaders had missed, so I read them three times for errors; then read them twice more in order to rewrite passages that I didn't like.

Still, I somehow contrived to make a little progress, in spite of all my proofreading, revising, rewriting, Lice-Aging, fulminating against politicians, letter writing, and attempting to solve the apparently unsolvable mysteries connected with the life of Robert Rogers. By the end of May, I had finished twenty chapters and given the book a name— *Northwest Passage*. I thanked my lucky stars that no one had ever before thought of using those pregnant words as the title of a novel. But twenty chapters were a mere scratching of the surface: the slightest budging of the mass against which I was impotently butting my head.

I had even failed to assemble much of the information I needed in order to get along with the book. One of those pieces of information, vital to my story, was the court-martial of Major Robert Rogers. Only by examining the testimony in his trial could I ever hope to know accurately why Rogers had behaved so strangely at Michilimackinac.

Allan Nevins, who had written the only comprehensive account of Rogers' life, had stated unequivocally that no copies existed, but I refused to believe it.

For months Miss Lucy Drucker, one of the erudite young English-women accredited as "searchers" by England's Public Record Office, had been on my pay roll, ransacking War Office records, Colonial Office records, for that court-martial.

She reported several times that it had probably been destroyed. I continued to insist that several copies must have been made of a trial as important as that of Major Rogers, and not *all* of them would have been destroyed. At my request she searched private libraries, and investigated repositories to which War Office and Colonial Office records had been transferred because of space requirements in the Public Record Office.

She hunted and hunted and hunted. And at last she found it! A copy had been filed and forgotten in a Colonial Office repository in the city of Canterbury.

That court-martial opened up a new line of investigation, and called for more searching, more documents, more books and journals. My library had grown to such proportions that I dared not leave it all in one place; so when we packed to return to America, I took only such source material as I had borrowed from the Congressional Library, and from friends and other libraries. The remainder I left in Porto Santo Stefano. Then if either part were lost, the book could still be finished.

Mrs. Roberts listed the books we left behind: *Encyclopaedia Britannica;* four-volume *History of London; Hunting with a Bow and Arrow;* set of Defoe; set of Cooper; *Montcalm and Wolfe;* Nute's *Voyageur; Life of Jonas Hanway; Toronto During the French Regime; Rocher Fendu (Split Rock); 18th Century in London; History of the American Frontier;* French's *First Year of the American Revolution; Algiers & the Scourge of Christendom; Rambles About Portsmouth,* I and II; *Annals of Portsmouth; Early Portsmouth History; Memoirs of Buckminster; Conspiracy of Ponteach; French Regime in Wisconsin;* Vol. I of *Life of Sir William Johnson;* Vol. 4 of Walpole's *Letters;* Elliot Coues, *New Light,* etc.; *Journals of A. Henry the*

Younger; The Veil Removed (Putnam); *The Fleet* (prison); *Michigan Fur Trade; Remarkable History of Hudson's Bay Company;* Carver's *Travels;* copy of the Rogers court-martial—and several hundred volumes that had nothing whatever to do with Rogers or Indians.

At the bottom of the list I find the note: What an innocent I had been when I graduated from Cornell, mistakenly regarded myself as educated, and thought I wanted to write! The mere preparation of this book has been equivalent to three college educations put together; and when it's finished I'll be able to pass a stiff series of examinations on the political situation in England prior to the American Revolution, the economic state of England's submerged nine tenths during that period, the foreign policies of Pitt, Bute and North, the French and Indian wars, Northwest Passage exploration, Indian trade and Indian tribes before the Revolution, trapping and trading practices in use in 1760, English prisons, New England society, painters and methods of painting in the eighteenth century, the relations between Algiers and the rest of Europe, conditions in English prisons, Benjamin Franklin's life in London, and a number of other related subjects.

§

Incipient writers, it seems to me, seldom think of writing as entailing work other than rapidly transferring thoughts from the brain to paper.

They seem to make light of the little matter of reading scores of journals, diaries, memoirs, biographies, orderly books; of perpetually peering into encyclopedias, Roget's *Thesaurus* and Bartlett's *Familiar Quotations.* It is a fact, however, that no group of college professors would ever dare propose to their students that they should, in the course of a college year, digest the tomes that any conscientious writer must consult during the same period.

Then, too, the number of letters that must be written over and above the day's work is frequently staggering. I use the word "must," for a writer who wishes to deal with any period other than the immediate present cannot escape the need of constantly seeking from a throng of sources the little details necessary to his labors, thanking friends for prompt and generous assistance, expressing heartfelt appreciation of encouraging messages, replying to queries from readers who haven't facilities for research, rebutting letters of denunciation. They must be answered regularly, too, or the recipient will be swamped.

I kept a record, in 1935, of those to whom I pounded out letters on my enduring Corona; and I insert that boring record here, not to have it read, but as a sort of print-picture or illustration to be glanced at by those who want to write. My idea in doing so is to show them that they cannot count on spending all their evenings in dancing, movie-going, bridge-playing, dart-throwing or other diversions if they persist in their desire.

LETTERS WRITTEN DURING THE FIRST YEAR
OF *NORTHWEST PASSAGE*

January 3, 1935
Miss French
E. B. Hill
American Mag.
Carl Brandt

January 6
Mingazzi

January 7
Carl Brandt

January 8
Miss Claasen
Norm Mason
Curtis Brown
Ellsworth
Edson Smith

January 9
Hatchard[1]
Gluyas Williams

January 12
Miss Claasen

January 13
Sam Blythe
Claasen
W. H. Stone
Pell

January 14
Booth & Susie
Margaret Carr

Dale Warren
2 correspondents

January 15
Nester, Palermo
Miss Nerney
Alec Woollcott

January 16
Von Auw
Claasen
Nat'l. Blank Book

January 17
Sherwood
Adelaide Neall

January 18
Hatchard
Julian Street

January 23
Miss Vaughan
Dodd, Mead & Co.
Mrs. Briggs
Harwood Merrill
Joan Masson

January 24
Herb Corey

January 25
Miss Nerney
Kilham Roberts
Munger & March't

Pub. Rec. Office
Claasen
Ralph H. Wms.

January 26
Mildred Burrage
Hamilton Gibbs

January 27
Claasen

January 28
T. S. Bosworth
A. W. Dean
Bob Choate
Jim Campbell
Julian Street
J. D. Ryan
Hatchard
J. P. Hatch
L. F. Hagglund

January 29
Booth (2)
Claasen

January 30
Greenslet
Mother
Ives, Algiers

January 31
Miss Nerney
C. Ewing

[1]Hatchard & Co., or Hatchard's, are the great London bookdealers who were ransacking England for source material for me.

February 1
Kilham Roberts
Nerney
Claasen

February 2
Munger & March't
R. W. G. Vail
Rand McNally

February 3
Wes Stout
Mrs. Casey
Rupert Hughes

February 4
Booth
Margaret Deland
Carl Brandt

February 5
Sen. Hale
Geo. Hobbs
Kreigh Collins
Claasen
W. H. Stone

February 6
Booth
Pub. Rec. Office
Hodder & Co.

February 7
Nerney
Allen Lane
Pollinger

February 9
Tittmann
Frank King

February 10
Nerney
Pollinger
Elrick Davis

February 11
Henry S. Canby
Dodd of Dodd, Mead
Jackson Gregory
Claasen: Revision

February 12
Von Auw
Kilham Roberts
Miss Cleaveland
Pesenti: *Rex*

February 13
Lorimer
Graeme Lorimer
Ben Williams
Bob Hale

February 14
P.R.O. searcher
Hatchard
Hopkins-*Rex*

February 15
Mother
R. Doubleday
Claasen
Lane
Pollinger
Nerney

February 16
Lawrence, Phil.

February 18
Booth
Sen. Hale
Sen. White
Mrs. Vanamee
Herb. Smith
Wayne Dawson

February 19
Woollcott
Bosworth
Mrs. Robins
Eunice Perkins

February 21
Madeleine Burrage

February 23
Pell
Robins
Dawes
H. W. Auburn
T. R. Hyde
Portia Burt

February 24
Jim Campbell
Dorothy Vaughan

February 25
Brandt
Alfred McIntyre
F. Greenslet
Kilham Roberts

February 27
Mrs. Robins

February 28
Booth & Susie

March 1
Pollinger
Robins

March 3
Lucy Drucker
G. Ward
Robins

March 5
L. Kiefer
Robins
Braille Press

March 6
Robins
Karl Mosser
H. C. Grover
H. A. Sturges
F. A. Fenger
H. R. Hardwick
Greenslet
Tittmann
MacQuarrie

March 7
Booth & Susie
Ben Williams

March 8
Elrick Davis
Bob Hale
Sam'l Wolcott
H. Raymond
S. Unwin
Guidicini
Robins

March 9
Mother
Mrs. Currier

March 10
H. Tittmann
G. Ward
Miles
Julian Street

March 11
Robins
K. Collins
Mrs. Ames
S. Laurent
H. Howland

March 12
Lorimer
Graeme Lorimer

Goodspeed
Norris Eveleth

March 13
E. M. Hopkins
Robins

March 14
S. K. Chapter
Nerney
Kilham Roberts
Drucker
Choate
Hatchard's

March 15
Guidicini
Ruth B. Owen
G. Ward

March 16
Pollinger
Calder

March 17
MacVeagh
Claasen
Robins
Drucker
Pollinger
Goodspeed
Hatch
War Dept.

March 18
Ray Grant
Hatchard

March 19
Doc Prescott
Turin Cons. Gen.
Ventimiglia

March 20
Mother
Booth & Susie
Ann Thayer
Von Auw

March 21
Guidicini

March 22
Kemper
Jim Campbell

March 23
Booth
Kemper
Ward
Chapter—German
   contract
Hatchard
Robins

March 24
Jim Campbell

March 25
Pollinger—Lane
R. Doubleday

March 26
Robins
Prof. West
Goodspeed

March 28
G. A. E. Clarke
Ward & Co.
Von Auw
Hatchard

March 29
Hatchard

April 2
Robins (drawings)
Gosnell
Kemper
Flakup

April 3
Booth & Susie
Mother
Munger & March't
McKenna, London

April 4
Sam Blythe
Antinori
Orvieto Est Est

April 5
Hardwick

April 6
Sen. White
R. Doubleday
Russell
Hanes

April 8
Doubleday (*Lice Age*)
Antinori
Walsh
Allen Lane
N. Orleans L.L.

April 9
Kemper
Ward
du Bois
Robins
Von Auw
Ruth B. Owen
Drucker

April 10
Elmer Ward
Jim Campbell

April 13
Robins
Claasen

April 14
Lane (proofs)
Robins (titles)
McIntyre
John M. Taylor

April 15
Robins
Guidicini
McKenna
Hatchard's
Booth

April 16
Robins
Walsh
Persel

April 17
Robins (*L.L.*proof)

April 23
Robins
Hatchard
Lane
A correspondent

April 26
Karl Mosser
Robins
Doubleday

April 27
Mother
Chapter
Campbell

April 28
J. L. Kuethe
Schell
Von Auw
Booth

April 29
Robins (proofs)
Ward
Hatchard

April 30
Graves (Cal)
Dysart
Miss Allen
Dr. Allen
M. Deland
Burke
Howland
Lorimer

May 1
Ben Williams
Alan Hunt (Braille)

May 3
Munger & March't
Calder

May 4
Jim Campbell
J. D. Ryan

May 5
Charley Cole
Von Auw
2nd National
Travelers
John Hancock

May 6
Gurney
S. H. P. Pell
Mrs. Robins

May 7
Vanamee
Lorimer
Manley
Booth & Susie

May 8
Pesenti

May 9
M. J. Walsh
Saccone & Speed
J. D. Ryan

May 10
Munger & March't
Hatchard

May 11
Bob Choate

May 12
Booth
Robins
Sam Blythe

May 13
Ed. for Lorimer
Bob Choate

May 14
Mrs. Meloney
Appleton-Century
Hatchard

May 17
Pollinger
Ray-Whitcomb
Florence Deskman

May 19
Bob Hale
Robert McBride

May 21
Robins
Kreigh Collins
Ward
Palloni

May 22
Saccone & Speed

May 23
Supt., P.R.Office

May 26
Antinori
Robins
R. E. Haven

May 27
Robins

May 28
Mother
Robins

May 31
Chapter
Pell
McKenna

June 5
Katharine

June 6
Thomas, Wien

June 21
Exeter History
Robins
Smith Colby

June 23
Allen Lane
Prof. Rogers
Geo. Hurrell

Mark Lawler
J. L. B. Williams
Eliz. Ring
Robins
Jack Gregory

June 24
McKenney
Clark Williams
R. G. Adams
Allen Lane
Von Auw

June 25
Von Auw

June 26
Pres. Johnson
Sen. Hale
Sen. White
Von Auw

June 28
Easton
Von Auw

June 30
Sonia Chapter
Kilham Roberts
Page Cooper
Doubleday
Robins
Aunt Lutie
Mrs. Lorimer
Pell
Chilson Leonard

July 1
Harriet Swift
Dorothy Vaughan
Ham's
Taylor

July 2
Margot Street

July 5
Leonard (biblio.)
Doubleday

July 6
Robins

July 7
G. E. Lawrence

July 8
Leon Leighton
Wired Robins

July 9
Wired Robins
Robins

July 10
G. Enderis, Berlin
Choate
Sen. White
Tel., Robins
St. Geo. Assessors

July 11
Chil Leonard

July 14
Adelaide Neall
Pell

July 15
Von Auw
Ad. Coors
E. Ward
Robins

July 19
Von Auw
Edson Smith

Lewiston Jrnl.
Sam Blythe

July 20
Mrs. Robins

July 26
Herbert F. West
Lillian Robins
Wright & Ditson
Edson Smith
Chilson Leonard
C. H. Easton

July 27
Harrie Coe
John M. Taylor
Jack Crawford
S. H. P. Pell
Von Auw

July 28
Allan Nevins
McKenna

July 30
Prof. West
Ad Coors

July 31
Lorimer
Robins
West

August 1
Mary Dickey
Pell
Leonard

August 2
Hatchard

August 3
Lorimer
Von Auw
Doubleday

August 4
Ben Williams

August 11
Prof. West

August 14
Brooks Bros.
Chilson Leonard
Robins
Robins
Fullam
Gwen Williams
Bob Choate
R. F. James

August 15
Fullam

August 16
Pell
Dr. T. S. Burr
Shuttleworth
Prof. West
Dale Warren
Scaife
Who's Who
Robins
D. R. Walker
Walsh
Coggswell
J. D. Ryan
Ray-Whit.

August 18
Sen. White
Booth
Robins
Fullam
A. Frost Lord

August 19
Sonia Chapter

August 22
Chamberlain
Hansen
Brickel
Canby
A.L.S. Wood
Minot
Edson Smith
Louisville Journal
Hopkins
Robins
Street
Von Auw

August 23
G. Lorimer

August 25
Mother
N. C. Wyeth
Leon Leighton

August 30
V. W. Rich

August 31
Booth
Levenson
May Dwight
Lorimer
Miss Lord
Lewiston Journal
Bob Hale
Arthur Gibbs
M. J. Walsh
Ray-Whitcomb
F. Greenslet
E. D. Tomlinson
Miss Vosper
R. K. Hodgman
Aunt Lutie
Maine State Library

N. C. Wyeth
Horace Mitchell
Brooke Anspach

September 1
Von Auw
Chapelle
Kallio
S. K. Chapter
Robins
Prof. Rogers
Pres. Hopkins

September 2
Goodrich (Dart.)
De Merritt

September 3
A. Neall

September 4
Bob Warner
C. W. Thompson
Booth
H. B. Coe

September 5
Walsh
Allen
Smith
Lorimer
Lane
Leonard
Saltonstall
Gurney
Rankin
H. S. Oragon

September 6
Hatchard
Robins
Nevins
W. J. Ghent

September 8
Robbie
Paul Allen
Miss Allen

September 16
Pargellis
Meyers
H. Stevens
P. Rollins
Curtis Brown
Sheldon Howe
Shuttleworth
Bob Hunt
Bernie Warner

September 17
Claasen
Lorimer
Levenson

September 18
Robins
Booth

September 22
Leonard
Choate
Robins
Brooks Bros.

September 23
L. Perry
Mason
Robins
Mayflower D.
Rugg
Pell

September 24
Choate

September 26
Moody
F. W. Pinkham
Robins
Hunt
Lorimer
Chapter

September 28
Old Corner
DeWolfe & Fiske
Pell
West
Choate

September 29
Leonard
T. Roosevelt
Ore. Hist. Soc.
Wis. Hist. Soc.
Kroch

October 2
Lorimer
McIntyre
Burt

October 3
Rugg
Draper
Campbell
Pargellis
Robins

October 8
Robins (2)
Pell
Leonard
Library Bulletin

October 9
Robins
Curtis Brown

October 11
Robins
Gonya
Webb
Mrs. D. Reynolds

October 12
Dave Lawrence

October 13
Ben Williams
Lorimer
Robins
Dr. Dahlstrom

October 18
Carol Faber
T. R. Rollo
J. J. Cryderman
J. J. Haas
Dr. L. Silvers
O. U. Ahlers
L. Ulbrich
Dr. R. M. Graham
Dr. Van F. Barnes
R. A. Martineau
J. L. Waring

October 19
Alfred McIntyre
W. M. Hastings
M. Orr, Jr.
Colston Leigh
John Pell
Lester Jenks
Roscoe Hupper
Mrs. Bacque
Mother
V. P. Boyle
Dr. Johnson
Muriel Kalan
Ben Williams

A. J. Sheldon
Tom Sorenson
G. Halliday

October 20
F. H. Fassett, Jr.
(M.I.T.)

October 21
J. A. McNamara
Rugg
Margaret Deland
Claasen
Robins
Mother

October 22
Mother
F. H. Tyson
D. Vaughan
Stan Emery

October 23
Mrs. Lorimer
Adelaide Neall
Old Print Shop

October 24
Getchell
Claasen
McNamara

October 26
Ernest King
Claasen

November 11
White X Ins.
Hatchard
Curtis Brown

November 12
P.R.O., London
Hatchard

November 13
Hosmer

November 14
Francis Edwards
Bob Choate
Miss Vaughan

November 15
Nester

November 16
Robins

November 17
Booth

November 18
Lorimer
Julian Boyd
Lyman

November 20
Mrs. Cabot

November 21
Lucy Drucker
Chilson Leonard

November 22
Jim Campbell

November 23
Nester
A. McIntyre
Francis Edwards
Sam Blythe
Laurent

November 26
Leonard
Curtis Brown
Dobbs

November 27
Sen. White
Francis Edwards
Lucy Drucker
Edson Smith
Rom. Berry
Herbert F. West
Harrie Coe
Mrs. Cabot

November 30
Booth
J. Gibson, Naples
Pesenti

December 1
Ben Williams
Coert du Bois
Mother
Trieste Consul
Hotel, Grosseto

December 2
Booth

December 3
Robins
Dale Warren
Arnaldo Cortesi
Lagueglia

December 6
Francis Edwards
Gotlieb, Trieste
Lea Shippen Luquer
Frecchiarossa
H. S. Canby
Dr. H. Johnson
Aspergum Co.

December 7
Alfred Nester
Robins

F. G. Fassett
(M.I.T.)
Alfred McIntyre

December 9
Holle & Co.
Mrs. Pinkham
du Bois

December 10
Booth
Nester
Lee Keedick

December 11
Booth
Leonard
Cecil Smith (Va.)
Dr. Renaud
Cal. potato man
Myron Adams

December 12
Arnaldo Cortesi
Allen Lane
G. A. E. Clarke

December 14
Coert du Bois
Hatchard
Drucker
Curtis Brown (H)
Cortesi

December 15
E. M. Hopkins
Choate
Ewing
Mother
Mrs. Currier
Robins
Buton (Rome)
Tittmann

December 16

Kilham Roberts
Sonia Chapter
F. G. Fassett, Jr.
Mrs. Nye (Vermont)
White Cross

December 17

Graeme Lorimer
Adelaide Neall
Wes Stout
Lorimer
Drucker
Booth
Gotlieb
& 8 cards

December 18

Edson Smith
Coert du Bois
Chil Leonard

December 19

du Bois
Laurent
& 12 postcards

December 20

du Bois
Edson Smith
G. Ward, London

December 21

Booth

December 23

Dr. Imelen
Julian Street
Hatchard

December 24

Booth
Mother
D. Getchell
8 postcards

December 25

Edson Smith
Arthur Staples
Sen. White

December 26

Chilson Leonard
Lorimer
Stanley Pargellis
8 postcards

December 27

Bob Steinert
Alfred McIntyre
Pell
Herbert West

December 28

Robins
Halliday
Lanctot
Stewart
Vajda
Leonard
Frank Henry
Francis Edwards

December 29

Curtis Brown
 (Hebdon)
R. W. G. Vail
Jack La Gorce
Saltonstall
Ben Williams
John Pember
Mrs. E. Akerley

December 30

Booth & Susie
Francis Edwards

CHAPTER

30

THAT 1935 winter was bad enough, but the summer that followed was worse. I begrudged everything that kept me from going ahead with *Northwest Passage;* but as usual something continually interfered. The first interference was a pair of infected tonsils,—the ones that English doctors had assured me were responsible for aching hands, arms and shoulders; so I had them pried out at the Maine General Hospital. The prying made such an impression upon me that I was unable to return to thinking about *Northwest Passage* until I had dealt fully with my aversion to tonsillectomy in a *Saturday Evening Post* article, "It Must Be Your Tonsils." This was promptly published as a book, since my publishers vaguely hoped that it would rival the 200,000 circulation of Irvin S. Cobb's *Speaking of Operations. It Must Be Your Tonsils* sold the conventional 5,000 copies.

With my tonsils out of the way, I re-read the first chapters of *Northwest Passage,* preparatory to adding others, but found I couldn't proceed until the first four chapters could be rewritten. The characters were flat and unreal: unalive; and conditions were such that I couldn't do anything about it.

In the immediate vicinity of my home, that summer, there seemed to be more golfers, more gin drinkers, more callers, more barking dogs, more squealing children, an even greater determination to force me to "do my duty to society," more airplanes, more brawling caddies, more mowing machines, more whistling chauffeurs, more telephone calls, than on the preceding summer. I couldn't get Rogers and his Rangers and Langdon Towne securely in my mind's eye when my ears were constantly assaulted by a procession of four-ball matches, attended by club-rattling caddies, that hacked, slapped and shouted their way past my windows.

Since the family fortune was again running low, I had to finish that book; so I once more removed Mrs. Roberts and myself from all these delights of civilization, retreated to an ancient farmhouse in a mountain valley far to the northward—a farmhouse more primitive than the Half-Baked Palace, but even freer from distractions than any other work-room I had occupied.

In that mountain valley we split our wood, cooked our food, carried our water from a well supplied with equal parts of water and angleworms. The only daytime sounds were the fluttering of leaves, the distant rustle of the trout stream below us, the twittering of swallows in the chimney, the cawing of crows, the squalling of blue jays; the only nighttime sounds the occasional hooting of owls, the gnawing of porcupines at the bacon-impregnated sink outside the front door, and the rumbling of thunder in the mountains; and in those peaceful surroundings I rewrote the first four chapters; then forged ahead through Chapter 27.

How much those forested ramparts had to do with it I don't know. In just such surroundings Rogers and his men, Towne and Hunk Marriner, must have moved on moccasined feet; and suddenly all those people seemed to be alive in the woods around me. Cap Huff and Langdon Towne, Harvard undergraduates, shallow-brained Elizabeth Browne and her stuffed-shirted parents, Sergeant McNott, Robert Rogers, the green-clad Rangers, took on breadth and thickness. By the time frost had reddened the foliage that rimmed that mountain valley, I was sure—sure for the first time in my life—that I had written something satisfactory to me.

But I didn't know how I had done it, nor had I any confidence that I would ever be able to finish the fifty-odd chapters that lay before me, each one certainly destined to be revised or rewritten fifty or sixty times.

§

In order to return to Italy at the earliest possible moment, I avoided the necessity of hunting *Post* articles by agreeing, in return for a thou-sand-dollar advance, to write a book on Maine for Little, Brown & Co. Since there was no need to deliver the manuscript for another year, we packed three bags of precious source material in the bowels of the Ford, made our companionable and widely traveled terrier Serena Blandish comfortable atop our baggage, and on October 24, 1935, set off for an Italian liner and Italy.

This winter, I assured Mrs. Roberts, I would tend strictly to my knit-ting! I'd put aside all other distractions like letter writing, Lice Ages, politicians, feuding with publishers, and fussing with the revising of

former books when nobody cared whether I revised them or not. I was
buoyed in this determination by the persistence with which *Arundel,
The Lively Lady, Rabble in Arms* and *Captain Caution* were stirring
weakly and breathing steadily.

To be specific about it, the sales of those four books during the preceding six months had been:

1935	*Arundel*	*The Lively Lady*	*Rabble in Arms*	*Captain Caution*
July 2	67	28	75	37
9	15	7	19	8
16	98	33	70	29
24	21	32	33	3
31	45	22	35	11
Aug. 7	16	7	10	4
15	140	105	122	9
22	130	18	72	18
29	14	21	29	7
Sept. 3	79	15	89	8
10	27	19	34	13
17	41	11	42	3
24	93	33	101	10
Oct. 1	143	25	172	37
8	103	39	111	14
15	31	28	19	11
22	60	48	52	6
29	18	14	22	10
Nov. 7	35	3	62	7
14	33	67	54	9
21	121	63	115	31
28	38	27	33	18
Dec. 5	27	37	89	38
12	82	58	46	27
19	115	75	59	49
26	62	38	26	14

§

I had been serious in my promises to Mrs. Roberts; but it often seems
to a writer that Unseen Forces at times work tirelessly and with grim
determination to keep him from doing as he wishes.

I had always liked that Italian liner on which we sailed; but since
I had last traveled on her, she had been a troopship, carrying Italian

regiments to Abyssinia to further Mussolini's inexcusable war upon that helpless country. As a result, she was infested with fleas, which fell upon me eagerly—a fact that had no immediate bearing on my situation, and at the time seemed merely annoying.

Our old friend Coert du Bois, consul general in Naples, called our attention to the attempts England was making, late in 1935, to stop Mussolini's aggression, and to the resulting anti-English feeling that was blazing high in Italy. We'd do well, he told us, to spend as little time as possible on city streets; for most Italians, unable to distinguish between English and Americans, had taken to stoning those they disliked—stoning their belongings, too.

So we made the long run from Naples to Porto Santo Stefano in one day—November 7, 1935. Just at dusk, ten miles from our destination, a five-year-old boy darted from the roadside shrubbery before us. How so many things could happen in a second's time was beyond my understanding. I had a dozen thoughts as I yanked the emergency brake; the child came to a huddled stop, reared backward, then pitched straight ahead and vanished beneath our radiator. I felt the bumper jar against him, and a moment later had him in my arms. The car had stopped before the wheel had reached him; but the harm was done, for he was limp, unconscious, occasionally gasping a little, as a dying bird gasps.

The only building in the neighborhood was a sort of community affair for the families of small farmers—*contadini*—and people ran from it toward us. I shouted to them in miserable Italian—*Dove il pappa* [where is the father]—*questa piccolino* [this little one]—*pronto prego* [quickly, I beg]—*vado ospitale* [go hospital]!

I expected them to reach for stones, and wouldn't have cared much; because my lightning thoughts, when I set the brakes and jumped out, had anticipated trial for manslaughter in an Italian court, conviction, years in an Italian jail. But none of them, so far as I could see, had any intention of stoning me to death.

They shouted the name of the child's father, but he couldn't be found. A priest joined the throng, and I tried to explain to him how it had happened; the need for hurry—*à ospitale nell' Orbetello—presto, presto* [quickly, quickly]! A woman clutched a black shawl to her breast and told the priest, "I saw it from the window, and it is as he says, *veramente!* The *poverino* fell beneath the *macchina,* as if pushed! *Solamente* the little one was at fault!"

I begged the priest to take the obviously dying child and come with me to the hospital; but he refused, saying it was better to wait for the father; so we just stood there in the gathering darkness, waiting.

The father arrived after a few interminable minutes. He was unperturbed and well dressed, so that I knew he had been warned and had changed from work clothes to his Sunday suit. He took his unconscious and gasping son from me without comment and seemingly without emotion. Since the car was filled with books and luggage, Mrs. Roberts drove, the father sat beside her, holding the child across his knees, and I clung to the running board with an arm hooked through the window. The child was a soiled and jointless doll, eyes closed; and at intervals he gasped, as I had seen a girl gasp when dying of starvation in Vienna. Only ten minutes ago I had not only wanted to write, but was confident that some day I might learn how to do so. Now, in a sort of cold resignation, I knew I never would—not if that child died; and I knew he was already as good as dead. Step on it, I told Mrs. Roberts. Step on it!

That was a good Ford. It had once done seventy-two miles an hour on a German autobahn; even on those uneven Italian roads we made the nine miles to the barren hospital of Orbetello in ten minutes.

The only person in sight, when I unceremoniously burst into the receiving ward, was a black-robed white-coifed Sister, who unemotionally listened to my labored explanation that I had brought a dying child: that no time must be lost: that I implored her to tell the *dottore* that my *cognato*, my brother-in-law, was *direttore* of San Gallicano Hospital and a consul of Rome: that I begged in his name that the doctor would *vengo, vengo, vengo!* And *subito!*

She went away, placid and unhurried; then placidly returned, took the child from the father, laid the little body on an operating table and stripped off the single dingy garment. So far as I could see, he was dead —or just barely living. The doctor came almost immediately, donning a white jacket as he came—and for a doctor to come promptly, even when fully garbed, was an uncommon occurrence in Italy. To have one come both promptly and partially dressed was a miracle.

He felt the limp little boy from head to foot; lifted his eyelids and peered closely at his eyes; put an ear to his chest; sat him upright on the operating table and applied an ear to his back.

The child's eyes magically remained open.

Holding the child by the arm, the doctor turned to us with eyebrows raised and hand outflung in a characteristic Italian gesture. *"Niente,"* he said. "Nothing! There is nothing wrong! He was merely frightened —shamming!"

He spanked the little boy's back sharply. *"Sti attenti* [pay attention]," he said reprovingly. "Stay out of roads and cease pretending to be dead!"

The child uninterestedly submitted to having his diminutive Mother Hubbard pulled over his head, while we had a word with the doctor. I knew exactly how a man feels when reprieved in the shadow of the gallows, and I trembled to think what would have happened to us under similar circumstances in America. The doctor protested when I pressed half my supply of lire on him; and the father, suddenly enriched by the other half, showered us with blessings as we put him and the bored infant in an Orbetello taxicab and sent them off to the community dwelling at Tre Torreta.

§

The shock of that near catastrophe was bothersome: so, too, was a discovery. In Rogers' court-martial proceedings, Rogers had testified that a certain Dr. John Campbell was his agent. For months I had been trying to find out something about Dr. John Campbell; and almost immediately after hitting the child, I received a complete report on him.

He had been a celebrated Scot, an historian and intimate of the great Dr. Samuel Johnson. He had been the London agent, also, who acted for Henry Ellis and Arthur Dobbs, colonial governors of Georgia and North Carolina. Campbell had written long accounts of various expeditions that had gone in search of the Northwest Passage. Dobbs had financed one of them; and Ellis had sought that fabled thoroughfare in a vessel that belonged to Dobbs. All knowledge of these facts had hitherto been lost, and now, at one gulp, so to speak, I knew the motives and personalities behind Rogers' interest in the Northwest Passage: understood how Jonathan Carver had lied about his part in that venture: understood that with this added knowledge I must once more rewrite several sections of the work already done.

Again I put Miss Drucker to work running down information on all these men: searching, too, for the court-martial proceedings against Lieutenant Stephens, the officer who had been sent by General Amherst to carry provisions to Rogers' retreating men, but had run away when those starving Rangers were only a few hours from the appointed meeting place. If I could find that court-martial, which had never been unearthed, I would know the real story behind the unfathomable finish of the dreadful retreat of Rogers and his Rangers from St. Francis. I told her to hunt, too, for documents having to do with Jonathan Carver— something that would prove him to be the liar, trimmer and ingrate I was sure he had been.

While waiting for Miss Drucker to search the vast mass of unpublished documents in the Public Record Office, I examined the chapters

I had not had time to revise before leaving Maine. Their ineptitude seemed dreadful; and a month was devoted to rewriting the first twenty-seven chapters. The chapters as originally written had made 205 typed pages. Only twenty pages out of the original 205 remained on December 7, when the rewriting was completed: 185 pages had been wholly changed and the original pages destroyed.

I think I might have made rapid progress after December 7 except for two unexpected disturbances: one the necessity of reading, editing and correcting the bungled proofs of *Arundel,* which an English publisher had decided to publish, but in the secretive way peculiar to a number of British publishers; the other the distressing development of three fleabites that had appeared upon my thigh six weeks before. I mention all these things for just one reason: to demonstrate that anyone who wants to write must stay on the job every day and all day, in spite of hell and high water.

CHAPTER

31

On the first of January, 1936, I reached Chapter 33 and the spot where Robert Rogers, returning from the raid on St. Francis, divided his forces at Lake Memphremagog. To say that I was mentally disturbed would be to put it mildly. The task of reconstructing the route followed by Rogers in his retreat was baffling; Mr. Frank Lloyd and my publishers were showering me with cables, urging me to sell the film rights to *Captain Caution* for about the same amount a ham actor would receive for two months' work; I was wiring London bookdealers to find for me books, mezzotints and handwriting samples of Dr. John Campbell, Jeffrey Amherst, Arthur Dobbs, Henry Ellis, Jonathan Carver and other characters I needed to know more about, along with books on endocrinology that might explain the behavior of some of those gentlemen.

And then in came a letter from Lucy Drucker saying that she had not only located the Stephens court-martial, but had found Jonathan Carver's petition to be allowed to accompany Robert Rogers on a second expedition to discover the Northwest Passage! Wow! Let's go.

Unfortunately, distractions developed with painful rapidity:

January 16: Don't know what to do for the three bites I got on November 15, and that are not only swelling, but itching like Billy-be-damned. Received Henry Ellis' *Voyage to Hudson's Bay:* he shows up the Hudson's Bay Company's agents as true British lice; but none of his evidence is even mentioned in Bryce's supposedly important *Remarkable History of the Hudson's Bay Company.* Wired Drucker to hurry up with the Stephens court-martial, as I'm just bringing Rogers to the mouth of the Ammonoosuc. That trip home of Rogers' was horrible. Even writing about it is exciting.

January 17: Received the Carver petition and the Stephens court-martial at last. The latter shows a bewildering discrepancy in dates. Rogers' *Journal* has him reaching the mouth of the Ammonoosuc on October 30, 1759. In his testimony in the Stephens court-martial he testifies that he reached the mouth of the Ammonoosuc on October 20, so he stayed there ten days. It's not in character for Rogers to stay in any such situation for ten days. Must know the answer, so telegraphed Drucker to hunt for the report carried to General Amherst by McMullen, the orders from Amherst to Stephens, the verbal report made to Amherst by Captain Ogden, November 7 or 8, 1759, and any report or record of the Indians, Rangers and captives who left Rogers, went to Crown Point by way of Otter River, and arrived at Crown Point November 8. Can't go on until I find the reason for the conflicting dates in Rogers' *Journal* and the Stephens court-martial. Those three bites suppurate more and more, and itch intolerably.

January 19: Got Rogers, Towne, Ogden and the Indian boy to the edge of Wattoquitchy Falls, and tomorrow should see him safe at No. 4. It has taken me longer to write the journey down the Connecticut than it took Rogers to do it, and I feel as though I'd been on the raft myself.

January 20: Started Chapter 40, down the river to No. 4, but bothered by those three bites, which throb and burn both day and night, and yield to no antiseptic. Got Rogers into the fort. Heard from Stephen Laurent, the St. Francis Indian who still lives in Odanak, the modern name of old St. Francis. He sent me an Abenaki grammar written by his father, and writes a more scholarly letter than most college graduates I run across. Most people who yap about "civilization" don't know what they're talking about.

January 23: So irritated by the horrible itching of those three bites and reading the filth in Robert Briffault's *Europa* that I wrote Governor Cross, president of the Institute of Arts and Letters, offering $1.78 yearly for two prizes of $.89—a yearly National Institute Pornographic Prize, to be awarded just after the Pulitzer Prize, for "that novel, published in America, which shall most effectively convey an atmosphere of indecency and degeneracy, and best exemplify the prostitution of literature to profit or to lubricity"; and a similar award to the American publisher "who upholds the high ideals of his profession by publishing, without editorial supervision or alteration," the prize novel. Suggested to Governor Cross that Briffault be the first recipient.

January 24: Infuriated by Lane, London publisher, who refuses to let me have a statement of sales, supposedly due on December 31, until April 1. Unless forced to do so, publishers will *not* let their authors— who, of course, are the persons most interested in their books' progress—

discover anything whatever about that progress until the last possible moment. Struggled hard to get Towne out of Crown Point and started home toward Portsmouth. That's the worst feature of writing: *nothing's* easy: *everything's* difficult. Read Richardson's book on painting. What a damned old fool he was!

January 25: Worried beyond expression by the violent itching of those three swollen bites. Can't understand why, in spite of constant application of S.T. 37, they grow larger and larger, itchier and itchier, and more and more inflamed. Further inflamed by our dinner—one diminutive spike mackerel, three infinitesimal red mullet, salad, and a cheese called *I Promessi Sposi*. *I Promessi Sposi* (*The Betrothed*) by Manzoni, is Italy's most celebrated novel, and the dullest drivel ever written—a veritable piece of cheese; but I never thought any Italian would admit it by naming a cheese for it. *I Promessi Sposi,* as one might expect, smells bad, too.

January 26: Those damnable bites now have white cores, like miniature Vesuviuses. No doubt my Italian *cognato,* who was direttore of Italy's largest hospital for skin diseases, would make short work of them, but he died of angina last spring. Rewrote the start of Chapter 42, and seriously considered a suggestion from Booth that I make a trip to the American hospital at Neuilly to have these three horrible bites investigated. Feel as if the damned things might suddenly explode, covering me with a mass of eruptions.

January 27: Dr. Polvani, dean of Porto Santo Stefano's medical corps, came up to examine the three bites and pustules that are radiating from them to legs, arms, back, hands, shoulders. . . . Could they come from the shock of hitting the child? Emphatically not! Could they be the result of fretting over publishers and a difficult novel? Not at all! They were, he said, urticaria, brought on by eating shellfish. I must stop eating fish and eggs, stop drinking *vino,* and in a week all would go away. That would be fifty lire. Much relieved and did two full pages—2,500 words.

February 7: Polvani up again to inject *olio di Zimbali,* guaranteed to cure this blasted urticaria or—as Booth calls it—Eureka acid. I insisted the swellings were bites. Polvani denies it: they're from somep'n I've eaten. That will be fifty lire. Did 1,200 words.

February 8: Polvani sent word that he had investigated the most recent researches in the Eureka acid field. I must take three daily shots of milk of magnesia, continue to inject *olio di Zimbali,* and cease and desist from every sort of exercise. Did 1,000 words.

February 9: Pustules spread with alarming rapidity, and itch and burn horribly. Wired Arnaldo Cortesi to get me the best skin specialist in Rome and make an appointment with him for the following afternoon. Finished Chapter 42.

February 10: To Rome by the early train. The pustules so thick and inflamed that they burst, gluing my shirt to my back. Arnaldo met me and took me to the hot and airless office of Dottore Vincenzo Montesano. He was a stuffy man with a hell of a cold. After using a magnifying glass on my eruptions, he stated unequivocally that the pustules were caused by zeccas, or ticks, which had embedded themselves in me while I was carrying some sort of tick-bearing animal, such as a rabbit, a lark, or a howl—meaning owl.

I told him I'd carried nothing of the sort, and everything had started from three ordinary fleabites, without anything embedded in 'em.

He contemptuously brushed aside my denials. Zeccas, he insisted; and he coughed fruitily in my face, instructing me to renounce alcohol, sauces, coffee, tea, eggs, fish, asparagus, and take ichthyol in graduated doses. Also I must rub the pustules with lanolin salve, which he guaranteed would alleviate the itching immediately. He provided me with two small pots of salve. When I had used both pots, he said, I'd be cured. That would be two hundred lire.

Montesano's persistence in spraying me with cold germs, plus his insistence that I must have played host to a dead animal infested with zeccas, or ticks, convinced me that he didn't know what he was talking about, and that I would do well to check up on his diagnosis.

Rome, February 11: Saw Kirk at the embassy and told him my troubles. He said he didn't think there was a doctor in Italy worth a damn, but I might try Erwin Stückgold, a German-Jewish doctor who had been chased out of Germany by the Nazis. Called on Stückgold, who instantly diagnosed my trouble as acute eczema, and assured me he could effect a cure in two weeks by injecting Staphylo-Yatren, a new and magical German discovery. He gave me an injection of Staphylo-Yatren. The eruptions, he insisted, would not extend to my head, soles of my feet, or you-know-where. They were emphatically not urticaria or the result of zecca bites. I must not allow water to touch my body: no bathing at all except in the universal European bath adjunct, the bidet. Returned to Porto Santo Stefano slightly cheered but still erupting.

February 13: Came down with Montesano's cold. Abjectly wretched because pustules continue to spread and burn. Injected 2½ c.c. Staphylo-Yatren and wrote two paragraphs.

February 15: Pustules spreading with unbelievable speed, despite the infallible Staphylo-Yatren. Sent for Polvani, and told him what Montesano and Stückgold had said. Polvani sticks to urticaria, caused by eating fish. Pustules itch and burn like fire. Montesano's two pots of salve almost gone, so wired the English drugstore in Firenze for six more. Eruptions so extensive that I wear pajamas over my lanolined body so that clothes won't be smeared. Wrote half a page.

February 16: Hands puffed and swollen—200 to 300 pustules on each. Salved them, added cotton gloves to the under pajamas, and wrote 600 words. Also composed a poem for Anna, by way of predicting what Kennebunkporters would say:

> Listen, my dear! It's simply rich!
> Kenneth Roberts has got the itch!

February 17: Miserere! Just a mass of eruptions and discomfort, but squeezed out 1,000 words. Wired Firenze for six more pots of Montesano's salve, as I use half a pot a day.

February 18: A night of complete misery and salve-applying, and a morning of itching, squirming, scratching, burning and applying pressure to spots that seem to be sizzling. Wrote 1,000 words and started Chapter 47.

February 19: No reduction in misery. Smeared myself three times with salve, wrote 1,000 words, and vainly tried to lose myself in *Jane Eyre,* but failed because of the manner in which ten-year-old girls talk like octogenarians.

February 20: Utter and wholesale torment. Salve and Staphylo-Yatren are equally ineffective. Awake and scratched from five to seven. Did 1,000 words, in torment from burning and itching legs, chest, stomach, back and arms, and swollen pustulated hands, so puffed that no veins are visible.

February 21: No diminution in itching. Can't sleep at night without taking sodium amytal at eleven and again at 2 A.M. Interested to find a book by Bertrand Russell on what constitutes happiness, and to read in it that in his opinion, solitude is one of the primary ingredients. Not if you have the itch it ain't. All men who have accomplished anything worth doing, Russell says, have had to go into solitary confinement. I dunno how much I'm accomplishing, but we've got all the solitude there is, and only by means of solitude have I been able to be content—and to be content, I assume, is to be happy. But what this itch is doing to me shouldn't happen to Bertrand Russell!

February 22: Took half a Sedormid pill every hour, hoping to dull the itching. Almost crazy from it. Did 750 words.

February 23: Sent to Florence for more Staphylo-Yatren and a five-pound mess of ointment. Wrote 1,000 words.

February 24: Horrible and all-pervasive itching, though my arms and back seem a little less inflamed. The palms of my hands are thick and stiff, but veins are faintly visible on their backs. Wrote 2,000 words.

February 25: Itching seemed a little less, though have to apply grease from neck to feet. More at ease mentally, so did 2,000 words and finished Chapter 48, completing Rogers' exposition of his Northwest Passage scheme and introducing Nathaniel Potter, who will develop into a first-class stinker and give me profound pleasure. I've long been afraid something would happen to me, so that I'd pop off without leaving a complete sketch of my objectives, but now they ought to be clear. Finished *Jane Eyre,* a highly improbable book, filled with mugs, according to my lights.

February 26: Itching less violent, and got through the night without almost tearing myself to pieces scratching. Dr. Stückgold wrote that I should take castor oil every morning, and inject calcium daily. Read C. Brontë's *Shirley,* which was spoiled for me by a preface by Mrs. Humphry Ward, who should have been choked for writing it, and her publisher choked for printing it.

February 27: 1,200 words. No diminution in the extent of blotches, but the burning and itching seem a little less. Hands almost unswollen. Tried applying salve only once—in the morning.

February 28: Stückgold wrote he had now changed his diagnosis, and was sure my eruption was the result of shock from hitting the child and worry over the progress of my book; that I should therefore take a coffee-spoonful of calcium after each meal, a tablespoon of castor oil every morning, continue with Staphylo-Yatren in diminishing doses, and not use soap for four weeks. These goddam doctors! Started Chapter 50.

February 29: Up after my best sleep in a month, thanks to an amytal pill, and wrote 1,200 words. Tackled the dinner party for Rogers at Dr. Campbell's. Wholly at a loss and filled a sheet with impatient dialogue, just to get forward and have something to rewrite:

> When the butler ushered us into Dr. Campbell's parlor, we saw four bastards sitting before a cannel-coal fire, drinking port out of tin dippers.
>
> "Nuts," said one. "Don't tell me that all Americans have six toes on each foot!"

"I don't recognize the voice," I whispered to Rogers, "but the words are familiar."

Rogers scratched his head. "I ain't quite sure, but I think it's a feller named Edmund Burke who's going to have Francis Burke-Roche for a descendant."

March 1: Smeared myself with lanolin salve and couldn't straighten out the dinner party. Wished repeatedly I'd never undertaken to write such an intricate piece of tripe. Then I learned that Joshua Reynolds was pock-marked, deaf, and had a badly scarred upper lip. That information, somehow, brought them all to life and resulted in 1,800 words.

March 2: Went without grease last night and this morning, under the impression that I was improving, but around noon pustules burst out all over me. Had to cover myself with salve, and itched terribly all evening, but wrote 2,000 words.

March 3: A miserable day of burning and itching. Smeared myself so thickly with lanolin that I had to put on two pajama tops under my clothes. Wrote 2,000 words. Haven't smoked for days; but all my non-smoking, non-drinking, non-bathing, bidet-ing, injecting, purging, calcium-taking, milk-of-magnesia-ing, castor-oiling and greasing have done me no good whatever.

March 4: Booth forwarded a letter from a nosy friend who thought I shouldn't be allowed to write American novels unless I live in America, and insisted I'm unpatriotic because I spend winters in Italy. The son of a bitch was serious, too! Greased all over, itched almost insupportably. Wrote 2,000 words, finishing Chapter 50. Sent to Rome for Cuticura ointment at Booth's suggestion. Booth's letters, commenting on the progress of my distressing ailment, were cheerful:

> Cern'y got us worried about your leprosy—pressure to cable you start for Mass. Gen. Hosp. by way Amer. Nursing Home at Neuilly—and general idea that you and Anna always heretofore so healthy you got no pract. experience how to handle yourselves when stricken. Also guessing that Dermatosa might be right ab't tick itch—or maybe not —or parasites that finally got their family really going—and also pressure to cable "Use Cuticura Ointment"——
>
> Hope you've got down to work—won't be hard to finish *if you don't make it so*—If you get into a jam, go out and whistle and sing, and the thing'll straighten out in your mind without bothering you to *think* about it. Just *wait* for it. Don't *force*.

March 5: Smeared myself with grease at 5 A.M. and discovered more pustules. Greased again on retiring. Frantic at my inability to obtain surcease from this damned outburst. Only did 1,000 words, in spite of going out and whistling and singing, in pursuance of Booth's suggestion. Hands too swollen to hold a book, so Anna read me excerpts from Lawrence's *Seven Pillars of Wisdom,* which show that Lawrence and his brother officers were regularly indulging in activities reminiscent of those peculiar to Taormina.

March 6: Indescribably weary of scratching, greasing, being miserable, and going without wine, preprandial snorts, cigarettes and ordinary foods. Exasperated beyond words at the inability of these damned doctors to agree on what I've got or to prescribe anything that will cure it.

March 7: Itching worse than in many days, but did 1,500 words and had my first long walk since November 7.

March 8: Best night since this damned thing started, but after I'd done 750 words, the fireworks started around my ankles and by dinnertime I was in abject misery again. Dictated fourteen letters to Anna.

March 9: Such frightful itching, arms and legs, at 2 A.M. that I had to grease all over. Stückgold wrote from Rome that I should at once start taking a German remedy called Uricedin, guaranteed to cure everything. Telegraphed to Florence for it, and bet Anna ten dollars it wouldn't cure anything at all.

March 10: 750 words. Itched like hell last night. Hope to God the Uricedin will help.

March 11: Got the Uricedin from Florence, took a shot of it, did 1,000 words, but seem to be getting nowhere. I think I've lost my story. It certainly is a dud. Wish to God I'd never embarked on it. Started wearing white greased stockings to ameliorate the itching and swelling that afflict my legs every night.

March 12: Smeared myself with ointment at 8 A.M. and 1 P.M. and peeled off 1,000 words. Two weeks ago England was howling for sanctions against Italy, and France was protesting. Now France is howling for sanctions against Germany (for entering the Ruhr), and England won't play ball. They're all a bunch of bastards—all! Felt distinctly better today. Read in C. Brontë's *Villette,* in which everyone is so blastedly refaned, as the English say, that they can't eat a piece or slice of toast—only a morsel of toast. Morsel!

March 13: Conscious of improvement, but still had to cover myself with grease. Booth wrote, expressing sympathy for my leprosy. Did 1,250 words.

March 14: Tried to get along without ointing, but burned and itched so violently that I had to apply salve again at 6 and 10 P.M. Wrote 1,000 words, said to hell with it, and had our first cocktails in two months.

March 15: Eruptions beginning to clear up, and hands look almost normal. Wrote 1,250 words.

March 16: Started Chapter 54 and wondered why in hell I ever tackled such a hopeless white elephant as *Northwest Passage!* Tried to read Santayana's new book, which is receiving rave front-page reviews in all lit'ry publications, but was bored by it. I guess I'll never learn to write.

March 17: Had to oint all over again, but cheered by a letter from Admiral Sims asking if I'd write his biography, and urging me not to say No until he'd had a chance to talk with me. Further cheered by a letter from a professor of English saying that he considers Santayana's new book dull, uninspired, incoherent and chaotic. Maybe I *can* learn to write, after all. Maybe Santayana ain't as good as the critics say he is.

March 18: The specialist in Rome, Montesano, said my itch would be gone after I'd used two jars of his ointment. I have now used thirty-six jars, and today sent to Florence for ten more. Five weeks ago Stückgold said I'd be cured in two weeks. If I'd ever gone that far astray when working for the *Saturday Evening Post,* I'd have deservedly been cut in small pieces and flushed down the toilet. Why does the world continue to endure those who are always wrong? Before every prize fight, each fighter's manager always predicts victory, and one is always wrong. Before every election everywhere, every campaign manager always predicts overwhelming victory for his side, and fifty per cent of them are always wrong—usually overwhelmingly so. Why not relegate such dopes to the side lines—not only in politics and athletics, but in every line of endeavor? Wrote 1,000 words, considerably encouraged by knowing I can't possibly be as incompetent as an author as is Rome's greatest skin disease expert as a diagnostician. Booth's letters continue to be cheering:

> Hope you're larfing reminiscently about the dermatolic hell by the time this reaches you and that your letter was written at the climax of it. It *does* sound like eczema—or like what Jack Thomson had in Rome in 1906. He was there with George Ade, and Ade was eloquent about living in the same suite. Jack's clothes had to be burned and the Doc wanted to take him to the Pest House, but the authorities there declined to receive him. It was a form of itch peculiar to Sunny It., and like nothing any American ever heard of—but it didn't last long, so I spose can't be related to yours. Jack was himself—meaning drunk again—by the time he left for Paris, ab't 2 weeks later.

Can't say Doc Dermatosa seems appetizing with check coat and unchecked cold all over the patient. Weren't there no Amer. docs in Rome? Top one used to be my cousin, Baldwin—grand ole party; limousine, fur coat, silk hat, white mustache—Royalties from all over coming to see him. He's the one who gave one of his patients a letter to Doc. Baldwin of Florence, his brother: "Dear Bill: This is a fat goose. Pluck her." Only the patient steamed the letter open. Doc used to laugh and holler over that.

Certainly is tough for Anna and not agreeable for you either! No good docs in Florence? Wonder why not having one come over from there? Eng. or American. Bum feeling, being away from Docs you know and have sized up—and with somepn you don't know. Wonder if they'd a-reckanized catsup poisoning. Bet they wouldn't! Li'l ole Doc Prescott pounced on it like lightning—landed on Eureeka like spider on a fly, so anyhow I had the gloomy satisfaction of knowing what I had—I mean what had me. Why do we speak of our ills possessively—maybe to be proud of 'em later?

32

NORTHWEST PASSAGE continued to progress at the rate of about 2,000 words a day through March and half of April, by which time I had finished Chapter 58.

April 12: Tried to evolve the transition of Rogers from Oswego to Michilimackinac, but only squeezed out two lines. I'm fed up: fed up with the novel, eczema, dieting, incompetent doctors, smearing myself daily with a disgusting mass of grease, and the impossibility of blowing off steam. In desperation wrote a burlesque transition:

> We left Oswego for Michilimackinac on the 7:49 express. The Pullmans were hot and smelled of bananas. We arrived in Michilimackinac at 3:45 the next afternoon, and the Red Caps were horrified by Elizabeth's luggage. "Good God, Boss," they said, "you'll need 'leven men for that! We ain't strong enough to carry more'n one bag apiece!"

On our way from Porto Santo Stefano to Naples, we stopped in Rome to call on Dr. Stückgold, who examined me superficially and announced that my trouble was not eczema at all, but *acido urico: intossicante di ricambio.* I pressed him as to the source of this *intossicante di ricambio*—this *acido urico* or Eureka acid. Was it in the blood?
No!
In the stomach?
No! It was in the *fegato*—the liver.
I told him I had been informed by an eminent Boston physician that starch baths were indicated for such a disorder.
Stückgold indignantly denied it. Starch baths are terrible for *intossicante di ricambio!* Do not drink! Do not smoke—not more than two or three cigarettes a day.
Could I have wine?

Yes, I could have two glasses of white wine; no more! But no red wine and no cocktails. None!

Would cocktails bring back the *intossicante*—the Eureka?

They would!

How about beer?

Well, I could have beer.

Could I have two bottles a day?

No! One: one only!

What, he wished to know, was my diet?

I said it was a diet that Montesano had given me. All the eggs I wished; lamb, lettuce and onions.

Stückgold was disgusted. All of these, he said, were bad—oh, but bad! No lamb, no lettuce, no onions, no strong cheeses, no shellfish, no antipasto, no eggs!

No eggs under *any* circumstances!

That will be one hundred lire, thank you so much.

We pressed on to Naples, where I consulted the eminent Dr. de Amicis, reputed by the American Consulate General to be the outstanding skin specialist in all Italy. He scrutinized me, front and back, through a magnifying glass. Yes, Dr. de Amicis said, my trouble might truly be *intossicante di ricambio,* but there was no possibility that it could have originated in a tick bite. All the remedies I'd been using were worthless. I must at once start taking Piperizina and Ca Wassermann, obtainable at Roberts' Drugstore.

How about eating and drinking? I asked him.

He shrugged his shoulders and raised his eyebrows. I could eat and drink whatever I wished. In cases of this sort, nothing makes no never mind! My distemper, in all likelihood, would pass away by itself with a change of air and of people! That will be two hundred lire, and one thousand thanks.

On the good ship *Vulcania* I had a few words with Dr. Gasparini, the ship's doctor, asking him whether he had any suggestions. Did he! I must not drink beer, I must eat lettuce and onions, I must take starch baths, I mustn't eat eggs. Nor should I bother with Piperizina or Ca Wassermann, as both were worthless. I could take a little white wine, but no red wine. Emphatically no red wine! He added that I could consult ten specialists on *intossicante di ricambio* and get a different opinion from each one, which was a profound understatement.

§

During our return to America, while trying to rid myself of accumulated correspondence, I came across a number of reviews which spoke contemptuously of my bad habit of writing novels in the first person. I found myself unable to understand their contempt, or their insistence that the use of the first person was "cheap writing." *Sherlock Holmes, Treasure Island, St. Yves,* Mark Twain's *Personal Recollections of Joan of Arc, Connecticut Yankee at King Arthur's Court, Lorna Doone, War of the Worlds, Jane Eyre, Villette* and *Looking Backward* are written in the first person, and no critic can call them "cheap" without cheapening himself.[1]

Boston, April 30: Called on Dr. Emery at the Harvard Medical School. After giving me a thorough going over, he said he suspected Montesano had been the nearest right of all the doctors who had guessed what was wrong with me. He could only guess that I'd picked up a fungus growth—some sort of tropical disease, and that it would be a waste of time and money to see specialists. His recommendation was to return to good Maine foods and good Maine customs with no loss of time.

Called on Admiral Sims, explained that I had a long book to finish, and couldn't touch his biography until I'd finished *Northwest Passage,* but that I'd rather write his life and that of General Billy Mitchell than any other men of whom I knew, because both of them had received such raw deals. He said he felt Arnold's case, in many ways, paralleled his. I'd done justice to Arnold in *Arundel* and *Rabble in Arms,* he said, so he knew I could do justice to him. Mrs. Sims urged me to do the biography if I possibly could, because he had repeatedly told her he had set his heart on having me do it. He hadn't considered anyone else, because no other writer, to his way of thinking, had the sense of the sea that I had. I was more encouraged by that statement than I could have been by a dozen formal awards.

Since doctors had been unable to supply me with remedies to cure eruptions, I turned to household cures recommended by State-of-Mainers. Jimmy Smith, our purveyor of thick steaks and groceries, strongly urged the application of brine from a pickle barrel, and immediately supplied me with a quart. Reg Harford, another local purveyor of comestibles, advocated gallons of orange juice. A local horseman urged me to swallow a few lead pellets from a shotgun shell every few days. I mustn't use chilled shot, but could use any size I wanted. My contractor friend, Raymond Grant, brought me a bottle of mange cure that a Sanford veterinarian insisted would cure any sort of human eczema.

---

[1] A sample of this sort of criticism is on p. 437, Appendix.

Lorimer wired me that his editorial staff was being bombarded with protests because of an article written by a lady contributor—"I Like Men with Money." He wanted an article in answer to it, and quick. So I did a piece called "I Like Girls with Simple Tastes" which, Lorimer gaily reported, put an end to the deluge of angry letters, and swamped the office with communications from grateful readers.

I include this essay in the Appendix, because anyone who wants to write will never be able to do so if he is unfortunate enough to marry a woman whose tastes are not simple.[2]

That summer of 1936 was another summer of harassment—a large part of it due to the increasing number of people who flatteringly sent packages of books to be autographed, and even stacked them on the front porch, with notes stating bluntly that the owners would call on the following day to pick them up. When I refer to these requests for autographing as "flattering," I'm using the word in its true sense; for it seems to me that an author who isn't delighted to know that his books are read by persons willing to take the trouble to have the author's name inscribed in them is saying, in effect, that his ambition is to write books that nobody will buy, read or like.

There comes a point, however, when the average household is unable to cope with the daily unwrapping, signing, re-wrapping and conveying of large numbers of books. I eventually solved the problem by having bookplates struck off, and sending them, autographed, to those unknown friends who thought enough of my books to want them autographed. Thus my friends were saved labor and postage, we were saved time and labor, and everybody seemed pleased.

But golfers, summer vacationists, distractomaniacs, cocktail-party-givers, airplane motors and all the other concomitants of a summer resort were even more in evidence in 1936 than they had been in 1935, so again we took to that secluded farmhouse in the mountain valley. There I again learned, to my horror, exactly what I had discovered the preceding summer. The rewritten early chapters of *Northwest Passage* were not yet satisfactory and must once more be rewritten.

The strangeness of that calling known as writing was further impressed on me that summer by a widely read novel, *Jamaica Inn,* by Miss Daphne Du Maurier.

In *Jamaica Inn* an uneducated Cornish farmer and a girl with no advantages at all speak thus: "It were a pity did I not appreciate the rare spirit that prompts you to such generosity."

It were indeed! I might not *know* much about writing, and certainly

---

[2]P. 417.

the American reading public preferred the output of Miss Du Maurier to my books in the ratio of ten to one; but I was despondently certain that if *that* was writing, I'd never make the grade.

On August 11 Booth, who had also been ill for several months with Eureka acid, sent word that he'd like to have me read *Northwest Passage* to him from the beginning; so we abandoned the mountain valley, and on the following evening, August 12, I started reading to him.

There were interruptions, of course—intrusions by idle people who, poor wretches, had nothing to do but break in upon others; but in spite of the interferences Booth contrived to spend fifty-eight evenings between August 12 and November 19 listening to the first fifty-one chapters of *Northwest Passage.*

On some evenings he'd stop me at the end of almost every sentence, and we'd examine that sentence and push it around and rephrase it, clearing it up and sharpening it and smoothing it: adding a little to it —sometimes adding three or four explanatory paragraphs. I'd go on reading, only to be drawn back to that troublesome sentence and told to try it again.

At the end of our fourteenth evening of reading, we had disposed of only 170 typed pages, which led me to remark to Booth that I could see, from the amount of rewriting he wanted me to do, that I had done much worse on *Northwest Passage* than on my preceding books. He said emphatically that I had never made a greater mistake: *Northwest Passage* was a marked advance over anything I had yet done, which was exactly why he stopped me so often. If he had urged me to alter everything in *Arundel* that had been a little out of kilter, I'd have been discouraged, and we could never have got through it.

§

On September 11 Lorimer wrote me he was retiring as editor of the *Post,* that Wes Stout would succeed him, and that he wanted me to come to Philadelphia and see Wes before the retirement. He added that he'd like very much to see the first part of *Northwest Passage* with the idea of cutting it up into a few short stories. When I queried Booth as to whether he thought it advisable to let any such hacking be done, he told me not to worry. Lorimer would never, he assured me, cut it into sections; and he said that if I was in any doubt about it, he'd be glad to bet me any amount that Lorimer would use it as a serial.

October 1: Boxed the first half of *Northwest Passage,* sent it to Lorimer, and made a start on the Michilimackinac episode in the last part of *Northwest Passage*. In the evening to Booth's and made slow progress, reaching the spot where Natty Potter tells Towne about the existence of his daughter Ann. I have high hopes for Ann.

October 5: A telegram from Lorimer: "Graeme and Brandt vote Yes on your story. I have read only half of it, but shall probably vote Yes as well. Suggest coming Philadelphia now to expedite cutting and piecing." Replied: "Will be in Philadelphia tomorrow morning." That's the end of our financial worries for at least a few years!

Philadelphia, October 6: To the sixth floor of the *Post* and found Graeme taking his father's place. Tried to find out what's the matter with Lorimer. He's sick, all right, because nobody'll talk. Graeme said they were going to use the first half of *Northwest Passage* in seven installments, and that I would have to cut approximately thirty pages from each installment. He had already indicated the spots where he thought cuts could best be made, but said that I could be the final judge of that. Also, his father wanted me to write a new and condensed introduction, and write joints to bridge the cuts that I made. He asked what I thought of changing the name to *Rogers' Rangers*. I said it made no difference to me, because when the entire book was published, it would be *Northwest Passage*. Asked that Jacovleff, Langdon Kihn and Winold Reiss, in that order, be considered to do the illustrations, and said I thought the *Post* ought to find some way of being less insistent on cutting, because the elimination of those two hundred pages would leave *Post* readers in ignorance of a lot of things they really ought to know about American history—things they probably would never otherwise learn. Graeme said there was nothing he could do about it: seven installments was the limit, and the cutting had to be done in order to get it into seven; but he added that he knew how I felt, and it might cheer me up a little to know that his father considered it the best serial he'd had in many years.

It cheered me more than I could say; and when he handed me the manuscript and gave me an office in which to work, I wrote a new opening, ripped twenty-seven pages from the first installment, and made all the required joints before lunch time.

After lunch got halfway through the second installment; then drove out with Adelaide Neall to Wyncote to see Lorimer. Can't find out what's the matter with him. Something is, but to me he looks, sounds, acts and talks just as he always has. He said he'd sent word to the office that the last episode of the last installment mustn't be cut by so much as a word. It's exactly right. He also said the staff had tried to talk him into using one of Bud Kelland's serials to wind up his editorship of the *Post,* but he'd told 'em that Wes Stout could start his regime with a Kelland story: he preferred to close his career with *Northwest Passage,* and they could all get busy and see that the art work, typesetting, checking and proofreading were rushed through in record time.

Let the other boys have the prizes! I'll take this remark of Lorimer's in preferance to any of 'em!

October 7: Out to King's Oak with Lorimer and had cold pheasant and beer for lunch. He swears he's glad he's leaving the *Post:* that he's been brooding over a novel for years, and now he'll be able to get at it; but he's too defiant about it. Extremely difficult to act pleased at his apparent pleasure when I know it isn't pleasure at all. He sent me back to the *Post* right after lunch, and I was given Lorimer's office to work in. Constantly interrupted by the reading staff and researchers, all expressing high enthusiasm for *Northwest Passage.* Maybe New Englanders really *will* find out how their ancestors fought Indians! Finished two more installments and spent the night with Adelaide Neall and her sister. Worked in bed from midnight to 3 A.M., revising, cutting and piecing.

October 8: Up at six after three hours' sleep, and finished installment 6. After breakfast Adelaide went to Philadelphia, leaving me to finish cutting the dreaded seventh installment. Must have become hardened to it, because I finished it in an hour and a half, cutting out thirty-five manuscript pages instead of the required twenty-nine. Left the manuscript for Adelaide and took the ten-twelve train to New York, feeling hollow-eyed from overwork, and depressed by Lorimer's approaching resignation.

In New York met my publishers, who proposed that I agree to a cheap edition of the Chronicles of Arundel, mostly for the benefit of the Dollar Book Club. Refused on the ground that retail bookdealers were doing all right with all those books, and that cheap editions and book-club distribution would penalize the dealers. They believed that the cheap editions would advertise *Northwest Passage,* whereas I felt that they had the cart before the horse: that all they needed to do was to sell *Northwest Passage.* By so doing, I held, they would automatically boost the sales of *Arundel, The Lively Lady, Rabble in Arms* and *Captain Caution*—which would be far better for them, for me and for booksellers than any number of cheap editions could possibly be. They said they saw my point, and they were amiable about it when they hinted that I was being unreasonable. Since that was the last thing I wanted to be, I suggested that we take a taxi to the Authors' League and put our respective cases before Miss Luise Sillcox, the League's secretary. If she could find anything unreasonable in my position, I told them, I'd yield on every point and consent to everything they suggested. Since my publishers are good publishers, they changed the subject by calling a waiter and ordering another round.

Stray notes from Kennebunkport, October 9–December 5, 1936:

October 9: Went on reading to Booth, and almost exploded at his insistence that I rewrite passages that already seem pretty good to me. He sees it, too, and explains his meticulousness by saying that he's tremendously interested in the handling of the London slums and in the character of Ann Potter. He wants just a little more added to almost every sentence, almost every paragraph. I scratch three or four additions in the margins and read them to him, but they aren't what he wants. After contemplatively smoking two or three of those cigar-size cigarettes of his, he says, "How would it be to do it something like this?"—and then he talks off a sentence that sounds better than anything I've done. Then he says, "That's just a suggestion. You rewrite it and see what you get out of it and we'll look at it tomorrow."

October 11: Booth sent Collier Young, Carl Brandt's moving picture representative, over to see me. Young said that Bill Counselman, the Hollywood scenario writer, wanted very much to do *Arundel,* and what would I take for the movie rights? Told him I'd practically give away the rights to any company that would use Wally Beery as Cap Huff, and consent to give the rights back to me after making the one film.

October 12: Up early and hard at work on Booth's suggested rewriting of the scene between Natty Potter and the solicitor. Worked all day on it and finished it at four-thirty. To Booth's at seven, only to find that he'd decided he'd given me a bum steer, so all the rewriting I'd done was thrown away and my original version used.

October 13: Patched and hacked at sections that have already been revised about twenty times. In the evening read to Booth, and again we stumbled around with four or five paragraphs. Told Booth I'd been doing some serious thinking about the enormous amount of time he had given to helping me, and suggested that if he really thought the book had merit, he let me put his name on the title page with mine and take half the royalties. He let out a howl that brought Susie running to the room in which we were working. When he'd allayed Susie's fears, he told me explosively that he had done nothing except act as an editorial adviser. Maxwell Perkins of Scribner's, he said, had done a million times more for each of Tom Wolfe's books than Booth had done for all of mine put together, but Perkins would never dream of letting himself be considered as a co-author. The whole conception of *Northwest Passage,* he said, was mine; it was I who had worked three years on it; and I was to get it out of my head that he had done anything except edit it. He took a good deal more pleasure in being an editor than in playing backgammon with me and getting beaten most of the time. Why wouldn't it be pleasure for him? he demanded. It was a big story: much bigger than I realized, and a great piece of character drawing. Tried to tell him that I could never have written any of my books without his help and encouragement; but he refused to listen: said he'd never heard such nonsense. Hadn't I always said in the middle of each book that the book wasn't worth a damn? But I'd kept on under my own steam, hadn't I? Hadn't I always sworn I'd never write another long one? Maybe I didn't know it, he said, but he knew from things I'd said to him that I was already subconsciously planning two other books that probably would be even longer than *Northwest Passage* or *Rabble in Arms;* so let's have no more talk, he said, about his having had any hand in the writing!

October 14: Received galleys from the *Post* and worked all day on them. At night to Booth's, and went ahead reading manuscript. He advised against the entire episode in which Langdon Towne visits Lord Bremerton at Breem in order to see his collection of La Tour pastels. It seemed to me to be good color and amusing; but Booth said No, so out she went.

October 18: An editorial in the *Boston Herald* quoting my *New York Herald Tribune* comments on Roosevelt's Wisconsin speech in 1920 and pointing out that I had been right and Roosevelt wrong.

October 26: Completed the Appendix, which contains the Rogers and Stephens courts-martial, and is to run as a separate volume in a Limited Edition of *Northwest Passage.* Autographed several hundred tip-in pages for the Ticonderoga edition of *Rabble* and *Arundel,* and to Booth's after a hasty dinner. We had done only three lines when we were interrupted by two young men who devoted the rest of the evening to discussing—in spite of knowing nothing about it—the reported engagement of the King of England to Mrs. Simpson, whose divorce case comes up tomorrow. Greatly distressed at getting nowhere.

October 29: Received from Doubleday the galley proofs of Book I of *Northwest Passage*—ninety-seven galleys—and went to work correcting them. Also corrected installment 7 of *Post* proofs and removed all the hells and damns by request. The *Post* is certainly touchy about such

things. Anna found a lot of mistakes that I had missed in the Doubleday galleys, and I had already found a raft of them that Doubleday
had missed. I can only suppose that the Doubleday proofreaders must
be dreadfully overworked, because any good proofroom ought to
catch every typographical error in a book, and leave the author free
to hunt for repetitions and obscurities. To Booth's for our fifty-fifth
night of reading. He thinks I ought to compress the end into an extremely short space, but I just can't do it—not if it's to end the way I
think it ought to end.

October 31: Corrected through galley 77 of the Doubleday proofs.
It's a shame the *Post* couldn't have run this without cutting.

November 1: Finished correcting Doubleday's galley proofs of Book
I, and Anna, working after me, found many errors I'd missed.

November 3: Received a German edition of *Arundel* and *Rabble*
combined—1,500 pages—together with a brochure quoting reviews
from leading German newspapers. Strange that I should get a better
break in Germany than in my own country. Matt Clark, selected by
the *Post* to do the illustrations for *Northwest Passage,* telegraphed to
find out how Rangers slung their blankets, whether their Scotch caps
had poms or not, whether Rangers' muskets had sling straps, whether
Ranger officers were differently uniformed than their men. The answers were: (1) over their left shoulders; (2) Glengarries, which could
also be used for water dippers and wouldn't catch on twigs; (3) muskets resembled Kentucky rifles in having no straps; (4) officers and
men dressed alike.

November 6: The president of M.I.T. wrote to ask whether they
could have my *Arundel* manuscript and source material to display in
the Tech Library. They certainly can. Don't know how to account for
it, but all four books seem to be doing better and better. Last week's
sales were: *Arundel,* 382; *Lively Lady,* 250; *Captain Caution,* 63;
Rabble in Arms, 263.

November 13: Sent off the first two hundred manuscript pages of
Book II, *Northwest Passage,* to Doubleday, partly to stop myself from
perpetually tinkering with them instead of progressing, and partly to
make sure the manuscript is safe. Almost impossible to get forward.
Got Towne as far as seeing Elizabeth at Michilimackinac: it all seems
sketchy and unsatisfactory: no texture to the stuff. Utterly exhausted
when I quit at twenty minutes of nine. I certainly can't work the way
I used to; and in spite of what Booth says, I'm sure I'll never again be
able to stand the strain of writing a book as long as this one.

November 17: The thermometer hit twelve above last night, making work extremely difficult, even with blankets around legs and shoulders; yet succeeded in advancing 2,500 words. Interesting to note the analogy between mental and physical effort: if I play a bum round of golf— 97 or thereabouts—I'm exhausted and depressed: if I knock off an 82 or 83, I feel swell. If I spend a day sweating and groaning over a few hundred words, my back aches and I'm a wreck. If I peel off two or three thousand words, I'm merely lively and stimulated when I quit for the day.

November 18: Kilham Roberts, secretary of the British Society of Authors, wrote me he was unable to obtain any accounting from my English publisher and sent me a form to fill out, so that the society could start proceedings against him. Nothing, he thought, would have any effect on the publisher except the threat of a writ! Yet publishers like to encourage the idea that it's always the authors who are the temperamental stinkers.

November 19: Eight above zero, and the cold wind seeps through all the windows, so that we have to wrap ourselves in comforters. In spite of numb fingers, and thanks to knowing exactly what I wanted to say, wrote 4,800 words, slammed them into the big manuscript book, scrambled into a clean shirt, revived myself with a slug of scotch and dashed for Booth's, getting there at six-twenty our time, seven-twenty his time. After dinner read Booth what I'd done. It's okay, he says— fine. He's a liar by the clock. The damned book is just petering into nothing.

November 27: Received 1,050 sheets to be autographed and inserted in the special edition, so wasted the day numbering and signing them.

November 28: Six above zero, and had to spend the day dictating letters about the details connected with front matter, back matter, Appendix, and phoning Doubleday's advertising manager about the book-autographing séance that he wants me to stage in the Jordan Marsh Book Department next Saturday. Told him I wouldn't do it unless I could go to all the other bookshops in Boston at the same time. To discriminate against any of them would be a dirty trick. The advertising manager said Jordan's wouldn't consent to let it be done that way, so said to hell with the whole business. So I'm unreasonable! The advertising manager contacted Jordan's, and Jordan's graciously agreed to let me do it *my* way. I can imagine about ten people showing up for autographs. Tried to get down to work, hoping to do 3,500 words, but could only do 2,400.

November 29: Tried to finish the Fleet episode while Anna slugged away on a hazy outline of the end of Book II that had been requested by the *Post.* When she'd finished it, I tore it up and wrote Stout that there was no way of telling how the book was going to end. To Booth's at seven and read him the Fleet episode, which was different from the way he'd suggested doing it. He said my way was better and that I shouldn't touch it. Ran out of ink and had to make my last few notes by spitting on the pen. Booth in a rage because the high cockalorums in the Institute of Arts and Letters have started to recommend the election of certain nominees, instead of letting the members judge for themselves.

November 30: Wrote a new layout for the finish, but can't get it right.

December 1 and 2: Thermometer stood at zero. Spent both days trying to anticipate a last chapter. I can't do it properly, and Booth can't help me, because I cannot satisfy myself as to the truth of Rogers' claim, made to Eleazer Wheelock of Dartmouth, that he had fought two battles for the Dey of Algiers—information that I hope to be able to get in Algiers.

December 3: Closed the Maine house and set off for Boston.

Boston, December 4: Visited the Old Corner Book Store, Lauriat's, DeWolfe & Fiske and the book department of R. H. White's, signing about three hundred copies of my books in all.

December 5: The newspapers full of the probable abdication of King Edward because of Mrs. Simpson—the best news story since the war. Since the ousting is being done by Stanley Baldwin, and since Stanley Baldwin is the king of stuffed shirts, I'm all for young Mr. Windsor. To the Bay Colony Book Shop and autographed ten books, Women's Educational and Industrial Union and did about thirty, then stumbled into a little bookshop on Bromfield Street and asked the girl who ran it whether she wanted me to sign any of my books for her. She had only one copy of *Lively Lady* and one of *Captain Caution* in stock. She asked whether I'd wait long enough to let her get a few, so tended shop while she went out. Stumbled on *Houses of Stone,* by Frazier Forman Peters. After I'd read ten pages in it I knew I'd found the sort of house I was going to build, and build quick. A customer came in and asked me to suggest a book for a young girl who had just gone to the hospital. Strongly urged him to take both *The Lively Lady* and *Captain Caution,* which he did. He suspected knavery when I asked the girl's name and wrote it in both books with my own, but he paid and left without protest. The salesgirl came back with ten books, and after signing them I relieved her of *Houses of Stone*.[3] Went on to Jordan's earlier than the announced hour, as there were mail orders to be autographed. As I suspected, no book buyers were in sight. Went into the manager's office and was considerably surprised to find a list of 157 persons who had ordered autographed books, and a gang of young ladies to slide books to me and snatch 'em away. When I came out into the book department again, I was considerably more surprised. There must have been 200 people standing around a table tucked into a niche in the bookshelves, and damned if all of 'em hadn't come to see me! Me, for God's sake! Some of them had copies of *Arundel* that were worn to tatters. Never was so touched—or embarrassed—in my life. It was almost five o'clock when I stopped autographing. I was hoarse from talking, my fingers felt permanently cramped, I was dog-tired—but I was profoundly grateful for the things those people had said to me; and I knew I'd never again swear that I wouldn't write another long book.

December 6–16: Sailed on the *Vulcania* for Algiers and Italy with Anna, Major A. Hamilton Gibbs ("Arthur" to his friends) and Jeannette, his sympathetic lady. Fortunate to find that the wife of Ernest Ives, our consul general at Algiers, was aboard. She radioed her husband to round up the head of the National Museum and Archives in Algiers and find out whether Rogers or anybody resembling him had led any Algierian troops early in 1770. In Algiers I had a long talk with the old gentleman, and learned that it was common practice, in those days, for Germans, Scots, French, Americans to take service in Algiers, Tripoli and so on—as witness Peter Lyle, who was Tripolitan admiral at the time of Eaton's Derna expedition. Invariably, though, such gentlemen wore Arab clothes, embraced (or pretended to embrace) the Moslem faith, and were given Arabic names. Lyle, for example, was Murad Rais. Thus it would have been possible for Rogers to have served in the Dey's army under some name other than his own—

---

[3]We never know our luck! If it hadn't been for stumbling into that bookshop, I'd never have learned about a method of building that is far more beautiful, far less expensive and far more satisfactory than any other I have seen. In this method, carpenters build cement-forms, working upward three feet at a time from bedrock, outlining the circumference of the house. Day laborers, following close on the heels of the carpenters, set field stone against the front of the forms and prop them in place with ordinary kindling wood. On the heels of the rock handlers come cement bearers, tossing grout (liquid cement) into the forms behind the rocks. The grout hardens overnight, and the next day the carpenters add another three feet of forms. The process is unbelievably rapid. The walls of my Kennebunkport home were poured in fourteen days; the walls of a stone barn in two days. When the forms are knocked away from the rock walls, they are taken to pieces and used again for constructing the inside of the house.

though the only actions which had taken place at the period in question were forays against mountain tribes who had been backward about paying their taxes.

On December 19 we returned to Porto Santo Stefano and the beautiful hilltop of Lividonia to find that in our absence a long line of telegraph poles had been run straight across the hilltop on which the Half-Baked Palace stood, so that those unrivaled views of Tuscan hills and Ligurian Sea were defaced by gaunt poles and sagging wires. The heat boxes of our Italian stoves, too, had corroded to uselessness. So the first week, when I should have been plunging ahead on the 50,000 words that still remained to be written, were spent in pursuing plumbers and writing letters to the town marshal, to the chief of the Italian Marine, the district engineer, the district judge in the neighboring town of Orbetello, and even to Mussolini himself, offering to buy new telephone poles if they would only move them off our place and set them out of sight beside the road, where they belonged. Our rights, I argued, had been invaded, our peace of mind ruined, and the beauty of the countryside outrageously and unnecessarily destroyed. By the end of the year I had accomplished practically nothing except correct, re-correct and make inserts in the first half of the galley proofs of Book II. But finally, on the thirty-first of December, "I squeezed out half a page of tough going, where Rogers receives the letters from Townsend and Campbell and prepares to open them. There must be some sort of curse on my books when *Drums Along the Mohawk* sells 150,000 copies and *Rabble* only 26,000. Celebrated the departure of the old year with champagne cocktails, backgammon and lamb and rice. This past year we have paid all our debts, but that's about all—and maybe that isn't a whole hell of a lot to be thankful for."

THE REAL home stretch of *Northwest Passage* started on the first of January 1937, when I undertook, come what may, to deliver the last 80,000 words of manuscript, revised and ready for the linotype machines, by the end of February.

January 1, 1937: Worked in bed till twelve forty-five and did almost a page. This Elizabeth Rogers woman was a stinker and no mistake, and I think I've got her dead to rights, thanks to discovering a few of her letters. Back to work at three-thirty, worked till seven-thirty and dined at eight on the toughest veal cutlets ever encountered by a human tooth. This town goes out of its way to get tough animals. Read *Reader's Digest* for last May and found in it a quote from a piece on England I wrote in January 1934.

January 2: Wrote ⅓ of a page before lunch and another third after lunch. Greatly discouraged, as the whole book seems to be falling to pieces at the end, instead of tightening up. The only bright spots are Elizabeth and Ann. Ann is a pip, and for a nickel I'd cut Elizabeth's throat, yet a great many critics will come out with their tattered old battle flags: "He cannot write about women," and "All his women are lay figures: wooden." Like hell they are! Ann and Elizabeth are no more wooden than I am.

January 3: Squeezed out ⅓ of a page before lunch, and tore Carver's *Travels* to pieces. I can prove from his book and the Rogers courtmartial that Carver was a liar, trimmer and ingrate. After lunch wrote 1,000 words, and after dinner read the *Atlantic* and *Blackwood's.* Wrapped and sent off the galley proofs of the first section of Book II.

January 4: Did 1,000 words before lunch and 1,000 words after.

January 5: Stumbled through half a page before lunch: then read Catlin, Carver's *Travels* and various commentators on Carver. Had intended to have Towne winter among the Mandans, but they lived too far south on the Missouri; so went back and re-did McNott's squaw as a Sioux captured by Chippeways: then it became natural for Towne and McNott to winter among the Sioux on the St. Peter's River, where Carver would reveal himself as a liar and trimmer, and turn back with Tute from the Northwest Passage expedition as conceived by Rogers—which is unquestionably what happened, though nobody ever found it out before.

January 6: Wrote 900 words before lunch, but only 400 after lunch because of the difficulty of reconstructing the big land deal that Carver must have made with the Sioux.

January 7: Dissected Keating's *Travels to the Source of the St. Peter's River,* which was only released today by the Italian censor, after being held ten days for no known reason. Found it extremely helpful, and did 1,500 words.

January 8: Another page before lunch, and after lunch started Towne off for his winter with the Sioux.

January 9: Couldn't do more than 1,200 words, largely due to my determination to work the Carver story into the narrative. He trimmed Rogers high, wide and handsome, has never been called for it, and he's just *got* to be called.

January 10: Peeled off 1,300 words. Drucker wrote she had found the suit for damages that Rogers had brought against General Gage, and the excerpts she sent sounded as though Rogers, when he made his claims, was either half drunk or half crazy—which he probably was.

January 11: 1,000 words, greatly cheered by receiving a column and a half review of *Rabble* from the *London Morning Telegraph.* For generous appreciation, it beat any American review I ever received, and makes up for the scamped and shoddy ones I've seen too often in English papers.

January 12: Worked in bed and was almost completely stumped by the approach to the episode where Carver and Tute turn homeward, and in despair over the dullness and stupidity of everything I write. It'll be God's wonder if I don't go cuckoo trying to finish this book. Wasted a lot of time making notes for a burlesque mystery story:

An Englishwoman writer of detective stories is found dead in her home, to which three other couples had been invited. All the invited couples are under suspicion and capable of doing the job. The solution is that the writer, overcome by the futility of all her stories, decides to end it all and so plants evidence on her guests—all of whom she hates and all of whom deserve to be murdered—and then seemingly kills herself. In the end her publisher would turn out to be the murderer, his motive being that the authoress had sewed him up so tight in a contract that he was afraid his other authors might learn about it and cut his profits.

January 13: Encouraged by letters from people who have read *Rogers' Rangers* in the *Post;* and Simon & Schuster complimented me by asking to see the manuscript of the completed book, "in case the book rights hadn't been contracted for." That's an excellent commentary on the book sales of my last four books. Simon & Schuster think I'm a newcomer in the fiction field and ain't had nuthin' published yet. Stumbled and groped onward for 1,200 words. Can't help feeling that it's incredibly rotten; yet I'm reasonably certain that it's better than ninety per cent of the junk I read, though that isn't saying much.

January 14: Tried to complete the split between Towne and Tute, making hellish going of it, and hellish reading. Saw by the morning papers that *Gone With the Wind* has sold 1,000,000 copies, and had a letter from Doubleday saying that *Arundel* had just passed 25,000. When, they demanded, would *Northwest Passage* be finished? Damned if I know! Never, I fear! If I hadn't made myself stay in bed every morning for the past two weeks, I wouldn't have got anywhere at all, and yet I don't seem to have arrived anywhere. Anna started typing the last section. Too discouraged after dinner even to sign a couple of letters.

January 15: Worked in bed and peeled off 3,000 words of conversation between Towne and Tute, but its value is only in my mind —the desire to bring out the ridiculousness of Carver's statements in his *Journal* as to why he, Tute and Goddard turned back. I'm afraid Booth would order it out: yet if the passage makes a point that no Carver commentator has ever thought of making, oughtn't I to go ahead and make it? I dunno! All I know is that I wish I'd never tackled the goddam book. I don't really mean this. I'd be miserable if I couldn't keep on with it and in the end lick it.

January 16: Got through 900 words before lunch. Wrote Doubleday that I didn't see how I could put the finished manuscript into their hands before March 1, and pointing out it wasn't much use to try to hurry *Northwest Passage* off the presses if *Gone With the Wind* was going to continue to sell 100,000 copies a month for the next year. That would be like fighting an avalanche with bare fists.

January 17: An enormous mail forwarded by the *Post,* but refused to look at it until I'd written 1,000 words. Read the letters after lunch and found them extremely touching in their enthusiasm—not only for

Rogers' Rangers, but for other books of mine that the writers seem to have read and re-read.

January 18: Awake at five o'clock, as has become my habit, and unable to get back to sleep because of fretting and fuming over the difficulties of tying together the threads I've left dangling in preceding chapters. They've got to be tucked in, but in such a way that the last few chapters will read smoothly. So far I'm not coming within a mile of doing it. How in God's name do writers of detective stories preserve their sanity? Squeezed out 900 words before lunch. After lunch went back to Anna's typed manuscript and hacked it all to hell. Too damned bad if the book on which I've worked the hardest should turn out to be the most complete flop. After dinner wrote fourteen letters and to bed at eleven, tired and discouraged, to read in the Lewis and Clark expedition. Discovered that Thomas Jefferson once thought of having two men, all alone, make just such a trip as Towne and McNott are trying to make.

January 19: Wrote another load of letters and got forward about 1,500 words.

January 20: Wrote ¾ of a page in bed before lunch. My nerves seem to be getting more and more shot over this damned book. The terrific wind howling in the electric wires attached to the house is almost insupportable. Anna's records show she has taken eighty-one letters for me in the month we've been here, typed 40,000 words from my manuscript and written fifty letters of her own. Then bridge players at home express surprise that we're able to find anything to occupy our time in such an out-of-the-way place as Porto Santo Stefano. I can only say it's a godsend to have a hole like this to crawl into and be free from interruptions. Either of us, trying to do this amount of work at home, would be in a strait jacket by now.

January 21: Strange how many people seem to delight in reading a book for nothing but picayune errors; then writing offensive letters to the author. Two such letters turned up this morning. One insultingly rebuked me for referring to dollars in a year when no United States Mint existed, and the other contemptuously hauled me over the coals for mentioning envelopes in 1759. Could only point out that Spanish trade dollars were in use all over the world long before 1759, and that the *Encyclopaedia Britannica* stated that envelopes were in common use in 1653.. Did 2,000 words and am just about ready to plunge into the return to Michilimackinac. When that's behind me, I can plow into the final London episode.

January 22: Strengthened myself with a breakfast of Brie cheese and coffee, got through 1,500 words, and finished making the joint to the Michilimackinac jail episode. If I had access to Camembert or Limburger for breakfast, I'd probably be able to do 5,000 words a day.

January 23: Wrote another 1,500 words and started hacking at the beginning of the typed manuscript, so Anna can retype it. It seems a complete mess, and I feel it's driving me plumb nuts. Struggled all afternoon to straighten out the pages pasted up in the big blankbook so it'll be readable, and though I closely follow Zagloba's battle cry in *Fire and Sword*—"Cut! Slash!"—I can't seem to improve it. To bed at nine-fifteen in deep despair, and woke up four times during the night, stewing and fretting over the rotten job I'm doing.

January 24: Those long waking hours last night showed me a way to rearrange the Tute-Carver-Rogers material so it won't drag quite so much. Did it; then got forward 300 words.

January 25: Fretted all night over the final stages of *Northwest Passage* and finally got two hours' sleep with the aid of a sleeping pill. Read and admired the account of the Lewis and Clark expedition. Rogers could have done it half a century earlier if he'd only been given the help for which he asked—if only he hadn't been trimmed and framed by General Gage, Sir William Johnson, and those lesser trimmers, Carver, Tute and Goddard. Two big packages of letters forwarded by the *Post*. Their enthusiasm is tremendously encouraging.

January 26: Planes from Orbetello started at daybreak to fly over the house, and continued to do so all day. Did 1,000 words in spite of them, and again received a mass of letters from *Post* readers. Three of them took me severely and contemptuously to task: (1) only a fool would say that Matlin would walk from Portsmouth to Boston and back in one day; (2) William Whipple could never have been a slave trader because he was a noble signer of the Declaration of Independence; and (3) Bologna sausage couldn't possibly have been known to Robert Rogers in 1759. Sent them the sources—the first two from Brewster's *Rambles About Portsmouth,* and the third from Rogers' journals; but it's a waste of time: they'll go around telling everyone the book's no good because it's full of mistakes. Anna handed me a bill from S. S. Pierce. I had ordered a pound of fresh caviar sent from Pierce's to Booth at Christmas. Instead of obliging with a pound, they had delivered an ounce! Imagine the look on the faces of the Tarkingtons and their guests when a whole ounce of caviar was drawn from the wrappings! Sent him a cable: "Rectifying horrible Christmas blunder. Embarrassment, anguish, fury, love." Wrote S. S. Pierce, asked them what they had been thinking of to send only an ounce, and told 'em to send Booth two pounds instead of the original one I had ordered.

January 27: Re-read Towne's start from Michilimackinac to the north-west, and found it impossible as I'd done it, so rewrote it. Received from Drucker the papers in the Rogers-Gage suit. Carver's shadow falls across them during the period when Rogers was under arrest, but Carver, the louse, completely ignores that episode in his book. There are samples of Spiesmaker's manner of talking, too, such as "Nord-west passage." Dug into a score of sources for enlightenment on Chip-peway divinities, and almost went nuts trying to get them straight. Wrote Lillian Robins and Clara Claasen at Doubleday's that they were altogether too optimistic about the probable success of *Northwest Passage,* and that I'd make each of them a present of a case of sherry if it had an advance of 30,000 copies.

January 28: Revised and threw away most of the early Indian stuff, and tried to chop and revise the Wanotan episode. Torrents of rain, which flooded the floor of my workroom.

January 29: Kept on slugging at the revision, throwing away ten or twelve pages, making it step along fairly rapidly and more interestingly by comparison with the first draft—though it's still far, far from being properly swift or sufficiently interesting. Anna pasted up the first fifty revised sheets, starting with Rogers' arrival at Michilimackinac, and took oath it was excellent.

January 30: Revised all morning, cutting out the messy third visit to Prairie du Chien and the even messier scene with Tute and Carver. Transposed the Carver grant material and the letters from Rogers and Ann, laying the action at the Falls of St. Anthony. This greatly improves it, and brings the revision up to Michilimackinac and Rogers in jail, so turned that portion over to Anna for retyping. The revising has given me a pain in both eyes and the neck; but I'm more worried for fear it'll do the same to those who read it. After lunch changed Anna's type-writer ribbon, then tried to get going again on the Michilimackinac-London episode, but failed completely. Could *not* figure how Towne would get word from Claus about Ann and Potter, or whether he would have learned of Rogers' arrival before or after Claus. The far-off ending preys on me day and night.

January 31: Up and at it after horrible dreams, but somehow the dreams straightened out something in my mind, because the McNott-Towne-Claus episode fell rapidly and neatly into place.

February 1: Jittery beyond words, and can't average more than three hours' sleep a night. Wrote 2,000 words and got Rogers into Montreal for his court-martial. An enormous mail from the *Post,* overwhelming and unexpected—stuff like "I read and re-read *Rabble in Arms* along with *Kim, The Three Musketeers* and *The White Company*"! Getting to the end of a long book while part of it is running in the *Post* is a sort of assault on nerves, heart and brain, and indescribably exciting.

February 2: Wrote 1,500 words in bed—the sergeant of the 60th describes Rogers' departure from Michilimackinac—and after lunch did another 1,500, polishing off McNott and getting a start on Towne's arrival in London. At last I'm at a point where I can see light. Now I know the finish. Numb from work, and went to bed without opening a book—something that hasn't happened to me for a long, long time.

February 3: Wrote 1,200 words before lunch—Towne's reunion with Mrs. Martin in London, just before he sees Ann do her stuff. After lunch Ann did her stuff. Maybe it's good and maybe it isn't. Anyway, it's the way she'd have done it, and I'm so desperate and so near the end of my rope that it sounds all right to me.

February 4: The sparrows and airplanes were in full cry this morning; but in spite of 'em, she keeps moving! In the morning got Ann into Towne's arms: in the afternoon got Towne married to Ann, and started on the rapid résumé leading to the Fleet episode. It may be faulty, but I'm getting there; beginning, even, to see there may perhaps be a few thrills in it—a few.

February 5: Before breakfast revised eight pages of the Michilimackinac episode. By typing all day yesterday, morning and afternoon, Anna reached Michilimackinac, and needs more work. After breakfast wrote 1,000 words and reached the point where Ann persuades Towne to visit Rogers in the Fleet. After lunch revised ten more pages of the Michilimackinac episode, gave them to Anna; then renewed my effort to make the joint with the Fleet episode. Tore off nearly 5,000 words in an almost delirious rush, making the joint a little after seven o'clock. Celebrated with champagne cocktails.

February 6: Worked all morning re-revising the Michilimackinac and Fleet episodes and longed mightily for Booth's guidance. In utter despair all afternoon because the whole episode from the arrival at Michilimackinac to the end seems so atrocious, so amateurish, so sophomoric. I thought I had written it fairly adequately last autumn, but now that I've reached it, it's worthless—unusable.

February 7 and 8: Struggled fruitlessly over the last chapter and tried to cope with a staggeringly large mass of letters forwarded by the *Post* and several by Adelaide Neall herself. I gather from her that the story has brought the biggest comeback a *Post* serial ever had. In the *Paris Herald* read Mark Sullivan's account of Roosevelt's announcement that he proposed to retire all Supreme Court justices at seventy, and have a fifteen-man court which would make him a virtual dictator. It was the best character news story I ever read, describing the "voluptuous pleasure" with which Roosevelt read his plans to the press, and the "cruelty" of his attacks on the Old Men of the Supreme Court.

February 9: Wrote nearly 1,000 words before lunch, and re-introduced Sam Livermore, in London, hunting for Rogers. Un-stabled the Hudson for the first time since our arrival and drove slowly towards Orbetello, where Arthur and Jeannette Gibbs were arriving by train from Taormina. Kept on struggling with the last chapter while waiting at the station. Arthur was voluble over the pansies he'd encountered in Taormina—he having been unaware, up to that time, of their prevalence in that resort as well as on the beautiful Isle of Capri. Escorted Arthur and Jeannette to their room, then went back to work, and kept at it until I heard a rapping on the wall, which is Anna's way of signaling me to come to dinner. Emerged to find the rapping had been caused by Arthur knocking out his pipe against the back of the fireplace, so rushed back to work again and did ⅓ of a page.

February 10: Revived myself with two aspirins and two cups of coffee: then finished the Livermore-Towne-Ann episode and got a start on the last picture before rising at one-ten. Back to work again at three-thirty, struggled forward and cracked the last scene in Towne's home after the war, cutting fast toward the finish. I'm afraid it's terrible. There's no way of telling: I'm too close to it. Talked with Arthur until midnight: then to bed and brooded over the last paragraphs.

February 11: Lit the lamp at 4 A.M. and wrote a vague outline for the last paragraph. Fell asleep and woke again at six to write two more lines. Turkey hash for breakfast; then went at it again, struggling with a rough and sketchy scene of Ann, Towne, Cap Huff, Ogden and Sam Livermore talking about Rogers. Got what looked like the last paragraph at twelve-thirty. Looked like it enough, that is, to lead me to print "The End." Now there's nothing to do but cut and revise—that's all! Just cut and revise!

Having had all I could take for one day, we decided to have the Hudson tuned up and embark on a full day's trip tomorrow. Surely I'm entitled to one day off a year. Got the Hudson out of hock and took it to Grosseto for a tune-up, had a few *grappas* (a lethal Italian beverage tasting like wet straw), bought forty liters of gas, had the tires checked and the oil renewed; then home by way of the beautiful little clifftop town of Talamone, which crowns the opposite horn of the Bay of Orbetello. We had admired its loveliness from a distance for ten years, but when we got into it, it was horrible. The beautiful cliff was the town dump and its base a stinking welter of tin cans, garbage, ordure and dead dogs: its street encrusted with filth—like some books that seem, in retrospect, to be beautiful, but prove, on re-reading, to be tripe! Home well content with our Tuscan hideaway. Enjoyed a dinner of fresh sardines, *pizza alla Napolitana* and *zuppa Inglesi,* all washed down with white Corvo that Alfred Nester had sent us from Palermo.

February 12: A vacation at last! Concetta announced that the day would be *brutta,* but since the wind was west and the fishing fleet on its way out, told her to pipe down. "Let's go," I told Arthur, and off we went to the southward, turning inland at Tarquinia through acres of Etruscan ruins. Crossed the hills into an enormous plain where we came unexpectedly on the walled town of Tuscania—one that looked to be straight out of the Middle Ages. We couldn't find it in the guidebooks and wondered why. Picked up a peasant girl who obligingly got in beside me, directed us around the town, and set us on the Viterbo road. At noon into Montefiascone. Climbed the hill on foot and had spaghetti, cheese, coffee and white wine in a little dining room looking down on Lake Bolsena, whose name I remembered from high school days because its Etruscan inhabitants, the Volsinii, had fought three wars with Rome —wars in which I was so profoundly uninterested that I couldn't even think of them without losing my appetite. Pressed on at one-thirty and unexpectedly stumbled on the Bigi winery—best of the producers of that delightful Orvieto wine called Est Est Est—located in an ancient monastery from which we looked across a wide valley to Orvieto on its hilltop—a gorgeous spectacle. (All true Orvieto comes from within three kilometers of that town.) Tried to buy wine from Bigi, but he wasn't allowed to sell until the tax had been paid. At Pietro Urbani's in Orvieto I could buy it, because there the tax would have been paid. On into Orvieto, got two cases of true Orvieto Secco, and had a second lunch of green spaghetti. The Orvieto cathedral, it seemed to me, was the most spectacular sight I'd seen in Italy. Jeannette located a beautiful bronze Etruscan figurine corroded to a peacock blue, exposed in a watch repairer's window. Where had he got it? It had been plowed up in a field a week before. What was it worth? Ah, signore, who could tell! It was beyond price! Observe the grace of the figure, the tilt of the Phrygian cap, the sweeping long sleeves of the figure's jerkin, the shapely curves of the urn. A museum, perhaps, would pay ten thousand lire. Surely two thousand lire—ah well, let us say seven hundred lire. When I said that two hundred lire seemed to me nearer the right price, the watch repairer shrugged his shoulders philosophically and handed it to me. As a matter of fact, I'd have paid him whatever he asked, because I wanted it to give Booth,[1] who I knew would take as much pleasure in it as I did. Started home at four and at dusk reached the hill town of Pitigliano, underlain with six or seven layers of residential caves burrowed into the hillside. Had two carafes of wine in one of the caves for one lire sixty (eight cents). It was the most dramatic and satisfactory short ride I ever had in Italy. Reached Porto Santo Stefano at seven-twenty to dine sumptuously on a six-pound turkey and a generous amount of Est Est Est. Arthur hesitantly said that if I'd let him read my manuscript he might possibly be able to make a few helpful suggestions—provided, of course, that I wished him to do so. If I wished him to do so! The whole twenty pounds of *Northwest Passage* was instantly deposited on a table in the living room, where he couldn't avoid it.

February 13: Finished revising the first of the four blankbooks which contain the last quarter of *Northwest Passage.* Smoothed and quickened it a good deal. Arthur spent all day reading, and almost finished Book I by dinner time. His comments to me were restrained, but Anna says he really let go when he told Jeannette about it. After dinner we were treated to a detailed history of the literary Gibbs family—Sir Philip, Cosmo Hamilton, and the others. There's a great story for a biography, provided it's done by someone who pulls no punches.

February 14: Spent the entire morning revising, while Arthur, having finished all the proofs, started on the typed portion. Wes Stout wrote and asked to see the completed *Northwest Passage:* there has evidently been a tremendous demand from *Post* readers to know what happened to Rogers in his later years. Now I find myself in a peculiar position: I won't let the second half be published as a serial, because I won't allow a word of it to be cut. Yet if the *Post* wants to see it again, I don't quite see how I can refuse. Arthur finished the book this afternoon and said he'd like to go to bat with me tomorrow on it. "I don't know whether or not you know it, old bean," he said, "but there's quite a wallop there at the end, where Towne finds Ann."

Quite a wallop, eh? Coming from the undemonstrative Major Gibbs, that means that a good many of the boys and girls are going to reach

---

[1] I examined that little figurine a thousand times during the remainder of our stay in Italy: kept it on my desk until we left Porto Santo Stefano, and then wrapped it in a silk handkerchief and put it in the glove compartment of the automobile. When the car was unloaded in New York, the little figurine was gone—taken by somebody who needed it far less than I did: a somebody who probably pawned that lovely two-thousand-year-old figurine for the price of a drink of whisky.

surreptitiously for their handkerchiefs when they come to that passage
—and they won't find any hokum in it, either.

February 15: Lighted the lamp a little before dawn and went to
revising. Arthur came in at ten and indicated a number of places where
he thought cuts should be made at the end of chapters—all obvious
improvements. After lunch to work with him again. He thought there
should be no silences between Towne and Ann in the pre-Fleet chapter; also he thought I should cut the few lines after Ann goes to the
window and says, "Ah, no, you can't kill what was in that man." He
was right and no question about it. Whether or not I can clean up the
whole job tomorrow, I don't know; but I can come pretty close to it.
A damned fine book, Arthur says. That's good enough for me, whether
she sells or doesn't sell. Decided I had to have a rest, so said we'd take
a trip to Perugia and Florence the second I wrapped up the manuscript and sent it off.

February 16: Up at 5 A.M. and went to transcribing my changes
into the carbon copy, finishing at eleven. Then tackled the pre-
Fleet chapter and polished it off at one-forty—8½ hours of grueling
labor on just one cup of coffee. Set Anna to typing the pre-Fleet chapter and the last two pages of the book. Took each page from her as it
came from the typewriter and corrected it. Wrapped up the finished
job, boxed it, smeared it all over with sealing wax, addressed it to
Doubleday, and wrote a cable for Robbie: "Manuscript shipped *Europa*
February 20. 80,000 words. Gibbs says it's a natural." Anna requested
Arthur and Jeannette to remove their hats, stand at attention and chant
"How can we leave thee: how can we bear to part" while the manuscript was being wrapped. Back to the Rot-Haus, which was cold and
fireless because the stove smoked. Cleaned off my desk and wrote a long
letter of instructions to Robbie. In for dinner at seven-fifteen, feeling
as though I'd been pounded with hammers.

February 17: An early breakfast, sent for the plumber to fix the stove,
and all of us piled into the Hudson for a three-day vacation. After kiss-
ing the manuscript and wishing it good luck, I dropped it in the Porto
Santo Stefano post office, only to be handed three packages of page
proofs of the first half of Part II (which had been sent off January 3
to make the *Rex* on January 7). This meant that I would keep right on
working during my vacation. As soon as we turned onto the Orvieto
road, a black fog shut down—one so heavy that we could only crawl.
Reached Orvieto at one o'clock, crept onward to Todi, a town that
enraptured Arthur but left me cold; then drove all afternoon through
a fog like cotton wool. The road was on a ridge, so one of us would

drive for fifteen minutes, and the other diligently polish the windshield to give us visibility to keep going. Fortunately made the Brufani at Perugia just at dusk through a Niagara of rain. Worked until 2 A.M. correcting proofs.

February 18, 19, 20: Assisi, Florence, Pisa and back to Porto Santo Stefano in the rain, correcting proofs early each morning and late at night.

February 21, 22, 23: Bade the Gibbses farewell, completed the page proofs of the first half of Book II, and sent them off to Doubleday ticketed to catch the *Bremen* March 3.

February 24: Assembled material for the book on Maine I'd promised to write for Alfred McIntyre, wrote the opening paragraph, and settled on a title—*Trending into Maine.*

§

March 7: There's no use saying that chivalry and high-mindedness are extinct in Boston, for on March 7 I received a letter of profuse apology from S. S. Pierce, saying that they were rushing Mr. Tarkington two pounds of caviar for the price of one. They explained their mistake by saying caviar, in Boston, was usually ordered by the ounce, and they therefore thought I must have accidentally written "pound" when I really meant "ounce."

§

March 9: A reader in Wisconsin discovered that in the *Post's* version of the first half of *Northwest Passage* I'd given Jennie Coit brown eyes to start with and blue at the finish, so wrote him that she really had one brown and one blue eye—but cabled Robbie to make Jennie's eyes brown throughout the book. That goes to show how mistakes creep in, even after scores of readings by author, expert *Post* readers and the *Post's* famed staff of editors, checkers and researchers.

March 10: Anna read me a book about the island of Giglio, written by an Italian priest who had lived there. Giglio lies twelve miles straight out from our front door. The residents of Giglio, he said, were among the laziest people on earth because of the ease and frequency with which they obtained relief from the Dukes of Florence, who held sway over the island for centuries. Anybody who thinks that history doesn't repeat itself needs only to watch what will happen to those who are going to get government relief for the next fifty years or so—or until intolerable taxes bring about another revolution in America.

March 11: A rush cable from Robbie: "THREE PACKAGES FIRST CLASS

LRIGEUG SAILING GIUTH MILGICHT." That's a representative sample of Italian efficiency. Translated, it means that three packages of proofs are being sent first-class mail on the *Bremen* leaving New York at midnight tonight. Chilson Leonard of Exeter sent me a page from a rare book catalogue in which a first edition of *Rabble* is listed at $12.50.

March 18: All three packages of proof, first part of Book II, arrived, and again Anna and I resumed the hectic pursuit of errors, which have an agonizing way of eluding the eye unless the proofs are read at least five times.

March 21: Shocked (but delighted) to have a letter from Harold Rugg of the Dartmouth Library, saying I had been elected to membership in the Dartmouth Chapter of Phi Beta Kappa. Thanked him enthusiastically, but had to tell him I couldn't possibly wear a vest on which to display the key. I certainly never thought, when I matched Freddie Townsend, back in 1907, to see which one of us would be president of Kappa Beta Phi, that I'd one day be in a position to wear a real key if I wanted to. Also had a letter from my old friend of Siberian days, Montgomery Schuyler, saying I'd been made an honorary cousin of the Schuyler family.

March 27: Packed a 500-pound crate of source books for shipment to America by the *Vulcania,* on which we will travel, and sent it to a shipping agent in Trieste. Received the first unfavorable review of *Rabble* to come out of Germany. The pundit who wrote it objected strongly to my treatment of Von Woedtke (though I have a score of proofs that he was exactly as I described him), and to my inconsistency in referring unkindly to Hessians, but in the same breath speaking highly of Virginians. This, the Kraut reviewer pointed out, was a shtupidity, because Virginians are descended from the same ancestors as the Hessians of whom I speak disparagingly. I wonder what Virginians would have to say to that—especially such well-known Hessians as the Randolphs, Custises, Lees, Washingtons and Byrds?

March 30: Counted up wordage on *Trending into Maine.* I have 50,000 words. Also I have a bumpy, palpitating-heart feeling most of the time, can hardly force myself to sit down at my desk, and drowse all day and lie awake all night. I've had enough, and made up my mind to waste time for two weeks. Finished *Gone With the Wind* today—a bully book: one that well deserved to sell the 1,300,000 copies it's already sold.

April 6: Closed the door of the Rot-Haus for the last time. Piled our precious books into the back of the Hudson and headed north to Florence, across the Futa Pass to Bologna (where we discovered the best restaurant in all Italy, the Pappagallo d'Oro, or Golden Parrot); then to Modena and Verona.

From Verona we went on north again, through Peschiera, Gardone on Lake Garda, where that little bastard D'Annunzio had a villa that he stole from an Austrian; through Limone, where miles of terraced lemon trees are enclosed in vast glassed boxes, and on to Trento and Bolzano. From Bolzano, we swung around through the majestic Dolomites to Cortina and then south again to Vittorio Veneto, Treviso, Venice, and Trieste, where we met friends who were joining us for a hasty vacation. Then, since the ship didn't sail for another four days, we made the same trip all over again, returning to Fiume on the fourteenth and sailing from Trieste for America on April 15.

Day after day, on that homeward trip, I was bombarded with cables from the Doubleday office, asking whether I could verify statements I had made in *Northwest Passage;* but I could do little about them because all my sources were deep in the ship's hold. One such message was handed to me just as I was about to go ashore at Algiers with our friends, hopeful of investigating Arab manners—information that would be usable in another novel to which I had given some thought while lying awake in the still watches of the night. The wireless query was three pages long and urged an immediate reply, so I excused myself from my friends, explaining that my day would have to be spent in local museums and libraries. One of the friends said—more than incredulously—"Gee, I never knew you had to do so much work when you wrote a book!"

That's the way of it with those who know nothing about writing, those who want to write, and those who could write if only they had time: they think that books practically write themselves, require no exertion, and permit the authors to indulge in long idle spells and a vast number of cocktail parties.

My LABORS were far from over when I received my first copy of *Northwest Passage* on May 22, 1937, a month and a half before the official publication date, and simultaneously read in the morning paper that it was the July choice of the Book-of-the-Month Club—a bit of publicity that brought a shower of telegrams and letters. One, from Mr. John F. Royal, who had introduced me to the onion soup of Boston's Province House, read, "Congratulations. It's a long way from Professor Kilgallen."

For the next five days I was busy reading that first copy for mistakes and unfortunately found fourteen, which necessitated the replating of fourteen pages.

Then there was *Trending into Maine* to be finished, and a decision to be made as to the novel on which I should next embark.

A score of puzzling matters had wormed their way into the books on which I'd worked for the past nine years. Since a complete knowledge of those matters hadn't been essential, I'd never got to the bottom of them; but I'd thought of them often, and knew I ought to find out all about them and make the information available to others.

When, for example, my great-grandfather had been committed to Dartmoor Prison by the British Navy, he had been quartered in Prison No. 4, which was ruled by a gigantic Negro, King Dick, who exercised police powers, so to speak, over American privateersmen as well as the many Frenchmen who also inhabited Prison No. 4. Most of those Frenchmen had been captured in San Domingo—and my great-grandfather, before he had gone privateering, had been captain of a vessel that sailed to San Domingo and brought home cargoes of rum—a bit of family history that distressed my grandmother beyond words. How had all those Frenchmen got to San Domingo in the first place? The books didn't say. And what—and who—had my great-grandfather seen when he sailed to San Domingo? There was no way of knowing without going to scores of sources, and most of those sources were confused, unintelligible and unreliable.

Then, again, Maine captains and ships were constantly being annoyed by Barbary pirates; and numbers of Maine people, headed by Wadsworths and Prebles, had spent years patrolling the Mediterranean; but I couldn't find the whys and the wherefores of these mysteries. Nobody in Kennebunkport or Portland knew anything whatever about the experiences of those Maine men in the Mediterranean, or what they'd seen, or done, or heard, or how they'd lived and acted. There was a square in Portland named after Preble, and the Wadsworths' name had been immortalized by Henry Wadsworth Longfellow; and they were vaguely connected with a place called Derna, which had a street named after it in Boston; but all the details were lacking. I wanted to find out about those things and tell about them so that at least a few residents of Kennebunkport and Portland could—if they wished--have easy access to and full knowledge of the reasons behind the naming of Preble Square and Henry Wadsworth Longfellow and Derna Street.

Then, again, there'd been three Nasons at the Siege of Louisburg, concerning which none of my Nason relatives knew anything whatever. Well, why didn't they? Why had the experiences, the labors of those Nasons and their friends, been forgotten—and why should they remain forgotten if I could bring them to light?

Even while I was writing *Arundel,* I was bothered because a certain Dr. Sylvester Gardiner kept peering out at me from the shrubbery of my story. He was obviously a gentleman of parts, with large holdings on the Kennebec River. Arnold, when he first appeared in *Arundel,* was on his way to pay a call on Dr. Gardiner. I knew from occasional references to Dr. Gardiner that he had been a wise man, greatly admired throughout New England; yet he became a Tory and was obliged to flee to England. Apparently many admirable citizens of Maine and every other state had been Tories. Well, if they were admirable, why had they been Tories, when everyone instinctively knew that Tories were fiends in human shape? My curiosity became even sharper, when I was writing *Rabble in Arms,* by passages between Peter Merrill, an ardent American patriot, and his younger brother Nathaniel, who had Loyalist leanings. At that time I made desultory attempts to investigate the Loyalist side of the American Revolution, but it was like hunting a needle in a haystack. Nowhere could I find any over-all presentation of the Tory case—though it was apparent that the intellectual cream of America were Loyalists—Tories—and that they had been driven from their country by a wave of intolerance little different from the waves of intolerance I had seen at first hand while covering Europe for the *Post*. That was a story that had never been written, and that most emphatically should be—and soon, since Franklin Roosevelt was making frequent references to Economic Royalists, and contemptuously implying that all such Royalists (or Tories or Loyalists) had always deserved extermination, which emphatically had not been the case.

I couldn't make up my mind which of those stories I ought to try to tell next, and as a result I began to collect source material for all of them. I glanced occasionally at my notes on *Forty on the Emu;* but I didn't like them. They were too far from Maine and the experiences of Maine men.

The *Post's* editors, to my great relief, had found it impossible to pry a serial from the second half of *Northwest Passage;* but they were insistent on having one, because *Post* readers had been inordinately interested in Robert Rogers, and wanted more of the same.

I had learned by now that I had no desire to write serials, couldn't hold a story to any definite length, and had no intention of ever trying to do so. I made an effort to fill the *Post's* needs by sending the editors a carbon copy of *Trending into Maine* with the suggestion that they take a few chapters from that book. Only one of the chapters struck them as usable. That, fortunately, was the one dealing with my recollection of the foods I had eagerly devoured, as a boy, in my grandmother's Maine kitchen. I say fortunately, because the flood of correspondence that followed the publication of that one chapter encouraged me to insist that my niece, Marjorie Mosser, write a cookbook—*Good Maine Food*—which, in my considered opinion, is the best cookbook in the world.

But that wasn't enough for Wes Stout, who had taken Lorimer's place: he wanted a serial; so I wrote him that I hadn't made up my mind definitely, but among the stories I was contemplating was one that might possibly contain a usable sequence. The novel would cover, generally speaking, the Prebles and the Wadsworths in the Mediterranean, against a background of Eaton's expedition to Derna. The story of the expedition, I thought, was the part he might be able to use. So Wes urged me to come to Philadelphia and talk it over, and I was glad to do so.

In all the years I had worked for the *Post,* I had dealt only with Mr.

Lorimer. I told him my ideas, which he instantly rejected or accepted (except in the case of *Captain Caution*). The price to be paid for a story was never discussed, and Lorimer was always generous.

With Lorimer not only retired but openly acknowledged to be too ill to receive callers, all this was changed, and I found the change both strange and uncomfortable—though I was greatly attached to all those *Post* editors: Wes Stout, Adelaide Neall, Erd Brandt and Graeme Lorimer . . .

In place of a comfortable, friendly talk with Lorimer, I was summoned to an editorial board meeting—something I'd never before experienced. It was almost a formal affair: a sitting-at-table; and when I'd joined the group, I was asked by Wes to outline my contemplated story to the assembled editors. I said I'd already told him all I knew about it, but he said he wanted it explained again, so the others could hear it.

I could only repeat that there was nothing to explain: I had long been interested in the activities of Maine seamen in the Mediterranean, and Erd Brandt had given me a book on General William Eaton by Francis Rennell Rodd (later Lord Rennell of Rodd) that had intensified that interest. Eaton had organized an expedition in 1805 to put the Barbary pirates out of business, and I had in mind a novel which would contain that expedition as one of its incidents. That was all I knew about it, I said, because I didn't know how the story would start, where it would end, or what would happen to anybody in it.

Wes said he thought that would make an excellent serial, and asked the others what they thought. They thought so, too: thought, with Wes, that they'd like to see it when it was finished. No promises were made on either side, however. Wes then produced the manuscript of the chapter taken from *Trending into Maine* and said that after due consideration, the editors had decided that a thousand dollars would be the proper price for it.

That sudden introduction of an atmosphere exactly opposite to the one I'd known under Lorimer, whom I had greatly admired, had a curious effect on me. That impersonal, indecisive board of editors, by comparison with Lorimer's warm and understanding toughness, was so comic that I wanted to laugh—until I glanced at Adelaide, Erd and Graeme, saw that their eyes were downcast and their faces expressionless, and realized that they were ill at ease and embarrassed. I had to tell Wes that I saw no reason for any such reduction, since he and everyone else on the *Post* must know that my former rate had been two thousand dollars for a story.

Wes reminded me that the piece under discussion was merely a chapter out of a book: had not been written as a contribution for the *Post*, and that my real return would come from the book: consequently, I shouldn't expect regular article rates for it.

I reminded him that the first part of *Northwest Passage* had been written as a book, too, but that Lorimer hadn't seen any reason to cut my rate for that or any other reason.

Wes said that if I felt that way about it, they'd boost the price to twelve hundred dollars, but that was the absolute limit they could afford.

It seemed to me that Adelaide, Erd and Graeme were looking more uncomfortable with each passing minute, so I reached for the manuscript, flipped through it, and found that it had been cut from its original length of some 7,000 words to about 3,500 words, which—to my way of thinking—made it worth about a hundred and twenty dollars instead of twelve hundred. So I told Wes that if the *Post* was really hard up, I'd make him a present of the story for old time's sake. He said no: they were glad to pay for it, but he wanted to be sure I was satisfied.

I assured him I wasn't satisfied, but would take the twelve hundred dollars if he was certain that was all the *Post* could afford—and it was eleven years before I found time to write anything for the *Post,* though my affection for Wes Stout, Adelaide Neall, Erd Brandt and Graeme Lorimer remained as strong as ever.

Five weeks later George H. Lorimer died, to my deep sorrow. In stature, in perception, he surpassed any statesman, any ruler, any prime minister, any leader of his generation. Those who knew him best felt themselves incapable of writing adequately about his insight, his generosity, his remarkable qualities. Fortunately, while many of Lorimer's friends were still alive to express a little of their deep admiration for him, it occurred to John Tebbel to undertake that difficult book. To would-be writers, Tebbel's *George Horace Lorimer and the Saturday Evening Post* should be an inspiration and a guiding star. To me Lorimer is still alive: I can see him and hear him, as clearly as we could hear him after his funeral, when seven of us sat around a table at Adelaide Neall's—Adelaide, Mary Roberts Rinehart, May Wilson Preston, Sam Blythe, Garet Garrett, Eddie Le Fevre . . . It was what Lorimer would have liked to see: we talked about the Boss, and what he'd said to one man and what he'd done about another, and where he'd been, and what he'd thought—and we laughed till we cried, and pushed the scotch back and forth across the table, and back and forth, and I'll swear Lorimer was in the room with us. . . .

§

I made a genuine effort during that summer and autumn to do something about that Eaton-Derna-Barbary pirate novel; but when I came to dissect the Derna episode, I found that it had three sides: one a military, one a naval, and one a political. The political story and the military story occurred at widely separated periods, as well as simultaneously, thousands of miles from each other. The military end of the expedition couldn't be told in fictional form unless the political end could be woven into it and made clear; but the intricate politics that preceded, encouraged, obstructed and then wrecked the expedition seemingly couldn't be introduced without obliterating the military story—which explained to me why Americans knew so little about an episode that so glaringly taught the incredible folly of allowing any average American politician to meddle with foreign affairs.

I racked my brains for weeks, talked about it and talked about it with Booth, wrote outline after outline, and so far as I could see, the story just couldn't satisfactorily be made into a novel.

I found myself thinking more and more, too, about the experiences of the Loyalists in the books I was gradually accumulating. I began to discover characters of whom I'd never heard, incidents, campaigns and battles that were wholly strange, Loyalist regiment after Loyalist regiment, fighting with astounding bravery and routing triple their numbers of Continental troops and militia. I knew that in all likelihood that story couldn't be adequately and accurately told in fiction form— knew I couldn't outline the story—until I'd done at least a year of intense research.

When I mentioned a few of these things to Booth, he said he had known, when I was writing *Rabble in Arms,* that I was unconsciously laying the foundation for just such a book—it was apparent, he said, at the very beginning, in the scene where Peter and Nathaniel Merrill return from England to find that their father has been suspected of being a Loyalist. That state of affairs had irritated me to such a degree, he said, that he knew I'd eventually have to write about it.

And so, Booth asked, what was I waiting for? It would take three years to write, so hurry up!

I went to work in earnest, and as soon as I did so I gave up all thoughts of returning to Italy to work; for my first discovery was that the most exhaustive and essential source of Loyalist material was contained in sixty manuscript volumes of Loyalist Claims on the shelves of the Manuscript Room of the New York Public Library—and only a super safe-cracker can remove anything from the Manuscript Room of the New York Public Library, for it has an iron-barred gate which is locked whenever anyone enters or leaves.

The entire autumn of 1937 was also made hideous for me by a three-months' wrangle with a motion picture company to which I had unwisely agreed to sell the rights of *Northwest Passage*. The less said about that miserable experience, the better, and I'll content myself with remarking that it taught me one great lesson: If you ever write anything that any motion picture company wants, *never* sell. Lease it for a term of years, but never sell outright.

December 3: Made a start on the Loyalist novel and got 3⅓ typed pages. Masses of Loyalist books rolling in. Greatly helped by Belcher's *First American Civil War* and Stark's *Loyalists of Massachusetts.*

December 5: Booth enthused over the Loyalist book. Discovered *Lord Percy's Letters,* the Vose, Rowe and Andrews *Journals.*

December 9: Learned that *Northwest Passage* had been the choice of the English Book Society, and that they had spoken with enthusiasm of the English scenes in it. This was pleasing, since Allan Nevins, in his review of *Northwest Passage,* had pontifically said that my handling of the English scenes had been painfully inadequate, and that I wasn't competent to write about Englishmen of culture or refinement.

December 13: Before leaving for Indianapolis, Booth gave me a lecture on the Loyalist book. I wasn't to give a thought to what critics might say about it, what the D.A.R. might do to me, pay no attention at all to anything except the job I'd outlined for myself, not give a damn whether the book would sell or not, or whether a serial could be made out of any part of it. He'd be back soon, he said, and by that time I'd be far enough along so that we could get the story straightened out in case I'd gone wrong anywhere. The day when he doesn't come back will be a sorry one for me.

December 20: Books are pouring in from Goodspeed, Dauber & Pine, American Antiquarian Society and the New York Historical Society. I've already accumulated more than I used for *Northwest Passage.*

December 24: Letter of advice from Sam Blythe.

I observe in the "Keeping Posted" department of the *Saturday Evening Post* that came in today that you are listed as being a forthcoming serial producer for 1938; and standing here on Sunset Hill, overlooking the Pacific, with roses blooming on this side and a lot of new-mown Chinks festering along the Yangtze on the other side, I raise my Ebenezer and shout: "Wait a minute!"

Now, listen, Kid:—

You have just made a prodigious hit with your *Northwest Passage.* Unless you have blown it in on bum stocks and wine, wimmen and song, you have plenty to keep you going. Don't be so goddam greedy. You've gotta go pretty far to beat your present reputation, and you might put a dent in it with another story at present, as well as put a damper on *Northwest Passage.*

You've gotta make a home run when you come up next time. No single or two base hit will suffice. Otherwise, the great Roberts, author of *Northwest Passage,* plainly shows by this new novel that he is on the down grade. It is disappointing, after the excellence of *Northwest Passage,* and so on, and so on, and so on.

Don't let your Yankee yen for money lead you to trying to do the grab game. Be calm. As I say, you've got enough now for a spell, and it is quite probable that all future dough will not be worth a damn, anyhow. But supposing it is to its extreme, but 59 cent degree, what of it? You are sitting on top of the world now. Why take the chance of pushing yourself into a crevasse? You might, you know. Mebbe the next one won't be a *Northwest Passage.* Such things have happened. Anyhow, why crab the present orgulous situation by hurrying to get out another book? Plenty of time. Don't get excited by these guys, like Wells, say, who have printed 167.5 books and shouldn't have printed 143.9 of them.

You sit down on your Plymouth Rock fanny, look at the sea (too bad you haven't got one to look at like the one I am eyeing at the moment), write an article or so if you like, play some golf, shoot some partridge, partake of a reasonable number of snorts of Scotch, and don't be in a hurry. There's cider and pippins to come.

All of which is set down by Old Doc Blythe, who hears all, sees all, knows all, as a preliminary to the wish for a Happy Christmas for you two. Salud y pesetas, as we say in our local patois.

§

I have no intention of telling, in boring detail, my three-year struggle with *Oliver Wiswell* and the ensuing five-year battle with *Lydia Bailey.* The former, unnamed, was begun in Kennebunkport on January 14, 1938, given a name on January 24, and had progressed to Chapter 15 on March 15. On that day I digressed to begin putting together the original diaries of the officers and men of Arnold's March to Quebec, one of which—and that one the most important—had been lost and never before printed. This was done partially to pass the time while Miss Drucker hunted in London for firsthand records of the Battle of Bunker Hill, the Siege of Boston and the retreat of the British and Loyalists to Halifax. But I had another reason for wanting to do it: when I had insisted on accumulating all those diaries before starting *Arundel,* I was four years doing it, and they had cost more than I liked to contemplate. I felt they should be made available to students of Revolutionary history under one cover and at moderate cost. My publishers—though they expected to make no profit from the book— willingly agreed to publish all of them together, with maps and annotations, so that they would hereafter be easily accessible to anyone. Only the best of publishers do things of that sort.

Wiswell was finished on September 28, 1940, published late in November, and produced an astounding diversity of critical opinion. The critics were unanimous in only one thing: their reviews were given leading positions by the editors of the *Times,* the *Herald Tribune,* the *Saturday Review of Literature, Time* and other critical journals. Most of the critics were, as usual, kind; but the things that some of them said about the book were as puzzling as they were untrue.

To set forth in a novel the Loyalist side of the American Revolution, I had been obliged, of necessity, to project myself into the mind of a Loyalist. Having put myself there, I necessarily told the story as a Loyalist would have told it. But for some reason or other, many critics persisted in confusing me with my characters, and argued that my characters' thoughts were my thoughts.[1] They contemptuously charged that *Oliver Wiswell* was too one-sided. I couldn't, of course, write these gentlemen that practically all novels concerning the American Revolution had been grossly one-sided, and that *Oliver Wiswell* was the first novel to cover it without one-sidedness, since it told the truth about the Revolutionaries, about the British, and about the Loyalists, who had suffered almost as much from bad British leadership as from Rebel persecution.

One reviewer in particular came to my defense—one who was in somewhat the same position as Olin Downes had been before the *New York Times* had taken him from the *Boston Post.* This was Jay Lewis of the *Norfolk Ledger-Dispatch,* a gentleman for whose literary judg-

---

[1] See p. 434, Appendix.

ments I had long had great respect, though he had no standing in bookish circles in larger centers of population, and book reviewers had small opportunity to read what he had to say. He repeatedly berated critics who, to his way of thinking, failed to understand things that to him had seemed obvious from the beginning; and a short time before he died, he put all his kind beliefs into one long essay. I have added it to this book to show why I so often had occasion to be grateful to Jay Lewis for brightening days so dark that work seemed impossible.[2]

---

[2] See p. 439, Appendix.

CHAPTER

35

THERE SEEMS to be an impression in some quarters that writing is like almost anything else: that with constant practice, it becomes easier and easier. In my case this was not so. The actual writing of *Rabble in Arms,* aside from several years of research, took eighteen months. That of *Northwest Passage,* in addition to the research, took two years. *Oliver Wiswell* consumed two years and a half; and the difficulties in writing it had been far greater than those I'd encountered in *Northwest Passage,* which I often thought I'd be obliged to abandon. *Northwest Passage* was much more troublesome than *Rabble in Arms,* which I'd repeatedly despaired of finishing.

I had practiced assiduously in writing all those books, and *Lydia Bailey* should have been easy for me. Instead of that, it was the hardest of all. One of the great stumbling blocks in *Lydia Bailey* was the character of Tobias Lear, who single-handedly wrecked the expedition of General William Eaton. Lear couldn't be satisfactorily explained until I understood him myself; and the way in which he wrecked Eaton's expedition could only be made clear if his behavior in Washington and Haiti could be made clear to the reader.

I had his handwriting analyzed by handwriting experts; secured copies of all his letters from the files of the National Archives—498 closely typed pages; got the records of his expenditures from the State Department. After all, Lear had acted as George Washington's secretary for a number of years, little was known about him, and I didn't want anyone to charge me with misrepresenting him or drawing an unfair picture of him.

The digging out of Lear's letters took months. So did the attempt to work out the details of the battle of Crête à Pierrot. So did the method of telling simultaneously the story of Eaton's march to Derna, and Lear's destruction of that expedition by corrupting the mind of a sick

American commodore in a safe and comfortable retreat far from the men he betrayed. So did the translation of hitherto untranslated French books dealing with the French occupation of Haiti—and the translation of *Moreau de St. Méry's American Journey, 1793–1798*, which contained facts elsewhere unobtainable about the life of French refugees in New York and Philadelphia during the *Lydia Bailey* period. This proved to be one of the most difficult tasks I ever tackled; for Moreau's French was involved, tortuous, beyond belief; and I almost went insane trying to turn Mrs. Roberts's literal translation of his muddy, twisted sentences into clear and understandable English.

When I'd settled on a manner in which *Lydia Bailey* could be told, and had produced three or four opening chapters, they weren't satisfactory. They didn't sound right. I hacked them to pieces and had them retyped. They still didn't sound right. I hacked them to pieces again and had them retyped, and they seemed to me to sound worse than ever. At my request Mrs. Roberts offered suggestions; my niece, who is also my secretary, offered suggestions. I rewrote and hacked, rewrote and hacked, and had the chapters retyped. There was still something wrong—something lacking. I called in A. Hamilton Gibbs to give judgment. Then I again rewrote the chapters, only to find them still wholly unsatisfactory. I called in Ben Ames Williams and told him to go the limit with criticism. He did as requested, and I rewrote the chapters again, trying to act on his suggestions. The results were no better. I went on with the book, but I constantly returned to the beginning, tinkering and rewriting, cutting and revising, until by the time the book was finished I had rewritten the opening chapters more than forty times.

No, practice doesn't make perfect in writing.

During 1946, when I was approaching the end of *Lydia Bailey*, my publishers decided to produce an illustrated edition of *Rabble in Arms* with eight portraits, by the talented Esta Cosgrave, of Cap Huff, Ellen Phipps, Doc Means, Peter Merrill and their fellows.

This idea met with the approval of the Literary Guild, which undertook to offer the remade *Rabble* as one of its gift books.

Since the remaking necessitated resetting, I stipulated that I should be allowed to revise the book wherever revision seemed necessary.

So, while waiting for proofs of *Lydia Bailey* to be returned, I began reading *Rabble in Arms* to see where it needed revision. Somewhat to my surprise, I reached page 133 without coming across anything that seemed to call for change.

Then the proofs of *Lydia Bailey* came tumbling in, and *Rabble* was laid aside. Those proofs were a nightmare, and my home was in a turmoil for a month, with everyone reading proof day and night. Part of the agony was due to the constantly rising price of paper, and my effort to save money for my publishers by eliminating one-word last lines from every paragraph in the book. I saved 575 lines—which resulted in the saving of seventy tons of paper. It also taught me more about proofreading than I had hitherto known.

When the frenzied task of seeing *Lydia* through the presses was finished, I boarded a plane to the West Indies, and resumed the reading of *Rabble* by way of occupying those monotonous hours. Page 133 and all subsequent pages, I found to my puzzlement, contained redundancies, repetitions, awkwardnesses, that kept my pencil constantly busy. I couldn't understand it, in view of the fact that the first 132 pages had seemed satisfactory; so I went back to those first 132 pages and re-read them. This time I found something to change on almost every page; yet those pages had passed muster only a month before. My violent exertions on the *Lydia Bailey* proofs had opened my eyes to things I had hitherto overlooked.

That rewriting of *Rabble in Arms,* and the corrections made in the resulting galley and page proofs—corrections which unfortunately and unexplainably were as numerous as on the galleys and pages that I'd corrected during those frantic days in 1933—took from November 5, 1946, to February 27, 1947: nearly four months. Work of this sort is infuriating and exhausting, but considerably more gratifying and exhilarating than golf, tennis, poker, cocktail parties, movies or The Game —provided the person who does it really wants to write.

§

Wise critics, who exercise their critical faculties before a book is published, can be enormously helpful and tremendously encouraging.

Destructive or unsound criticism before the publication of a book can be as harmful as it is impudent, ignorant and idiotic. When Booth Tarkington, Ben Ames Williams or A. Hamilton Gibbs tackled my manuscripts before publication, they willingly pointed out my shortcomings; and since I had great faith in their judgment, I always followed their advice. They never suggested changes in plot or in the use of facts; and the changes that I made because of their suggestions were always an improvement. On the other hand, when *Oliver Wiswell* was nearly finished, I had to hear it argued that sales might be damaged if I persisted in telling how Loyalists viewed the Declaration of Independ-

ence: that the D.A.R. and other patriotic organizations would be antago-
nized. I had to close my ears to hints that Wiswell, instead of remaining
true to his first love and going with her to New Brunswick at the end of
the Revolution, should marry the pretty Virginian with whom he
traveled Boone's Wilderness Road, suddenly turn into a devoted patriot,
and spend the rest of his life patriotically drinking mint juleps
in Kentucky.

I had to explain as patiently as possible that my reason for writing
the book was to tell exactly how the Loyalists felt about everyone and
everything, as well as what they did. They had strong feelings about
the Declaration of Independence, and if I couldn't clearly convey what
they thought and why, readers would keep right on thinking that they
didn't think at all. The opinions of the Sons and Daughters of the
American Revolution didn't interest me: all I cared about was painting
a complete and truthful picture of the Loyalist side of the American
Revolution. I had to explain further that Wiswell was a man of principle, a fighter. Like all the rest of those unfortunate Loyalists, he was by
nature loyal, not a weak-spined opportunist who would abandon the
cause for which he'd fought for seven long years, jilt the girl he loved
for a chance acquaintance with a Southern accent, and desert his brothers in arms just to lead an easy and more convenient life.

I have never felt any of the aversion to book critics that most writers
pretend to feel, because I have found them almost universally kind,
perceptive and appreciative. Only occasionally did I come across one I
couldn't understand. While I was bafflingly enmeshed in the opening
chapters of *Oliver Wiswell,* an eager acquaintance hurried to me with a
copy of *Newsweek* containing a review of *Northwest Passage* by Burton
Rascoe. Rascoe was not only bitter about the defects of the book, but he
depressed me by saying openly that I couldn't write novels and had
never created a character. I wondered what had ever induced Mr.
Rascoe to make such a statement, and how a critic who called himself
a critic could willingly sign his name to it with the accusing eyes of a
jury containing Phoebe Nason, Cap Huff, Jeddy Tucker, Richard
Nason, Corunna Dorman, Sergeant McNott, Elizabeth Brown and Ann
Potter upon him. I wondered whether Rascoe had ever read Thoreau's
opinion of character-inventing in his *Week on the Concord and Merrimack Rivers*—"We can never safely exceed the actual facts in our narratives. Of pure invention, such as some suppose, there is no instance. To
write a true work of fiction even is only to take leisure and liberty to
describe some things more exactly as they are." If Rascoe *had* read it,
he must have known that Robert Rogers in *Northwest Passage,* in spite

of having a "real" name, was created out of a few bare facts and a few scraps of information. If he didn't know that, he didn't know much about writing.

But when the *Saturday Review of Literature* for April 2, 1938, polled outstanding critics from coast to coast on the novel that should receive the Pulitzer Prize for 1938, 19 critics threw their votes for *Northwest Passage,* 9 for *Of Mice and Men;* 5 for *To Have and Have Not;* 3 for *The Late George Apley;* 3 for *American Dream;* 2 for *Paradise;* 2 for *Children of Strangers;* 1 for *Slogum House;* 1 for *Imperial City;* 1 for *Life and Death of a Spanish Town.* I knew, when *Northwest Passage* did *not* get it, that I would never again allow any book of mine to be submitted for a Pulitzer award. I'd already been amply rewarded.

Kindly critics even went out of their way to express pity, with the publication of *Oliver Wiswell,* over the harsh things that the Daughters of the American Revolution were going to do to me. Their sympathy was wasted, for never a Daughter of the American Revolution assaulted me, either by letter or word of mouth. Many wrote me reassuringly, and the Sons of the American Revolution even asked me to banquets and dances—which should be instructive to editors who are so fearful of offending the book-buying public if they publish a few unpalatable truths.

The few critics whom I found completely incomprehensible were those who bitterly and persistently insisted that the characters in *Oliver Wiswell* were expressing my beliefs—which was nonsense. There is no way in which the Loyalist side of the American Revolution can be adequately told unless the narrator enters the brain of a Loyalist and sees the Revolution through Loyalist eyes; but a few critics evidently thought fretfully that there was another way to do it. No words of mine can convey the depression that follows the reading of unfair and contemptuous reviews, but every writer is bound to have his share of them. In pages 434–38 of the Appendix I include two of the sort of reviews that unfailingly brought Jay Lewis of the *Norfolk Ledger-Dispatch* angrily to my defense.

But most critics, I am happy to say, weren't like that; and adverse reviews by angry reviewers were always more than balanced by readers who took the time and trouble to write letters as helpful and touching as they were welcome and encouraging. The same day I received an infuriated anti-*Wiswell* blast from a Chicago newspaper,[1] I opened a letter postmarked Liverpool, Nova Scotia. It was from

---

[1]See p. 434, Appendix.

Thomas H. Raddall, whose stories of Nova Scotia Loyalists I had long admired in Scotland's *Blackwood's Magazine:*

Let me add my congratulations to the flood which must be pouring in upon the author of *Oliver Wiswell*. Not all good books have a soul, and not all souls are honest; the honest soul of *Oliver Wiswell* will keep it alive when most of the writing of this generation (historical and otherwise) has been very properly forgotten. This was a book that needed to be written, that yelled to be written. I confess I had hoped to write it. The true story of the Loyalists (who were far too busy fighting and working for their lives to write it themselves) has seemed to me all my life a job that must be done. Well, you've done it, and done it with such a thoroughness and such passionate sincerity that I give up my dream actually with pleasure.

Too much historical fiction nowadays is nothing but a re-gilding of old bones. The greatness of *Oliver Wiswell* is that it fills a gap where nothing was before, a gap created by the policy of "letting the dead past bury its dead." Of all inane maxims that's the worst; it's stuffed our heads with so much shoddy "history."[2]

With the publication of *Oliver Wiswell,* there was again considerable talk on the part of kindly critics to the effect that it should be given a Pulitzer award. I hoped it wouldn't, because I had made up my mind to refuse that award if offered; and this would be embarrassing, since I knew some of the committee members and didn't like the idea of hurting their feelings. I needn't have worried, for in the opinion of the committeemen no novel that year was regarded as having sufficient merit to receive a Pulitzer award. Later, in a roundabout way, I learned why. *Oliver Wiswell* had been proposed, and had been ruled out on the ground that it wasn't really a novel, but history disguised as fiction. Even still the diary-page on which I entered that discovery has a scorched odor:

"Disguised as fiction? What does that mean? Lamb disguised as lamb stew? Beef disguised as hamburger? Fish disguised as chowder? Wool disguised as cloth or Harris tweed or Persian rugs? What a picture: all those prize-awarders sitting around a table, nodding their heads portentously, flicking their cigarette ashes delicately to the floor and meaninglessly mouthing 'history disguised as fiction'!

"Apparently the Pulitzer Committee considers itself privileged to change the rules on literature as well as Pulitzer's prize rules; but no

---

[2]Compare this letter with the review on p. 434.

matter what the Pulitzer Committee thinks or says, *Oliver Wiswell* will continue to be a novel as well as history."

§

With the publication of *Lydia Bailey*[3] the critics were again kind; but some amateur reviewers who were also regarded as historical experts professed to be pained by what they called my unfairness to Tobias Lear. Since I'd worked hard over Lear, and since none of these gentlemen could have had access to more than a small fraction of the Lear material I'd unearthed, I was inclined to be discouraged—and again I was rescued from that discouragement by a letter from a reader I had never anticipated.

The foremost student of General Eaton's expedition to destroy Tripoli was Francis Rennell Rodd, son of a former British ambassador to Italy, Lord Rennell of Rodd. Francis Rennell Rodd was a North African explorer, and in 1932 he published an excellent biography of General Eaton and a minutely detailed account of Eaton's North African campaign. When his father died, around 1942, he became Lord Rennell of Rodd, and because of his familiarity with the North African deserts he served with the British Army in the campaigns against Rommel.

At the height of my depression over the failure of some of the historical critics to understand the difficulties I'd had in presenting Lear honestly, and in making clear an expedition that had been only vaguely understood by anyone—barring Francis Rennell Rodd—I received an envelope stamped "London, E.C.2." The enclosed letter read:

23 Great Winchester Street,
17th February 1947.

Dear Mr. Roberts,

My friend and partner in New York, Mr. T. S. Lamont, was good enough to send me a copy of your *Lydia Bailey,* since he knew of my continuing interest in any publication dealing with General William Eaton. May I, at the outset, say that much as I liked *Northwest Passage,* I cannot over praise *Lydia Bailey.* It is not only a great piece of story telling, but records a wealth of historical detail in the picture which you have drawn, unusual even in a formal history.

---

[3]Publisher's note: *Lydia Bailey* was one of the few books to have been selected by the Literary Guild and also used as a gift book by the Book-of-the-Month Club. *Lydia Bailey* was selected for the Basic Book List as compiled by the American Booksellers Association, 1948, as were *Arundel, Rabble in Arms, Captain Caution, The Lively Lady, Northwest Passage, Oliver Wiswell, March to Quebec, Trending into Maine, Moreau de St. Méry's American Journey*—an unequaled record.

I am particularly gratified to find that your conclusions on the subject of Colonel Tobias Lear were entirely those which I had reached myself on, of course, much less extensive evidence. As an Englishman I did not feel that it was possible for me to express more strongly than I did my views about Lear's conduct: it falls much more appropriately on you to use the language that you have done which I do not feel is in any way exaggerated.

I am very glad to see the interest which has grown in America about General William Eaton since I published my biographical sketch of him many years ago. I am proud to have been among the first to have drawn attention to this great and tragic story.

Believe me
Yours sincerely
RENNELL
(Lord Rennell of Rodd)

§

There isn't much an author can say to a person who wants to write, except "go ahead and write."

Thoreau, who was so determined to write that he refused to let cocktail parties or anything else interfere with his labors, spoke often of writing. "How vain it is," he wrote in his *Journal,* "to sit down to write when you have not stood up to live! . . .

"A writer," he points out, "who does not speak out of a full experience uses torpid words, wooden or lifeless words, such words as 'humanitary', which have a paralysis in their tails. . . .

"How much forbearance, aye, sacrifice and loss," he reminds himself, "goes to every accomplishment! I am thinking by what long discipline and at what cost a man learns to speak simply at last."

And "we cannot write well or truly but what we write with gusto. The body, the senses, must conspire with the mind. . . . The intellect is powerless to express thought without the aid of the heart and liver and of every member. . . . A writer, a man writing, is the scribe of all nature; he is the corn and the grass and the atmosphere writing. It is always essential that we love to do what we are doing, do it with a heart."

And "say what you have to say, not what you ought. Any truth is better than make-believe."

That's the truth.

APPENDIX

A GENTLEMAN FROM MAINE AND INDIANA

By Kenneth Roberts

Travelers who wish to view the small Maine town of Kennebunkport must first cross a narrow bridge over which there hangs a rich and perpetual odor of fish, then twist perilously through the serpentine purlieus of Dock Square, and finally emerge on a road parallel to the unimpressive river which the early and not easily discouraged residents of Maine somehow utilized as a port, launching in its meager channel a host of schooners, brigs and ships that sailed to every quarter of the globe.

Today the traveler finds but one reminder of the early maritime importance of this more or less quiet town. Near the seaward end of the river road, within easy sight of the long stone piers that protect the river mouth from storms, two tall masts rise beside a high and angular boathouse—a late-Victorian boathouse, so perched on piles emerging from the mud that it seems almost to lean for support against the masts that tower over it. The masts are those of the ancient coasting schooner *Regina;* and her long and fingerlike bowsprit and jib boom, thrust out over the sidewalk of the river road, point upward toward the nearby home of Booth Tarkington.

This fact provides excellent brooding material for resident and visiting philosophers; for it was Booth Tarkington who combed the seaports of Maine until he located and purchased the *Regina;* and those given to a flowery manner of speaking have been heard to remark that although the ships and brigs of Kennebunkport have vanished from the seas, the bowsprit of the *Regina* points to the home of a man whose literary argosies have sailed farther and borne weightier and more pleasing cargoes than all the vessels that once sailed in and out of that narrow river.

By literary argosies they mean a fleet of novels and tales so numerous as to cause the more skeptical and ignorant to wag their heads and declare that Booth Tarkington cannot be an individual but must be a syndicate. The fleet is as stately as it is large, and contains such staunch craft as *Alice Adams, Beasley's Christmas Party, Beauty and the Jacobin, Cherry, The Conquest of Canaan, Gentle Julia, Harlequin and Columbine, His Own People, In the Arena, Mirthful Haven, Monsieur Beaucaire,* three Penrod books, *Ramsey Milholland, Seventeen, The Beautiful Lady, The Flirt, The Gentleman from Indiana, The Guest of Quesnay, The Magnificent Ambersons, The Man from Home, The Midlander, The Plutocrat, The Turmoil, The Two Vanrevels,* and *Women.*[1]

One who lurks patiently in the neighborhood of the *Regina* on almost any afternoon of late spring or summer or early autumn is fairly certain to see the tall, slightly stooped figure of Mr. Tarkington descending the hill with a somewhat nautical roll, to embark on his long, low, rakish-looking motorboat, or climbing the companionway of the *Regina* to snatch what is euphemistically known as forty winks in her snug cabin, or emerging from the ship-model-decorated interior of the late-Victorian boathouse for an hour of sun absorption and conversation on the boathouse porch. He shares that boathouse with his friends, his French poodle, Figo, and a hundred supercilious sea gulls. Thus lurking, one is apt to hear Mr. Tarkington refer jocosely to his eyesight and general health, which at times had made it advisable for him to be partially supported by friends when out of doors. Residents of Kennebunkport, seeing him thus depending on others for guidance, have been heard to remark dismally: "Gosh! If I had to go through what that feller's been through, you wouldn't hear me laughing about it any!" Mr. Tarkington, however, refers to his infirmities almost with levity, sometimes even expressing the opinion that he is becoming so fragile that he might knock off an arm or a leg unless he exercises unusual care. When, after several months of almost complete blindness, one of his eyes was operated on for cataract, he carried the cataract about with him in a small bottle and eagerly displayed it to interested friends.

At the end of five months the retina of the repaired eye detached itself, so that he was obliged to hurry back to Baltimore, completely blind again, for a series of operations designed to save the detached retina. These operations not only failed to save his eye but they also failed to quench either his gaiety or his energy. He persisted in referring to the Wilmer Institute, where his operations were performed, as an educational institution. When he first went there, he "matriculated."

---

[1]Subsequent to the time when this was written, Mr. Tarkington wrote fourteen other books, among which were: *Mary's Neck, Presenting Lily Mars, Little Orvie, Rumbin Galleries, Image of Josephine* and *The Show Piece.*

Between classes at Old Wilmer—when, that is to say, he was not on the operating table—he dictated a full-sized novel; a fact which ought to be an object lesson in something or other to the serious-minded young literary aspirants who are taking a couple of years in Paris to write a short story. He hoped to "graduate" early in 1931; and so he did, for when repeated operations failed to save the first eye, the second eye was operated on. The operation was wholly successful, and he is now not only an active member of the Wilmer Alumni Association but a trustee of Wilmer Institute as well. He was there so long, he says, that "something had to be done about it."

Mr. Tarkington's methods of work have altered considerably of late. For years, during the spring, summer and fall, he sat hunched over a drawing board at one end of a high balcony in his lofty Kennebunkport study, consuming quantities of enormous cigarettes, looking down on twenty-odd ship models of various sizes and rigs, and scrawling almost indecipherable words diagonally across extra large sheets of thick yellow paper.

Today, due to his long months of blindness, he evolves his books by sitting on a couch on the same balcony, and dictating and re-dictating to an amanuensis. He has been heard to say that this method of work removes all labor from literary endeavor. Careful observers, however, noted that *Mirthful Haven* was patiently cut, revised, re-cut and re-revised before it left his hands; and that the proofs of that same novel were read to him six times, and a thousand changes laboriously dictated, before the proofs were finally released for publication.

The room on which he looks down from his balcony has changed as completely as have his methods of work. He visualized the change during his first months of blindness, when it occurred to him that if he recovered his eyesight, he "wanted something to look at." Consequently, all the ship paintings and ship models, barring three unusual specimens, were sent down the hill to the late-Victorian boathouse; the rough plaster walls of the earlier study were replaced with elaborately carved wainscoting and panels; the somewhat nondescript furniture gave way to a carefully selected assortment of Louis XV and Louis XVI chairs, settees and cabinets grouped around an elaborately carved and decorated Louis XV table desk; while the ultimate touch in "something to look at" was provided by the colorful and, in some cases, celebrated paintings, by eighteenth-century artists, that hang on the walls.

Among these are the Duchess of Marlborough, by Kneller; the Countess of Sunderland, by Sir Peter Lely; the first—and naughtiest—Duchess of Portsmouth, by Wissing; Isaac Newton, by Riley, court painter to

William and Mary; and the portrait of an unknown gentleman by Joseph Highmore, all of them acquired by Mr. Tarkington subsequent to his first attack of blindness.

There seems to be an impression, among persons who see Mr. Tarkington steering his motorboat between the piers through which Arundel brigs and ships once sailed, or supervising the placing of a new ship model or figurehead in his boathouse, or ambling about in white flannels, or indulging in fierce and controversial games of checkers or mah-jongg in the evening with his friends, that authors never work. There seems, even, to be a vague idea extant that there is something disgracefully easy about writing. Some years ago a distressed mother approached Mr. Tarkington on behalf of her deluded son. "Oh, Mr. Tarkington," she told him, "if only you'd give Edwin some good advice! He won't listen to me, but he admires you tremendously, and I think he'd listen to you! He wants to write, Mr. Tarkington; and I wish you'd tell him not to do it! I don't want him to write, Mr. Tarkington; I want him to *do* something!"

If, however, one of those misguided persons should be fortunate enough to back Mr. Tarkington into the balcony of his workroom or into a corner of his boathouse—where escape, because of his natural politeness, would be difficult—and pry ruthlessly into his past, he would soon discover that Mr. Tarkington has worked somewhat harder than a pre-war bricklayer, oftentimes with less to show for his labors.

For many years he went to work immediately after breakfast, had his lunch placed outside the door of his workroom, dragged it in when he felt like it, worked until dinner, and after dinner worked again until midnight. At midnight he snatched a little relaxation and dissipation by reading for an hour, after which he went to sleep, only to be back at work at nine-thirty the next morning. *The Turmoil,* due to this semi-perpetual-motion method of laboring, was written in sixty days.

One further discovers that he was afflicted with the urge to write almost as far back as he is able to remember—as far back, in short, as the age of six. It might be remarked in passing that Mr. Tarkington daily demonstrates that his memory is in some ways as remarkable as that of the most expert lightning calculator; and he goes so far as to claim an undimmed recollection of occurrences that took place when he was six months old. This statement is occasionally challenged by skeptical acquaintances, but Mr. Tarkington persists in his claim, declaring that he distinctly recalls being clothed in a white dress and a blue sash at the age of six months, being exhibited to a company of banqueters and encouraged to drink part of a goblet of champagne, as a result of which he suffered a temporary indisposition—to the more permanent impairment of the blue sash. It might also be remarked in passing that he has touched no sort of alcoholic beverage since 1912, though he touched several sorts prior to that time.

At all events he was six years old, and unable ᴛo read or write, when he dictated his first literary effort to his sister. Stories had been read to him—stories of the sloppy and evasive English school, so much admired in the 1880's; so his story was an English story, starting, "As twilight approached, a solitary horseman was seen approaching over uneven ground." He finished one page of this masterpiece.

For the ensuing seven years he continued to dabble desultorily in the arts, writing and drawing with equal facility; but it was not until his thirteenth year that his efforts were enthusiastically acclaimed—and in that instance the acclaim was limited to close relatives.

He was a neighbor of James Whitcomb Riley at that period, and a frequent caller on Riley; and Riley, having produced a poem, would try it out, with gestures, on young Tarkington. He even assisted Riley with a cover design for a book of poems. The original cover, designed by Riley, showed a bottle of ink exploding, with the words of the title appearing in the midst of the explosion. Master Tarkington suggested the addition of an imp applying a match to the fuse that caused the bottle to explode. The suggestion entranced Riley, and was instantly adopted, so that Tarkington jumped to the conclusion that illustrating was not only easy but his forte.

Riley, however, was a poet; so out of loyalty the youthful Tarkington felt that he should not abandon literature entirely. It was while he was in this frame of mind that he produced a poem—a powerful piece entitled *The Trees*. It contained, he recalls, the line, "But my soul answers not passion's call." He illustrated it with pictures of a jester caught in a severe storm—a jester who for some obscure reason had been obliged to seek out a priest in order to have something soothed in him. The admiration felt for this poem by his parents was such that copies were sent to his grandparents, but Mr. Tarkington freely admits he was unable to think of himself as a finished writer, even then. His life work, he felt, was illustrating.

Financial returns from his early labors were not high, which may account for the clarity with which Mr. Tarkington recalls them. He and a friend earned fifteen cents shoveling snow, seven cents going to each shoveler and the remaining penny being invested in a stick of candy which was equally divided. Later, for perpetrating a portrait of his grandfather in crayons, he was rewarded with one dollar, though there is some doubt in his mind as to whether or not the portrait was worth it. He entered a prize contest held by *St. Nicholas* and received honorable mention but no money; and when he went to Exeter Academy he hopefully submitted literary material to the school magazine, the *Lit,* only to have it enthusiastically rejected.

From Exeter he went to Purdue, for reasons that are not quite clear. Purdue is a coeducational institution, located in West Lafayette, Indiana; and there is reason to believe that Mr. Tarkington, like many other young Americans, settled on a college because he knew someone —possibly a young lady—who was going there. At Purdue he followed in the footsteps of George Ade and contributed a column a week to a Lafayette newspaper—a column that contained news and what Mr. Tarkington now recalls as "attempts at being very humorous." Since Ade had been highly successful with the column, Mr. Tarkington suspects that he imitated George. He received nothing for it, however.

After one year at Purdue he transferred to Princeton; and it was in Princeton that he made his first big killing. He had no sooner arrived there than he learned that an undergraduate magazine was running a prize-story competition. Inflamed by this news, he wrote and submitted a story, won the competition and received fifteen dollars.

He was a busy young man in Princeton; for he followed up, as the saying goes, his early success by drawing and writing for two undergraduate publications, the *Bric-a-Brac* and the *Tiger,* as well as by collaborating with Post Wheeler, then an instructor but now a diplomat, in writing a musical comedy for the Triangle Club, an undergraduate dramatic organization of which Mr. Tarkington was president, in addition to being actor, author, stage manager, and selector of costumes and scenery. He wrote, too, the words of a song which he rendered amid enthusiastic applause as soloist of the Princeton Glee Club—a song called "It's All Over Now." And in his senior year he received thirty-five dollars for writing the words of a prize song, "Princeton Days," which has had hard usage ever since at the hands of undergraduate songbirds, but is still giving good service.

Thus, after toying with literature from his sixth to his twenty-second year, with total receipts of $51.07 and half a stick of candy, Mr. Tarkington departed from Princeton in 1893, minus a degree because of having entered with a condition in Greek—a condition which he had never made up "because of having too many other things to do." Mr. Tarkington's early indifference to the Greek classics did not meet with permanent disapproval; for but the fact is that Princeton, a few years later, presented him with the degree of Master of Arts, and completed the job in 1918 by giving him the degree of Doctor of Literature.

At all events, he went back to Indianapolis in 1893 and seemed to the old home folks to be leading the unproductive life of a social butterfly. Having a small income, he gadded around in a red-wheeled runabout, and participated so frequently in balls, theatricals and other diversions that neighbors shook their heads despondently and remarked that what with the wildness and frivolity of the young people and all, there wasn't any way of telling what the world was coming to. Actually, however, he was working at all hours of the night—and morning—writing and drawing pictures—"fumbling," he says.

One of his classmates started a magazine called *John O'Dreams;* an arty little magazine of the sort calculated to appeal to really intelligent people, but doomed from the start to appeal to nobody except its own editorial staff. He wrote and drew pictures for *John O'Dreams,* imitating French and English seventeenth- and eighteenth-century literary forms. He sent a varied assortment of material to *Life,* and within a year he had something accepted. It was a two-line joke. He received $2.50 for it, and Charles Dana Gibson illustrated it. This was considered something of a triumph; and his hopes of becoming an author were raised slightly—not very far, but a little—half an inch, say, or even an inch. Later—this was in 1894—he sold a longer piece to *Life,* and this time there was a picture with it. For the picture he received thirteen dollars; for the text accompanying it he was paid seven dollars.

The deduction that he drew was inevitable—his drawing must be to his writing as thirteen is to seven. This pretty well decided him to be an artist; so he buckled down to work and completed thirty pictures in quick succession. They were rejected almost violently, and he began to think of abandoning drawing entirely and going in for writing in a big way.

It was around this time—also in 1894—that *John O'Dreams* went the way of all arty little magazines, and busted. The busting threw back on Tarkington's hands a few pictures that seemed thoroughly valueless. One was a drawing of a smallish man in knee breeches and a long coat, showing a playing card to a larger, oafish-looking man whose face was marred by an expression of disgust, not to say loathing. He brooded over this picture and over some of the others.

One of the others suggested a novel to him—a novel to be called *The Gentleman from Indiana;* so, between balls, theatricals and gadding around in his red-wheeled runabout, he went to work on this novel.

He found it extremely troublesome; for somewhere in it he got off what he calls "the straight road," and couldn't seem to get on again. Consequently he laid it aside, half done, and took up the picture of the small man showing the card to the large oaf. After he had ruminated and fumbled for a time, he used the sketch as the basis of a tale called *Monsieur Beaucaire.*

Competent critics have called *Monsieur Beaucaire* the greatest short story ever written. As a book it has had an enormous circulation. It has been made into a play, into operas in English and Italian by different composers, has been given as a motion picture in several forms, and has brought Mr. Tarkington as much grief and as little return as might be expected to accrue from something criminally libelous—all of which is another and highly distressing story.

In the beginning, however, when *Monsieur Beaucaire* first came to life from Mr. Tarkington's pen, it attracted as little editorial notice as would have been given to an 11,000-word essay on "Plumbing Methods in Vogue Among the Early Phoenicians." It bounced out of editorial offices as energetically as though written on rubber.

While it was bouncing, Mr. Tarkington wrote *Cherry,* which joined *Monsieur Beaucaire* in racing back to Indianapolis from editorial offices. The year 1895 came and went, as did 1896. A number of short stories joined the bouncing brotherhood of *Monsieur Beaucaire* and *Cherry.* Even today Mr. Tarkington wags his head in amazement at the speed with which these stories were shipped back to him by editors.

In addition to turning out his stories, he dabbled in the drama, writing two plays that were given by the Indianapolis Dramatic Club, and a comedy melodrama of the eighteenth century—"boyish pieces," he now says. A New York play agent read them with some approval, and Mr. Tarkington went to New York "to try to rewrite them," but the attempt brought no reward.

He went back to Indianapolis, deposited *Monsieur Beaucaire, Cherry* and the short stories in a drawer, and turned again to *The Gentleman from Indiana.* It was now 1897, and three years had elapsed since he started it and "got off the straight road." Somehow he got back on the straight road and was able to go ahead once more. Why he went on with it, he now says, he doesn't know. Apparently nobody, barring his immediate family, read anything he wrote. He didn't like to talk about what he was writing; for it was bound to be, it seemed to him, just another rejection. He was so used to rejections, he says, that he expected nothing else. He "supposes," now, that they disappointed him at the time, but the disappointment was not sufficiently severe to stop him.

Dubious glances were cast at his seeming lack of occupation. An old lawyer, a friend of his father, eyed him condescendingly at the country club and remarked: "Well, Booth, your father says you're one of these damned literary fellers!" But he went ahead with *The Gentleman from Indiana*. He had no hope that anyone would accept it. It would be, he thought, "kicked right out." He was obviously a sad case, and his family felt sorry for him.

Moved by this sorrow, his sister exhumed *Monsieur Beaucaire* from the drawer where it reposed, and departed for New York. Arrived there, she took the manuscript to the office of *McClure's Magazine* and raised an outcry for Mr. McClure himself. She was finally persuaded to state her business to an assistant editor; and the assistant editor, casting a quick glance at the manuscript, said without hesitation that it wouldn't do.

This answer only served to bring a grim, set look to her mouth, and she at once announced at great length and with firmness verging on violence that she wanted Mr. McClure. Exhausted by her conversation, the assistant editor weakened and promised her that if she would leave the manuscript it would be brought to Mr. McClure's attention. So she left it and went away muttering darkly.

The next day she returned, to the deep distress of everyone in the office. Had Mr. McClure read her brother's book? He certainly had, the assistant editor said; and his secretary handed her the manuscript. It was not, she was told, suited to the needs of *McClure's Magazine*. This answer seemed to carry no conviction to her. What, she demanded, was the matter with it? She was told that there was too much description.

"Then it's not the little poems at the heads of the chapters?" she asked.

She was assured that it wasn't the poems; it was the overabundance of description.

"So the poems are all right?" she persisted.

They told her wearily that the poems were all right—very pretty and appropriate, as a matter of fact—very nice indeed.

"Well," she told them, "there aren't any poems in it—neither at the heads of the chapters nor anywhere else. No poems at all! You haven't read it! Mr. McClure hasn't read it! Nobody's read it! I came here to have this read, and here I stay until it is read! Where's Mr. McClure? I want Mr. McClure! You—yes, you! You go up and tell Mr. McClure I want to see him! Poems at the heads of the chapters, indeed! Poems! I want Mr. McClure! I want——"

Mr. McClure declared later that no angrier woman had ever been seen by the staff of *McClure's Magazine*—that in her rage she virtually tore the office to pieces. Pale and trembling employees laid the case before Mr. McClure, and he came to their rescue by emerging from his sanctum and giving the infuriated lady his solemn promise to read the manuscript. This he did; and when Mr. Tarkington's sister again returned, she was told that while *Monsieur Beaucaire* hadn't been accepted, it was being retained until Mr. McClure could see more of Mr. Tarkington's work.

This news came just as *The Gentleman from Indiana* had been at last finished—110,000 words long. Mr. Tarkington wrapped it up and shipped it to Mr. McClure; and soon he had a letter telling him to come to New York and cut it down to a 60,000-word serial—to make out of it what Mr. McClure's associate, Frank Doubleday, called a cablegram. At the same time Mr. McClure conquered his early aversion to *Monsieur Beaucaire* and decided to risk publishing it.

So he was launched at last, though to himself he seemed to be sticking on the ways. He thought *The Gentleman from Indiana* would never sell as a book.

Those who think of Mr. Tarkington as having instantaneous success with all his novels would discover, if they should inquire, that many of his books, in addition to his earliest ones, have distressed him by seeming to be sickly flowers in their early days.

He had, for example, hoped that *The Turmoil,* a comparatively recent book, would quickly make its way in the world; but for a long time it seemed to him to be dead. Soon after it was published he went to a large gathering of influential and bookish people, hoping to hear favorable mention of *The Turmoil.* Instead of that, he heard no reference to any book except *The Harbor,* which had been published at the same time. The gathering, in fact, appeared to be dominated by an excessively busy woman who rushed from group to group, exclaiming eagerly: "Have you read *The Harbor?* You must read *The Harbor!* Don't fail to read *The Harbor* as soon as you get home! *The Harbor* is just wonderful! Now don't forget the name—*The Harbor!* Harbor— no, no, not Barber! Harbor! Yes, *The Harbor!*" Nobody, he thought, would ever hear of *The Turmoil.*

Similarly, he was certain that *The Gentleman from Indiana* was doomed because its circulation moved coyly to 7000 and hung there. Eventually, however, it came to life and surged majestically to 40,000. Then it jumped briskly to 100,000—and continued to jump.

Mr. Tarkington went home then, to receive modestly the plaudits of the home folks for his kindly delineation of dear old Indiana. Unhappily he found them in a state of rage, filled with the idea that he had held Indiana up to ridicule as a rube state, populated by yokels. County-seat newspapers throughout Hoosierdom wrote bitter editorials attacking this insulting young pup, while the Indianapolis papers copied all attacks, to say nothing of elaborating them gleefully. He was accused of having "assaulted the sacred altars." The Hoosiers preferred the sugary output of Mr. Charles Major, who had just flowered, not to say ripened, with that sterling Hoosier interpretation of life in the Age of Chivalry, *When Knighthood Was in Flower.*

Following this, Mr. Tarkington made the disconcerting discovery that he didn't know how to write. He rewrote *Cherry,* and then essayed a story about the Terre Haute of his mother's youth—a story designed to capture the loveliness his mother had seen in the town. This, *The Two Vanrevels,* failed, he thinks—failed because he didn't know how to write. The craftsmanship, to him, seems "youthful," and "maladroit."

He insists that he fumbled for years, and that the first person who made him see the difference between a grammarian's English and the English of an artist was Mrs. Robert Louis Stevenson. The best illustration he ever saw of those two forms of English, he thinks, was contained in a paper on Thackeray by a scholarly and extremely academic college professor. In the paper the professor dealt contemptuously with the opening paragraphs of *Vanity Fair,* and rewrote them, making them correct from a rhetorician's viewpoint. In so doing, the professor utterly ruined the effect that Thackeray had achieved. He took all the life out of the opening paragraphs, and was only successful in implying that he knew a great deal, whereas Thackeray knew very little. What he failed to realize was that Thackeray knew all that the professor knew, but discarded it in order to get an artist's picture.

What Mrs. Stevenson definitely made him realize, Mr. Tarkington says, was that there are plenty of words that are good usage according to the dictionaries, but that would never have been used by Stevenson because they weren't his sort of English. He had vaguely felt this before Mrs. Stevenson came along, but only vaguely. Then Mrs. Stevenson took a copy of *The Gentleman from Indiana* and annotated it heavily to show him where he had slipped. He had, for example, used the phrase "back of" in one place. It had slid into the manuscript, and he had never thought of examining it. On the margin beside it, Mrs. Stevenson wrote: " 'Back of!' Dear me! 'Back of!' " On that, says Mr. Tarkington, he examined the phrase for the first time, and was horrified by it.

A person, he thinks, must develop an ear for the sort of English that ought to be written; and he must, too, be "born with something." Some people can't develop an ear for music; others can't develop an ear for writing. There's a cadence in prose, just as in verse; so the natural ear should always be developed—not only for the kind of words used but for balance in phrases and sentences.

There isn't, Mr. Tarkington thinks, much pleasure in writing. The chief pleasure he gets out of it, he says, is the occasional feeling of "that does it" or "that says it"—the feeling that a passage has been well handled. He admits, however, that there is also pleasure in receiving, now and then, a letter that shows he has been able to communicate with somebody—has amused somebody in a hospital, say, or "been of use" to someone.

He has apparently "been of use" to more persons than he is willing to admit. Just before Christmas of 1930, while he was slowly recovering his strength after repeated insertions of white-hot cauterizing needles into his eye—and you "haven't smelled anything," he says, until you have "smelled your own eyeball being frizzled"—his friend, Julian Street, had the thought of assembling a Golden Book for him—a book containing signatures and Christmas greetings from his admirers. It is a big, heavy book; and a glance at it shows that among those to whom he has given pleasure, aid and comfort, obviously in the highest measure, are most of America's leading educators, dramatists, editors, musicians, novelists, painters, sculptors, theatrical managers, actors, opera singers and illustrators, as well as the President of the United States, his entire Cabinet, the Supreme Court, and the leading representatives of both parties in the Senate and the House.

If you catch him late at night on the balcony that overlooks the glowing canvases in his workroom, he will, before vanishing through the nearby door to be read to sleep by Mrs. Tarkington, speak at some length about why people write, and why they write what they do, and why readers read what is written, and what writing is—though he isn't overeager to do so. Literary conversations, in fact, are apt to make him squirm internally, whereas the mere thought of addressing a gathering on any subject, literary or otherwise, almost nauseates him.

"The natural writer," he will tell you, "can hardly tell why he writes. He just writes. A painter, while he's painting, paints for himself, though he hopes and expects his painting to be seen. The same is true of a writer—the critic in him edits what he writes; it is in his mind that somebody beside himself is going to read it, or else he wouldn't edit his writing. Therefore he not only writes for himself but hopes to communicate—to present to somebody else his interpretation of life.

"He is not just an entertainer, manufacturing stories of the entertainment type of which Stevenson said the use might as well be for a turn in vaudeville—a useful and pleasant way of serving his fellow creatures and making a living, but not art, though often there is craftsmanship in it, and occasionally art incidentally.

"A writer who is seriously, and often in the humorous manner, engaged in the interpretation of life doesn't edit his writing with the idea that he's offering entertainment, no matter if he be by nature and in manner a humorist. He may often disappoint some types of readers; and the bulk of them, if he have many, will fall into types, as he'll discover by the letters he has from them through a period of years.

"One type of avid novel reader seeks to escape from life itself by the reading of romances—a very numerous type. These readers love to repeat over and over vicariously in their reading the sensations of youthful love. Such a reader may never have had a love affair in one sense—that is, with both parties playing happy roles in it. Such a reader may have been disappointed in love or have had an unhappy marriage; but what she wants in her reading is almost always a love affair with difficulties that have to be overcome and always must be overcome in the end of the book. Such a reader demands the same thing of any play she goes to. She doesn't want an interpretation of life, though she does ask that the characters be plausible enough for her to accept them as real while she's reading. Even if she be fifty, she identifies herself with the heroine of the book, who may be twenty. If the reader is a young man, he identifies himself with the hero; and sometimes even elderly men readers are able to do that.

"A woman of this type, no matter how disappointed she may have been in an actual lover or husband, is very impatient if a writer, trying, for instance, to write of just such a case as her own, has in his book a disappointed lover for his heroine, or if the two fail to come together under perfectly ideal circumstances. That is to say, she wants a novel to repeat for her and let her live for a time in the repetition of the romantic dreams of love and a lover that she had in her youth before she knew the disappointing kind of things that may have happened to her.

"This type is the largest class of reader, and sometimes it may happen that a serious writer writes a book that just by chance satisfies and pleases this enormous class of readers; but it probably won't happen often, since, being serious—which is nearly always to say humorous, too —he can't please them any more than their own lives do, since what he's doing is trying to paint life as truthfully as he can, and not to tell children bedtime stories.

"Then there is a kind of book talk that speaks of serious reading and light reading, and usually rather contentedly classifies all fiction as light reading, and everything else as serious reading. Another glib distinction among the bookish and semi-bookish people classifies some fiction as serious reading, and usually means the Russian and French fiction that deals with realism and tragedy. Anything written with a light touch or with humor is called light reading.

"I think those definitions are shallow. They might as well be applied to painting, so that gloomy painting and architectural and archaeological drawings and geometrical propositions would be called serious pictures, while Frans Hals's *Laughing Cavalier* would be called a light picture, and not to be considered at all seriously as a picture in comparison with an engraving of the viscera in a medical work.

"One type of critic, held to this definition, would be obliged to define *Huckleberry Finn* as light reading, and the dullest of statistical, historical essays on the *Decline of the Federal Party in Montclair, New Jersey,* as serious reading. And for those who divide fiction into serious and light reading according to the elements contained of gloom—Zola realism—deftness and humor, they would be obliged to call *An American Tragedy* serious reading and *A Midsummer Night's Dream* light reading.

"I think the proper way to define serious reading is by the serious intention and successful accomplishment of the writer. And light reading is writing done to please the romantic reader—writing done for the purpose of being entertaining. That is, Ade's *Fables in Slang, Pink Marsh* and *Doc Horne* are serious reading; and much of the modern writing that pleases readers by giving them a vicarious thrill in what some of them think of as their sex lives is the lightest of reading, though it's almost never written with a light touch.

"And there you come to another type of reader out of whom the modern entertainment writer—the lowest form of writer—seeks to make a living. I speak of this writer as the lowest type of writer, because for the type of writing he does, the least craftsmanship is needed. All he needs to know how to do is to describe scenes of sexual excitement with a few gross details, and he immediately clutches the kind of reader he is after. No serious writer, of course, could belong to this class, and no reader who cares for writing could bear to read a book of this type. In order to excuse itself, this type of book calls itself realism, and so far as the action of the lovers is concerned ends in tragedy. So it makes a pretense of being art for those who feel that only gloom is art.

"What kind of reader can a serious writer communicate with? He can fully communicate with those whose critical reading selves are most like his own most critical writing self."

MAJOR SAMUEL I. JOHNSON

When Major Johnson was finished with the Russian Military College for officers, he spent a year in the Cossack cavalry: then went in the Russian Navy and was assigned to a warship. I never got around to asking why his tour of duty in the cavalry was so brief, but I sensed that it was due to an impulsive streak peculiar to his family—as was clearly shown by the experience of one of his uncles: the one who was commander in chief of the Russian Armies and later governor of Irkutsk.

The general, while in favor with the Tsar, fell in love with the beautiful wife of another important officer. They were dancing together at an official ball when their feelings, in the phraseology of the times, got away from them, and they defied convention by walking out of the ballroom and vanishing. The secret police located the happy pair several days later, and the love-sick general was led off to durance vile: then exiled to Siberia, where he rose to be governor of Irkutsk and died in 1908.

I think the whole family must have been impetuous, for Johnson had another uncle who was governing a Siberian province; and that uncle, too, I have reason to think, had not willingly migrated to Siberia, but had been the recipient of government transportation to the salt mines.

At all events, the major soon found himself in difficulties on the Russian warship, for an officer had occasion to strike him. Johnson thoughtlessly struck back—a dangerous form of indulgence in the Russian or any other navy—and was immediately thrown in the brig, as a ship's cooler is called.

When the ship touched at a French port, Johnson's social error was reported by wire to the Russian Admiralty. The Admiralty, scandalized, tersely directed that Johnson should remain in the cooler for the duration of the cruise.

The vessel proceeded from France to Philadelphia. In Philadelphia

Johnson and eleven dissatisfied fellow brig dwellers contrived to gain access to an aperture through which they lowered themselves to the waters of the Delaware during the still watches of the night, and swam ashore in the shadow of a large brick building that happily proved to be a brewery staffed by a Finnish night watchman. Through the kind offices of the watchman, Johnson joined the brewery's vat department with the privilege of drinking green beer with his lunch.

A short term of scouring beer vats at a dollar a day, coupled with his understandable aversion to green beer, dampened any illusions he may have had about achieving prosperity or social advancement in Philadelphia; and he severed his connection with brewing interests to ship as a seaman on a coasting schooner plying between Philadelphia and Portland, Maine.

In Portland he followed the old nautical custom of resorting to the public square across from City Hall, public squares usually having benches on which sailors can sit without expense, take their bearings and borrow a newspaper.

The bench selected by Johnson was partly occupied by a man with a strangely distorted ear and a singular habit of making short, tense punching motions at intervals. Johnson, fascinated by the motions, engaged the man in a lingua franca conversation and found that he, too, was a sailor, answering to the name of Liverpool Joe. When the occasion offered, he confided to Johnson, he added to his income by demonstrating the manly art of self-defense in the prize ring. His punching motions, constantly indulged in, were a part of his training program.

He not only explained his manner of punching to Johnson, but successfully urged its advantages upon him. Johnson's first punch knocked Liverpool Joe off the bench, and resulted in Liverpool Joe's developing such a strong affection for Johnson that he signed up on Johnson's ship and sailed back to Philadelphia with him. The two, as they sailed, punched each other whenever they had a spare moment.

Johnson, like Liverpool Joe, had a yearning for the wide-open spaces; so when their schooner returned to Philadelphia, Liverpool Joe and his young protégé toured the waterfront until they located a windjammer about to sail for South America. Her destination being strongly to their liking, they solicited berths aboard her, were accepted, and punched each other steadily from Philadelphia to Buenos Aires.

In Buenos Aires they encountered a bit of good fortune: a revolution had broken out and the government, threatened with the loss of its treasury, was recklessly offering fantastically high wages and free uniforms to all who joined the government army. Johnson and Liverpool

Joe lost no time in joining. Johnson, because of his cavalry training, was made a cavalry scout, was nearly killed when he stopped a saber with his forehead and received a gash that left in his skull a permanent indentation about the length and depth of a rifle cartridge.

His wound won him a decoration for services over and above the call of duty, but put an end to his career in the Argentinian Army; and when he was discharged from the hospital, his faithful mentor Liverpool Joe, preaching the restorative virtues of a sea voyage, arranged for the two of them to be signed as seamen on a ship bound for Barbados. Early during the voyage the mate, a surly fellow who saw no reason to make concessions to an ordinary seaman just because he had recently emerged from a hospital, accused Johnson of malingering, slugged him until he was down and almost unconscious; then kicked him in the face, providing him with a companion scar to his saber cut.

Liverpool Joe, distressed by his companion's misfortune, started him on a rigorous regime of training. At the end of the seventy-five-day voyage, when the ship swam serenely into the jewel-like harbor of Bridgetown, Johnson, in prime condition, lurked inconspicuously in the bow until the mate came forward to superintend the dropping of the anchor. When that happy moment arrived, Johnson took the mate by the elbow, briskly turned him around: then rammed a brine-toughened fist into the mate's stomach, following it with a shattering right hook to the Adam's apple. When the mate was on the deck, groaning but still conscious, Johnson lectured him briefly on his shortcomings as an officer and his total failure as a human being, after which—knowing he'd be put in chains if he remained on the ship—he did a neat jackknife dive over the bow and lightheartedly puffed his way to shore.

From Barbados Johnson and Liverpool Joe shipped to Pensacola, where Liverpool Joe decided he had become too creaky to lay aloft in a howling gale, and should turn to a gentler profession, such as the tutoring of aspiring pugilists. Johnson, however, in high spirits because of his recent training course, again signed on as a seaman for South American ports and thence to England.

In England his eye was so taken by a splendid new barque, the R. P. Rithit, that he went to her shipping office, only to learn that she was bound for Honolulu, and that only Scandinavians were acceptable as crew.

The word "Honolulu" struck a chord within him. It sang to him: lured him: sweetly ululated through the corridors of his brain, like the chords from a vast and irresistible organ.

Somehow he must get aboard the R. P. Rithit. Men were being signed for the voyage. Johnson observed and listened. All were Swedes—all. They spoke their names Swedishly: Ole Oleson, Gustav Gustavson, Gunnar Bigvig.

Johnson fell in behind them, and when the shipping clerk asked his name, he wiped all Russian consonants from his mind and tongue, looked the clerk in the eye with a bland and candid gaze, and Swedishly said, "Sam Yonson. Finland."

Before the *R. P. Rithit* was ten miles at sea, Sam Yonson discovered that all those who had spoken Swedishly and given Swedish names were Americans, and that he was the only foreigner aboard.

Mark now how Truth can put Art and Invention to shame:

At the moment he arrived in Honolulu, penniless and without trade or profession on which to rely, save that of scouring beer vats, the white residents of Hawaii rebelled against Queen Lil and her native subjects. The whites, having more money than adherents, offered forty dollars a month for experienced gunmen, together with free meals at Honolulu's leading hotel.

To Sam Yonson this was manna from heaven, and he made the cause of the whites his own without loss of time. The white forces were little more than disorganized bands of guerrilla fighters, but they were soon organized into an army whose personnel was formally enlisted. On Sam Yonson's re-enlistment his captain, a stickler for military formality, insisted that he use his true Russian name. Sam was happy to oblige, and the captain essayed to enter the name on the rolls. After five efforts to spell it, he grudgingly and desperately said, "I'm putting you down as Sam Johnson, and that's who you are from now on."

I know how the captain felt, because I had the same trouble, later, in pronouncing the name of a stout Russian linguist, Dr. Sorokoletoff. I couldn't manage it. It stumbled from my lips as Sokkleotoff, Sokolorotoff, Solokolotoff, Sorotolokoff, Soffolokoffoff. . . . Until my tongue became adjusted to Russian words and letters, I was forced to address Dr. Sorokoletoff as "Dr. Forty Years," which is what Sorokoletoff means.

So from then on, until about 1915, it was Sam Johnson. But when he was confronted with signing orders as commanding general of Hawaiian Militia, plain "Sam Johnson" struck him as too abrupt: not sufficiently military; so he adopted the middle name Ignacio, which allowed him to sign, more suavely, "Sam'l I. Johnson, Brig. Gen."

When the rebellion was over, he remained in the Army because of the greater opportunities it gave him to indulge in his favorite pastimes— swimming, rifle shooting and pistol shooting; and he concluded, too, that his English needed refining if he intended to give orders and have them understood. So he went to night school every night for two years.

The quality of night schools in Honolulu must be high, for Johnson mounted steadily from private to brigadier general, won the twenty-five-mile swimming championship of Hawaii, held the rifle championship of the islands for eighteen years, and married a charming Hawaiian lady to whom Mrs. Jack London refers in her book as the Pearl of the Islands.

A CENSOR IS CLEARED FOR REFUSING TO CENSOR

WAR DEPARTMENT

OFFICE OF THE CHIEF MILITARY CENSOR

WASHINGTON

Military Intelligence Division
In reply refer to
M.I.10-1
C-16-25

November 19, 1918

From: Director of Military Intelligence, Chief Military Censor.
To: Major General William S. Graves, American Expeditionary Force,
Vladivostok, Siberia.

Subject: Censorship.

1. Though cablegrams have been sent answering your queries, you will perhaps desire fuller information of the status of censorship.

2. The Cable Censor's office first called our attention to what it considered indiscreet utterances in cablegrams from Vladivostok. One of the first of these was an allusion to the Swedish Red Cross as an organization of German spies. This statement was submitted to the State Department, authorized and passed.

3. References to the free sale of vodka were cut out, and the mention of receptions to certain troops as giving military information of their arrival or departure.

4. None of these elisions was suggested by this office, but attention was called to them over the telephone from New York by Walter S. Rogers of the Committee on Public Information, by the Cable Censor's office, and by Capt. Leech, Military Intelligence officer stationed in the Cable Press Censor's office. In one or two instances this office acquiesced in the deletions suggested.

5. On November 4 we received the following notice of action by

Lieut. J. G. Winslow, supervisor of the Cable Press Censorship Office, New York, at the direction of the Chief Cable Censor.

Pending establishment of adequate military censorship on news from Vladivostok and some means of accrediting correspondents with expeditionary forces there and possibly also to Asiatic fleet, we must exercise extreme care in censorship of all incoming press despatches dealing with any Allied movement in Siberia. Certain despatches dealing with delicate international problems as well as others concerning troop movements and military statistics have to be referred either to State Department or Chief Military Censor. This is being done with such despatches reaching Press New York for New York addresses from Vladivostok, Tokio or Shanghai. Similar despatches may reach Press Censor San Francisco for delivery at San Francisco or Chicago and these should first be forwarded to Press New York in order that their contents may be referred to the proper higher authorities. As soon as Vladivostok military censorship proves efficient will notify you. In the meantime please exercise great care in censoring despatches herein outlined, referring to Press New York any despatch which should in your opinion be seen by higher authorities.

6. This action and your cablegrams seemed to justify a reference to the Chief of Staff of the whole matter with quotations of deletions and a request for a decision on policies. This resulted in a memorandum from the Chief of Staff as attached confirming your opinion and the matters let pass by your censorship.

7. The sudden acceptance of the armistice terms by Germany altered the whole censorship situation so abruptly that the Censorship Board met and passed resolutions which, as revised and approved by the President, were as follows:

Whereas the question of the continuance of the Censorship has been raised, it is the unanimous opinion of the Board that the cable, postal, telegraph and telephone censorship shall continue with the following changes only:

That the voluntary censorship agreement entered into by the Press of the United States shall be discontinued forthwith, and that the press censorship in connection with the postal, cable and land lines censorship shall be discontinued forthwith.

8. This simplifies the censorship situation almost to the point of extinction, but we should be glad to be advised of your activities as it is

proposed to keep up an observation of the press until peace has been definitely signed.

> (*Signed*): M. CHURCHILL
> Brigadier General, General Staff
> Director of Military Intelligence
> Chief Military Censor

1 encl.

i a v

§

WAR DEPARTMENT

OFFICE OF THE CHIEF OF STAFF

WASHINGTON

November 14, 1918

MEMORANDUM for
Director of Military Intelligence:

The question of policy brought up by General Graves' cable No. 71 as to censorship brings up two questions concerning which it is desirable to make a decision:

1st. The despatches from Rome, signed Buckey, relating to plan of censorship of news regarding matters in Siberia, while obscure, clearly indicates in the despatch dated September 23rd, Buckey's No. 236, that the scheme proposed cannot be approved, and if any approval, tacit or otherwise, has been conveyed by the Military Intelligence Division it will be revoked.

2nd. The despatch which is given in letter signed by Captain Leech, dated November 2d, in which censorship was exercised over the statement concerning the sale of vodka and also concerning the statement of the organization of a training school for officers, indicates a misunderstanding on the part of the censor as to what is desired in such cases. There is no objection whatever on the part of the War Department to both of these censored statements being published.

3rd. As a matter of policy, the War Department has no objection whatever to the publication of newspaper articles of the kind under consideration, whether the statement of opinions by correspondents is in co-ordination with the opinion of the War Department on public matters or not, as long as the facts stated do not tend to reveal military operations. It is desired that the utmost latitude be extended to correspondents in Siberia to say what they please. As stated by General Graves, there are no military operations and there is no necessity for their being censored.

4th. I am directing the Adjutant General to reply to General Graves as follows:

"Reference your No. 71, the whole question of censorship has been brought to the attention of the Chief of Staff and he states that your attitude concerning censorship is wholly correct."

(*Signed*): MARCH
Peyton C. March
General, Chief of Staff

DIARY OF HENRY SEWALL

(WITH COMMENTS IN ITALICS BY KENNETH ROBERTS)

Marched from Boston to Ticonderoga, starting August 8th, 1776. 8th, Roxbury. 10th, Watertown Waltham Westown. 10th, Lincoln: Concord: Acton. 11th, Littleton to Groton. 12th, through Lunenburg to Fitchburg. 13, Ashburnham. 14, Winchendon. 15, through woods to Fitzwilliam. 16, Swansey. 17, Keene Surry Walpole. 18, Charlestown (NO.4). 19, Whitcomb's Regiment marched for Ti. 21st, marched from No.4 at 9 o'clock into Springfield. 22, Cavendish (a camp of bushes). 23, lodged in woods in rain. 26, 4 or 5 miles to Otter Creek. 27, 28, got over the creek on a raft. 29, Castleton. 30, Poultney River. Sept. 1, Skenesboro. A rogalley launched in the lake. 2 more on the stocks. [*From no other source can the state of the fleet on this date be established.*] Sept. 2, by Batteau to Mt. Independence.

Sat. Nov. 9, Gave in my name to tarry during the war under Col. Brewer as a 1st lieut.

Thurs. Dec. 12. Drummed a shemale out of camp. [*A detail and a bit of Revolutionary slang nowhere else mentioned.*] A small flirt of snow.

Wed. Feb. 26, 1777. Set off from Gorham. Got to the Widow Pattens at Arrundel. 27th, Breakfasted at Capt. Merrill's and proceeded to Uncle Titcomb's at Kennebunk, where I lodged. [*Since Sewall reached Arundel before he reached Kennebunk, he must have traveled by the shore road.*]

Fri., June 26, 1777 (Ticonderoga). Very hot. Capt. Merrill arrived with some recruits.

Sat. July 5th. In the evening had orders to strike all tents, etc. Upon the whole we found that we were to evacuate the post which we did very reluctantly, at Day Break and very precipitately. [*This shows the panic in which the American forces retreated.*]

July 6th. Retreated within 5 or 6 miles of Castleton.

July 7. The Regulars, Hessions and Indians attacked us a little after sunrise and after a heavy fire, obliged us to retreat. Our loss not ascertained. I received 2 balls in my clothes. Retreated precipitately through the woods over the mountains and arrived in the evening at a house in Rutland. Our party consisting of about 400 composed of different Regts. promiscuously collected, under command of Col. Warner.

July 11 . . . Marched on but could not overtake the main body, they marched exceeding fast, two men dropped down dead. [*This brings horribly to life the speed and terror of the retreat.*]

July 22nd (Fort Edward). Genl. Arnold arrived with Continental Troops from the Southward. [*No way of establishing this from source books.*]

July 28th. The Indians among our camp daily, skulking within the sentries and inhumanly killing and scalping our men.

Thurs. Aug. 7 (Stillwater) Col. Long's Regt. of militia discharged. [*Source books don't sufficiently show the undependable and unpatriotic quality of the American militia regiments. This regiment went home when the American Army was dangerously near extermination.*]

Thurs. Aug. 28th. Had certain intelligence of the Enemy's precipitate and total retreat from Fort Stanwix. . . .

Monday Sept. 8 . . . Gen. Arnold's Division with a large force of militia joined us above ½ Moon. [*Had never been able to dig this up anywhere else.*]

Fri. Sept. 19 (Stillwater) The action lasted 3 hours without intermission. Killed, field officers 2, line 10, privats 51; Wounded, officers 35 privats 182; Missing, officers 9; privats 29.

Tues. Oct. 7 . . . an action was brought on by the riflemen . . . we finally drove them with precipitation . . . had one killed and one wounded in our company. [*Such small losses tell better than any book how completely the American forces routed the British and with what exuberance they must have done so.*]

§

Friday Dec. 19, 1777. Marched about 5 miles into the rear at a place called Valley Forge in order to make ourselves Winter Quartars. [*Establishing the fact that Merrill and Nason were also there.*]

§

Sept. 22, 1778. Col. Brewer's Courtmartial came on.

October 1. Col. Brewer's dismission from the service published in G.O. [*Court-martialed for what? This is news, mentioned nowhere else. It must have been something pretty serious. Wrote the War De-*]

partment for the court-martial records, but the War Department reported they were not in the files. Our old files, State, War, Navy and all of them, are in a shameful condition, because relatives or descendants abstracted and destroyed records that reflected on relatives and ancestors who were far from being heroes.]

Nov. 26 1778 Thanksgiving . . . Was invited to a Ball in the evening. Attended but without relishing such trifling Boyish amusements. [*Sewall could moralize on the evils of dancing, and at the same time remain silent on matters of the most profound interest.*]

March 1, 1780. Capt. Williams presented me with a new shirt, and Capt. Hitchcock with new linen to make another. . . .

Mar. 22. Paid $500 for a sword. [*The sword was worth about ten dollars in "hard" or silver money.*] Paid $100 to mend it.

Fishkill July 7. Settled the expense of the feast and find it to be 65 dollars per man.

July, 1780. Got a pair of silver buckles of Mr. Bailey for three silver and 165 paper dollars. Got my watch put in repair for 105 dollars.

Thurs. Aug 31, 1780. (Fort Lee). Ensign Nason got a discharge.[1]

Sat. Sept. 2, 1780 Rode to the auditors office at Tarrytown with Mr. Nason. . . . [*Establishes the fact that Nason and Sewall were friends.*]

[*In 1780 Sewall was reading Hervey's* Meditations among the Tombs; *the fifth and last volume of* The Fool of Quality, *(*"this volume is very beautifully interspersed with moral and religious sentiments, and the tender sensibilities of humanity"*), Something New, 2* vols.; *Thompson's* Seasons; "Lucy Mary Worthly Mantaigue's" (*meaning Lady Mary Wortley Montague*) Letters. *In 1781, Yorick's* Letters to Eliza; *the first volume of* Telemachus. *1782, Abbé Raynal's* History of the Revolution in America. Dobbs's *Thoughts* and the constitutions of the several states. He wrote "lines"; those on autumn published in a Fishkill paper: those on the King's Address in a London paper. He considered card playing and dancing a disgusting bait for the unwary and viciously inclined; but when, in 1784, he went to storekeeping on Cobosseecontee, he purchased six hogsheads of rum and one of tea.*]

---

[1]There was little or no fighting in the North after the Battle of Saratoga, though most Americans aren't aware of the fact.

ANOTHER NASON, A MAJOR, FINDS HIMSELF
IN TROUBLE,
JUST LIKE CAPTAIN RICHARD NASON

OFLAG VII,
Germany.
September 13, 1940.

My dear Roberts: Family history has repeated itself and once more a Nason is a Prisoner of War. In order to cover the withdrawal of our main forces, and bolster up our allies (for whom I have supreme contempt) we had to fight it out to the end, and this proved a prison camp in my case. In fact the Highland Division was well named The Doomed Division. Since capture on the 13th June, no parcels from home have reached us, and I am writing to ask whether you would arrange with an American firm to send us each a parcel of food once every week. To simplify payment could this order be placed with a firm with business connections in London. We could then pay the London representative by bankers order, as we have no money here, and only £2 per month can be sent out of England. We would like each parcel to contain Golden Syrup or honey, 1 lb., plain eating chocolate, 1 lb., biscuits (non sweetened to replace bread) 2 lbs., preserved meat, 1 lb., castor sugar, ½ lb., tobacco, ¾ lb., cigarettes, ¼ lb., addressed individually to Lt. Col. I. C. Barclay MBE (Prisoner of War Number 1159), Lt. Col. Shaw-Mackenzie (No. 1176), Major J. M. Grant (No. 1160), Major R. F. Nason (No. 1467), Major I. R. L. Fraser (No. 1232), Major G. P. Murray (No. 1184). The P.O.W. number (Gefangennummer) must be quoted on each address. I do not know if the Atlantic Route will be possible, but if not possibly they could be sent via Siberia. I feel that I am presuming very much on a distant kinship, but if you could do this we will be inexpressibly grateful.

LETTER FROM A BATTLEFIELD

Captain Daniel Merrill, campt at Saratoga, October 15th, 1777, to the Rev. Silas Moody at Arundel in the county of York, New England: to be left at Capt. Merrill's town:

Reverend Sir: As I have a few moments time I will send you a line or two to acquaint you of the proceedings of the Northern Army from the 7th Instant to this Day. At Stillwater the Enemy marcht out of their lines twas said to take Possession of a height adjoining our Encampment on our left wing. Our General sent out a party to meet them under the Command Majr. Gl. Arnold who held a wound in his leg and Brigadier Gls. Lennard and Lincoln who Drove them and kild a vast number and took a number of prisoners. Our men forst their lines by guidance of Divine Providence with the loss of a few men and took a considerable number of tents and field pieces, ammunition and camp furniture; a number of haversacks, blankets and clothing.

Turned the Cannon Round and Drove the Enemy with their own Cannon. The Same Night the Enemy evacuated the next redoubt. Our men immediately took Possession of the Same.

The Constant fire of our men and the Enemy, the Shouts and Huzzas of our army, the Cries and Groans of the wounded and Dieing men, the sight of prisoners both well and wounded, some walking with crutches or staves; some supported between two leading them in, some held in on waggons: these things were terrible to behold, and much easier to be conceived of than written or spoken. It is positively affirmed there were thirty Waggons loaded with dead and wounded men, chiefly belonging to the Enemy, before night, besides hundreds that lay on the ground the next Day; and by the Enemies burying places they must have lost some hundreds that they Buried themselves; our losses I cannot give any account of, Not yet. Except 3 in our own Regiment and 2 wounded and Major Lithgow of Frances Regt wounded, Our townsmen are in general in health. I have lost but two men by death out of the company: one kild and one dead by sickness.

The 8th our army marcht Round the Enemy some went forward up the river and Some Surrounded the Enemy by the river who were preparing all day to Retreat. At Night effected the Same, and burnt all the houses on the road as they went off, and left 12 markees in their Encampment with all their sick and wounded. On the 8th General Lincoln Rec'd a wound in his leg twice. Both Genls must lose their left legs.

The 9th It was a Very Rainy Stormy Day. No fireing all day.

The 10th our army marcht at 12 o'clock and found the Enemy Encampt at Saratoga round where our barracks stood, which they had burnt, together with General Schuyler's houses, mills and barns. We Encampt as fast as we possibly could all round the Enemy within 80 rods of their lines: on one side opened 4 batteries immediately. Kept up a constant fire on both sides for three days. The enemy kild some of our men and wounded some officers and soldiers.

The 14th, cessation of arms, and the 15th no fireing at all. Our Generals were Capputelateing all these Days.

Additional remarks: The 16th at 9 o'clock our general gave Burgoyne one hour more to Consider whether he would sign his Proposals or not; which was to Resign themselves as Prisoners of War with all their baggage then in their possession (which was but a part, for they had burnt the greater part).

The 17th at 9 o'clock Recd orders from the General to be under arms and had orders not to plunder in the Enemy's Camps nor on their march, and the man Detected for the breach of these orders and convicted should suffer immediate Death. At 11 o'clock ordered to strike tents and march. I am not able to say where at present but you no doubt will hear. I have no time to add any more; only Desire to return thanks in public to God for his goodness to me, and Desire Prayer that we may still be preserved and our lives and health spared.

Subscribe my Self, with all due respect, yours etc, etc,

DANIEL MERRILL

SOMETHING EVERY WOULD-BE WRITER
OUGHT TO KNOW

For ten winters, in order to make an almost non-existent income go as far as possible during the writing of books so lengthy we were sure nobody would ever buy them, we lived in a small town on the Tuscan seacoast, halfway between Rome and Leghorn and abreast of the southern tip of the island of Elba. From our Italian neighbors we learned something that everyone ought to know but doesn't—that practically everything is edible, and that any person who wants to write ought to be able to get along on a fraction of the food he now consumes.

As a beauty spot Porto Santo Stefano was almost without a peer; as a place to work it was beyond compare; but it was blessed with few gastronomical delicacies of the sort that Americans regard as essential to health and happiness.

Butter and cream were not available. Meat was always eaten the day it was killed, and consequently had to be sliced to paper thinness and stewed for hours with tomato sauce, garlic and olive oil to eradicate its leathery quality.

There was a plethora of fresh fish—many of them contemptuously discarded by Americans—skate, dogfish, squid and octopus, for example. All these fish, properly cooked, are delicious. Fillets from a twenty-inch dogfish taste like a cross between sole and halibut.

America has no universally used staple that compares with the many forms of dried dough known to Italians as pasta—spaghetti, vermicelli, fettucini, or the romantically named capellini d'angeli, or angel hairs; with ravioli or gnocchi; with the various regional forms of thick soup known as *minestrone*—or "minestrony," as it should be spelled when Anglicized. Any one of these things is a meal by itself, and a satisfying one, as it is economical; and all of them somehow contrive to emerge successfully from the hands of even an incompetent cook.

Our cook was Maria Nobile, a pinheaded young woman unable to read or write, and with a mentality that left much to be desired. She was warned, however, that our resources were limited and that we must, perforce, live as Italians live; and Fanny Farmer couldn't have done better for us than did Maria on a food budget that averaged seventy-five cents a day. She did it by giving us fettucini, gnocchi, ravioli and minestrony day after day.

Why it is that all those dishes baffle so many American households I cannot say; nor can I say why an Italian, in his homeland, is able to eat four times as much spaghetti as an American. I have no idea why Americans cannot think of spaghetti without meat balls. In all the winters that Mrs. Roberts and I lived in Italy, I never heard of meat balls being served with spaghetti or any other form of pasta. Italians take their spaghetti straight on the theory that the lily needs no gilding.

Italians never allow pasta to cook until it becomes glutinous, as so often happens in America, but stop it from boiling while it still retains a slight tooth-resistant quality. Also they deluge their pasta with semi-lubricant sauces made from mashed salt pork or bacon, tomato paste, mashed garlic and water.

To make sure of Maria Nobile's procedure in cooking pasta, I went repeatedly to our Porto Santo Stefano kitchen and watched her operate.

When preparing pasta for six people, she put six quarts of water in a kettle, and when the water was boiling hard, she dropped in a handful of coarse cooking salt and brought it again to a turbulent boil. If the salt had been finer, she said, she'd have used a mere tablespoonful. Why? *Ma che!* Why not!

The amount of pasta she used varied with the known pasta-eating habits of those for whom she cooked. If, for example, there were to be six people at the table, and two were true pasta gluttons—if, that is to say, they piled their plates high, picked up large forkfuls and drew them into their mouths with sonorous sucking sounds—she used a pound and a half. Cost, twelve cents.

Her cooking time for fettucini and spaghetti was thirteen minutes of brisk boiling, though she started fishing out pieces and nibbling them after ten minutes, so to find the exact moment when they were midway between chewy-hard and mushy-soft. Fettucini are often known in America as noodles, and noodles can be either dough noodles or egg noodles. Egg noodles cook more quickly than ordinary fettucini, usually in eight minutes.

American cookbooks are inclined to recommend that spaghetti be cooked twenty minutes and more. A leading American cookbook even wants them cooked thirty-five minutes. Such overcooking makes spaghetti too soft and slippery to handle effectively; and overcooked pasta of any sort makes the eater feel extraordinarily distended.

American cookbooks also insist that spaghetti or fettucini be washed in cold water when removed from the stove. Maria Nobile unhesitatingly condemned spaghetti-washing as *pazza,* or cuckoo. Italians don't wash spaghetti. They cook them, drain them and serve. Washing is not for what has been cooked! *Ma che!* Washing is for garments!

Having cooked the pasta thirteen minutes, Maria Nobile drained it in a colander, spread it on a heated platter, dappled it with butter, sprinkled over it four tablespoonfuls of grated Parmesan cheese, and stirred and tumbled the mass with a fork and a spoon until the butter and cheese were evenly distributed. Then she rushed it to the table with a tureen of tomato sauce and a dish of grated Parmesan cheese. Total cost for six persons, forty cents.

The double application of butter-and-cheese and sauce-and-cheese—first by the cook and then by the eater—is by no means universal in Italy, but it's the way good cooks handle pasta.

Alfredo, in Rome, made an international reputation as a restaurateur because of the thoroughness with which he personally and violently worked butter and cheese into his platters of fettucini just before serving them. His fettucini were no better than anybody's fettucini; but the mere fact that he thoroughly buttered and cheesed his product before turning it over to his customers for a final saucing and cheesing somehow made it more toothsome.

The sauces used by Italians on pasta vary as widely as recipes for ketchup in America. In some parts of Italy thick meat sauces are the rule: in other parts thin tomato sauces. Italian cookbooks seem chary of revealing anything about such matters, probably because all Italian cooks are supposed to understand from birth how to make them. American cookbooks never handle the subject satisfactorily.

I collected recipes for pasta sauces from Maria Nobile and her compatriots, and set them down here for the benefit of those who want to write. Tomato sauces preponderate in Italy; and even our modest household, during our stay in Porto Santo Stefano, necessitated the presence, in the kitchen, of a five-gallon tin of tomato paste. Thus our daily expenditure for tomato sauce was four cents. The same sort of tomato paste is obtainable in America, especially from shops which specialize in Italian foods.

A satisfactory but more costly sauce can be made by adding 1 tablespoon of butter, 1 tablespoon of grated onion and 1 cup of boiling soup stock to 2 cans of tomato purée. Every Italian cook knows that the longer a sauce simmers, the better it tastes.

§

To make Everyday Sauce, put in a saucepan 1 tablespoon of butter or 2 tablespoons of olive oil; ½ onion cut fine; a single stalk of celery; 1 finely chopped carrot. Add a paste made of a 2-inch cube of salt pork, a mashed-up clove of garlic and a bunch of parsley, and place over a moderate fire, stirring frequently. Add an occasional tablespoon of water so the herbs will cook and become golden without burning.

When this is ready, add 2 heaping tablespoons of tomato paste and 2 cups of water, stir well and season with salt and pepper. Cook 20 minutes, or until the sauce thickens. If fresh tomatoes are used instead of paste, use 3 pounds. This sauce can be made larger, richer and more expensive by adding a can of mock turtle soup, 2 more cups of water and 1 more tablespoon of tomato paste.

§

To make Whole Tomato Sauce, mix 1 quart of fresh or canned tomatoes, ½ sliced onion, a handful of herbs (parsley and celery), 1 tablespoon of olive oil (or a corresponding amount of butter), and salt to taste.

Put on the fire, and when well cooked, rub through a sieve. Add twice as much oil or butter as originally used, cook a little more, and serve.

§

To make Simple Tomato Sauce, put a piece of butter in a casserole, add 2 cups of boiling water and ½ cup of tomato paste, a bunch of parsley, a single stalk of celery, a carrot, pepper and salt. Simmer slowly for 1½ hours, adding water as the original water evaporates. Before serving rub through a sieve.

§

To make Meatless Meat Sauce, make a paste of a 4-inch cube of salt pork, 2 sliced onions, and salt and pepper to taste. Put on the stove in a saucepan. When the onions turn golden brown, add a 1¼-pound piece of lean pork or beef. Cook for 15 minutes; then add ½ glass of wine. When boiling again, add enough tomato purée or diluted tomato paste to cover the meat. Continue cooking over a slow fire until the meat is done. The meat is removed from the sauce, thinly sliced, and served as a part of the sauce.

§

To make Meat Sauce, make a paste of a 2-inch cube of salt pork, 1 onion, 1 carrot, 1 stalk of celery, ½ clove garlic. Put in a saucepan with 1 tablespoon of butter. Salt and pepper to taste. Add ¼ pound of hamburger. Add any sort of meat scraps or chicken livers cut in small pieces. Sauté well, stirring to prevent burning. When well cooked, add ½ cup of tomato paste and 4 bouillon cubes dissolved in 2 cups of boiling water. Cook until thickened; then put in double boiler so it won't boil away. The longer it simmers, the better. Before serving, add ½ cup red or white wine.

§

No dish is more satisfying than spaghetti or fettucini, provided sauce and grated cheese are used with proper Italian abandon. An Italian, when confronted by a plate of fettucini or spaghetti, covers the mound completely with tomato sauce, works it in with a sensuous movement of his fork, and adds more sauce for good luck. He then reaches for the grated-cheese container and gives the mound a dusting. After working the cheese into the pasta, he adds more cheese for good luck, plunges his fork into the heap, as a farmer stabs a pitchfork into a stack of hay, and hoists the forkful to his mouth with a twisting motion. As the Italians say, *non cé male!* Not half bad!

The regulation cheese used by Italians for grating and sprinkling on pasta is the wheel-shaped Parmesan or Parmigiano. Excellent replicas of Italian cheeses are made in Wisconsin and Vermont. An American-made Romano is obtainable at all Italian-American food stores. It keeps as well as Parmesan, and when freshly grated is as satisfactory on pasta or rice. The ready-grated cheese available in envelopes and cartons is a miserable substitute for freshly grated Romano or Parmesan.

§

Another Italian dish that was as easy on the pocketbook as it was to eat was the country-style gnocchi that Maria Nobile sent to the table once a week as our sole luncheon dish. Her gnocchi was made from yellow corn meal—the same sort of corn meal from which johnnycake is made.

Maria mixed 1 cup of corn meal with 1½ cups of cold water. Then she put 2 cups of cold water in a saucepan, set it on the fire and brought it to a boil. When it was boiling, she poured into it the corn meal and cold water, added ½ cup of any sort of grated cheese, 2 heaping table-spoons of butter, 1 teaspoon of salt and a pinch of paprika. When it boiled she stirred it 5 minutes with a wooden spoon, then removed it from the fire and poured it evenly on a board, a scoured table top or any other flat surface. Five minutes later she cut it into oblong cakes 2 inches long, 1 inch wide and ½ inch thick. These cakes she arranged in a baking dish in three layers, sprinkling grated cheese and dots of butter over the two bottom layers. The little rectangles, she said, must be stiff or they'd run together, and to put cheese on the top layer was inadvisable, because it might burn.

The baking dish was placed in the oven until the exposed surfaces of the squares showed signs of browning. It was then whisked out and rushed to the table, where it was handled like spaghetti or fettucini: each individual helping was covered generously with tomato sauce, then dusted with grated Parmesan cheese. The cost of such a luncheon, for six people, came to fourteen cents.

§

Maria Nobile was past mistress of the art of making leftovers go a long way, and what she was able to accomplish with just one turkey leg was gratifying to a would-be writer.

First she made rice in the Italian manner by putting 2 meat cubes into 1 quart of boiling, salted water; then adding 1 cup of rice. At the end of 20 minutes the rice had absorbed the liquid, but was still juicy. She added a dash of saffron powder—as much as could be picked up on the end of a penknife blade. This gave the rice a yellowish tinge, and eliminated the flat taste of boiled rice. She also added 1 clove of garlic chopped fine and 1 tomato cut in small cubes.

She then minced the meat of a turkey leg on her chopping board and mixed it with 1 cup of mashed potatoes and ½ cup of turkey gravy, salting and peppering the mixture to taste.

She put a layer of this mixture into the bottom of small oval baking dishes, covered the layer with a layer of cooked rice, and on top of the rice broke a raw egg. The baking dishes were put into the oven until the eggs were cooked; then served with the conventional side dish of grated cheese. This fed six people at a cost of sixty cents.

She also made what she called *Gnocchi alla Tacchino,* or Turkey Nyocki. First she broke the turkey bones, covered them with cold water, and boiled them an hour, after which she strained off the liquid and picked off all the meat scraps. These she chopped fine with 1 cup of celery, added ½ cup of turkey fat, 1 quart of dried bread crumbs, a sprig of sage, a finely chopped clove of garlic, 1 cup of giblet gravy, 1 teaspoon of celery salt and pinches of salt and pepper. All these ingredients she chopped and mashed and re-chopped and re-mashed; then added to the broth from the turkey bones and set it on the stove to simmer.

When it simmered well, she poured into it 1½ cups of corn meal, continued the cooking till the mixture thickened; then poured it into bread pans, filling the pans to the top.

When cooled, it could be sliced, and in a cold room would keep three weeks. When served, it was sliced and browned in a frying pan with a little olive oil or butter; then served like nyocki—with tomato sauce and grated Parmesan cheese.

A welcome time-, labor- and knuckle-saving rotary device for grating cheese has fortunately been invented—a Godsend to devotees of Italian cookery: the Mouli grater, handled by J. C. Varkala & Co., 602 Pennsylvania Avenue, Washington, D.C. Price, $1.00.

§

So far as I was able to learn, every Italian cook had the knack of making a filling minestrony for six or eight people out of fourteen cents' worth of meat and three cents' worth of beans. When Maria Nobile made minestrony, she soaked 1 cup of white beans overnight. The next day she boiled them with a 2-inch cube of salt pork in 2 quarts of water for 2 hours. Then she added a pinch of rosemary, a finely chopped clove of garlic and 2 cups of diced potatoes and cooked them another half hour. She then added 2 cups of broken macaroni. When this had boiled 10 minutes, she put in any scraps of meat, chicken or chicken gizzards that she was able to find, ½ cup of grated cheese, 1 tablespoon of olive oil and pinches of salt and pepper. After a final 5 minutes of boiling, she sent it to the table, where each consumer added grated cheese to taste. The average cost of a minestrony for six people was thirty cents.

As a matter of fact, an Italian minestrony is any or all vegetables obtainable, cooked with rice, beans or macaroni, or with all three, and blended with salt pork. An Italian can live, and live well, on minestrony every noon for years on end. We did it, and so can anyone else who wants to write.

MYSTERIES AND THE PULITZER PRIZE

Mysteries, seemingly, are easily solved. English detective novels, for example, are laden with insoluble mysteries. Yet in the end they are all unraveled.

Let us take one at random. The dead body of Sir Hector Branksome-Gower, clad in immaculate evening kit, monocle still in place, is found suspended from a chimneytop in Gower Towers, apparently suffocated by smoke.

Police Inspector Crabbe of Branksome-on-Wye is called in. Death, he states, was accidental: due merely to Sir Hector's natural desire, on the evening of his demise, to see that all of Gower Towers' many doors, windows and other apertures were securely fastened against intruders.

This theory is satisfactory to the occupants of Gower Towers, barring Miss Enid Branksome-Gower, Sir Hector's beautiful daughter. To Miss Enid it proves vaguely disturbing. She is not a particularly bright girl, so cannot account for her unrest. She only knows it seems odd to her that her father should have climbed to the roof to look down the chimney when he might more easily have stood in a fireplace and looked up.

Fortunately one of the guests at Gower Towers at the time of Sir Hector's mishap is Arthur Yarrow, a rising young solicitor, who has come down from London to take an inventory of Sir Hector's pheasants. To him Miss Branksome-Gower imparts her doubts.

On investigation, Mr. Yarrow discovers a significant fact, overlooked by Inspector Crabbe. Sir Hector's monocle, it is true, was in place when the body was discovered; but Sir Hector was right-handed, whereas the monocle was found in the body's left eye. In other words, Sir Hector had not inserted the monocle. It had been done for him, and the person who did it had thrust it in the wrong eye.

To Arthur Yarrow, and to any other English gentleman, the inference is obvious. If Sir Hector had been alive, he would never, never, never have placed his or any other person's monocle in the wrong eye, or permitted it to be done for him. Better death than the slightest deviation from good form. Therefore, Sir Hector must have been dead when the monocle was inserted. The monocle had unquestionably been adjusted for one purpose and one alone: to divert suspicion. Instead of falling, Sir Hector was necessarily popped into the chimney by the same person responsible for the misplaced monocle. In a word, Sir Hector had been murdered.

Here is what is technically known as a mystery of the first water. I am not exactly sure of the meaning of the words "first water," so frequently applied to English mysteries; but I take them to mean "ripe" or "odorous"—as would be the case with water sufficiently venerable to be regarded as the first water anywhere.

At all events, here is a mystery of the first water. It is as murky and fragrant as the first water to emerge from an old aquarium. Let us examine its fascinating features. A murdered baronet; no motive for the murder; no clues; a police inspector who cannot read the address on an envelope without moving his lips; a heroine so thick-witted that she suspects everyone of the murder, including herself; an amateur detective whose free hours are few because of his gentlemanly willingness to clarify Miss Enid's unfailing misunderstanding of every situation that confronts her.

Anybody with a working knowledge of detectives or other fact-finding agencies will say at once that this mystery is insoluble. In real life, so far as I know, genuine mysteries are never solved by professional or amateur detectives unless the person responsible for the mystery goes out of his way to call the attention of the police to the solution.

In the case of the Monocle Murder, however, Mr. Yarrow achieves the impossible. He not only explains all the intricate details to Miss Enid in such a way as to make them clear to her almost non-existent intelligence, but he solves the mystery.

His task is to find a culprit capable of putting a monocle in the left eye of a right-handed man. This turns out to be none other than the butler, a disguised American, who—being an American—naturally lacks that instinctive age-old knowledge, common to every Englishman, of the amenities of monocle-wearing.

Mr. Yarrow discovers that the butler is in reality a notorious counterfeiter, who has been carrying on his nefarious work at the bottom of a chimney in the cellar of Gower Towers. Mr. Yarrow even learns the motive for the murder. Sir Hector, sniffing about the chimneytops at closing-up time, scents the powerful acids used by the butler-counterfeiter. He complains about them to the butler, in the belief that something has gone wrong with the drains. So the butler kills him.

That is the way of it in British detective stories. No mystery is so dark or devious as to defy solution. The unfailing insight revealed in them fills me with admiration. I am unable to state the exact number of detective novels produced in England each year, but the output is large—larger and more effectively standardized, I have been led to believe, than those two other popular products of Great Britain: scotch whisky and Chippendale furniture. Yet no matter how many there are, there's never a one of them in which the mystery isn't solved.

In a British detective story everything is fully explained—everything, that is to say, except the abysmal stupidity of the heroine. Since no attempt is ever made to explain why these females are invariably mental deficients, I gather that no explanation is needed. Not only, apparently, does England expect every man to do his duty, but she also expects the heroine of every detective novel to be a cretin.

In a detective story by that Henry Ford of English detective-story writers, Mr. E. P. Oppenheim, is a beautiful cretin named Félice. Félice, though the heroine and innocent, prefers to be thought guilty of several dreadful crimes rather than tell the simple truth. It is axiomatic that an English mystery-story heroine should never clear herself of suspicion, just as it is axiomatic that English detective-story writers should never use the simple word "while." There is an unwritten law in England that writers of detective stories must make it "whilst."

Quoting from Mr. Oppenheim's study in feminine stupidity:

> Félice stole into her husband's room whilst he was dressing for
> dinner that evening. He dismissed his servant at once and made her
> comfortable in an easy chair whilst he brushed his hair.

The question at once arises: why should a wife steal into her husband's room? There was no reason for concealment. She could have entered beating a snare drum without offending the proprieties. But she preferred to steal in. Why? Because she was a true British heroine, devoid of all reasoning power.

§

The point of the matter, however, is this: England is full of detective-story writers who are no more baffled by the most intricate murder mystery than they would be by a hot cross bun. That being so, I have one or two mysteries of a minor nature that I wish to submit to their searching analysis.

I am mystified as to why every British author of any standing, for many years, has apparently considered it a sacred duty to introduce a made-in-England American into every book he writes, whether the plot needs him or not.

Let us suppose that an Englishman turns out a novel dealing with the mental distress of a little group of English people residing in a remote section of Africa.

(That, incidentally, introduces another mystery. The characters in all recent English novels, barring mystery novels, are usually undergoing a tremendous amount of internal agony over something pretty unimportant. In the mystery novels, all characters deserve immediate extermination. Why should this be so?)

In the novel concerning an English group in darkest Africa, the group is suddenly visited, for no reason at all, by an American and his son, both described as wearing derbies, stiff collars and badly fitting suits of heavy black cloth. The father is a wealthy Detroit manufacturer, traveling for no apparent reason.

He says, "Wa-al, I reckon I guess we ain't fur from the lion-huntin'!"
The son says, "Sure, I guess I reckon we ain't!"

Then, having added nothing to the plot, or to any situation or character, these two representative Americans depart humorously from the picture in a small, noisy automobile. I take this example from the work of Mr. R. W. Garnett, a distinguished contributor to *Blackwood's Magazine*.

No matter where the modern English novel is laid—whether among the country houses of the Shropshire hunting set or on the outermost fringes of the British Empire—it contains an American whose talk is as accurately and painstakingly depicted as though the author had hired it done by a seller of jellied eels from Whitechapel.

One of the unfortunate features of calling an English author's attention to the misuse of American dialogue lies, it seems to me, in an Englishman's inability to recognize the misuse when it is brought to his attention. Not even when it is forcibly hammered into his attention is he able to get more than a vague glimmering of what he has done.

Recently I tried to argue the point with an English author; but the proceeding struck me as futile. My argument was based on the speech of the Detroit businessman mentioned above—"Wa-al, I reckon I guess we ain't fur from the lion-huntin'!"

That, I assured him, was not the way Detroiters talked. Back in 1760, I said, the rude trappers who traded glass beads with the Indians for beaver skins might have garbled the English language in that manner; but at the present time, thanks to Detroit's public schools, universities, libraries and what not, such garbling is as extinct as Indians and beavers. I further suggested that a book so inaccurate and untruthful in reproducing the speech of a Detroiter might be equally worthless in other respects.

"But, my dear chap!" the author said. "You Americans are hypersensitive! Forgive me for mentioning it, I mean to say, but really, you know: really, you shouldn't be so quick on the triggah! I mean to say, it's not an insult to your entire nation, you know, when we make one of your American chaps speak naturally."

I hesitatingly advanced the thought that there was nothing natural about the speech of the Detroiter in question: that he wouldn't have said "Wa-al" or "I reckon I guess" or even "we ain't fur."

The Englishman's reply was politely skeptical. "Really! And what would he have said?"

Probably, I told him, he'd have said, "We're not far from the lion country, are we?" or possibly he might have added a touch of piquancy to his inquiry by asking, "What's the lion situation this morning?"

"Oh, but I mean to say," the Englishman protested, "this Detroit chap is from the Western portion of the States. I mean to say, if he spoke as you say he'd have spoken, there'd be nothing about him to show he was from Detroit. I mean to say, one can't make an American, in a book, speak like everybody else, can one? He wouldn't be an American, if you know what I mean! And what a silly ass one would look if one wrote about an American in such a way that there was nothing American about him!"

In an attempt to clarify a situation that seemed to be growing hopelessly foggy, I asked my English friend to consider, for a moment, an American author who might wish to introduce into the pages of a book a conversation between the Earl of Herts and his son, the Hon. Vivyan

Montacute, concerning an American college professor who has presented a letter of introduction from the president of the Society for Furthering Anglo-American Friendship. Suppose, I said to him, that the dialogue between the two should run something as follows:

> The earl bit savagely at the end of a moist, black cigar. "Coo!" he said bitterly. " 'Ere's a ruddy nuisance! 'Oo's goin' to look after this blighter if 'e comes bargin' abaht?"
> The Hon. Vivyan smiled affectionately at his father. " 'Old your 'osses, guv'nor!" he said. "Don't get your blinkin' wind up over this Yank! 'E's nuffin to worry abaht, not 'alf!"

My English friend was pained. "But, my dear old bean!" he protested. "The thing's impossible! Fancy any writer chap being such a stupid! Why, it's positively sickening! I mean to say, who ever heard of an earl dropping his h's! And having him smoke a moist cigar! Why, the fellow knows nothing about our customs—nothing! A moist cigar, indeed! What I mean, there's no need making us out a lot of barbarians! I'll venture to say a member of our aristocracy wouldn't smoke a moist cigar if it were the last bit of tobacco in the world. I will indeed, by Jerve! A moist cigar's not fit to smoke! It must be dry, old fellow! So dry it crackles, I mean to say. Look here, old chap: you're having me on, eh? Why, no publisher would publish such drivel! And certainly no Englishman would read it!"

I agreed with him that every Englishman would probably resent, and rightly so, any such misrepresentation of the British upper classes. Probably, I suggested, an Englishman would feel differently about a novel, written by an American, laid partly among the honest peasants of the Cotswold Hills. A roughly clad shepherd, for example, sits before a peat fire in the quaint kitchen of a Cotswold cottage, discussing with his aged wife the American who has recently purchased the cottage for shipment to America.

> "Blimey!" he says in his rough, shepherd's voice, "blimey, but it's cruel 'ard to be chucked out of one's digs wivout a blarsted word! Eighty-two years come Michaelmas Oi'm lived in these 'ere digs, by Cripes, an' now 'ere Oi be, throwed out like a bloomin' old straw 'at! Oi'm a good mind to give yon American what for, that Oi be!"
> His gentle old wife, neat as a pin in her gray dress and white Cotswold cap, leans forward and pats his wrinkled hand. "Cruel 'ard, aye," she says, "but buck up, laddie! We're self-respectin' Cotswold

folk, an' blimey if Oi'll stand for givin' an American aught! Sure an'
ye're daft, laddie, to talk of *givin'!* They'll buy anything, yon Americans; an' he'll want your old Cotswold breeks an' your old smock for
local color. So sell 'em to him, laddie boy, an' we'll buy ourseils a
secondhand Austin an' get out of this bloomin' rut we're in, eh
what?"

My English friend stared at me. "Look here," he protested, "that's
not the way they talk in the Cotswolds! I mean to say, you could travel
through the Cotswolds for yahs and yahs without hearing anyone say
'Eh what!' Why, it's positively indecent! 'Blimey' and 'wivout a
blarsted word' and 'digs'—in the Cotswolds! No, no, my dear chap:
it won't wash! Absoballylutely not! Why, it's like dropping a bit of
carrion in Westminster Abbey! An author who'd write a thing like
that ought to be deported! In all sincerity, my dear fellow, he shouldn't
be allowed to associate with sportsmen, I mean to say!"

When I attempted to call his attention to the fact that nearly every
English author was guilty of a similar misrepresentation of American
speech, he adjusted his tie indignantly.

"It's all your American sensitiveness!" he assured me. "You're so
quick to take offense! Really, old chap, it's your great national fault. I
mean to say, we hardly dare mention your slowness in entering the
war, you're so sensitive about it! No, no, my dear fellow: there's no
similarity whatever between the two cases you mention and the
Americans our chaps put in their novels. Absolutely none! All we do
is attach certain well-recognized quirks of speech to our American
characters, so they won't be mistaken for some other nationality.
Surely, old chap, you must be able to see the difference between a
kindly little word picture, such as that of the Detroit manufacturer,
and a vicious attack on the entire aristocracy of England, as was implied in your quotation about the Earl of Herts."

As an afterthought he added, "Besides, old fellow, our best authors
have lectured in America. I mean to say, they're familiar with the
kentry; and you won't find 'em making the blunders that stay-at-
homes make."

I consulted my notebook, flipping over the leaves to locate the
British authors whose little mistakes concerning America had caught
my eye.

Mr. Charles Dickens had made mention of visiting an establishment
on either Long Island or Rhode Island—he had forgotten which.

Mr. Warwick Deeping had dealt with an American woman of culture, wealth and social position, and represented her as prefacing her remarks with such expressions as "Say, pardner!"

Mr. John Galsworthy had drawn an American scientist and college professor with the best of intentions, but had left rough edges here and there—edges sufficiently rough to give American readers the impression that the scientist-professor was a cross between a British ham actor and an Arkansas congressman of the coonskin-cap era.

Being a big masculine chap from Wyoming, Mr. Galsworthy's professor says, "I just love it," and, "Isn't that just wonderful!" and, "I don't want any grass to grow."

Mr. Galsworthy was trying to reproduce the phrase "Don't let any grass grow under your feet"; and he came fairly close. Fairly. Yet a miss is as good as a mile.

Mr. Galsworthy's professor-scientist, speaking to an acquaintance, asked, with professional tact, "Were you married in a stovepipe hat, Captain?" and, on receiving a negative answer, observed, "I'm sorry about that. They seem to me so cunning."

He also addressed ladies as "Ma'am," and, in the customary manner of American professors, slightly scrambled his Americanisms by remarking, "I'm just wondering whether that guy will be in? I've a kind of impression they do most of their business over food. We should do well to go and look at the ducks in the Park."

Mr. J. B. Priestley and Mr. A. P. Herbert had proved their powers of observation, as regards the speech of Americans, were not dependable. Mr. R. W. Garnett, son of the librarian of the British Museum, had seemingly exhumed his Americanisms from the Museum's dustiest recesses.

Blackwood's Magazine, which to me has seemed the most interesting monthly periodical published in the English language, made much of a serial by Mr. Hamish Blair, dealing with the possible state of affairs in India in the year 1957.

Mr. Blair introduced an American—Mr. Simmonds, a young consular officer—in the first chapter. The American, obviously, was a consular officer of career; a young man, that is to say, who must have trained for his position: first by spending four years in a university: then by undergoing an intensive course of study in the State Department and the Foreign Service School in Washington.

Mr. Simmonds was depicted as "a long-limbed, neatly dressed youth in mufti . . . clean shaven and good-looking in the American way."

I do not know how to differentiate between a youth who is good-looking in the American way and one who is good-looking in the British way or the Danish way or the German way. The author may have known, but he was careful not to let his readers into the secret.

Mr. Simmonds' first remark was, "We are hardly a noos agency, but if a citizen applies to us for information, why nat'rally we are very willin' to hand him any facts that have come to our knowledge."

He characterized certain noises as being "con-tinual," stated that the noises were "vurry simple," and assured his audience that "the consulate ain't goin' to take sides."

I closed my notebook and returned it to my pocket. Something told me that if I tried to argue with my British author friend over the likelihood of hearing, from the mouth of an American consul of career, the words "ain't goin'," I would nat'rally be vurry much out of luck. So far as I was concerned, the whole business was doomed to remain a dark mystery—unless England's detective-story writers should take the matter in hand and solve what, to Americans, must always be unsolvable.

It is barely possible, of course, that a solution of the mystery would serve no useful purpose. The Associated Detective Story Writers of England might conceivably get at the bottom of why it is that no English author can successfully reproduce the speech of an American; but at the same time the English authors might stubbornly refuse to profit by their discovery. From what I have seen and read of English authors, they would be almost certain to refuse to profit by it.

With that danger in mind, it occurs to me that those philanthropists —usually Americans—who are laboring so industriously to improve Anglo-American relations might reasonably devote some of their time and money to publishing a phrase book for British authors—a phrase book that would clear up, for all time, the British belief that a Boston clergyman talks as a Nevada bartender may have talked in 1855.

I am always pleased to see in the papers that a large number of Englishmen and Americans have met together at a dinner of the Pilgrim Society in London and exchanged compliments. Such dinners, no doubt, promote good feeling between England and America. At the same time I am conscious of the fact that while the dinner is in progress, it is being nullified by thousands of British authors—possibly by hundreds of thousands of them, now that innumerable English publications carry advertisements guaranteeing to teach any clerk or housemaid how to become a first-class author in twenty easy lessons.

While the diners exchange compliments, countless British authors hunch grimly over their desks, striving to introduce into novels, plays and short stories Americans who will fit their surroundings as easily and realistically as a hippopotamus would fit a Vermont trout stream.

Those who attend the dinner will doubtless be filled with Anglo-American good feeling; but those who read the novels and the short stories are almost certain to feel differently. I am not prepared to say they will feel like shooting a few British authors; but they will think several things about British authors, as well as about the English in general, that wouldn't look well in print.

It is, of course, a friendly gesture for wealthy Americans to contribute large sums toward the restoration of English cathedrals and manor houses, but personally I feel that Anglo-American relations would be considerably enhanced if the cathedrals and manor houses were allowed to take care of themselves, and the same sums devoted to setting up a series of prizes to be awarded to those English authors most nearly successful in depicting Americans who can be recognized by persons familiar with the subject.

These prizes should, it seems to me, be yearly prizes, awarded in perpetuity, like the Pulitzer Prize for Literature; but they would, necessarily, have to be more carefully guarded from encroachment than has been the case with the Pulitzer award. If they were not more carefully guarded, the award supposed to go to an English author for depicting a lifelike American would doubtless be pressed on a Czechoslovak author for a moving romance of the Swedish match factories, or even to an American for a stark and gripping tale of life and love among the Amber Hunters of the Baltic.

Here, incidentally, is another mystery. Perhaps the infallible mystery solvers who write the English detective stories can solve, for the benefit of American authors and critics, the mystery that hangs around the Pulitzer Award for Literature.

This is one of the thickest, richest mysteries of modern times; and it grows thicker and richer with each passing year.

It may be, for all I know, that the true mystery lies in the last will and testament of the late Joseph Pulitzer, the editorial genius whose eagerness to further the literature of America led him to establish the Pulitzer awards. It may be that the trustees of Columbia University, who dispense the Pulitzer prizes each year, are unable to explain Mr. Pulitzer's will to their own satisfaction. They may possibly be like the heroines of British detective novels, who must have everything explained to them, whether it needs explaining or not. In that case, any good writer of British detective stories should be able to clarify the matter to everyone's satisfaction.

The mystery about the Pulitzer Award for Literature, as I see it, is why it should be so frequently bestowed on books that would have seriously affected Mr. Pulitzer's blood pressure if he were still alive.

Mr. Pulitzer was a genius, but an irascible one. Because he knew what he wanted, he made the *New York World* into one of the most powerful newspapers that America has ever known. He had the misfortune to be blind, because of which he employed secretaries to read the news of the day to him and to carry out his orders. All of Mr. Pulitzer's many secretaries lived in constant fear of the cataclysm that invariably resulted whenever his desires were misinterpreted or stupidly executed.

This cataclysm was a sort of eruption or explosion. I have heard Pulitzerian explosions described by gentlemen who held secretarial posts under Mr. Pulitzer. These gentlemen were apt to be newspapermen, trained to describe accurately any type of natural phenomenon. They were unanimous in stating that Mr. Pulitzer's explosions, when his ideas or plans were bungled, were almost as dangerous and considerably more impressive than the 1907 eruption of Mount Vesuvius. The nervous systems of those within range, they said, were shattered and sometimes permanently ruined.

Years after Mr. Pulitzer's death, his close associates were unable to describe one of those explosions without turning pale and glancing nervously over their shoulders.

He was a positive gentleman, not only about his newspapers, but about everything else; and he was as patriotic as he was positive. One of his patriotic desires was "to further the welfare of the Republic in every possible way." It was this laudable desire that led him to establish the Pulitzer scholarships, the Pulitzer School of Journalism, and finally the Pulitzer prizes.

Having in mind Mr. Pulitzer's explosive nature when crossed, we will now proceed to an examination of Mr. Pulitzer's well-chosen words regarding the Pulitzer Prize to be conferred on one novel each year.

It is safe to take the original stipulations of that award from the *World Almanac;* for the *World Almanac* was published by Mr. Pulitzer's employees; and fear of being blown sky-high by one of Mr. Pulitzer's explosions would have kept them from committing noticeable errors. The prize, then, was to be given "for the American novel published during the year which shall best present the wholesome atmosphere of American life, and the highest standard of American manners and manhood."

That seems clear and simple. It sounds, to even an untrained mind, as though Mr. Pulitzer knew what he wanted. Apparently Mr. Pulitzer wished to encourage American authors to write about American scenes and themes. It doesn't necessarily imply that Mr. Pulitzer felt American authors were liable to go wrong if they tried to reproduce the conversation of the Earl of Herts, or write about the oriental mind, or tackle a powerful novel dealing with the psychological forces underlying the break-up of a Turkish harem. It makes no effort to hint that American literature would be better off, ultimately, if American authors stuck to things they knew most about, instead of evolving, say, romantic tales of the great love of an American reporter for a Balkan princess in the mountain-rimmed Balkan kingdom of Zikla. It merely intimates that he had no desire to provide prizes for American novels about Turkish harems or Balkan princesses.

There may be a mystery hidden away in the phraseology of Mr. Pulitzer's stipulation; but if there is, I cannot find it. I cannot extract from the words "American novel" any interpretation other than American novel; and when I read the proviso that wholesome American life shall be depicted, I cannot seem to make "wholesome American life" mean anything except wholesome American life. Certainly American life cannot possibly be construed as Russian or Chinese life; and the word "wholesome" has no double meaning, so far as I know.

As to the statement that the winning novel should also present the highest standards of American manners and manhood, Mr. Pulitzer apparently disagreed with the English authors who imply that there are no such standards in America. He must have felt that there are, and always have been, quite a few standards of this sort scattered around the country; and as I see it, he considered it a good idea to encourage American authors to write about them.

I cannot read into Mr. Pulitzer's stipulation the thought that the prize should go to a novel that ignores these high standards and devotes itself to glorifying the lowest standards of American manners and manhood. Mr. Pulitzer may have meant "lowest" when he wrote "highest"; but from what I know of Mr. Pulitzer, he probably meant exactly what he said. Apparently he didn't care how many prizes were won by novels that concentrated on low standards of American manners, so long as somebody else supplied the prizes.

Seemingly, therefore, Mr. Pulitzer was not responsible for any part of the mystery in which his prize has been repeatedly befogged.

The mystery is apparent when we examine four novels that won the Pulitzer Prize during befogged periods. For the sake of convenience let us call these novels *The Bridge of San Luis Rey, Scarlet Sister Mary, Laughing Boy,* and *The Good Earth.*

§

The Bridge of San Luis Rey was laid in Peru and dealt exclusively with Peruvians. Some of them were Spanish Peruvians, and some were straight or Peruvian Peruvians; but generally speaking, they could all be classed as native Peruvians. I wish it understood that I have nothing against *The Bridge of San Luis Rey* in the light of a straight novel with no prize strings attached. For all I know, it may be one of the great literary masterpieces of all time—though the chances are against it, since most great novels were written by people who knew what they were writing about. I am here treating it solely as a novel that received the Pulitzer Award for being the one novel published during an entire year that best presented the wholesome atmosphere of American life, and the highest standard of American manners and manhood.

Viewed in that light, *The Bridge of San Luis Rey* is one of the great mystery novels of all time.

Nowhere in *The Bridge of San Luis Rey* have I ever been able to find anything remotely suggesting the wholesome atmosphere of American life, or of Peruvian life either. Most of the characters, to be blunt about it, led strikingly unwholesome lives—so much so that although the author permitted a gratifying number to be destroyed in the collapse of the bridge, he could have allowed all of them to meet the same fate without hurting anyone's feelings.

§

Scarlet Sister Mary dealt with the life and loves of a colored person. Her upbringing, to put it conservatively, had not been of the best; and her surroundings, her companions and her habits were decidedly unwholesome. So far as I was able to discover, the standards of American manners and manhood in the book were so low that the slightest push would have sunk them without a trace.

§

Laughing Boy was a novel woven, as the saying goes, around the more or less idyllic life of two noble redskins from the great Southwest. The general tenor of the book was that the only good American is a

red one. The white Americans in the book were a singularly scurvy
crew; and even the Indians, noble as they were supposed to be, were
guilty of grave lapses from nobility. The Indian lady who played one
of the two leading roles was afflicted with a dangerous case of loose
morals. The two other Indian characters developed homicidal tenden-
cies, though only one of them proved to be a skilled murderer. The
other was more of a bungling amateur, even though his intentions
were serious. Wholesome? Highest standard? Well, really!

§

The Good Earth received the hearty approval of the gentlemen engaged in carrying out Mr. Pulitzer's plans to encourage American
authors in the writing of books on the American scene. It was laid
in China, the characters were Chinese, and it was given a Pulitzer Prize.
As in the case of *The Bridge of San Luis Rey, Scarlet Sister Mary* and
Laughing Boy, I have nothing against the book as a book. I have no
doubt that it is a good book, full of excellent Chinese character drawing
and splendid Chinese psychology.

Having been born and brought up in New England, I have never
succeeded in understanding the functioning of the oriental mind, in
spite of several favorable opportunities to observe it at close range. I
have found it so difficult to figure out what a New Englander would
do and say under a given set of circumstances that I am nonplussed at
the idea of trying to calculate what a single Chinaman would do and
say.

In my more despondent moods I sometimes think that no American
could possibly succeed in correctly interpreting the actions and reactions
of a whole bookful of Chinamen. I must admit, however, that a part
of this thought may be due to my knowledge of the inept manner in
which English authors deal with American characters. I must also
admit that Americans and Chinese have little in common; so an English author could probably write about Chinamen more skillfully than
about Americans. In fact, it wouldn't be possible, it seems to me, for him
to write about them less skillfully. If an English author can do it, there
is no reason why an American author cannot do it too: no reason why
an American author cannot treat a bookful of Chinamen in an emi-
nently accurate and satisfactory manner. So *The Good Earth* probably
presented a sufficiently wholesome picture of Chinese life, and gave
everyone quite an idea of certain standards of Chinese manners and
manhood; but Mr. Pulitzer's reaction to it, I will guarantee, would
have lacked enthusiasm.

In the awarding of the Pulitzer Prize, then, lies a mystery sufficiently baffling to place every English detective-story writer on his mettle and keep him there.

As in every first-class English detective story, almost everything is missing except the crime. The crime, as in all good mysteries, is prominently displayed. Mr. Pulitzer's original plan for improving American literature has had its throat handsomely cut.

The motive, however, is certainly not discernible to the naked eye. The outcome, too, is shrouded in mystery. We cannot tell how many philanthropists will refuse to lend a helping hand to American literature because of the almost certain suspicion that their efforts will be misdirected.

There is no way of knowing how far the sinister influence of the crime may spread. There is a Pulitzer Award for the best American biography teaching patriotic and unselfish services to the people; another for the best book of the year upon the history of the United States. Pulitzer Committees being what they are, the former might be awarded to a biography of Jack the Ripper, and the latter to a comprehensive account of the Swedish wars against Poland.

For the benefit of English authors who might wish to devote their energies to unraveling this mystery, I feel obliged to mention an occurrence which may or may not have some bearing on the matter. The awarding of the Pulitzer prizes, as I understand it, is in the hands of the trustees of Columbia University; and Columbia University once awarded a degree to Mrs. Alice Pleasance Hargreaves, of the Broaches, Westerham (Kent), on the ground that in her childhood days she had somehow stirred the imagination of Mr. Charles Lutwidge Dodgson in the writing of *Alice in Wonderland*. She was, it was said, the original Alice. She had no hand in the writing of the book, or any other book. In fact, her very existence had almost been forgotten until she achieved a sudden prominence by disposing of the original manuscript of *Alice in Wonderland* at a record-breaking price.

In addition to writing *Alice in Wonderland,* Mr. Dodgson was also the author of *A Syllabus of Plane Algebraical Geometry*. To be consistent, Columbia University should, it seems to me, have awarded a degree to a regular polygon of n sides, on the ground that it, also, had stirred Mr. Dodgson's imagination.

To reward the subject of a book, instead of the creator of it, seems to me to indicate a regrettable amount of confusion in high places. I would certainly have been distressed if the National Institute of Arts and Letters had elected Colonel Lindbergh's airplane, the *Spirit of St. Louis*, to membership. There would, however, be no doubt in my mind that in so doing, the National Institute of Arts and Letters had shown a lack of intelligence. On that point I would be clear and positive. Yet Colonel Lindbergh's airplane was a prominent character in the widely acclaimed book *We*, and therefore, it seems to me, as deserving of recognition as a lady whose name becomes a part of the title of any book. English detective-story writers, adept as they are at solving mysteries, may see some connection between Columbia's bestowal of a degree on the lady in question, and the befuddling manner in which the Pulitzer Prize for Literature has occasionally been awarded.

The least mysterious thing about this singular business, I believe, is what Mr. Pulitzer himself would have said on learning that *The Bridge of San Luis Rey, Scarlet Sister Mary, Laughing Boy* and *The Good Earth* had received his award for the novels which best presented the wholesome atmosphere of American life and the highest standard of American manners and manhood. We cannot, of course, know exactly; but we can get at the matter indirectly.

Let us suppose that both Mr. Pulitzer and the *New York World* are still alive, and that Mr. Pulitzer should decide to have published, on the front page, an attack on Democratic folly in wasting billions of dollars on insane theories of government. He would issue his orders in no uncertain language to the secretary who happened to be on duty; and the secretary would hurriedly transmit the order to whichever editor happened to be in charge of the *World* at the moment. On the following morning Mr. Pulitzer would impatiently command his secretary to read the attack on Democratic extravagance.

Let us further suppose that the managing editor of the *World*, on receiving Mr. Pulitzer's orders, had decided to interpret them to suit himself, in the mistaken belief that he was a better Democrat than Mr. Pulitzer, and therefore better qualified to know what the *World* needed.

Let us suppose he had decided that since Mr. Pulitzer was so emphatic about a pure Democracy, he must primarily be interested in an article on Democracy in America. He is at once reminded that a celebrated book entitled *Democracy in America* was written by a Frenchman named De Tocqueville in 1832 or thereabouts. And let us suppose that in consequence of all this, the managing editor embellished the front page of the *World* with a weighty article on De Tocqueville's visit to America in 1832, together with photographs showing the great strides made in America since the days of De Tocqueville.

Thus it would have been the sad duty of Mr. Pulitzer's secretary, on the morning in question, to read to Mr. Pulitzer the weighty piece about De Tocqueville. The reading, however, would have been brought to an untimely end by an awe-inspiring explosion, preceded by an impressive emanation of electric sparks from Mr. Pulitzer's beard. Police reserves would have hastened to the Pulitzer home to hold back the crowds attracted by the tumult within, and a score of glaziers would have been summoned to replace the windowpanes shattered by the eruption. When telephone receivers and transmitters had been mended, rugs straightened and torn paper picked up, it would have been discovered that the city's unemployed had been augmented by Mr. Pulitzer's secretary and several prominent members of the *World* staff, including one managing editor, one night city editor, four night-desk men, seventeen reporters, two sob sisters and an office boy.

The *New York World* under Joseph Pulitzer was a great newspaper, of inestimable value to the United States and its citizens. When the Pulitzerian hand and principles were removed, its greatness and its value vanished. It is as dead as an old almanac.

In this there should be a sort of suggestion or hint for those who have the awarding of the Pulitzer prizes. They may not, of course, feel like taking the hint. If they do, they will be doing what Mr. Pulitzer thought would be of great benefit to American letters. If they do not, there will be just one more mystery to turn over to the Associated Detective Story Writers of England for solving.

THE WIFE OF THE COMMISSARY

It is impossible to acknowledge adequately the willingness and eagerness with which librarians like Haraszty and Miss Swift of the Boston Public Library, Randolph G. Adams of the William L. Clements Library, R. W. G. Vail, Dorothy Barck and Marie Becker of the New York Historical Society, Sylvester Vigilante of the New York Public Library, Robert Gooch and Elsie Rackstraw of the Library of Congress, Clarence S. Brigham and C. K. Bolton of the American Antiquarian Society, dig into the records when they know their assistance will be put to use. They are far more conscientious than most alleged historians. Here is the way Haraszty ferreted out the lady who had always mystified the historians:

I believe [Haraszty wrote] "the wife of the commissary" or "the wife of *a* commissary"—"die Frau eines Commissar," as the original has it, was really just that: the wife of one of the commissaries. Now in the *Orderly Book of Lieut. Gen. John Burgoyne,* edited by E. B. Callaghan and printed at Albany in 1860, there is a list of British officers captured at Saratoga. The Commissary General was Jonathan Clarke, and there were five Assistant Commissaries, namely: J. Rousseau, Andrew Foster, L. Cromanteau, Nathaniel Collyer, and John Powell. I think we can discard Jonathan Clarke at the outset; for if the woman had been his wife, Baroness Riedesel would have mentioned her by name; the Commissary General was too important a person to refer to him as "a commissary." The question comes down to this: which of the five assistants was meant by the Baroness.

In Hadden's *Journal* we find, p. 198, under the date June 20, 1776, this entry: "Mr. Rousseau is appointed Quarter Master to the Commander-in-Chief at Head Quarters, and is to be obeyed as such." Horatio Rogers adds this note: "Assistant Commissary J. Rousseau was included in the Saratoga Convention and signed the Cambridge Parole. He was exchanged Sept. 3, 1781." In the *Orderly Book of Burgoyne* I found this single reference to Rousseau, in the order for July 10, 1777, p. 35: "The General Officers will send an Account to Mr. Rousseau, Commissary to the Staff, of the number of Rations they would chuse to be daily supplied with."

The Staff formed a separate unit in the Army. They usually were located together, had their meals—and drinks—together. What is more likely than that on the night in question, October 9, Burgoyne was amusing himself in company of the wife of the commissary, who was staying anyhow in his lodgings—the ample mansion that belonged to General Schuyler? His drinking with the wife of any other Commissary, located perhaps with an outlying regiment, would have been too conspicuous even for John Burgoyne.

Well, of course, this theory can be true only if J. Rousseau had a wife. At present there is no fact in my hand to show it—except the narrative of Baroness Riedesel.

Or, rather, there are a few more scraps which I shall quote for your convenience:

In *The Campaign of Lieut. Gen. John Burgoyne,* printed at Albany in 1877, William L. Stone writes, pp. 87–8:

"Burgoyne, however, would not think of a further advance that night; and while his army were suffering from cold and hunger, and every one was looking forward to the immediate future with apprehension, 'the illuminated mansion of General Schuyler,' says the Brunswick *Journal,* 'rang with singing, laughter, and the jingling of glasses. There Burgoyne was sitting with some merry companions at a dainty supper, while the champaign was flowing. Near him sat the beautiful wife of an English commissary, his mistress. Great as the calamity was, the frivolous General still kept up his orgies. Some were even of opinion that he had merely made that inexcusable stand for the sake of passing a merry night. Riedesel thought it his duty to remind his general of the danger of the halt, but the latter returned all sorts of evasive answers.' "

In Hadden's *Journal,* p. LXXXI, there is this passage by Horatio Rogers:

"The London *Chronicle* for Dec. 20–23, 1777, says—'There were many women and children in Gen. Burgoyne's camp when he surrendered, all of whom were ordered to be provided for by Gen. Gates; the women at a whole ration, the children at an-half.' A 'Return of the British Troops who draw Provisions, Prospect Hill 22 Nov., 1777' found among the Heath Papers, gives 215 women; while a Provisional Return of the German troops, about the same time, gives 82 women; making 297 women, besides officers' wives, and servants, with Burgoyne at Cambridge, a month after his surrender."

The wife of the commissary—whom I believe to be the wife of J. Rousseau—was undoubtedly among the latter.

§

Promptly on receipt of Mr. Haraszty's letter, I telegraphed Gustav Lanctot of the National Archives of Canada, Ottawa, to find out whether Rousseau had a wife. He did: a young and beautiful one, who had been captured by Indians when a girl, rescued from them by the celebrated Brant, and paddled alone from the head of Lake Ontario to Cataraqui, where she met and married Rousseau. Thus, I was justified in the use of Marie de Sabrevois at Burgoyne's headquarters.

I LIKE GIRLS WITH SIMPLE TASTES

As I grow older and more crotchety, I find myself becoming more and more intolerant of persons incapable of thinking straight, talking sensibly or behaving normally.

I find myself disliking moving picture producers who pay a feather-headed actress $150,000 a year for what is loosely known as her services, and at the same time offer an author $5000 for the motion picture rights to a novel in which the actress may exhibit those services.

I find myself revolted by officeholders who, in one breath, call me a brave defender of my country because I happened to participate somewhat remotely in the last war—who even force upon me a bonus which I do not want and to which I do not consider myself entitled; then, in the next breath, call me a Tory out of the horse-and-buggy age because I dare to speak contemptuously of their financial and political imbecilities.

I am wearied by those who cannot understand that America, in 1776, was full of politicians who would sacrifice their country to further their personal vanity, and that it is even fuller of such politicians at the present time.

I find myself irritated by society columns which tend to glorify the activities of young gentlemen and young ladies whose greatest contribution to the welfare of mankind seems to be a mild interest in motoring, cocktail drinking and divorce.

I find myself disgusted beyond words with the sheeplike idiocy of novel readers who, through literary snobbishness, make nation-wide best sellers out of literary detritus which they cannot understand, and through which not one person out of ten is able to wade. I am sick of those gentlemen who dub themselves publishers, but are in reality job printers with an almost uncontrollable desire to print dirty books, then to advertise that the reading of such drivel is a great emotional experience.

I detest neutrality advocates whose interpretation of "neutrality" leads them to be ardent denouncers of nations of which they know next to nothing.

Above all, I find myself disliking, with increasing heartiness, the appearance and ideas of the annoyed-looking girls who sit behind the steering wheels of automobiles during the summer months and drive rapidly around the country with a contemptuous and careless air. These young ladies, as I understand it, are conveying the impression of sophistication; and it frequently seems to me that this desire to seem sophisticated is at the bottom of much of the imbecility that is apparently permeating the United States of America and other nations with such rapidity.

Some years ago I visited Michigan University—an institution whose undergraduates like to think of themselves as more sophisticated than, and consequently superior to, the undergraduates of less-favored institutions, known locally as Cow Colleges. The young lady undergraduates of this institution particularly prided themselves on their sophistication. A group of sophisticated young things, finding me somewhat baffled by their yearning toward sophistication, kindly undertook to enlighten me.

There were twelve of us packed in the music room of the most sophisticated sorority in this sophisticated university—eleven amiable young ladies, all smelling delightfully of highly sophisticated perfumes, and one puzzled male, whose upper lip was perspiring slightly from embarrassment.

The young ladies were not only fragrant and easy on the eye: they were intelligent. Nowhere among them, I had been privily informed, was there a single dumb cluck. They were Big Gals on the Campus. One had attained to an eminent position in the super-club where all the young ladies of the university diverted themselves during their idle hours. One had so mastered the intricacies of golf that she had achieved something which eludes many male mental giants—she played regularly in the low eighties. One was a poetess able—according to my informant—to strum upon the heartstrings as an organist toys with the *vox humana*.

Occasionally, as a special treat, her friends were allowed to read her daily diary; and such was the beauty of its thoughts and language that those who perused it wept like hydrants.

Another read the *New York Times* from weather to ship news every

day, and was an authority on world affairs. Another held the undergraduate dating championship—on no day during her senior year had
she had less than four dates with male undergraduates. She had been
known to keep as many as nine dates in one day; and it was said, on
reasonably good authority, that she was the temporary custodian of
forty-two fraternity pins owned by young men who considered themselves—presumably with reason—engaged to her. In short, the eleven
young ladies were freely admitted to be the mental cream of the university.

"What I can't understand," I told them, "is your insistence on the
desirability of sophistication. Just what pleasure do you get from
sophisticated people and sophisticated pursuits?"

"And sophisticated clothes," one of the young ladies reminded me.

A chorus of charming voices assured me that sophisticated clothes
were most important.

"This university," said the young lady who read the *New York Times*
and knew all about Hitler, "prides itself on its sophistication in dress-
ing. If a girl wants to rate here, she must wear sophisticated things.
She must wear gloves and a hat to classes, and carry a handbag. She
must wear spectator sport clothes to football games in the autumn and
active sport clothes in the spring."

"Does that make her sophisticated?" I asked.

"Certainly," said the girl who read the *Times*. "What's more, sophisticated men wouldn't look at a girl unless she was sophisticated. Why, a
girl came here last year, and at first she had everybody fooled. The best
houses gave her a rush, and she had as many dates as she could handle.
Then, my dear, we found out she wore a slip at dances! A slip! Well,
really! No girl who's genuinely sophisticated would do such a thing!
We had to drop her."

I looked around the circle of young women. I could find nothing in
their faces but faint exasperation at the stupidity of the slip wearer.
"Isn't it possible," I said, "that there's some slight misconception as
to——"

The poetess interrupted me: "Not at all! Almost everybody, nowadays, knows that the most important things to be obtained from college are the friendships one makes there—the social contacts. What
chance would we have to make the proper social contacts if we didn't
wear sophisticated clothes and act in a sophisticated manner? Sophisticated men wouldn't have anything to do with us. We'd leave here at
the end of four years without having made any social contacts at all!"

"What puzzles me," I said, "is your use of the word 'sophisticated.'

Perhaps your ideas of sophistication aren't mine. Would you be willing to explain what you mean by 'sophisticated men'? What is a sophisticated man?"

The eleven young ladies looked at one another and delicately adjusted their skirts.

"A sophisticated man," said the reader of the *Times*, "is one who has been places and done things."

The poetess spoke to me a little sharply: "You know a sophisticated man as well as we do. He knows how to speak to a waiter so the waiter doesn't make you feel uncomfortable. He can order a dinner without making you feel embarrassed."

The all-time dating champion emitted an enlightening contribution: "A sophisticated man is seen everywhere. People talk about him. He knows almost everybody and can say 'Hi' to everyone he meets. He isn't hey-hey or high-schoolish, and he knows how to dress. His hair looks neat all the time, and he can hold lots of gin without showing it much."

"He's not an exhibitionist," a fluffy blonde added concisely.

"What do you mean by 'exhibitionist'?" I asked.

"Oh," she said carelessly, "he doesn't play chess or do queer things like that."

"A man who's sophisticated," said the poetess, with an air of finality, "knows what to do and when to do it. Isn't that sophistication?"

"I'm afraid it isn't," I said.

I didn't have the heart to tell those innocent young things the accurate meaning of sophistication, but I feel no such reluctance now that so many young ladies have come to think that sophistication consists of playing contract bridge snappily, drinking old-fashioned whisky cocktails, reading books which are fashionable instead of worth reading, painting their fingernails red, and discussing intricate viands and rare wines as though they knew what they were talking about. In fact, it strikes me that the ladies who think there is something admirable in being sophisticated are not unlike those who think there's something praiseworthy in insane theories of government. The latter think as they do because they know nothing about government. The young ladies know nothing about sophistication.

The most complete definitions of "sophistication" and of the verb "to sophisticate" are found in the Century Dictionary and Cyclopedia. The transitive verb "sophisticate" has five meanings: (1) To clothe or obscure with fallacies; to falsify: (2) To overcome or delude by sophistry; to pervert; mislead: (3) To adulterate; render impure by admixture: (4) To deprive of simplicity; subject to the methods or influence of art: (5) To alter, either to deceive a reader or hearer, or to make a fancied improvement.

The noun "sophistication" has substantially the same meanings: "the act of investing with specious fallacies; the process of perverting or misleading by sophistry; adulteration or debasement; a quibble or specious fallacy; that which is adulterated or not genuine."

From these definitions it is apparent that young ladies who talk about sophisticated men are in reality talking about young men who are misled; who are specious—who are, in a word, bogus. When they admire their own sophistication they are admiring something that isn't genuine; something not worth having. The more I see of young ladies who regard themselves as the acme of sophistication—who interpret "sophistication" as meaning worldly wisdom and a contempt for those who lack a surface polish—the more I like the simple ones who aren't so easily confused by half-baked opinions, or so quick to pick up new phrases and throw them at the heads of innocent bystanders.

I recently read an expression of opinion from a young thing—doubtless a sophisticated young thing—who had no use for men without lots of money. Her ideal man, she said, had to have the assurance, ease and arrogance that only money can give. She didn't explain under what circumstances her ideal man would exhibit his arrogance, but I feel free to say that if he displayed it to his elders, he deserved to be kicked; if he used it on his friends, he probably wouldn't have many friends left in a short time; if he was arrogant to his juniors or to servants, he was a pretty poor specimen; if he tried it on women, the less said about it the better. One was forced to the conclusion that if the lady was ever so fortunate as to locate her ideal, she was welcome to him.

Above all, said this sophisticated lady, her ideal man should be desirable to other women; for if there is one thing that a man and a woman have in common, it is a passion for parading conquests.

It may be, of course, that the lady knew what she was talking about, but I am inclined to question her ability as an observer. Sophisticated ladies who marry sophisticated men may have a passion for parading their conquests, and it may be true that desirable men are willing to be paraded. It has seemed to me, however, that men who amount to anything in this world have a strong aversion to being paraded. They can't afford the time. Twenty-four-hour days, as a rule, are a little too short for the amount of work which they would like to accomplish; and ladies who insisted on parading them would ultimately hear some truths about themselves that would sear unsightly holes in their sophistication.

Another great quality of the rich man, according to this sophisticated lady who only liked men with money, is that he dares to break an engagement at the last moment if he is offered an opportunity to participate in something more interesting. I am forced to assume from this that the breaking of commitments among sophisticates may, under certain circumstances, be regarded as a virtue rather than as a sign of weakness, unreliability and bad manners. I am willing to admit that the breaking of contracts, promises, treaties and covenants is more widespread today than formerly, but I still belong to the seemingly rapidly dwindling number of people who won't vote for a man who can't keep his word, or have anything to do with anyone—even with the most worldly-wise and socially polished young lady—who breaks a promise. The old New England belief that the person who trims you once will trim you again still seems sound to me, in spite of all the theories and campaign promises of all the sophisticates in public and private life.

The sophisticated lady who liked men with money stated clearly that she didn't like second-rate entertainment or food, but she didn't explain how she distinguished between what was first-rate and what was second-rate. By reading between the lines of her statements, I gathered that foods and entertainments which were fashionable and costly impressed her as being first-rate, and that those which were unfashionable and less expensive struck her as being second-rate.

In her remarks concerning her philosophy of life, she adhered closely to food, wines, dress and money. Nowhere did she mention anything as stupid as books, but I cannot refrain from remarking that if she applied the same standards to literature that she applied to food and entertainment, she would always prefer the moment's best seller to a cheap edition of one of Jane Austen's novels.

She had, apparently, been reared in Europe, and had come to have a high regard for the more luxurious hotels. Tastes, of course, differ. My experience has been that one sees less, encounters duller people and has a stupider time in the de luxe hotels of Europe than in less pretentious hotels. If I were unfortunate enough to be cumbered with a lady so sophisticated that she couldn't find pleasure in simple things— who frowned on small taverns, beer, sauerkraut and *Weisswurst* in Germany, for example, because of her uncontrollable desire for velvet curtains, doormen in baby-blue uniforms, champagne and crêpes Suzette —it wouldn't be long before the exigencies of my profession would make it necessary for me to travel alone.

"For me," declared the sophisticated young lady who liked men with money—"for me a dinner without wine loses half its flavor." She doesn't say how many dinners she had to eat before this blinding truth burst upon her, or how often she has been able to gratify her tastes since making the discovery, or what she will do when embonpoint, rheumatism or skin trouble force her to do without wine. In the latter case, won't she ever enjoy a dinner? Is she being truthful, or is she merely talking loosely, like other sophisticates? If she dined on oysters, sole, salad, Roquefort cheese and coffee, which part of it would lose its flavor unless accompanied by wine? She doesn't say, but probably only the sole would seem savorless. In that case, she could restrict her menu to oysters, salad, Roquefort and coffee, and have a full-flavored repast, even though wineless.

She gives us no gauge of her tastes in wine. We can only suppose them to be so catholic that she would prefer to drink a sickeningly sweet white wine of no particular vintage with a Chateaubriand—as the French laughingly call a first-class steak—than to ruin half its flavor with a glass of creamy beer. If so, she wouldn't make a satisfactory traveling companion.

The sophisticated admirer of rich men explained her system of winning over a reluctant male to her taste in foods and wine. He was, she said, a gentleman accustomed to dining in the back rooms of obscure speakeasies and drinking bad whisky.

"The first time we went out together," explained the sophisticated lady, "I was careful to make a tremendous fuss over the delicious food and take an interest in the selection of the wines. This was all new to him, and for once he really noticed what he was eating. Even the headwaiter was impressed. He already knew me, which had its value, because we were given a good table and excellent service in a restaurant that my escort patronized so seldom that he got kicked around and put in the back room, or Pariah Hall."

To me, this sounds highly sophisticated or bogus. What is a good table in a restaurant? What are the advantages in impressing a headwaiter? If the young man had been served badly in this particular restaurant, why should he return, unless he was feeble-minded? The fact that he had never before noticed what he was eating indicates that he was greatly below par mentally.

How were the wines selected? If the young man had been a drinker of bad whisky for a long time, he could have known nothing about wines. The sophisticated lady certainly didn't select them, or she would have said so, as she was obviously a person who would arrogate to herself all possible credit. Yet she claimed to have taken an interest in their selection. How was it done?

We must imagine the headwaiter bringing the wine list and presenting it to the baffled drinker of bad whisky. If the young man had known his business, he could have said, "Bring No. 27," and handed the list back. Not knowing his wines, he couldn't do it. Probably the headwaiter deferentially murmured something about a nice Montrachet and pointed it out with his pencil. The young man's eye, doubtless, wandered helplessly to the price column and saw that a bottle of Montrachet, 1927, was listed at $6.50, or three times its real value. There _____ he could do about it, because he wouldn't know _____ :e of it. As for the sophisticated young lady, she , "No, I think we should have some Nuits St. etter year and costs forty cents more." She had her men diplomatically, and such a remark would with the utterances of the most undiplomatic of she could have said would be, "Oh, won't that be trachet!" In other words, she couldn't have been n wine selecting as she'd like to have us believe. ;irls who are less pretentious and more appreciative. I returned from Europe with a friend who was l girl students from their school in Florence to ?y were under close restraint, I pleaded with the m come to the smoking room just once for a little ety. The chaperon finally softened her heart, on the ie of them should be allowed to have cocktails, and /as permitted to assemble.

harming group, and some of them were well worth looking at. In spite of their youth, they had an air of knowing a thing or two. One in particular was what is known in some circles as a knockout. She had frizzy hair and long meditative eyes that slid around and lingered a little. She looked to me as though she could down four cocktails without turning a hair. What a shame it was, I thought, that such a sophisticated young thing shouldn't be allowed a little more freedom.

When asked to name their poison, the young things named soupy sweet drinks, as young things usually do. When it came the turn of the fascinating lady with frizzy hair, she murmured softly that she'd have Château Yquem.

"You'll have what?" I asked.

She repeated it. Château Yquem.

"Château Yquem," I said, "comes by the bottle. You can't drink a whole bottle of Château Yquem."

She said she knew she couldn't, but she could drink some of it.

"How many bottles of Château Yquem have you had in your life?" I asked.

She said she'd never had any, but her brother had told her it was the best wine there was.

"That's a matter of taste," I assured her, and I added coarsely, "Did your brother tell you what it cost?" Since Château Yquem was quoted around ten dollars a bottle on that ship, I felt I was entitled to the information, even though, by demanding it, I shattered the young lady's faith in the universal generosity of hosts.

She slid her eyes around at me and said he did.

I saw the time had come to be blunt. "What," I asked her, "would you like if you can't have Château Yquem?"

She said she'd like some port.

"What sort of port?" I inquired.

"Just port," she assured me.

Port was what she got.

Sophisticates will probably brand this as a shocking exhibition of New England penuriousness. My claim, however, is that the young lady, for her own good, deserved to be treated as all sophisticates should be treated when their demands are inspired by a combination of ignorance and greed. My experience with ladies who claim to be unable to get along without the most expensive jewelry, food and drinks has been that they can't tell the difference between a cultured pearl and a genuine pearl at three paces, that the simplest of foods are highly enjoyable to them if they are genuinely hungry, and that their familiarity with fine wines and liquors is a pose—just as it's a pose with everyone who hasn't had innumerable opportunities over a long term of years to become familiar with such things.

To explain why it seems to me to be a pose, I must draw once more on experience. I am fond of sherry. On occasional visits to England I have toyed with my share of it, but probably all the drinks of sherry I have absorbed in England, when added together, wouldn't make enough bottles to fill anything larger than a trunk.

A few years ago I enlarged my sherry knowledge by a trip through Spain.

When I passed through Seville I disclosed my leanings toward sherry to my friend, Mr. Richard Ford, who was at that time occupying the American Consulate.

He urged me to take a postgraduate course in sherry-tasting by visiting the Jerez bodega of his friend Mr. Gonzales, one of the heads of the largest sherry-exporting firm in Spain. I lost no time in proceeding to Jerez and presenting myself at the bodega of Gonzales, Byass & Co.

A bodega is a collection of warehouses and sheds covering acres of ground. In each warehouse and beneath each shed are endless streets, rows, alleys and amphitheaters of casks as large as locomotive boilers, all arrayed in triple tiers. A particular brand of sherry may fill an entire warehouse. The best grade of that brand is in the lowest tier of kegs, the second-best grade in the middle tier, the third-best grade in the top tier. When one third of the sherry has been drawn from the lowest tier, the amount withdrawn is replaced by an equal amount from the second tier. Withdrawals from the second tier are replaced from the third. Since the sherry is mellowing with age, the quality of sherry in the lowest tier remains constant until the last drop is gone from all three tiers.

In the center of the array of sheds and warehouses is a sampling warehouse, where buyers and visitors come to sample sherry direct from the bunghole, so to speak. There are scores of unnamed sherries in this sampling warehouse, and in it one finds brands which have been dedicated to distinguished visitors who have retaliated by scrawling their names in chalk across the keg-heads. One sees the autographs of King Alfonso XII of Spain, Reina Mercedes, Victoria Eugenia, King Alfonso XIII, his son Don Jaime, Primo de Rivera; Edward, Prince of Wales; Queen Marie of Rumania, Princess Ileana, the Maharajah of Kapurthala—who, beneath his signature, added the words, "the best stuff in the world"—Guglielmo Marconi, and Franklin Roosevelt, Jr.

I was escorted through the sampling shed by José Galvez, a rotund and amiable Spaniard with a profound knowledge of sherry. In one hand he carried a four-foot whalebone wand, to the end of which was fastened a metal cup the size of a goblet. In the other hand he carried two sherry glasses. As he explained the different brands, he would flip the bung from a keg, drop the metal cup through the bunghole, withdraw it, filled, by its whalebone handle, and dexterously shoot the sherry into the glasses from a distance of two feet. Not a drop was spilled. Then he would hand me one of the glasses.

We roamed through the sampling warehouse. We sampled sherris-sack made in 1725—molasses-like in body, and so acridly sweet as to be undrinkable; heavy dessert sherries; sherries so dry that they threatened to pucker the tongue; forty-year-old sherries with the sourish, bitterish taste that sends the Spanish sherry connoisseurs into ecstasies; hundred-year-old Methusalem sherry, sweet and rich as fudge; eighty-five-year-old Pedro X sherry, of a honey-like taste and consistency, used as a base for brown sherries. By the time José Galvez had finished with me, his voice came to me dimly, as through a heavy fog, and I had learned more about sherry than I could have learned in ten years of assiduous sherry tippling.

My point, however, is this: Much as I learned from José Galvez and from a leisurely automobile trip through the sherry country, I still know very little about sherry. My tastes in it have altered. I take more pleasure in a moderately priced dry sherry than in a sweet sherry costing half again as much. If the occasion arose, I could probably pose as a sherry expert and write important-sounding monographs on the sherries which should be served under specific food and weather conditions. But if I tell the truth, I am forced to admit that if I feel like having a glass of sherry, almost any sort of genuine sherry answers the purpose admirably.

I also know that the same thing is true of brandies and wines. Sophisticated young ladies, I have found, like to pretend to an extensive knowledge of wines. Like the lady who admired men with money, they wish the world to think they know how to select wines, or can distinguish between the flavor of brandies. I have known them to make something of a point of having ordinary three-star brandy served in a sniffing glass, in order to demonstrate their knowledge of the fine points of brandy drinking.

If the beholder knows anything about brandy, such behavior leaves him as cold as the Muir Glacier. I have nothing against a three-star brandy. It serves its purpose almost as well as commercial brandies whose labels would have you believe they are sixty years older than a three-star brandy. But the person who insists on drinking it from a sniffing glass is comparable to a French-Canadian guide who might refuse to drink tin-can tea unless it was accompanied by doilies, sliced lemon and a tea cart.

Interesting experiments have been made on young ladies who considered themselves so sophisticated that they felt competent to judge between two makes of three-star brandy, or different vintages of champagne. I have seen them placed, blindfolded, before a tray on which were eight samples of liquor in numbered glasses—sherry, port, rum, rye whisky, scotch whisky, bathtub gin, an ordinary three-star brandy, and a so-called Napoleon brandy. Each, in turn, moistened her lips from one of the eight liquids, and as she did so, gave her decision as to what the different glasses contained. Many of these sophisticates confused the sherry with the brandy, thought the rum was sherry, couldn't tell the brandy from the rye, and pronounced the bathtub gin to be scotch. Not one sophisticate in a hundred, male or female—as any reader of these words can easily demonstrate—is able to call such a list correctly. The Napoleon brandy is particularly baffling. Hardly a sophisticated lady alive can, when blindfolded, distinguish it from sherry; but sophisticates—especially sophisticates who like men with money—will continue to insist that no meal is perfect unless topped off with Napoleon brandy at two dollars a glass.

I hope I make myself clear. I would fight bitterly to avoid gratifying the whims of a girl who argued that no brandy but Napoleon brandy is worth drinking, and that she, therefore, had to have it. I must confess, too, that I would consider it a waste to provide anything extra special in the brandy line for any young lady who stated frankly that she had never tasted good brandy and would like to learn why so much fuss is made over it. I can't get away from the old New England belief that girls who are healthy and properly brought up take what they can get and like it.

Personally I can't get along with girls whose tastes aren't simple— chiefly because I have found their beliefs so irritatingly dishonest. Scarcely a day passes that I don't read, in the newspapers, that some sophisticated young thing, married to a man with money, has obtained a Reno divorce and made an important statement to the newspapers on the eve of marrying another man with money.

"Yes," she says, "Mr. Pratt and I decided that a divorce was the only solution. I admire him enormously, and we shall always be dear, dear friends, but we just couldn't make a go of it."

Such interviews are hard on a reader's blood pressure. He longs to get the sophisticated young thing in a corner and inquire into her conception of marriage.

If she and her husband remain dear friends—if she still admires him enormously—why didn't she keep him? How could she ever hope to attain to a more satisfactory married state? Did she hope to find, eventually, a husband so deficient in good sense and decency that he would be willing to waste his life on a perpetual honeymoon? Was she so weak-minded as to think she could endure unending love-making?

Wasn't their trouble, as a matter of fact, due to her inability to think accurately and truthfully about anything—to her insistence on parading her conquests; on being arrogant because arrogance seemed smart; on wanting men just because other women wanted them; on having no objection to disregarding an engagement if she could find a more amusing one—or forgetting a husband at sight of somebody with a little more money?

The reasoning of the ladies who like men with money is too intricate, too irritating, for me. I prefer girls who think more accurately; who are sufficiently unspoiled to understand the beauty and good taste of simplicity.

FORTY ON THE *EMU*

(GROUNDWORK FOR A NOVEL)

Late in 1812 the brig *Emu,* lying at Deptford, ready to transport forty female convicts to New South Wales, had grave irregularities happen aboard. At first she was commanded by Captain Inglis; but Captain Inglis had been supplanted by his chief officer, John Brown, Captain Inglis having been jailed for causing a riot and committing an assault on a midshipman employed on the Impress Service in London. Acting Captain Brown's wife lived with him aboard the *Emu.*

Not until December 18, 1812, did the *Emu* sail for New South Wales; and on May 1, 1813, four and a half months later, the Transport Service learned that the crew and passengers of the *Emu* had been landed on the island of St. Vincents from the American privateer *Holkar* with provisions for four months. The *Isabella* transport was accordingly sent for them under convoy of the *Favorite.*

The forty women who were marooned on St. Vincents with Captain Brown, Mrs. Brown, ship's cook George Jackson Ward (a Negro), and the *Emu's* crew were as set forth here.

Isabella Anderson was twenty-eight years old when on January 22, 1812, she was sentenced to seven years for larceny. Later in New South Wales she worked in a Public Factory.

Sarah Baker was fifteen years old when on September 17, 1812, she was sentenced at the Old Bailey for seven years. Later in New South Wales she became a hospital nurse.

Mary Bruce was twenty-eight years old, and was convicted of larceny on the next day at the Old Bailey and given a seven-year sentence. She became a servant of Mr. Tayler at New South Wales.

Ellen Blake was twenty-two when she was convicted of larceny at the Old Bailey on July 7, 1812, and given seven years. She, too, later worked in a Public Factory in New South Wales.

Martha Banford, forty-three years old, received a similar sentence in the Essex Summer Assizes, 1811. In New South Wales she became a servant of Mr. J. Bloxland.

Ann Best, twenty-nine, received a seven-year term for larceny at the Lancaster January Session in 1812. In New South Wales she became a servant to Pat Flynn.

Ellen Chambers, twenty-five, was convicted of larceny in a dwelling house at the Old Bailey in May, 1812. She was sentenced to death. Later in New South Wales she married Hamless Watts.

Margaret Cunningham, thirty-five, was convicted at the Lancaster Lent Assizes of uttering a forged bank note and sentenced to death. In New South Wales she married: husband's name unknown.

Martha Entwhistle, forty, was sentenced to death in the same court at the same time and for the same crime. In New South Wales she became a nurse at Castle Hill.

Mary French, twenty-two, got seven years at the Devon Summer Assizes in 1811 for larceny. In New South Wales she worked in a Public Factory.

Hannah Fern, thirty-six, on March 3, 1812, appeared before the Warwick Lent Assizes, was found guilty of shoplifting and sentenced to death. In New South Wales she married James Jennings.

Elizabeth Griffiths, twenty-one, was found guilty of larceny at the Old Bailey, May 14, 1812, and given a seven-year sentence. In New South Wales she worked in a Public Factory.

Mary Gleaves, thirty-five, was given fourteen years at the Lancaster Lent Assizes in 1812 for receiving stolen goods. She became a hospital nurse in Sydney.

Harriet Ann Horne, twenty-six, appeared before the Essex Summer Assizes, found guilty of burglary, and sentenced to death. In New South Wales she became a servant to N. Bayley, Esq.

Elizabeth Holloway, twenty-four, was convicted of larceny on January 14, 1812, and given a seven-year sentence. In New South Wales she became a servant to Richard Kittle.

Jane Jones, seventeen, appeared before the Old Bailey on July 6, 1812, convicted of burglary and sentenced to death. In New South Wales she got a Ticket of Leave.

Priscilla Jones, twenty-five, was convicted of burglary in Sussex and sentenced to death. In New South Wales she worked in a Public Factory.

Sophia Kingsmore, nineteen, on the same day and in the same court was also convicted of burglary and sentenced to death. In New South Wales she, too, worked in a Public Factory.

Eliza King, twenty-six, appeared in the Old Bailey September 25,

1812, was convicted of larceny and given seven years. In New South Wales she lived in Parramatta and was unmarried.

Ann Lord, thirty-two, was given fourteen years by the Lancaster Lent Assizes for larceny in a bleaching field. In New South Wales she worked in a Public Factory.

Ann Lane, twenty-seven, got seven years at the Old Bailey for larceny. In New South Wales she married Francis Thomas.

Amelia Major, sixteen, found guilty of larceny, was sentenced on May 19, 1812, to seven years and transportation. Later she was given a Ticket of Leave, lived in Sydney and remained single.

Mary Ann McDaid, twenty-two, got seven years for larceny and in New South Wales worked in a Public Factory.

Ann Parsons was thirty-two when she got the regulation seven years for larceny on March 16, 1812. Later she worked in the Parramatta Hospital.

Margaret Proctor was twenty-four when the Lancaster Salford Sessions gave her seven years for larceny. In New South Wales she worked in a Public Factory.

Ann Rowley was eighteen when she got a seven-year sentence from the Warwick Lent Assizes on March 3, 1812. In New South Wales she was also a Ticket of Leave woman. She married Mic. Holligan.

Jane Robinson, thirty, received the same sentence in the same court at the same time. In New South Wales she became a servant to Mr. Bean.

Ann Rogers was fifteen when at the Old Bailey, July 6, 1812, she was found guilty of burglary and sentenced to death. In New South Wales she became a servant to Mrs. Badgerry.

Margaret Sullivan was eighteen when she was convicted of larceny and given a seven-year sentence. She was given a Ticket of Leave and settled in Sydney, where she remained single.

Ann Torritt was nineteen when the Gloucester Easter Sessions in 1810 sentenced her to seven years for larceny. In New South Wales she was a servant to Mr. Nash.

Alice Tomlinson, twenty-five, got her seven-year sentence from the Lancaster April Sessions. In New South Wales she married G. Eltham.

Alice Wallace, twenty-one. The Old Bailey on July 4, 1812, sentenced her to seven years for larceny. In New South Wales she married H. Shannon.

Jane White, twenty-eight. The Lancaster Lent Assizes on March 21, 1812, gave her seven years for larceny. In New South Wales she worked in a Public Factory.

A few of the women who returned from St. Vincents didn't go to New South Wales.

Susannah Eaton, thirty-one. The Old Bailey on April 9, 1812, found her guilty of burglary and sentenced her to death.

Sarah Grant, twenty-seven. At the Old Bailey, July 6, 1812, she was given seven years for larceny.

Elizabeth Hatherill, twenty-three. On April 8, 1812, the Old Bailey gave her seven years for larceny.

Mary Roberts, twenty-two. The Glamorgan March Sessions, 1812, gave her seven years for larceny.

Bella Janson, thirty-seven. The Lancaster Lent Assizes on March 21, 1812, gave her a fourteen-year sentence. No record after returning to England.

Mary King, twenty-one. The Middlesex Autumn Assizes in September, 1812, gave her seven years for larceny. No record after returning to England.

Susannah Lallament, eighteen. On July 1, 1812, the Old Bailey found her guilty of larceny in a dwelling house and sentenced her to death. No record after returning to England.

§

On October 13, 1813, the *Isabella* transport with thirty-nine female convicts aboard, arrived at Portsmouth from St. Vincents. One was missing. Which one? The records didn't say.

§

On November 4, 1813, the hospital ship at Portsmouth was ordered to receive on board Susannah Eaton, Mary French and Sarah Grant, now on board the *Isabella,* with Elizabeth Hatherill to take care and attend upon them. Their immediate removal from the *Isabella* was required. What had happened to them? Had they instigated a revolt and been beaten up for their efforts? Probably. The records didn't say.

§

On July 27, 1814, Susannah Eaton, Sarah Grant, Elizabeth Hatherill and Mary Roberts, being on board the hulks at Portsmouth, were granted free pardons in consideration of "some favorable circumstances."

Unaccounted for were Susannah Lallament, Bella Janson and Mary King. Since thirty-nine returned, one of those three must have died or remained on St. Vincents. Something told me that it was Susannah Lallament. I knew, even, what had happened to her.

HOW FASHIONABLE CRITICS
SOMETIMES GO OUT OF THEIR WAY
TO DISCOURAGE AUTHORS

OLIVER WISWELL. By Kenneth Roberts. (Doubleday, Doran. $3.00.)

REVIEWED BY ———— ————

Best Historical Novel of Our Time;
Most Outrageous Defense of Tories!

Kenneth Roberts has always considered Washington's men a Rabble in Arms. Scum, pock-marked brutes, *canaille*. He has always admired Benedict Arnold and felt sympathy for the Tory or "Loyalist" cause.

But he has waited until America is being threatened by a Fascist coalition throughout the world to vilify in 800 exquisitely written pages the entire American cause of 1776, to distort (when he bothers to mention) the ill-defined ideals for which underfed and ill-clothed men fought and died by the thousands, and to prettify the treachery of the Cliveden set, the Hoares, Lavals and Lindberghs of the American Revolution.[1]

My intense admiration for Kenneth Roberts' artistry is only equaled by my disgust for what he is pleased to imagine is his logic. *Oliver Wiswell* is, at once, the best-written historical novel I have ever read and the most outrageous apologia for Tory treachery since Munich.

Undoubtedly there were rogues and rascals in both camps, "mobsters" among the Americans as well as paranoiac imbeciles in the British high command. Kenneth Roberts reveals as much. But neither the Declaration of Independence (at which Roberts scoffs) or the military tactics of Washington (at which he sneers) were the product of the "stinking scum" and "rabble" who (after the "Loyalists" had scuttled for Canada) became the ancestors of the bulk of our present population.

---

[1]See p. 349.

I say that Roberts "scoffs" and "sneers" and not his *alter ego* Wiswell, for the very sound reason that this is no *tour de force*. There is no 800-page *tour de force* of such passion in the language. Only deep-seated belief can produce such property-loving eloquence.

The trouble with Roberts is that he got most of his training as one of Lorimer's trained seals writing for the ever-superficial *Saturday Evening Post*. Like Pegler, he was "bitten at an early age by an income tax." He is as incapable of understanding the economic reasons for the American Revolution as he is the reasons for the rise of democracy.

You simply can't beat Roberts on costumery and old silver. He can do a battle scene with all the finish and flourish of a court painter. He knows to a man how many died at Bunker Hill and in the Battle of Long Island. He can describe to a ribbon the seductive attire of Mrs. Loring, who dallied with Howe while the British lost an empire.

But ask him why the red coats of the British shone with bright buttons while the hickory-shirts of the rebels were in shreds. Why outnumbered, outequipped, and even at times outmaneuvered the "undisciplined," "loose-mouthed," anthropoidal types in Washington's army whipped England's crack regiments and pushed the invader into the sea. He doesn't know!

Roberts uses the oldest device in historical fiction to bring in the love interest. Oliver Wiswell (who like Frank Merriwell was a Yale man) falls in love with Sally Leighton, whose politics (you've guessed it) were purely rebel. Naturally the war comes temporarily between them. Oliver captures a sloop singlehanded, becomes a spy for Howe on Long Island, continues his espionage in London and Paris and joins Benedict Arnold for his campaign against the animalistic Americans in the Southern colonies. Then, the war over, he comes to get Sally.

The only other thing I wish to say about this brilliant and infuriating book is that it can't be put aside even for an hour. The story rides under full sail. The characters—particularly Wiswell and his diabolical side-kick Tom Buell—are as great creations in their way as Don Quixote and Sancho Panza. *War and Peace* has no more vigorous or minute descriptions of a country torn by conflict than are to be found in this surging novel. I would be amazed at the lack of perception of any reader who did not think *Oliver Wiswell* great writing, but I would be equally surprised if any intelligent reader were taken in by this obviously biased account of the Revolution as one-sided as D.A.R. propaganda and as passionate.

§

KENNETH ROBERTS CONTINUES HIS
REVOLUTIONARY CHRONICLE

RABBLE IN ARMS. By Kenneth
Roberts. (Garden City. Doubleday,
Doran. $2.50.)

REVIEWED BY ——— ———[1]

It seems too bad to interrupt the chorus of generous praise which has greeted *Rabble in Arms* (the term applied by Burgoyne to the Continental Army) which is a good, but by no means extraordinary, historical novel of the Revolution. For, in the first place, neither the historical nor the imaginative plots develop evenly. We jump rapidly from London to Arundel, Maine, with Peter and Nathaniel Merrill, and thence, without rhyme or reason, to Lake Champlain and Montreal. There Benedict Arnold barges into the story, which, from this point, becomes more and more confused, as Captain Peter watches his brother fall prey to the fascinating charmer, Marie de Sabrevois. Marie, as you may readily guess, is a British "agent provocateur," but her niece, Ellen Phipps, is a stanch American adherent, though temporarily blinded to the truth by her malicious aunt. How this too-often woven snarl of human relationships is unraveled does not matter; any schoolboy could disabuse Nathaniel of his infatuation and hand the beautiful Ellen to patriotic Peter, and enable Nathaniel to pass freely from American to British side and back again. The real merit of *Rabble in Arms* lies not in the weak plot but in the genuinely interesting and carefully authenticated historical background.

Captain Peter and his friends fight on lake and on shore with Benedict Arnold, finding him an ever alert and brave leader, the center, therefore, of an endless number of rumors which he brushes aside as well as he can. All the while Arnold is checking the British his American enemies are undermining him with Congress, and thus a perfect case is made by the author to justify his subsequent desertion to the British. The retreat from Canada is handled admirably by Arnold, who, almost unaided, builds and directs the small fleet which checked Burgoyne's troops for a short but vital period. It is in these scenes of action —the pain-racked retreat from Canada, the naval engagement on Lake Champlain, the year's imprisonment among the Indians, the bat-

---

[1] For condescending stupidity, this gentleman's critical ability leads all the rest. See p. 349.

tle of Saratoga—that Mr. Roberts excels himself. These episodes linger in the mind and thrill the spirit, though some might object to his over-use of superlatives in describing the hardships of the American troops; though some might think he labors the point of starvation, disease, desertion and defeat. But the story of the jerry-built flotilla, ill-manned and poorly equipped, which gave battle to Carleton's armada, is as good a yarn as has ever been written of fresh water naval battles. And the imprisonment of Captain Peter among the Western Indians, the Sacs and the Foxes, is amusingly related. The best third of the book, however, is the last, from the escape of Peter and his comrades and their escape from the doomed Ticonderoga to the final episode, the second battle of Saratoga—the only successful fight of the Continentals in this book.

Rabble in Arms would have been a better historical novel if it had been written in the third person. All the faults of Thackeray's *Henry Esmond* and *The Virginians*—dullness, verbosity, lack of continuity—appear in this book, without the saving grace of Thackeray's power of character delineation. Mr. Roberts never brings his chief actors to life, although the historical Arnold, Schuyler and Gates are interesting figures, but distorted by Mr. Roberts' pro-Arnold bias. Captain Peter is a reincarnation of the priggish Henry Esmond and his friends figures of straw. Scott, Dickens and Tolstoy, to name only the greatest masters of historical fiction, thought it best to write in the third person; what necessity is there for a first-hand narrative unless it is written by an actual eye-witness of inexperience; his previous novels, *Arundel* and *The Lively Lady,* are similar in form and composition to *Rabble in Arms.* The former is immediate predecessor to this—the story of Arnold's fruitless assault on Quebec in the first year of the Revolution, it bids fair to be the first in a long, long series of Revolutionary historical fiction, for Steven and Phoebe Nason, Cap Huff and Marie de Sabrevois roam through both novels. Since all of them are alive after Burgoyne's surrender, we may look forward to their periodical reappearance, with the Merrills and others, in at least three other equally long novels before the Revolution is ended. *The Lively Lady* looks ahead to the War of 1812, with Richard Nason, son of Steven and Phoebe, a privateersman, continuing his father's activities against the British. At this rate Mr. Roberts' possibilities of long distance novel writing are unlimited.

The major fault, then, with Mr. Roberts' novels is the confusion between historical events and fictional plot. The bloody retreat from Canada, the engagement at Valcour and the battle of Saratoga, well as they are told, are cast into the shade by the moralizing and pessimism of Peter Merrill and the buffoonery of Cap Huff. This is all the more to be regretted because Mr. Roberts, when he chooses, can write sharply, convincingly and even beautifully. His descriptions are accurate and noteworthy, his selections from historical source material sure and lucid. Could he turn steadfastly from this amorphous romantic history to sober fiction or lively history the results should amply repay him.

HOW A GREAT-MINDED CRITIC
HELPS AN AUTHOR FORGET SMALL ONES

AN APPRECIATION

By Jay Lewis

Keats, on first looking into Chapman's *Homer,* found a new planet had swum within his ken.

So it is with any reader, who for the first time opens a book by Kenneth Roberts. Any book, whether *Northwest Passage, Arundel, Rabble in Arms, The Lively Lady, Captain Caution* or *Oliver Wiswell.* He, too, will feel like some watcher of the skies who amazedly sights a blazing comet or new planet of the first magnitude. For Kenneth Roberts is one of the world's greatest writers, one of those immortals who weave words into tales.

And such tales! They abound in movement, they have vigor and color and they also have that mark of the master craftsman, comic relief. Moreover, they are flawlessly written.

The list of immortals is not so long. Defoe, Swift, Scott, Cooper, Hawthorne, Dickens, Balzac, Dumas, Hugo, Sienkiewicz[1] and Mark Twain are chief among the masters; if you wish to add Richardson, Fielding, Smollett, Thackeray, George Eliot, Charles Reade, Rider Haggard and Conan Doyle, few will care to dispute; include Jane Austen, the Brontës, Herman Melville, Harriet Beecher Stowe, Hardy and Kipling, too, if you like. Put in Tolstoy and the Russians if you must, although the Russians, like vodka, are an acquired taste and they write with the gloominess of the morning after the night before.

That Kenneth Roberts is among the great masters you recognize at once. He has the splendor and sincerity of Scott, the simplicity of Stevenson, the sweep and scope of Sienkiewicz, yet differing as they differ one from the other. He has an individuality all his own, a personality embossed on the printed page as distinct as that of Dumas or Hugo.

---

[1]See p. 193.

Or as that of Cooper of the Wood and Wave, to quote Stevenson, for Kenneth Roberts is equally at home on se~ and land.

All authors put their personalities into their books.

They reveal their inner selves rather than their outward.

They may create characters, using the traits they see in others through their psychological studies of self; but the trend of their thoughts is unmistakable, plain as footprints in the sand. Their manner of thinking crops out like specks in a ledge. The lode itself may be gold or base metal, but its presence is revealed.

The personality of Dumas, extravagant, exuberant, gaudy; his barbaric magnificence is not to be mistaken. Nor is the theatrical ego of Hugo concealed by his attempts at simplicity. The culture and gentle refinement of Thackeray are as apparent as the middle-class virtues and defects of Dickens.

Writers, women no less than men, reflect what is within them through a soul mirror, used consciously or unconsciously, and known to some as the subconscious. The personality of Emily Dickinson appears in her poems as plainly as that of Amy Lowell in her free verse. Sappho and Harriet Beecher Stowe are as clearly revealed.

The psychology of Proust or Guy de Maupassant is as plain in their writings as in those of O. Henry or Jack London.

Without having met or ever seen Kenneth Roberts it is clear that he is not only a great writer but a man of rugged honesty and virile patriotism.

That superb trilogy, the first three books of the Chronicles of Arundel, incidentally, compares favorably with the best three of The Leatherstocking Tales and still leaves *The Lively Lady* and *Captain Caution* to offset *The Red Rover, The Pilot,* or any other of Cooper's sea tales. *Oliver Wiswell* is a far more robust tale than *The Spy*. But, as Dogberry insisted, comparisons are odorous.

After all, a novel is but a story strung out for an Arabian, or Rainy, Night's entertainment, with the reader in the role of Scheherazade's tyrant. And there is but one true test, a trinitarian test, three in one:

Is the story worth telling?

Is it well told?

Is it worth rereading?

If the answer to all three questions is Yes, you have a book worth keeping, one for your permanent personal library, even if it be but a 10-foot shelf.

Still, a tale to have permanent value must have substance and upon the quality of that substance depends the worth of the book. Some call it the texture of the tale, the warp and woof of the fabric; but the finished product, pattern as well as weaving, also counts, with the result that superior quality is recognized as easily as shoddy is known for what it is.

There is substance, a superior quality, about the books of Kenneth Roberts, such as you will find only in those of the accepted great masters of English literature.

Cooper, as an instance, for it will never do to underestimate Cooper who, with all his faults, has a philosophic depth far greater than many realize, a philosophy simple yet profound, an awareness of the eternal law of compensation and retribution, the spiritual law that governs the universe, flowing like a Gulf Stream through the oceans of eternity, touching all shores of space and time. What Drummond called the natural law in the spiritual world but which is the spiritual law in the natural world.

Time alone is said to set an official seal upon the classics, whether fiction or otherwise; but there are established standards by which books may be judged, especially romances popularly called historical novels, among which are classed the Chronicles of Arundel.

Background, construction, development of the story to a fitting climax, delineation of characters by dialog, as well as by description; action, suspense, surprise and comedy, what the dramatists called comic relief, something to loosen the tension, relax the strain and afford contrast with the more dramatic situations, all have to be considered.

Comic relief breaks up the monotony, one of the noticeable many sins of modern novelists, who strike a keynote at the beginning and maintain the same pitch all through, much like modern composers who may vary the beat and orchestration, but who surge to a chaotic crescendo of dissonance that stirs the eardrums but not the emotions, except possibly annoyance. It may be stimulating, but it shows a lack of artistry, as well as a lack of consideration for the audience.

Others who strive for comic relief mistake bawdiness for comedy and gross vulgarity for humor. It may be expected, as Aristophanes said of his Athenian audiences; but few follow his example and apologize for descending to smut. They rather seem to like it, to judge from their persistence in using it.

The comedy in the books of Kenneth Roberts runs from roaring farce and homespun humor to classic wit and irony, often with a sardonic grotesque exaggeration, characteristic of rural America and, like the assumed innocence of Mark Twain, devastating in its effect.

The grim drollery of Tom Buell with his Perkins' Metallic Tractors, Sergeant McNott and his Indian spouse, Old Doc Means and his naïve seriousness are funny, but they only tend to emphasize the genuine, spontaneous humor of Cap Huff, the best comic character since Zagloba, probably the greatest in English literature, aside from Falstaff.

Cap Huff appears in *Northwest Passage, Arundel* and *Rabble in Arms,* reappearing in retrospect for a moment in *Captain Caution,* a regular Paul Bunyan in his gastronomical feats.

In many schools and universities the Chronicles of Arundel are required reading, but they are something more. They are necessary reading if you are to understand the true background of the Colonial, Revolutionary and War of 1812 periods, when the foundation for the building of the nation was laid.

We are apt to forget, in our joyous admiration of the Founding Fathers, that there were many great and good men who did not think separation from the mother country was necessary: that fear of France and of French intentions to regain control and dominate America influenced their minds.

Scholarly men, especially, were doubtful about Democracy, for they had in their mind's eye the fate of Greece and the Roman republic, which became a bureaucracy, next a dictatorship and finally an autocracy with an imperial tyrant on the throne of the Divine Augustus. From the deified Julius Caesar, we get Czar and Kaiser, with an occasional Tsar, borrowed from Slavic sources.

For the ideal is seldom practical, just something to be discussed, something to be brought forth on special occasions, so that each nation may see clearly the beam in another's eye while blind to the mote in its own eye. We are all great in telling others what they should do, while failing to correct our own shortcomings. We are big on talk but puny on performance, until thoroughly convinced and aroused.

Perhaps the ideal is impractical for the same reason that Chesterton gave for the failure of Christianity. It never has been tried.

The change noted by Oliver Wiswell when he thought of the leaders of the turbulent mob that attacked his home where his father lay bedridden, merely because he had played Good Samaritan to Tom Buell— tarred and feathered and ridden on a rail because he dared write and publish a pamphlet—and later Oliver's revised opinion when he reviewed the leaders most prominent in the rebellion against the crown, is something that can be studied with interest. It teaches, among other things, that you cannot win anything by tolerance and that the mob spirit may be right, even when it is most violent and deplorable.

Give the mob a slogan and it will carry everything before it, even if the slogan is forgotten and dropped on the way to victory.

No taxation without representation was the slogan for the War of the Revolution and John Hancock must have smiled benignly, knowing that he owed the British government nearly $500,000 in customs dues, one hundred thousand pounds in money of that day.

That slogan was obsolete in 1812 when Free Trade and Sailors' Rights was adopted and the 1812 slogan was utterly overlooked in the treaty that ended the war.

For nations, like human beings, are greatly given to self-deception and no little hypocrisy, to talking a grand idealism and then letting the whole thing drop for something immediately expedient.

So, in the Chronicles of Arundel, you will find all those things reflected—the rise of democracy, the fight for freedom, the intolerance and violence of mobs, the dismaying thought that tolerance has won few victories and that fear is a force to be reckoned with.

Fear of British vengeance inspired more than one patriot to fight to the death, and fear of the French alliance drove more than one thoughtful American into the British camp.

Benedict Arnold was one of those who believed Congress had sold America to France. He was wrong, but so was many another eminent American of that period, a jurist like John Jay, for instance, as you will find in the opening theme of *Oliver Wiswell*.

Those Founding Fathers saw also that what they had won they were likely to lose, just as today many fear that the freedom to be free is on its way out and that regimentation, dictatorship, imperialism, lie just ahead, with the fate of Rome to follow.

The necessity now to tolerate no shackles is just as imperative as in the days of the Chronicles of Arundel and *Oliver Wiswell*.

In the books of Kenneth Roberts you get more than a mere chronicle of those times. You get a true background with documented facts, for the tremendous amount of research, with the tediousness, the labor, the earnestness of accuracy implied is enough to exhaust a contemplative mind. It is almost beyond comprehension, so small wonder if it inspires awe. If genius is an infinite capacity to take pains, *March to Quebec* alone would award him that distinguished honor.

Bare bones of facts are clothed with romance and realism. His stories are more than mere historical romances, they are matter-of-fact, as realistic as those on which Charles Reade prided himself, not forgetting *The Cloister and the Hearth,* one of the greatest historical romances in any language.

His bac\`grounds are real, his characters are real, his facts are real and \` nas that convincing quality that Dumas so vividly possessed.

Jumas made the *Count of Monte Cristo* so real that present-day guides point out in the Château d'If, if it still stands near the harbor of Marseilles, the cells occupied by the fictitious Dantes and Abbe Faria.

Kenneth Roberts possesses the same magic. His picture of Hogarth's London, in the second book of *Northwest Passage,* is so vivid, so realistic, that you feel that if you ever visit London you are surely going to Vauxhall if only to see that gorgeous mural Langdon Towne painted of Amherst at Crown Point, with Robert Rogers, his scouts and the flaring colors of the Indians in all their garish glory. You feel that it still must be there, cherished among historical paintings.

Only the real masters possess that magic.

Dumas waves his wand and a barefooted Catalan girl, Mercedes, is transformed into a Parisian grande dame, the fisherman Fernand into the aristocratic Count de Morcerf, a ship's purser becomes the millionaire banker Baron Danglars, and the humble mate of a merchant ship is transformed into Monte Cristo, mephistophelean demigod.

And you never stop to question, never even pause to smile.

Kenneth Roberts transforms by the magic of his genius the backwoods child Mary Mallinson into an aristocrat, who, if she lacks the purity of the Mercedes of Dumas, has all the qualities of Miladi, the pythoness of *The Three Musketeers.* As Marie de Sabrevois she is a beauty, both dainty and dangerous, the perfect adventuress.

There is a reality about her, too. She is a type, to be sure, a temptress truly feminine, a distinct trait in all the women of Kenneth Roberts, despite the masquerade of Phoebe Marvin, who became Phoebe Dunn and finally Phoebe Nason, matriarch.

It has been said by one more hasty than accurate that Kenneth Roberts knows little about women and that there is a sameness about his female characters. Hoydens, the critic intimates, crude, given to uncouth garments and manners even cruder.

Yet, to those who have known mothers and sisters, not to mention aunts and kissable cousins, Kenneth Roberts knows women as well as he knows his men kinfolk. That his heroines are unfashionably chaste should not be held against him. There are chaste women even today, despite the fondness of writers for maids à la mode, unrepentant magdalens, shameless socialites, bawds, trollops, adulterous wives and dissolute dowagers.

Writers who deliberately smut up their books and those smug recorders of case histories, who delight in primly describing, with resignation, the infirmities and filth they encounter in welfare work and who are prone to believe the worst, instead of the best, about their neighbors, might be surprised if they ever got away from their surroundings and intimates, to discover the wide-spread, almost conventional family belief in chaste mothers, virtuous sisters, devoted wives and modest daughters. Incidentally, they are not as obsolete as supposed. They actually exist.

Kenneth Roberts, apparently, has been brought up among kinfolk who have not only honored their parents but have not, as Rudyard Kipling said, played tennis with the seventh commandment and disregarded the others, more or less important. His women, moreover, are of an infinite variety.

What could be more primitive than Jennie Coit, the captive white girl found among the St. Francis Indians. A slut. Yet, whose womanhood comes to the surface when she nurses the wounded Captain Ogden during the terrible retreat of the Rangers to safety on the Connecticut.

In the end, despite the urging of the grateful soldier, she returns to the primitive and her Indian husband, deaf to the pleas of the infatuated Ogden, who has learned to love her.

You find the other extreme in the French aristocrat, Mme. De Perigord, niece of Talleyrand, who comes to the aid of Captain Daniel Marvin. A type, you will say. Perhaps! Just as Victorine, self-appointed guardian to Corunna Dorman, is another type: just as Captain Lucien Argendeau is a typical Frenchman. They are as individual as Captain Thomas Boyle, thorough seaman, commander of a dashing privateer, yet a typical Southern gentleman.

Such characters are true to type, as typical as S'Roth, the detestable Englishman, husband of the adorable Lady Ransome in *The Lively Lady*. Just as Jeddy Tucker, Captain Eli Bagley, miserly downeaster, and Tommy Bickford, as nice a boy as you will ever find in fiction, are typical.

Indeed, you might say that the giant Negro, King Dick, ruler of the kangaroo court in Dartmoor Prison, is typical, or that the humane Irish surgeon is typical when, in fact, they are individual characters, as distinct as type cast from a new die, and marvelously well presented.

Langdon Towne's mother in *Northwest Passage* is just such a mother as you would expect him to have; and Elizabeth Browne, who becomes Mrs. Robert Rogers through ambition and a shrew, as Copley feared, was the sort young Langdon would have fallen in love with, before he met Ann Potter.

Ann Potter is a darling. Ellen Phipps, the heroine of *Rabble in*

Arms, is as sweet a lass as you will find in or out of a book. Corunna Dorman, the independent, is a girl to love, despite her foolish faith in Lurman Slade and her contempt, until her eyes are opened, for Captain Caution, who is Daniel Marvin, hero of that tale.

Sally Leighton, heroine of *Oliver Wiswell,* is a perfect specimen of loyalty and devotion. Aunt Ora, as they called Mrs. Belcher Byles, a real bit of New England lavender-scented acrimony, set off by the comely, placid, dumb but amiable Henrietta Dixon. Nor should Julia Bishop and Mrs. Benjamin Loring of *Oliver Wiswell* be forgotten. They, too, are sisters under their skins.

Still, Phoebe Marvin, heroine of *Arundel,* who reappears in both *Rabble in Arms* and *The Lively Lady,* is the masterpiece among all these women. The development of the impish child into the shrewd, calculating, indomitable woman is faithfully traced and easily understood. The girl skipper of the coasting schooner, and the intrepid camp follower who marched to Quebec, plays all her parts equally well. She knows what she is after and she attains it worthily, after travail and tribulation.

The assumed part is protective armor for the warmhearted, companionable, dependable, and utterly feminine Phoebe. She is Mother Eve, New England model; the eternal woman, timeless, self-sacrificing, but ever conscious of her rights: daughter, wife, mother, head of the house and the power behind the throne, wise counselor, mistress in her domain and queen of the household. She is as life-like as life.

In most historical novels you are taken from the present into the past, where you feel as unreal as the Connecticut Yankee at the court of King Arthur; but Kenneth Roberts brings the past to the present and you become a part of it. Things as they were become things as they are.

You are given close-ups of the people and the period, their problems, their motives, their attitude individually and collectively toward public questions, public opinion, pressure groups, political opportunists, idealists, patriots for profit, patriots through fear, false patriots and honest patriots.

At times you are given close-ups of Congress and its brave attempts to do the right thing, with one ear to the ground, the other to the blowing wind, making mistakes with the joyous enthusiasm of zealous public servants and at other times acting perversely, stubbornly, mulishly: one minute making major generals of strutting adventurers like the Frenchman Roche-Fermoy, and the next frowning upon Arnold, refusing him advancement, while promoting incompetents over his head. So much like our own Congress, pressure groups and practical politicians of our own period, that the unescapable comparison would be laughable if it were not grimly tragic and disheartening.

Still, the Colonies came through triumphant despite the disastrous outlook that dismayed so many faithful patriots, and that augurs hope for what lies ahead of any nation in travail.

History and historical novels based on conventional history present stories done in the accepted style; but Kenneth Roberts presents actual history, documented, backed by recorded evidence obtained by the most persistent and thorough research work.

His data for *Arundel* alone would be called a formidable volume were it not so full of interesting information from original sources that it became a book well worth publishing under the title *March to Quebec,* and which may well be called a collector's item.

There is no questioning the accuracy of Kenneth Roberts nor his fidelity to history. His facts are documented beyond any doubt.

Times change, environment furnishes new backgrounds; but human nature remains much the same from age to age, easily excited, easily fooled, easily tempted and as easily betrayed. With selfishness as characteristic as generosity, with slyness and trickery as common as honesty and integrity, with foolishness and absurdities as conspicuous as sound good sense and instability as well known as sturdy forthrightness, among those recognized as leaders. As it was, so it is.

It was not the most clamorous in the days of the Chronicles of Arundel who were the sincerest patriots, but rather the reticent, thoughtful and sometimes doubtful citizens who were the bulwarks of democracy; who followed Washington faithfully and with him were sorrowful over the apostasy of Arnold. It was they who were the real Founding Fathers, the builders of the nation, and Kenneth Roberts makes that fact clear to all.

In the Chronicles of Arundel Kenneth Roberts reveals the difference between conventional history and actual history.

Conventional history is biased, prejudiced, partisan but always patriotic. All that is excellent is praised. Faults are glossed over, errors excused. Virtue triumphs and is made glorious.

Just as in war, pomp and pageantry cover up misery and woe. Fighting qualities, magnificent courage and heroic deeds more than atone for suffering and death, maimed bodies, squalidness and filth, corruption and disease, carnage and chaos.

In conventional history, all that is evil is brushed aside or regarded as something that must be endured, as a part of the penalty for victory. Cheating and chiselling, profiteering and chicanery are to be expected, it seems, along with hypocrisy and those mercenaries who see in war an opportunity for personal gain, the patriots for profit.

Only the bright side of war is presented in conventional history, the darker side is left to poets and novelists. Actual history may be found in the records and the records reveal the base as well as the beautiful.

The fact that deified heroes had their faults is often granted, but that those whom conventional history has condemned may have had redeeming qualities, even virtues, is generally ignored, or grudgingly admitted.

In his Chronicles of Arundel it has been the purpose of Kenneth Roberts to be just, to present the base as well as the beautiful, to set forth actual history against a background of truth. Not only to write realism into romance, but to show how far conventional history may be from the facts.

In doing so he presented two supermen with human failings and faults, victims of vaulting ambition, as well as victims of their unbounded imaginations. Thwarted, balked, calumniated, humiliated, the poison of ingratitude first numbed and then destroyed them.

Although *Arundel* was written first, *Northwest Passage* preceded it in the actual order of the chronicles, including the trilogy that records the saga of Cap Huff, as well as its more important heroes.

Northwest Passage has Langdon Towne, American artist, for its historian; but its real story is the disintegration of a superman, Robert Rogers, leader of the Rangers who destroyed the St. Francis Indians and whose subsequent career is one of the most amazing known to mankind.

To gain his purpose of opening up the Northwest Passage to the Pacific, to the greater glory of Great Britain and his own personal aggrandizement, he went to London where he became a national hero. He wrote a play about the Indians and English in America in which justice was done the Redmen and the scheming whites were shown for what they were. He was put in the way to win fame and fortune; but his enemies, ever alert, trapped him. Yet such was his determination, so great his grit, so indomitable his spirit that no outrage could quell him.

Shackles and prison could not daunt him, but the poison of his disappointments entered his soul. He could assume a part and play it, deceive himself and others, face adversity heroically, take advantage of any opportunity; but toward the end of the book he gradually fades until he becomes a disembodied spirit, something to haunt his associates to the end of their lives.

In *Arundel,* second of the series, Steven Nason is the hero, but

Arnold pervades the book from the time he appears as captain of his trading brig, off the Maine coast, to its end, following the disaster at Quebec, where Steven Nason discovers the truth about Mary Mallinson and her abductor.

Of the march of Arnold's men through the Maine wilderness to the shores of the St. Lawrence, opposite Quebec, their sufferings, their endurance, their patriotism, much has been written; but it remained for Kenneth Roberts to make it real in a romance unmatched in American literature, save by such masterpieces as *Northwest Passage* and *Rabble in Arms,* third of the chronicles.

In that tale Arnold again dominates the story. He is pictured as an inspiring leader, generous, valiant, resourceful, unconquerable, never despairing, no matter how great the odds. Thwarted, hated, but carrying on despite his detractors, turning calamitous failure into wonderful success, he is the incarnate patriot, the unconquerable soldier.

The end of *Rabble in Arms* finds Arnold at the zenith of his glory. Wounded in the same leg which cost him Quebec he is hospitalized at Albany following victory at Saratoga won by him and his men, despite Gates.

Hero of the army, he bids farewell to his faithful followers, performing a final act of justice, no less generous because it was just, that brings joy to the hearts of those who trusted him.

Grit and determination are no less in evidence in the stories of *The Lively Lady* and *Captain Caution,* both of which belong among the Chronicles of Arundel, although of another generation and the War of 1812.

Yet young Richard Nason is the son of Steven Nason and Phoebe Nason and possesses qualities drawn from both, a sturdy patriotism and steadiness of purpose that recognizes no failure.

Kenneth Roberts, as said before, knows the sea as well as the shore, nor does he mistake a topsail schooner for a brigantine, or a sloop of war for a single sticker, errors that have crept into more than one nautical narrative.

There are seafights in both *The Lively Lady* and *Captain Caution,* realistic seafights and scenes ashore equally exciting. The account of Dartmoor prison, with big, black King Dick and his satellites, is painted with the vividness of a modern mural. The horrors of that dread prison are appalling and the supineness of the American representative in London is enough to stir to wrath and indignation the most complacent reader.

As romance it would be hard to choose between *The Lively Lady* and

Captain Caution; for Daniel Marvin, with his Gangway Pendulum which makes for accurate shooting that batters his enemy into submission, is as daring as young Richard Nason.

Corunna Dorman, self-opinionated young woman, discovers that fact in the end, after much mortification of spirit over the mistake she made in admiring the suave but sinister Slade and accepting his advances.

The Old Grenadier of a duenna and the loquacious Captain Lucien Argandeau, who admits that he is a Don Juan and even boasts about it, form a grand contrast to honest Daniel and equally honest, if impulsive Corunna. Both stories, while romantic enough to suit the most sentimental, have a sturdy patriotism which shows that the main purpose is to make plain what sort of folk our forebears were.

Nor is that purpose absent from *Oliver Wiswell,* although that novel presents the Loyalist side. It is now an accepted fact that the most esteemed men in America, including Washington himself, were for conciliation with the Crown; and only the diehards and demagogues, those fearful of the vengeance of the British and their adherents—the mob— were for separation from Great Britain.

Those who die in a good cause are often ennobled by death and finally deified; but it is a matter of record that the martyrs of the Boston massacre were so tough a lot that the soldiers responsible for the so-called massacre were defended by the best of the patriot lawyers.

Oliver Wiswell, without doubt, is Kenneth Roberts at his best. It would be hard to name a better novel in all English literature. There may be more popular books: many, perhaps, more attractive in theme to readers in general; and many readers may dislike the fact that Oliver Wiswell never saw the errors of his way or became converted to the patriotic cause. But that was not the purpose of the author. His idea was to show that there was another side to the conventional story of the American Revolution and ably did he carry out his plan.

Regarded fairly, without prejudice, as the product of an American author, *Oliver Wiswell* is the finest work in the entire list of American fiction.

It does not properly belong with the Chronicles of Arundel, already claimed as classics by educators, and to be even more highly esteemed as Time ticks away the years.

Legends of heroes and their heroic deeds are destined to become a part of the folklore of the American people; and the sturdy independence of those pioneers may yet be remembered with a sigh for lost liberty. The future alone holds the spinning of that thread.

It should be pointed out that the work of Kenneth Roberts is not wholly confined to fiction: that his *March to Quebec* is a remarkable collection of historical data; that *Trending into Maine* is not only historical but biographical and historical. Not to say whimsical.

But it is in his romances, novels, Chronicles of Arundel, that Kenneth Roberts is at his best, for in them is written himself.

Great writers write what they feel. The others merely feel what they write.

Many, including best sellers, are meteorites. Kenneth Roberts is a fixed star in the literary firmament.

INDEX

INDEX

MANUSCRIPTS OF KENNETH ROBERTS'
BOOKS ARE DISPLAYED IN THESE LIBRARIES:

Arundel . . . . Massachusetts Institute of Technology

The Lively Lady . . . . Colby College

Captain Caution . . . . Episcopal Academy of Philadelphia

Rabble in Arms . . . . Fort Ticonderoga Museum

Northwest Passage . . . . Boston Public Library

Oliver Wiswell . . . . Bowdoin College

Moreau de St. Méry's American Journey . . . . Free Library of
Philadelphia

ARUNDEL

A CHRONICLE OF THE PROVINCE OF MAINE

RABBLE IN ARMS

A CHRONICLE OF ARUNDEL

BUFFALO EVENING NEWS:

"*Rabble In Arms* is epic in scope, epic in grandeur, epic in atmosphere. It is indispensable to anyone who wishes to know the true story of the War for American Independence. For the first time this country has produced an historical novelist of the first rank. His books are destined to take a permanent place in the great literature of war of all times." —*W. A. Martin.*

CHRISTIAN SCIENCE MONITOR:

"*Rabble In Arms* is a long yet breathless tale. The work is gloriously performed."

RUPERT HUGHES:

"*Rabble In Arms* is magnificent. In both the beauty and the horror of his story, Kenneth Roberts reaches supreme heights and can defy comparison with any author that ever lived and wrote in any language I ever read in the original or in translation. They talk big talk of Tolstoi, Victor Hugo, Stephen Crane and a few others, but I put Kenneth Roberts up with the best of them. He is a great author who has actually written great novels."

MARC CONNELLY:

"I have seldom closed a book with more regret."

BOSTON TRANSCRIPT:

"Nothing we have ever read has made us see and feel the American Revolution with the vividness of this novel. In it history becomes alive. The actual purpose of the historical novel is that it shall translate fact into human experience, and *Rabble In Arms* is a supreme justification of that." —*Dorothea L. Mann.*

NEA SERVICE:

"A magnificent picture on a great, glowing canvas. Some day the reading public will wake up to the fact that Kenneth Roberts is writing American historical novels that are as fine as any in existence."

THE NEW YORKER:

"A fine murmurous forest of a book." —*Alexander Woollcott.*

RICHMOND TIMES DISPATCH:

"Valuable as biography, invaluable as history, and almost unsurpassed as spirited narrative, *Rabble In Arms* has all the old fashioned virtues of Scott and Thackeray while escaping the slightest suspicion of tedium. It has all the breezy freshness of early American vigor."

AMERICAN ANTIQUARIAN SOCIETY:

"*Rabble In Arms*, with *Arundel* and *The Lively Lady,* should be on the required reading list of every course in American History in every college in America." —*Robert W. G. Vail, Librarian.*

MANCHESTER (England) GUARDIAN:

"*Rabble In Arms* is magnificent work . . . a feast of good reading."

NEW YORK SUN:

"*Rabble In Arms* is my candidate for the best novel of American history." —*P. M. Jack.*

CHRONICLES OF ARUNDEL

THE LIVELY LADY

CAPTAIN CAUTION

NORTHWEST PASSAGE

NEW YORK TIMES:

"It is the eternal pageant of the 18th Century that keeps one reading *Northwest Passage* to the very end. Of Robert Rogers Ann says: 'Ah, no! You can't kill what was in that man!' And it seems you can't—not with Kenneth Roberts to bring him back out of the star dust and make him again so real."
—*R. L. Duffus.*

SATURDAY REVIEW OF LITERATURE:

"The first half of *Northwest Passage* deals with one of the most agonizing marches in history. The second half you will read with as much satisfaction as you ever got from *The Virginians.* The hunger and desire of the nation just about to break westward into the untrodden lands, the tangle of cupidities and venalities and stupidities that in great part conditioned them—they are in *Northwest Passage* as they have not been in our fiction before. The second half is not only a good story; it moves on a plane of understanding and perception that only the best kind of historical fiction achieves."
—*Bernard De Voto.*

ATLANTIC MONTHLY:

"*Northwest Passage* is a great novel, since in its pages an era comes to life, complete with people and with things. When Kenneth Roberts wrote *Arundel,* he produced a novel which for most writers would have been a culmination. In *Rabble In Arms* and in *Northwest Passage* he has proved that *Arundel* was no more than a promise now bountifully fulfilled."
—*Ben Ames Williams.*

PROVIDENCE JOURNAL:

"So rich is *Northwest Passage* that I can do no more than recommend it with all my heart. In it Mr. Roberts has created an unforgettable figure. Robert Rogers has come to stay, to be despised, loved, abhorred and warred about, and withal saluted as an undoubted hero."
—*B. K. Hart.*

CLEVELAND PRESS:

"Kenneth Roberts' *Arundel* proved that he was the best historical novelist now practicing in America. Its sequel, *Rabble In Arms,* continued the proof. Consensus of critical opinion still is that each of these books should have received the Pulitzer Prize. *Northwest Passage* proves him to be not only the best historical novelist now practicing in America; but as far as American readers are concerned, the best that ever practiced anywhere, used any subject matter."
—*Elrick B. Davis.*

BROOKLYN EAGLE:

"*Northwest Passage* is accurate history, graphically told. Here is scope and power of writing. Here is the accuracy of a camera, the warmth and life of oils, the detail of an etching; the story of great men attempting great deeds."
—*Virginia Bird.*

MINNEAPOLIS JOURNAL:

"Towering above all else in the swirling 700 pages of *Northwest Passage* is that indestructible giant, Robert Rogers, a prodigious creation, a character bristling and sounding with life, a vivid portrait for your literary gallery. *Northwest Passage* will give you three novels' worth of entertainment."
—*Charles Lee.*

CHICAGO HERALD TRIBUNE:

"*Northwest Passage* chronicles a hero of gargantuan proportions and brings alive scenes and people from the forgotten pages of history. It is an enormous tale in every sense of the word—in length, breadth of action and intensity. The pages that describe the raid on St. Francis are as tense and lyric as a taut harp in a gale. It is a memorable and impressive book—a tremendous story."
—*Fanny Butcher.*

BOSTON POST:

" 'Magnificent' is the word for Kenneth Roberts' glorious story, *Northwest Passage.*"

WORCESTER TELEGRAM:

"The clarity with which the characters emerge from the past, the drama of its campaigns, will fix the period in our memories for all time. The pictures in this story of gallantry and endurance are more vivid and unforgettable than any set pieces of fireworks."
—*Helen Beals.*

OLIVER WISWELL

LYDIA BAILEY

TRENDING INTO MAINE

BOSTON HERALD:

"Roberts knows his Maine, its history, geography, literature, legend, tradition, and people. It is his other Eden, his more than demi-paradise. For him it has a better than happy breed of men. It is the one spot beloved over all. He writes, therefore, something more than a native's appreciation, something better than a nicely tempered panegyric, a something which in its masculine passions disproves the old notion that a Maineman's reach cannot exceed his grasp. *Trending into Maine* is an exhilaratingly lyrical book, with a warm glow over it, and a clean wind through it, and an unspoken challenge and invitation in it that sets a man's eyes gazing northward."—*Charles Lee.*

NEW YORK TIMES:

"Readers who have made Mr. Roberts' acquaintance in one of his novels will recognize him in *Trending into Maine,* but with a difference. Freed from the trammels of plot, sustained character, and stylistic pattern, he lets his hair down, puts his feet up, and talks about what interests him most. He can't look at a bit of Maine scenery without having his mind filled with stories and people: 'Red men puttering about their lodges'; 'long, unhappy lines of women and children . . . trudging silently through the snow to the eastward and to Canada, pushed and shouted at by painted Indians'; 'wives and children of sea captains, waiting patiently through long Winters for those sailing on far-off waters'; 'Arnold's men, hunkered uncomplainingly among their bateaux on the river bank above Augusta . . .' It's a rambling, eloquent, colorful, lovable book."—*R. L. Duffus.*

SATURDAY REVIEW OF LITERATURE:

"When Kenneth Roberts isn't writing an historical novel (which isn't often), he takes one peck of ripe tomatoes, puts them through a sieve, and adds vinegar, allspice, mustard, and powdered cloves. The result is ketchup. Or he rows out between the ledges at half tide and fishes for cunners. Or he retraces Arnold's route to Quebec. Or he mixes up a batch of letters, notes, and clippings and produces a book like *Trending into Maine,* into which he pours some of his ketchup, most of his great-great-grandmothers, and every ounce of his passionate admiration for the state of Maine. *Trending into Maine* is not so much a book as it is a visit with Kenneth Roberts. He takes you into the kitchen, sits you down by the stove, hands you a doughnut, and stuffs you full of Arundel, Maine traditions, Maine smells, Maine people, the hardships of soldiering, the pleasures of ducks' breasts, the bravery of sea captains' daughters."— *E. B. White.*

MARCH TO QUEBEC

BOSTON EVENING TRANSCRIPT:

"Bringing together, in *March to Quebec,* the journals of the Quebec Expedition is an exceedingly valuable contribution to the Americana of the Revolution. . . . Many have been practically inaccessible. . . . Only a few libraries in the country have them all, and he who would buy them for himself would be obliged to spend a large sum of money and wait for a year or so before some dealer in rare books could accumulate all of them."

NEW YORK TIMES:

"Readers who enjoy weighing evidence ought to find much in *March to Quebec.* It has a suggestion of the thrill of a mystery story, not because the main outlines are in question but because motives and characters are deeply involved."

MOREAU DE ST. MÉRY'S AMERICAN JOURNEY (1793-1798)

Translated and edited
by
Kenneth Roberts and Anna M. Roberts

THE PHILADELPHIA INQUIRER:

"It is impossible to do more than hint at the wealth of detail which is in this book about life in Philadelphia. Frank details seldom recorded are abundant. The reader can learn much of love, morals and marriage, the frigidity of the American women, of the bringing up of children, the treatment of servants, bound and slave. . . . Every page is a combination of guide-book and social analysis."—*Roy Franklin Nichols*

NEW YORK TIMES:

"In MOREAU'S pages we see Talleyrand, the man who virtually ruled Europe for three decades, cavorting around Moreau's bookstore until dawn while La Rochefoucauld Liancourt wrestled with Moreau's son. With him we observe Washington, dressed in black with a turned-up hat and sword and his hair in a bag, opening the sessions of Congress; and we talk with Alexander Hamilton, a small, slightly furtive-looking man who spoke French 'very incorrectly.' Here is a cross-section of a nation in the process, to use Moreau's apt phrase, of being born."—*William Peden*

CHRISTIAN SCIENCE MONITOR:

"Early in Kenneth Roberts' research in connection with his novel, *Lydia Bailey*, he became aware of the need for more information about the five-year sojourn of Moreau de St. Méry in the New World. Mr. Roberts became so convinced of the importance of this record that he suspended work on his novel for six months while he and his wife made a translation. The result—MOREAU DE ST. MÉRY'S AMERICAN JOURNEY (1793-1798), translated and edited by Kenneth and Anna M. Roberts, with an introduction by Stewart L. Mims—is a volume valuable to the historian and fascinating to the layman."—*Ralph Adams Brown*

SATURDAY REVIEW OF LITERATURE:

"So stimulating and so curious did Kenneth Roberts find Moreau's book, that he and Mrs. Roberts set about translating it for the rest of us. We owe them both a debt of gratitude, for not only is it the absorbing book they say it is, but it is one which gives us the serious and trivial facts of our early Republican days in a fashion at once unique and quite unobtainable elsewhere."—*Harry Hatcher*

KNOXVILLE NEWS-SENTINEL:

"The diary of M. de St. Méry is satisfactory and salutary reading. We may reflect on the one hand how greatly we have improved and on the other ask ourselves if the improvement has gone as far as it might. Its translation is a notable addition to the early literature of this country."—*Lucy Curtis Templeton*

NEWSWEEK:

"Colorful, racy, and brilliant, Moreau's 'Journey' is delightful reading."

HARTFORD COURANT MAGAZINE:

"Kenneth Roberts has done a real service to historical research by making available in translation the key work of this almost forgotten Frenchman. Contemporary comment on the mores and foibles of the past is always a fruitful and comforting study. . . . And this translation succeeds in preserving the vividness and Gallic clarity of the original."—*Joseph J. Frank*